Nottingham Trolleybuses

David R H Bowler

First Published 2006

ISBN 0-904235-20-3
ISBN 978-0-904235-20-3

Published by:
Trolleybooks
24 Heath Farm Road
Ferndown, DORSET
BH22 8JW
www.trolleybooks.co.uk

This publication is in no way an official publication either of Nottingham City Council or Nottingham City Transport although due acknowledgement is made to both the Council and the Company as sources of official information contained herein. Acknowledgement is also made to the City Council for permission to use the city coat of arms.

Graphics and Book design by: Ashley Bruce, 156 High Street, Bildeston, Ipswich, IP7 7EF
Typesetting by: Lateral Concepts, 22 St Paul's Gate, Wokingham, RG41 2YP

Printed and bound in China

TROLLEYBOOKS is the Joint Publications Panel of:

BRITISH TROLLEYBUS SOCIETY

and

TROLLEYBUS MUSEUM COMPANY

For further information on the activities of these organisations please contact:

Mr A J Barton
Membership Secretary
British Trolleybus Society
2 Josephine Court
Southcote Road
READING
RG30 2DG

www.britishtrolley.org.uk

Mr I G Martin
Membership Secretary
Trolleybus Museum Company
2 St John's Close
Claines
WORCESTER
WR3 7PT

www.trolleybus.co.uk/nta

Photo captions

Front cover:

Top left — Railless No 4, in original livery, outside the Prudential Insurance building at the apex of the junction between King Street and Queen Street, terminus of the Nottingham Road services. *GHFA & JMB*

Upper left — Ransomes No 15 seen at full deviation, passing road works in Lower Parliament Street, at the junction with Milton Street in March 1934. *GHFA & JMB*

Lower left — Karrier E6 No 25 in a coloured publicity photograph. *Park Royal*

Bottom left — A row of three BUT9641Ts headed by 511 stand beneath the "slip" wires at Carlton Post Office Square terminus in Cavendish Road. *Martin Eady*

Centre right — An early colour image of Ransomes Sims & Jefferies D6 39 posed, without passengers and still with Brush bodywork labels on the windows, on Middleton Boulevard in the summer of 1931. *Roy Marshall*

Crest — The Nottingham coat of arms as used on the Corporation's trolleybuses throughout the lifetime of the system. The motto Latin 'VIVIT POST FUNERA VIRTUS' which translates as "Virtue survives death".

Title Page: On a beautiful summer's day in 1932 one of the latest examples of modern railless electric traction Ransomes D6/Brush 44, just some six months old, stands in the northbound carriageway of Middleton Boulevard at Fairham Drive. Note the driver's white-topped cap and summer dustcoat. *BTS*

Back Cover: BUT9641T 517 at the much photographed junction of King Street and Queen Street. *MJ Russell*

Contents

Foreword

Prior to reading this book I, like many in my profession, had only a rudimentary knowledge of the history and development of the public transport industry in the UK prior to 1970.

David Bowler has in his book set in a historical context the development and operation of the Nottingham Trolleybus. The book also sets out, almost as a by-product, the needs, history and development of our Towns and Cities during the mass production, labour-intensive period stretching from the late Victorian era through to the latter part of the 20th century.

It is clear from the book that the Nottingham Trolleybus has formed an integral part of the development of Nottingham as a City, conurbation and economic centre.

David traces the development and gestation of the Trolleybus in Nottingham from the earliest comments made by the Vice Chairman of the Tramways Committee in October 1908. He continues to the earliest official reference in the Nottingham Corporation Act 1913. Then to the final journey on that Friday morning in July 1966 when Driver, Albert Parish and Conductor, Fred Cooper drove vehicle 506 with its party of dignitaries out of King Street, watched by members of the public, along to Nottingham Road before returning but a few short minutes later to King Street and then passing into history.

David has covered the intervening period in minute detail and provides the reader with a fascinating historical account of the workings and interrelationships in local politics that lead to the success of Trolleybuses in Nottingham and the decisions which lead to them not being introduced in some adjacent authorities.

David's attention to detail and ability to convey the information in a way which will delight the enthusiast and casual reader alike is extraordinary. I for one as a successor to some of the names mentioned in this book have been educated, enlightened and amused.

Mark J Fowles
Managing Director
Nottingham City Transport
April 2006.

Publisher's note

This book is the second extensive trolleybus history researched and written by David Bowler and is a worthy successor to his book on Bournemouth Trolleybuses published by the Panel in 2001. It also marks the first effort of a totally reconstituted Trolleybooks Panel that came together for the first time in late 2003.

Nottingham may be considered to be one of the pioneer UK trolleybus operators having commenced operations as early as 1927. It was inevitable therefore that there would be much more data and general information to be extracted from the various archives than say for many other UK systems. In preparing this history David Bowler has been as meticulous as ever and we feel certain that readers will be delighted with the wealth of information that David has unearthed as well as the variety of excellent photographs from various sources that complement and enhance this important history.

This latest volume from Trolleybooks is by far the largest book published by the panel to date and will we hope set new standards in the layout and presentation of the Panel's publications.

2006 marks the fortieth anniversary of the demise of Nottingham's trolleybuses in June 1966. This publication is a fitting tribute to an excellent trolleybus system that served the city well for almost forty years. Nottingham's trolleybuses deserve to be remembered for the significant part that they played in the life of Nottingham in general and its transport system in particular.

Carl F Isgar, Chairman, Trolleybooks. April 2006.

Author's Acknowledgements

As the human being ages, so time seems to pass faster and faster, yet can it really be forty years since the last Nottingham trolleybus disappeared from the city's streets? Certainly the fruits of my efforts, mainly unsuccessful, to make contact with those hundreds of employees who kept the trolleybus service running efficiently in all weathers, indicate that it was a long time ago.

The foundation upon which this book has been written is based on historical documents covering the trolleybus era cared for by the efficient and helpful teams at Nottingham's Local Studies Library and at the Nottinghamshire Archives, which is entrusted with the safekeeping of Nottingham City Council's records. I am also grateful to City Councillors and staff at the Council House for unbureaucratically giving me access to the Members' Room Library and its documents on a number of occasions.

During the course of my five years' research, I have gradually got to know, and received tremendous support from, a number of trolleybus enthusiasts with a particular interest in the erstwhile Nottingham system. In alphabetical order, Peter Badgery who, prior to National Service, was employed at Trent Bridge Works, where he kept an enthusiastic record of Nottingham City Transport's activities. He subsequently joined the West Bridgford undertaking retaining his interest in most public transport operations in the immediate area and further afield. Rodney Bramley, a leading light in the erstwhile Nottingham Trolleybus Group of the 1960s, has contributed his extremely detailed notes of the system's last ten years and patiently corrected my own lack of local knowledge. Michael Elliott, Human Resources Manager at today's Nottingham City Transport Ltd., who has invested many hours in massaging the undertaking's remaining archives and records into useable material, and solving apparent contradictions and mysteries. Roy Marshall who, as a Carlton schoolboy, recorded developments and events throughout the 1940s before entering the passenger transport industry, first with Skills Coaches, later with Nottingham City Transport and subsequently in a number of senior management positions in other undertakings. To these gentlemen I extend my most sincere thanks.

"A picture paints a thousand words". Road passenger transport enthusiasts in the East Midlands have reason to be thankful to Geoffrey Atkins, a Nottinghamian now in his nineties, who meticulously photographed developments in his native city throughout the trolleybus era. I have been fortunate to gain access to his clear and well-composed views through the generosity of John Banks.

A host of other individuals, too numerous to mention all by name, have assisted me with my research, often in respect of very specific points or uncertainties. These include Ashley Bruce, Geoff Burrows, Brian Deans, Martin Eady, Philip Groves, Robert Hall, Bernard Jefford, Neil Lewin, John Lowrie, Geoff Lumb, Jack Morris, Alan Oxley and John Whitehead, to name but a few.

I also wish to place on record my thanks to Mark Fowles, Managing Director of Nottingham City Transport for writing the Foreword to this book, for his support and for permitting me to use photographs and plans from the undertaking's records.

Finally my thanks go to John Gillham for preparing the revised tramway track map and providing a host of valuable inputs, and to the many photographers, on occasion unknown by name, whose illustrations appear in the book.

A note about the pictures

Many photographs in this book are by GHF Atkins. The main collection is held by John Banks and all these photographs are marked GHFA & JMB. We are extremely grateful to John for kindly making the Atkins photographs available and acknowledge rights thus – GHF Atkins/© & Courtesy John Banks Collection. Other Atkins photographs are from Roy Marshall, Photobus, WJ Haynes (BTS Collection) and Peter Badgery.

Other photographs are from -

BTS	British Trolleybus Society Collection (WJ Haynes, RF Mack, David Hall, RMS Simpson, J Burrows or C Carter)
NTA	National Trolleybus Association Library (Ian Hill, London Trolleybus Preservation Society)
TLRS	Tramway and Light Railway Society
TMS	Tramway Museum Society
MERL	The Museum of English Rural Life courtesy of JR Whitehead
NCT	Nottingham City Transport
Nottingham Libraries	
STA	Senior Transport Archive
EE/Beilby	John Beilby Collection (Alstrom/English Electric Archive)
Geoff Lumb	Geoff Lumb Collection (Railless Archive)
John Aldridge	John Aldridge Collection (Leyland Archive)
Roy Marshall	Roy Marshall Collection, including G Pulfrey
Photobus	Photobus (courtesy Arnold Richardson)

Alan Oxley
Joan Marvin
Richard Delahoy
Fred York
Jack Morris
Neil Lewin
Rod Bramley
Martin Eady
Bernard Jefford
Peter Badgery
John Lowrie
MJ Russell
Martin Jenkins
Charles Bedgley
Images from Brush Coachworks Ltd and Brush Electrical Engineering Co. Ltd., held by John Bath, John Lowrie and Nottingham City Transport

Introduction

My first recollections of Nottingham's trolleybuses must date back to the mid-1950s when, as a six year old, I accompanied my parents on an autumn weekend staff outing to Buxton organised by my Father's employers. We travelled from our family home at Oakham, Rutland to the meeting point in Low Pavement, Nottingham from whence our Barton's coach set out for the Peak District. I recall traversing the city streets with their trolley wires above shining in the dark and the electric buses bustling past one after another. A couple of summers beforehand we had spent a holiday at Llandudno, North Wales where I had been fascinated by the trams running to Colwyn Bay and that evening I was perhaps, as a child, trying to puzzle out the relationship between the electric tram and the trolleybus.

The largest shopping centre in the immediate area and my Father's local head office ensured that we visited Nottingham from time to time, each trip by mainline train through Melton Mowbray being something of a special event, to be crowned by lunch at Lyons on Long Row or perhaps afternoon tea at the "Black Boy." In 1962 my parents bought their first car and we started to travel further afield more frequently whilst my own interests in public transport had been furthered by the discovery of Bournemouth's trolleybuses and, through an article in the Meccano Magazine, the infant tram museum at Crich. My pestering for Sunday trips to Crich often led to outbound journeys through Derby with a return through Nottingham yet although both cities then boasted trolleybuses I paid them no special attention. After all trolleybuses were a permanent fixture, weren't they? Only when it was almost too late and the London Road route already closed did I start to investigate the Nottingham trolleybus system although I was never to become as familiar with it as with that in distant Bournemouth!

Following the appearance of my history of Bournemouth's trolleybuses, published by *Trolleybooks* in 2001, it was suggested to me that it was surprising that I had not attempted a record of my former "native" system, Nottingham. I had enjoyed the preparation of that volume despite the logistics and expense involved (I have lived in Switzerland for the last thirty years), and thus here is my second attempt at a chronology of a British trolleybus system.

My researches have been left me with contradicting impressions of the development of Nottingham's trolleybus system. Those tram and the few motorbus routes which it had been decided to convert to trolleybus operation in the eight-year period 1927-1934 provided Nottingham with one of the largest networks in Britain at that time over which a high-frequency service was offered until the mid-1960s. A change of policy from 1934 saw an end to these conversions whilst Nottingham's younger suburbs were never to benefit from electric traction in the manner that other provincial cities saw their trolleybuses extend well beyond the limits of their rail-bound predecessors. Throughout the trolleybus era, the Labour Party, then closely linked with coal mining and power generation industries, was predominantly in the majority on the City Council and it is surprising that they were not more successful in defending their own supporter's interests and thus trolleybus expansion against the motor vehicle lobby. During the Second World War and the period immediately thereafter, Nottingham's trolleybuses appear to have been simply tolerated, almost as a necessary evil, until new motorbuses became freely available, equipment was life-expired and oil supplies from the Middle East could be guaranteed.

If Nottingham's transport policies had not changed in 1934; if the electric power supply had remained in municipal hands; if "clean energy" had been discovered earlier; if the public had been ecologically-minded; etc., the city might still be benefiting from fume-free, silent and efficient trolleybuses.

Despite the departure of the trolleybus from both the streets of Nottingham and the United Kingdom, the city still benefits from, by British standards, an excellent public transport network, recently supplemented by a reincarnation of the electric trams albeit primarily along the route of erstwhile or existing railways. In other countries the private car has been shown to be an unsustainable mode of urban transport that is slowly destroying the very environment essential for human life. It is to be hoped that Nottingham's citizens realise their good fortune and that they can be tempted, or if necessary forced, out of their private cars to use the affordable, quality services available to them.

David Bowler,
Pfungen, Switzerland
September 2005

Notes for Guidance – Terms and expressions

For the benefit of non-enthusiast the more obscure terms used in connection with trolleybuses, and in particular the trolleybus overhead line installations, are explained:

Bracket Arm: A tubular steel support bolted to the upper section of the *traction pole* at right angles and projecting over the road, from which to suspend the *trolley wire* as an alternative to a *span wire*. Usually employed where the length of span wire between traction poles would be unduly long or along straight stretches on narrow roads to reduce the number of traction poles. Also referred to as a single bracket arm to differentiate from a *gantry* or double bracket arm.

Converter: Rotating electromechanical device, like a motor or a generator, used to convert alternating current (AC) into direct current (DC).

Composite (body): In this form of bodywork, the main framework constructed from hardwood, reinforced as necessary with steel flitches, supports and brackets, and panelled in metal.

Curve Segment: A special curved fitting replacing several separate *pull-offs* in the *running wire*, which gave a smoother passage for the *trolleyheads* on sharp curves.

Drop light: A type of opening side window employed in the main side bays of the lower and upper saloons of bus bodies whereby the entire pane of glass dropped downwards into a recess within the side panels below.

Frog: The overhead line equipment equating to railway points where one pair of running wires left or joined another, know as facing frogs where the lines diverged or trailing frogs where the lines converged. Facing frogs were operated either by hand (the conductor leaving the vehicle and pulling an operating handle, connected by cable to the frog mechanism, on an adjacent traction pole) or automatically by the trolleyheads of a trolleybus energising a solenoid through a contact fitted to the overhead line a short distance before the frog. The direction of the frog could be changed by the trolleybus drawing power as the trolleyheads passed beneath the contact. Trailing frogs were spring loaded.

Gantry: A tubular steel support joining the upper section of two *traction poles* on opposite sides of the roadway, from which to suspend the *trolley wire* as an alternative to *span wire*. Also referred to as a double bracket arm.

Half-drop: A type of opening side window employed in the main side bays of the lower and upper saloons of bus bodies whereby the window was divided horizontally into two, the upper pane of glass dropped downwards outside the fixed lower pane.

Hanger: The attachment which, by use of a mechanical grip or "ear" and a porcelain insulator, supported the *trolley wire* beneath a *bracket arm* or *span wire*.

Metal framed: In this form of bodywork, a steel or aluminium frame was built with timber packers (body) and wooden inserts to accept the many screws needed to hold the interior finishers and exterior panels. Also referred to as an "all metal" body.

Motor generator: An electric motor using the traction power supply as its source of energy, driving a generator to produce power for a vehicle's low tension lighting.

Pull-off: A span wire or wires providing additional support or securing a correct alignment of the trolley wires on bends under the correct tension, creating a curve consisting of a series of short straight sections.

Quarter light: A separate, roughly triangular, side window situated between the driver's cab door or main cab side window(s) and the front pillar.

Railless: See *trolleybus*.

Rectifier: A device for converting alternating current (AC) into direct current (DC).

Reversing Triangle: An arrangement in the overhead line to enable vehicles to turn by means of a three-point reversing procedure into and out of a side turning.

Rosette: An anchor fitting, rag-bolted or otherwise fixed to the face of a building, used instead of a *traction pole*. To which a *span wire* or wires was attached.

Route: The way or series of roads and streets between two points.

Running Wire: See *trolley wire*.

Section insulator: An overhead line assembly containing a short length of non-conductive material of the same profile as the *trolley wire* to break the route up into electrically isolated half-mile sections as required by law in the United Kingdom.

Service: The timetabled frequency of vehicles identified by a service number along a stipulated route.

Span wire: The load-bearing wire erected across the width of the roadway (usually between opposite or diagonally opposite *traction poles*, but sometimes anchored to buildings by a wall *rosette*) from which the trolley wires were suspended.

Top light:	A type of opening window employed in the main side bays of the lower and upper saloons of bus bodies whereby the upper portion of the window was divided vertically into two, one or both sections sliding horizontally. On earlier vehicles top lights could be found above other windows, including the driver's cab windscreen and rear platform, some being fixed and others opening inwards by use of bottom-mounted hinges.
Trackless:	See *trolleybus.*
Traction pole:	A steel tubular pole used to support bracket arms, gantries and span wires, usually about 31 ft long, set 6ft into the ground at the roadside at a 5° rake away from the road (to compensate for the weight supported) and embedded in concrete. There were four grades of pole, light, medium, heavy and extra heavy, varying in girth and used according to the weight and/or strain they were expected to carry.
Trolleybase:	The point at which the *trolleypoles* were attached to the roof or a roof-mounted gantry of the vehicle. The trolleybase enabled the *trolleypoles* to move laterally and vertically, whilst large inclined springs more or less parallel to the *trolleypoles* provided the tension necessary to keep the under-running skid or wheel in contact with running wires.
Trolleybooms:	See *trolleypoles.*
Trolleybus:	A public passenger transport vehicle with rubber tyres which travels along ordinary roads and is powered by electricity that is collected from a pair of conductor wires hung above the road by means of a under-running wheels or skids attached to sprung *trolleypoles.* Contrary to a tramcar, a trolleybus does not require tracks laid in the road surface and was accordingly initial known as a *railless.* or *trackless.*
Trolleyhead:	The retention and swivel device at the extreme end of each *trolleypole* which held the under-running current collecting skid or wheel.
Trolleypoles:	The roof mounted tubular booms which, by means of a sprung base permitting lateral and vertical movement, kept the under-running skid or wheel in contact with the running wires in order to draw current to propel the vehicle.
Trolley Vehicle:	The official term used in legislative documents for a *trolleybus.*
Trolley Wire:	The conductor wire along which the under-running wheels or skids ran. The pair of wires were kept laterally apart and suspended about 20 ft above the surface of the road. The wire nearest the centre of the road had positive polarity and that nearest the edge of the road had negative polarity.
Twin line hanger:	A spacer assembly designed to clamp the two *trolley wires* the correct distance apart (generally 2ft) when supported by *bracket arm* or *span wire.* The *trolley wire* itself was held by "ears" bolted to and insulated from the hanger assembly.
Turning circle:	An arrangement in the overhead line to turn vehicles back along the route by means of a U-turn.
Wheel trim:	An ornamental pressed steel ring, normally chromium plated, fitted over the exterior face of the wheel hub. Also referred to as. *dress rings.*

Abbreviations

The following abbreviations are used in the text:

AA	Anti-Attrition Metal Co. Ltd.
ABEJR	Ambergate, Nottingham, Boston and Eastern Junction Railway
AEC	Associated Equipment Company
AEU	Amalgamated Engineering Union
ARP	Air Raid Precautions
BICC	British Insulated Callender's Cables Ltd.
BoT	Board of Trade
BS	British Standard
BTH	British Thomson-Houston
BTS	British Trolleybus Society
DC	Direct Current
EMEB	East Midlands Electricity Board
FP	Feeder Pillar
GCR	Great Central Railway
GNR	Great Northern Railway
GPO	General Post Office
hp	horse power
kW	kilowatt
kWh	kilowatt-hour
LMS	London Midland and Scottish Railway
LNER	London and Northern Eastern Railway
MCW	Metropolitan-Cammell-Weymann
MCCW	Metropolitan-Cammell Carriage, Wagon and Finance Company
MGOC	Midland General Omnibus Company
MoS	Ministry of Supply
MoT	Ministry of Transport (known as the Ministry of War Transport between 1939 and 1946, and the Ministry of Transport and Civil Aviation between 1946 and 1959)

MoWT	Ministry of War Transport
MP	Member of Parliament
MPTA	Municipal Passenger Transport Association
MR	Midland Railway
MTTA	Municipal Tramways and Transport Association
N&D	Nottinghamshire and Derbyshire Traction/Tramways Co.
NCC	Nottinghamshire County Council
NCT	Nottingham City/Corporation Tramways/Transport
NDTC	Nottingham and District Tramways Co. Ltd.
NFVT	National Federation of Vehicle Trades
NJIC	National Joint Industrial Council
NSR	Nottingham Suburban Railway
NTA	National Trolleybus Association
OAP	Old Age Pensioner
pa	*per annum*
PSV	Public Service Vehicle
RTC	Regional Traffic Commissioner
RTS	Reading Transport Society
TGWU	Transport and General Workers Union
TIM	Ticket Issuing Machines Ltd.
Trent	Trent Motor Traction Co. Ltd.
UDC	Urban District Council
UK	United Kingdom

At various points in the text use has been made of a standard code (which will be familiar to enthusiasts) when referring to the type of body and seating capacity of a particular type of trolleybus. The code usually consists of two figures separated by an oblique stroke to indicate, respectively the upper and lower-deck seating capacity. Letters are prefixed to indicate body type and suffixed to indicate doorway positions. The elements of this code used in connection with Nottingham's trolleybuses are as follows:

Prefix letter(s): B Single-deck bus
H Highbridge double-deck layout i.e. with centre as opposed to side gangway in upper saloon.
Figures: Indicate the number of seats in the upper and lower saloons respectively.
Suffix letter(s): C Centre doorway position.
D Dual-doorway vehicle; both the ex-Southend-on-Sea purchases and the Glasgow demonstrator featured entry at the rear and exit through the forward doorway.
R Rear doorway with open platform.
OS Open staircase.

For example, Karrier E6s 51-60 (TV9307-16) were H34/30R, i.e. highbridge bodywork with 34 seats upstairs, 30 seats downstairs and a single rear doorway.

Conversion Factors: Units and Currency

During the period in which the trolleybuses operated, Britain used Imperial units of measure and pre-decimal currency. These traditional units are used throughout this book as no useful purpose would be served in providing conversions in the text. The following table will be of use to readers wishing to convert any figures quoted to metric units and decimal currency.

Length: 1 inch (in) = 25.4 millimetres (mm)
1 foot (ft) = 12 inches = 30.5 centimetres (cm)
1 yard = 3 feet = 91.4 centimetres
1 chain = 22 yards = 20.1 metres (mt)
1 furlong = 10 chains = 22 yards = 201 metres
1 mile = 8 furlongs = 1.6 kilometres (km)
Area: 1 acre = 4,840 square yards = 4,046.86 square metres
Weight: 1 quarter (qtr) = 127 kilogrammes (kgs)
1 hundredweight (cwt) = 4 quarters = 50.8 kgs
1 imperial ton = 20 hundredweights (cwt) = 1.02 metric tonnes
Currency: 1 penny (d) = 0.416 pence (p)
1 shilling (s) = 12d = 5 pence (p)
1 pound (£) = 20 shillings (s) = 240d = 100p

Chapter 1

Setting the Scene

Nottingham is the largest centre of population in England's East Midlands located at the southeast corner of the extensive Derbyshire, Nottinghamshire and Yorkshire coalfield, which provides the eastern boundary of the Pennines, where it meets the agricultural uplands of Leicestershire, Lincolnshire, Northamptonshire and Rutland gently sloping to the east. The two dissimilar areas are separated by the flood plain of the Trent, a river that rises in the Southern Pennines and flows north-eastwards to enter the North Sea through the Humber Estuary. Easy waterborne communications, a river crossing point where a cliff above the Trent providing a defensible site and a plentiful supply of soft well water ensured the early location for industries to develop.

Human beings settled in Nottinghamshire thousands of years ago, indeed excavations at Creswell Crags, a group of limestone caves some 25 miles north of Nottingham, have revealed continuous human occupation from 40,000 – 28,000 BC whilst Iron Age relics have been found beneath today's City.

The Romans colonised the immediate area but there is nothing to suggest that there was a Roman town although there were undoubtedly individual houses, small settlements and forts within a few miles distance. Several Roman roads crossed the surrounding countryside but none passed through today's Nottingham.

In the 6th century the Saxons settled in *Snotingaham*, the "ham" indicating that this was the home of a man bearing the unfortunate name of Snot, but its development is more likely to stem from the arrival of the Danes in 877. The settlement, on a steep outcrop overlooking the lower reaches of the River Lean and the marshy Trent floodplain, developed into a fortified borough covering about 39 acres in the area known later as the Lace Market. In 918 the Saxons recaptured it but some Danish influence survived most obviously in certain street names such as "*gata*" or "*gate*", meaning street. The settlement grew initially in the east around Barker Gate and then northwards bordered by ramparts roughly encompassing Fletcher Gate, Goose Gate and Carter Gate, with sandstone cliffs to the south.

By the time of the Norman Conquest the settlement had grown into a modest semi-agricultural town with a population approaching 1,000. The Normans constructed a wooden fortress in 1067-68 on a rocky ridge, a little to the west of the established Saxon borough, thus sparing the Saxon population the loss of property which generally accompanied the Norman army of occupation's castle building. A new Norman borough grew up in the shelter of the castle, leaving the Saxons largely undisturbed on St. Mary's Hill. This situation resulted in Nottingham developing twin French and English boroughs, in peaceful coexistence and with different legal customs, both under Norman protection. In the shallow valley between the two settlements the Market Square was established.

In 1155 King Henry II granted the town a Charter, which recognised it as a borough with the privilege of holding a market for traders from Nottinghamshire and Derbyshire. This market soon became a focal point of town life. At certain times of the year, often coinciding with pilgrimages or local festivals, it would become a fair, attracting people from far and wide. This royal patronage increased Nottingham's prosperity and it became important enough for Richard I and Edward III to hold parliaments there.

Over the following centuries, the wooden castle was rebuilt in stone and its fortifications and accommodation were improved. Politically, Nottingham Castle represented the monarch's power base in the Midlands and North, as it controlled the bridge over the River Trent, where a major road to the north crossed the river. Socially, the castle was a favourite royal residence throughout the medieval period as it provided access to Sherwood Forest, famous for the legends of Robin Hood, and for hunting.

In medieval times the town walls ran roughly along today's Park Row and Parliament Street whilst industry was characterised by cloth manufacture and dyeing. By 1449, Nottingham's population had risen to about 3,000, a sizeable number for those times, and King Henry VI granted the town it's Great Charter, elevating it to "Town and County of the same Town", and making it independent of Nottinghamshire.

During the Civil War, Charles I raised the Royal Standard in Nottingham in August 1642 to rally support. However, the town remained loyal to Parliament throughout the conflict although it did not play an important role. In 1651, with the Civil War over, the Parliamentarians destroyed much of the castle as part of their policy to denude the country of all fortifications.

In 1720 Daniel Defoe described Nottingham as *"one of the most pleasant and beautiful towns in England"* yet half a century later the influx of frame knitters to serve the growing hosiery industry had been so great that housing conditions were described as *"hardly to be surpassed in misery by anything to be found within the entire range of our manufacturing towns"*. The flow of workers continued throughout the century and was encouraged further when in 1768 Richard Arkwright, who had developed a water-powered cotton spinning and carding machine producing a stronger yarn and requiring less physical labour, moved from Lancashire to Nottingham in an effort to avoid machine-breakers. The fears of mechanisation soon followed Arkwright; Nottingham's Industrial Revolution of the late 18th and early 19th century becoming closely associated with the Luddite rioting amongst hosiery workers. Rioters smashed the knitting frames and spinning machines, which they blamed for their plight.

Prosperity, albeit short-lived, returned in the early 1820s when the hosiers, stimulated by the efforts of Flemish immigrants, turned their attention to knitting other materials and Nottingham rapidly developed into the largest lace-making centre in the world, the streets in the area to the west of Lower Parliament Street, now known as the Lace Market, being lined with towering Victorian lace warehouses.

Attracted by the chance to work in the new industries, the population grew almost six-fold between 1750 and 1850 to around 57,000. But with no increase in the residential area, resulting in Nottingham changing from a spacious market town into an overcrowded health hazard. The overcrowding was primarily due to the continued existence of large tracts of common land or grazing pastures, jealously protected by leading townsmen, in the area beyond the old city walls. This situation continued until the Municipal Reform Act 1835 forced them to relinquish their rights and the Enclosure Acts 1839 allowed development of the erstwhile common land. Extensive areas of terraced housing, such as the appropriately named Meadows, were rapidly developed, only to become the slums of a later era, and by the time the borough boundary was extended in 1877, much of the freed land had already been built on.

The appalling overcrowding of the workers' "back-to-back housing" and the lack of sanitation led to the Royal Commission on the State of Large Towns and Populous Districts targeting Nottingham in its investigations of 1844/45. The high population density suffered from a lack of clean water, daylight, fresh air and proper sanitation, and ensured that cholera broke out frequently until 1865. The construction of such housing was prohibited from 1845, although many examples survived until the slum clearances of the 1920s and 1930s. William Booth born in Sneinton in 1829 said it was witnessing the *"degradation and helpless misery of the poor stockingers of my native town"* which led him to found the Salvation Army.

Understandably, the population over spilled into the surrounding area, particularly the villages north and west of Nottingham, such as Basford, Bulwell, Lenton and Radford, along the River Lean. Located next to a ready source of running water for the mills and closer to the coalfield, these villages became more and more industrialised, with frame knitting for the hosiery trade and lace manufacture being most prominent.

In 1845 further Enclosure Acts released some 600 acres for housing, attention being paid to the construction of semi-detached housing and the retention of some green space, notably the Arboretum. Nonetheless new housing began to fill the open spaces between the surrounding villages and industrial satellites, the municipal boundaries being extended in 1877 to bring these areas under unitary control.

New industries widened Nottingham's prosperity although the lace industry continued to flourish with exports peaking in 1906. Raleigh Cycles and the tobacconist John Player built factories in the late 19th century whilst Jesse Boot, later Lord Trent, built up his business from a family herbalist's shop in Goose Gate to a national chain of chemists and lending libraries.

Throughout urban England a steadily growing population and the birth of industrialisation called for improved communications. The Great North Road running some 20 miles east of Nottingham became the main road to the north in the days of the stagecoach, the post for Nottingham being

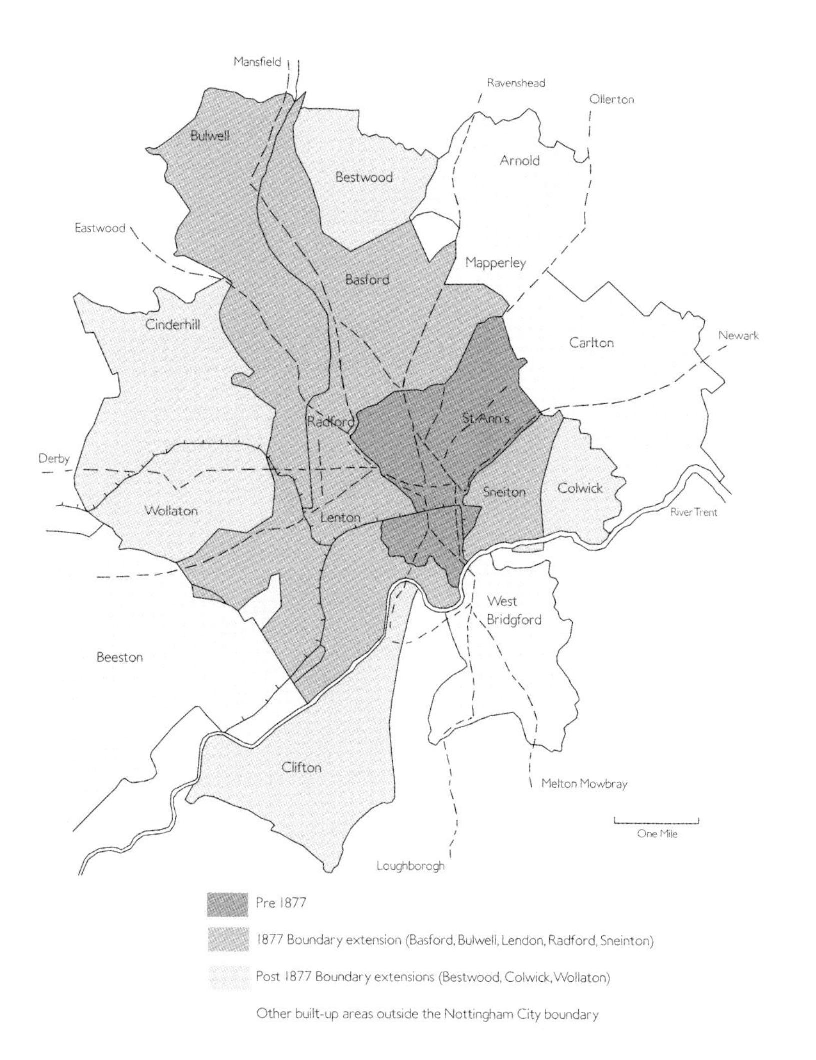

delivered from Newark. Nottingham was already a noted river port by the 14th century. By the 18th and early 19th century goods were conveyed from Nottingham to the Humber Estuary for South Yorkshire or London, and to the Fossedyke for the port of Boston for onward shipment to London and France. The growth of the railways led to a decline of river traffic but dredging, and the construction of locks and weirs at the end of the 19th century, enabled powered vessels with cargoes of up to 150 tons to reach Nottingham.

Coal mines appeared in the area as early as the late 13th century, those at Wollaton proving particularly profitable, and towards the end of the 16th century Sir Francis Willoughby built a wooden wagonway from his Wollaton coal pits to Nottingham, thereby financing the construction of Wollaton Hall. Over the ensuing years a number of wagonways and tramways were built linking the collieries with wharfs on the navigable River Trent and later the canals.

In 1778 the Erewash Canal opened, linking the area around Langley Mill with the Rivers Soar and Trent at Long Eaton, just seven miles upstream of Nottingham. Six miles further southwest, at Shardlow, the Trent and Mersey Canal offered a through route to the Black Country and Liverpool, whilst the Soar Navigation provided waterborne access to Leicester. The success of the Erewash Canal led to calls for an extension to the mines further north and the Cromford Canal opened in 1794. Nottingham colliery owners became increasingly anxious about these new competitors to the west and promoted a 14¾ mile long canal between Nottingham and Langley Mill. The Nottingham Canal, which left the River Trent just downstream of Trent Bridge and followed the course of London Road into the city before turning west through Lenton and along the eastern edge of Wollaton Park, opened in April 1796. By then work had started on the Beeston Cut, from the River Trent at Beeston to Lenton where it joined the Nottingham Canal, enabling barges to by-pass shallows near Clifton Grove and the difficult to navigate old Trent Bridge. The Grantham Canal, which joined the Trent immediately opposite the entrance to the Nottingham Canal, opened in 1797, giving local colliery owners and other industrialists access to further new markets.

The canals made the transport of bulk goods efficient and reliable, over greater distances than ever before, contributing to Nottingham becoming a flourishing industrial centre but the colliery owners became increasingly frustrated by the canals' monopoly status and tolls. This led them to finance construction of the Midland Counties Railway between Derby and Rugby, where it joined the London and Birmingham Railway, with a branch from Long Eaton to Nottingham which opened on 30 May 1839. The waterways immediately lost traffic and from 1840 the Nottingham Canal began to reduce its rates. There was great competition between the Midland Counties Railway and the Birmingham and Derby Railway for the lucrative coal traffic to London and to avoid bankruptcy, the two companies, together with the North Midland Railway, merged in 1844 to form the Midland Railway (MR). As its receipts continued to fall, in May 1845 the Nottingham Canal opened negotiations with the Ambergate, Nottingham, Boston and Eastern Junction Railway (ANBEJR) resulting in the Railway offering to buy both the Grantham and Nottingham Canals once it started operations.

Initially the sole railway connection between Nottingham and London was via Derby using the MR but in 1852 the Great Northern Railway (GNR) opened its East Coast mainline through Grantham where a junction was made with the ANBEJR. There was now an alternative route and competition for traffic to the metropolis. The first direct route to London was the MR's Nottingham – Melton Mowbray – Oakham – Kettering line which opened for goods traffic on 1 November 1879 although express passenger services did not commence until 1 June 1880.

In January 1855 the ANBEJR took over the Grantham and Nottingham Canals, whilst in 1861 it was absorbed into the GNR. Thereafter canal traffic declined dramatically, commercial traffic finally ceasing on the Grantham Canal in 1929, on the Nottingham Canal in 1937, on the Cromford in 1944, on the Erewash in the late 1940s.

In 1893, the Manchester, Sheffield and Lincolnshire Railway started construction of a new mainline commencing at Annesley, 12 miles north of Nottingham, and terminating at London Marylebone. Its dynamic General Manager, Edward Watkin built as direct a route as possible, laid out to the continental loading gauge with the intent of providing a through route to the Continent by way of the South Eastern Railway and a Channel Tunnel. This direct route gave the company its new name, the Great Central Railway (GCR), but also involved considerable demolition work in the middle of Nottingham. The line lanced directly through the city centre, the impressive Victoria Station laying in a cutting in a cleared slum area, with tunnels at each end of the platforms running south as far as Weekday Cross and north to Carrington. Britain's "last mainline" opened for coal traffic in July 1898 with express passenger services between London and Sheffield commencing in March 1899 and Nottingham Victoria opening on 24 May 1900. Thereafter the GNR ceased to use its London Road station and extended its services into Victoria Station ensuring connections to a wide selection of destinations.

The heavily engineered 3¼ mile long Nottingham Suburban Railway (NSR) was opened in 1889 between Basford and Netherfield (Trent Lane Junction), both on the GNR, mainly to serve Mapperley and Thorneywood brickworks, but with intermediate stations at Daybrook, Thorneywood, St. Ann's Well and Sherwood to provide a commuter service into the city. It was worked from the outset by the GNR. Thus by 1900 Nottingham was well served by railways, Bulwell for example having four stations: Bulwell Market (MR), Basford & Bulwell and Bulwell Forest (both GNR), and Bulwell Common (GCR), and a halt Bulwell Hall (GCR) whilst by 1910 three lines ran north in parallel from Basford to Sutton-in-Ashfield.

Urban passenger transport first appeared on Nottingham's streets in 1848 when horse buses were introduced between the "Maypole Inn" (later the site of the "Black Boy Hotel") in Long Row East and the Midland Station to connect with train arrivals and departures, and from the "Unicorn Inn", on the corner of Milton Street and Upper Parliament Street, to Arnold five times daily. Buses and carrier's carts to nearby towns and villages also carried local passengers within the suburbs for a negotiated fare. By 1853 services had started between the "Black Boy" and Arnold, and the "Shoulder of Mutton", Smithy Row, and Beeston and Bingham, both hostelries also serving as the terminus for services to outlying towns and villages.

A group of local businessmen formed the Nottingham and District Tramways Co. Ltd. (NDTC) in 1875 to bring rail-born street transport to the city and its suburbs. They were authorised by the Nottingham and District Tramways Order 1877 to construct and operate tramways in Nottingham and the then independent suburbs of Basford, Lenton and Radford.

The horse tramways opened on 17 September 1878 with a 4ft 8½ins gauge line from St. Peter's Square, some 150 yards south of the Market Place, running southwards along Albert Street, Lister Gate and Carrington Street to the Midland Station where there was a junction. One tramway continued along Arkwright Street to Trent Bridge and the other followed the length of Station Street to terminate at the junction with London Road opposite the GNR station. In August 1879 another line was opened from Long Row East on the north side of the Market Place, then up the steep gradient of Market Street, along Upper Parliament Street to Milton Street and Mansfield Road to the junction with Watcombe Road, Carrington. There was no link between the two lines. By the end of 1879 the NDTC was running 20 tramcars, using 192 horses and carrying around 55,000 passengers per week.

Thereafter the following horse tramways were opened, between Market Place and Basford (Church Street) via Derby Road and Alfreton Road in June 1881, and Alfreton Road and Mansfield Road via Forest Road, in September 1881. The Basford terminus was located at the junction of Church Street with Radford Road just south of Basford (MR) railway station, the track being at the side of the road next to the gas works' wall. The Forest Road line was initially served by through cars running between the Market Place and Mansfield Road but this was curtailed later date to a single deck car shuttling between the Basford and Carrington routes.

The NDTC operated services along 7 miles 40 chains of double track and 3 miles of single track (Board of Trade (BoT) annual returns 1887-97) and owned a total of 46 different trams during its lifetime although it would appear that there were never more than 38 cars in the fleet at any one time. A single Wilkinson steam tram "dummy" locomotive with a top-covered bogie trailer ran on the Basford service 1883-1889; thereafter the trailer was converted into a smaller 4-wheel car and the system reverted to horse operation. Each service was identified by a unique colour scheme and the terminal points were listed above the saloon windows: cars on the Station Street and Trent Bridge services were painted yellow, Carrington and Forest Road cars red, and Basford cars blue. A green livery was applied to summer toastrack cars.

As the horse tramways flourished a network of urban horse bus services sprang up serving other areas which did not warrant construction of a tramway. By 1899 there were services to Arnold, Basford, Bulwell, Carlton, Colwick, Lenton, St. Anne's Well Road, West Bridgford and Wilford. As illustrations, St. Anne's Well Road was served by ten different operators offering a combined seven minutes service whilst the horse buses between St. Peter's Square and West Bridgford ran every ten minutes. The NDTC also operated horse bus services between the Market Place and Gawthorne Street, New Basford, and along Vernon Road to connect Basford tram terminus with Bulwell Market Place every 30 minutes.

In 1897, Queen Victoria's Diamond Jubilee year, Nottingham, with a population approaching 240,000, was elevated in status from "Town and County of that Town" to "City and County of that City". The Corporation decided to exercise its powers under the 1877 Act to purchase the NDTC as a going concern at the end of its 21-year term, 23 July 1898. This was provided for in the Tramways Act 1870 whereby a local authority could require a company tramway promoter to sell them the undertaking within 6 months of the expiry of 21 years from the date upon which the promoters had been granted construction powers. Agreement was reached to take over operations early, on 16 October 1897, for the sum of £80,000, the purchase comprising all track, 3 depots and 316 horses, 37 tramcars and 14 omnibuses.

The only immediate changes were the introduction of a uniform maroon and cream livery, improved employees' working conditions and the opening of a tramways head office in Exchange Walk. Alfred Baker, the NDTC Manager remained as the Corporation Tramway's first General Manager. Under the Nottingham Improvement Act 1897 the new Nottingham Corporation Tramways (NCT) were granted powers to use mechanical propulsion but for the time being horse traction remained whilst Mr Baker prepared his proposals for conversion.

By spring 1898 the newly constituted Tramways Committee had decided to double the single track sections of the horse tramways and extend the Basford and Carrington lines to Bulwell Market Place and Winchester Street, Sherwood respectively. After further deliberations they agreed on a number of additional routes:

1. Mansfield Road, Carrington – Gregory Boulevard – Sherwood Rise – Nottingham Road (Vernon Road)
2. Upper Parliament Street – Lower Parliament Street – King Edward Street – St. Ann's Well Road – The Wells Road (St. Bartholomew Road)
3. Lister Gate (Carrington Street) – Greyfriar Gate (outbound)/Canal Street (inbound) – Castle Boulevard – Lenton Boulevard – Radford Boulevard (Hartley Road)
4. Castle Boulevard – Wilford Street – Wilford Road – Wilford Bridge
5. Mansfield Road (Milton Street) – Woodborough Road – Mapperley Plains (Porchester Road)
6. Market Place – Wheeler Gate – St. Peter's Square (linking the two horse car systems)

On 3 October 1898 the City Council resolved to promote a Parliamentary Bill including all the above extensions although no decision as to the form of motive power had been reached. Amongst other things, the Nottingham Corporation Act 1899 authorised construction of over 14 miles of new tramways and the use of electrical power. Following the publication of a number of newspaper articles promoting cable traction, the Tramway Committee wavered in its enthusiasm for the overhead trolley system of electric traction and deputations visited Edinburgh's cable tramways. Still undecided, the City Engineer and Electrical Engineer were despatched on a fact-finding mission to the USA in April 1899.

Based on their visits to nine tramway networks embracing travelling cable operation, and the underground conduit and the overhead trolley system of electric power collection, a report, relating US experience to future developments in Nottingham, was presented to the City Council on 11 September 1899. Although the two engineers favoured the underground conduit system they realised that it was neither affordable nor suitable for Nottingham. They argued that the demand for cheap fares and the high cost of conduit construction would result in uneconomic electric tramways. Citing Glasgow, Hull, Leeds, Liverpool, Manchester and Sheffield they added that *"The Overhead Trolley System is the most widely adopted, the most economical, and its status has most clearly been determined"*. The Tramways and Electricity Committees jointly decided on 2 October 1899 that the overhead trolley system was best for Nottingham. The General Works and Highways Committee would conduct all street work under the direction of the Tramways Committee. Electric power would initially be supplied from Talbot Street power station but a new generating station, purpose built for tramway traction power, would be constructed on a site acquired by the Council near the Old Gaol.

Tenders were invited for electric tramcars, equipment and track work but at this stage Mr Baker resigned to take up the challenging new post of Chief Officer with the London County Council Tramways, who were also planning a major conversion of the horse tramways in their area to electric traction. He was succeeded by John Aldworth who had been Manager of the pioneer Isle of Man Tramways & Electric Power Co. Ltd.

Treading carefully, the tender of Dick, Kerr & Co. for 12 double-deck open-top 4-wheel electric trams was accepted and thoughts turned to the conversion of the Market Place – Carrington route and its northwards extension along Mansfield Road to Winchester Street, Sherwood where a new purpose built depot was constructed. The prevailing national boom in tramway construction led Dick, Kerr to warn that their workload was such that they could only guarantee to deliver tramcars in 1901 if firm orders were placed by January 1900. This prompted the Corporation to increase their order to 25 and subsequently to 57 cars although delivery proved slow.

Test runs began on 17 November 1900 and a successful Board of Trade (BoT) inspection on 16 December 1900 heralded the public opening on 1 January 1901 with a tram every five minutes between the Market Place and Sherwood at a fare of 2d.

The system expanded rapidly: by the end of 1901 there were 67 electric trams operating and by 1903 the fleet had grown to 105 trams which covered 2,117,000 miles and carried 24,552,000 passengers pa.

The last horse cars ran on the Forest Road line, which was never converted to electric traction, on 30 April 1902. On the same date operation of the Corporation's remaining horse

The "Nottingham Evening Post" recorded:

"After a delay of more than 2 months, the Market Place to Sherwood section of the new Nottingham electric tramways was opened for public use this morning and, in spite of the inclement weather, the cars were very extensively patronised. The first car was timed to leave Sherwood at 7.15, a large crowd assembled to witness its departure and enjoy the novelty of the first journey. Indeed it would have been quite possible to fill four cars with the people anxious to travel. For some time afterwards there was a falling off in the demand, due entirely to the rain, but with the weather clearing up at dinner time there was again a great rush. From every point of view the opening of the section marks a vast improvement upon the old order. The length of the journey has been extended from Carrington Church to Winchester Street, Sherwood, the fares are arranged upon a cheaper basis, the service of cars has been reduced from one every 7 minutes to one every 5 minutes, and the hours of running have been extended. In the future the first car will leave Sherwood at 07.15 am and the last at 10.55 pm while from the Market Place end the respective times are to be 7.35 am and 11.15pm. Nine cars each capable of accommodating 56 passengers – 22 inside and 34 outside – are in use, and it will be seen that an average of 20 minutes is allowed for each journey".

bus services were taken over by a private operator who continued to run them until 1910. Thereafter the growth of the electric tramway network slowed and by 1910 was limited to short extensions of existing routes further into the suburbs.

Market Place – Chapel Bar – Derby Road – Alfreton Road – Bentinck Road – Radford Road – Basford – Bulwell Market Place (horse tramway conversion and extension), 23 July 1901.

Market Place – St. Peter's Square – Albert Street – Lister Gate – Carrington Street – Arkwright Street – Trent Bridge (horse tramway conversion and extension), 21 October 1901

Carrington Street – Station Street – London Road (horse tramway conversion), 21 October 1901

Market Place – Upper Parliament Street – Lower Parliament Street – King Edward Street – St. Ann's Well Road – The Wells Road (St. Bartholomew Road) (replacing a horse bus service), 21 February 1902

Mansfield Road (Milton Street) – Woodborough Road – Mapperley Plains (Porchester Road), 13 May 1902

Mansfield Road, Carrington – Gregory Boulevard – Sherwood Rise – Nottingham Road (Vernon Road), 7 July 1902

Lister Gate (Carrington Street) – Greyfriar Gate – Castle Boulevard – Lenton Boulevard – Radford Boulevard (Hartley Road) (replacing horse bus services over parts of the route), 30 September 1902

Castle Boulevard – Wilford Street – Wilford Road – Wilford Bridge (replacing a horse bus service), 20 November 1902

Bentinck Road (Alfreton Road) – Hartley Road (Radford Boulevard) (creating a circular route around the Boulevards), 30 July 1903

King Edward Street – Bath Street – Southwell Road – Manvers Street – Sneinton Hermitage – Colwick Road, 14 March 1907

Manvers Street – Pennyfoot Street – London Road – Trent Bridge, 14 March 1907

Southwell Road (Bath Street) – Carlton Road – Standhill Road, 16 December 1910

Church Street, Basford (Radford Road) – Percy Street – Stockhill Lane – Dark Lane – Nuthall Road – Cinderhill (operated by the Nottinghamshire & Derbyshire Tramways Co.), 1 January 1914

Standhill Road – Carlton Hill – Carlton, 14 June 1914

Alfreton Road (Zion Hill) – Derby Road – Lenton – Gregory Street, 25 September 1914

Sherwood (Winchester Street) – Mansfield Road – Daybrook Square – Nottingham Road – Front Street – Arnold, 1 January 1915

Mapperley (Porchester Road) – Mapperley Plains – Mapperley (Westdale Lane), 7 June 1926

Gregory Street – Derby Road – Wollaton Park Lodge Gates, 15 April 1927

Rather than terminate all services at the Market Place by 1903 through cars ran Bulwell – Trent Bridge, Mapperley – Trent Bridge, Nottingham Road – Lenton and Sherwood – Station Street (Trent Bridge on Sundays). The most remunerative route was that to Trent Bridge with annual receipts of £7,399 1s 2d per single track mile. The fleet grew progressively to 125 trams in 1908, 155 in 1914 and finally 200 in 1927, not a single car being disposed of until 1931. Two further tram depots were built at Bulwell and Trent Bridge in 1901, both of which survived through the trolleybus era and beyond.

In October 1908 the Vice Chairman of the Tramways Committee provoked discussion as to the use of "Trackless trolley vehicles as used on the Continent" and mentioned how other British local authorities were carrying out evaluations but the matter was deferred.

The 16 February 1912 edition of "The Light Railway and Tramway Journal" recorded that *"at a dinner held in the Arboretum Rooms to celebrate the "coming of age" of the Nottingham branch of the Amalgamated Society of Tramway and Vehicle Workers, Councillor R.H. Swain, Chairman of the Tramways Committee, made an interesting reference to the possibility of introducing the new railless trams into the city. He said he was making a special study of the system, and intended visiting every town where the railless trams were working. He could not make any definite announcements at this juncture, but there was reason to hope that the new system might be introduced into Nottingham when the existing system required extension".*

The Town Clerk reported to the 2 April 1912 Tramways Committee meeting that existing legislation gave the BoT no powers to grant a Provisional Order to enable tramway authorities to operate trams (sic) on the trackless trolley system. A Parliamentary Bill was the only means of acquiring permission. The Municipal Tramways Association had informed the Committee that the BoT had submitted a general Bill into Parliament to amend the Light Railways Act to include trackless trolley vehicles. If passed this would authorise the Light Railway Commissioners to grant Provisional Orders empowering tramway authorities to equip and work trackless trolley systems. The Tramways Committee supported this move and requested that the Town Clerk write to the City's MPs asking them to support passage of the Bill in Parliament. However when the Light Railways Bill was enacted in 1912 it concentrated on financial matters and did not include the hoped-for authorisation, indeed apart from the period of the Second World War, a local Act of Parliament remained necessary for the construction of any trolley vehicle route throughout the trolleybus era.

Meanwhile, another trackless trolley proposal was being mooted to the south of Nottingham. West Bridgford was a small residential community, virtually an independent suburb, on the southern boundary of Nottingham, across the River Trent, whose transport needs were inevitably linked to those of the neighbouring city. Horse buses operated along Musters Road and to Lady Bay, off Radcliffe Road, whilst in 1911 Barton Bros had considered introducing motorbus services. In January 1912 West Bridgford Urban District Council (WBUDC) negotiated with a Mr E.L. Fleetwood of London to provide motorbus services in the District subject to a 21-year monopoly clause but although approval was granted, he decided not to proceed. By June 1912 a motor landaulette was operating scheduled journeys on Radcliffe Road.

Although Nottingham Corporation had assured the UDC earlier in the year that they had no plans to commence services to West Bridgford, on 5 November 1912 Nottingham's Tramways General Manager John Aldworth reported to the Tramways Committee as to the possibilities of running motor buses or trackless trolleys in the District to connect with the Corporation's trams at Trent Bridge. They resolved to promote a Parliamentary Bill and appointed a subcommittee to meet the WBUDC on 8 November 1912. The Bus Service Subcommittee of WBUDC's General Purposes Committee, by then in the final stages of preparing a Parliamentary Bill to run their own motor buses, were surprised to learn of Nottingham's proposals to run services into West Bridgford. The Nottingham representatives made it clear that they would object to any WBUDC plans to run its own bus services. This led the WBUDC to immediately contact their parliamentary agent and they rapidly reconfirmed their intent of promoting their own Bill in the ensuing session.

On 12 November 1912 the Nottingham Tramways Committee resolved to seek powers to reach, by way of West Bridgford, Nottingham's Southern Cemetery in the Parish of South Wilford. WBUDC's parliamentary agent had established that until 20 November 1912 the UDC could object to Nottingham's aspirations by filing a Parliamentary Notice and still promote its own Bill by 17 December 1912. The agent was only aware of one case in which an authority had been given powers to run in an adjoining authority's district and he was optimistic that the UDC would succeed. As Nottingham proposed to run over Trent Bridge into West Bridgford, he recommended that WBUDC should also apply to run over Trent Bridge into Nottingham. He went on that "in view of the residential character of the district, its good and level road, the district is one in which the trolley system should not be introduced" and he suggested that *"the application should be for motorbuses".* The UDC's opportunity to operate trolley vehicles was thus lost.

The Nottingham Town Clerk wrote to WBUDC to inform them that the Corporation would proceed with a Bill to obtain powers to run trolley vehicles and requested the UDC to inform him as to the manner in which public notices should be posted along the proposed routes. The Clerk to the West Bridgford UDC responded on 16 November 1912 with his Council's views. Within the WBUDC it was noted that as they proposed to operate motor buses without tracks or trolleys there was no necessity to post notices along the intended routes.

At a public meeting attended by some 300 people held at the Exchange Hall on 3 January 1913, the Mayor, Thomas Ward; the Chairman of the Tramways Committee, Councillor R.H. Swain and the Town Clerk, Mr A.J. Board, explained the proposals contained in the Nottingham Corporation Bill 1913. It was explained that powers were sought for *"The provision of a trolley vehicle system for the running of trackless motor vehicles to serve the West Bridgford District and the new Southern Cemetery. The system will start on Beastmarket Hill, in the Great Market Place, and thence run via Wheeler Gate, Albert Street, Lister Gate, Carrington Street, Arkwright Street, and London Road over Trent Bridge into West Bridgford.*

From the City Boundary three lines will run, videlicit (namely):

(a) Along the Radcliffe Road, Holme Road, and Trent Boulevard as far as Adbolton Avenue.
(b) Along Bridgford Road, Musters Road, and Chaworth Road to Loughborough Road
(c) Along Loughborough Road as far as the new Southern Cemetery on Wilford Hill".

The plan was to operate trolley vehicles from the Market Place to West Bridgford along Arkwright Street, paralleling the busy tram route, and over Trent Bridge. In 1913 and indeed until the 1951 boundary revision in connection with the acquisition of the Clifton Estate, parts of the south bank of the River Trent opposite Meadow Lane, Trent Bridge and Victoria Embankment, were within the City of Nottingham. This included the site of the present-day Nottingham County Council (NCC) County Hall and Nottingham Forest Football Ground, together with a number of sports grounds (but not the Nottinghamshire County Cricket Ground). The boundary then lay just north of the junction with Radford Road. Once in the area of West Bridgford UDC, three routes would have fanned out to the east and south.

The Bill, which included a variety of topics other than public transport, also sought approval for a tramway extension along Derby Road from the existing Alfreton Road line at Zion Hill (known later as Canning Circus), through Lenton Sands, crossing and connecting with the Lenton Boulevard tramway and terminating at Wollaton Park Lodge Gates. Other tramway extensions requested were from Bulwell Market toward Hucknall Torkard (part of which was later to become the Bulwell Hall Estate trolleybus route); from Mansfield Road, Carrington along Hucknall Road as far as Bagthorpe Hospital (later Nottingham City Hospital); and from Southwell Road along Sneinton Road to Sneinton Dale. An extension of time was sought in the bill, for the purchase of land and the construction of tramways authorised by the Nottinghamshire and Derbyshire Tramways Acts 1903 and 1908 but which were to be constructed by the Corporation, that is the Basford – Cinderhill line, and due to expire in August 1913. Furthermore the Corporation sought the right to run motor buses anywhere in the city, along the proposed trackless trolley vehicle route and any other route in West Bridgford agreed on between the Corporation and the UDC, and additionally beyond the city boundaries in Carlton along Carlton Road, Carlton Hill and Main Street East to its junction with Newgate Street; in Mansfield Road to Daybrook and thence along Nottingham Road and Front Street (both in Arnold) to its junction with Spout Lane; and along Mapperley Plains Road to its junction with Spout Lane, Mapperley. In principle the first three motor bus proposals referred to the routes of the subsequent tramways extensions to Carlton (opened 14 June 1914), Arnold (opened 1 January 1915) and Mapperley Plains (opened 7 June 1926).

West Bridgford UDC found Nottingham's moves unacceptable and promoted its own Bill to

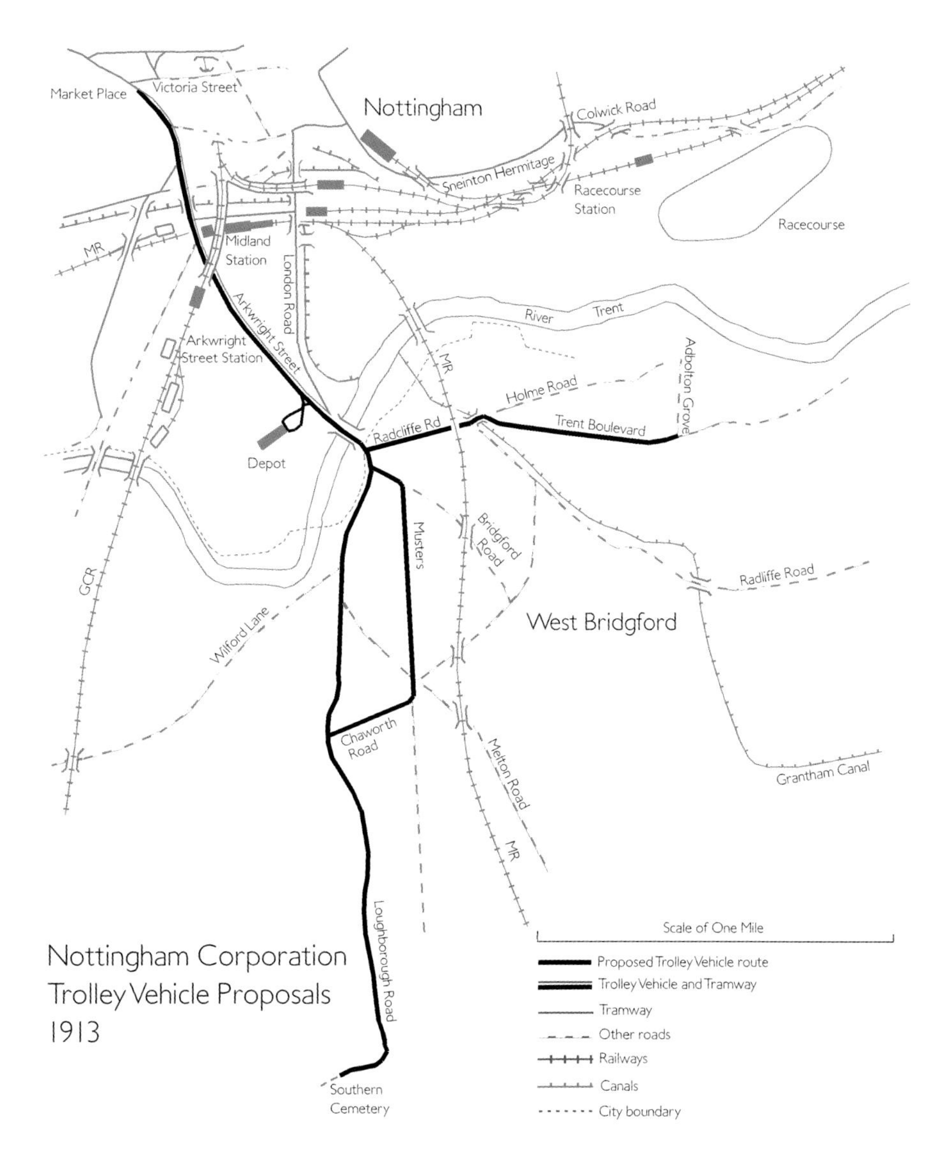

Nottingham Corporation Trolley Vehicle Proposals 1913

run motor buses within its own boundaries connecting with Nottingham's trams at their Trent Bridge terminus. In a classic example of municipal pique the Nottingham Tramways Committee resolved that the City Council should oppose the WBUDC Bill and the Town Clerk was authorised to take the necessary steps to prepare a petition in Parliament against the UDC's Bill. These opposing positions led to a further meeting between a Nottingham Tramways Subcommittee led by Councillor R.H. Swain and representatives of WBUDC. Notes from this conference are sparse but Nottingham's Tramways Committee recorded:

"In answer to certain questions from the West Bridgford UDC representatives, the Chairman of the Tramways Committee intimated the attitude which the Corporation would adopt in the event of West Bridgford withdrawing the clauses in their Bill relating to Motor Bus services and undertaking not to oppose the Bill of the Corporation. The Conference then terminated".

The Nottingham Corporation Bill was read for the first time on 12 March 1913. Both Nottinghamshire County Council (NCC) and West Bridgford UDC placed objections and although at one stage a compromise whereby NCT would have operated a trial motorbus service along Loughborough Road was discussed, no agreement could be reached. As a result all references to West Bridgford were struck out of the Bill. On 15 August 1913 Nottingham Corporation was granted trolley vehicle operating powers for those portions within the city boundaries subject to the vehicles being limited to a maximum laden weight of 5 tons. They were also granted powers to make any future applications to operate trolley vehicles along roads defined by the Tramways Act 1870 through the easier process of a BoT Provisional Order. The prime traffic purpose for Nottingham's first trolley vehicle aspirations was thus lost; no action was taken and the powers were allowed to lapse. It should be mentioned that railless electric traction in the UK was still in its infancy and if Nottingham had become an operator at this stage it would have joined a small illustrious band of undertakings which at the beginning of 1913 consisted of just Bradford, Dundee, Leeds and Rotherham Corporations.

West Bridgford UDC's Bill, granting them rights to operate motor buses both within their own boundaries and also across Trent Bridge some two hundred yards over the Nottingham boundary as far as the tram terminus was passed on 14 July 1913. As a pioneer municipal motor bus operator WBUDC commenced services on 28 January 1914 with five Dennis vehicles having Dodson double deck open-top 33-seat bodies running between Trent Bridge and Julian Road via Radcliffe Road and Trent Boulevard. A second service, between Trent Bridge and Caernarvon Road via Musters Road and Melton Road opened on 30 January 1914, whilst on 14 February 1914, a third service to North Road via Loughborough Road commenced.

As far as the tramway portions of the Nottingham Corporation Act 1913 were concerned, solely the Derby Road extension was built. The line as far as Gregory Street opened on 25 September 1914 and the extension to Wollaton Park Lodge Gates, where trams terminated on a double track reservation to the north of entrance lodge, on 15 December 1927. Trams never ran to Bulwell Hall Estate or along either Hucknall Road or Sneinton Road.

As a preliminary to constructing a tram route, NCT started to run motor buses between the Market Place and Carlton Road (Crown Hotel), just east of the junction with Thorneywood Lane at the city boundary, on 26 March 1906. Frequent mechanical breakdowns ensured that the motor buses soon received a negative reputation and gained a number of derogatory nicknames such as "The Tupenny massage". The service was withdrawn on 15 June 1908, albeit taken over by a private operator until the Carlton Road tramway opened on 16 December 1910. There were no further corporation motor buses until May 1920.

By the outbreak of the First World War Nottingham's tramways had almost reached their maximum extent with 155 tramcars operating 9 services on a 24¼ route mile network of which 1⅓ miles were leased to N&D. Thereafter short extensions to the Derby Road, Mapperley and Sherwood lines increased the length of the network to 25¾ miles by 1926 and the fleet grew commensurately to 200 cars. In 1912 service numbers began to augment and then replace the destination plates which used different coloured lettering and/or backgrounds to designate each service:

1. Trent Bridge – Arkwright Street – Market Place – Upper Parliament Street – Milton Street – Mansfield Road – Sherwood
2. Trent Bridge – Arkwright Street – Market Place – Upper Parliament Street – Milton Street – Woodborough Road – Mapperley
3. Trent Bridge – Arkwright Street – Old Market Square – Derby Road – Alfreton Road – Hyson Green – Radford Road – Vernon Road – Bulwell Market Place
4. Colwick Road – Sneinton – Bath Street – King Edward Street – Upper Parliament Street – Market Place – Derby Road – Alfreton Road – Hyson Green – Radford Road – Vernon Road – Basford
5. Nottingham Road (Vernon Road) – Mansfield Road – Milton Street – Market Place – Derby Road – Alfreton Road – Hartley Road – Lenton Boulevard – Castle Boulevard – Market Place – Upper Parliament Street – Milton Street – Mansfield Road – Nottingham Road (Vernon Road) (unidirectional)
6. St. Ann's Well Road (Ransom Road) – King Edward Street – Upper Parliament Street – Market Place – Castle Boulevard – Lenton Boulevard – Hartley Road – Alfreton Road – Derby Road – Market Place – Upper Parliament Street – King Edward Street – St. Ann's Well Road (Ransom Road) (unidirectional)
7. Wilford Bridge – Wilford Road – Market Place – Upper Parliament Street – King Edward Street – Bath Street – London Road – Trent Bridge
8. Market Place – Upper Parliament Street – King Edward Street – Bath Street – Carlton Road – Carlton (Post Office Square)

With the completion of the Derby Road extension on 25 September 1914 and the Daybrook Square – Arnold, Coppice Road extension on 1 January 1915 a further tram service was introduced:

9. Derby Road (Lenton Boulevard) – Market Place – Upper Parliament Street – Milton Street – Mansfield Road – Arnold

As far as the local railway network was concerned, the economic success of the Nottingham Suburban Railway (NSR) proved short lived; indeed by 1901 it had been severely affected by competition from the tramways to Sherwood, and the GCR's suburban services. Train services included a 10-mile long circular "outer ring" which operated Basford – Daybrook – Gedling & Carlton – Netherfield – London Road (High Level) – Victoria – Basford; however in 1916 wartime economies led to the withdrawal of passenger services. Those through passenger services which were subsequently reinstated ceased altogether in 1931. The remaining goods service (largely for bricks from the local brickyards) ended in the early 1950s, and the track was lifted.

Many other Nottingham suburban stations closed in the electric tramway or trolleybus era:

Basford & Bulwell	(GNR/LNER)	September 1964
Basford Vernon	(MR/LMS)	January 1960
Bulwell Common	(GCR/LNER)	March 1963
Bulwell Forest	(GNR/LNER)	September 1929
Bulwell Hall Halt	(GCR/LNER)	May 1930
Bulwell Market	(MR/LMS)	October 1964
Gedling and Carlton	(GNR/LNER)	4 April 1960
Radford	(MR/LMS)	October 1964
Thorneywood	(GNR/LNER)	1916
St. Anns Well	(GNR/LNER)	1916
Sherwood	(GNR/LNER)	1916

The extensive Nottinghamshire coalfield attracted tramway promoters in the early years of the twentieth century. Plans included the Erewash Valley Light Railway with an 18 mile network, the Derby and Nottingham Light Railways based on Long Eaton, and a 20 mile extension of the Mansfield & District system. All three proposals were unsuccessful and superseded by the 1902 Nottingham and Derbyshire Tramways Co. (N&D) Bill which sought a 79 mile network of standard gauge tramways based on Alfreton and Long Eaton. Included in the proposals were Alfreton – Cinderhill; Trowell – Wollaton – Nottingham; Cinderhill – Radford; Bulwell – Hucknall Torkard; Sherwood – Arnold and Sneinton – Carlton routes, all abutting or crossing the Nottingham city boundary. The last three were proposed extensions to NCT routes as they then existed: the Hucknall Torkard route never saw trams although it was, in part, covered by the Bulwell Hall Estate trolleybus line; the other two however were subsequently covered by extensions of the city tramways.

The 1903 N&D Act authorised a Hucknall-under-Huthwaite – Ripley – Belper line (which would have connected at its northern extremity with the Mansfield & District Light Railways); Alfreton – Somercotes – Pye Bridge; Swanwick – Somercotes – Pye Bridge; Ripley – Heanor – Cinderhill – Radford; Beeston – Lenton; Sherwood – Arnold and Sneinton – Carlton. Some 8½ miles of these powers were transferred to Nottingham Corporation in 1908 and of the remainder solely the 11⅜ mile Ripley – Heanor – Cinderhill section was actually built. The N&D retained the remainder of its powers until 1911 when the Hucknall-under-Huthwaite – Butterley, Ripley – Belper, Alfreton – Pye Bridge and Swanwick – Pye Bridge plans were abandoned,

No 179, an open-balcony top-covered tramcar with platform vestibules built in 1919/20 by English Electric and mounted on Preston Flexible Axle 4-wheel trucks. ***TLRS***

and 1920 when the Butterley – Ripley powers were also given up.

In early 1913 the Corporation and the N&D discussed arrangements to permit trams on the Company's Ripley – Cinderhill route, upon which construction was about to start, to continue over the city boundary and run over NCT tracks into the city centre. Construction work commenced at a number of locations along the N&D route in February 1913 and the first passenger services ran between Cinderhill and Crosshills on 7 August 1913, these being extended to Ripley on 15 August 1913. Nottingham Corporation constructed 1⅜ miles of predominantly double track tramway connecting with the NCT network at Radford Road, Basford, as far as the city boundary at the junction of Bell's Lane with Nuthall Road, Cinderhill, including a private reserved track along Dark Lane, on the N&D's behalf in the second half of 1913, the Company's services being extended to Nottingham, Upper Parliament Street on 1 January 1914, by way of Basford, Radford Road, Alfreton Road and Derby Road to a crossover just west of Theatre Square. The Basford – Cinderhill tramway remained in the Corporation's ownership throughout its life but was used only by the N&D, which paid the cost of its construction by annual rental together with a fee per passenger representing 50% of the Upper Parliament Street – Cinderhill fare for through-running powers over the city system Upper Parliament Street – Basford. No NCT tram service ever operated along the Cinderhill line.

The 15½ mile through service between Ripley and Nottingham offered the longest through tram journey in England outside London. The N&D had a depot for its 24 four-wheel double deck tramcars at Langley Mill. On 16 November 1916 the N&D assumed control of the moribund Ilkeston Corporation Tramways which ran 13 trams on a 3¾ mile, 3ft 6ins gauge system. In 1922 the N&D promoted another Bill to convert the Ilkeston lines to standard gauge and construct a 2½-mile link from the existing Heanor line to join the Ilkeston system at Shipley Common but this was never carried out.

Once the First World War was over Nottingham sought to recommence motor bus services and extended their existing general powers to operate within the city boundaries with the Nottingham Corporation Act 1920. This Act permitted the operation of their motor buses outside the city boundaries subject to the consent of the Ministry of Transport (MoT) and the local authorities concerned. Although passing reference was made to trolley vehicles no routes had been sought, whereas powers for tramway extensions along Derby Road to Beeston Road, south westwards on a cross-country reserved track to the city boundary with Beeston UDC, within Beeston, and from Highbury Road to the city boundary with Hucknall UDC were granted.

The City Engineer reported to the 2 September 1921 Tramways Committee meeting that the construction of Valley Road, a new road running north-eastwards from Basford Station to Mansfield Road, Daybrook, would require a re-grading of Nottingham Road at its junction with the new thoroughfare. He recommended that the tram rails should be renewed at that point and moved towards the centre of the road. This was followed by a proposal to widen Nottingham Road between its junction with Haydn Road, and Basford Cemetery just to the south of Valley Road, it being suggested that at the same time the existing single line and passing loop tramway should be replaced with a double track layout. This work was carried out when the road was widened, probably in 1923. As the tram track in Nottingham Road south of the junction with Haydn Road did not require relaying in the immediate future, this section was left unchanged.

Despite the expense of laying double track, the Tramways Committee were satisfied with this solution as the Nottingham Road tram route operated through a densely populated area and involved narrow streets from where it branched from Mansfield Road at Gregory Boulevard through to its terminus at Vernon Road. There was a six-minute tram service throughout the day and a five-minute service during peak hours but the single track with passing loop layout hindered time-keeping and made it impossible to operate a warranted, more frequent service.

Nottingham was not alone in its concerns about finding an economic solution to the replacement of life-expired single line and passing loop tramways in narrow city streets after the First World War. Birmingham took the brave decision to replace their urban Nechells tram service with double deck Railless trolley omnibuses and on 27 November 1922 the first conversion of a tramway to railless electric traction in the UK took place. Alfred Baker, the Birmingham General Manager, who had started his managerial career at Nottingham, presented a paper to the Municipal Tramways Association Conference in September 1923 in which he discussed the relative merits of tramways, petrol omnibuses and railless electric traction, stressing that *"for dealing with large volumes of traffic, tramways still hold the field, and there are no signs at the present time of any other system being developed which is likely to supersede them"*. Mr Baker saw the trolley omnibus as a means of developing routes for conversion to tramway operation at a later date utilising the same overhead equipment and traction supply, or as a substitute for single track and passing loop tramways where the width of the road made reconstruction with double track impossible or where traffic volumes did not warrant such an investment. Where suburban services were unlikely to be converted to tramway operation or for radial routes, he felt that the motor bus was the preferred solution.

Amongst the audience was Alderman Arthur Turney, Vice Chairman of Nottingham's Tramways Committee and at one time Chairman of the municipal Electricity Committee. In the ensuing question time he defended trolley omnibuses from negative comments such as "they would increase wear and tear on the surface of city streets" or that "maintenance of much of the width of the road, as required by the Tramways Act 1870, would cease to be the responsibility of the public transport operator". *"It will be safe to claim that the adoption of the trolley omnibus would not play such havoc with the roads, and therefore, even if some contribution were made towards the upkeep of the roads, it would not be nearly as much as in the case of tramways"*. In respect of Mr Baker's statement he added, *"the trolley omnibus gives a better and more comfortable ride than could be got with a single line of track with crossovers (sic) here and there"*.

Alderman Turney added another perspective. *"I happen to live in a very nice house, the gable end of which comes very nearly up to a single line of tramway track, and I can tell you this much, gentlemen, that the house is worth £2,000 less today than it would be if there were no single line of tramway track there at all. I would defy anyone to sleep there the first thing in the morning or the last thing at night. I am not far from a crossover (sic), and it is really impossible to sleep at these times. The other day I made an appeal against the assessment, and I may say that the Assessment Committee in Nottingham sympathised with me to such an extent that I sustained my appeal, purely on the ground that the value of the house had been destroyed as a residence by reason of the single line of tramway track and the crossover"*. Clearly the Nottingham Tramways Committee already included a trackless trolley enthusiast!

Market Square and four covered top trams seen before the building of the iconic Council House in 1929. *NCT*

The Minutes of the 14 November 1923 Tramways Committee meeting record that *"The attention of the Committee was called to the advisability of adopting the trackless system of tramways on the Nottingham Road route before proceeding with the relaying of the track as already decided upon. It was resolved that consideration of the matter be deferred to the next meeting and that in the meantime the City Engineer be asked to defer the carrying out of this work of relaying the track pending receipt of further instructions. A Subcommittee consisting of the Chairman Alderman Pendleton, Vice Chairman Councillor Radford, and Councillors Ashworth, Freckingham and Kidde was appointed to go into the suggestion and report after inspecting the trackless system in other cities"*.

By early December 1923 the City Engineer was urging a decision due to the deterioration of the tram track in the southern part of Nottingham Road. This prompted the Subcommittee to visit Birmingham on 10 January 1924 to inspect that city's Nechells trackless trolley route. Following the introduction of trolley omnibuses, receipts on that route had reportedly risen by over 50% and the vehicles had been an immediate success with the passengers, who appreciated the smooth and almost noiseless ride. Until then the BoT had been reluctant to allow double-deck buses to be top-covered but the Birmingham Corporation Act of 1922 and the introduction of the 12 top-covered Railless trackless trolley vehicles, overcame these inhibitions. The Subcommittee's report on their Birmingham visit *"recommended the adoption of the Rail-less (sic) system in lieu of all single line tramway routes in the city"*.

Mr Aldworth, Nottingham's General Manager, was authorised, in consultation with the City Engineer, to submit estimates of the cost of converting the Nottingham Road route to the "rail-less system" as soon as possible. He was also asked to investigate the advisability of operating in and out of the city along Sherwood Street, which runs almost parallel to Mansfield Road and Milton Street, with a terminus in Theatre Square.

The Town Clerk was instructed to prepare a Provisional Order to operate railless cars on the Nottingham Road, St. Ann's Well Road and Wilford Road tram routes which were of single track and passing loop construction. He was urged to obtain MoT consent for the Nottingham Road tramway conversion immediately and an exploratory meeting between the Town Clerk accompanied by Mr Aldworth, and the MoT took place in mid-February 1924. This led to a resolution to submit the Tramways Committee's proposals to the MoT as soon as possible whilst Mr Aldworth was authorised to obtain advice as to the most suitable type of vehicle for the Nottingham Road route and seek tenders for the conversion work.

The Subcommittee received two representatives of the Trackless Vehicle Company Ltd. on 16 May 1924. They stated that the Nottingham Road route was quite suitable for any of the three types of trolley vehicle recommended and that delivery would be possible within 6 months. Representatives of Railless Traction Ltd also visited Nottingham that month, however the matter was deferred until a full comparison between the costs of a conversion to railless traction and relaying the tram track was available. In early July 1924 however the Tramways Committee reviewed the alternative of using motor buses instead of trolley vehicles. This provoked questions on a general tramway abandonment, the operation of both trolley vehicles and trams along on same route, that is there would be no commitment to the MoT to remove tramlines, and a requirement that trolley vehicles should only run along the tram tracks in the crown of the road, rather than closer to the kerb on the main carriageway. Nonetheless it was resolved to adopt the Subcommittee's 3 July 1924 recommendation to convert the Nottingham Road tramway to trackless operation.

The northern portion of tram service 5 covered the route between the Market Place and a terminus at the north end of Nottingham Road at Vernon Road, a distance of 2½ miles. It followed the Mansfield Road route to Sherwood and Arnold for about one mile, as far as the junction with Gregory Boulevard, Carrington, and then branched off north westwards along the narrow Sherwood Rise and Nottingham Road. For about half a mile from Gregory Boulevard there was a continuous climb, including a gradient of 1 in 14, followed by a descent for a further half-mile at 1 in 13.

Under the Nottingham Corporation Act 1913, powers had been granted for the operation of railless trolley vehicles not exceeding 5 tons laden weight, effectively precluding the use of trolley vehicles having sufficient seating capacity to replace a double deck tramcar. The Town Clerk applied therefore in July 1924 for MoT consent to run trolley vehicles not exceeding 10 tons laden weight but in September 1924 it was learned that they were not prepared to sanction more than a maximum of 9 tons. In order to achieve their aim the Corporation had no alternative but to apply to Parliament, in the form of a Parliamentary Bill, to rescind the weight restriction clause of the 1913 Act.

The 10 October 1924 Tramways Committee meeting resolved to add provisions for railless traction into the Parliamentary Bill which *inter alia* sought extensions of the Derby Road tram route to the second lodge at Wollaton Park, built into the south side wall of the Park on Derby Road opposite today's Beeston Lane (then a main road to Beeston) and the Mapperley route along Mapperley Plains as far as Westdale Lane.

Alderman Pendleton said that the Tramways Committee had come to the conclusion that single line tramways with passing loops had seen their day, and that the trackless trolley system was the most suitable alternative for such routes. If the Corporation was successful in gaining permission to operate vehicles weighing up to 10 tons they would be able to carry 12 more passengers. Giving evidence to the parliamentary commission reviewing the Nottingham Corporation Bill 1925 and specifically the wish to repeal the weight limit in Section 13 of the 1913 Act, Birmingham's General Manager was interviewed with respect to the unladen weight of his trolley vehicles, which approached 10 tons, and any road damage that they may have caused.

The Nottingham Corporation Act 1925 granted permission for the following trolley vehicle routes:

Route A – Commencing in Vernon Road at the intersection of the centre lines of Nottingham Road and Vernon Road thence proceeding along Nottingham Road Sherwood Rise Gregory Boulevard Mansfield Road Milton Street Upper Parliament Street King Street and Queen Street and terminating at the junction of King Street with Long Row:

Route B – Commencing at the junction of King Street with Long Row thence proceeding along Long Row the Market Place South Parade and Exchange and terminating at the junction of King Street with Long Row:

Route C – Commencing in Upper Parliament Street at a point eighty feet or thereabouts measured in a westerly direction from the intersection of the centre lines of Upper Parliament Street and Milton Street thence proceeding along Upper Parliament Street Lower Parliament Street King Edward Street St. Ann's Well Road and The Wells Road and terminating at the junction of The Wells Road with Kildare Road:

Route D – Commencing in the Market Place at a point fifty feet or thereabouts measured in a north-westerly direction from the intersection of the centre lines of Friar Lane and Wheeler Gate thence proceeding along the Market Place Wheeler Gate Albert Street Lister Gate Greyfriar Gate Canal Street Wilford Street and Wilford Road and terminating at the junction of Wilford Road with Colliery Road.

Importantly the Nottingham Corporation Act 1925 repealed the 5 tons maximum laden weight limit and stipulated that the maximum laden weight should not exceed 10 tons. The use of the selected Railless double-deck trolley vehicles, seating up to 56 passengers, was thus possible. On 18 September 1925 the Tramways Committee reconfirmed the conversion decision and instructed Mr Aldworth to obtain tenders for the latest type of railless vehicles.

A posed manufacturers picture of the first double deck Railless LF, No 10, before delivery to Nottingham and still displaying a Birmingham registration, OK1935 and an exhibition livery. *Geoff Lumb*

In view of the profit made by the Electricity Department in 1923, the Tramways Committee informed the Electricity Committee in August 1924 that if they were not granted a reduction in the price of traction current, they would have to refer the matter to the City Council. Mr Aldworth was instructed to send details of the electricity charges paid by other tramway undertakings to the Electricity Committee. This led to the charge being reduced by 1½d to 2¼d per unit from July 1925 and an almost annual decrease for the rest of the decade.

In July 1925, having inspected uniforms supplied to the Birmingham, Glasgow, Leicester, Manchester and Sheffield Corporation Tramways, it was decided to re-issue traffic staff with green uniforms having red piping of the same colour and quality as used in Glasgow. Inspectors wore uniforms of a somewhat darker green cloth.

By 1925 West Bridgford UDC's motorbus services were under attack from private operators, including Barton Brothers who operated a direct service from private land in Nottingham, Greyfriar Gate to West Bridgford. They sold pre-paid books of tickets for the journey thereby circumventing the stage carriage provisions and avoiding a change from tram to bus or *vice versa* at Trent Bridge. Barton charged just 2d whilst the separate tram and bus tickets combined cost 3d. This so affected the finances of the two municipal transport undertakings that the neighbouring authorities entered into a joint running agreement, commencing on 18 March 1928 with the introduction of motor bus service 11 between Nottingham, Greyfriar Gate and West Bridgford, Melton Road. There were subsequently five joint services. Although, from 1934, the joint motorbus service paralleled NCT's trolleybus route as far as Trent Bridge, there is no record of a route extension or joint trolleybus operation into West Bridgford ever having been discussed.

The 20 November 1925 Tramways Committee meeting considered a tender from Railless Ltd. (a subsidiary of Short Bros) for 10 trackless trolley cars with the latest equipment:

Single motor vehicles	£ 2,234 delivered
Tandem motor vehicles	£ 2,402 delivered

subject to 2½% discount for cash

The tender for 10 tandem (twin) motor trolley vehicles at an estimated total cost of £25,000 was accepted subject to the plans for the vehicles being approved by the MoT.

MoT approval of the plans of the proposed trolley vehicles was still outstanding at the end of December 1925, and on 1 January 1926 the Tramways Committee resolved that the contract for ten Railless trolley vehicle chassis, equipped with Short Bros bodywork, should be placed immediately without waiting any longer. Only on 12 February 1926 was their approval finally received. The 1926 General Strike delayed delivery as the manufacturers could not obtain certain parts.

Possibly prompted by the manufacturer, embarrassed at being unable to deliver promptly, the General Manager reported that Railless had exhibited one of their low frame trolley vehicles with a Short Bros double-deck body exactly in

Two of Nottingham's 1926 English Electric enclosed cars are seen at Mansfield Road, Villiers Road. Car 195 continues its journey north to Arnold whereas 199 has turned back at the end of the double track and will return to the City on service E. *TMS*

The following tram services were then in operation:

1 Trent Bridge – Arkwright Street – Carrington Street - Market Place – Upper Parliament Street - Victoria Station – Mansfield Road – Sherwood (Villiers Road)

2 Trent Bridge – Arkwright Street – Carrington Street – Market Place – Upper Parliament Street - Victoria Station – Mansfield Road – Woodborough Road – Mapperley (Westdale Lane)

3 Trent Bridge – Arkwright Street – Carrington Street – Market Place – Derby Road – Alfreton Road – Hyson Green – Radford Road – Vernon Road (Nottingham Road) – Basford – Bulwell Market

4 Colwick Road – Sneinton – Manvers Street – Bath Street – Upper Parliament Street – Derby Road – Alfreton Road – Hyson Green – Radford Road – Vernon Road (Nottingham Road) – Basford (extended to Bulwell Market in peak hours)

5 Nottingham Road (Vernon Road) – Mansfield Road – Victoria Station – Upper Parliament Street – Theatre Square – Derby Road – Alfreton Road – Hartley Road – Radford Boulevard – Lenton Boulevard – Castle Boulevard – Market Place – Upper Parliament Street – Victoria Station – Mansfield Road – Nottingham Road (Vernon Road) (anti-clockwise around the Boulevards)

6 St. Anns Well Road (Ransom Road) – King Edward Street – Upper Parliament Street – Market Place – Castle Boulevard – Lenton Boulevard – Radford Boulevard – Hartley Road – Alfreton Road – Derby Road – Upper Parliament Street – King Edward Street – St. Anns Well Road (Ransom Road) (clockwise around the Boulevards)

7 Trent Bridge – London Road – Pennyfoot Street - Manvers Street – Southwell Road - Bath Street – King Edward Street – Upper Parliament Street – Market Place – Wilford Road – Wilford Bridge

8 Carlton (Post Office Square) – Carlton Road – Bath Street – King Edward Street – Upper Parliament Street – Market Place – Carrington Street – Station Street – London Road – Pennyfoot Street – Manvers Street – Sneinton – Colwick Road (only every third car continued beyond the Market Place to Colwick)

9 Wollaton Park (Lodge Gates) – Derby Road – Market Place – Upper Parliament Street – Victoria Station – Mansfield Road – Sherwood – Daybrook – Arnold

A Carlton (Standhill Road) – Carlton Road – Bath Street – King Edward Street – Upper Parliament Street – Market Place (assumed to be a peak hours only service)

H Nottingham Road (Haydn Road) – Mansfield Road – Victoria Station – Upper Parliament Street – Market Place (assumed to be a peak hours only service)

accordance with Nottingham's specifications at the 1925 International Commercial Motor Exhibition held at London's Olympia. Railless could deliver it immediately for road testing and staff training purposes if the Tramways Committee wished, although use would have been limited until fixed infrastructure was available. It is likely that this vehicle, foreseen for use in Birmingham, was offered at a discount price. The vehicle was subsequently delivered to Nottingham as fleet number 10 and the original order reduced to 9 units.

At the 12 March 1926 Tramways Committee Meeting it was suggested that the red and green colours of the City's coat-of-arms should be used as a basis for a new livery. Railless provided a panel showing a possible green livery. It was agreed that all future bus or trolley vehicle acquisitions, together with existing vehicles on overhaul, should be finished in a two tone green and cream livery with red wheels. The trolley vehicles thus introduced a new fleet livery although the tramcars retained the maroon and cream colour scheme until final closure.

On 7 June 1926, the new tram track from Porchester Road to Westdale Lane, Mapperley, was brought into operation, service 2 Trent Bridge – Arkwright Street – Market Place – Woodborough Road being extended accordingly, bringing the tramway system to its maximum extent of 25.9 route miles. This figure was maintained for just ten months due to the replacement of the Nottingham Road line by railless traction. Tramways were still seen as the prime mover, as evidenced by the opening of another tramway extension, along Derby Road from Gregory Street to Wollaton Park Lodge Gates, on 16 April 1927. Indeed the future of the tramways seemed secure with the new Carter Gate Depot providing capacity for 80 trams under construction, 20 fully-enclosed 4-wheel tramcars on order and a new track layout in the Market Place, including an additional access from the east along Hockley and Pelham Street, in the final planning stage.

The Nottingham Road tram service 5 did not terminate at the Market Place but continued in an anti-clockwise direction along a circular route comprising Derby Road, Alfreton Road, Hartley Road, Radford Boulevard, Lenton Boulevard, Castle Boulevard, Lister Gate and Wheeler Gate back to the Market Place. The clockwise service was provided by tram service 6 which operated to and from St. Ann's Well Road. It was decided to replace this circular portion of tram service 5 by extending the Carlton Road tram service 8 beyond the Market Place anti-clockwise around the Boulevards when the trackless trolleys were introduced. The infrequent extension of tram service 8 beyond the Market Place to Colwick Road via Station Street was replaced by an unnumbered service running between the LMS Midland Station and Colwick Road only at 15-minute intervals.

In the meantime the Tramways Department erected the trolley vehicle overhead wiring along the new route with a 2ft 6ins gauge between the positive and negative running wires although this was, in the main, narrowed to the customary Nottingham 1ft 6ins separation during the 1930s (and widened again later to the national standard of 2ft). On that portion of the route which paralleled the tramways, that is as far as Gregory Boulevard, Carrington, separate overhead wiring for trolley vehicles and trams was employed.

The northern portion of tram service 5 from the Market Place to Nottingham Road (Vernon Road) was converted to trackless trolley vehicle operation on 10 April 1927, the last tram being on the day before. Trolley vehicles ran between King Street and the junction with Vernon Road by way of Upper Parliament Street, Milton Street, Mansfield Road, Sherwood Rise and Nottingham Road. The city terminus took the form of a one-way loop via King Street, Queen Street and Upper Parliament Street, adjacent to the Market Place. Around the terminal were situated the main Post Office, the Theatre Royal and Empire Theatre, with the Guildhall a few minutes' walk away. Trolley vehicles terminated in the apex of the junction between King Street and Queen Street. From Upper Parliament Street the route turned northwards into Milton Street and Mansfield Road passing Holy Trinity Church, the Mechanics' Hall and the LNER's Victoria railway station. Leaving Mansfield Road at Gregory

The tramcar fleet numbered 200 passenger cars and two departmental vehicles:

1-57 Open-balcony top-covered cars originally built in 1900/1 as open-top by the Electric Railway & Tramway Carriage Works mounted on Brill 21E 4-wheel trucks.

58-67 Open-balcony top-covered cars originally built in 1901 as open-top by G.F. Milnes mounted on Brill 21E 4-wheel trucks.

68-75, 77 Open-balcony top-covered cars originally built in 1902 as open-top by G.F. Milnes mounted on Brill 27G equal wheel bogie trucks.

76 Totally enclosed top-covered car originally built in 1902 as open-top by G.F. Milnes mounted on Brill 27G equal wheel bogie trucks.

78-83 Open-balcony top-covered cars originally built in 1902 as open top by G.F. Milnes mounted on Brill 21E 4-wheel trucks.

84-89 Open-top cars built in 1902 by G.F. Milnes mounted on Brill 22E maximum traction bogie trucks. Never top covered, by 1927 these cars were normally only used for running extras for sporting events.

90-105 Open-balcony top-covered cars originally built in 1901/2 as open-top by the Electric Railway & Tramway Carriage Works mounted on Brill 21E 4-wheel trucks.

106-115 Open-balcony top-covered cars built in 1907 by Milnes Voss mounted on Mountain & Gibson 21EM 4-wheel trucks.

116-125 Open-balcony top-covered cars built in 1908 by the United Electric Car Co. mounted on Brill 21E 4-wheel trucks.

126-135 Open-balcony top-covered cars built in 1911 by the United Electric Car Co. with full-drop windows and mounted on Brill 21E 4-wheel trucks.

136-145 Open-balcony top-covered cars with platform vestibules built in 1914 by the United Electric Car Co. mounted on Preston Flexible Axle 4-wheel trucks.

146-155 Open-balcony top-covered cars with platform vestibules built in 1914 by Brush mounted on Peckham P22 4-wheel trucks.

156-180 Open-balcony top-covered cars with platform vestibules built in 1919/20 by English Electric mounted on Preston Flexible Axle 4-wheel trucks.

181-200 Totally enclosed top-covered cars with platform vestibules built in 1927 by English Electric mounted on Peckham P22 4-wheel trucks.

1-2 Works cars available for carrying equipment, snowplough and street sweeping duties, built in 1902 by the Electric Railway & Tramway Carriage Works on Brill 21E 4-wheel trucks.

\- Snowplough, built in 1911 by the undertaking (details and fleet number not known).

\- Snowplough and stores van, built in the 1920s from the original lower saloon of a passenger car and placed on a high mounted truck (details and fleet number unknown).

The cars in the series 1-57, 78-82, 90-105 had all been rebuilt with open-balcony top-covers. Many of these cars and other earlier deliveries had by now received replacement lower saloons and subsequently replacement upper saloons whilst from 1920 platform vestibules were added to many 4-wheel cars. It can be seen that the Corporation was endeavouring to keep the fleet up-to-date by successive rebuilding nonetheless, as with so many municipal tramways at that time, over half the fleet had its origins with the start of electric operations some 25 years previously.

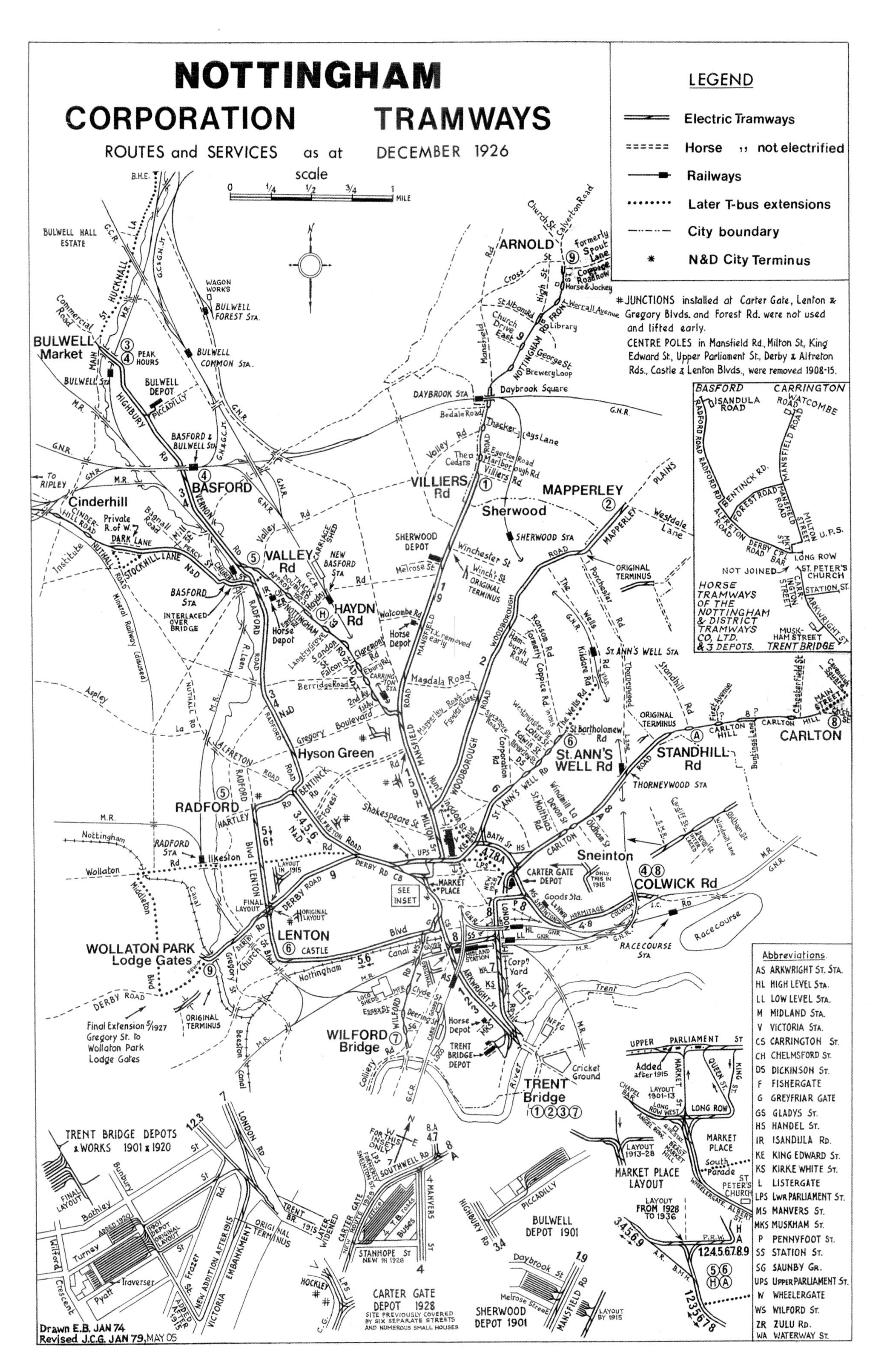

NOTTINGHAM
CORPORATION TRAMWAYS
ROUTES and SERVICES as at DECEMBER 1926
scale
0 1/4 1/2 3/4 1 MILE
LEGEND
Electric Tramways
Horse ,, not electrified
Railways
Later T-bus extensions
City boundary
N&D City Terminus
JUNCTIONS installed at Carter Gate, Lenton & Gregory Blvds. and Forest Rd. were not used and lifted early.
CENTRE POLES in Mansfield Rd., Milton St, King Edward St., Upper Parliament St., Derby & Alfreton Rds., Castle & Lenton Blvds., were removed 1908-15.
HORSE TRAMWAYS OF THE NOTTINGHAM & DISTRICT TRAMWAYS CO, LTD. & 3 DEPOTS.
BASFORD
CARRINGTON
NOT JOINED
TRENT BRIDGE
BULWELL HALL ESTATE
BULWELL Market
BASFORD
Cinderhill
VALLEY Rd
HAYDN Rd
VILLIERS Rd
Sherwood
MAPPERLEY
ARNOLD
Daybrook Square
Hyson Green
RADFORD
LENTON
WOLLATON PARK Lodge Gates
WILFORD Bridge
TRENT Bridge
St. ANN'S WELL Rd
STANDHILL Rd
CARLTON
Sneinton
COLWICK Rd
MARKET PLACE
SEE INSET
SHERWOOD DEPOT
BULWELL DEPOT
CARTER GATE DEPOT
TRENT BRIDGE DEPOT
Final Extension 5/1927 Gregory St. to Wollaton Park Lodge Gates
ORIGINAL TERMINUS
TRENT BRIDGE DEPOTS & WORKS 1901 & 1920
CARTER GATE DEPOT 1928
SITE PREVIOUSLY COVERED BY SIX SEPARATE STREETS AND NUMEROUS SMALL HOUSES
SHERWOOD DEPOT 1901
BULWELL DEPOT 1901
MARKET PLACE LAYOUT
LAYOUT 1913-28
LAYOUT FROM 1928 TO 1936
UPPER PARLIAMENT ST
Abbreviations.
AS ARKWRIGHT St. Sta.
HL HIGH LEVEL Sta.
LL LOW LEVEL Sta.
M MIDLAND Sta.
V VICTORIA Sta.
CS CARRINGTON St.
CH CHELMSFORD St.
DS DICKINSON St.
F FISHERGATE
G GREYFRIAR GATE
GS GLADYS St.
HS HANDEL St.
IR ISANDULA Rd.
KE KING EDWARD St.
KS KIRKE WHITE St.
L LISTERGATE
LPS LWR PARLIAMENT St.
MS MANVERS St.
MKS MUSKHAM St.
P PENNYFOOT St.
SS STATION St.
SG SAUNBY Gr.
UPS UPPER PARLIAMENT St.
W WHEELERGATE
WS WILFORD St.
ZR ZULU Rd.
WA WATERWAY St.
Drawn E.B. JAN 74
Revised J.C.G. JAN 79, MAY 05

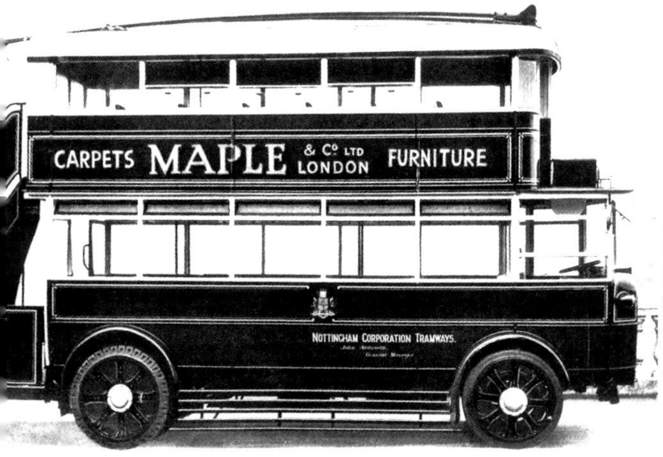

An official pre-delivery view of an unidentified Railless LF possibly photographed by Short Bros in the grounds of Rochester Castle. The balustrade behind the trackless trolley vehicle are evident in other of Short's publicity photographs.

BTS

Boulevard, Carrington, the route proceeded north westwards along Sherwood Rise and Nottingham Road to a turning loop in the junction of Nottingham Road with Vernon Road and thus the Bulwell – Hyson Green tramway, opposite Basford railway station (LMS).

Those trolley vehicles operating the full length of the route displayed service 5 whereas those turning short at the Haydn Road turning circle during peak hours displayed service H, offering a combined railless service along Nottingham Road every 3 minutes. The maximum permitted speed was 12 mph. The new vehicles received fleet numbers 1 to 10 and pending completion of Carter Gate Depot, they were housed at Trent Bridge Depot, which they accessed along Arkwright Street using their positive trolley boom on the overhead wire and a negative return skate in the tram track. The new operation was identified to the public as a "Railless" service and white stop flags so annotated in green were affixed along the route.

5 Queen Street/King Street – Upper Parliament Street – Milton Street – Victoria Station – Mansfield Road – Nottingham Road (Vernon Road)

H Queen Street/King Street – Upper Parliament Street – Milton Street – Victoria Station – Mansfield Road – Nottingham Road (Haydn Road)

The belated MoT approval for the operation of Trackless Trolley Vehicles was received at the beginning of June 1927.

Soon Alderman Turney was quoted as saying that *"the trolley omnibuses had been a colossal success"*. He omitted to mention that there had already been complaints that they caused wireless interference. In May 1927 it was decided to remove the Nottingham Road tram track between Mansfield Road and Haydn Road, and lay a tarmacadam road surface. Passenger loadings on the route increased to such an extent that it became necessary to order more rolling stock and permission was granted to order a further two double-deck trolley vehicles from Railless. However on 3 June 1927 it was learned that the company had declined to quote or give a date for future deliveries. Railless ceased trading soon afterwards, and Nottingham's 1-10 were the last vehicles to be constructed by the company. Alternative quotations from other manufacturers were considered in August 1927 and the additional vehicles were subsequently ordered from Ransomes, Sims & Jefferies Ltd. of Ipswich.

In July 1927 the Markets and Fairs Committee asked that a temporary trolley vehicle terminus be erected on Upper Parliament Street during the three day annual Goose Fair, which until that year was held in the Market Place, in the same manner that tram services were cut back to temporary crossovers in Upper Parliament Street and Wheeler Gate but this was refused.

By now the Tramways Department were being charged 1½ d per unit for electric current supplied for traction purposes and it was felt that a further reduction was due. Following an investigation to establish if any commercial undertakings were being charged less, the Electricity Department reduced the amount from 1½ d to 1¼ d per unit from 1 October 1927. It was estimated that this would save the Tramways Department £9,000 pa. When the report on electricity charges came before Nottingham Council on 3 October 1927, Alderman Turney said that there had been one rate for lighting and one for power, indeed at that time domestic customers had two meters. Now a third rate for traction current had been introduced albeit at a higher rate than power, meaning that the Electricity Committee still charged the Tramways Committee (its best customer) more than private consumers. The Electricity Committee replied that they could not sacrifice further revenue at that time.

From the autumn of 1927 posting boxes were placed on designated inbound tram departures scheduled to reach the city centre at around 10 pm Monday-Friday, the destination blinds on these journeys displaying "POSTAL" in red lettering whilst a special remark was printed in the relevant timetables. This service was extended to the trolleybuses as the network developed and in 1936 to tram replacement motor bus services. Letters could be posted at any compulsory stop en route, the posting boxes being removed at the nearest stop to the GPO in Queen Street.

The City Engineer reported to the 13 January 1928 Tramways Committee Meeting that repairs to the single track and passing loop tram track in Wilford Road were urgently required. Before carrying out any repairs he sought guidance as to any plans to withdraw the tram route and replace it with another form of traction. It was decided to carry out only those repairs necessary for safety reasons and to seek an estimate for removing the tram track and reinstating the road surface in preparation for either railless or motor bus operation.

In January 1928 Mr John Aldworth, who had been the Tramways General Manager since 1898, applied for retirement. The Tramways Committee accepted his request and expressed their admiration of his excellent services. They asked him to remain as a consultant to the undertaking at a fee of £600 pa.

It will be recalled that the interurban Nottinghamshire & Derbyshire Tramways Co. (N&D), which was owned by the Midland Counties Electric Supply Co. Ltd., part of the Balfour Beatty Group, operated an interurban tram route through the coal mining communities to the northwest of Nottingham. Since the end of the First World War their Nottingham – Ripley service had suffered from severe motor bus competition and reduced fares to Nottingham on market days (Wednesday and Saturday) had been introduced in 1922 to stimulate traffic. This had proportionately reduced

Nottingham's first excursion into railless electric traction involved nine identical Railless LF trolley vehicles featuring an open staircase and rear platform, and solid rubber tyred wheels, delivered in early 1927. No 4, still in original livery, is seen outside the Prudential Insurance building in the apex of the junction between King Street and Queen Street, terminus of the Nottingham Road services.

GHFA & JMB

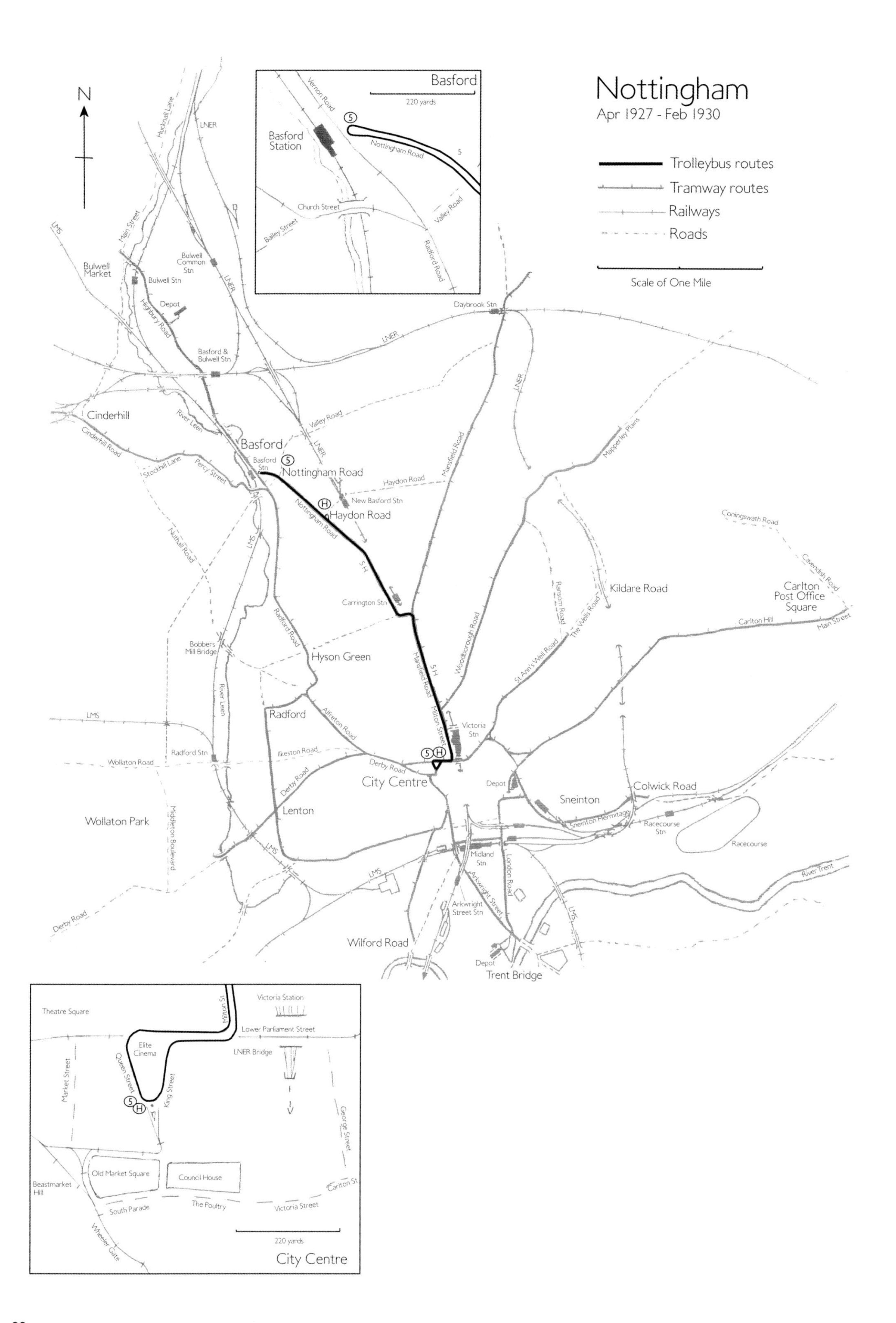

Nottingham
Apr 1927 - Feb 1930
Trolleybus routes
Tramway routes
Railways
Roads
Scale of One Mile
N
Basford
220 yards
Basford Station
Vernon Road
Nottingham Road
Church Street
Bailey Street
Valley Road
Radford Road
Bulwell Market
Bulwell Stn
Bulwell Common Stn
Depot
Highbury Road
Hucknall Lane
Main Street
LNER
LMS
Basford & Bulwell Stn
Daybrook Stn
Cinderhill
Cinderhill Road
River Leen
Stockhill Lane
Percy Street
Basford
Basford Stn
Nottingham Road
Haydon Road
New Basford Stn
Valley Road
Mansfield Road
Mapperley Plains
Nuthall Road
Carrington Stn
Kildare Road
Ransom Road
The Wells Road
St Ann's Well Road
Woodborough Road
Coningswath Road
Cavendish Road
Carlton Post Office Square
Carlton Hill
Main Street
Bobbers Mill Bridge
Hyson Green
Radford
Radford Road
Alfreton Road
Milton Street
Victoria Stn
Radford Stn
Wollaton Road
Ilkeston Road
Derby Road
City Centre
Depot
Colwick Road
Sneinton
Sneinton Hermitage
Racecourse Stn
Racecourse
Lenton
Wollaton Park
Middleton Boulevard
Midland Stn
London Road
Arkwright Street
Arkwright Street Stn
River Trent
Derby Road
Wilford Road
Depot
Trent Bridge
Victoria Station
Theatre Square
Milton St
Lower Parliament Street
Elite Cinema
LNER Bridge
Market Street
Queen Street
King Street
George Street
Old Market Square
Council House
Beastmarket Hill
Carlton St
South Parade
The Poultry
Victoria Street
Wheeler Gate
220 yards
City Centre

the revenue which Nottingham Corporation received for the use of their tracks between Cinderhill and Upper Parliament Street. At the beginning of July 1925 it was reported that despite the fares reduction, passenger figures had continued to decline to such an extent that N&D losses were averaging £30 per week.

Mr Aldworth informed the Tramways Committee on 9 October 1925 that the fall in N&D's receipts had led to a serious reduction in the through-running fees due to Nottingham. Discussions with N&D had taken place and their management was preparing a further reduced fare scheme to encourage traffic. The company enquired if NCT would reduce the through-running fees in proportion to any fare reduction. The prevailing fare between Cinderhill and Upper Parliament Street was 3½d from which the Corporation received 1¾d for the privilege of N&D running from the junction of Church Street and Radford Road, Basford to Upper Parliament Street. He recommended that the total fare be reduced to 2d with the Corporation receiving 1d of this fare and it is believed to have been introduced however by 9 April 1926, N&D receipts showed a loss over the preceding 5 months of £1,007 3s 11d.

As a result of these continuing losses, the N&D announced its intention to promote a Parliamentary Bill seeking powers to convert its tramways to trolley vehicle operation, to operate motor buses and to change its name to the Nottinghamshire & Derbyshire Traction Co. (N&D). In an initial reaction on 27 January 1928 the Nottingham Town Clerk instructed the Council's Parliamentary Agents to prepare a petition against the Bill. On reflection he noted that unless the company was successful in obtaining an Act, it would probably be forced to go into liquidation with losses to the Tramway Committee of £10,590 3s 4d. This was the amount still outstanding from the cost of constructing the tramway from the junction of Church Street and Radford Road, Basford to the city boundary at Nuthall Road, Cinderhill specifically for the use of the N&D and leased by the Company since 1913. The Council subsequently resolved not to oppose the Bill.

Agreement was reached between the two parties for Nottingham Corporation to convert their Church Street, Basford – Nuthall Road, Cinderhill tramway, which had always been operated solely by the N&D, to trolley vehicle operation. The Company would pay the outstanding amount for the original construction, together with the cost of removing the redundant track and for the reinstatement of the road surface. N&D was to remove the traction poles and overhead equipment along the reserved sleeper track between Nuthall Road and Stockhill Lane at its own expense and hand over the traction poles to the Corporation for use elsewhere on the new trolley vehicle route.

Nottingham Corporation agreed to apply for trolley vehicle powers from the City Boundary in Nuthall Road, Cinderhill, along that road, Stockhill Lane, Percy Street, Alpine Street, Church Street and Fairfax Street to join the existing Corporation trolley vehicle system at the junction of Fairfax Street and Nottingham Road, Basford, in the 1929 Session of Parliament to enable N&D vehicles to reach the city centre. The N&D trolley vehicles would thus follow the same route into the city centre as NCT's railless services 5 and H, rather than along Radford Road and Alfreton

One of the Ransomes D4s believed to have been photographed at Ransomes, Sims & Jefferies' Ipswich factory prior to delivery.
John Whitehead

Road as their tram service did. It should not be forgotten that at this time NCT had no plans to convert its double track trunk tram route to Bulwell to trolley vehicle operation. All receipts for passengers travelling on the N&D routes within the City, less a sum to be paid or retained to cover the Company's working expenses would pass to Nottingham Corporation. Fares and Stages were to be agreed between the respective Managers from time to time. The initial response of the N&D was to suggest that the trams be replaced by motor buses instead but they subsequently withdrew this proposal.

The N&D Bill had a difficult passage through Parliament primarily due to the company's insistence on having protection against competition, a so-called "Monopoly Clause", along the entire route as a compensation for investing some £91,000 in the tram to trolleybus conversion and continuing to offer reduced workmen's fares, provoking opposition from both Derbyshire and Nottinghamshire County Councils. Following consideration by a House of Lords Select Committee at the beginning of May 1928 there followed a third passage through the House prior to the Royal Assent of the Nottinghamshire & Derbyshire Traction Act on 19 September 1928. In the meantime, to satisfy the request for a more frequent service from many of the local authorities along the line of route, a combined schedule of N&D trams and Midland General Omnibus Company Co. Ltd. (MGOC) motorbuses was introduced between Nottingham and Ripley, both companies being under the same ownership.

By now the City Engineer was becoming increasingly concerned about the condition of the tram track in Wilford Road and the Tramways Committee accordingly instructed the General Manager to submit a detailed report on the conversion of this tram route and all other single track with passing loop routes to trackless trolley vehicle operation. As a result of this report, the Town Clerk was authorised to apply for powers to run trolley vehicles on all such tram routes in the city. However on the debit side the Finance Committee noted on 8 June 1928 that the Nottingham Road trolley vehicles were wearing the sides of the roads badly and requested that, like the trams before them, they should keep to the more substantially surfaced centre of the road instead!

In his report on the state of the undertaking in September 1928, Mr Aldworth noted that tram services 1-4 operated along double track throughout whereas the others were of single track and passing loop construction. Following a total redesign of the city centre track layout carried out in conjunction with the removal of the covered market and construction of the Council House, services 1, 2, 4 - 9 operated along Queen Street northbound and King Street southbound between the Market Place and Upper Parliament Street, the Market Street line being abandoned. The network was based on through services between areas having *"a similar class of residents"* and having similar traffic demands at each end.

The following trolley vehicle operating statistics for the year ending 31 March 1928 were published in "Tramway & Railway World" for 16 May 1929:

Miles authorised:	6.45
Miles in service:	2.58
Total number of cars:	10 (52-seaters)
Number of passengers carried:	5,265,175
Miles run:	383,801
Vehicle hours worked:	49,589
Average speed:	7.74 mph
BT Units consumed	730,000 (1.90 per car mile)
Fare per mile:	ordinary 0.94d
	workmen 0.62d

Traffic income per car mile 17.68d, per route mile £10,962.
Working expenses per car mile 11.66d operating ratio 65.94.
As can be seen from the financial statistics below, the profit margin on the railless services exceeded that of the tramways which they replaced and gave a higher return than motor buses:

	Trams	Railless	Motorbuses
Total Receipts	£373,136	£28,283	£62,481
Working Expenses	£260,053	£18,649	£60,237
Balance	£113,083	£9,634	£2,244
Capital Charges			
(interest & redemption)	£32,522	£3,466	£11,218
Surplus	£80,561	£6,168	
Deficit			-8,974
Average fare per mile	0.77d	0.94d	0.91d
Av. Workmen's fare p/m	0.47d	0.62d	0.51d
Av. speed including stops	7.32 mph	7.74 mph	9.36 mph

It was noted that the loan repayment period for trams was 20 years, railless cars 10 years, motor buses 8 years, and that for every £1 of capital expended on the purchase of rolling stock the annual sum required for redemption charges was trams 1s, railless cars 2s, and motor buses 2s 6d.

Tram services operated satisfactorily where double track was available but elsewhere *"it is impossible to keep a regular service running or to avoid congestion under the present day conditions of traffic"*. The two tram routes to which this specifically applied were Wilford Road (service 7) and St. Ann's Well Road (service 6), the track on Wilford Road being absolutely worn out. St Ann's Well Road was in better condition but the portion of that thoroughfare beyond Corporation Road (about half way between the junction with Bath Street and the terminus at Ransom Road) was very narrow and laid with single track and passing loops making the operation of a regular, frequent service impossible.

He recommended that neither routes be re-laid with single track and passing loops but that as reconstruction with double track was impossible, the alternatives of running motor buses or trackless trolleys should be investigated. This would enable the St. Ann's Well Road service to be extended north-eastwards from Ransom Road to Kildare Road, the Statutory Powers for such an extension having already been obtained in the 1925 Parliamentary Act. To avoid vehicles terminating in the busy Market Place they could be run through Long Row and Wheeler Gate or across the front of the new Council House which was nearing completion on the site of the former Exchange Building, and along South Parade into Wheeler Gate the return journey being made by Long Row. If this was not acceptable the vehicles running from St. Ann's Well Road could branch off at the bottom of Parliament Street and run through George Street down Victoria Street and along Poultry and South Parade into Wheeler Gate.

Discussion then centred on an alternative through routing of trams should a conversion take place, by linking the circular portions of tram services 6 and 7 around Derby Road, Alfreton Road, Radford Boulevard, Lenton Boulevard, Castle Boulevard and Wheeler Gate with the London Road (Trent Bridge) service along a new road, subsequently to be named Lower Parliament Street, to be built between King Edward Street and London Road.

In September 1928, General Manager John Aldworth reported that *"In further consideration of the relative merits of the Motor Bus and Railless Car, it should be noted that the bus is a single unit independent of Power Station and Trolley Wires, and more mobile in not being confined to any particular road: whereas the Railless vehicle is dependent upon power supplied from a Central Station along overhead wires suspended over certain roads, with a liability of a complete stoppage of the service by a failure at the Power Station or a breakdown of the overhead equipment. There is also considerable difficulty in reversing the direction of the Railless Vehicle in the case of an obstruction on the Road, except at properly constructed Turning Circles".*

"During the busy periods of the day there are 218 tramcars and railless cars passing through Parliament Street between Milton Street and the top of King Street per hour. The suggested diversion of the St. Ann's Well Road Railless Cars through George Street would reduce this number by 15. This diversion would necessitate obtaining Parliamentary Powers".

"The only other single track routes serving Arnold and Carlton are less restricted by the limitation of single track".

The Tramways Committee resolved to replace the Wilford Road and St. Ann's Well Road tram routes with trackless trolleys and to extend the latter to Kildare Road. The Town Clerk was authorised to apply for Powers for the operation of railless cars southbound along George Street, Victoria Street, Poultry, South Parade and Wheeler Gate, enabling trolley vehicles to follow a one-way system around the Old Market Square (the northbound wiring from Wheeler Gate followed Beastmarket Hill, Long Row East and King Street to join the existing trolley vehicle overhead wiring at Queen Street). It was estimated that an additional 15 trolley vehicles costing £2,250 each would be required.

In October 1928, the City Engineer reported that in places it was no longer possible to patch the tram track in Wilford Road and that there was no alternative but to lay new rails in certain places. He was instructed to carry out such repairs as were immediately necessary.

Following competitive interviews for the position of General Manager upon the retirement of Mr Aldworth, a short list of applicants comprising Walter Marks, General Manager Chesterfield Corporation Transport; William Boot, Nottingham's Rolling Stock Superintendent; and Richard Hoggard, Manager Lincoln City Transport, were invited for interview by the Tramways Committee on 26 October 1928. Mr Marks was appointed at a commencing salary of £1,200 pa, effective 1 January 1929. At the time of his appointment Mr Marks was 45 years old and had 27 years of experience in public transport, including some 8 years as Assistant

The Wolverhampton demonstrator was a high-built three axle Guy BTX with Rees Stevens motor and Christopher Dodson H33/28R body of a rather dated design, delivered in 1929 with fleet number 59. It is seen here at the city centre terminus of the Nottingham Road services in the apex of the junction between Queen Street and King Street. The spire of the erstwhile Holy Trinity Church can be seen behind the buildings on Upper Parliament Street. *GHFA & JMB*

The exit roads from Parliament Street Depot into Manvers Street, seen in later years. *Martin Eady*

From Doncaster was a 1928 Karrier Clough E6 with a domed roof and enclosed rear staircase Roe H32/28R body typical of the fleet at that time, carrying fleet number 8. Passengers clamour to board the "foreign" vehicle at Kings Street terminus. *Roy Marshall*

Having reached Wilford Road terminus the driver of English Electric E11 19, the first of the class delivered in December 1929, reaches up in his cab to change the destination indicator to Wells Road in the mid-1930s. *BTS*

Manager of Rotherham Corporation Tramways, a pioneer trolleybus operator, and four years as General Manager at Chesterfield where he had introduced trolleybuses. He was to become the prime mover of Nottingham's tram to trolleybus conversion programme.

On 31 December 1928 Mr John Aldworth retired after some thirty years of service as General Manager having led the undertaking through the construction of the electric tramways (although the "ground work" had been prepared by his predecessor) through to the introduction of trackless trolley vehicles.

The reconstruction of Nottingham's Market Place, at 5.5 acres the largest market square in England, was by now complete and it was decided to rename it as the Old Market Square. The Exchange Building at the east end was demolished and replaced by a new impressive municipal building, the Council House, which was ceremonially opened by the then Prince of Wales on 22 May 1929.

On 8 April 1929 the Tramways Committee inspected the tram route along King Edward Street, Bath Street, Sneinton Market, Manvers Street, Pennyfoot Street and London Road which had been built or remodelled in conjunction with the construction of the new Carter Gate Depot. They also visited the site of the new road, later to be named Lower Parliament Street, between Upper Parliament Street and London Road, and decided that tram track would not be laid in it. The reasons for this decision are not known. Double junctions had already been laid from Carter Gate into Lower Parliament Street and from that street into Hockley to provide an alternative route to/from the Market Place, and the City Engineer was instructed to remove them, unused, together with short connecting stretches of track.

The Lord Mayor in the presence of the Tramways Committee and other guests officially opened the Carter Gate Depot complex on 30 April 1929 although administrative staff had relocated from Beastmarket Hill to the new Carter Gate offices on 14 June 1928. There was accommodation for 4-roads of trolley vehicles in addition to the trams and motor buses. The office block to the northwest of the depot became the Department's headquarters. Upon the exodus of vehicles to Carter Gate the original 1901 Trent Bridge Depot and Workshop, the southern of the two depot buildings, bounded by Pyatt Street and Turney Street, ceased to be a running shed. It was converted into a maintenance and repair Works with three times its previous capacity by adding 31,500 square feet to the existing 17,000 square feet of workshop space. The northern 1921 building was retained as a running shed.

At a luncheon to celebrate the opening, Alderman Arthur Turney, Chairman of the Tramways Committee, paid tribute to the previous manager Mr John Aldworth for the loyal and often strenuous service he had rendered to the Corporation during the years that they had seen the traffic grow from the seven million passengers, which the tramways had carried in his first year (1899), to the eighty millions carried during his last year (1928). Although not advocating any particular type of vehicle, Alderman Turney went on to state that he was out to give the best possible service to the people, so that, until they were able to give as frequent and as cheap a service by some other system, the case for the tramways would remain. They had found out that a well-conditioned tramcar was a good commercial proposition. So far as the future policy was concerned, the Committee would face the facts, cut out all prejudice, not be advocates for any one system but experiment in all, with a view to adopting that which proved successful in meeting their requirements. He wanted, however, to see the time when every vehicle on the road was a flexible one. The design was improving at such a pace that the time may come when the railless car would prove the solution. Having got the workshops right, they must get the fleet right, and then the services right. They were also determined to get the staff right. Both he and Mr Marks were doing all they could to promote the spirit of goodwill among the employees. They wanted the best from the men and were prepared to encourage them in their sports, as well as welfare and ambulance work, classes for which had already been established.

Brand new, registered, but not in service, an empty Ransomes D6 18 is probably on a test run, in late 1929 or early in 1930. *NCT*

At the 3 May 1929 Tramways Committee Meeting authority was given to tender for railless trolley vehicles and overhead equipment for the conversion of the Wilford Road and St. Ann's Well Road tram routes. The Committee studied details of the proposed trolley vehicles and accepted the suggestion that they should inspect the various types already in operation in Doncaster, Maidstone and Wolverhampton, as well as at the English Electric works at Preston, before deciding on which type of vehicle to order. It was arranged to visit Wolverhampton on 21 June 1929. Trolley vehicles were also hired from Doncaster and Wolverhampton for evaluation.

In anticipation of the parliamentary powers being granted, six vehicles each were ordered from the English Electric Co. Ltd. and Ransomes, Sims & Jefferies Ltd., both types being similar in appearance to Maidstone's 11-18. These vehicles were delivered in 1930 and numbered 13-18 (Ransomes, Sims & Jefferies) and 19-24 (English Electric).

At the same time as making a further appeal for reduced prices for electricity for traction purposes, the 12 July 1929 newly retitled Transport Committee meeting resolved to seek powers for Trolley Vehicles routes as follows:

1. Trent Bridge – London Road – Fisher Gate – Carter Gate – Lower Parliament Street – Upper Parliament Street 1.35 miles
2. Lower Parliament Street – Huntingdon Street – Mansfield Road to form a junction with the existing trolley vehicle system 0.68 miles
3. Carter Gate – Southwell Road – Carlton Road – Carlton Hill – Carlton (Church Street tram terminus) 2.31 miles
4. King Edward Street Junction – Bath Street – Handel Street – Carlton Road 0.37 miles
5. a. Carlton (Church Street tram terminus) – Main Street – Burton Road – Shearing Hill Road – Gedling Road 1.92 miles
   b. Carlton (Church Street tram terminus) – Station Road – Conway Road – Burton Road 0.81 miles
   c. Burton Road – Manor Road – Station Road 0.12 miles

Mr Marks reported on the overhead equipment tenders and recommended the acceptance of the lowest tender complying with Municipal Tramways and Transport Association (MTTA) standards at £670, together with a supply of cadmium wire from British Insulators at approximately £2,250.

On 14 June 1929 the Tramways Committee decided to appoint Mr Harry Citford Godsmark, Chief Technical Assistant of the Rolling Stock Department of Manchester Corporation Tramways to the position of Assistant Rolling Stock Superintendent. During the course of 1929 the name of the undertaking was changed from Nottingham Corporation Tramways to Nottingham Corporation Passenger Transport Department.

Traffic congestion in Main Street, Carlton, was making use of the single track and passing loop terminal arrangements for service 8 trams there increasingly difficult thus when Carlton UDC asked if the trams could be extended to a more suitable reversing location Nottingham's Transport Committee suggested that the trams should be replaced by trolley vehicles, in which case they would do all possible to assist.

The trolley vehicle scheme as presented to the City Council encompassed the following:

	Existing Tramways to be converted to Trolley Vehicle System INSIDE City Boundary	Miles	Furlongs	Chains
1.	Commencing in Mansfield Road at its junction with Gregory Boulevard thence proceeding along Mansfield Road to its Junction with Woodthorpe Drive (*west end*).	1	2	4.55
2.	Commencing in Woodborough Road at its junction with Mansfield Road; thence proceeding along Woodborough Road and Mapperley Plains to its junction with Woodthorpe Drive (east end).	2	0	3.64
3.	Commencing in Bath Street at its junction with King Edward Street, thence proceeding along Bath Street, Southwell Road, Manvers Street, Sneinton Hermitage and Colwick Road to the LMS railway level crossing.	1	3	5.14
4.	Commencing in Carlton Road at its junction with Southwell Road thence proceeding along Carlton Road to the City Boundary near Lancaster Road.	1	1	4.00
5.	Along Handel Street for its entire length.	0	1	0.6
6.	Along Southwell Road.	0	0	5.3
7.	Commencing in Pennyfoot Street at its junction with Manvers Street, then proceeding along Pennyfoot Street, Fisher Gate, London Road, to the junction with Arkwright Street near Trent Bridge.	1	0	0.25
8.	Along Station Street for its entire length.	0	2	4.23
9.	Commencing in Carrington Street at its junction with Grey Friar Gate, thence proceeding along Carrington Street, Arkwright Street to the Victoria Embankment.	0	7	5.0
10.	Commencing in Castle Boulevard at its junction with Wilford Street, thence proceeding along Castle Boulevard, Lenton Boulevard, Radford Boulevard, Hartley Road, to the junction with Alfreton Road.	2	1	5.73
11.	Commencing in Derby Road at its junction with Alfreton Road, thence proceeding along Derby Road to its junction with Hill Side (Wollaton Park Gates).	1	1	1.00
12.	Commencing in Long Row West at its junction with Market Street, thence proceeding along Long Row West, Chapel Bar, Derby Road, Alfreton Road, Bentinck Road, Radford Road, Vernon Road, Highbury Road, to Bulwell Market Place.	4	0	2.75
13.	Along Beastmarket Hill.	0	0	4.6
14.	Commencing in Upper Parliament Street at its junction with Queen Street, thence proceeding along Upper Parliament Street to its junction with Derby Road.	0	1	4.1
	Proposed Extension of Trolley Vehicle System INSIDE City Boundary	Miles	Furlongs	Chains
15.	Commencing in Sneinton Road at its junction with Carlton Road, thence proceeding along Sneinton Road, Dale Street, Sneinton Dale, Cardale Road, Thorneywood Lane, Porchester Road,to its junction with Woodborough Road.	2	7	0.27
16.	Commencing in Huntingdon Street at its junction with Mansfield Road, thence proceeding along Huntingdon Street, Windsor Street, St. Michael's Street, Milestone Lane, Cross Street, Parliament Street extension, (New Road) Leen Side, Canal Street, to its junction with Wilford Street.	1	4	5.73
17.	Along Parliament Street extension, between King Edward Street and Cross Street.	0	1	0.6
18.	Commencing at Abbey Bridge at its junction with Castle Boulevard then proceeding along Abbey Bridge, Abbey Street, Beeston Road, to the City Boundary in University Boulevard.	1	0	6.36
19.	Commencing in Derby Road at its junction with Hill Side (Wollaton Park Gates) then proceeding along Derby Road, Woodside Road, Manton Crescent, to the City Boundary in Manton Crescent.	1	3	9.68
20.	Commencing in Ilkeston Road at its junction with Derby Road, thence proceeding along Ilkeston Road, Wollaton Road, and Middleton Boulevard to its junction with Derby Road.	2	0	3.64
21.	Commencing in Gregory Boulevard at its junction with Mansfield Road, thence proceeding along Gregory Boulevard and Radford Boulevard to its junction with Hartley Road.	1	2	0
22.	Commencing in Main Street, Bulwell, at Bulwell Market Place, and proceeding along Main Street and Hucknall Lane to Moor Bridge.	0	7	8.77
	Existing Tramways to be converted to Trolley Vehicle System OUTSIDE City Boundary	Miles	Furlongs	Chains
23.	Commencing in Mansfield Road at its junction with Woodthorpe Drive, thence proceeding along Mansfield Road, Nottingham Road, Front Street Arnold, to its junction with Spout Lane.	1	4	4.23
24.	Commencing in Mapperley Road on the City Boundary thence proceeding along Mapperley Plains to its junction with Beech Avenue.	0	1	7.41
25.	Commencing in Carlton Road at the City Boundary thence proceeding along Carlton Road, Carlton Hill to its junction with Church Street (Carlton).	1	0	1.82
	Proposed Extension of Trolley Vehicle System OUTSIDE City Boundary	Miles	Furlongs	Chains
26.	Commencing in Church Street, Arnold, at the junction with Spout Lane thence proceeding along Church Street, Mellors Road, Redhill Road, and Mansfield Road to its junction with Nottingham Road (Arnold).	1	4	7.27
27.	Along Woodthorpe Drive for its entire length.	0	6	8.18
28.	Commencing in Mapperley Plains at its junction with Beech Avenue, thence proceeding along Mapperley Plains to its Junction with Spring Lane.	1	0	9.36
29.	Along Westdale Lane for its entire length.	1	6	6.95
30.	Commencing in Main Street, Carlton, at its junction with Church Street thence proceeding along Main Street, Gedling Road, Arnold Lane, Shearing Hill Road, Burton Road to its junction with Main Street, Carlton.	1	6	8.45
31.	Commencing in Station Road at its junction with Main Street thence proceeding along Station Road, Conway Road to its junction with Burton Road.	0	6	6.64
32.	Along Manor Road, between Main Street and Station Road.	0	0	9.36
33.	Commencing in University Boulevard at the City Boundary, thence proceeding along University Boulevard, Broadgate (Beeston), High Road (Beeston), Wollaton Road, Abbey Road, Marlborough Road, Hetley Road, Wensor Avenue, Manton Crescent back to the City Boundary.	2	1	4.23
34.	Commencing in Chilwell Road at its junction with Wollaton Road, thence proceeding along Chilwell Road to its junction with Bramcote Lane.	1	0	8.00

The Town Clerk reported on 9 August 1929 that as far as those routes within the city boundaries were concerned trolley vehicle operating powers would be granted on application to the MoT for a Provisional Order under the provisions of the Nottingham Corporation Act 1913. However Proposal 5 to extend the Carlton service beyond the current tram terminus was outside the city boundaries and thus required full Parliamentary Powers. He added that the city was not seeking any other powers requiring a Bill in the 1930 Parliamentary Session and asked if he should specifically promote a Bill for trolley vehicles in Carlton. The matter was accordingly adjourned until the General Manager had prepared a comprehensive scheme for trackless trolleys.

Mr Marks' scheme involved the complete abandonment of the tramways system (together with a number of routes for which construction powers were held) and its replacement by trolley vehicles. Many extensions into the more distant suburbs were suggested whilst several motor bus routes would be converted to electric traction.

The City terminus of the Nottingham Road services was located in the apex of the junction between King Street and Queen Street until March 1942. Here 1929 Ransomes D4 11 waits for passengers in July1931.

GHFA &JMB

The suggested network would have given Nottingham one of the largest trolleybus systems in the country, requiring a fleet in excess of 200 vehicles. Coincidentally the Electricity Committee granted another reduction of ¼d per unit, bringing the average cost of traction current down to 1d per unit, effective from 1 October 1929. The Transport Committee considered the scheme on 6 September 1929 and resolved to carry out all of the General Manager's recommendations.

The City Council informed the Transport Committee on 29 November 1929 that they had approved the recommendations in their entirety and that the Town Clerk had been instructed to promote a Bill in the next Session of Parliament.

The residents of Woodthorpe Drive, which runs eastwards from Mansfield Road, Sherwood to Plains Road, Mapperley, prepared a petition protesting against the running of trolley vehicles and suggested motor buses as a preferable alternative. There were a number of exclusive residences at the Mansfield Road end near the entrance to Woodthorpe Grange Park. This would have made up part of an "outer circular" route linking the Arnold tram route at Mansfield Road, just south of the Villiers Road short-working terminus, the Mapperley tram route at Mapperley Plains and Woodborough Road, and the Carlton route at Cardale Road and Thorneywood Lane, and again closer to the city centre opposite Bath Street (proposed extensions 15 and 27).

The two additional trolley vehicles, built by Ransomes, Simms and Jefferies were delivered in September 1929 and given fleet numbers 11 and 12. They were supplied with pneumatic tyres, as were the department's latest motorbuses, but it proved impractical to replace the solid tyres of the Railless trolley vehicles 1-10.

In December 1929 the local press recorded that the overhead equipment for the St. Ann's Well Road – Wilford Bridge conversion had been in place for some time but that the new trolley vehicles had not yet been delivered. On 10 January 1930 Mr Marks informed the Passenger Transport Committee that by the end of the month, the MoT would have inspected the route and the new trolley vehicles would be delivered. The tram service could be replaced and he asked for instructions as to an opening ceremony. One of the two English Electric trolley vehicles which had been delivered at the end of December 1929 ran

Ransomes D4 12 joins Mansfield Road at the east end of Gregory Boulevard on a wet day in August 1930. Today the presence of two roundabout makes the location is hardly recognisable. As a guide the tall telegraph pole behind the trolley vehicle in Sherwood Rise. *GHFA & JMB*

The number of inquisitive onlookers suggest that that this photograph of brand new English Electric 21 at The Wells Road, Kildare Road terminus was taken on the first day of passenger operations on service 10, 23 February 1930. The bridge in the background carried the Nottingham Suburban Railway. *GHFA & JMB*

Left: The tight turning circle providing the northern terminus of service 5 at the junction of Nottingham Road with Vernon Road required modifications to accommodate 3-axle vehicles in early 1930. In May 1929 Railless 7 turns on to the east side of Nottingham Road prior to returning to King Street. *GHFA & JMB*

Right: English Electric E11 19 speedily demonstrates its agility on St Ann's Well Road, 1930. *NCT*

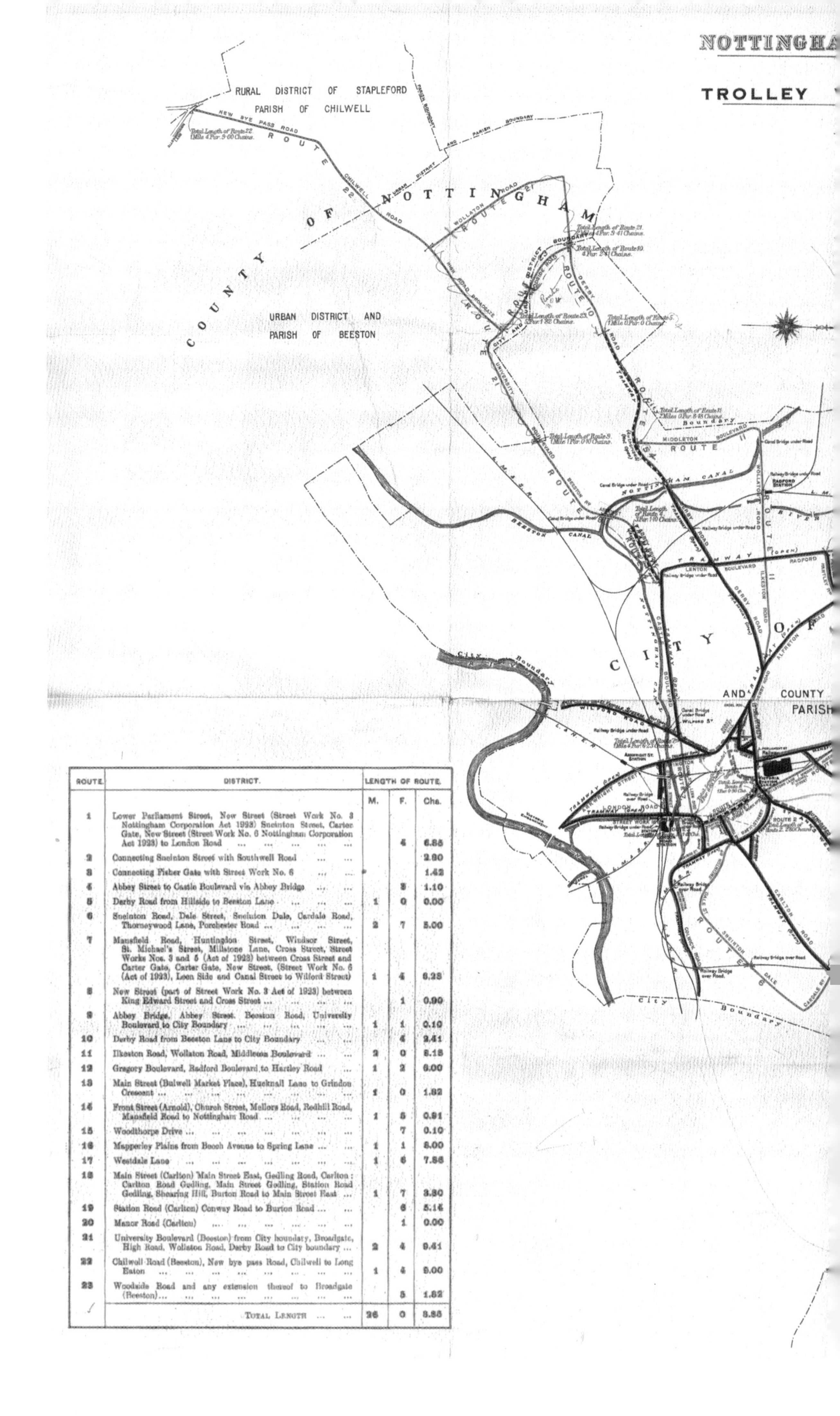

ROUTE.	DISTRICT.	LENGTH OF ROUTE.		
		M.	F.	Chs.
1	Lower Parliament Street, New Street (Street Work No. 3 Nottingham Corporation Act 1923) Sneinton Street, Carter Gate, New Street (Street Work No. 6 Nottingham Corporation Act 1923) to London Road		4	6.85
2	Connecting Sneinton Street with Southwell Road			2.80
3	Connecting Fisher Gate with Street Work No. 6			1.42
4	Abbey Street to Castle Boulevard via Abbey Bridge		3	1.10
5	Derby Road from Hillside to Beeston Lane	1	0	0.00
6	Sneinton Road, Dale Street, Sneinton Dale, Cardale Road, Thorneywood Lane, Porchester Road	2	7	5.00
7	Mansfield Road, Huntingdon Street, Windsor Street, St. Michael's Street, Millstone Lane, Cross Street, Street Works Nos. 3 and 5 (Act of 1923) between Cross Street and Carter Gate, Carter Gate, New Street, (Street Work No. 6 (Act of 1923), Leen Side and Canal Street to Wilford Street)	1	4	6.28
8	New Street (part of Street Work No. 3 Act of 1923) between King Edward Street and Cross Street		1	0.90
9	Abbey Bridge, Abbey Street. Beeston Road, University Boulevard to City Boundary	1	1	0.10
10	Derby Road from Beeston Lane to City Boundary		4	2.41
11	Ilkeston Road, Wollaton Road, Middleton Boulevard	2	0	8.18
12	Gregory Boulevard, Radford Boulevard to Hartley Road ...	1	2	6.00
13	Main Street (Bulwell Market Place), Hucknall Lane to Grindon Crescent	1	0	1.82
14	Front Street (Arnold), Church Street, Mellors Road, Redhill Road, Mansfield Road to Nottingham Road	1	5	0.91
15	Woodthorpe Drive		7	0.10
16	Mapperley Plains from Beech Avenue to Spring Lane	1	1	8.00
17	Westdale Lane	1	6	7.86
18	Main Street (Carlton) Main Street East, Gedling Road, Carlton: Carlton Road Gedling, Main Street Gedling, Station Road Gedling, Shearing Hill, Burton Road to Main Street East ...	1	7	3.30
19	Station Road (Carlton) Conway Road to Burton Road		6	5.14
20	Manor Road (Carlton)		1	0.00
21	University Boulevard (Beeston) from City boundary, Broadgate, High Road, Wollaton Road, Derby Road to City boundary ...	2	4	9.41
22	Chilwell Road (Beeston), New bye pass Road, Chilwell to Long Eaton	1	4	9.00
23	Woodside Road and any extension thereof to Broadgate (Beeston)...		5	1.82
	TOTAL LENGTH	26	0	8.85

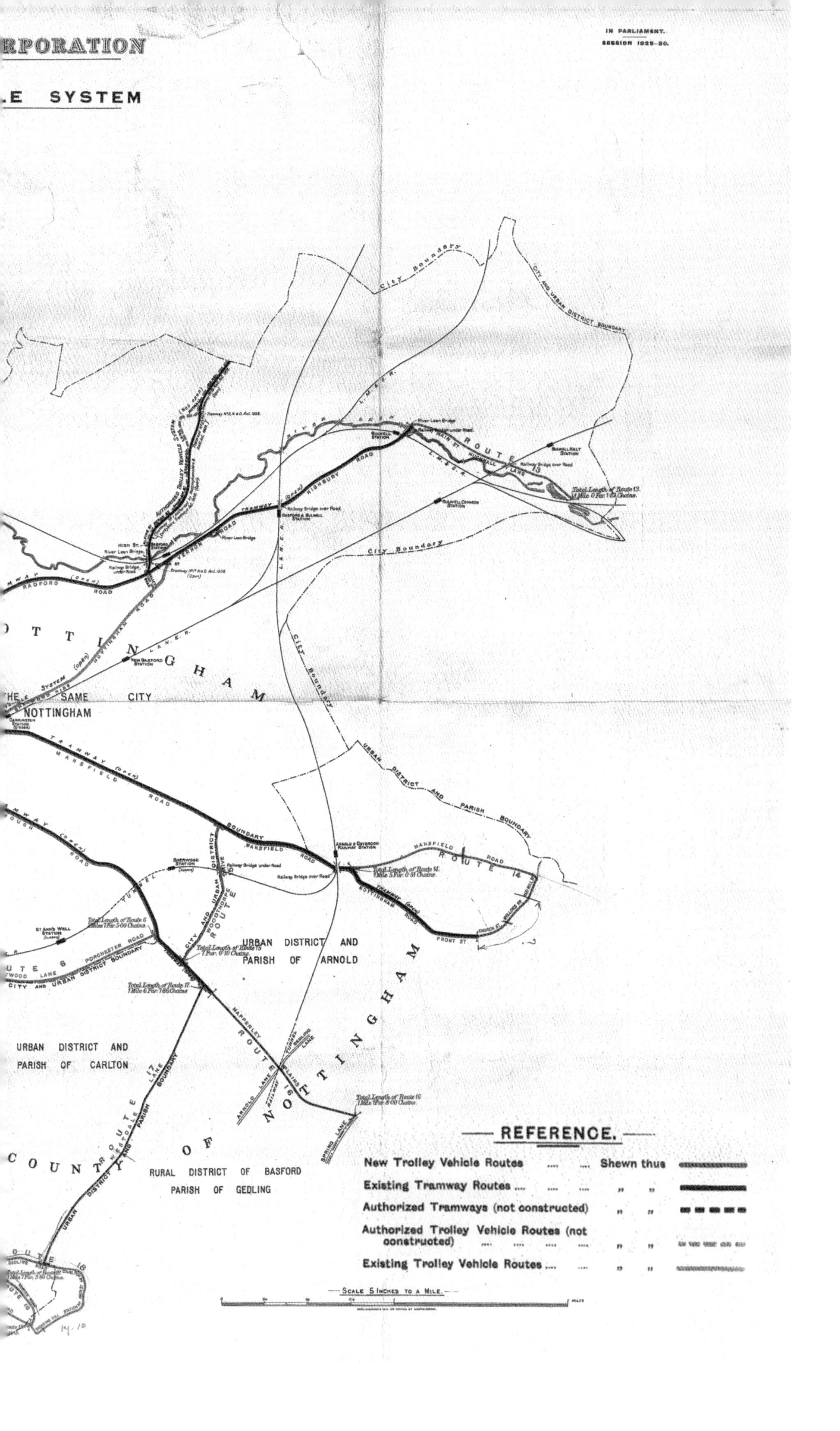

RPORATION
.E SYSTEM
IN PARLIAMENT.
SESSION 1929–30.
REFERENCE.
New Trolley Vehicle Routes .... Shewn thus
Existing Tramway Routes .... ,, ,,
Authorized Tramways (not constructed) ,, ,,
Authorized Trolley Vehicle Routes (not constructed) .... ,, ,,
Existing Trolley Vehicle Routes .... ,, ,,
SCALE 5 INCHES TO A MILE.
URBAN DISTRICT AND PARISH OF ARNOLD
URBAN DISTRICT AND PARISH OF CARLTON
RURAL DISTRICT OF BASFORD
PARISH OF GEDLING
URBAN DISTRICT AND PARISH BOUNDARY
CITY AND URBAN DISTRICT BOUNDARY
City Boundary
MANSFIELD ROAD
MAPPERLEY
Total Length of Route 13. 1 Mile 0 Fur. 1·82 Chains.
Total Length of Route 14. 1 Mile 3 Fur. 0·51 Chains.
Total Length of Route 16 1 Mile 1 Fur. 8·00 Chains.

Ransomes D6 13 entered service on Sunday 23 February 1930, the day that Railless service 10 opened. The vehicle is seen here at The Wells Road, Kildare Road terminus with a goodly crowd of onlookers and would-be joy-riders on that first day. *GHFA & JMB*

In February 1930 Ransomes D6 14, in this re-touched view, is seen outside the "Fifty Shilling Tailor" in Angel Row being tested with one trolley boom pole on the tram positive wire and a skate trailing in the tram rail. *Roy Marshall*

In its 13 March 1930 edition, "Tramway & Railway World" recorded *"At a luncheon afterwards Mr John Aldworth the recently retired General Manager responsible for the first introduction of trolley vehicles into the city proposed success to the city's latest development. Alderman A. Turney, Chairman of the Transport Committee, said that they have had to face the fact that although the tramway was still the "supreme crowd shifter" the time had come when flexibility and speed were two factors of which they had to take more notice. In Nottingham they had 24 trolley omnibuses, and the newest vehicles were the best examples that the manufacturers could offer. The Corporation were putting forward a Bill for further powers to convert the whole of their system into trolley omnibus routes as time went on. No municipality of the size of Nottingham, it was safe to say, had done anything approaching what they had done, and within the next ten years it was very likely that Nottingham would have the most up-to-date system of trolley omnibuses in the country".*

on test on 12 January 1930 identifying the need for changes to the overhead layout at Vernon Road turning circle, to accommodate the larger 3-axle vehicles. Mr Marks said that the new route would have a 6-minute frequency throughout the day with a 3-minute frequency at peak times.

The section of tram service 7 from Wilford Toll Bridge, known as the "Halfpenny Bridge", referring to the toll fee for pedestrians, to Old Market Square and part of tram 6 from the Old Market Square to St. Anns Well Road, Ransom Road, became railless service 10 on Sunday 23 February 1930, numbered in the same series as the tram services. Overhead equipment had been extended some 600 yards up The Wells Road beyond the tram terminus as far as the junction with Kildare Road. The new route was just over 3 miles long and the conversion cost £29,000. The running time was 21 minutes end to end.

10 The Wells Road (Kildare Road) – St. Anns Well Road – King Edward Street – Upper Parliament Street – Old Market Square – Wilford Road – Wilford Bridge *(northbound via Queen Street, southbound via George Street – Carlton Street – Victoria Street – The Poultry – South Parade)*

In conjunction with the conversion, several tram services were amended:

Tram 1 – withdrawn completely

Tram 6 – the Old Market Square – St. Ann's Well Road northern portion of service 6, which continued to operate clockwise around the Lenton and Radford Boulevards, was withdrawn and diverted to Sherwood (replacing tram service 1)

Tram 7 – the Wilford Bridge – Old Market Square western portion of service 7 from Trent Bridge via London Road was withdrawn and diverted along Upper Parliament Street and Derby Road to Wollaton Park Lodge Gates (replacing the western end of service 1 (Daybrook – Wollaton Park) which was cut back to the Old Market Square).

Tram 9 – the Old Market Square – Wollaton Park Lodge Gates southern portion of service 9 was withdrawn and diverted to Trent Bridge.

After some experience had been gained with these new routings, the tram service along Mansfield Road was further amended:

Tram 1 – reintroduced Old Market Square – Mansfield Road – Daybrook Square (peak hours)

Tram 6 – extended at its northern end from Sherwood (Winchester Street) to Villiers Road

Tram 9 – the frequency beyond Villiers Road to Arnold was reduced.

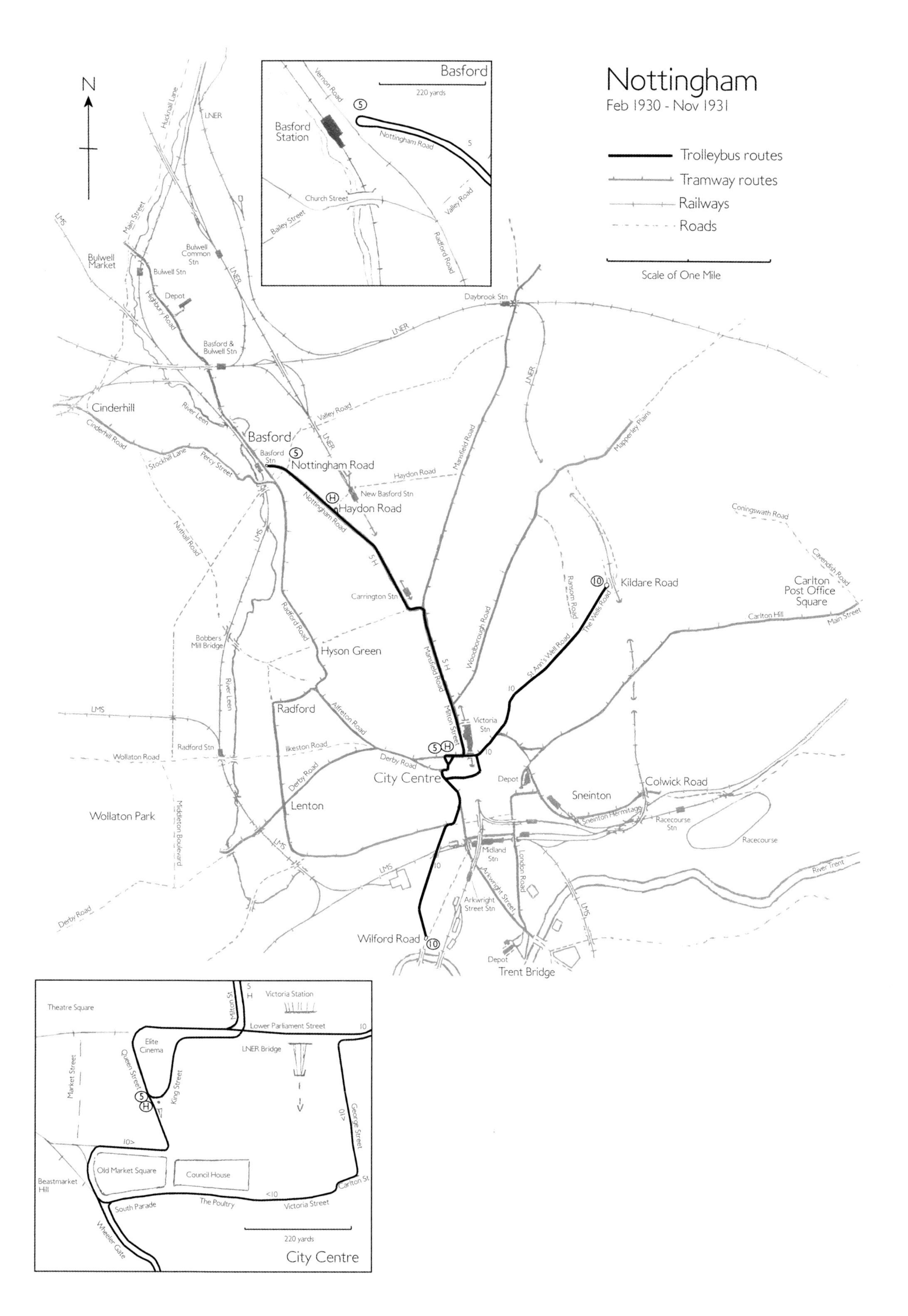
Nottingham
Feb 1930 - Nov 1931
Trolleybus routes
Tramway routes
Railways
Roads
Scale of One Mile
N
Basford
220 yards
Basford Station
Nottingham Road
Church Street
Bailey Street
Valley Road
Radford Road
Vernon Road
Hucknall Lane
LNER
Main Street
LMS
Bulwell Market
Bulwell Common Stn
Bulwell Stn
Depot
Highbury Road
Basford & Bulwell Stn
Daybrook Stn
Cinderhill
Cinderhill Road
River Leen
Basford
Basford Stn
Nottingham Road
Stockhill Lane
Percy Street
Valley Road
Haydon Road
New Basford Stn
Haydon Road
Mansfield Road
Mapperley Plains
Coningswath Road
Cavendish Road
Nuthall Road
Carrington Stn
Kildare Road
Carlton Post Office Square
Ransom Road
The Wells Road
Carlton Hill
Main Street
Bobbers Mill Bridge
Radford Road
Hyson Green
Woodborough Road
St Ann's Well Road
River Leen
Radford
Alfreton Road
Victoria Stn
Milton Street
Wollaton Road
Radford Stn
Ilkeston Road
Derby Road
City Centre
Depot
Colwick Road
Sneinton
Sneinton Hermitage
Racecourse Stn
Racecourse
Wollaton Park
Middleton Boulevard
Derby Road
Lenton
Midland Stn
London Road
Arkwright Street
River Trent
Arkwright Street Stn
Wilford Road
Depot
Trent Bridge
Theatre Square
Victoria Station
Milton St
Lower Parliament Street
Elite Cinema
LNER Bridge
Market Street
Queen Street
King Street
George Street
Old Market Square
Council House
Beastmarket Hill
Carlton St
South Parade
The Poultry
Victoria Street
Wheeler Gate
220 yards
City Centre

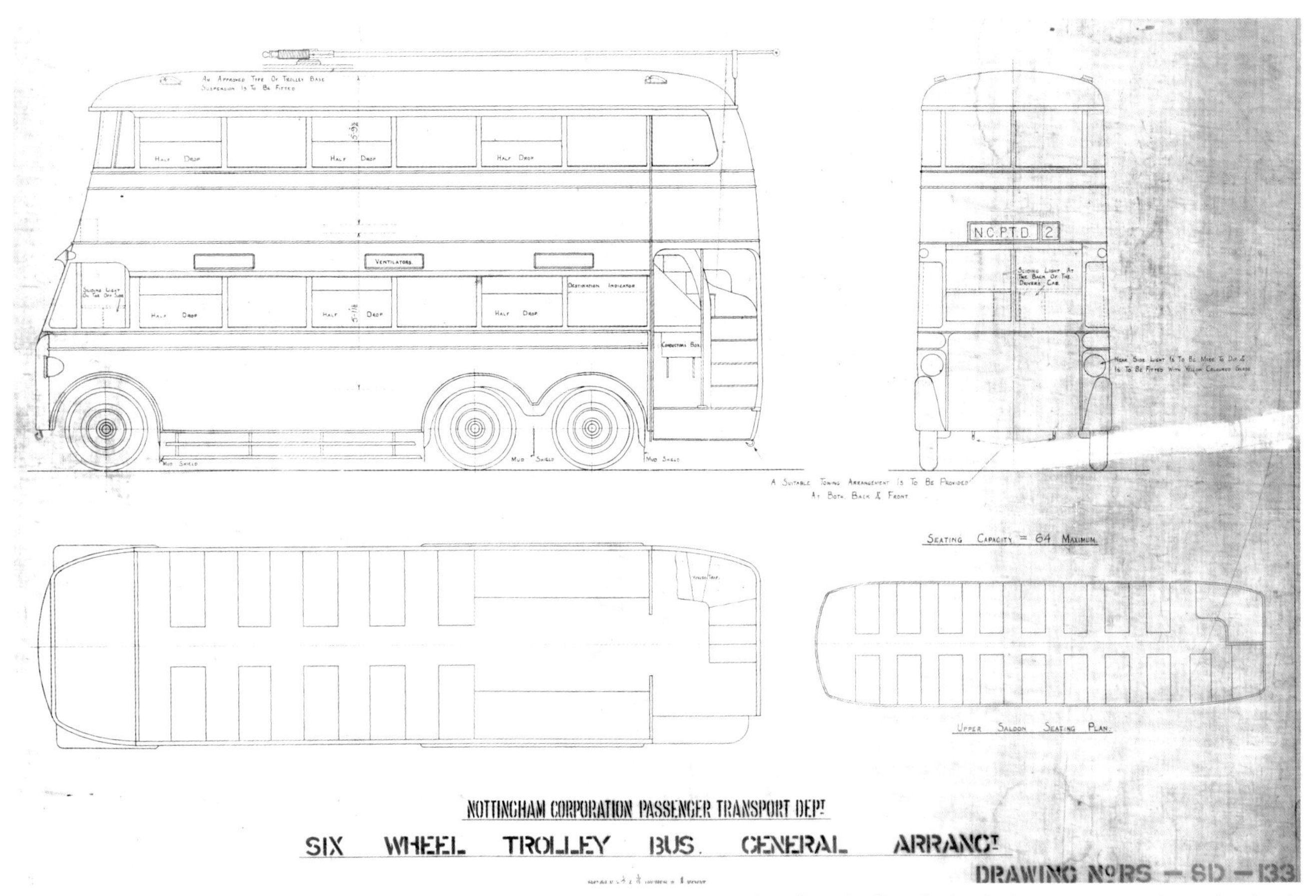

In the early 1930s the NCT Drawing Office produced a general arrangement drawing for a "standard" trolleybus body incorporating the undertaking's preferred fittings e.g. half-drop saloon side windows, and equipment e.g. towing brackets at front and rear. Although many of Nottingham trolleybus deliveries of this period appeared similar, no bodywork complying exactly with this design was ever constructed. *NCT*

On 7 February 1930 the Town Clerk reported that the Nottingham Corporation Bill was now before Parliament and that he expected several Petitions would be made against it. He considered it essential that these Petitions be opposed and, after discussion with the Chairman and Mr Marks, he had retained Sir Henry Maybury, formerly Chief Road Officer of the MoT, to appear and give expert evidence on behalf of the Transport Committee.

In 1921 Sir Jesse Boot, the founder of Boots the Chemists, offered Highfields Estate in Lenton, as the location of a new Nottingham University. The remaining 35 acres were landscaped into a public park with a new dual carriageway road, University Boulevard, along its southern boundary. A tramway extension on private right of way, roughly along the route of the Boulevard, had been pegged out immediately before the First World War had caused work to cease. These generous gifts were valued at around £450,000, a phenomenal amount at that time, but were, of course, subject to certain conditions. Once the war was over Sir Jesse Boot successfully objected to the construction of a tramway along the Boulevard.

Unfortunately this benefactor, since 1929 Lord Trent, had not been informed in advance of the proposal to run "Trackless Trams" along University Boulevard. Only in February 1930 was his Agent informed about the Bill's provisions and, hardly surprisingly, Lord Trent decided to oppose both

Ransomes D6 15 is seen at Walter Fountain, loading a winter crowd, possibly soon after the opening of service 10 on February 23rd 1930. *NCT*

Railless 7 stands outside the erstwhile Carrington Station, Gregory Boulevard (between Sherwood Rise and Mansfield Road) heading citywards in May 1930. *GHFA & JMB*

their operation on the Boulevard and the proposed "Monopoly Clause" intended to give NCT fare protection. In debate, Alderman Huntsman, attacked the Boulevard proposals as the road had been financed by Lord Trent and the Committee had not consulted him in advance as to what he thought of them. Alderman Turney replied that trackless trolley vehicles would not run along the Boulevard without Lord Trent's consent. As this was not forthcoming, in view of the legal difficulties involved, the proposal to run trackless trolley vehicles along University Boulevard was deleted from the Bill. Lord Trent then withdrew his formal opposition against the Bill's clause relating to public transport along the Boulevard, it being noted that he wished it to be regarded more or less as a private road although it was subsequently to become the main artery between the City and Beeston and Chilwell.

On 10 April 1930 the "Guardian Journal" newspaper reported on the Bill's progress. Witnesses were quoted as having said that the roads in Arnold were unsuitable for trackless trolley vehicles whilst Trent Motor Traction would be able to serve all foreseeable transport needs, and their service between Gedling and Nottingham rendered the proposed trolley vehicle route unnecessary. It was already clear that Nottingham Corporation's trolleybuses would not be granted a monopoly outside the city boundary.

Apparently in a MoT inquiry in 1928, NCT and Trent had agreed that municipal buses should not run beyond the White Hart, Mansfield Road, Daybrook. Trent's counsel now suggested *"Do you not think it is a little hard for the Corporation to come along now and say 'we won't run buses, but we will apply for trolley vehicle powers."* Mr Marks responded *"But the conditions have changed considerably since then"*. On 23 April 1930 Carlton UDC decided to oppose the Nottingham Corporation Bill in the House of Lords although Beeston UDC decided to take no action.

The City Engineer reported at the 2 May 1930 Transport Committee meeting that the tram track in Derby Road and on Arkwright Street needed to be re-laid, whilst track repairs in Mansfield Road were necessary. Pending any tram retention policy, he would keep the work to a minimum and was authorised to obtain tenders for the necessary rails.

Arrangements were made with AEC, Guy and Karrier-Clough to have one of each type of vehicle on protracted trial, it being only necessary to pay a small mileage rate for the period the vehicles were in service. Four demonstrators arrived in the second half of 1930 and were allocated fleet numbers 25-28. Two complete vehicles, the AEC 663T (26) and the Guy BTX60 (25) were eventually returned to the manufacturers, as was the chassis of the fourth, a Brush Thornycroft (28). The body of this vehicle was retained as was the

The AEC 663T demonstrator parked alongside Guy BTX60 demonstrator 25 just inside the Stanhope Street entrance to Parliament Street Depot probably in July 1930. Although in a basic version of the Nottingham livery, the AEC is as yet unregistered and carries neither insignia nor fleet number. *GHFA & JMB*

Guy BTX60 demonstrator 25. Despite the destination 25 is turning out of Milton Street into Upper Parliament Street city bound. *GHFA & JMB*

Busily unloading in the middle of the road, Wolverhampton Corporation Guy BTX/ Dodson 59 is seen in its home town. *NCT*

third vehicle (27), a Karrier E6 fitted with Park Royal body featuring a then fashionable dummy radiator, the latter subsequently being taken into stock as number 50.

Interviews for the position of Assistant Manager were held on 23 May 1930, Mr H.C. Godsmark, Assistant Rolling Stock Engineer, NCT, and Mr C.P. Paige, Traffic Manager, Yorkshire (West Riding) Electric Tramways Co. Ltd., being short-listed. Mr Godsmark was promoted to the position effective 1 June 1930.

On 30 May 1930 the Minister of Transport, Herbert Morrison, opened Lower Parliament Street, a new thoroughfare curving south eastwards between King Edward Street and Carter Gate. It was announced that trams would not be introduced on the new street but in due course trolleybuses would. The undertaking's Carter Gate Depot was henceforth officially known as Parliament Street Depot although it took some years for the new title to stick!

The Wollaton Park Estates Committee met the Transport Committee on 13 June 1930 to discuss proposals to run trackless trolley vehicles along Middleton Boulevard, a dual carriageway road running between Derby Road and Ilkeston Road to the west of the city, later making up part of the ring road. Also in June 1930 the Derby Road trams were cut back some 700 yards from the Wollaton Park Lodge Gates terminus to the Johnson Road, Lenton crossover on the east side of the bridge over the LMS Wilford-Radford railway line whilst the bridge was rebuilt and widened. Motorbus service 6 Upper Parliament Street – Middleton Boulevard, Scalford Drive via Ilkeston Road was extended in early August 1930 along Middleton Boulevard and Derby Road to Wollaton Park Lodge Gates to cover the curtailment. Trams were never reinstated on this portion of Derby Road.

Meanwhile the Nottingham Corporation Bill 1930, less the University Boulevard and Woodthorpe Drive proposals, which had already been deleted due to opposition from Lord Trent and the local residents respectively, had reached the House of Commons Committee stage. The NCC decided not to object to the conversion of the existing tram routes outside the city boundary to trolley vehicle operation, however Arnold and Carlton UDCs lodged objections to extensions beyond the tram termini in their districts. The Committee of the House of Commons struck out the Mapperley Plains and Westdale Lane (Carlton – Mapperley) proposals (28 and 29) and passed the rest of the Bill in its

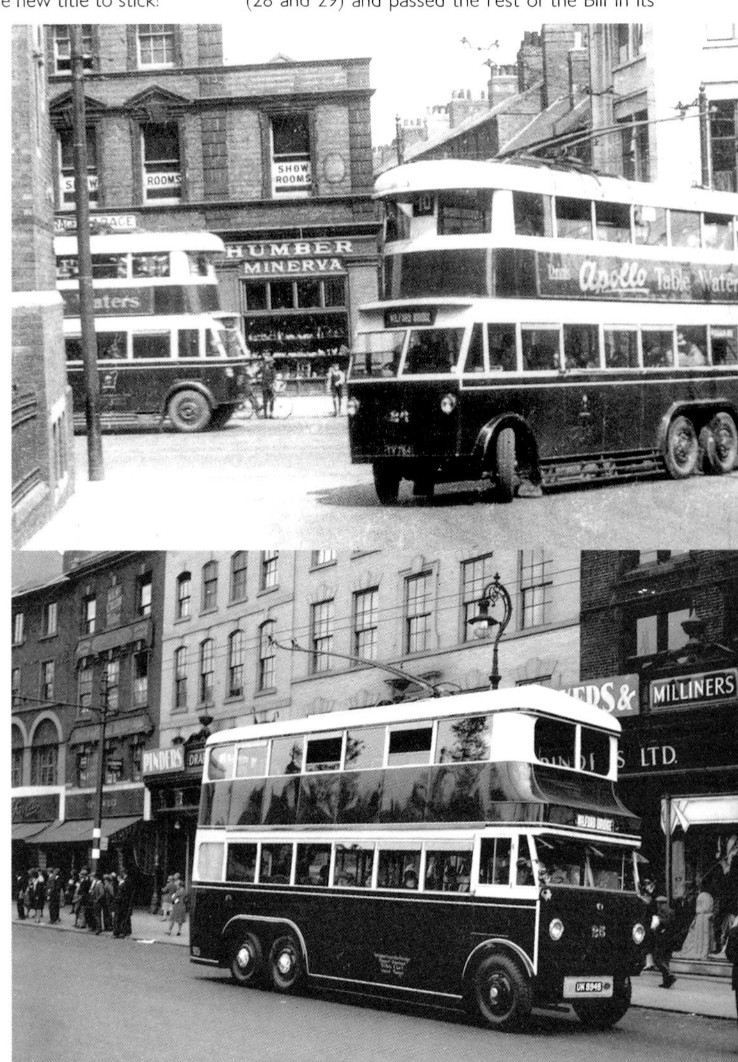

English Electric No 24 turns into George Street while sister vehicle No 20, with cream beading across the lower front panel, speeds east along Lower Parliament Street in June 1930. *GHFA & JMB*

Guy BTX 60 Demonstrator 25 loads passengers at the South Parade stop in Old Market Square en route to Wilford Bridge in October 1930. *GHFA & JMB*

The crew of Railless 8, clad in their new summertime linen dustcoats and with white cap covers both introduced in June 1930, stand in front of their charge close to the Nottingham Road, Vernon Road terminus looking south i.e. prior to using the turning loop. *Alan Oxley*

entirety. This proved a somewhat theoretical exercise however as those routes outside the city boundary not already served by trams were rejected by the House of Lords Committee due to opposition from the NCC and Trent Motor Traction. The remainder were approved subject to a 12-ton maximum weight limit being applied to the trolley vehicles used. The Nottingham Corporation Act 1930 received Royal Assent on 10 July 1930 and additionally a loan of £781,000 for the conversion, including road reinstatement.

Although not mentioned in Mr Mark's conversion scheme as referred to the City Council or in the Parliamentary Bill, the following additional trolley vehicle route proposals were actively suggested during the period now under review -

Aspley Estate, to be served by a loop from Cinderhill or linked as a circular service to the Cinderhill service.

Beeston (High Road) – Queens Road – Attenborough

Bulwell Market – Coventry Road – Cinderhill Road – Cinderhill (Nuthall Road)

Derby Road – Woodside Road, Lenton Abbey Estate, as a branch from the Derby Road – Beeston route.

Wollaton Road – Western Boulevard – Valley Road – Mansfield Road, offering an "Outer Circle" service, presumably in conjunction with the Woodthorpe Drive, and Thorneywood Lane and Porchester Road proposals.

By autumn 1930 the arrival of more trolley vehicles had made Parliament Street Depot increasingly congested. As Trent wished to extend their premises facing the NCT depot, it was suggested that Trent's premises be taken over at a price to be agreed whilst other land belonging to the undertaking in Manvers Street, Pennyfoot Street and Lower Parliament Street would be offered to Trent. Agreement was reached in September 1931. Trent received £23,000 for their existing premises including the machinery, etc. on site, and took on a lease of 5,288½ sq yards of NCT land for their new premises at a rental of 2s 6d per sq yard. The remaining strip of land between Trent's boundary and that leased to Atkey Motor Engineers was leased to Messrs Atkey. It should be noted here that this latter company was owned by Alderman Albert Atkey, a prominent member of the Transport Committee.

In March 1931 the junction of Alfreton Road, Ilkeston Road and Derby Road, known until then as Zion Hill, was renamed Canning Circus to commemorate the statesman, George Canning.

Shortly after its arrival in Nottingham (note the shining clean trolley booms) Karrier-Clough E6/Park Royal demonstrator 27 descends Upper Parliament Street heading east at Milton Street. *GHFA & JMB*

Having outlined his proposals to extend the trolley vehicle network at the previous Passenger Transport Committee meeting, on 6 February 1931 Mr Marks presented details of those petrol bus and tram routes, comprising 6 routes to be converted in 3 stages, which should now be converted to trolley vehicle operation:

1) Carlton – Wollaton Park via both Derby Road and Ilkeston Road.
2) Hartley Road and a circular route via Castle, Lenton, Radford and Gregory Boulevards, Mansfield Road, Huntingdon Street, Lower Parliament Street, Leenside (later renamed Canal Street) and Canal Street.
3) Bulwell – Trent Bridge, Bulwell – Bulwell Hall and Cinderhill.

His recommendations were adopted and the City Council was asked to consider applying for a loan to cover the cost of the new trolleybus system at an estimated expenditure of £156,400 for vehicles and £45,525 for equipment. In practice the Carlton Road conversion took place some 4 months later than the rest of Stage 1 due to difficulties in finding a suitable location for a turning point, Stage 2 was deferred due to the economic depression and subsequently cancelled, whilst the pressing needs of N&D ensured that the Cinderhill route was given priority over the rest of Stage 3. On 2 March 1931 the full Council approved the conversion of all remaining tram routes to trolley vehicle operation in due course and authorised borrowing of £203,925 (an inexplicable £2,000 more than the estimate).

Speeding down Mansfield Road at the junction with Woodborough Road, Ransomes D6 14 heads towards the city centre in the early 1930s. Note the drinking trough for horses beneath the street lamps and the car showroom to the left; MG only went out of production recently whilst Singer were also well known for their sports cars well into the 1960s. In the background an open-balcony tram grinds up the hill near Forest Road.
BTS

Tenders for 25 new trolley vehicles and overhead equipment for the first stage (Carlton and both Wollaton Park routes) were invited in March 1931. On 1 May 1931 the Passenger Transport Committee considered tenders for complete vehicles from AEC, Brush, Clough Smith, English Electric, Guy, Karrier and Ransomes Sims & Jefferies, together with separate offers for chassis only and bodywork only. Tenders for bodies were received from Brush; Cravens; Eastwood & Kenning; English Electric; Guy; Metropolitan-Cammell Carriage, Wagon & Finance; Park Royal Coachworks; Ransomes Sims & Jefferies; Short Brothers; Strachan; and Weymann.

Cammell Laird's Nottingham factory on King's Meadow Road was on the verge of closure due to the trade depression and the owners had great hopes that they might win the tender with their Metro-Cammell steel bodies whilst local politicians suggested that the Corporation should place the order with the company and thus rescue many jobs. The Passenger Transport Committee felt however that the use of steel bodies for double-deck passenger vehicles was still only in its infancy and that there was a risk of excessive wear, and consequent rattle and discomfort in service. Following discussions between Mr Marks, the City Electrical Engineer and the Ministry of Transport, the MoT advised that they would not approve the use of all-steel bodies on trolley vehicles due to the risk of electrical short circuits, etc. This contradicted prevailing legislation abroad; Turin for example having recently introduced steel bodied trolleybuses. In view of the Department's previous experience with timber bodies it was decided not to experiment, not least as Metropolitan Cammell would have required a substantial order to keep their local employees at work.

The following tenders, as recommended by the General Manager, were accepted:

a) Chassis Only
   1. Ransomes Sims & Jefferies, 13 vehicles at £1,236 each
   2. Karrier Motors, 12 vehicles at £ 1,239 each
b) Bodies Only
   1, Brush Electrical Engineering, 13 bodies at £897 each
   2. Park Royal Coachworks, 12 bodies at £ 890 each

These orders materialised as Karrier E6 Park Royal bodied 25-36 and Ransomes D6 Brush bodied 37-49.

Karrier Clough E6/Park Royal demonstrator pulls away from the Wilfor Road services stop on South Parade, Old Market Square in the winter of 1930-1931. In the background a West Bridgford UDC AEC motorbus and the columns of the Council House can be seen. *BTS*

Brush Thornycroft demonstrator 28 is seen at The Wells Road, Kildare Road terminus in spring 1931. *BTS*

Tenders for the supply and construction of overhead equipment for the Carlton and both Wollaton Park routes were received from British Insulated Cables, Clough and Estler. The lowest tender from Estler Bros. Ltd., London E16 at £11,891 was accepted although they sub-contracted the traction pole planting, using defective concrete in places, which was subsequently replaced. Later, Estler's purchased the tower wagon, which the undertaking had used since 1917, for £65.

The MoT asked when the undertaking planned to convert its solid tyre Railless trolley vehicles to pneumatic tyres. As the conversion would have cost about £140 per vehicle with the new larger tyres projecting 5 ins beyond the bodywork, the MoT was informed that no conversion was planned and that they would be used solely as spares as the network expanded.

The first stage of the N&D tram to trolleybus conversion involved the erstwhile Ilkeston Corporation Tramways; all trams ceased on 7 February 1931 with MGOC motorbuses providing services until single deck English Electric trolleybuses started to run between Cotmanhay and Hallam Fields on 7 January 1932. The link from Ilkeston to Heanor, which had never been operated by trams, together with Heanor – Loscoe portion of the main Nottingham – Ripley tram route opened on 2 August 1932. Work then switched to the remaining two portions of tramway: from the Nottingham city boundary at Cinderhill to Heanor, and Loscoe to Ripley, N&D paying substantial sums for road reinstatements and the lowering of the road surface beneath the six railway overbridges en route to accommodate high bridge trolleybuses. The Ilkeston – Loscoe trolleybuses were temporarily extended to Ripley in November 1932 although the Nottingham – Ripley tram service continued to run.

In preparation for the conversion programme, a call for tenders to rebuild the pits and remove the end wall facing Manvers Street in that portion of Parliament Street Depot accommodating trams to provide addition space for trolley buses was issued in May 1931. The tender of A. Green for the conversion of the pits, at £525, and the offer of G. Brady & Co. for the installation of electric roller shutter doors, at £475, being accepted. The shutters proved so satisfactory that in April 1933 they were asked to replace further roller shutters there at an estimated £25-£35 per shutter.

The Works & Ways Committee approved the proposed positions of traction poles along Middleton Boulevard on 12 June 1931 subject to the poles being erected in line with the existing trees, except at junctions where the poles were to be placed about two feet up the side streets, and receiving a scale drawing of their design. The Estates Committee had already approved the design of the ornamented bracket arm traction poles whilst the Passenger Transport Committee had no objections to these proposals.

Introduction of trolleybuses to Wollaton Park was delayed by the reconstruction of the railway bridge on Derby Road, Lenton, work only being completed at the end of September 1931.

It had been suggested that higher fares should be applied on the trolley buses operating on the Nottingham Road route where these paralleled the trams but no changes were made. It was argued that the fares on the trolley vehicles were the same as on the trams, yet the longer distance passengers were benefiting from a better service on the trolley vehicles,

Further negotiations with N&D concerning the conversion of their tram route into Nottingham took place in April 1931. As the Company were now contemplating operating motor buses instead of the trolleybuses originally proposed, a meeting to discuss their plans took place between the Passenger Transport Committee Chairman (Alderman Turney), Vice Chairman, the Town Clerk and the General Manager, and Sir Joseph Nall, Chairman N&D, in early July 1931. It is worthy of mention that Colonel Sir Joseph Nall MP (1887-1958) was also Chairman of Mansfield & District Tramways Ltd., Midland General Omnibus Co. Ltd., Lancashire United Transport Co. and Llandudno & Colwyn Bay Electric Railway Ltd., as well as a Director of the Midland Counties Electricity Supply Co. Ltd. and the Leamington & Warwick Electrical Co. Ltd.. The provisional agreement reached in these negotiations was confirmed in the Passenger Transport Committee's letter of 13 July 1931, namely that:

1) *The Tramways from Church Street, Nottingham, to the City Boundary at Cinderhill to be abandoned forthwith.*
2) *Your Company to pay the Corporation on the abandonment of the tramway the amount of capital outstanding in the books of the Corporation in respect of the construction of the Tramway with interest to date of payment (it is understood that this amount of capital is at present £8,441).*

Karrier E6/Park Royal 30 (TV4688) heading west on service 8 to Wollaton Park in Lower Parliament Street. Some 60 yards behind a 1930 English Electric is pulling out of King Edward Stree. *GHFA & JMB*

The professional magazine "Bus & Coach" featured an article on systematic fleet maintenance written by Mr Marks in their July 1931 edition:

"The Nottingham Corporation, in addition to 200 trams and 100 petrol buses, operates a fleet of 24 trolley vehicles including four and six wheelers over three separate routes covering 5½ miles, all of which are converted tram routes. The financial results have fully justified the conversion, the average traffic revenue having increased from 15d per car mile on tramway operation to 16.7d per car mile on trolley vehicle operation, in spite of the fact that the services in each case have been increased from a headway of 10 minutes ordinary and 5 minutes peak load to 6 minutes ordinary and 3 minutes peak load.

All six wheeled vehicles are equipped with air brakes and electric brakes. The electric brakes were fitted for the purpose of reducing the cost of maintenance on the brake linings, which are operated by the air and mechanical brakes, but from experience gained during the operation of these vehicles it is not now deemed necessary to incur the expense and additional weight entailed by the fitting of an electric brake, because by the correct combination of brake drum metal and brake shoe liners it has been found that the latter can be made to last considerably over 60,000 miles before relining is needed and with an entire absence of scoring of the drums.

At Nottingham we have put into operation three classes of overhaul, which are designated A, B and C Docks. These are designed to cover all contingencies and take place as follows: A at the end of each 5,000 miles; B at the end of each 15,000 miles and C at the end of each 100,000 miles. In a Class C Dock, which really constitutes a complete overhaul, the body is removed from the chassis and passed forward on a special truck to the body shop where it is thoroughly overhauled and then transferred to the paint shop. Immediately the body has been removed, the chassis is passed over to the chassis shop and is completely dismantled, the electrical equipment being passed forward to the electrical shop. The various units are dealt with on the "unit system" by specialists and the vehicle is reassembled and turned out thoroughly reconditioned and to all intents and purposes a new vehicle.

Pneumatic tyres are the subject of constant attention. Each tyre pressure is tested daily and if necessary inflated to the correct pressure of 110lb. Experience has taught us that constant care and attention in this direction is true economy, this being demonstrated by the fact that pneumatic tyres on the six-wheel vehicles during past years have only cost 0.45d per vehicle mile run.

A further important factor in the maintenance of tyres is that of wheel alignment and in order to maintain this correctly all vehicles are tested fortnightly and adjustment made where necessary. It is very desirable whenever possible to arrange the ordinary running shed for trolley vehicles with entrance and exit at opposite sides in order to facilitate the despatch of vehicles from the shed with a minimum of shunting. It is further very desirable that all roads should contain pits, well lighted and drained in order that inspection of the chassis and brake adjustments, etc., can be made nightly. Each vehicle on entering the running shed on the completion of duty is inspected in accordance with the driver's report sheet and such adjustments made as are necessary. The vehicle is then swept out, washed, dusted, greased and tested for electrical leakage. In addition to the nightly cleaning, each vehicle is soap washed once a month during the day. The normal tramcar practice is very closely followed in regard to inspection and cleaning of electrical equipment, controllers, commutators, trolley heads and bases.

All vehicles are fitted with Chamberlain and Hookham car meters and very careful record is kept of the current consumed by each vehicle. They are also fitted with mileometers which have been adopted as giving the most accurate mileage record after testing various types of mileage recording instruments. By this combination very accurate data is obtained showing the units consumed per vehicle mile. These are carefully tabulated both with reference to the vehicle, the driver and the journey. Thus it is a very easy matter at any time to pick out a vehicle or driver using an excessive amount of current.

Another interesting and very useful item in maintenance work is the "History Book". Every person who attends to a vehicle in any way whatever records the fact on a daily report sheet by giving the number of the vehicle and the work done. This is entered by a clerk in the history book under the appropriate vehicle number and thus is kept a complete record of the troubles of each particular machine. The clerk takes note of excessive use of any particular item, such as trolley wheels, brake linings, or glass for broken windows and immediately draws the attention of the Rolling Stock Engineer to the fact. Furthermore, it is possible to read back at any time and so – when considering the purchase of new vehicles – obviate the recurrence of similar troubles ".

3) *The Company to have the whole period of their existing powers to decide whether or not they shall run Trolley Vehicles on the route outside the City to connect the Corporation's authorised route at Cinderhill.*
4) *The Corporation not to apply for Omnibus Powers outside the City for routes in competition with the services of the Company before August 1933, provided that this restriction shall not apply if the Company are not giving an adequate service of Omnibuses within the meaning of Section 42 of the Nottinghamshire and Derbyshire Tramway Company's Act of 1928.*
5) *If the Corporation obtain Trolley Vehicle powers for services into the City by way of the new Bobbers Mill Bridge the Corporation will be prepared to consider the question of an arrangement enabling the Company to run their Trolley Vehicles over such route.*

The N&D replied that they were generally in agreement but proposed slightly different wording, significantly adding *"if and when the Corporation provide and equip their proposed trolley vehicle route between the Cinderhill district of the City at or near Stockhill Lane and the centre of the City via the new Bobbers Mill Bridge, the Corporation shall, if so requested by the Company, provide junctions at Stockhill Lane, Cinderhill and Parliament Street with the trolley vehicle routes of the Corporation as described in Section 10 of the Act of 1928, and shall afford to the Company running powers over such route via Bobbers Mill on the terms and conditions of Section 10 of the Act of 1928".*

These proposals were rejected on 17 July 1931, the Passenger Transport Committee insisting on retaining the original version. Only on 13 May 1932 could the Town Clerk report that N&D had decided to convert their route at Cinderhill to trolley vehicle operation and that agreement had been reached. It was resolved that the agreement be approved and that the conversion of the tram route from Cinderhill, Bell's Lane to Basford, Fairfax Street, for trolleybus operation be proceeded with to finish simultaneously with the N&D work. The agreement with N&D was completed in late August 1931 and the balance of the outstanding capital paid to the Corporation. The City Engineer was asked to take up the tram rails on Nuthall Road from the City Boundary immediately in conjunction with the road widening in progress, whilst he was asked to discuss what was to be done with the remainder of the track, that is between Church Street and Stockhill Lane, with the General Manager.

Carlton UDC had been promised that the Carlton tram route would be the next to be converted to trolleybus operation, it being intended to operate the Carlton Road trolleybuses through the city and then by two routes, namely along both Derby Road and Ilkeston Road, to Middleton Boulevard, Wollaton Park. This circular routing would replace the Ilkeston Road motorbus service and the truncated Derby Road tram route. It proved difficult however to find a suitable location for the Carlton terminus turning circle, the original plans submitted to the MoT in June 1931 being disapproved. The Department again suggested a one-way loop line along Main Street, Manor Road and Station Road but this was still not acceptable to the UDC. It was deemed prudent to continue work on the Wollaton Park routes for a timely inauguration but postpone the opening of the Carlton Road portion.

The trams terminated near the National Schools in Main Street and in further negotiations with Carlton UDC, the Department proposed that the narrow thoroughfare beyond the terminus be widened sufficiently to allow trolleybuses to reach Post Office Square where there would be space for a turning circle. Carlton UDC agreed to carry out the widening subject to Nottingham Corporation contributing £1,000 towards the cost of the improvement and NCC approval (as the road authority). This was felt to be a cheaper solution than purchasing other land at the terminus. The Passenger Transport Committee approved the proposal and suggested an on-site meeting with the NCC as soon as possible as the next County Council meeting was only due on 13 October 1931. Negotiations continued until March 1932, it being finally agreed that Carlton UDC would widen and improve Main Street as soon as practicable and that Nottingham would pay one third of the cost. The arrangement was approved by the MoT. A small shop in Post Office Square had to be demolished to make way for the turning circle, £150 compensation being paid in settlement of all claims.

Following test runs the previous day, Col. Woodhouse, MoT carried out an official inspection of the Wollaton Park routes on 25 November 1931. They opened on Sunday 29 November 1931 with a circular service from the Central Market turning circle at the junction of Glasshouse Street, King Edward Street, Lower Parliament Street and Upper Parliament Street outside the Palais de Danse, via Upper Parliament Street and the eastern end of Derby Road, continuing alternately via Derby Road or Ilkeston Road to Middleton Boulevard and then back to the City. There was no turning point whatsoever on Middleton Boulevard and all vehicles followed a continuous circular routing changing their service number at their Wollaton Park timing point. The nominal terminus, timing point and fare stage in both directions was Fairham Drive (a short residential road on the east side of Middleton Boulevard) although trolleybuses travelling in a clockwise direction would layover just north of Scalford Drive (which branched off Middleton Boulevard to the north-west) about 30 yards south of Fairham Drive on the opposite side of the dual carriageway. Through passengers were carried.

The Derby Road service was numbered 8 and the Ilkeston Road 9, however it appears that, in view of the common city centre terminal point, the number blinds were not changed before

A publicity image of Karrier-Clough 25. *Park Royal*

returning to Central Market. It is unclear if this was official policy or not. The already truncated tram service 7 ran along Derby Road for the last time on Saturday 28 November 1931 and thereafter was further foreshortened to run Old Market Square – Trent Bridge via London Road only. The Ilkeston Road motor bus service (6), including its temporary tram-replacement extension to Wollaton Park Lodge Gates, Derby Road, was withdrawn entirely.

8 Central Market – Upper Parliament Street – Derby Road – Wollaton Park (Middleton Boulevard, Fairham Drive)

9 Central Market – Upper Parliament Street – Ilkeston Road – Wollaton Park (Middleton Boulevard, Fairham Drive)

The two new trolleybus services each operated at 12-minute intervals throughout the day (giving a combined service every 6 minutes between Central Market and Canning Circus) and at 6-minute intervals at peak periods, Monday – Saturday. This was reduced to a 20-minute frequency on Sunday mornings, increasing to a 10-minute/5-minute frequency later in the day. Services were provided by 12 Karrier E6s 25-36 and 13 Ransomes D6s 37-49 both with 60 seat bodies. Thereafter, with the exception of the 1935 Leyland TTB4s, the latest deliveries were always placed in service on the Carlton route, probably due to its demanding schedule and topography.

In November 1931, 10,072 yards of 4/0 SWG and 562 yards of 3/0 SWG grooved cadmium copper trolley wire was ordered from White Cross Co. Ltd. at £74 per ton according to MTTA specifications.

On 30 November 1931 a special meeting of the Passenger Transport Committee recommended that a reserve and renewal fund should be set up and that amounts should be transferred from the trading profits annually. The City Treasurer

Heading west along Lower Parliament Street Ransomes D6/Brush 39 which entered service on 29 November 1931 crosses the junction with King Edward Street. Note that the Central Market, Palais de Danse turning circle is still aloft and that for a short period there was obviously no westbound overhead wiring in Lower Parliament Street between King Edward Street and Southwell Road. *GHFA & JMB*

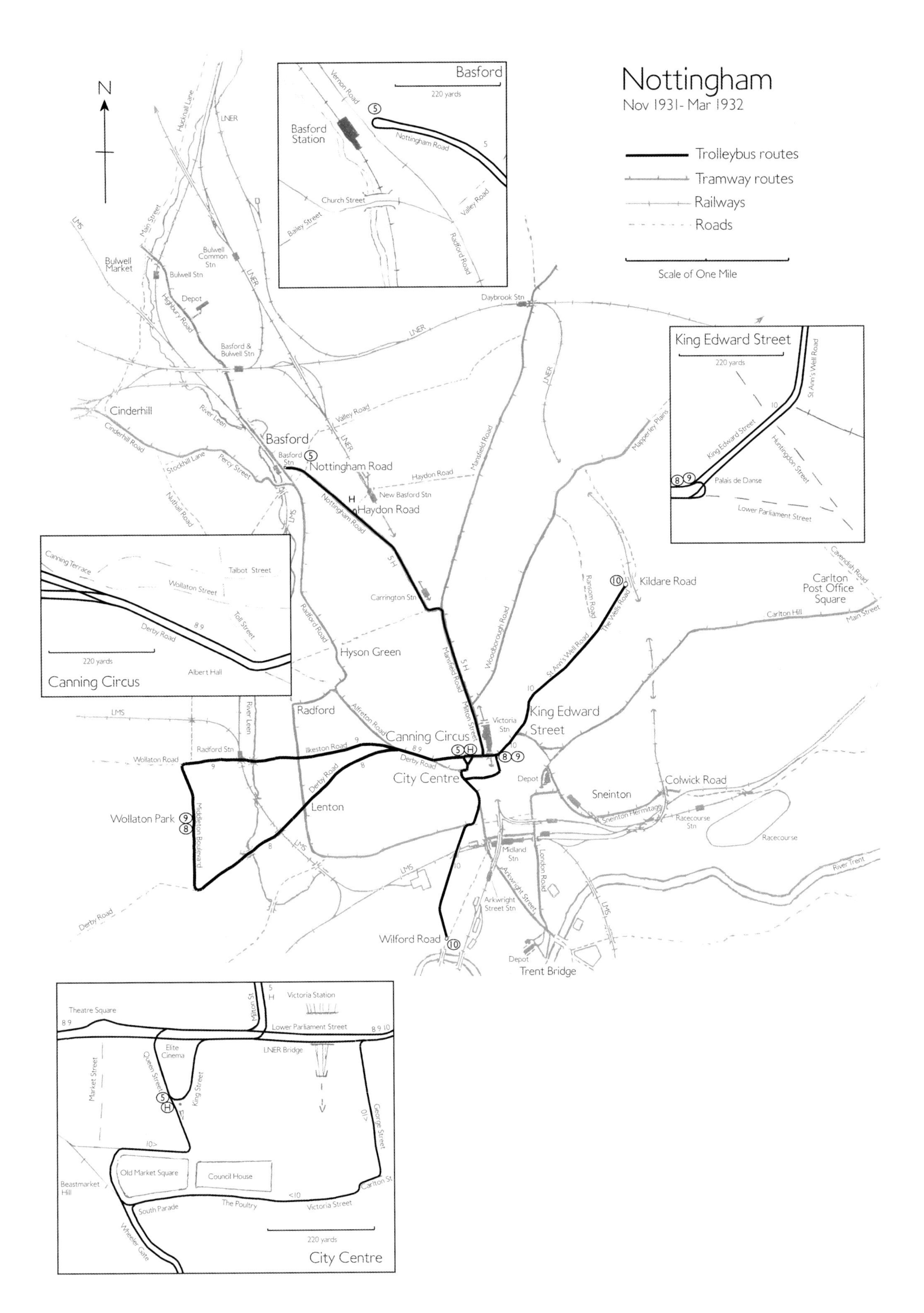

Nottingham
Nov 1931- Mar 1932
Trolleybus routes
Tramway routes
Railways
Roads
Scale of One Mile
Basford
220 yards
Vernon Road
Basford Station
Nottingham Road
Church Street
Bailey Street
Valley Road
Radford Road
King Edward Street
St Ann's Well Road
Huntingdon Street
Palais de Danse
Lower Parliament Street
Canning Circus
Canning Terrace
Talbot Street
Wollaton Street
Derby Road
Toll Street
Albert Hall
City Centre
Theatre Square
Victoria Station
Lower Parliament Street
Milton St
Elite Cinema
LNER Bridge
Market Street
Queen Street
King Street
George Street
Old Market Square
Council House
Beastmarket Hill
South Parade
The Poultry
Victoria Street
Carlton St
Wheeler Gate
Bulwell Market
Bulwell Stn
Bulwell Common Stn
Depot
Highbury Road
Basford & Bulwell Stn
Cinderhill
Cinderhill Road
River Leen
Basford
Nottingham Road
Haydon Road
New Basford Stn
Carrington Stn
Mansfield Road
Woodborough Road
Mapperley Plains
Daybrook Stn
Kildare Road
The Wells Road
Ransom Road
Carlton Post Office Square
Carlton Hill
Main Street
Cavendish Road
Hyson Green
Radford
Alfreton Road
Ilkeston Road
Radford Stn
Wollaton Road
Wollaton Park
Middleton Boulevard
Lenton
Canning Circus
City Centre
Victoria Stn
King Edward Street
Depot
Sneinton
Sneinton Hermitage
Colwick Road
Racecourse Stn
Racecourse
Midland Stn
London Road
Arkwright Street
Arkwright Street Stn
Wilford Road
Depot
Trent Bridge
River Trent
Derby Road

questioned the policy of purchasing additional vehicles out of revenue. The General Manager commented that the first ten railless vehicles were now four years old whilst the loan period was ten years; before the loan period was over the vehicles would be obsolete due to the rapid development of trolley vehicles. It was resolved that the loan charges should be paid off in eight instead of ten years.

The Karrier demonstrator (27) had by now been on loan for 12 months and had proved most satisfactory. Karrier had been paid £450 for the hire at a rate of 3d per mile and was now offering to sell the vehicle to NCT for £2,129 less the £450 hire charge. Mr Marks was successful in negotiating a 5% discount, less the cumulated hire charge of £473 6s 4d, making the price asked £1,549 4s 8d. This was accepted, the vehicle being paid for out of the existing loan. In January 1932 an accounting error in the hire charge was discovered which increased the final purchase price to £1,555 13s 1d.

The experiment of filling in and tarring over the disused tram rails in St. Ann's Well Road was deemed a success and the Works and Ways Committee recommended this solution for all other abandoned track including Derby Road, where the rails were already proving detrimental to other traffic, adding that sooner or later the Passenger Transport Committee would have to pay for its removal.

Mr Godsmark presented a paper on City Transport Problems to the Nottingham Society of Engineers in which he stated that the modern tramcar was superior to the modern omnibus for city work except that it was less mobile. Since trams had been introduced to Nottingham's streets they had contributed almost £500,000 in rate relief. If that money had been put into a reserve fund and used for tramway modernisation all the needs of the new housing estates could have been met. He spoke of the advantages of the trolleybus, its speed and its powers of acceleration and braking. At 20 mph the trolley wheel made 2,000 rpm and there was a pressure of 28 to 32lbs per square inch against the trolley wire. Thus lubrication was a serious matter, especially as too much oil led to bad electrical contact. Mr Godsmark added that the department had vehicles in service which had completed 75,000 miles without new brake linings.

In December 1931 the continuing economic depression led the City's Finance and General Purposes Committee to instruct that no Committee was to proceed with work involving capital expenditure without their consent. In March 1932, following a recommendation by Alderman Sir Albert Ball, the father of the World War I flying "ace", the City Council decided that the trolley vehicle conversion scheme should be spread over four years instead of three.

The need for a turning circle on Middleton Boulevard for vehicles from Derby Road was becoming evident and on 4 March 1932 the Works and Ways Committee asked if it could be constructed at Scalford Drive, Wollaton Park, instead of at the junction with Wollaton Hall Drive where two additional traction poles would be necessary. The Department had no objections to this change. They also pointed out that as the bus stop signs were mounted on the traction poles in Middleton Boulevard, passengers were walking onto the grass spoiling its appearance. The Passenger Transport Committee decided that identifying squares should be marked out on the road surface at bus stops and that the stop signs should be relocated.

The necessary work to convert the Carlton tram route and construct the short extension to the new, Post Office Square, terminus was completed on 15 March 1932, Lt.Col. Trench carried out a successful official MoT Inspection on 18 March 1932 and trams ceased to operate on service 8 after the last car on Saturday 19 March 1932. From Sunday morning 20 March 1932, Carlton was served by extending both Wollaton Park trolley vehicle services eastwards beyond Central Market. An amended timetable provided improved frequencies along Derby Road, serving Raleigh Cycles' Faraday Road factory, at peak periods and a reduced frequency on Ilkeston Road, and thus a balanced number of journeys on both services to/from Wollaton Park. The new turning circle at Scalford Drive, Middleton Boulevard, a "U" shaped turn-back between the northbound and southbound overhead wires through a gap in the dual carriageway central reservation, also came into use on 20 March 1932 and was served by additional peak hour journeys along Derby Road to and from Central Market. These changes improved revenue on the Wollaton Park services by approximately 2d per vehicle mile whilst the first revenue statistics on the Carlton route were most encouraging.

Ransomes D6/Brush 41 (TV4479) delivered in October 1931 climbing Derby Road out of the Old Market Square towards Canning Circus in January 1932. *GHFA & JMB*

8 Carlton (Post Office Square) – Carlton Road – Upper Parliament Street – Central Market – Derby Road – Wollaton Park (Middleton Boulevard) *(eastbound via Central Market – King Edward Street – Bath Street – Handel Street, westbound via Southwell Road – Lower Parliament Street)*

10 Carlton (Post Office Square) – Carlton Road – Upper Parliament Street – Ilkeston Road – Wollaton Park (Middleton Boulevard)

Karrier Clough E6/Park Royal 35 waits at Middleton Boulevard, soon after entering service in 1932. *NCT*

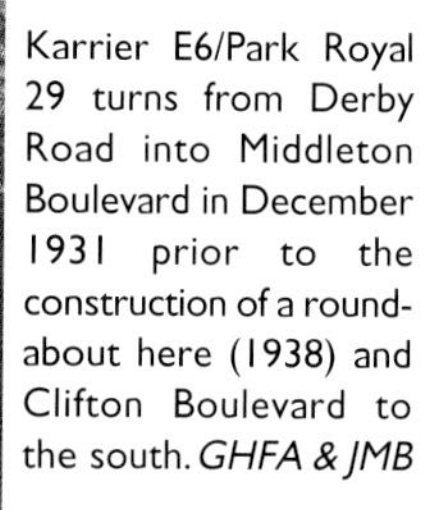

Karrier E6/Park Royal 29 turns from Derby Road into Middleton Boulevard in December 1931 prior to the construction of a roundabout here (1938) and Clifton Boulevard to the south. *GHFA & JMB*

Ransomes, Sims & Jeffries D6 39 heading west on service 8 outside the Leyland depot in Derby Road at the erstwhile Wollaton Park Lodge Gates tram terminus in January 1932. Note the orange lens of the nearside fog light and the large sidelights (above the driver's windscreen). *GHFA & JMB*

(eastbound via Central Market – King Edward Street – Bath Street – Handel Street, westbound via Southwell Road – Lower Parliament Street)

It is understood that the practice of not changing the service number display at Wollaton Park on these circular routings continued and that trolleybuses returned to the city centre still showing the service number corresponding to their outward journey along Derby Road or Ilkeston Road, as the final destination, Carlton, or Central Market beforehand, did not vary. This situation continued throughout the lifetime of the 8/9 and 38/39 circular routings.

Trolleybuses operating towards Carlton continued from the Central Market via King Edward Street, Bath Street and Handel Street to Carlton Road and in the reverse direction via Carlton Road, Southwell Road and Lower Parliament Street to Central Market. Although the trams had operated a short working to Standhill Road no trolleybus turning arrangements were installed here although the destination was included on the vehicles' indicator blinds.

The following tram services were amended:

Tram 7 – the Trent Bridge – Old Market Square service was extended to operate anti-clockwise around the Radford and Lenton Boulevards, replacing the western portion of tram service 8. Clockwise journeys around the Boulevards to/from Sherwood (Villiers Road) continued to be provided by tram service 6.

Tram 8 – withdrawn completely

The Police had expressed their concerns about the number of vehicles using the tight Central Market turning circle, located at a busy road junction. Following the extension of the Wollaton Park services to and from Carlton this figure was reduced from 296 to just 23 per day. It is not known exactly when the turning circle, which is known to have been short-lived, ceased to be used and when it was removed. Photographic evidence shows the frog in place in May 1933 but it had gone by March 1934. Vehicles continued to terminate at Central Market although they physically continued around the loop provided by King Edward Street, Bath Street, Southwell Road and Lower Parliament Street or vice versa for turning purposes.

Fares had been increased on the introduction of the Ilkeston Road trolleybuses but following complaints from the Wollaton Park Householders' Association a revised fares structure for the Carlton – Wollaton Park services was introduced on 3 April 1932. The Passenger Transport Committee informed a deputation from the Association that with the completion of the conversion to trolley vehicle operation, it was possible to revise the fares and stages on this route, and with the exception of the new 1d Scalford Drive Workman Fare, which was shortened from Upper Parliament Street (an above average length) to Canning Circus, the revised fares and stages met most of the Association's objections. Also at some date in 1932 the times of the last trolleybuses from the City were extended to around 11 pm.

On 29 April 1932 Forest City signal lights were installed in Carlton to prevent trolleybuses passing in the narrow Main Street. Trolleybuses waited just past St. Paul's Church of England Primary School, almost opposite the junction with Church Street, until the one at the terminus passed on its way back to the city centre.

Some economies were recorded in the paint shop by simplifying the livery to all-over medium green with cream bands, and giving up the lighter green lower deck waistband. The financial crisis affected the employees as well as the Department. At the Passenger Transport Committee meeting of 25 April 1932 the Chairman reported that consideration of the National Joint Industrial Council for the Tramway Industry's recommendations as to a reduction of wages and conditions of service had been adjourned in order that Mr Marks could investigate what other authorities had done and also the undertaking's financial position. The Chairman stated that the matter had already been considered by the Midlands group of the Municipal Tramways and Transport Association (MTTA) which had asked its member authorities to put the reduction into force but this had not been implemented in Nottingham as the wage levels for many employees were already below the national standard for comparable undertakings. Mr Marks' investigations showed that Nottingham's wage rates had been below those of similarly sized undertakings from 1924 to 1928, and it was accordingly decided not to make any reductions (although these proved necessary in 1933).

The passenger waiting shelter at the junction of Mansfield Road with Gregory Boulevard in March 1933. Open-balcony top-covered tram 177 dating from 1920 pulls away on its journey to Villiers Road, Sherwood as Railless 5 pulls on to Mansfield Road heading for the city centre. Somewhere behind the stone wall the railway tunnel from Victoria Station surfaced at Carrington Station. *GHFA & JMB*

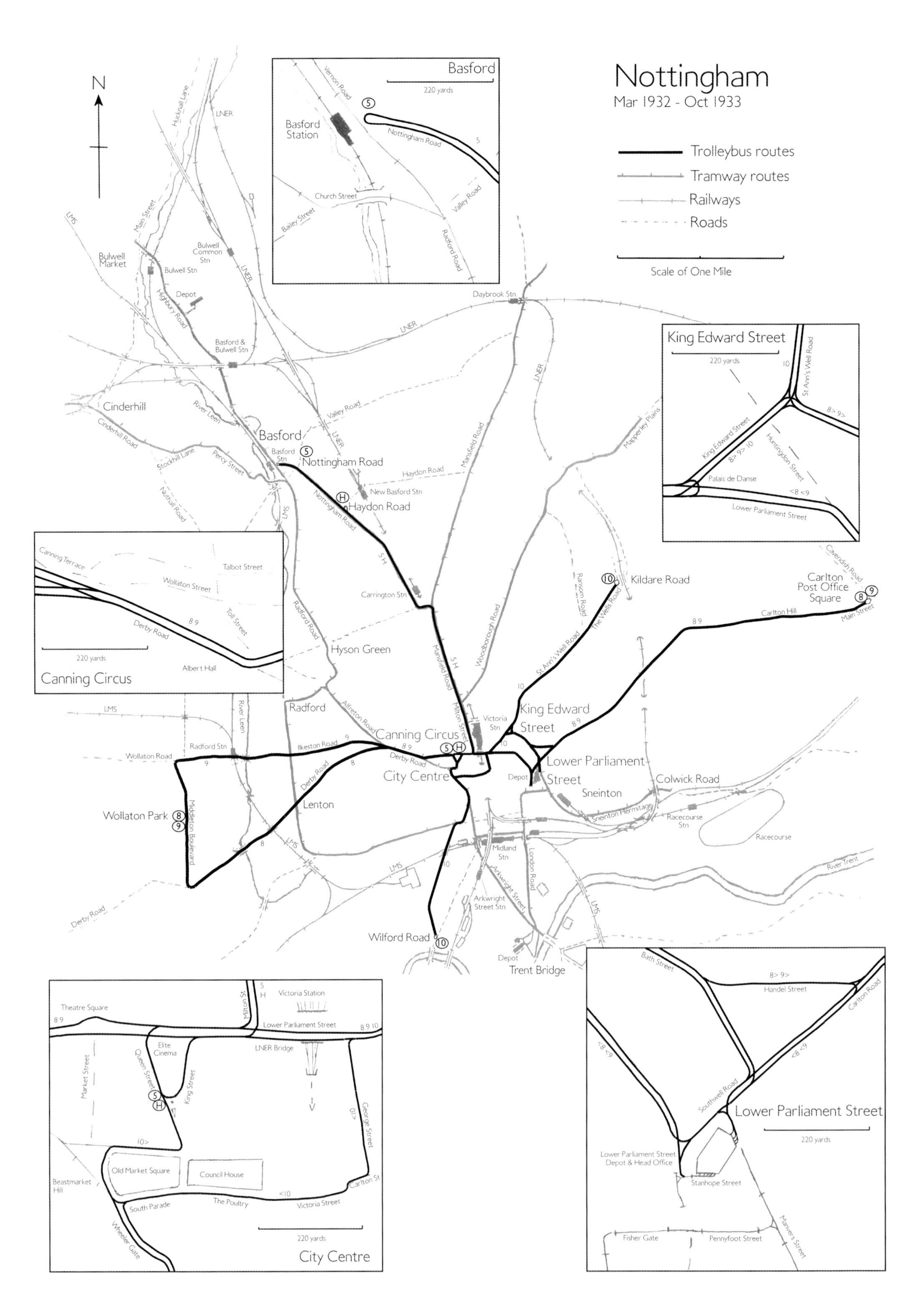
Nottingham
Mar 1932 - Oct 1933
Trolleybus routes
Tramway routes
Railways
Roads
Scale of One Mile
N
Basford
220 yards
Basford Station
Vernon Road
Nottingham Road
Church Street
Bailey Street
Valley Road
Radford Road
King Edward Street
St Ann's Well Road
King Edward Street
Huntingdon Street
Palais de Danse
Lower Parliament Street
Canning Circus
Canning Terrace
Talbot Street
Wollaton Street
Toll Street
Derby Road
Albert Hall
Bulwell Market
Bulwell Stn
Bulwell Common Stn
Depot
Highbury Road
Basford & Bulwell Stn
Daybrook Stn
Cinderhill
Cinderhill Road
Stockhill Lane
Percy Street
Nuthall Road
River Leen
Basford
Basford Stn
Nottingham Road
Haydon Road
New Basford Stn
Mansfield Road
Mapperley Plains
Carrington Stn
Hyson Green
Radford
Alfreton Road
Ilkeston Road
Canning Circus
City Centre
Victoria Stn
King Edward Street
Lower Parliament Street
Kildare Road
The Wells Road
Ransom Road
Carlton Post Office Square
Cavendish Road
Carlton Hill
Main Street
Woodborough Road
Milton Street
Radford Stn
Wollaton Road
Wollaton Park
Middleton Boulevard
Lenton
Derby Road
Depot
Sneinton
Sneinton Hermitage
Colwick Road
Racecourse Stn
Racecourse
River Trent
Midland Stn
London Road
Arkwright Street
Arkwright Street Stn
Wilford Road
Depot
Trent Bridge
City Centre
Theatre Square
Victoria Station
Milton St
Lower Parliament Street
Elite Cinema
LNER Bridge
Market Street
Queen Street
King Street
George Street
Old Market Square
Council House
Beastmarket Hill
South Parade
The Poultry
Victoria Street
Carlton St
Wheeler Gate
Lower Parliament Street
Bath Street
Handel Street
Carlton Road
Southwell Road
Lower Parliament Street Depot & Head Office
Stanhope Street
Fisher Gate
Pennyfoot Street
Manvers Street
LNER
LMS

In 1912, a tram services numbering system, consecutively from 1, had been introduced and the replacement trolley vehicle services were numbered in this same series until now whereas motor buses had their own separate series, also starting from 1. During the tram to trolleybus conversion programme service numbering changed frequently and included several duplications, for example at one time there were three different services displaying the number 8! The tram Carlton – City – Lenton and Radford Circle; trolleybus City – Wollaton Park via Derby Road and motor bus 8 Trent Bridge – Sneinton Dale via Meadow Lane.

A new universal numbering system was introduced on Sunday 5 March 1933 to avoid duplication, motor bus services being designated 1-35 and later 51 and above, trolleybuses 36-50 and trams displayed letters instead of numbers. The existing trolleybus services were renumbered as follows:

36 (5) Old Market Square (Queen Street/King Street) – Upper Parliament Street – Milton Street – Victoria Station – Mansfield Road – Nottingham Road (Vernon Road)

37 (H) Old Market Square (Queen Street/King Street) – Upper Parliament Street – Milton Street – Victoria Station – Mansfield Road – Nottingham Road (Haydn Road)

38 (8) Carlton (Post Office Square) – Carlton Road – Central Market – Upper Parliament Street – Derby Road – Wollaton Park (Middleton Boulevard) *(eastbound via Central Market – King Edward Street – Bath Street – Handel Street, westbound via Southwell Road – Lower Parliament Street)*

39 (9) Carlton (Post Office Square) – Carlton Road – Central Market – Upper Parliament Street – Ilkeston Road – Wollaton Park (Middleton Boulevard) *(eastbound via Central Market – King Edward Street – Bath Street – Handel Street, westbound via Southwell Road – Lower Parliament Street)*

40 (10) The Wells Road (Kildare Road) – St. Ann's Well Road – King Edward Street – Upper Parliament Street – Old Market Square – Wilford Road – Wilford Bridge *(northbound via Queen Street, southbound via George Street – Carlton Street – Victoria Street – The Poultry – South Parade*

The remaining tram services were given alphabetic codes:

A (2) Trent Bridge – Arkwright Street – Old Market Square – Upper Parliament Street – Milton Street – Woodborough Road – Mapperley

B (2) Old Market Square – Upper Parliament Street – Milton Street – Woodborough Road – Mapperley

C (3) Trent Bridge – Arkwright Street – Old Market Square – Derby Road – Alfreton Road – Hyson Green – Radford Road – Vernon Road – Bulwell Market Place

D (4) Colwick Road – Sneinton – Bath Street – King Edward Street – Upper Parliament Street – Old Market Square – Derby Road – Alfreton Road – Hyson Green – Radford Road – Vernon Road – Basford

E (6) Villiers Road, Sherwood – Mansfield Road – Milton Street – Old Market Square – Castle Boulevard – Lenton Boulevard – Hartley Road – Alfreton Road – Derby Road – Old Market Street – Milton Street – Mansfield Road – Villiers Road, Sherwood *(unidirectional)*

F (7) Trent Bridge – London Road – Bath Street – King Edward Street – Upper Parliament Street – Old Market Square – Derby Road – Alfreton Road – Hartley Road – Lenton Boulevard – Castle Boulevard – Old Market Street – Upper Parliament Street – King Edward Street – Bath Street – London Road – Trent Bridge *(unidirectional)*

H (1) Old Market Square – Upper Parliament Street – Milton Street – Mansfield Road – Daybrook

J (-) LMS Station – Station Street – Sneinton – Colwick Road

K (9) Trent Bridge – Arkwright Street – Old Market Square – Upper Parliament Street – Milton Street – Mansfield Road – Arnold

On Sunday 20 March 1932 trolleybus service 9 was extended eastwards from Central Market to Carlton. Families take their first trip and an excited school boy peers out of upper deck front window as 42 turns out of Southwell Road into Lower Parliament Street with the curved facade of the undertaking's head-quaters on the nearside. As its a Sunday the blinds of the shop to the offside are drawn down. *GHFA & JMB*

The Annual Report for the year ending 31 March 1932 showed that trams ran 4,306,286 miles, the 50 trolleybuses 1,082,004 and motorbuses 4,305,437; a total of 9,693,727 miles and an increase of 785,945 during the year.

	Tram	Trolleybus	Motorbus
Receipts per mile run	15.10d	15.84d	12.41d
Working expenses per mile	12.55d	12.16d	10.33d
Profit	2.55d	3.68d	2.08d
Ordinary Fares	0.76d	0.94d	0.92d
Workmen's Fares	0.48d	0.67d	0.56d

In August 1934 Ransomes D6 17 pulls out of King Edward Street into Lower Parliament Street with the main entrance of Central Market evident on the left and the Palais de Danse (still extant in 2005) on the right. Although only 4 years old, the "trackless" appears dated in comparison with the AEC Regent. In this view all evidence of the short-lived Central Market turning circle has disappeared. *GHFA & JMB*

The point duty policeman complete with white gloves and cuffs controls traffic in Theatre Square as Ransomes D6/Brush 38 races past westwards along Upper Parliament Street to Wollaton Park via Derby Road. This view must have been taken in 1932-33 following the extension of trolleybus service 8 and 9 to Carlton as there is a number 7 tram displaying Radford as its destination in the background. The delivery boy is either looking for a gap in the traffic to move across to Wollaton Street or he is admiring the modern trolleybus. *BTS*

Rushing for Railless No 2 at a stop in Sherwood Rise during February 1933. *GHFA & JMB*

Service letter G (8) had been reserved for the Carlton tram route but this was by now trolleybus operated. There were no further tramway abandonments until 12 May 1934.

By the early 1930s the nation's railways were complaining that, in addition to the economic recession, they were suffering from indiscriminate road competition. In their opinion motor traffic needed to bear the real costs of the roads it used, something still not corrected seventy years later! Eventually the MoT called a special conference, consisting of an independent chairman, Sir Arthur Salter, four representatives of the railways and four representatives of the road haulage industry, to consider competition, the division of functions and the incidence of highway costs. It was estimated that the real cost of roads in 1930-31 was some £66.4 million. The MTTA anticipated that passenger carrying vehicles, apparently excluding trams but inherently including trackless trolley systems, would potentially have to pay a higher rate of duty or fuel tax. A 6-fold increase in the cost of trolley vehicle licence duty to compensate the Exchequer with a sum equivalent to that paid in petrol duty by a motorbus was rumoured, which, in isolation, would have removed the financial advantages of electric traction over motorbuses.

At their 2 September 1932 meeting the Passenger Transport Committee considered the Salter Report and, aligned with the MTTA's interpretation, feared that it sought to impose additional duties on municipal transport undertakings. Nationally, for a short period undertakings viewed the introduction of trolleybuses with caution; but later in the autumn it was clarified that the Salter Report's recommendations referred only to road goods vehicles. Mr Marks had recently attended an MTTA Midlands group meeting that had discussed government proposals for an Area Joint Transport Board and decided that this was neither necessary nor desirable due to the geographical isolation of the municipal undertakings. Mr Marks had also unofficially attended a meeting of local company operators to discuss the revision and standardisation of fares. He asked for, and was granted, permission to attend future meetings so that he could report upon developments. Assuming some kind of nationalisation, Nottingham committed to support the MTTA Council and stated that the Salter Report was contrary to continued municipal ownership and would reduce the number of passengers.

The Gas Department was considering lighting Radford Boulevard, Hartley Road and Gregory Boulevard corner and enquired if the Passenger Transport Committee would be planting traction poles along this route for a conversion to trolley vehicle operation. In view of the Salter Report it was felt that the Passenger Transport Committee might need to review its tramway conversion programme and that the Lighting Committee should pay the interest on the necessary capital expenditure on traction poles until such time as they were required for their true purpose.

At 6 pm on 13 May 1932 Railless 9 pulling out of Queen Street on a service 5 working, collided with a service 8 trolley vehicle leaving the Elite Cinema stop on Upper Parliament Street *en route* to Wollaton Park, and was damaged sufficiently as to require a new body. It was decided to scrap the body but retain the chassis as a source of spares for the remaining chassis of that type, and replace it with a new larger vehicle. The "paper transaction" to accomplish this was provided by the purchase of the Brush body formerly mounted on the Thornycroft demonstrator chassis which had operated, as fleet number 28, in Nottingham until June 1931. Originally priced at £897, it proved possible to purchase the body for £650. A new Karrier E6 chassis, suitable for the body, was bought for £1,189 15s, the resultant Karrier Brush bodied vehicle being delivered in 1933 and receiving the fleet number 1.

On 25 November 1932 the Passenger Transport Committee accepted the tender of John Spencer Ltd., Wednesbury, amounting to £982 (40 heavy poles at £12 6s each and 50 medium poles at £9 16s) for the Nottingham Road (Valley Road) – Church Street, Basford – Percy Street – Stockhill Lane – Nuthall Road – Cinderhill route which was being converted from tram to trolleybus operation on behalf of N&D.

On 6 January 1933 the Passenger Transport Committee considered a report on trolley bus interference with wireless (radio) reception. The trolley vehicle fleet could be equipped with suppressor coils costing £16 each plus fitting leading to a total expenditure of ca. £1,000. Mr Marks felt that such coils would not obviate the alleged interference with wireless reception. Although there had been a meeting with representatives of the Wireless Traders Association, who appreciated the Department's efforts to help, a Mr A.W. Lymm protested at the casual manner with which the subject of trolleybus interference had been handled. In an "Evening News" report he was quoted as saying that interference *"was so bad on the No. 8 route that one resident in Wollaton Park had told how he caught his bus daily by the noise created in his receiver as the trolley bus approached along Middleton Boulevard!"* He dismissed the statement that not more than 10% of interference in Nottingham was due to trolleybuses as "perfectly absurd". Quite 95% of interference was due to the trolleybuses. The experimental coils had been a great success and the cost was not significant. On 3 February 1933 it was resolved that the Town Clerk contact the Secretary to the Post Office upon the matter and that the Chairman make a press statement.

In the meantime the N&D had curtailed their Nottingham – Ripley tram service to the city boundary at Cinderhill, Bell's Lane on 3 September 1932, the delay causing Nottingham some problems with the MoT in repeatedly extending the grant for road reinstatement along Nuthall Road, until after the trams had been abandoned. No direct replacement of the through service was offered whilst the tram to trolleybus conversion was carried out. In January 1933 NCT loaned N&D a Karrier Clough E6 trolleybus in order that the company could confirm that double deckers were really suitable for their system. Its apparent success led the company to order 15 AEC661Ts with 55-seat MCCW bodies. The normal service of trams was then withdrawn in stages; Langley Mill Depot – Ripley ceasing at the end of January 1933, Cinderhill – Eastwood on 13 February 1933 and Eastwood – Langley Mill on 9 March 1933. Motorbuses provided a replacement service on these portions of the route although one tramcar per day continued to run between Cinderhill and Heanor for legal reasons until a through trolleybus service commenced.

On 25 July 1933 Col. Woodhouse inspected the route to be followed by the N&D trolleybuses within the city boundary from Nottingham Road (Valley Road) along Church Street, Alpine Street, Percy Street, Stockhill Lane and Nuthall Road, in place of the tramway reservation along Dark Lane, to Cinderhill, Bells Lane. As in the case of the Carlton-Wollaton Park

No longer in original livery Railless 5 waits outside St. Andrew's Church, Mansfield Road, at the traffic lights controlling the Forest Road East, Mapperley Road crossroads in November 1933.
GHFA & JMB

route, "Nottingham" catenary suspension overhead equipment was used on this extension. The through N&D trolleybus service 1 between Nottingham, Queen Street and Ripley via Cinderhill, Nuthall, Kimberley, Eastwood, Langley Mill, Heanor and Loscoe commenced on Thursday 5 October 1933 in time for the Goose Fair, utilising NCT overhead wiring along Upper Parliament Street, Milton Street, Mansfield Road, Sherwood Rise and Nottingham Road through Basford then as above to Cinderhill. This completed the construction of the N&D trolleybus system, the ½ mile link along Church Street, Cotmanhay, providing an alternative through route between Ilkeston and Heanor having opened on 1 October 1933.

The N&D trolleybus service operated every 15 minutes, increased to every 10 minutes on Saturdays, but there were a variety of motorbus and trolleybus operated extra and short workings, many of which turned back at Cinderhill where, as the name suggests, there was a large colliery, throughout the life of the system. The newspapers placed great store on the fact that the company's new half-cab AEC661T MCCW bodied double-decker trolleybuses were equipped with wireless interference suppression coils. The 15½-mile trip offered the longest interurban trolleybus service in the UK, being noted for its high speeds and hilly topography for which the vehicles were ideally suited. The "posting box" hitherto conveyed by the 9.04 pm MGOC bus from Ripley was now carried by the 8.52 pm trolleybus.

As a turning circle, accessible from both the Basford and Kimberley directions, was included at Bells Lane, the Corporation used this opportunity to introduce their own peak hour only trolleybus service as far as the city boundary at Cinderhill:

41 Old Market Square (Queen Street/King Street) – Upper Parliament Street – Milton Street – Victoria Station – Mansfield Road – Nottingham Road – Stockhill Lane – Cinderhill (Bells Lane)

The N&D trolleybuses provided the sole example in Nottingham of a company operator's service that was permitted to pick up and set down passengers within the city boundaries, local passengers being carried within the city boundaries at applicable Corporation fares. There was a combined timetable for services 36, 37 and 41 that referred to a joint Corporation and N&D operation between King Street and Nottingham Road, Vernon Road, although N&D schedules to/from Cinderhill were not coordinated with those of the 41. All revenues collected on N&D trolleybuses between King Street and the city boundary passed to the Corporation, less 10½d per mile working expenses. A proposed joint service as far as Kimberley (some 3 miles beyond Cinderhill) was never implemented although some NCT trolleybuses had Kimberley on their destination blinds.

The February 1934 NCT timetable curiously shows solely northbound (outwards) journeys on service 41, scheduled to operate just in front of N&D departures, the company perhaps fearing that local, short stage traveller might "crowd out" long distance passengers, but no inbound workings! It is not known if the vehicles working these journeys returned towards the city empty or in service but not timetabled. Subsequent editions made less and less mention of a joint operation with N&D, and by September 1934 service 41 journeys to Cinderhill were no longer mentioned in the timetable, schedules only reappearing in 1939 whilst service number 41 was dormant until 1941.

Throughout the 1920s the Tramways Committee had asked that they be granted reduced rates for traction power to align them with bulk commercial consumers but on each occasion the Electricity Committee had refused until the North Wilford Power Station came on line. A reduction of ¼d per unit had at last been granted from 1 October 1929 but, having reviewed the amounts paid in other towns, it was decided to ask again for another reduction. In March 1933, the Electricity Committee proposed a reduced tariff structure for traction current commencing at 0.85d per unit for the first 10,000,000 units used and then on a sliding scale reducing by 0.05d for each 2,500,000 units with a minimum charge of 0.70d for all consumption in excess of 15,000,000 units pa. As the prevailing price was 1d per unit, these proposals were estimated to offer the Transport Department savings of up to £10,937 if 15,000,000 units were used. In the absence of the Electricity Committee, the Passenger Transport Committee resolved that as from the end of the March quarter the standard price would be 0.70d per unit subject to a coal clause adjustment of 0.15d per unit for every 6d per ton rise or fall on the average annual price of coal delivered into the power station above 12s per ton. The Electricity Committee appears to have accepted this although throughout the 1930s NCT's traction power consumption never exceeded 13 million units.

In April 1933 the City Engineer was asked for an estimate for removing disused tram rails on Nottingham Road from Haydn Road to Vernon Road, and on St. Ann's Well Road between Bath Street and the terminus, with a view to providing work for the unemployed. The amounts of £2,360 and £5,500 respectively amounted to ca. 11s 8d per square yard whereas other undertakings were being charged considerably less e.g. Dundee 4s 3d, Halifax 5s 6d, Llanelly 3s to 4s, N&D 5s 6d, whilst the Nottingham Corporation Act 1930 foresaw 5s 6d to 7s. As liability under the Tramways Act was limited to putting the roads back into the condition that they were at the time the tram track was laid and not to the condition in which the rest of the road now was, the Works and Ways Committee were asked to reconsider the matter.

There were a series of senior staff changes in the spring of 1933. Mr Godsmark, Deputy General Manager and effectively chief engineer, was appointed General Manager of Huddersfield Corporation Transport, effective 1 May 1933. Mr W. Boot, Rolling Stock Superintendent, wished to retire, and the Assistant Superintendent had proved unsatisfactory and had been asked to seek alternative employment. Solely the position of Rolling Stock Engineer was advertised, the post of Deputy General Manager being abolished, the

AEC/EE's official picture of one of the 661T double deckers for Notts & Derby, before registration.
Geoff Lumb

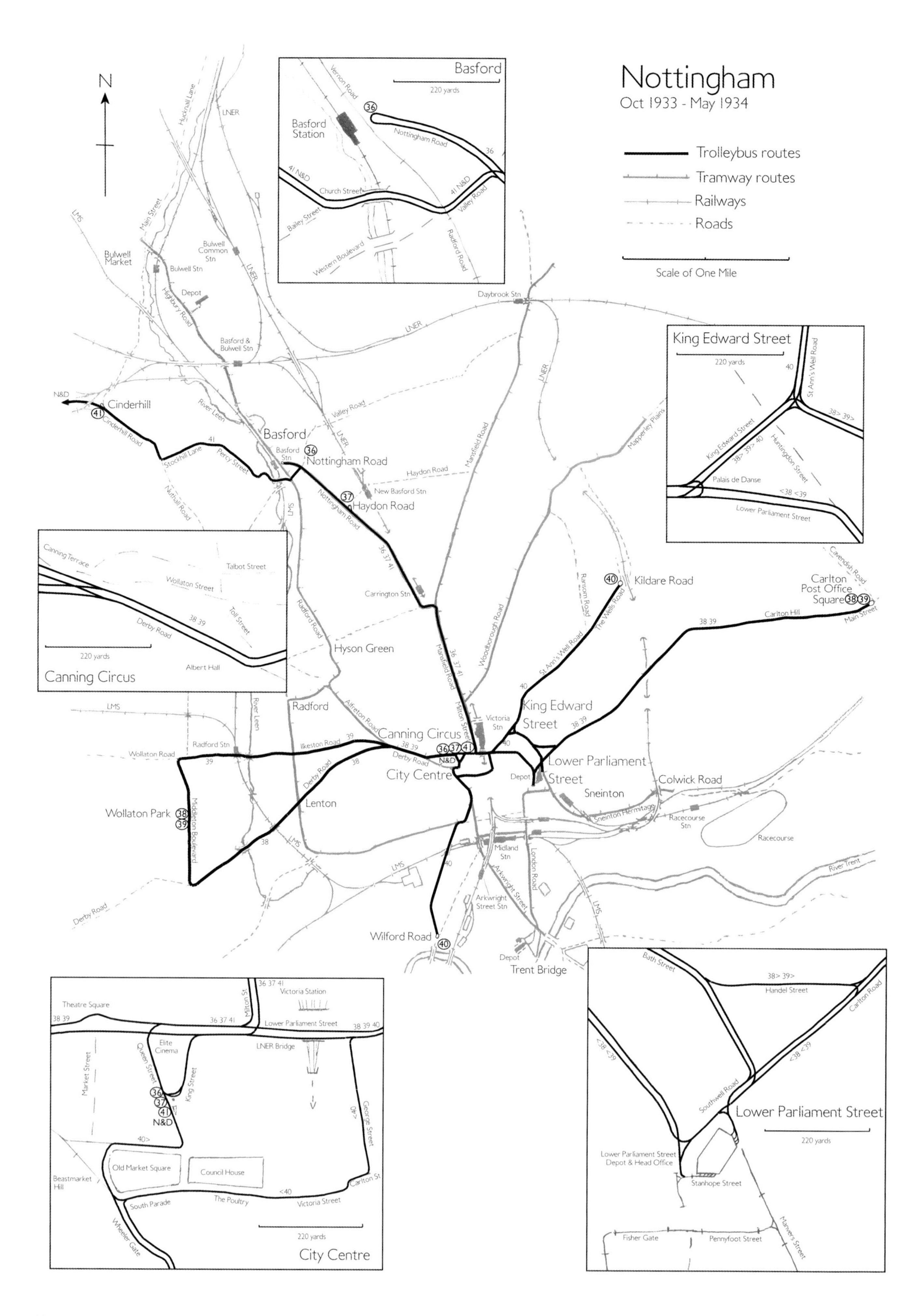
Nottingham
Oct 1933 - May 1934
Trolleybus routes
Tramway routes
Railways
Roads
Scale of One Mile
Basford
220 yards
Basford Station
Vernon Road
Nottingham Road
Church Street
Bailey Street
Western Boulevard
Valley Road
Radford Road
King Edward Street
St Ann's Well Road
King Edward Street
Huntingdon Street
Palais de Danse
Lower Parliament Street
Canning Circus
Canning Terrace
Talbot Street
Wollaton Street
Toll Street
Derby Road
Albert Hall
City Centre
Theatre Square
Victoria Station
Lower Parliament Street
LNER Bridge
Elite Cinema
Queen Street
King Street
Market Street
Milton St
George Street
Old Market Square
Council House
Beastmarket Hill
South Parade
The Poultry
Victoria Street
Carlton St
Wheeler Gate
Lower Parliament Street
Bath Street
Handel Street
Carlton Road
Southwell Road
Lower Parliament Street Depot & Head Office
Stanhope Street
Fisher Gate
Pennyfoot Street
Manvers Street
Cinderhill
Basford
Nottingham Road
Haydon Road
Kildare Road
Carlton Post Office Square
Hyson Green
Radford
Canning Circus
City Centre
King Edward Street
Lower Parliament Street
Colwick Road
Sneinton
Lenton
Wollaton Park
Wilford Road
Trent Bridge
Bulwell Market
Bulwell Stn
Bulwell Common Stn
Basford & Bulwell Stn
Daybrook Stn
New Basford Stn
Carrington Stn
Radford Stn
Victoria Stn
Midland Stn
Arkwright Street Stn
Racecourse Stn
Racecourse
River Trent
River Leen
Mansfield Road
Woodborough Road
Mapperley Plains
Ransom Road
The Wells Road
Carlton Hill
Main Street
Cavendish Road
Alfreton Road
Ilkeston Road
Wollaton Road
Middleton Boulevard
London Road
Arkwright Street
Sneinton Hermitage
Stockhill Lane
Percy Street
Cinderhill Road
Nuthall Road
Highbury Road
Hucknall Lane
Main Street
Depot
N&D
LNER
LMS

Karrier E6A No.1 resplendent with the Brush body from the Thornycroft BD chassis, travelling west on route 39 in Upper Parliament Street by Theatre Square, soon after entering service in May 1933. *GHFA & JMB*

duties being divided between the still to be appointed new Rolling Stock Superintendent and a Statistician (Mr E.S.H. Eales). Shortly thereafter the Salaries Committee suggested that a new Rolling Stock Superintendent and the open accountancy position should not be appointed pending a salary and grade decision.

There were 45 applications for the position of Rolling Stock Superintendent, 4 being short-listed. On 22 May 1933, Mr George H. Pulfrey from Sheffield Corporation Tramways was appointed at a commencing salary of £550 subject to his residing within the City.

The Chairman of the 21 April 1933 Passenger Transport Committee Meeting asked as to the advisability of converting the remaining longer tram routes to trolleybus operation. The immediate conversion of the Bulwell route was confirmed at a special meeting that same day. The General Manager was instructed to prepare a report and estimate of the cost of the conversion of the tramways on the whole of the western side of the city.

The Committee inspected the Bulwell tram route on 12 May 1933, travelling first from Lower Parliament Street to Bulwell Depot where they viewed the building with Mr Marks indicating the alterations which would be necessary to house trolley vehicles. The City Engineer who accompanied them was instructed to prepare a plan and estimate of the necessary alterations. They then inspected the rest of the tram route to Bulwell Market Place, paying special attention to the possibilities of erecting a turning circle in the Market Place. Proceeding along Main Street to the Bulwell Hall Housing Estate, they inspected a plot of land at the City Boundary upon which a turning circle could be built. The Town Clerk was asked to make enquiries with a view to acquiring the site.

They returned via Main Street, Coventry Road, Cinderhill Road, Nuthall Road, Alfreton Road to Gregory Boulevard, Mansfield Road, Huntingdon Street and Lower Parliament Street, stopping to inspect the railway bridge above Cinderhill Road. Mr Marks pointed out it would be necessary to lower the road about 18ins at this point to enable trolley vehicles to operate along this road. They then continued along Manvers Street as far as the railway bridge close to the junction of Port Arthur Road and Colwick Road. Here, the General Manager explained that there were no houses between the railway bridge and the level crossing where the tram terminus was situated, and only 6 small houses just over the crossing and thereafter no further houses until the village of Colwick. He drew attention to very bad state of the Colwick Road tram track. In view of the lack of housing between the railway bridge and the city boundary he suggested that the trolleybus terminus should be located at Port Arthur Road.

Having inspected the remaining tram track in St. Ann's Well Road, the Committee continued along Pennyfoot Street, Lower Parliament Street and London Road to the Cattle Market. The entrance was considered to offer a suitable location for a turning circle to serve the Notts County Football Ground. Continuing to Trent Bridge terminus, it was felt that by demolishing the ticket office there, sufficient space would be available for a turning circle.

It was resolved to seek the City Council's approval to continue with the tram to trolleybus conversion programme, together with a number of additional routes:

Tram Route Conversions:

Bulwell Market Place – Canning Circus via Highbury Road, Vernon Road, Radford Road and Alfreton Road

Colwick – City Centre via Sneinton Hermitage

Trent Bridge – Old Market Square via Arkwright Street and Wheeler Gate

Additional Routes:

Bulwell Hall Housing Estate (City Boundary) – Bulwell Market Place via Hucknall Lane and Main Street

Cinderhill Road (sic, assumed to be the junction of Nuthall Road with Stockhill Lane, Cinderhill), – Bentinck Road Corner via Nuthall Road, Bobbers Mill Bridge, Alfreton Road, linking up with the Alfreton Road route

Huntingdon Street (near Elm Avenue) – Lower Parliament Street.

On 22 May 1933 Mr Marks pointed out that it would be inappropriate to leave trams operating along London Road or Station Street and these were included on the list of conversions.

The City Council approved all the recommendations on 31 July 1933, for immediate conversion or construction, together with any

Nottingham Corporation Transport Department's drawing number 534 of a 'Standard' 6 wheel trolleybus, a guide to manufacturers of what was required. The document is thought to date from 1932-3, and shows a body similar to Brush and MCCW bodies delivered in 1934. ***NCT***

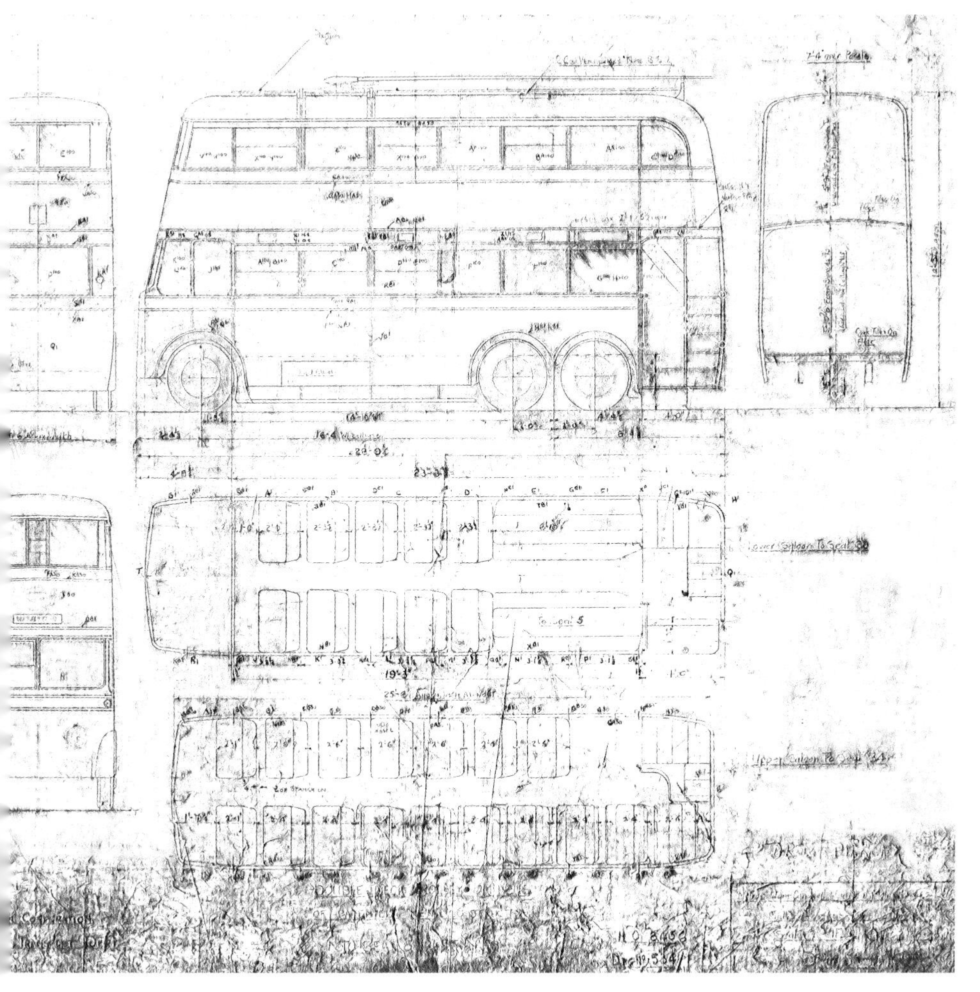

At sometime in 1933 or 1934 the prematurely withdrawn Ransomes LF/Shorts 6 manoeuvres prior to turning north out of Gregory Boulevard into Sherwood Rise en route to Haydn Road on a 37 working. The trolley vehicle is in Livery 2 of 1930. The original overhead wiring is constructed at 30ins separation and there is a rather clumsy splice in the outbound positive wire immediately behind the vehicle.
Roy Marshall

other outstanding tram to trolleybus route conversions which had been approved on 2 March 1931 but subsequently postponed for economic reasons, that is. the circular route along the Boulevards, Huntingdon Street and Canal Street. The additional costs, over and above that already approved in 1931, were:

Overhead equipment	£6,561
Trolley Vehicles	£32,472
Depot alterations	£3,500
Purchase of land for turning circles	£1,500
Total estimated costs	£44,033

The Finance Committee approved the expenditure based on a 10-year loan for the trolley vehicles and a 20-year loan for the equipment, and tenders were invited for 64 miles of trolley wire and 56 trolleybuses. The tenders for wire were all at the same amount whereas the large number received for the vehicles and bodies varied widely in respect of delivery period and price. Tenders were received from AEC, Bristol, Brush, English Electric, Gloucester Railway Carriage & Wagon, Guy, Karrier, Leyland, Ransomes Sims & Jefferies and Sunbeam for the chassis; Brush, English Electric, Gloucester Railway Carriage & Wagon and Metropolitan-Cammell Weymann for metal bodies; Beadle, Brush, English Electric, Gloucester Railway Carriage & Wagon, Park Royal, Roe, Short Bros. and Metropolitan-Cammell Weymann for composite bodies, and several combinations of the above offered as complete vehicles.

Twenty-five of the three-axle Karrier chassis were equipped with 64-seat Brush composite bodies whilst the other 10 had MCCW all-metal 64-seat bodies, and all 21 Ransomes, Sims & Jefferies three-axle chassis were fitted with 64 seat Brush composite bodies. Experience showed that the additional cost of the all-metal bodywork was well justified. At the end of 1933 Mr Marks requested the body builders to incorporate a more substantial type of destination indicator winding gear into the design at an extra cost of £1 3s 6d per vehicle.

The increasing quantity of overhead equipment required an additional tower wagon and the body was removed from recently delivered 1932 AEC Regent motorbus 48. The chassis was converted from side control to normal control, that is the driving position was moved from beside to behind the engine, and an Eagle Engineering body and tower costing £234 5s were fitted.

Following a meeting between the Lord Mayor, the Passenger Transport Committee Chairman, Town Clerk and the Postmaster General concerning wireless (radio) interference, the GPO offered the Corporation six suppression coils for a six month trial on one route. The Corporation viewed wireless as something new which needed to be compliant with existing technology, that is trolleybuses. The GPO stated that they were receiving some 20,000 complaints per year and that other towns had fitted their trolleybuses with coils at their own expense (ca £12 per vehicle) for example Birmingham, Derby, N&D and Southend-on-Sea, whilst others were investigating this solution. The Corporation accepted the offer without accepting any responsibility, considering the coils to be an incomplete solution.

Having approved the Passenger Transport Committee's recommendations of 31 July 1933, by mid-November 1933 the City Council instructed the Town Clerk to obtain a Provisional Order to operate trolley vehicles from the junction of Bentinck Road with Alfreton Road, along Alfreton Road and Nuthall Road to the junction with Stockhill Lane. This was noted as being primarily to the benefit of N&D by providing a more direct route into the city centre.

Mr Marks informed the Committee on 20 August 1933 that he intended to apply for the position of General Manager at Liverpool. Following the selection procedure, he was recommended for the appointment subject to confirmation by Liverpool City Council on 6 December 1933 and the vacancy for a General Manager at Nottingham was advertised. Having had his appointment at Liverpool confirmed, Mr Marks tendered his resignation on 5 January 1934. There were 24 applications for the Nottingham vacancy and the following applicants, all of whom were or had been General Managers, were invited for interview: Mr J. Austin Baker, South Shields; Mr. James L. Gunn, Aberdeen; Mr Frank Lythgoe, Rawtenstall; Mr Charles Stafford, Burnley, Colne & Nelson and Mr G.V. Stanley of London Transport but previously General Manager of Croydon Corporation Tramways. Mr Tattam of Bradford who had also been short-listed subsequently withdrew his application.

Mr Gunn, who proved to be no enthusiast of trolleybuses, was appointed at a salary of £1,500 pa. Having toured the depots and works, one of his first actions was to suggest that consideration of the 57 applications for the position of Deputy General Manager, advertised in October 1933, should be held in abeyance. On 2 March 1934 Mr Marks was presented with a silver salver as a mark of the Passenger Transport Committee's esteem and friendship during his period of office with the undertaking.

The General Purposes Committee asked the Passenger Transport Committee and the Works and Ways Committee to expedite their decision on the questions of tram track removal and finding work for the unemployed. It was resolved on 15 November 1933, prior to agreeing on a price for this work with the Works and Ways Committee, that the City Engineer should proceed with the removal of the remaining rails on the Nottingham Road route. On 1 December 1933, the City Engineer pointed out that where rails were removed, the tramway authority was liable to pay the cost of reinstating the road to the condition prevailing when the tram rails were first laid. His records showed that in nearly every case the roads from which the rails were about to be removed were made of setts at the time the tram track was initially laid. Using regular labour the cost of paving a square yard was 9s 6d to which had to be added 1s 6d for taking up the track but less a credit of 1s from the resale value for the scrap rails. The Works and Ways Committee suggested a revised contribution of 7s per yard to the Passenger Transport Committee, plus the cost of taking up the track and less credit for the material recovered. This methodology was approved in March 1934 and following a further inspection of the St. Ann's Well Road tram track it was recommended that the track between Lotus Street and the terminus be removed.

By the end of August 1933 some 449 square yards of land had been acquired for a turning circle at Colwick Road, about 100 yards west of the railway level crossing rather than at Port Arthur Road, from the Agent for Earl Manvers Trustees at a price of £100 plus surveyors and

The following orders were placed immediately:

a) Chassis only

Karrier Motors Ltd.	35 vehicles at £1,045, 16 weeks delivery
Ransomes Sims & Jefferies Ltd.	21 vehicles at £1,043, 24 weeks delivery

These were not quite the lowest offers received (AEC, Brush and Leyland had tendered up to £4 less) but included the shortest delivery times. It was unclear if Karrier's offer of £1,045 included the cost of £10 per meter per vehicle and the General Manager took this up with the company. The possibility of taking 1 or 2 AEC chassis was discussed but this idea was given up at the end of July 1933.

b) Bodies only

Metropolitan-Cammell Weymann Motor Bodies Ltd.	10 all metal bodies at the price of £738 each, plus £42 for extras, delivery commencing in 10 weeks with delivery thereafter at the rate of 7 per week.
Brush Electrical Engineering Co. Ltd.	46 composite bodies at the price of £650 each, delivery commencing in 3-4 weeks with delivery thereafter at the rate of 6-8 per week.

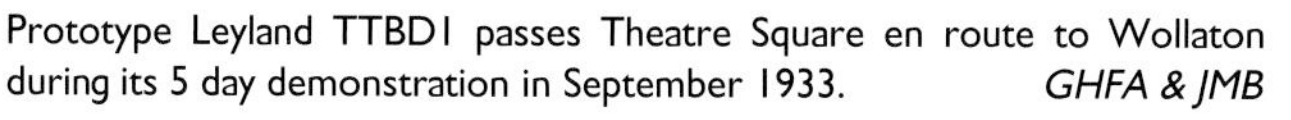
Prototype Leyland TTBD1 passes Theatre Square en route to Wollaton during its 5 day demonstration in September 1933. *GHFA & JMB*

Railless 10 in Lower Parliament Depot in February 1934. The oldest trolleybus in the fleet, and once an exhibition piece, it would soon be withdrawn after 7 years of service, together with No 3 behind. *GHFA & JMB*

solicitors costs. Negotiations with the Nottingham Cooperative Society to purchase 830 square yards of land near the northern end of Longford Crescent in Hucknall Lane for the Bulwell Hall Estate turning circle were finalised in late September for £525. The rebuilding plans for Bulwell Depot had been approved.

Tenders were invited for 200 heavy poles and 120 medium poles for the conversion of the Canning Circus-Bulwell route to trolleybus operation, the lowest tender of British Mannesman Tube at £11 9s 6d (heavy) and £9 3s 6d (medium) being accepted.

A large number of fares were being lost on the short stage routes from the city centre due to the conductor's inability to collect them and issue traditional Bell Punch tickets from a ticket rack in the time at his disposal. In the autumn of 1933 experiments were carried out with mechanical ticket machines, two "Verometer" machines being hired from Clayton Dewandre of Lincoln. The tickets were printed on paper rolls, the value of the tickets being printed by depressing buttons of different values. Shortly afterwards machines manufactured by Ticket Issuing Machines Ltd. (TIM), which printed the ticket, indicated the date, stage and direction of travel and which used a dial instead of buttons were experimented with. As a result 50 TIM machines were ordered and delivered by the end of the year being introduced on 22 January 1934 on the 38, 39 and 40 trolleybus services and a number of motor bus services. A further 118 TIM machines were purchased during the course of 1934.

The order for 56 additional vehicles now made it necessary to halve the tram capacity in Parliament Street Depot from eight lines to four in order to accommodate trolley vehicles. On 27 November 1933 Mr Marks showed the Passenger Transport Committee plans for a proposed traverser. There were four tenders varying between £244 and £350 for the traverser, whilst those for the pit conversions and cleaning galleries varied between £1,515 and £1,964. It was decided to omit a traverser and accept the lowest tendered price from A. Green at £1,255 for the conversions. Having received tenders for extensions and alterations to Bulwell Depot to permit trolley vehicle access at its eastern end whilst retaining the single tramcar access at the west end as the new trolley vehicle exit, the lowest tender of Gilbert & Hall Ltd. at £1,539 was accepted whilst that for work on the pits at £580 from Thomas Fish & Sons, one of two lowest tenders at the same price, was also accepted. The lowest tender for modifying Trent Bridge Depot pits, £425 from Mr A. Green, was additionally accepted.

Councillor Braddock suggested that a circular trolley vehicle route should be constructed from Bulwell Market Place to Cinderhill but as there was a low railway bridge in Coventry Road (LMS) and another in Cinderhill Road (LNER) this would require the road surface to be lowered. The matter was referred to the General Purposes Committee for consideration with a view to adapting the road for trolley vehicle purposes.

Trams reversed on a single-track stub in Bulwell Market Place at the southern end of Commercial Road. In February 1934 agreement was reached on alterations to the existing traffic island in the Market Place to accommodate a trolleybus turning circle at a cost of £550.

By March 1934 the 35 Karrier E6 trolleybus chassis had been delivered to the bodybuilders and some complete vehicles had already reached Nottingham but Ransomes, Sims & Jefferies were three months in arrears with their deliveries causing much inconvenience at Brush who had already completed the 21 bodies. The Town Clerk was instructed to enforce any penalty clause in the contract. English Electric renewed the electrical equipment in five 4-year old trolley vehicles for £100 per vehicle.

In view of the large amount of business related to the trolley vehicle conversion, the Passenger Transport Committee resolved on 23 March 1934 to meet fortnightly for the next 3 months. On 6 April 1934 Mr Gunn attended his first meeting and suggested that the Lenton and Radford Boulevards tram services should be replaced by motor buses; this was approved once the Traffic Commissioners' permission had been granted.

In April 1934 the Department sought permission from Carlton UDC to install a reversing triangle at the top of Carlton Hill at the junction with Standhill Road, the location of a short working in tramway days. Permission was refused; however the UDC suggested the junction with Hooton Road as an alternative location subject to the undertaking paying for the road widening, estimated to cost £40. Shortly afterwards they withdrew this proposal, something which Mr Gunn considered unreasonable in view of the Corporation's powers under the Nottingham Corporation Act 1930, and nothing further was done for the time being.

It was also suggested that a second turning circle, on this occasion to serve vehicles operating along Ilkeston Road, be built between the carriageways of Middleton Boulevard at Fairham Drive (a short distance north of the Scalford Drive turning circle) and that services 38 and 39 between Carlton and Wollaton Park which were operating at a common frequency at this period despite having different loadings, should operate separately.

It was realised in April 1934 that although the MoT had sanctioned the form and the construction of the 56 trolley vehicles on delivery, their maximum weight was still limited by the Nottingham Corporation Act 1930, Section 5, to 12 tons for three axle vehicles, originally imposed by the 1925 Act, whereas Clause 23 of the Trolley Vehicle Regulations permitted a maximum weight of 13 tons. On legal advice, legislation in the form of a "late" Bill in Parliament was immediately promoted to alter the section in the Act of 1930 relating to weights of trolley vehicles and to obtain power to run trolley vehicles of such weight, form and dimension as the MoT might approve. The local maximum weight limit had originally been imposed to protect bridges over railways and, following consultation with the railway companies, it proved possible to waive this clause. The 1935 Nottingham Corporation Act allowed the operation of vehicles complying with the normal MoT construction and weight conditions subject to providing the respective railway company prior notice of the weight of the trolleybuses to be used on the route over their bridges. The City Council delegated the powers under Part 3 of the Nottingham Corporation Act 1935 relating to the weight of vehicles to the Passenger Transport Committee in November 1935.

Under the Road and Rail Traffic Act 1933, the railway companies were empowered to schedule any bridges with a limitation of the weight of vehicles which may pass over them. In November 1934 the LMS scheduled Wilford Road Bridge, amongst other bridges in the city, at a proposed limit of 5 tons total weight and 3 tons axle loading. The Town Clerk asked for guidance as trolley vehicles used the bridge and the railways would do nothing to improve or strengthen the bridge. The City Engineer took up the matter with the railway company.

Mr Gunn reported to the Passenger Transport Committee Meeting on 20 April 1934 that in connection with the imminent opening of the Bulwell trolley bus route the question of the motorbus service to Hucknall and the protection which the Corporation had under the 1930 Act should be considered. A meeting with Trent was arranged at which their General Manager asked if the Corporation were interested in taking over their Hucknall service. By January 1935 Trent suggested that they should operate the Hucknall route alone and all receipts over a certain figure per mile be given to the Corporation, the figure per mile to be arrived at by adding an amount of 3d per mile to the company's net operating costs. This was accepted for a one-year trial period.

Under close inspection, Ransomes 15 inches passes roadworks in Lower Parliament Street by Milton Street junction, in March 1934. *GHFA & JMB*

Causing a queue of tramcars and with inspectors in attendance, English Electric 23 squeezes past the junction with Milton Road on Lower Parliament Street, a little after No 15 has passed in March 1934. *GHFA & JMB*

A coffee stall from which a Mrs Chapman had traded for several years on the site of the proposed Hucknall Lane, Bulwell Hall Estate, trolleybus turning circle was moved to a portion of the land outside the turning circle. She was a widow with a crippled son; the stall was her sole means of livelihood and as she had agreed to pay a 5s per week rent for the privilege of having her stall on the Corporation's land a licence was granted.

Prototypes, 51 (Karrier E6/MCCW), 61 (Karrier E6/Brush) and 90 (Ransomes D6/Brush), of the three types of vehicles to be used on the Bulwell services were inspected by the MoT and their official approval received on 23 February 1934. A trial run along the new route was made, concerns being expressed about clearance beneath the LNER railway bridge in Arkwright Street particularly if both trams and trolleybuses were to operate on this portion of route. It was accordingly decided that the Arnold and Mapperley tram services which also followed the route between the Old Market Square and Trent Bridge would be curtailed to the city centre when the Bulwell – Trent Bridge tram service ceased. The cost of lowering the road at that point was investigated. Lt. Col. E. Woodhouse of the MoT inspected the Bulwell trolleybus route on Tuesday afternoon 8 May 1934 and despite questions as to the height of the Arkwright Street railway bridge, MoT consent was given. The Bulwell conversion would have left solely the Lenton and Radford Boulevards tram route, which Mr Marks had intended to convert to trolleybus operation before the Bulwell services, operating on the west side of the city. However on Mr Gunn's recommendation it was decided to convert them to motorbus operation on the same date as the Bulwell tram to trolleybus conversion.

The fares table for the Bulwell – Trent Bridge trolley vehicle services was approved by the Passenger Transport Committee, including a range of transfer fares between the Arnold and Mapperley trams, and the trolleybuses operating to and from Trent Bridge. Single transfer fares were already offered on trams services but workmen's single and return transfers were now added. These remained in place until tramway operation finally ceased and through journeys, by motor bus, were reintroduced.

Trolleybuses replaced tram service C Bulwell Market Place – Trent Bridge, on Sunday 13 May 1934, and the trunk tram route from Bulwell

Karrier E6 58 seen new in 1934. *NCT*

On 11 May 1934 the "Nottingham Evening Post" published the following article:

BIG TRANSPORT SPEED-UP
IN THE CITY
WEEKEND TO WITNESS BULWELL – TRENT BRIDGE CONVERSION
TRAMS REDUCED FROM 200 TO 83

Nottingham passenger transport services will, on Sunday, undergo the greatest change experienced for a long time. By the conversion of the Bulwell and Trent Bridge tram services to operation by trolley vehicles of the latest type, and the replacement of trams by buses between Old Market Square and Lenton and Radford, the only routes in the city, after Saturday, to be served by tram cars will be:

Between the Old Market Square and Mapperley, Old Market Square and London Road and Colwick, and the Old Market Square and Arnold. The changeover does not involve an alteration to fares.

BIG SAVING OF TIME

Following the inspection on Tuesday by Col. Woodhouse, the official inspector to the Minister of Transport, of the route for the new trolley vehicles, he impressed his approval in the terms that "Nottingham had left him little to criticise, and indeed he had always regarded Nottingham as one of the most enterprising districts in overhead equipment".

It will be of interest and value to know that a Bulwell resident will, under the new system, do the journey each way in seven minutes less time, a total economy of 14 minutes, apart from the fact of the greater comfort in travelling.

In this changing aspect of transport in Nottingham, it is worthy of note that there were originally a maximum of 200 tramcars in service in the city. These have been reduced to 127 today by the previous conversion of the Nottingham Road and Carlton routes, and, following the conversion this weekend, when 44 tram cars are taken off the road, there will be only 83 trams left in the city. These will have a comparatively short life owing to the policy of the Corporation Passenger Transport Committee in giving a more efficient and speedy transport service to the travelling public. Indeed, it is hoped to convert the London Road and Colwick Road route in September, which will then leave only Arnold and Mapperley routes on tram equipment.

LOOKING BACK

The first trams to operate in Nottingham were on January 1st, 1901, on the Sherwood route, and this was followed by the Bulwell to the Market Square route in July 1901. In October, 1901, the Trent Bridge to Market Square tramway route was commenced.

It is interesting to note that the longest route from the city centre is that to Bulwell, 4.66 miles, and will be extended a further 1.12 miles from Bulwell Market Place to the Bulwell Hall Estate.

In addition to the Bulwell conversion, the trams will be taken off the Lenton and Radford circle on May 12th and replaced on the 13th by oil-engined double decker buses. Each of the new vehicles will be equipped with the new self-printing, time-punching ticket machines, and in each of these districts (subject to a few "teething" troubles) the public will have a much better service.

Almost the whole of the new vehicles will be fitted with Brush bodies, of semi-local manufacture, and on May 13th Nottingham will possibly be the largest operator in Great Britain of the Trolley Vehicle system.

On Monday May 14th the total equipment of the fleet of the Nottingham Corporation Passenger Transport department will be: 83 trams, 106 trolley vehicles, 131 petrol and oil vehicles - something over 50 per cent increase on the original complement of trams.

Old residents will recollect that the now redundant trams superseded the old horse trams.

ECONOMIES

The remaining conversions will take place as soon as reasonably possible with consequent economies on maintenance on tramway vehicle which, of recent years, have been a heavy burden on the Transport Department, for in addition to paying something like £90 per vehicle for licence duties the department has had to bear a heavy charge in road maintenance.

The new routes will absorb 37 of the new vehicles on permanent duty, leaving 19 for the time being in reserve as excess traffic vehicles, for football matches, cricket matches, and abnormal traffic to Trent Bridge at holiday time.

With the greater mobility and flexibility of the trolley vehicles, picking up and depositing passengers on the kerb, an unmeasured advantage will be silently given to transport generally in the city, enabling other forms of traffic to proceed on their journey with less frequent interruption.

With its gradients and curves, Nottingham is not the easiest city to give an efficient transport service to the public, but during recent years, repeated and almost continuous experiments have been made with the improved and different forms of transport vehicles. This month there will be put into operation the first large complement of the most improved vehicles, and the committee hope, at no distant date, to give Nottingham ratepayers a service which will bear comparison, as to fares and efficiency, with any in the country.

In future the Bulwell Hall Estate and Trent Bridge route will be known as Number 42, and that from Bulwell Market to Trent Bridge as Number 43.

The first trolley bus to leave the Hall Estate from Mondays to Fridays will be at 6.09 am and the last at 10.54 pm. The first and last from Bulwell Market will be 5 am and 11.25 pm. The return times from Trent Bridge will be 5.55 am (for the Hall Estate) and 5.35 am (for the Market) and the last 10.47 pm and 11.15 pm respectively. On Saturdays the first trolley bus from the Hall Estate will be at 6.09 am, the last at 11.04 pm and from Bulwell Market the first at 5 am. The first and last buses from Trent Bridge on that day will be 5.55 am and 10.51 pm (for the Hall) and 5.35 am and 11.17 pm (for the Market).

At the peak periods on weekdays, buses will be running on the route at intervals of two, three and five minutes.

On Sundays the first bus to leave the Hall Estate will be at 9.08 am, and the last at 10.42 pm (for Trent Bridge), and 10.39 pm (for Old Market Square). The first bus to leave Bulwell Market will be at 9.00 am, and the last at 10.35 pm (for Trent Bridge), and 11.05 pm (for Old Market Square).

From Trent Bridge the first on Sundays will be at 9.08 am, and the last at 10.42 pm (for the Hall), and for Bulwell Market 9.08 am and 11.07 pm.

On the new bus route between the Old Market Square and Lenton and Radford, the first bus on week-days will leave Old Market Square at 5.30 am and the last 11.15 pm. On Sundays the first will be at 9.15 am and the last at 11 pm.

From Addington Road to the city centre the first and last buses on week-days will be at 5.10 am, and 11.15 pm (Saturdays), and 11.10 pm (other days). On Sundays the times will be from 9.10 am, to 11 pm.

TRAMCAR TIMES REVISED

The times on the remaining tramcar services have been revised, and full details of these and other routes and services are being posted in Corporation vehicles forthwith.

It is also announced that the service of tramcars (Route J) between the LMS Station and Colwick Road is being replaced by a service of omnibuses (Route 27). There will be no alteration of times on this route.

through Basford, Hyson Green and Canning Circus to the Old Market Square, and onwards to Trent Bridge by way of Arkwright Street, was abandoned. On the same date motorbuses replaced trams along Station Street (tram service J) and around the Boulevards (tram services E and F), the routes being abandoned. Tram services B, D, E, F and K were curtailed to the Old Market Square, turning back at the single crossover on the short section of reserved track in Long Row East. Tram service A was withdrawn, the basic service to Mapperley being henceforth provided by the B. The frequency of these services led to considerable congestion at the terminus and within a fortnight a second crossover, made up from unused junctions laid at Carter Gate for the abortive extension along Hockley, had been installed.

42 Bulwell Hall Estate – Bulwell Market – Basford – Vernon Road – Radford Road – Hyson Green – Alfreton Road – Derby Road – Chapel Bar – Old Market Square – Carrington Street – Arkwright Street – Trent Bridge

43 Bulwell Market – Basford – Vernon Road – Radford Road – Hyson Green – Alfreton Road – Derby Road – Chapel Bar – Old Market Square – Carrington Street – Arkwright Street – Trent Bridge

This led to a major tramway abandonment including all remaining routes in the western suburbs:

Tram A (2) – withdrawn completely. Trolleybuses replaced the portion south of the Old Market Square. The northern portion was replaced by tram service B which continued to operate between Old Market Square and Mapperley only.

Tram C (3) – withdrawn completely

Tram D (4) – the Basford – Radford Road – Hyson Green – Alfreton Road – Old Market Square western portion of service D was withdrawn and replaced by trolleybuses. The eastern portion of tram service D continued to operate between Old Market Square and Colwick Road via Bath Street.

Tram E (6) – the Castle Boulevard – Lenton Boulevard – Radford Boulevard – Hartley Road – Alfreton Road western portion of service E, which operated clockwise around the Lenton and Radford Boulevards, was withdrawn completely and replaced by motorbus service 26. The northern portion of tram service E continued to operate between Old Market Square and Villiers Road, Sherwood.

Tram F (7) – the Alfreton Road – Hartley Road – Radford Boulevard – Lenton Boulevard – Castle Boulevard western portion of service F, which operated anti-clockwise around the Radford and Lenton Boulevards, was withdrawn completely

A "puzzle" photograph of 1930 English Electric 22 at the Processional Walk, Old Market Square stance. Service 10 never operated to Wilford Bridge along Long Row and Processional Walk nor are any southbound overhead wires evident (these were only erected when the Bulwell-Trent Bridge tram route was converted to trolleybus operation in May 1934). Presumably 22 used one trolley boom and its trailing skate to get there. *GHFA & JMB*

In February 1934 English Electric E11 trolley vehicle 21 is seen heading towards the city centre in Mansfield Road at the junction with Woodborough Road. The prefabricated telephone cabin and post box pillar, complete with sign pointing to the nearest post office, add to the period atmosphere. The Nottingham catenary overhead wiring supports both the wide spaced pair of trolleybus wires and the single tram wire in each direction at this point. *GHFA & JMB*

and replaced by motorbus service 26. The southern portion tram service F continued to operate between Old Market Square and Trent Bridge via London Road.

Tram J (-) – this isolated remainder of tram service 8 operating between Midland Station and Colwick Road via Station Street was withdrawn completely and replaced by motorbus service 27. Although wired, no trolleybus service ever operated regularly along Station Street.

Tram K (9) – the Trent Bridge – Arkwright Street – Old Market Square southern portion of service K was withdrawn and replaced by trolleybuses. The northern portion of tram service K continued to operate between Old Market Square and Arnold.

Motorbus service 7 was cut back from Longford Crescent, adjacent to the Bulwell Hall Estate trolleybus terminus, to operate between Bulwell Market Place and the Old Market Square via Bobbers Mill Bridge and Alfreton Road.

The conversion was one of the largest to have been carried out in the UK until that date and was just predated by Birmingham Corporation's conversion of their Coventry Road group of services on 7 January 1934 which had brought their fleet up to 66 vehicles. Nottingham however now operated 106 trolleybuses making it the largest fleet in the country at that time whilst some 52 tramcars were withdrawn for scrap leaving a fleet of 83 passenger cars and two works cars to operate the remaining four tram routes, Arnold, Colwick Road, Mapperley and Trent Bridge via London Road. Bulwell and Trent Bridge Depots ceased to operate trams. Mr Marks had ordered 56 trolleybuses, sufficient to convert the Bulwell – Trent Bridge and the Boulevard circular routes, but now only 37 were required for the normal operating schedule, the remainder being used for special services and extras. As the Transport Department no longer required traction poles along Castle, Lenton and Radford Boulevards, 198 poles were sold to the Lighting Department at £1 each.

An anti-clockwise turning circle for trolleybuses travelling from Trent Bridge was erected around the traffic island provided by the Queen Victoria Statue at the west end of the Old Market Square. Both trolleybuses operating a short working to or from this point and through journeys continuing northwest up Chapel Bar used the single pair of wires erected above Long Row West to the north of the erstwhile tram loading island.

The Nottingham Corporation (Trolley Vehicles) Provisional Order 1934 granted powers to operate trolleybuses from Bentinck Road to Stockhill Lane via Alfreton Road, Bobbers Mill Bridge and Nuthall Road, to provide a direct route to Cinderhill. As it was perceived that this would only advantage N&D in providing a faster connection between Ripley and the city centre, and the route was already served by motorbus service 7, no immediate action was taken by the Corporation to erect the necessary equipment. It was noted that N&D trolleybuses were suffering more dewirements than Corporation vehicles, this being attributed to their use of 5-ins trolley wheels deemed suitable for the higher running speeds beyond Cinderhill, whereas NCT employed 4-ins wheels. The Company was loath to change in case this should lead to problems on their own network where dewirements were considered as being within acceptable norms. The problem was never entirely solved and although the Corporation replaced wheels with slider heads in the early part of the War, the N&D continued to use trolley wheels until the close of trolleybus operations.

An attempt to abolish workman's single fares failed. On 8 June 1934, a one-penny fare was introduced on trolley vehicles between Old Market Square and Muskham Street, and between Trent Bridge and the Walter Fountain at the junction of Carrington Street with Greyfriar Gate. On the same date penny fares for dogs were introduced.

The MoT enquired if the undertaking wished to revise the authorised speeds and compulsory stopping places prescribed by the existing Regulations and Byelaws, and asked for confirmation that all the trolley vehicles used on the system were fitted with pneumatic tyres on all wheels. The Passenger Transport Committee replied that no revision was contemplated and that all vehicles in service were now equipped with pneumatic tyres (although vehicle records show that the remnants of the solid-tyred Railless fleet, numbers 2, 4 and 8 at least, were officially only withdrawn on 31 May 1935).

Don Bradman's presence at the First Test Match at Trent Bridge increased receipts by £1,072 (182,000 more passengers). Loading barriers were erected at Bentinck Road and Alfreton Road. Following the installation of several poorly positioned traffic islands which were too large for trolley vehicle operations the Works and Ways Committee promised to install temporary islands first.

An official anxiously watches Karrier E6/Brush 80 as it leaves the passenger loading island at the Queen Victoria Statue for Chapel Bar in May 1934. His concern is probably related to both the Bulwell trolleybus route and the vehicle being brand new that month. The buildings on the north side of Long Row are little changed today: the Talbot survives as Yates Wine Lodge whilst Griffin & Spalding's is now one of Debenham's stores. *GHFA & JMB*

Karrier E6 58 seen new in 1934. *NCT*

A number of new cinemas, such as the Futurist on Valley Road and the Savoy on Derby Road, had been built in the suburbs producing additional late evening traffic and thus on 22 July 1934 many services, which until then had ceased between 11 pm and 11.15 pm, were extended by half an hour until between 11.30 pm and 11.45 pm.

It proved necessary to make further alterations to Trent Bridge Depot to enable it to deal with the trolley buses. Tenders were invited to remove the west end (rear) wall of the building and demolish one of the sheds at the rear to enable trolley vehicles to enter the depot at the rear and leave at the front. The lowest tender from Mr Thomas Bow of £542 was accepted.

Inexplicably, the Passenger Transport Committee was informed at the beginning of August 1934 that the London Road trolley bus route to and from Trent Bridge would commence operations in time for the start of the football season later that month as the MoT had authorised their operation without inspection. It is a matter of conjecture if there were plans to operate a full timetable or simply special journeys for football matches only using the prevailing surplus of vehicles but trolleybus services only commenced on 2 June 1935. Further vehicles were however required for the Colwick Road conversion and tenders for these were only invited in August 1934. It is possible that London Road was seen as an intrinsic part of the LMS Station – Colwick tram service and that it was felt appropriate to convert the Colwick Road, London Road and Station Street tram routes in one transaction.

As a further stage in the tram to trolleybus conversion programme on 16 August 1934 the Town Clerk was authorised to apply for Trolley Vehicle Powers for a circular route from the Arnold tram terminus in Front Street, by way of Cross Street (sic – it is likely that Church Street was intended), Mellors Road and Mansfield Road rejoining the existing tram route at Daybrook Square, as originally applied for in the 1930 Bill. Together with other proposals unrelated to public transport, the necessary Bill was promoted in 1935.

On 31 August 1934 it was resolved to call for tender for 30 vehicles and the tenders, from Karrier, Leyland and Ransomes, Sims & Jefferies, received were passed to the General Manager for his consideration on 5 October 1934. Mr Gunn recommended the lowest tender received, that of Leyland Motors Limited at the price of £957 (total £28,710) plus an extra amount for low voltage lighting sets. The 16 October 1934 Passenger Transport Committee Meeting, recalling the visit of the Leyland TTBD1 demonstrator (TJ939) in September 1933, asked Mr Gunn to seek Birmingham Transport's experiences with their Leyland vehicles. If these were deemed unsatisfactory, the order was to be divided (15 each) between Ransomes, Sims & Jefferies at £997 per chassis and Karrier Motors at £1,001 per chassis both plus an extra amount for low voltage lighting. The order was placed with Leyland and the tender of Metro-Cammell Weymann Ltd at £813 per 64-seat all metal body for all 30 bodies was accepted. Upon delivery these vehicles were given fleet numbers 107-136. They differed from previous deliveries in having a deeper destination screen at front and rear of the same type as that fitted to motorbuses from 1935 onwards.

There was a delay in signing the contract for the chassis, the cause of which is unknown, and further negotiations took place with Leyland in December 1934. The matter was resolved by Christmas with the first deliveries expected, over-optimistically as it transpired, at the end of February 1935 with completion by the end of March. Newspaper reports indicated that delivery of these trolleybuses would permit the conversion of the Colwick Road and London Road tram services.

It was decided that the tram track between Valley Road and Bulwell Market Place should be removed at an early date and the road surface restored, with the section Colwick Road to Manvers Street and Pennyfoot Street being dealt with later in 1934.

At the end of August 1934 the Passenger Transport Committee visited the site of the Queen Victoria Statue on Beastmarket Hill at the west end of the Old Market Square. The impracticalities of loading vehicles heading in opposing directions at one point resulted in a decision to reconstruct the turning circle for clockwise instead of anti-clockwise use, vehicles unloading on the west side of Beastmarket Hill, turning east into Long Row West and then almost immediately south at the foot of Market Street to load at the Procession Way stop. The northbound pair of through overhead wires was relocated closer to the Queen Victoria Statue, trolleybuses effectively following the route of the unused tram tracks. They resolved that the former tram loading island on the north side of the statue was no longer required in its present form and could be removed, resulting in a much wider roadway. The Works and Ways Committee were asked to widen the pavement on the north side of the statue as large numbers of people collected there at rush hours for westbound trolleybuses and in October 1934 experimental queue barriers for services to Bulwell were introduced here. These were deemed successful and similar barriers introduced throughout the system.

A trolley vehicle request stop was introduced on Derby Road between the stop at

East Circus Street and the top of Derby Road, near the entrance to the Cathedral, and that at Upper College Street discontinued.

Three tenders for external vehicle advertising were reviewed on 23 November 1934 that of Frank Mason, London for 5 years at £4,176, with a maximum of £5,000 should the number of vehicles in crease considerably, accepted. In February 1935 Frank Mason asked for permission to place a Bisto advertisement on the large rear panel at the rear of each motorbus and trolleybus, for an additional £4 pa per vehicle.

The first Ransomes D6/ Brush trolley vehicle to be delivered, 37, is seen being pulled by an LMS tractor on 21 October 1931. *Nottingham Library*

Ransomes 87, newly built and during delivery, but with blinds fitted, in 1934. *STA*

Railless LF/Shorts 9 at the Nottingham Road, Vernon Road terminus of service 36 in 1933-34. The disused Nottingham Road tramway, double track immediately prior to the junction with Vernon Road, is still in situ.. *BTS*

This view can be dated as having been taken between 1930 and 1933 as at least eastbound trolleybus overhead wiring is already in place in Lower Parliament Street whilst service H was renumbered 37 on 6 March 1933. Railless LF/Shorts 8 heels over as it pulls out of Milton Street into Upper Parliament Street heading for King Street terminus. *Photobus*

A nearside view of Brush Thornycroft demon-strator 28 at The Wells Road, Kildare Road terminus in spring 1931. *GHFA & JMB*

In the autumn of 1934 Karrier E6/Brush 76 is pictured heading over the disused tram tracks towards the city centre past Canning Terrace on Canning Circus. *GHFA & JMB*

During its first few days in service Karrier E6 55 (TV9311) with MCCW & F all metal body leaves the Old Market Square for Trent Bridge in May 1934. Immediately behind the trolley booms can be seen the trailing frog from the short-lived anti-clockwise turning circle at the Queen Victoria Statue on Beastmarket Hill. *GHFA & JMB*

In September 1933 Leyland TTBD1 demonstrator passes along Upper Parliament Street on the south side of Theatre Square at the top of Queen Street. Open balcony English Electric tram 177 has halted at the Elite Cinema stop to take up passengers for Radford and the Boulevards. *GHFA & JMB*

Brand new Leyland TTB3s/MCCW & F stand, as yet unused, on 31 May 1935 in Trent Bridge Depot looking towards the new rear entrance. The first of the batch, 107 displays an interesting "CITY POSTAL" destination display. *GHFA & JMB*

Chapter 4 A Premature End to Expansion 1935-39

Whilst there is no evidence that Walter Marks showed a personal favouritism for any specific mode of transport, as shown by his rejuvenation of Liverpool's electric tramways by miles of grassed-over sleeper track reservations and fleets of "Streamliner" tramcars, although a wholesale conversion to trolleybus operation had been mooted, he was certainly an advocate of electric traction. The same could not be said for James Gunn, indeed during his five year tenure at Aberdeen, he had overseen the replacement of the Duthie Park and Torry tram routes by motorbuses whilst tramcar construction and modernisation came, albeit temporarily, to an end. In the national championship league of municipal transport management it was necessary to "make a name for oneself" and in this respect Mr Gunn was seen as an enthusiast of the motor bus and a follower of Stuart Pilcher. It is fair to assume that he soon found an ally in Alderman Sir Albert Atkey, JP, an established member of the Passenger Transport Committee, active in the motor trade and an opponent of the trolleybuses.

Ransomes D4 11 seen in Parliament Street Depot in the mid-1930s. Behind the trolley vehicle work is in hand to fill the tramcar inspection pits. *Peter Badgery*

On 22 February 1935 the Passenger Transport Committee learned of the progress of the Nottingham Corporation Bill, which included plans to replace the trams to Arnold with trolley buses. Nottingham already had authority to replace its tramways in the Arnold UDC area with trolleybuses and additionally use any street(s) in Arnold for turning purposes under the provisions of the Nottingham Corporation Act 1930, and these plans referred to another attempt to gain operating powers along the circular route provided by Church Street, Mellors Road, Redhill Road and Mansfield Road, which had been deleted from the 1930 Bill. Petitions had been lodged against this part of the Bill and having considered the circumstances, the clause in the Bill for a trolley vehicle route was withdrawn.

Whether Mr Gunn anticipated similar difficulties in finding a suitable location for a trolleybus turning circle at the Mapperley terminus outside the city boundary, or if he was simply pursuing his motorbus ideology is unclear, but at the beginning of April 1935 he recommended that the Mapperley tram route be converted to motor bus operation. The Passenger Transport Committee appears to have accepted his recommendation without any discussion of trolleybus substitution although the gradient of Woodborough Road and the frequent service would have made the route an ideal candidate for trolleybus operation. He requested authority to purchase 17 oil-engined AEC double deck buses similar to the undertaking's last order, at an estimated cost of £26,000. Although a loan for this amount was approved, an order was not placed due to a major increase in diesel fuel tax and because the Finance Committee, on considering the report, reminded the City Council that statutory powers were already in existence for the conversion of tramway routes to trolley vehicle operation. Under the circumstances, they suggested that the decision between motorbuses and trolley vehicles on the Arnold and Mapperley routes should be left to the Council.

The evening newspapers of 4 June 1935 reported on the City Council's lively debate on the merits of trolleybuses and oil (diesel) motorbuses as replacements for the Mapperley tram route. The Committee considered *"without committing themselves to any policy, that the oil vehicle would most economically meet their needs"* and recommended the Council to approve the proposal and instruct the Town Clerk to make application to the MoT for sanction to borrow the £26,000. At that time there were 40 tramcars, including the 20 fully enclosed cars delivered in 1927; 125 petrol buses; 100 trolley vehicles and 15 oil (diesel) buses in service; and 25 oil buses were in the process of delivery. *"The conversion of the trams would take place as soon as possible. It would be possible, shortly after they removed the trams, to offer to the Nottingham ratepayers what they were entitled to have, an equal fare on every vehicle for an equal stage"*. Despite the recently increased diesel fuel tax, oil motorbuses were still the cheapest option.

Alderman Bowles contended *"so far as taxation was concerned it did not matter very much whether oil or petrol buses were put on the Mapperley route"* and added *"Taxation on petrol and on oil had not yet reached its limit – there would be further taxation on both – and the Committee must take that in consideration in future developments"*. He continued, *"The Committee had either been wrong in the past or were wrong now. If the past conversions from tram routes to trolley vehicles routes were right*

The last Ransomes D6/Brush, 106, waits outside the Barclays Bank local head office on Beastmarket Hill in February 1935 prior to circumnavigating Queen Victoria's Statue and setting off in the opposite direction to Trent Bridge and thus the Nottingham Forest FC ground. *GHFA & JMB*

that policy was right now. The trolley bus had shown more than double the percentage of profit per mile than was made on the petrol and oil-driven vehicle". Referring to the cartel or "ring" within the fuel supply industry he suggested that the comparative cost of running a trolley bus, a petrol bus and an oil bus on the Mapperley route should be given. *"A trolley bus services used a local commodity manufactured on their own doorstep, with their own labour, using coal got from their own coal pits. Buses could not run a single yard without foreign oil or foreign petrol".*

Alderman Sir Albert Atkey, a local champion of the motor industry, suggested, *"that the electric trolley bus was only a transitional stage in transport. Nobody wanted to see Nottingham like a spider's web, as it would be if the trolley system was extended".* As his businesses, A.R. Atkey and the Carter Gate Motor Co., held the local agencies for Ford and Austin cars respectively, he probably had his private interests in mind too.

"Mr E.A. Braddock seconded Alderman Bowles's amendment, stating that it was surprising the Committee which replaced the Trent Bridge – Bulwell trams (the best paying tram route) with trolley vehicles should now tell them the bus was the cheapest form of transport and the safest. He submitted the chairman of the committee knew trolley buses cost less to run than petrol buses" whilst the steep gradients of the Mapperley district were ideally suited for the hill-climbing abilities and superior brakes of the trolleybus. The Mapperley route had the overhead equipment already, and required only small additions. *"Alderman Farr, touching on the margin of profit made on trolley buses, suggested that this was not due to superiority or more economical running, but to their running on the most profitable routes. If trolley buses had been used on the Mapperley route instead of trams last year there would have been a loss of £2,055, if the same number of passengers had been carried; while if oil vehicles had been used there would have been a profit of £4,014".* It has proved impossible to correlate these figures as the Annual Report for the year ending 31 March 1935 showed that for the network as a whole trams generated profits of 1.271d per mile, trolley vehicles 4.793d and motorbuses 2.946d. Even Mr Gunn's accompanying report showed that the working expenses and net surpluses per mile run were tram 12.9d (3.74d), trolley vehicles 12.6d (1.742d) and motorbuses 10.2d (0.479d) but it must be added here that he was an expert at manipulating statistics to support his aims. All these arguments conveniently ignored the fact that motor bus fares were higher than those applicable on the trams and trolleybuses at that time. Alderman Sir Albert Atkey continued that there was no suitable location for a trolleybus turning circle at Mapperley, *"A trolley vehicle, not having an engine at each end* (sic), *could not turn. Turning circles were expensive, and sanction was necessary. In this case it might be two or three years before they were allowed to turn a circle".*

Regarding the complete revision of fares Alderman Farr, Chairman of the Passenger Transport Committee said *"There will be the same fares on all vehicles throughout the city if we can get on with the conversions without interruption".* Undoubtedly this argument strengthened the case for motorbuses with the general public but thereafter there was no rush to achieve this aim, indeed the common fares policy for all types of vehicles by increasing all trolleybus fares to the level applicable on motorbuses was only implemented on 3 April 1949.

The amendment was defeated by 25 votes to 22, and the City Council declared the Passenger Transport Committee's report as adopted. On 5 July 1935 the General Manager was granted authority to apply to the Traffic Commissioners for motorbus licences for the Mapperley route, basing the fare structure in the application on the prevailing tram fares. The Chairman also confirmed that the Arnold trams would also be converted as soon as possible with the decision as to the type of vehicle being left to the Passenger Transport Committee. Mr Gunn was instructed to invite tenders for the vehicles required and a further order for 12 AEC motorbuses for the Arnold tram route conversion was accordingly placed.

The removal of the remaining tram rails on the Bulwell route, from Valley Road to the Grand Theatre, was agreed to on 1 February 1935, providing further work for the gang of men then engaged and ensuring continuity until they could be transferred to the Colwick Road route.

Four tenders for five of the remaining original Railless LF trolley vehicles, withdrawn to avoid conversion to pneumatic tyres, were received. The second highest of £60 from J. Abbott, Ashover was accepted as their offer included the removal of the vehicles whereas the highest tender from W. Forrest & Co. Ltd., Sheffield was based on dismantling at the depot.

In February and April 1935, following articles in the local press, MoT officials carried out successful tests with radio-interference suppression coils. As a result the entire trolleybus fleet was so equipped, the suppressor being mounted centrally on the roof immediately in front of the trolleybases, so ending the question of radio-interference. The General Manager, soon to become a member of the MTTA committee on broadcasting interference, submitted a report at the beginning of May 1935 on wireless interference by trolley vehicles and recommended that filter units should be fitted in all new trolley vehicles.

The lowest tender for traction poles from British Mannesman Tube Co., at £578 5s for 60 medium type and £362 5s for 30 heavy type for the Colwick Road and London Road conversions was accepted. However by March 1935 it was evident that the alterations to Bulwell Depot had cost more than expected, nonetheless the bill of £580 from Messrs T. Fish & Sons, an overspend of £9 9s, and for £1,539 from Messrs Gilbert & Hall Ltd., an overspend of £205 14s 11d, were settled.

After a number of meetings the Fares Subcommittee provisionally fixed maximum fare stage points for all routes on 29 May 1935. Having considered the General Manager's figures for a "Central Free Area" Scheme and used these for comparison purposes, they provisionally adopted a 3d maximum fare to all standard distance points. As a result on 7 June 1936 a maximum fare of 3d between the city centre and the city boundary (except to Bulwell Hall Estate) came into operation, and the ½d child trolleybus fare was extended to motorbus services. On 9 December 1935 it was decided to retain a maximum fare of 3d to all termini for a further 12-month period.

The City Council suggested that the Old Market Square should be simply referred to as "City Centre" on destination screens. In response the Passenger Transport Committee suggested Old Market Square should be renamed as "City Square" but this was not proceeded with.

In May 1935 the N&D approached the Passenger Transport Committee prior to promoting a Parliamentary Bill for a second, more direct route into Nottingham in addition to that along Nottingham Road and Mansfield Road, and ordering more vehicles. This would have branched from the existing NCT route at Cinderhill, Stockhill Lane, and continued along Nuthall Road, Bobbers Mill Bridge and Alfreton Road to link up with the existing city network at Bentinck Road, a proposal which had been made several times previously. The Corporation objected to N&D's request for running powers over this proposed new route which would have been entirely within the city boundaries, was already served by NCT motorbuses, and for which the Corporation already held trolleybus operating power under the Nottingham Corporation (Trolley Vehicles) Provisional Order 1934. In support of their request the N&D then endeavoured to prove to the MoT that their passengers were being crowded out of the King Street terminus by short stage NCT passengers, adding that their vehicles were only permitted a 3-minute waiting time. On 10 September 1935 N&D offered to run a local service from Bentinck Road to Cinderhill at an agreed frequency in addition to that along Nottingham Road. If this was not acceptable they were prepared to lease such a new line and run trolley vehicles in place of their motorbuses currently using that route to/from Nottingham. In the second half of November 1935 the Chairman and Vice Chairman of the Passenger Transport Committee met Sir Joseph Nall, Chairman of the N&D and Mr Douglas Hayes, Engineer and Manager, to discuss the company's proposals. They argued that as the Corporation's trolleybus network was still incomplete they could not accede to the N&D proposals at that time and on 9 December 1935 refused N&D's proposal to run local services.

When the N&D did apply for parliamentary powers, in December 1935, these referred solely to additional trolley vehicle routes *outside* the city boundaries and Mr Gunn considered that NCT would not be affected. However they also requested powers to enable the company to apply to the MoT for a Special Order authorising N&D to provide, maintain, equip and use trolley vehicles upon any road as defined by the Tramways Act 1870. Nottingham's Town Clerk considered that this included any road in the City and accordingly a Petition against the Bill to exclude the City was made. Those parts of the N&D Bill that were approved, including route alterations in Heanor and Ilkeston, received the Royal Assent on 21 May 1936.

On Tuesday 30 April 1935 Lt. Col. Trench of the MoT inspected the new Colwick Road, London Road and Station Street trolleybus routes, official operating approval being received on 22 May 1935. During the same visit, he also inspected the turning circles at Eland Street, Basford; Fairham Drive, Middleton Boulevard and Old Market Square, Beastmarket Hill. On Sunday 2 June 1935 trolleybus service 44 replaced tram service D Old Market Square – Colwick Road, all tram track in Manvers Street, Pennyfoot Street, Sneinton Hermitage and Colwick Road being abandoned:

44 Bulwell Hall Estate – Bulwell Market – Basford – Vernon Road – Radford Road – Hyson Green – Alfreton Road – Derby Road – Old Market Square – Upper Parliament Street – Lower Parliament Street – Bath

Street – Manvers Street – Sneinton – Colwick Road *(southbound only from Bulwell Hall Estate to Colwick Road, all northbound journeys from Colwick Road to Bulwell Hall Estate displaying service 42 or 43 if operating to Bulwell Market).*

The Bulwell group of services was completely rearranged on unidirectional basis as follows:

Southbound

42 Bulwell Hall Estate to Trent Bridge

43 Bulwell Market to Trent Bridge

44 Bulwell Hall Estate to Colwick Road

Northbound

42 Colwick Road or Trent Bridge to Bulwell Hall Estate

43 Colwick Road or Trent Bridge to Bulwell Market

There was no service 44 northbound.

Alternate journeys on service 42, which until then had operated in both directions Bulwell Hall Estate – Trent Bridge, were withdrawn and the vehicles thus released used to strengthen the combined frequencies on the Arkwright Street and Radford Road group of services. The reduced frequency of trolleybuses along Arkwright Street resulting from the diversion of alternative northbound 42s to operate from Colwick Road instead of Trent Bridge, was compensated for from Sunday 2 June 1935 by the introduction of service 46 which, operating daily, used the new turning circle at Beastmarket Hill and loaded at Processional Way:

During the period that services 42 and 43 interworked, Leyland TTB3/MCCW & F 120 heading north on a 43 between Colwick Road Railway Crossing and Bulwell Market Place passes NCT 1930 AEC Regent/ Shorts motorbus 26 loading for Beeston on South Parade, Old Market Square. *BTS*

46 Old Market Square – Arkwright Street – Trent Bridge

Also on 2 June 1935 trolleybus service 45 replaced tram service F Trent Bridge – London Road – Old Market Square, the new service continuing into the western suburbs along Derby Road to the Scalford Drive, Middleton Boulevard turning circle:

45 Trent Bridge (Globe Cinema) – London Road – Pennyfoot Street – Manvers Street – Bath Street – King Edward Street – Upper Parliament Street – Derby Road – Middleton Boulevard – Wollaton Park, Scalford Drive

A review of PM peak services between Old Market Square and Trent Bridge via Arkwright Street shows however an almost constant capacity offer each hour:

Timetable	Vehicle	Origin	No. p/hour	Comment
02.1934	Tram	Arnold	6	
		Bulwell	12	
		Mapperley	15	
			(Total 33)	
09.1934	Trolleybus	Bulwell	20	Arnold & Mapperley tram services cut back to Old Market Square.
04.1935	Trolleybus	Bulwell	30	Frequency improved to combat a lack of capacity.
10.1936	Trolleybus	Bulwell	20	Inter-working of services 42, 43, 44 had started.
	Motorbus	Arnold	5	Tram replacement motorbus services 20, 35 extended to Trent Bridge.
	Motorbus	Mapperley	5	
			(Total 30)	

In addition, several joint NCT/WBUDC motorbus services also operated over the route but with protective fares.

Brand new Leyland TTB3/MCCW & F 116 stands at the former tramway loading island by the Queen Victoria Statue at the west end of the Old Market Square probably in June 1935. In the background one of the fully enclosed 1927 English Electric trams, Nottingham's last traditional tramcars subsequently sold for further use in Aberdeen, can be seen on the private right of way (later to become the southern carriageway of Long Row East) which from May 1934 provided the city centre terminus of the Arnold and Mapperley services. *BTS*

Brand new Leyland TTB3/MCCW & F 117 entered service on 2 June 1935 and is seen at the junction of Bath Street with St. Ann's Well Road and King Edward Street – a most unusual location for a westbound service 38! The destination display clearly reads "Wollaton Park via Bath Street, Parliament Street, Derby Road. During the summer of 1935 the then newly introduced London Road trolleybus service 45 (Trent Bridge – Wollaton Park) operated alternately in both directions around the Wollaton Park loop for the duration of the Pageant and Northern Command Tattoo in Wollaton Park with service number 38 displayed when operating westbound along Derby Road. *BTS*

At Trent Bridge, passengers boarded trolleybuses outside the Globe Cinema, which stood in the apex of the junction between Arkwright Street and London Road. Outward journeys terminated at Turney's Factory on the eastern side of London Road before the vehicle turned around a small traffic island (upon which a Departmental cash office stood) located in front of the cinema and between the two main roads. Service 45 trolleybuses thus avoided difficult manoeuvres and congestion at the convergence of Arkwright Street and London Road. The tramway in Pennyfoot Street, Fisher Gate and London Road was abandoned (indeed trolleybuses never ran along Fisher Gate and the northern end of London Road but followed Lower Parliament Street), although at least one track remained intact to provide a rail connection to Trent Bridge Works.

Tram D (4) – the truncated portion of this service between Old Market Square and Colwick Road via Bath Street was withdrawn completely and replaced by trolleybus service 44.

Tram F (7) – the truncated portion of this service between Old Market Square and Trent Bridge via London Road was withdrawn completely and replaced by trolleybus service 45.

These two tram to trolleybus conversions were the final "Trollifications", an unusual expression coined by the "Nottingham Journal" (according to the July 1939 edition of "Transport World"), in the city, and effectively marked the premature end of expansion to the trolleybus system. There were now just tram services B and K remaining serving the northeastern suburbs from the Old Market Square.

It is assumed that from Sunday 2 June 1935 different frequencies were introduced on trolleybus services 38 and 39 to relate better to the different passenger loadings on Derby and Ilkeston Roads, and that, as the new 45 service reinforced the existing Derby Road frequencies, the additional journeys between Central Market and Scalford Drive introduced on 20 March 1932 were withdrawn. For the duration of the Pageant and Northern Command Tattoo in Wollaton Park, that is until 18 August 1935, the new service to and from Trent Bridge operated alternately in both directions around the Wollaton Park loop with service number 38 displayed when operating westbound along Derby Road and 39 when running westbound along Ilkeston Road, whilst all journeys from Wollaton Park to Trent Bridge via either route showed 45.

The 30 Leyland TTB3 Metropolitan-Cammell bodied trolleybuses 107-136, which had been approved for service on 24 May 1935, entered service on 2 June 1935 from Bulwell Depot, the vehicles which they displaced there being transferred

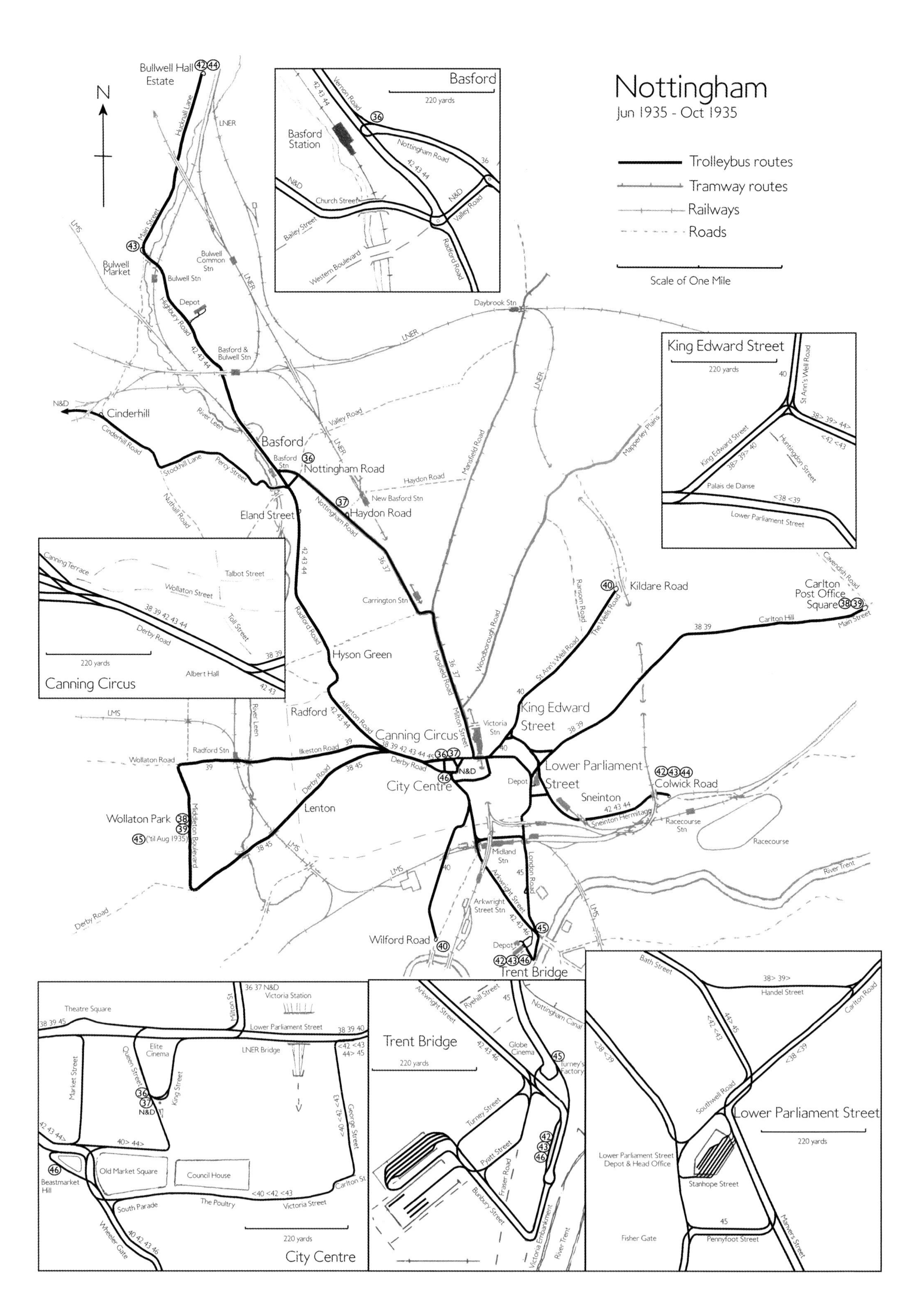
Nottingham
Jun 1935 - Oct 1935
Trolleybus routes
Tramway routes
Railways
Roads
Scale of One Mile
Basford
220 yards
King Edward Street
Canning Circus
City Centre
Trent Bridge
Lower Parliament Street
Bullwell Hall Estate
Bulwell Market
Cinderhill
Basford
Nottingham Road
Haydon Road
Eland Street
Hyson Green
Radford
Canning Circus
City Centre
Lenton
Wollaton Park
Kildare Road
Carlton Post Office Square
King Edward Street
Lower Parliament Street
Sneinton
Colwick Road
Wilford Road
Trent Bridge

An overcast wet day in September 1935. Leyland TTB3/MCCW & F 117 awaits departure time at Processional Walk, Old Market Square. One of NCT's "camel back" roof motorbuses is visible in the background. *GHFA & JMB*

Ransomes 39 makes its stately way down Mansfield Road into Milton Street immediately to the north of Victoria Station in September 1935. In 2005 the public house still remains but the Victoria Shopping Centre has replaced the mainline railway station. The wide 30 ins separation between the two trolley used for the early tram to trolleybus route conversions, the separate single trolley wire for the Arnold and Mapperley trams which continued to operate along Mansfield Road, and the typical additional spanwire supporting a Wembley Lantern street light are all clearly visible.
GHFA & JMB

Christmas shopping on a Saturday afternoon in December 1935. Leyland TTB 109 passes beneath the wiring leading from South Parade onto Beastmarket Hill as it heads off down Wheeler Gate to the Midland Station and Trent Bridge. The three substantial rear bumper bars, the application of the registration number to the rear platform window and the detailed destination blind display typified this class of vehicle. Unusually a double bracket arm traction pole supports the overhead wiring at the top of Wheeler Gate. The gentleman on the right has more than a passing resemblance to Walter Marks!
GHFA & JMB

to Trent Bridge Depot. Purchased primarily with the Colwick Road and London Road conversions in mind, the excess of vehicles permitted the withdrawal of the three remaining Railless LFs, 2, 4 and 8 (although their solid tyres had ensured that they had been little used of late). All trolleybuses delivered in the 1930s including the Leyland TTB3s featured air-operated bells which necessitated a small bore pipe on both decks connected to a bell with a plunger inside in the driver's cab and a number of "push" plungers in the saloons and on the rear platform. A sharp "thump" made the plunger in the driver's cab ring the bell, although this was hardly necessary as the "thump" could be heard all over the trolleybus! Communications came to an end if there was any leak in the pipe and the usual check was to light a cigarette, then blow smoke into the body of the bell "push" plunger and see where the smoke came out of the internal panelling before sending for a coachbuilder!

Once the Pageant and Northern Command Tattoo in Wollaton Park ended it was considered that the 38 provided sufficient capacity on the Derby Road section and from 18 August 1935 the 45 trolleybus service was cut back to operate solely between Trent Bridge and the city:

45 Trent Bridge (Globe Cinema) – London Road – Pennyfoot Street – Manvers Street – Bath Street – King Edward Street – Upper Parliament Street – Old Market Square (Queen Street/King Street)

The outer portion of both the Arnold tram route, almost 1 mile long from Daybrook Station to Coppice Road, Arnold, and the Mapperley tram route, about 750 yards along Mapperley Plains from Porchester Road to Westdale Lane, lay beyond the city boundary within the jurisdiction of Arnold UDC. In 1935 Arnold UDC stated that they did not wish trolleybuses to replace the tram routes in their area.

The resurfacing of parts of Arkwright Street in July 1935 provoked a question as to the removal of the disused tram tracks. However, the City Engineer advised that these were solely minor repairs and that no unnecessary expense would be incurred by removing the rails at a later date. Soon afterward two fatal accidents in Arkwright Street were attributed to the tramlines whilst on 13 September 1935 a female cyclist who fell from her bicycle due to the wheel catching in a projecting disused tram rail was run over and killed by a van. As a consequence the City Council were asked for authority to raise £25,000 for tram track removal and reinstatement of the road surface. At the same time £5,000 was requested for depot building alterations for trolley vehicle operations.

By the end of November 1935 the City Engineer had estimated that the removal of all remaining tram tracks would cost £56,000, and suggested:

i) All tramway tracks were to be handed over to the Works and Ways Committee, together with the remainder as they were abandoned,
ii) The Passenger Transport Committee to pay for the cost of removal and reinstatement on the fixed estimate figure of £56,000 spread over a period of 4-5 years,
iii) Programme of works to be arranged
   - All defective track not in use to be dealt with immediately
   - Additional sections to be dealt with in conjunction with road surfacing operations in the vicinity

– Remainder to be scheduled for dealing with in the period referred to in ii) above.

Between the Cattle Market and Ryehill Street at the southern end of London Road, a short length of German overhead wiring was strung employing a flexible insulating dropper fitting, which hung from a span wire 9-ins higher than usual, to support the running wire. These fittings, which were of three types, vertical for straight runs, and two patterns of angle droppers for use on curves of small and large radii, and supplied by the Equipment & Engineering Co., were more flexible and gave less noise beneath the ears, whilst vibration from one pair of wires was not transmitted to the other pair. Despite the advantages, the equipment proved less satisfactory than normal fittings and was replaced early in the Second World War. It may be remembered that for the majority of the period that this overhead wiring was in use, Nottingham's trolleybuses were equipped with trolley wheels and not slider heads, additionally from 1939 replacements were impossible to obtain.

On Tuesday 1 October 1935 Lt. Col. Woodhouse inspected the new route along Huntingdon Street between Mansfield Road and Lower Parliament Street, together with the reconstructed Vernon Road, Basford turning arrangements at the junction of Nottingham Road, which now included a double junction with the Bulwell route. MoT Approval was granted on 9 October 1935. The Huntingdon Street wiring was foreseen as a part of the inner circular trolleybus route that was never constructed. At the end of November 1935 the MoT approved a further strategic connection along Lower Parliament Street commencing at the junction with Southwell Road as far as the junction with Pennyfoot Street. Also in November 1935 it was agreed that the final tram route, to Arnold, would be converted to motorbus operation.

Tram service B operating between Old Market Square and Mapperley was withdrawn on Saturday 1 February 1936 and the Woodborough Road tram route closed, motorbuses on service 31 between the same two points taking over the next morning. It is understood that Sherwood Depot ceased to house trams that night, its allocation being transferred to Parliament Street Depot, and that the work of conversion to accommodate motorbuses, which had already started, was rapidly completed. Some 28 tramcars were retained for the Arnold service (K) based at Parliament Street Depot, whilst 12 passenger cars surplus to requirements and a rail-grinder, assumed to be works car 1, were sold. The tramways still had a debt of £65,000 and repayment continued at the rate of £24,000 pa.

An attempt was made to sell the two remaining two-axle Ransomes D4s 11 and 12, the last open-staircase trolley vehicles in the fleet, in running order but as no offers were received they were put into store in the tower wagon garage. As they were already obsolete, the undertaking was authorised to sell them for scrap on 3 April 1936 whilst the City Treasurer was asked to write-off the sum of £152 14s 6d outstanding on the two vehicles. They were officially withdrawn at the end of May 1936.

The City Engineer now estimated that removal of all remaining tram track would take some 3 years and suggested that the agreed sum of £56,000 should be paid in instalments of two annual amounts of £20,000 followed by a final amount of £16,000 in the third year. As he aimed to remove all the worst sections in the first year this estimate could be exceeded whilst completion could take longer than 3 years. It was agreed that payment would be made as and when the work was actually carried out.

The only known photograph of the German flexible trolleybus overhead installed in London Road in 1935. *NCT*

Belatedly the North Midland Area Committee of the Coal Utilisation Council wrote in June 1936 to ask the Passenger Transport Committee to seriously reconsider the conversion of the Arnold and Mapperley tram routes to trolley vehicle operation, pointing out that the use of electricity provided work for local miners. In the same month, the official name of the undertaking was changed from "Nottingham Corporation Passenger Transport Department" to simply "Nottingham City Transport".

During August 1936 the Notts & Derby and Midland General Group of companies introduced a new service numbering system on their network, the Nottingham – Ripley trolleybuses service being allocated the number A1. Prior to this, those N&D trolleybuses having a number aperture had displayed a blank.

Nottingham's last traditional electric tram operated on service K Old Market Square – Upper Parliament Street – Mansfield Road – Sherwood – Daybrook – Arnold late in the evening of 5 September 1936. The official last tram was driven to

The "Nottingham Journal" recorded *"With triumphant jangle of the bell the car started off, headed by a police car and followed by well over a hundred private cars in three lines of traffic. Two or three motor-cyclists and a score of pedal cyclists did the whole journey behind the tram. Inside all were hilarious and fully entered into the spirit of gaiety.*

Soon the souvenir hunters got busy. The conductors' bells were detached, straps cut off, mirrors "acquired", everything portable removed and even the upholstered spring seats were taken. The warning gongs were removed after the car reached the depot, also for souvenirs. In the scramble for mementoes lights were turned off and the driving switch pulled over to bring a compulsory stop which baffled the aldermanic driver for a moment.

A big crowd waited the passing of the car through Sherwood amid prolonged cheers, led by the workmen at the Sherwood depot. The residents of Mapperley Park turned out in force and scores of people collected at the various stops, Hucknall Road and Gregory Boulevard being packed with people.

Another huge crowd waited at the Milton Street crossing and ran with the tram down King Street into the Old Market Square for the return via Queen Street, Parliament Street, Central Market, Bath Street, Sneinton and into the depot.

The biggest crowd of all had gathered at the depot and after a stop for photographs, Ald. Farr drove the car over the pit without having made one mistake throughout the drive"

It added, "Not a single tramway employee lost his job with the final conversion".

A scene dating from 1933-34 of English Electric car 194 on service C at the Valley Road, Radford Road "Shoulder of Mutton" crossroads in Basford. In the background, Basford gasworks and above, the trolleybus overhead wiring between Church Street and Valley Road completed in July 1933 for N&D access to Nottingham. *TMS*

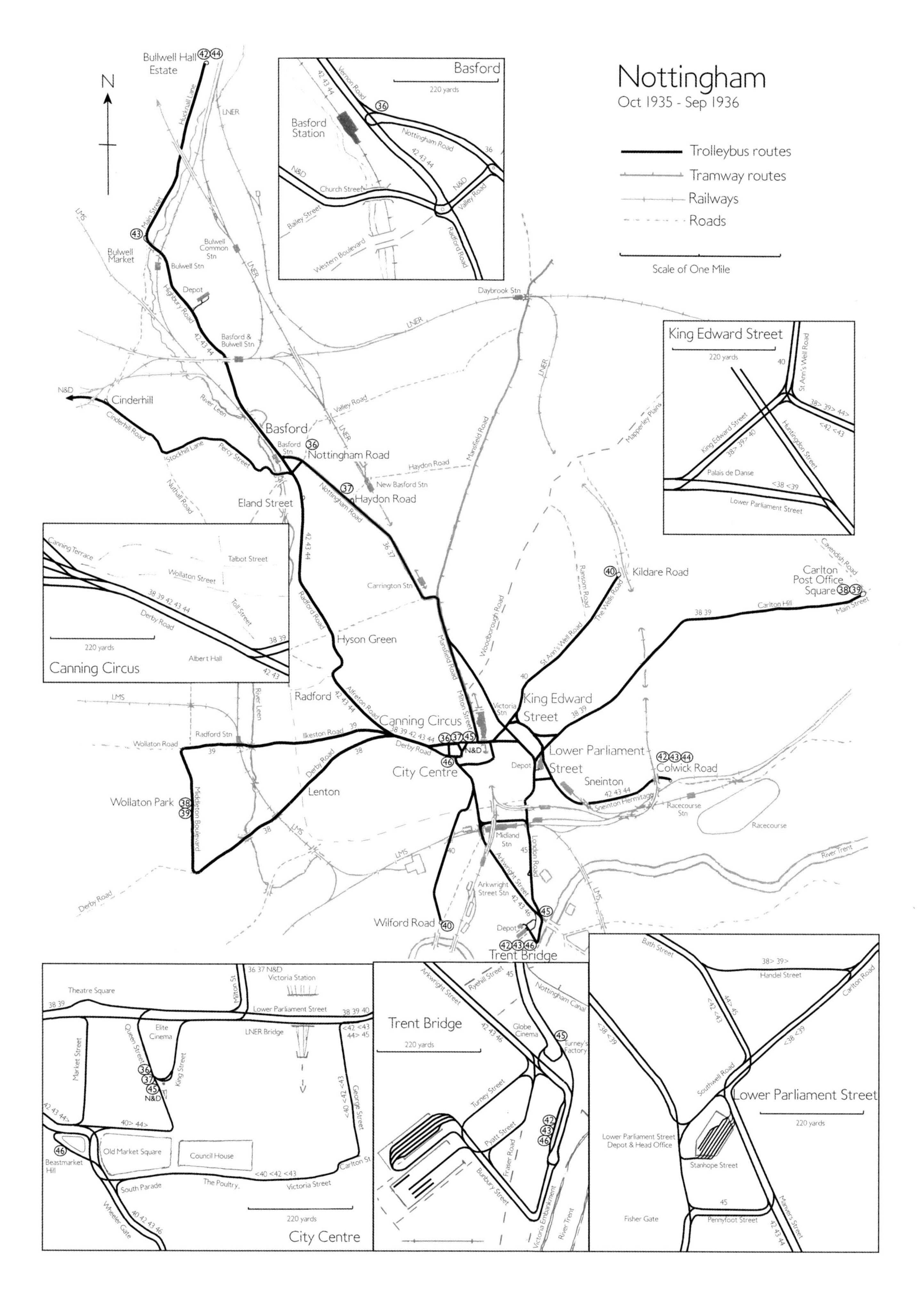
Nottingham
Oct 1935 - Sep 1936
Trolleybus routes
Tramway routes
Railways
Roads
Scale of One Mile
N
Bullwell Hall Estate
Bulwell Market
Bulwell Stn
Bulwell Common Stn
Depot
Basford & Bulwell Stn
Cinderhill
Basford
Basford Stn
Nottingham Road
Haydon Road
New Basford Stn
Eland Street
Carrington Stn
Hyson Green
Radford
Radford Stn
Canning Circus
City Centre
Lenton
Wollaton Park
Victoria Stn
King Edward Street
Lower Parliament Street
Depot
Sneinton
Sneinton Hermitage
Colwick Road
Racecourse Stn
Racecourse
Kildare Road
Carlton Post Office Square
Daybrook Stn
Midland Stn
Arkwright Street Stn
Wilford Road
Trent Bridge
Mansfield Road
Woodborough Road
St Ann's Well Road
Carlton Hill
River Trent
Basford
220 yards
Basford Station
Church Street
Nottingham Road
Western Boulevard
Valley Road
Radford Road
King Edward Street
220 yards
St Ann's Well Road
Huntingdon Street
Palais de Danse
Lower Parliament Street
Canning Circus
220 yards
Canning Terrace
Talbot Street
Wollaton Street
Derby Road
Tolll Street
Albert Hall
Theatre Square
Victoria Station
Lower Parliament Street
Elite Cinema
LNER Bridge
Market Street
Queen Street
King Street
George Street
Old Market Square
Council House
Beastmarket Hill
South Parade
The Poultry
Victoria Street
Carlton St
Wheeler Gate
220 yards
City Centre
Trent Bridge
220 yards
Arkwright Street
Ryehill Street
Nottingham Canal
Globe Cinema
Turney's Factory
Turney Street
Pyatt Street
Fraser Road
Bunbury Street
Victoria Embankment
River Trent
Bath Street
Handel Street
Carlton Road
Southwell Road
Lower Parliament Street
220 yards
Lower Parliament Street Depot & Head Office
Stanhope Street
Fisher Gate
Pennyfoot Street
Manvers Street

Daybrook by Chief Inspector Ellison (32 years service) with Inspector J.W. Vale, the longest serving traffic employee with 43 years of service who had joined the undertaking as a horse tram driver, as conductor. The Passenger Transport Committee travelled by motorbus to Daybrook Square where they joined the car, which departed at 12.10 am and ran direct to Parliament Street Depot. The final car, 190, inched into the depot in the early hours of Sunday 6 September 1936 driven by the Committee Chairman, Alderman John Farr, J.P, who had received tram driving lessons and had been issued with a licence the day before. Also on the platform were the Lord Mayor, Alderman Sir Albert Ball; the Sheriff; the Town Clerk; and the General Manager, Mr Gunn. Special tickets were issued with "RIP" in red letters and by the time the tramcar reached the depot it had been stripped of most of its fittings by souvenir takers!

As they followed the last tram into the depot Mr Gunn and Councillor J. Willbery fell into an inspection pit, and Mr Gunn was absent from work for some time as the result of the accident, indeed his health never fully recovered.

There were 26 tramcars available for service on the final day, cars 185 and 200 having been withdrawn in the meantime:

1914 Brush	146, 149-151, 153, 155
1919 English Electric	179, 180
1927 English Electric	181-184, 186-199
1902 ERTC	works car, presumed to be 1

During the next two weeks the remaining tramcars were driven from Parliament Street Depot to Trent Bridge Works utilising the remaining tracks in London Road. The last survivor, 146, made a fast and furious one-way journey on Monday 21 September 1936. The eighteen fully enclosed English Electric cars of 1926-27, together with partially cannibalised 185, were sold to Aberdeen Corporation Transport, where Mr Gunn had formerly been General Manager. Here, after renovation, 18 cars re-entered service and remained at work until 1950. The remaining older tramcars were sold to A. Devey & Co. Ltd. Birmingham for £715 the lot.

The trolleybus "shuttle" service 46 between Trent Bridge and Old Market Square last ran on Saturday 5 September 1936 and was replaced by an extension of the Arnold tram replacement motor bus service 20 which was extended through the city centre to Trent Bridge via Arkwright Street on a daily basis from 6 September 1936. On the same day some journeys on the Mapperley tram replacement motor bus service 31 were also extended from the Old Market Square to Trent Bridge via Arkwright Street, displaying service number 35.

With the completion of the tramway conversion programme, the Nottingham trolleybus system had, although much smaller than envisaged by Mr Marks, in principle already reached its maximum size. In September 1936 the following services were in operation over a system of 23.2 routes miles operated by 125 three-axle vehicles:

36 Old Market Square (Queen Street/King Street) – Upper Parliament Street – Milton Street – Victoria Station – Mansfield Road – Nottingham Road (Vernon Road)

37 Old Market Square (Queen Street/King Street) – Upper Parliament Street – Milton Street – Victoria Station – Mansfield Road – Nottingham Road (Haydn Road) (Monday – *Friday peak hours, including lunch time, all day Saturday)*

38 Carlton (Post Office Square) – Carlton Road – Central Market – Upper Parliament Street – Derby Road – Wollaton Park (Middleton Boulevard, Scalford Drive) *(eastbound via Central Market – King Edward Street – Bath Street – Handel Street, westbound via Southwell Road – Lower Parliament Street)*

39 Carlton (Post Office Square) – Carlton Road – Central Market – Upper Parliament Street – Ilkeston Road – Wollaton Park (Middleton Boulevard, Fairham Drive) *(eastbound via Central Market – King Edward Street – Bath Street – Handel Street, westbound via Southwell Road – Lower Parliament Street)*

40 The Wells Road (Kildare Road) – King Edward Street – Lower Parliament Street – Old Market Square – Wilford Road – Wilford Bridge *(northbound via Queen Street, southbound via George Street – Carlton Street – Victoria Street – The Poultry – South Parade)*

42 Bulwell Hall Estate – Bulwell Market – Basford – Vernon Road – Radford Road – Hyson Green – Alfreton Road – Derby Road – Chapel Bar – Old Market Square – Arkwright Street – Trent Bridge *(alternate northbound journeys commenced at Colwick Road running Sneinton – Manvers Street – Bath Street – Lower Parliament Street – George Street – Victoria Street to join the normal route at Old Market Square. There were no southbound journeys to Colwick Road, all southbound vehicles travelled to Trent Bridge)*

43 Bulwell Market – Basford – Vernon Road – Radford Road – Hyson Green – Alfreton Road – Derby Road – Chapel Bar – Old Market Square – Arkwright Street – Trent Bridge *(alternate northbound journeys commenced at Colwick Road running Sneinton – Manvers Street – Bath Street – Lower Parliament Street – George Street – Victoria Street to join the normal route at Old Market Square. There were no southbound journeys to Colwick Road, all southbound vehicles travelled to Trent Bridge)*

44 Bulwell Hall Estate – Bulwell Market – Basford – Vernon Road – Radford Road – Hyson Green – Alfreton Road – Derby Road – Upper Parliament Street – Lower Parliament Street – Bath Street – Manvers Street – Sneinton – Colwick Road (unidirectional) *(this service operated southbound only from Bulwell Hall Estate to Colwick Road, all northbound journeys from Colwick Road to Bulwell Hall Estate displaying service 42)*

45 Trent Bridge (Globe Cinema) – London Road – Pennyfoot Street – Manvers Street – Bath Street – King Edward Street – Upper Parliament Street – Old Market Square (Queen Street/King Street)

During the 1920s and 1930s some twenty municipal housing estates were built, mainly on the northern and western fringes of the city, additional land being annexed from the bordering parishes by a further boundary extension in 1932. The housing programme was accompanied by the construction of a dual carriageway ring road, in stages from Valley Road (1925) to Clifton Boulevard (1938), to serve the new estates and keep the growing volumes of road traffic out of the congested city centre. The public transport needs of these estates and orbital roads, although eminently suitable for electric traction, were served entirely by motorbus. Indeed, Nottingham must be one of the few provincial cities where the trolleybus route network was hardly extended beyond the bounds of its railed predecessors.

After the War further housing estates were built on those few undeveloped areas still remaining within the city boundaries, namely at Bilborough and Bulwell, after which it became necessary to extend the boundaries on the south side of the River Trent within which the extensive Clifton Estate was constructed. Again trolleybuses never served these new centres of population nor was it ever proposed that they should.

In October 1936 the Lighting Engineer took over 123 traction poles on the Mansfield Road route in consequence of the motor bus conversion and 6 poles on London Road at £1 each. The trolleybus stop four traction poles beyond Chatham Street on Mansfield Road was moved to one pole north of the "Belisha" pedestrian crossing. Nottingham Chamber of Commerce submitted a list of other trolleybus stops where they prevented a clear view of pedestrian crossings and recommended a policy of removing stops from street corners. It was decided to generally permit litter bins to be attached to traction poles.

Just south of The Wells Road, Kildare Road terminus of service 10, English Electric E11 24 swerves to avoid a car pulling out of a side street. The embankment and overbridge of the Nottingham Suburban Railway is visible in the background. This photograph was used in the trade press of the period to demonstrate the manoeuvrability of the trackless trolley vehicle. *BTS*

English Electric E11 23 at Wilford Bridge turning circle in what has certainly become an atmospheric shot of a crew able to pose in the middle of the road. *NCT*

On 23 November 1936 there were two separate trolleybus fires, one on Ilkeston Road and the other on Mansfield Road. There was thick fog that day and it is assumed that the incidents were due to overheated resistances resulting from the continued use of low speed notches.

The City Treasurer and the General Manager reviewed capital expenditure planned for the next 5 financial years, that is until 31 March 1942, at the beginning of December 1936. This was foreseen as totalling £250,000 made up of £126,000 for new motorbuses and £70,300 for trolley vehicles if purchased out of revenue (if purchased on a loan the cost would rise to £90,000 during the period in question) with a further £34,000 anticipated for depots, shelters, etc. By 9 July 1937 the trolleybus requirements had become more concrete as:

1939/40	£22,800	12 vehicles
1940/41	£47,500	25 vehicles

still at a cost of £70,000 whereas other expenditure was now estimated at £135,000 for motorbuses, £22,000 for road reinstatement and £25,000 for a new depot.

On Saturday 9 January 1937 service 38 was discontinued, the Carlton trolleybus service henceforth being maintained solely by the 39, which continued across the city to Wollaton Park via Ilkeston Road. To compensate for the reduced trolleybus service along Derby Road, the 45, which had been cut back from Wollaton Park to the Old Market Square on 18 August 1935, was re-extended the next day along Derby Road to Wollaton Park, Scalford Drive:

39 Carlton, Post Office Square – Carlton Road – Central Market – Upper Parliament Street – Ilkeston Road – Wollaton Park (Middleton Boulevard, Fairham Drive) *(eastbound via Central Market – King Edward Street – Bath Street – Handel Street, westbound via Southwell Road – Lower Parliament Street)*

45 Trent Bridge (Globe Cinema) – London Road – Pennyfoot Street – Manvers Street – Bath Street – King Edward Street – Upper Parliament Street – Derby Road – Wollaton Park (Middleton Boulevard, Scalford Drive)

Both services used their respective turning circles on Middleton Boulevard and returned along the reverse route, the 39 operating more frequently than the 45 to accommodate the heavier loadings on Ilkeston Road. The layover point for service 39 at the side of the western carriageway of Middleton Boulevard was moved somewhat northwards to a point about midway between Scalford Drive and Selston Drive but still virtually opposite Fairham Drive. From Sunday 9 May 1937 improved frequencies were introduced on services 44 and 45.

In April 1937 it was decided that the forthcoming Coronation of HM King George VI and Queen Elizabeth would be celebrated by illuminating a motorbus and a trolleybus, and that the offices and depots be decorated at a cost of £132 5s. English Electric E11 trolleybus 24 was decorated and toured the system at specially advertised times although there is no evidence that passengers were carried. A Bank Holiday service was run on Coronation Day, 12 May 1937, holidays and wages for staff being handled as for Christmas Day.

It was decided to carry out alterations to Bulwell Depot, which had previously only operated electric traction, in order to accommodate some of the additional 50 motor buses and on 11 July 1937 a separate rota, known as the "bus side" as opposed to the trolleybus rota (known as "the track"), took over the operation of motorbus services 1, 7 and 22. Soon after the decision was taken, increased petrol and diesel prices, estimated at costing the department £5,700 pa, were announced although the Department was able to secure a £2,100 income tax rebate on its general administration expenses, this being credited to rate relief.

The N&D again asked the Passenger Transport Committee on 30 April 1937 if they would consider constructing a route via Nuthall Road and Alfreton Road solely for the use of the Company's through traffic. In June 1937, Carlton UDC asked that a passenger waiting shelter be built at the Post Office terminus but this was refused. That same month a further 80 TIM ticket issuing machines were ordered.

The Electricity Committee increased the price of traction current by 0.015d from 0.7d to 0.715d per unit on 9 July 1937 due to wage increases in the mining industry having increased the price of coal. The General Manager was asked to investigate the cost of traction current in other towns. At this time there were also two increases in the cost of diesel fuel oil and petrol. On the positive side it was announced on 1 October 1937 that the rateable value of the undertaking had

Fred Parr, a trolleybus driver in the early 1930s, reminisced that on one occasion when he should have been going to Wollaton Park via Ilkeston Road he took the wrong exit at Canning Circus and turned off down Derby Road. His conductor and passengers soon made him aware of his mistake. The trolleybus was de-poled and the more able-bodied passengers pushed it across the carriageway into one of the side roads e.g. Seely Road or Douglas Road, that run from Derby Road to Ilkeston Road. Fortunately these side roads are on a down gradient to Ilkeston Road and it was merely a case of getting everyone back on board, letting the handbrake off and coasting down to Ilkeston Road, where the trolleybus was re-poled and carried on its way none the worst for its 'off route experience'. Other driver's recall similar escapades including one who thus managed to avoid an Inspector standing at the Canning Circus end of Ilkeston Road. The Inspector couldn't believe his eyes when a trolleybus which he had not seen heading out to Wollaton Park returned to the City!

1934 Karrier E6 52 at the Queen Victoria Statue, Beastmarket Hill loading island (at the west end of the Old Market Square) prior to departing on a 43 working to Bulwell Market in January 1937. *GHFA & JMB*

Electric E11 trolleybus 24 newly decorated for the Coronation of HM King George VI and Queen Elizabeth 12 May 1937 with proud officials. *NCT*

On 21 June 1937 English Electric E11 22 heading for Wells Road descends from the Wilford Road bridge over the approach to the LMS Nottingham Midland Station to the Nottingham Canal and Castle Boulevard passing the entrances to the LMS Goods Station and Heavy Goods Depot. *BTS*

been reassessed following the abandonment of tramway operations, leading to a fall from £29,215 to £25,000 backdated to the financial year ending 31 March 1937.

Workmen's Returns were available for use Monday-Friday up to 9pm and on Saturdays up to 3pm with exchange tickets being issued against the return portion for the return journey. On 21 June 1937 the Fares Subcommittee resolved that they should be available up to any hour on the day of issue.

At the first Passenger Transport Committee Meeting of 1938 it was estimated that a further 46 trolleybuses would be required in 1942/43 costing £92,000. These figures were submitted to the Finance Committee. A call for tenders for a Ticket Office at Parliament Street Depot, to be paid for out of the reserve fund, was issued.

In order to reduce the amount of empty mileage operated on works specials, in February 1938 the construction of turning circles at the junction of Derby Road and Gregory Street, Lenton, at an estimated cost of £140, and at the junction of Middleton Boulevard with Ilkeston Road were recommended. That opposite the end of Gregory Street, used by works specials serving the Raleigh Cycles factory, was constructed later in 1938, but no action was taken in respect of a turning circle at the north end of Middleton Boulevard.

Perhaps provoked by news of the forthcoming closure of Chesterfield's one route trolleybus system (which occurred on 25 March 1938) a question on the abandonment of Nottingham's trolleybuses was tabled at the March meeting of the City Council. Alderman Sir Albert Atkey stated that he would like the Passenger Transport Committee to consider at its next meeting whether the time was not now opportune to abandon all trolley vehicle routes and substitute motorbuses. The Committee subsequently asked Mr Gunn to prepare a detailed report. Alderman Atkey disregarded the fact that Chesterfield's stated reasons for the withdrawal of their successful trolleybuses were high electricity costs and the difficulty of extending the routes. All possible out of town extensions were bedevilled with low railway bridges whilst GPO trunk telephone lines strung at low height along the route across main roads had prevented the use of span wires. The entire cost of the system had been amortised by 1937 but modernisation was by now necessary.

Despite Mr Gunn's lack of enthusiasm for the trolleybus, the Nottingham system was still considered as providing a glowing example of the advantages of this mode of transport in part due to Mr Pulfrey's enthusiasm. A group of Belfast officials had visited Nottingham to inspect the trolleybus system and in a reciprocal gesture the General Manager and the Passenger Transport Committee Chairman were invited to participate in the opening celebrations of the Belfast system on Monday 28 March 1938. Representatives of the Tramways Board from Bergen, Norway visited Nottingham on 29 April 1938 to inspect the trolley vehicle system and were entertained to lunch. Bergen's first trolleybus route only opened on 24 February 1950; the city continues to operate trolleybuses and took delivery of a fleet of new vehicles in 2003.

Mr Gunn presented his report, which stressed the economy and flexibility of the motorbus, to the Passenger Transport Committee on 17 June 1938. It was the guarded recommendation from a professional transport manager to his civic policy makers to abandon trolleybus operation. Considering the widely prevailing enthusiasm for the trolleybus in the UK during the late 1930s, the far-reaching plans for extensions to the network only a few years previously and the proximity of a major coal mining industry this was a surprising step, no doubt influenced by the combined lobbying efforts of Alderman Atkey and the General Manager himself. Nottingham thus became the first major trolleybus operating city in the country to actively consider abandonment of this mode of transport. Interestingly Mr Pulfrey wrote comments on the manuscript of the report to the effect that certain items were "incorrect" when applied to Nottingham.

The report and its argumentation make interesting reading and can be found in appendix L. Alderman Atkey asked for an item to consider the complete substitution of trolley vehicles by buses be placed on the agenda of the next meeting of the Passenger Transport Committee with the General Managers report as evidence. Mr. Gunn predicted that the debt for all 125 trolleybuses would be paid by 1943, the overhead by 1954 and the depot alterations by 1955. He calculated the replacement cost of the trolleybuses as £300,000, (£2,400 each) to be bought between 1939 and 1945 and assumed a service life of the newest vehicles of only 10 years. The cost of buying motorbuses instead, over the same period, was calculated as 140 vehicles (to give the same seating capacity) at £1,965 each, totalling £275,000, a saving of £25,000. Mr Gunn then presented a comparative cost of operation table, based on figures for 1936-37.

Not included (see below) were figures for Bradford, Darlington, Hastings, Ipswich, Llanelly, London, Mexborough&Swindon, Notts&Derby, South Lancs and Teeside, although some of these operators did not operate motorbuses. Despite admitting that existing motorbuses in Nottingham operated at 1.040 mph faster than trolleybuses because they were not running through densely populated areas, Mr. Gunn was of the opinion that they would still average .75 mph faster service speeds on the trolleybus routes. This, together with the loan charges,

Undertaking	Trolleybus operating costs per mile d.	Motor Bus operating costs per mile d.	Undertaking	Trolleybus operating costs per mile d.	Motor Bus operating costs per mile d.
Ashton-under-Lyne	12.985	9.898	Pontypridd	9.67	9.40
Birmingham	12.248	10.967	Portsmouth	12.045	11.761
Bournemouth	10.780	11.290	Reading	13.348	12.389
Chesterfield	8.850	9.010	Rotherham	7.520	7.750
Derby	12.144	12.826	St. Helens	9.721	8.287
Doncaster	10.100	7.451	Southend	12.251	10.333
Grimsby	10.219	9.174	South Shields	8.275	6.983
Huddersfield	10.209	8.252	Walsall	11.529	10.120
Maidstone	11.972	10.437	West Hartlepool	9.790	8.200
Newcastle	10.930	9.761	Wolverhampton	10.354	10.194
NOTTINGHAM	12.984	10.516	AVERAGE	10.854	9.762

enabled him to claim an annual saving of £4,761 in favour of motorbuses. Whilst maintenance and crewing costs would be more, power costs and income from the rates (as trolleybuses, like trams, were rateable) would be less. The report stated that electricity costs were currently "extremely high" but that a war might have an adverse effect on fuel prices. Other points were that traction poles were in good condition and could be used for lighting purposes, motorbus fares were 25% higher and that through running with N&D would "have to be taken into consideration". The report claimed not to be one-sided, despite dubious estimates for service life and speed ability actually being asserted as advantages for motorbuses. More usual, general claims were stated, such as the manoeuvrability and flexibility of motor buses and that "trolleybuses cannot overtake" and "are slow over crossings where congestion usually arises". Mr Gunn wanted "unification of transport" that would, over a number of years, produce economies. No advantages for trolleybuses were stated.

On 1 July 1938 the Passenger Transport Committee decided to defer any decision about trolleybus operations until September 1938 when it was again postponed for consideration until 1939, (see later) a particular point being the price paid to the city's own Electricity Department for traction current. It should be added here that in Nottingham the position of Chairman of the Passenger Transport Committee was considered non-political, a change of local political control not necessarily leading to a change of Chairman.

The number of accidents involving the Department's vehicles was leading to an unenviable reputation which was gradually gaining national proportions, indeed an article on the safety of Nottingham Corporation's Omnibuses prompted by two recent fatalities involving trolley vehicles was published in the 22 May 1938 edition of the "Sunday Dispatch". A few days later, on 27 May 1938, a trolleybus hit William Breffitt as he crossed the road near the junction of Derby Road and Parliament Street. His claim was settled "out of court" in November 1938 with £100 compensation and 20 guineas costs. Another fatality in St. Ann's Well Road prompted the City Council to request a review of the number of fatal accidents involving trolley vehicles and their average speed, which was presented on 1 July 1938.

It went on to stress: *"The area in which the greatest number of accidents have occurred, namely St. Ann's Well Road, is a densely populated area and that all along the road there are steep and narrow gradients running into this narrow road. There are always innumerable children playing and running about and very often these children dash from the side streets into the main thoroughfare, thereby increasing the risk of accident. The density of this area and the liability of accident was taken into consideration when the Schedules were prepared and that the statutory speed as laid down by the Ministry of Transport in St. Ann's Well Road is 16 mph. The average schedule speeds for other municipal operators throughout the country are given below from which it will be noticed that Nottingham operates with practically the lowest speed"*

Town	mph
Rotherham	11.21
Doncaster	10.78
Walsall	10.624
Bradford	10.54
St. Helens	10.45
Newcastle upon Tyne	10.38
Portsmouth	10.0
Huddersfield	9.758
Ipswich	9.72
Birmingham	9.39
Wolverhampton	9.272
Bournemouth	8.87
Darlington	8.79
Derby	8.59
NOTTINGHAM	**8.571**
Southend on Sea	8.437

The report concluded: *"in the twenty fatal accidents before referred to, an inquest was held in each case, and the verdict recorded was 'Accidental Death' and the driver exonerated in each case. The Committee desire to record in their report their appreciation of the services rendered by the drivers employed in the Department, and they are quite satisfied with the manner in which these employees carry out their onerous duties".* Nothing appears specifically to have been done to alleviate the situation and accidents inevitably continued to happen. Mrs Louisa Mason was knocked down and killed by a trolleybus near the junction of Forest Road and Alfreton Road on 6 September 1938. A claim for funeral expenses £24 1s 6d plus pain, suffering and loss of expectation of life was subsequently received and settled with a sum of £200 damages plus 30 guineas solicitor's costs. On 19 October 1938 Conductor Cyril Staniforth died of injuries incurred when he fell into a trench at the junction of George Street and Parliament Street when attempting to rewire a de-wired trolleybus. Subsequently a verdict of accidental death was returned and his widow was paid £300 compensation. At lunchtime on 18 July 1939 an unidentified Ransomes/Brush trolleybus heading into the City collided with a traction pole on St. Ann's Well Road near the "Cavendish" cinema, injuring some 28 persons and bringing down the overhead wiring. On 26 July 1939 a dewired trolley boom struck the Walter Fountain monument and dislodged masonry that fell and fatally injured a 73-year old man walking past.

Mr Gunn reported that 7¼ miles of copper wire was required to renew the Bulwell route and that 6 identical quotations had been received 93⁄16d per lb. This was not necessarily indicative of excessive wear, although there was a 2-minute service on this portion and the vehicles used trolley wheels. The original conversion had probably retained the tram positive wire for trolleybus use and it was this that now needed replacement. Generally during the tram to trolleybus conversion programme separate

Extract from the report presented to the City Council 1 July 1938;
Annual number of fatal accidents involving Trackless Vehicles since their introduction

Service	Route	Years/months in operation	Fatalities	Av. fatalities per annum	One fatality every Passengers	One fatality every Miles
36, 37	Nottingham Road	11 yrs 2 mts	1929 - 1 1933 - 2 1936 - 1	0.358	10,610,000	907,000
39, 45	Carlton - Wollaton Park	6 yrs 3 mts	1932 - 2 1934 - 1 1935 - 1	0.64	23,280,000	2,053,000
	and London Road	3 yrs	Nil			
40	St. Ann's Well Road	8 yrs 3 mts	1931 - 3 1932 - 1 1933 - 1 1937 - 1 1938 - 2	0.970	6,330,000	421,000
40	Wilford Road	8 yrs 3 mts	1933 - 1			
42, 43, 44	Bulwell - Trent Bridge	4 yrs 1 mt	1934 - 2 1937 - 1	0.735	29,810,000	2,273,000
	and Colwick	3 yrs	Nil			
			TOTAL		13,615,000	1,049,000

Time Schedules (1938) and Average Speed in MPH

Service	Route	Mileage	Running Time incl. Stops	Scheduled Speed
36	King Street – Vernon Road	2.39	19 - 24 mins	7.55 - 5.97
37	King Street – Haydn Road	1.83	17 mins	6.46
39	Carlton – Wollaton Park	5.12	31 - 34 mins	9.91 - 9.03
40	Kildare Road – Wilford Bridge	2.93	20 - 25 mins	8.79 - 7.03
42, 43	Bulwell Hall Estate – Trent Bridge	6.50	43 mins	9.07
44	Bulwell Hall Estate – Colwick Road	7.20	43 mins	10.05
45	London Road – Wollaton Park	4.04	30 mins	8.08

Leyland TTB3/MCCW & F 107 pulls out of narrow Chapel Bar into Derby Road at the junction with Upper Parliament Street en route for Bulwell Hall Estate in 1938. *GHFA & JMB*

trolley wires were used when the two modes of transport operated along the same street, Bath Street being a known exception where trams used the trolleybus positive trolley wire. There were however many examples of the new trolleybus positive trolley wire being used by trams prior to the introduction of trolleybus services and the complete withdrawal of the tram route e.g. Carlton Road, Vernon Road.

The fleet numbering scheme which until then had consisted of a separate series for motor buses and trolleybuses was simplified by adding 300 to the trolleybuses' existing numbers. Announced in 1938, the process is thought to have been completed by September 1939.

On 18 November 1938 Mr Gunn asked for instructions as to a possible renewal of the Nottingham Corporation (Trolley Vehicles) Order Confirmation Act 1934 powers which had been granted to equip and run trolley vehicles along Alfreton Road, across Bobbers Mill Bridge and along Nuthall Road to Stockhill Lane. These powers were due to expire on 11 July 1939 and, perhaps in part due to an enquiry from Ripley UDC asking if Nottingham were intending to approve the N&D's plans to run through trolleybuses between Cinderhill and Bentinck Road, it was decided to apply for a 5-year renewal.

A suggestion that bell boys or an additional conductor should be employed on the St Ann's Wells Road service was looked into and it was found that only Manchester had adopted, and after a trial discontinued, such a practice. No action was taken. However having heard what other undertakings were collecting from this source, red-painted uncollected fare boxes were fitted to the side of the staircase on trolley vehicles and motorbuses commencing in November 1938. They rapidly justified their cost and upkeep.

In January 1939 the City Engineer released proposals to install a roundabout at the west end of the Old Market Square on Beastmarket Hill at the bottom of Market Street necessitating the removal of the Queen Victoria Statue. Although the Passenger Transport Committee approved of the removal of the Statue they asked that any traffic islands constructed on the site should initially be of a temporary nature. They also saw this as an opportunity to provide WC accommodation for both staff and the general public but the MoT would make no grant towards the roundabout if a building was erected on it. It would also be necessary to move the Department's telephone kiosk which stood on the island at the base of the Statue. Use of shop premises in Angel Row was rejected as too expensive, however the rental of a room at the back of this shop for £25 pa was authorised in May 1939. The toilets were subsequently situated underground on the east side of Beastmarket Hill, also known as New Street, beneath the ornamental gardens in the Old Market Square.

Further traffic islands or roundabouts were planned for Nottingham including one near the Walter Fountain at the junction of Carrington Street and Greyfriar Gate necessitating the purchase of about 470 sq yds of land at the junction (although the Fountain would be retained) and an elongated island on Long Row East effectively creating a dual carriageway. The Passenger Transport Committee asked that the Long Row proposal be deleted. In respect of a traffic island at the junction of Canal Street with London Road, the City Engineer planned to acquire a 102 sq yd plot of land at the north-east junction of London Road and Lower Parliament Street and also a 223 sq yd plot of land at the south-east junction of London Road and Lower Parliament Street. Subject to MoT approval, the Passenger Transport Committee again resolved that the island should initially be of a temporary nature.

The Electricity Committee agreed effective 1 January 1939 to reduce the charge per unit from 0.70d to 0.65d, subject, as before, to a coal clause adjustment of 0.15d per unit for every 6d per ton rise or fall in the average annual price of coal delivered to the power station bunkers above 12s per ton.

At the 3 February 1939 Passenger Transport Committee Meeting, Councillor Rees referred to traffic delays in King Street when trolley vehicles terminating there arrived before schedule and had to wait until other waiting trolley vehicles had moved off. It was agreed that this could be solved by the construction of a clockwise loop around

Passengers hurry to board another 43, operated by Karrier E6/MCCW & F 54, at the Processional Walk "Railless" stop in Old Market Square. In 2005 the scene has changed surprisingly little. The compass design in the pavement, Griffin and Spalding's department store, now named Debenhams, and Yates Wine Lodge at the Talbot still remain, whilst Nottingham's second-generation electric trams pass exactly this spot before turning into South Parade. *GHFA & JMB*

Trinity Square, which lay immediately to the west of Milton Street. The matter was referred for costing but the loop was never built. An additional turning circle on the edge of the city centre for vehicles from the north would have been a sensible precaution as the risk of war grew.

A special Passenger Transport Committee meeting finally considered Mr Gunn's 17 June 1938 report into trolleybus abandonment on Friday 24 February 1939. Speaking at a political event a few days earlier Councillor Littlefair stated: *"there was a suggestion that the Committee should scrap the trolleybuses and go over entirely to petrol driven vehicles. He did not think such a move would be made while there was a feeling in the air that this country might be involved in an international disturbance, for petrol supplies might be curtailed in the event of war breaking out. Such a position of affairs would make the conveyance of the public a chancy matter. So, for a time, the Committee would probably pursue the policy of having two separate forms of transport, and running buses on electricity generated 'on the spot'"*.

The Town Clerk pointed out that under Section 13 of the Nottingham Corporation Act 1930 the Department's trolleybuses enjoyed protection against the operation of competitive motorbus services, although similar protection under prevailing legislation would have been granted for trolleybus-replacement motorbus services. Mr Gunn warned that 12 new trolleybuses would be required in June 1940 to replace the 1930 Ransomes D6s 13-18 and English Electric 19-24, which could be considered as obsolete. Bearing in mind the outstanding loan debt on the trolleybus fleet, overhead equipment and related depot infrastructure, which then amounted to around £106,000, and the relative youth of many of the trolley vehicles, it was decided that trolleybus operation should continue. There is no doubt that this question would have been revisited within the ensuing 12 months had the outbreak of the Second World War not intervened. It is noteworthy that no immediate action was taken to order 12 replacements for the vehicles referred to above.

With this major decision behind them plans to extend the trolleybus service from Wilford Road to the Royal Ordnance Factory in King's Meadow Road off Queens Drive were discussed in March 1939. New overhead equipment would have cost about £1,007 although an alternative proposal envisaged dismantling the overhead in Huntingdon Street and its re-use to reach the factory at a considerable economy, but the matter was not pursued.

General traffic congestion, "Belisha" or "zebra" crossings and pedestrians overflowing from the pavement particularly in the relatively narrow, busy shopping streets of Wheeler Gate and Lister Gate led to complaints about irregular trolleybus services between the Old Market Square and Trent Bridge by way of Arkwright Street. At this time all motorbuses to/from West Bridgford, together with the tram replacement services to/from Arnold and Mapperley, ran along this artery as well as several trunk trolleybus services, some of which had a three minute service at busy times.

Carlton UDC had complained of excessive wear and tear to the road surface at the Carlton Post Office Square terminus. The Town Clerk stated that the only relevant statutory provision affecting trolley vehicles was Section 55 of the Tramways Act 1870 under which the promoters were liable to a road authority in respect of "accident, damages or injuries happening through their act or default". As this only covered negligence and did not cover damage arising from normal wear and tear, the Corporation were under no liability to the UDC. It was agreed that the City Engineer should discuss options for reinforcing the road surface with the UDC and if this was possible, Nottingham would make a contribution to the cost. Having reviewed the options, the resurfacing with reinforced concrete although this was the most expensive solution at £750 or alternately scarifying followed by resurfacing with 4ins bituminous asphalt macadam at £375 were suggested. Carlton UDC accepted the 4ins bituminous solution and Nottingham contributed ⅓ of the cost.

In May 1939 Carlton UDC asked if the Corporation would extend the trolley vehicle system beyond Post Office Square over the routes for which the Corporation had sought powers under the Nottingham Corporation Bill 1930. At that time the UDC had opposed these extensions and the Passenger Transport Committee now refused the request for the time being although they were prepared to reconsider the matter at a later date.

Questions were again raised in the City Council's 6 June 1939 meeting about continued trolleybus operation in Nottingham. Alderman Young *"could not conceive that the fears as to scrapping trolleybuses were well founded"*. Alderman Halls thought one anomaly they should wipe out, however, was a different fare over the same route on different types of vehicle. Alderman Sir Albert Atkey once again emphasised that the time was coming when the Passenger Transport Committee would have to consider if the electric system of transport was to be of a permanent character. He was anxious that they should consider this matter. *"It would be wise to take time by the forelock, because in the course of a year or two the Committee would have to contemplate spending many thousands of pounds on renewing the trolleybus system of transport, and if at that time the system was not permanent it would embarrass the Committee and involve expenditure which might not be justified. There were advantages and disadvantages of the electric trolleybus system. One disadvantage was that it was immobile – you could not direct the transport over other routes when roads were up. Again it was not a system which could be extended. No county authority would consent to the desecration of the highway by putting up overhead wires. The city, from a transport point of view, presented a fine spectacle to all who saw it, and they could be justly proud of it. He hoped the Committee would keep an open mind as to the future of the trolleybus"*. Mr Cox asked how the recent budget would affect the transport undertaking and suggested that before scrapping the trolleybus system they should consider what the price of petrol would be in the event of war.

The July 1939 timetable again showed journeys to, and additionally from, Cinderhill, Bells Lane, every 15 minutes off-peak and 10 minutes during peak hours, as a part of the joint operation of the Nottingham Road services with N&D. There is no evidence that these were additional trips operated by NCT but simply part of the N&D through service timetable.

By the end of March 1939 it was clear that Mr Gunn was critically ill, reportedly due to heavy drinking and the after-effects of his fall into an inspection pit at Parliament Street Depot on the night of the last tram, and Mr H.G. Morley, Traffic Superintendent was appointed Acting General Manager. Mr J.L. Gunn, the General Manager since February 1934, died on 10 April 1939, at the early age of 42. The vacancy for a General Manager attracted 24 applications and a short list was prepared consisting of Mr. B. England, General Manager and Engineer of Leicester Corporation Transport; Mr. H.C. Godsmark, General Manager at Huddersfield and formerly Deputy Manager at Nottingham; Mr G.H. Pulfrey, Rolling Stock Superintendent at Nottingham; Mr F. Lythgoe, General Manager at Middlesbrough; Mr G.A.Cherry, General Manager at Rochdale and Mr H.G. Morley, Traffic Superintendent and Acting General Manager at Nottingham. On 12 June 1939 Benjamin England, FRGS; MIAE; AMI Mech E.; M.Inst T., was appointed General Manager at a starting salary of £1,350 pa. He committed not to apply for any other position for 3 years.

In recognition of his services as Acting General Manager, Mr Morley was appointed Deputy General Manager at a salary of £750 with immediate effect. Perhaps in disgust at having failed to secure promotion or a salary increase shortly beforehand, Mr Pulfrey resigned to take up the position of General Manager at St. Helen's. Following interviews on 13 July 1939 with a short list of 6 applicants which included a number of personalities such as W.J. Evans and William Little, who rose later to senior managerial fame, Chaceley Thornton Humpidge, B.Sc., AM Inst T, of Portsmouth Corporation Transport was appointed at £600 pa.

At lunchtime on 18 July 1939 an unidentified Ransomes/Brush trolleybus heading into the City collided with a traction pole on St. Ann's Well Road near the "Cavendish" cinema, injuring some 28 persons and bringing down the overhead wiring. On 26 July 1939 a dewired trolley boom struck the Walter Fountain monument and dislodged masonry that fell and fatally injured a 73-year old man walking past.

Chapter 5 The Challenge of War 1939-45

Nottingham City Council decided in August 1939 *"that in order to concentrate on the work in connection with air raid precautions as required by His Majesty's Government, this Council instructs all Committees to defer all schemes (unless the prior consent of the Special Air Raid Precautions and Emergency Committee to proceed has been obtained) except those works which are at present in hand and the subject of a formal contract"*. Nonetheless the MoT had only granted a 6-month extension of time for the exercise of the powers conferred by the Nottingham Corporation (Trolley Vehicles) Order 1934 covering the Nuthall Road, Bobbers Mill Bridge and Alfreton Road extension until 12 January 1940. This allowed little time for construction in view of the City Council's ruling although the N&D were pressing for work to start as they were keen to operate through services along the route. The Council's parliamentary agents asked the MoT if they would accept a request for a further extension of time but due to the political situation their positive response was not received until late November 1939. An application for an extension of the powers to equip the route within 12 months of the declaration of peace was submitted before the end of the month but MoT consent to a one-year extension i.e. until 12 January 1941 was only given in January 1940.

As the international crisis worsened, Mr Morley, the Acting General Manager used his initiative to prepare the undertaking for "black-out" conditions by buying sufficient exterior and interior lamp screening, blue lacquer for use on the windows and light bulbs for the 340 vehicle fleet. On a more serious note first aid, fire fighting, decontamination equipment and sandbagging to the value of £1,700 was purchased. Thereafter he ordered an enlarged stock of replacement parts including gear oil, brake liners, timber, trolley and span wire in anticipation of a shortage of materials, and, anticipating the effect of a war on labour, material costs and revenue, started work on an application for higher fares.

Nottingham was seen as a regional centre and industrial city of strategic importance, making it an attractive target for the enemy. Whether small engineering works or the huge Royal Ordnance Factory, which produced heavy guns, mountings and ancillary equipment, or the Boots drugs and Players tobacco factory, they all played an important role in the war effort.

Public parks offered a possible refuge during air raids and appropriate direction signs were fixed to city centre traction poles together with a further 40 signs directing to air raid shelters. It soon became difficult to arrange duty rosters as 71 employees had been conscripted for military service or specialist war work, and it was expected that an additional hundred employees would be "called-up" immediately if general mobilisation took place. This was expected to require the employment of female conductors. Until the end of September 1939, around 80 men would be absent each week on their summer holidays, and the Passenger Transport Committee cancelled all holidays in view of the

Karrier E6/Park Royal 330, newly renumbered from 30, shows its repositioned sidelights and headlamp masks fitted in 1939.
NCT

At the outbreak of war, Nottingham's trolleybus fleet comprised:

301	TV8473	Karrier E6/Brush	1932
313-318	TV743-748	Ransomes D6/Ransomes	1930
319-324	TV749-754	English Electric E11/EEC	1930
325-336	TV4463-4474	Karrier E6/Park Royal	1931
337-349	TV4475-4487	Ransomes D6/Brush	1931
350	VH3305	Karrier E6/Park Royal	1930
351-360	TV9307-16	Karrier E6/Metro Cammell	1934
361-385	TV9317-42	Karrier E6/Brush	1934
386-406	TV9343-63	Ransomes D6/Brush	1934
407-436	ATV170-199	Leyland TTB3/Metro Cammell	1935

(351-406 were not registered in numerical sequence.)

On the outbreak of war Nottingham's 125 trolleybuses were operating the following services:

36 Old Market Square (Queen Street/King Street) – Upper Parliament Street – Milton Street –Victoria Station – Mansfield Road – Nottingham Road (Vernon Road)

37 Old Market Square (Queen Street/King Street) – Upper Parliament Street – Milton Street – Victoria Station – Mansfield Road – Nottingham Road (Haydn Road) *(Monday – Friday peak hours, including lunch time, and all day Saturday)*

39 Carlton (Post Office Square) – Carlton Road – Central Market – Upper Parliament Street – Ilkeston Road – Wollaton Park (Middleton Boulevard, Fairham Drive) *(eastbound via King Edward Street, Bath Street and Handel Street, westbound via Southwell Road and Lower Parliament Street)*

40 The Wells Road (Kildare Road) – King Edward Street – Upper Parliament Street – Old Market Square – Wilford Road – Wilford Bridge *(northbound via Old Market Square – Queen Street – Upper Parliament Street, southbound via Upper Parliament Street – George Street – Carlton Street – Victoria Street – The Poultry – South Parade – Old Market Square)*

42 Bulwell Hall Estate – Bulwell Market – Basford – Vernon Road – Radford Road – Hyson Green – Alfreton Road – Derby Road – Old Market Square – Arkwright Street – Trent Bridge *(alternate northbound journeys commenced at Colwick Road running Sneinton – Manvers Street – Bath Street – Lower Parliament Street – George Street – Victoria Street to join the normal route at Old Market Square. There were no southbound journeys to Colwick Road, all southbound vehicles travelled to Trent Bridge)*

43 Bulwell Market – Basford – Vernon Road – Radford Road – Hyson Green – Alfreton Road – Derby Road – Old Market Square – Arkwright Street – Trent Bridge *(alternate northbound journeys commenced at Colwick Road running Sneinton – Manvers Street – Bath Street – Lower Parliament Street – George Street – Victoria Street to join the normal route at Old Market Square. There were no southbound journeys to Colwick Road, all southbound vehicles travelled to Trent Bridge)*

44 Bulwell Hall Estate or Bulwell Market – Basford – Vernon Road – Radford Road – Hyson Green – Alfreton Road – Derby Road – Upper Parliament Street – Bath Street – Manvers Street – Sneinton – Colwick Road (unidirectional) *(this service operated southbound only from Bulwell Hall Estate to Colwick Road, all northbound journeys from Colwick Road to Bulwell Hall Estate displaying service 42)*

45 Trent Bridge (Globe Cinema) – London Road – Pennyfoot Street – Manvers Street – Bath Street – Lower Parliament Street – Upper Parliament Street – Derby Road – Wollaton Park (Middleton Boulevard, Scalford Drive)

national emergency. Arrangements were made to evacuate the city's school children should the need arise, needing virtually the whole motorbus fleet and their crews for one or two days with some 50 additional employees to act as marshals and thus the complete suspension of all motorbus services.

The European tension, which increased during the summer, culminated in the German invasion of Poland on 1st September 1939. At 11.15 am on Sunday 3 September 1939, the Prime Minister Neville Chamberlain broadcast to the nation, *"as a result of Germany's invasion of Poland, a state of war existed between Great Britain and Germany"*. The Second World War had begun.

On 1 September 1939 the frequency of trolleybus services was cut by 50% between 9 pm and 10 pm, whilst on Sunday 17 September 1939 motorbus services were similarly reduced by 50% after 9 pm. In both cases, services ceased entirely at 10 pm. It should be noted that during this "phoney war" period virtually all evening entertainment stopped and in any case public houses closed at 10 pm (10.30 pm at weekends). The RTC allocated a fuel ration based on 50% of the Department's 1938 mileage thus when diesel oil and petrol rationing commenced on 24 September 1939, 13 motorbus services, including all cross-suburban routes but one retained for workers in the various factories in the area, were withdrawn entirely and the remainder cut by 50%. Motorbus services ceased entirely at 9 pm although works services remained unchanged and trolleybus services continued until around 10pm.

Motorbus services 20 (Arnold – Trent Bridge) and 35 (Mapperley – Trent Bridge) were cut back to the Old Market Square on 23 September 1939 as they were paralleled by a trolleybus route south thereof, and trolleybus service 46 was reintroduced on Monday 25 September 1939, operating on a daily basis, along Arkwright Street to Trent Bridge:

At some time between the introduction of interworking of service 43 and 44 in June 1935 and mid 1939, Leyland TTB3s 128 and 133 take their layover in Bulwell Market Place outside the "Horse and Jockey" public house. *BTS*

46 Old Market Square (Processional Way/Beastmarket Hill) – Arkwright Street – Trent Bridge

In the course of September 1939 trolleybuses were modified to comply with "black-out" requirements; all saloon windows and internal light bulbs were lacquered blue, resulting in a gloomy interior, whilst shades prevented light from the rearmost bulbs filtering through to the rear platform. By mid-October 1939 work began to remove the lacquer from one window each side and to equip that window with a "black-out" roller blind. At the same time the nearside cab bulkhead blind was removed to give passengers a view of the road ahead. By Christmas 1939 all 85 trolleybuses with high-tension lighting i.e. those with composite bodies, had been equipped with blinds throughout and the window lacquer was in the process of removal. Supplementary sidelights were fitted to the front mudguards and those vehicles still having sidelights above the driver's windscreen had them moved to the waistband beneath the side windows to the driver's cab. Those trolleybuses equipped with a single red rear light at cantrail height had them lowered to a more conventional position on the rear platform panelling (work on both the cantrail mounted sidelights and the rear light position having commenced before the outbreak of war). Additional brackets for emergency paraffin lamps were fitted to the base of the offside and, in some cases, the nearside front mudguards for use when the trolleybuses were parked at the roadside with their trolley booms down or when there was any disruption to the power supply.

It is difficult, in retrospect, to imagine just how difficult it must have been for the driver of any vehicle, let alone a trolleybus, which had to respect the limitations of its overhead line equipment, to navigate the darkened city streets with virtually no external lighting through the years of the "black-out". Newspaper advertisements instructed would-be passengers how to signal a bus driver to stop by briefly shining the beam of a torch onto the road surface but under no circumstances towards the cab. Whilst these conditions prevailed a sad record of fatal accidents involving pedestrians crossing the street or trying to board vehicles appeared with monotonous regularity in the newspapers. An approaching trolleybus could neither be heard nor seen, and they quickly gained a new euphemism "silent death"!

A decision by the City Council's Emergency Committee that all Corporation buses should stop when air raid sirens sounded was roundly criticised by the Regional Traffic Commissioners (RTC) as no other operator followed this practice. By the third week of September 1939 motor and trolleybus drivers were experiencing difficulties with the prevailing lighting restrictions evidenced by the collision between a trolleybus and a parked car in St. Ann's Well Road on 9 November 1939.

In early October 1939 J.H.Stirk, the Regional Traffic Commissioner, stated that Nottingham was the only operator in the area to have withdrawn motorbus services as early as 9 pm and that he felt they should continue until 10 pm with a skeleton service after 9 pm. An additional 3,000 gallons of fuel were granted to permit the operation of 68% of the pre-war services and on 7 October 1939 the last motorbuses were extended until 10 pm. Wherever possible

Karrier E6 301, carrying the Brush body previously mounted on Thornycroft demonstrator 28, passes 329 (TV4467) at Gregory Boulevard in January 1940. *GHFA & JMB*

additional journeys were trolleybus-operated but it is noticeable that Nottingham, unlike many other undertakings, did little to divert suburban motorbus services to "feed" the trolleybus routes. Both Aberdeen and nearby Leicester provided good examples of motorbus services being curtailed at the outer termini of their tram routes. On 15 October 1939 new schedules came into operation giving 60% of the 1938 mileage on the restricted services and by day-to-day alterations it was possible to run 68% of the 1938 mileage by 31 January 1940.

In November 1939, Nottingham's cinemas approached the undertaking with a request for later evening services to combat a fall in customers but this had to be refused as the RTC refused to allocate more motorbus fuel. However on 19 November 1939 revised trolleybus services came into operation giving an improved service between 9pm and 10pm.

In a demonstration of how "a new brush sweeps clean" Mr England suggested a number of improvements to the Passenger Transport Committee Meeting of 1 December 1939. In June 1936 the Department had been renamed "Nottingham City Transport" and he suggested that the Committee should shorten its own title and delete the word "Passenger". This was agreed. He went on to unsuccessfully suggest that, at no extra cost, a brighter shade of green paint should be used for the fleet livery.

The undertaking lacked a properly equipped breakdown tender and used 116 (TV4949) a de-licensed 1931 double-deck petrol bus laden with breakdown equipment instead. Mr England's suggestion to rebuild this motorbus with an 8-ton crane and the necessary equipment, at a cost of £176 plus £76 for labour, was approved. It became known as "Mathilda"! On 5 January 1940 he was also granted permission to replace Dennis lorry TO6093 dating from July 1927 and which was in poor condition by placing its body on the chassis of AEC double deck petrol bus 122 (TV4955).

The official titles of certain senior positions were changed: that of the Rolling Stock Superintendent (Mr C.T. Humpidge) became Chief Engineer, the Assistant Rolling Stock Superintendent (Mr D.P. Martin) became Assistant Engineer and the Deputy General Manager (Mr H.C Morley) was re-named Assistant General Manager and Traffic Manager. Chief Mechanical Inspector D. Machin was promoted Traffic Superintendent at £300 pa reporting to the Assistant General Manager and responsible for the services on the road.

On 31 January 1940 fire broke out in the cab of an empty trolleybus, possibly 362 which later appeared with sliding windows instead of half drops in the upper saloon, on Lower Parliament Street close to the junction with Milton Street. Flames appeared through the side of the vehicle just above the door of the driver's cab and a hole was burned right through the metal sides. Fortunately the trolleybus was empty but seating and interior fittings at the front of the upper deck were badly burned. Driver Pearce suffered burns to his face and hands, and received further injuries getting out of the cab. He was discharged from hospital later that day but on alighting from another trolleybus near his home he received an electric shock and was thrown to the ground. Driver Pearce was still off work in April 1940 receiving Workmens Compensation at £1 10s per week when the TGWU applied to the Transport

In February 1940 Karrier E6 376 suffered a fire in London Road on a 45 journey to Trent Bridge. *NCT*

Fire damage to the upper saloon roof of Karrier E6 376 in February 1940. *NCT*

Upper saloon of Leyland TTB3/MCCW 420 showing wartime "black-out" light canisters. *NCT*

The upper saloon of 399 clearly demonstrates the anti-blast netting on each side window with appropriate allowances for the half-drop openers and central grippers, canister light bulb covers and "black-out" roller blinds above each pane. *NCT*

Committee on his behalf for full wages whilst off work or an ex gratia payment. The latter was subsequently granted to the value of £20. Only a few days later there was a fire beneath the cab of a trolleybus at Sandon Street in Nottingham Road whilst later in February a fire broke out on trolleybus 376 at London Road (High Level) Station.

In an effort to increase revenues by £30,000 to meet additional wage costs, caused by wartime inflation, a package of fare increases was proposed. In February 1940 the matter was discussed with the RTC and approval was given to the increased motorbus fares from Sunday 14 April 1940. As far as the trolleybuses were concerned the 2d maximum fare between the city centre and outer termini was increased to 3d ordinary and 2d workmen's single with some intermediate increases.

The maximum length of the 1d ordinary stage was reduced thus:

Trolleybuses:	from about 1.33 miles to about 1.06 miles
Motorbuses:	from about 1.00 mile to about 0.80 miles

Commencing in 1940 a new style of metal bus stop "flag" featuring plain white lettering on a green background for trolleybus services and on a red background for motorbuses, began to replace the earlier white flags. This colour differentiation (which had also applied to the trams) between trolleybus and motorbus stops was retained until the end of trolleybus operation.

The blue lacquer on the saloon windows and internal light bulbs was abandoned early in 1940 in favour of "black-out" blinds to all windows in certain trolleybuses of the 313-318 and 361-406 series and clear light bulbs. Shortly afterwards experiments were carried out with clear windows and very subdued lighting during the hours of darkness and this was later adopted throughout the fleet. Some improvement was effected later by "saw cut" shades that projected the light towards the ceiling and thence downward. Laboratory tests produced a shade which Mr England considered to be the first satisfactory fitting of its kind. This was greatly improved by a new regulation allowing 0.1-foot candle of light at the seat level.

Nottingham's trolleybuses, with the exception of the Karrier E6s 51-60, Leyland TTB3s 107-136, and from October 1940 the ex-Cleethorpes vehicles, had high-tension lighting and the internal light bulbs were equipped with a new type of canister which threw the light downwards and onto the ceiling. The bulbs were arranged into two circuits of eight each.

The trolleybuses with high-tension lighting were fitted with a headlamp mask that threw the light downwards until Hartley multi-slot masks were fitted. There was no requirement to screen low-mounted fog or spotlights but they could only be used when it was foggy and they had to be switched off during "alerts". In October 1940 revised lighting regulations permitted two low-mounted spotlights that were also appropriate for foggy weather. At the time only trolleybuses 407-436 were equipped with spotlights but these were soon fitted to 351-360 followed by 361-385 in 1944 and 325-349 in 1945.

As an aid to drivers and pedestrians, queue barriers were painted white and white bands were painted around all traction poles, those at stops having the whole of the lower portion and the ground around the base of the pole painted

The experimental microphone system suspended in front of drivers of two trolleybuses in 1940. *NCT*

One of two speakers installed on both decks of two trolleybuses to announce stops at night but which transmitted drivers flowery frustrations at not being able to see during blackouts! *NCT*

A sketch made by Roy Marshall shows how the low voltage type was improved in 1943-4 by the fitting of higher-powered bulbs. Towards the end of 1944 the three lower pieces of metal (A + B + G) were removed. When higher-powered bulbs were fitted to the high-tension type it was found necessary to fit a shield (C) to the shades. It was subsequently found necessary to remove the shield and seal parts of the two slits up (D + E). Late in 1944 the piece marked E was removed and in some cases that marked F. Early in 1945 up to 4 shades in both decks of the vehicles were removed giving pre-war lighting standards from these lights

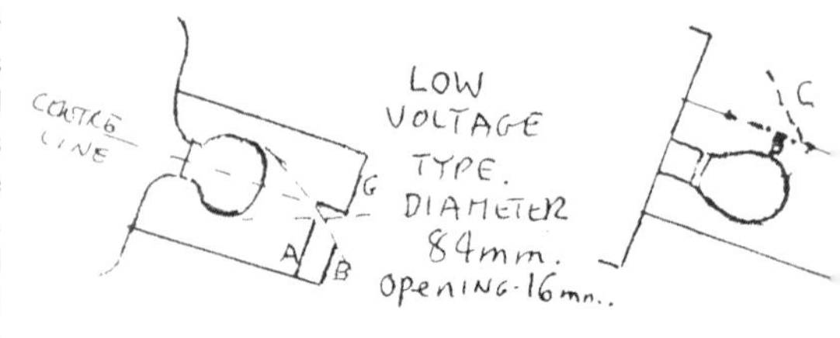

Wollaton Park, Fairham Drive boarding point for service 39 to Carlton Post Office Square. Karrier E6/Park Royal 326 has just turned through the central reservation of the dual carriageway Middleton Boulevard to wait at the "railless" stop in the northbound carriageway. The white circle painted on the road surface immediately behind th e trolleybus was a wartime aid to drivers of the trailing frog above so that they could coast and thereby avoid sparks which might give away their location to enemy aircraft during hours of darkness. *BTS*

Ransomes D6/Brush 338 waits in The Wells Road at Kildare Road terminus of service 40. White stripes are painted around each tree trunk close to the roadside. *BTS*

Ex- Cleethorpes AEC663T/Park Royal 437 dating from 1937 stands at the Nottingham Road, Vernon Road terminus of service 36. Note the "black out" blinds and the taped windows in the house behind. *Photobus*

Ransomes No 316 seen renumbered and in wartime livery in August 1940 on Gregory Boulevard. *GHFA & JMB*

The smartly uniformed lady conductress assists the driver to align the destination blind immediately above the cab windscreen before Ransomes D6 387 in full wartime guise makes another trip to Carlton. The sign on the adjacent traction pole directing would-be passengers to the nearest air raid shelter whilst the curiously-shaped metal tubes along the verge appear to be smoke-generating incinerators for use in the case of an aerial bombardment, there being factories of considerable strategic value in the vicinity. *GHFA & JMB*

Viewed from the Nottingham Suburban Railway embankment Ransomes D6/Brush 338 waits in full wartime livery complete with head lamp masks and emergency paraffin lamps at The Wells Road, Kildare Road terminus of service 40 ca 1940. *GHFA & JMB*

An ex-Cleethorpes AEC 661T 439 loads at the Nottingham Road, Haydn Road stop (the turning circle and "slip" wires are visible behind) before continuing its journey from Vernon Road, Basford to King Street in this wartime view. *BTS*

white. Traction poles in Wilford Road were experimentally painted aluminium instead of green whilst the impressive double bracket arm pole at the junction of Queen Street and King Street appeared in silver but this was not generally adopted. Vehicle wings, rear bumpers where fitted, and platform edges were painted white.

In April 1940 trolleybuses 404 and 424 were experimentally fitted with a microphone in the driver's cab and two loudspeakers with which to announce stopping points during the hours of darkness. The press recorded that: *"Loudspeakers have been fitted in a Nottingham bus and two trolleybuses, through which the stopping places on the route are announced to the passengers in blackout conditions. The scheme is at present in its experimental stage, Mr. Ben England, General Manager of the Transport Department, has stated that the scheme worked quite well, but it was rather expensive, costing about £20 to equip each vehicle. A microphone is fitted in the drivers cabin, and he announces the stops by means of loudspeakers on the upper and lower deck".* The experiment was discontinued due to the expense and reportedly the bad language used by drivers as they endeavoured to pick their way along the darkened streets.

An application from Frank Mason, the advertising contractor, to add a 19 ins diameter circular "spot" advertising space to the offside rear platform corner panel of the entire fleet was refused on 5 April 1940 although the Corporation would have earned £910 pa. Shortly afterwards tenders for advertising on the fleet for the next five years were reviewed, interest having been expressed by Frank Mason, J.W. Courtenay, Henry Squire, Darby's Advertising Agency, Blakeborough Publicity, and Griffiths and Millington. Mason's tender was accepted. However on 26 May 1940 the Ministry of Supply (MoS) prohibited the printing and display of paper posters but this could be circumvented by employing a signwriter to hand paint the advertisements.

Tenders were invited for the 64 miles of copper trolley wire needed for renewals during the next 12 months: British Insulated Cables Ltd., Richard Johnson & Nephew, The Whitecross Co. Ltd. and Thomas Halton & Sons all submitted identical tenders of 113/8d per lb whilst Frederick Smith & Co. Ltd. asked for 117/16 per lb. As BIC could offer the shortest delivery times their tender at £7,756 4s 8d was accepted.

The RTC rejected an application to extend motorbus and trolleybus services until 10.40 pm outwards for the summer of 1940 but did agree to consider an extension until 10.15 pm in July and August, dependent on the prevailing fuel supply, at a later date. On 28 April 1940 trolleybus services were extended for the summer period until 10.30 pm. In May 1940 the RTC granted additional fuel supplies enabling motorbus services to be extended until 10.30 pm in the months of June, July and August. Sunday services had been starting at 1 pm but from May 1940 a skeleton morning service was introduced for workers. Eventually the RTC were able to grant a further fuel allowance enabling the extended motorbus services to continue to operate until 28 September 1940.

There was an increasingly wasted trolleybus mileage on the Carlton route due to the absence of a short-working turning point. Carlton UDC had objected to the construction of a reversing triangle at Hooton Road before the war but by early June 1940 they had approved a renewed approach subject to the necessary alterations to the footpath and carriageway being at the Transport Department's expense and the provision of a passenger waiting shelter at the turning point. These conditions were accepted although it is known that no shelter was built.

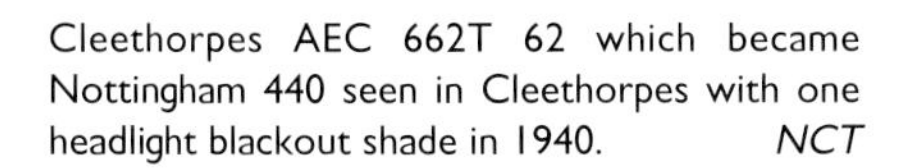
Cleethorpes AEC 662T 62 which became Nottingham 440 seen in Cleethorpes with one headlight blackout shade in 1940. *NCT*

Ex-Southend-on-Sea English Electric E11 302 repainted into Nottingham livery on Victoria Embankment, Trent Bridge.
Richard Delahoy

Ben England was keen to move the engineering administration from Trent Bridge Works to Parliament Street thus in June 1940 the Department took over first and second floor premises rented by Civic Clothiers at 2A Southwell Road, next to the Head Office, for use by the Rolling Stock Engineer and his staff. Shortly afterwards Meadow Dairy Co. Ltd., which also leased Departmental property at 4 Southwell Road, gave up two rooms above their shop.

Varnished bills directing the public to the nearest Air Raid Shelter began to appear on traction poles whilst as fear of an invasion grew, during May 1940, precautions were introduced to promote anonymity throughout the country. The word Nottingham was removed from the lower panels of all vehicles and for a short time in June and July 1940 no destination displays at all were carried, passengers having to rely solely on service numbers. It was decided to remove timetables and any destination information as part of a national campaign, however destination displays were reintroduced by the end of July. Indeed no timetable booklets were issued during the Second World War, service changes being announced in the local newspapers and by issuing leaflets. White circles were painted on the road surface to indicate to trolleybus drivers when passing underneath overhead equipment where they should coast to reduce flashing that could potentially attract enemy aircraft. Carbon insert slider heads were progressively introduced from January 1940 to replace trolley wheels thereby further reducing the risk of flashing and reducing wear on the overhead equipment. Some 35 trolleybuses were equipped by March 1941 at a cost of £10 a set. N&D vehicles however continued to use trolley wheels as slide inserts could apparently be worn away by ice on more exposed parts of their system in a single journey. Councillor Littlefair stated that the wisdom of the Committee in not scrapping the trolleybuses had been clearly revealed.

The Police instructed that unnecessary entrances to and from public utilities buildings, including the Department's depots, should be closed to protect them from sabotage. At Parliament Street Depot, Stanhope Street was temporarily blocked at each end by immobilised motorbuses, more permanent barricades with gates being fitted later, whilst access to Trent Bridge Depot and Works was restricted by the careful positioning of withdrawn vehicles.

The "Nottingham Journal" joked "It is prophesied that Nottingham will have women bus conductors before the war ends – the fare sex" and indeed the increasing shortage of fit men led to a decision in May 1940 to employ unmarried women conductors. The first entrants soon started work and, based on an Industrial Court award, were paid 90% of men's rates for the first 6 months and full rates thereafter. It soon became impossible to recruit conductors, not least as until June 1940 the small grant made during their two-week training period was less than unemployment benefit. In July 1940 the employment of married women whose husbands were serving in HM Forces until the end of the war or until their husbands are demobilised whichever was earlier, commenced. Labour became increasingly scarce and from August 1940 the discretionary employment of married women whose husbands had not actually been called up or indeed were unlikely to be in the armed forces was permitted. From September 1940, employees over 65 years of age could also be retained in service for one year.

In June 1940 the Emergency Committee recommended the dismissal of all conscientious objectors from the Corporation's service, one of the Department's employees being discharged later. The Transport Committee agreed that military service be considered as continuous service with respect to merit pay as in the First World War. On 5 July 1940 the Emergency Committee instructed that all suitable skilled and semi-skilled men should be released for war work, NCT having already released 25 men. The continuing suspension of holidays meant that the Department had 50 temporary conductors surplus to requirements and the Emergency Committee considered that if the Transport Committee agreed these surplus employees could be discharged. In September 1940 the Emergency Committee, stressing that the previous suspension of leave had been in the national interest, granted all employees one week's paid holiday to be taken by 31 March 1941 for the sake of their health.

The RTC recommended that all vehicles should carry equipment in case of air raid injuries to passengers. Green painted metal plates, supporting a first aid box with an advertisement beneath, were fitted to the front bulkhead below the waistband behind the driver's cab, the whole being provided by Frank Mason, the advertising contractor.

In September 1940 the introduction of a parcels service using pre-purchased stamps for payment was approved. It was foreseen that the sender would place the parcel on the vehicle and the receiver would meet it and collect the parcels; yet although the scheme was discussed with the RTC it was not proceeded with.

Although the petrol-engine AEC Regent motorbuses, withdrawn in September 1939, were progressively returned to service in late 1940 and early 1941, ever increasing passenger loads meant that more vehicles, particularly trolleybuses, were needed. The trolleybuses served the main traffic arteries and were not dependent on oil-based fuels, imported to Britain at great risk by the crews of the Merchant Navy, but the fleet was beginning to suffer from wartime conditions. The 38 English Electric, Karrier and Ransomes trolleybuses dating from 1930 – 1932 needed a thorough overhaul, whilst the younger vehicles were deteriorating due to the heavy loadings and low running speeds made necessary by the "black-out".

Exceptionally for Nottingham, some if not all of the first batch of Karrier Ws supplied in 1943-44 with Weymann bodies arrived in primer paint. Masking tape surrounds the windows.
Roy Marshall

In full wartime livery complete with emergency paraffin lamps, Karrier E6/Park Royal 326 is seen standing in the northbound carriageway of the Middleton Boulevard dual carriageway at Wollaton Park, Fairham Drive terminus of service 39. *Nottingham Libraries*

A low angle shot of AEC 661T 439 on a foggy day passing over a cobbled street. One of a series shot by the Corporation in the 1940's. *NCT*

Having investigated opportunities to buy second-hand trolleybuses from other operators, four Park Royal bodied 56-seat two axle double deck AEC661T trolleybuses dating from 1937-1938 were purchased from Cleethorpes, an East Coast holiday resort with a surplus of vehicles. Cleethorpes Corporation calculated with a 12 year depreciation valuing the four vehicles at £6,490 3s 2d. Following an inspection they were deemed suitable and purchased for £1,705 each, the cost being charged to the Reserve and Renewals Fund. The "Nottingham Journal" quoted Ben England as saying that they *"could have been sold 12 times over"* due to national need for trolleybuses. The Department towed them to Nottingham in September 1940 and, following a repaint into fleet livery, they entered service in October 1940 numbered 437-440. These comfortable and speedy vehicles became the newest trolleybuses in the fleet and operated all-day schedules on the Nottingham Road services, where their lack of air brakes sometimes proved an embarrassment. They remained in use until 1953.

Less modern were the two 1930 English Electric double-deck trolleybuses bought, together with £200 worth of spares, from Southend on Sea Corporation Transport in October 1940, at a bargain price of £575. Following overhaul, re-upholstering and general reconditioning, costing £200 each, they were repainted and entered service in November 1940, numbered 302-303. Due to their age they were restricted to peak hour extras from Parliament Street Depot.

The introduction of a new air raid warning "purple", indicating enemy air activity in the general area, in which the headlights and vehicle interior lights had to be extinguished immediately, made it impossible for the conductor to see the tickets, collect fares (being wary of passengers tendering "dud" or foreign coins), or make up waybills. The Department purchased 700 Oldham "Conductalites" rechargeable lamps, which were attached to the conductor's equipment to assist them in their "black-out" duties, for £301 8s 9d.

Motorbus services were cut back to 10 pm on 29 September 1940 but trolleybuses continued to run until 10.30 pm. However due to a lack of passengers after 10 pm it was decided to cease running trolleybuses at 10 pm the change taking place on 20 October 1940.

The January 1940 Extension to the Nottingham Corporation (Trolley Vehicles) Order 1934, covering the Bobbers Mill proposals, was due to expire on 12 January 1941 but the Town Clerk's parliamentary agents felt that it would be considered as a special case under the Special Enactments (Extension of Time) Act 1940. This allowed the extension of parliamentary powers for up to 3 years. On 15 November 1940 the Transport Committee instructed him to make such an application, it being learned in early March 1941 that the Nottingham Corporation (Extension of Time) Order 1941 had been approved by the MoT extending the time limit for the commencement of running of trolley vehicles along Route No. 1 authorised by Section 3 of the 1934 Order by three years.

Negotiations started with the City of Portsmouth Passenger Transport Department, no doubt due to "insider" information provided by Mr Humpidge who had recently moved from that undertaking, to buy the four 1934 three axle 60-seater trolleybuses from that city's trial fleet that were considered surplus to requirements, not least due to their lack of traction batteries, and which were in store out of service. These were AEC 663Ts, 212, with English Electric equipment and bodywork, 215, with English Electric equipment and Metro Cammell bodywork; and Sunbeam MS3s 213, with BTH equipment and English Electric bodywork, and 214 with BTH equipment and Metro Cammell bodywork. Nottingham's Transport Committee approved their purchase for £3,885 in November 1940 but following a delay, during which the naval city suffered a major air raid which brought

Ransomes Sims and Jefferies D6 399 repainted in wartime livery and with window mesh fitted, probably at the time of re-motoring in 1941-3. *NCT*

Could life really go on as normal? White paint and uniforms everywhere, the signs for an Air Raid Shelter, etc. Leyland TTB3 435 heads a column of vehicles at the "Railless" stop at the Queen Victoria Statue at the west end of the Old Market Square. The trailing frog of the turning circle in the width of the road (Long Row West and Angel Row) is evident. ***BTS***

trolleybus services to a halt, Portsmouth decided in February 1941 that the trolleybuses could not be spared. These same trolleybuses were subsequently loaned to Pontypridd UDC from August 1942 until 1945.

On 4 January 1941 the purchase of an almost new ex-demonstrator Daimler CTM4 trolleybus for £1,875, compared to its original price of £2,169, from Transport Vehicles (Daimler) Ltd. was approved. The vehicle had been built in 1938 and demonstrated in Hull equipped with high specification Weymann body to the style of Kingston upon Hull Corporation Transport. This luxurious trolleybus entered service in Nottingham on 1 February 1941 numbered 441. Like the ex-Cleethorpes vehicles, it could usually be found on the Nottingham Road services.

Motorbus service 13 was curtailed on 4 November 1940 to run as a feeder to the 39 trolleybus service at Wollaton Park, operating between Hollington Road, Enthorpe Street and Radford Canal Bridge only instead of into the city centre.

On 15 November 1940 the Transport Committee decided under what circumstances services should continue during air raid alerts:

During daylight: all motorbuses and trolleybuses would continue to operate after the sounding of public air raid warnings until such time as in the opinion of the driver and the conductor aerial activity in the vicinity constituted a danger. If and when it became necessary to stop, vehicles had to stop as near as possible to a public air raid shelter to enable passengers to take cover. Two minutes thereafter traction current would be cut off. Detailed instructions of the procedures to be adopted in the event of it becoming necessary for a vehicle to stop were issued to every Departmental employee.

During the hours of darkness: all motorbuses and trolleybuses had to stop on the sounding of public air raid warnings with the exception of motorbuses conveying passengers to works engaged on work of national importance.

The RTC objected to this decision which was stricter than the practice of other operators and thus at the beginning of December 1940 the Transport Committee resolved that motorbuses should continue to run until gunfire or the dropping of bombs was heard; there was no change to the instructions for trolleybus operations. The RTC responded that if trolleybuses were not run during alerts, permission would be given to Barton and Trent to pick up passengers during such periods on the trolleybus routes at Corporation fares. It was noteworthy that whenever practicable N&D trolleybuses stranded in Nottingham during alerts when the power was off were towed to Cinderhill from whence their own traction power supply was available. Fearing the loss of its monopoly the Transport Committee then instructed that trolleybuses should also continue in the same manner as motorbuses.

This provoked the Emergency Committee to ask in January 1941 if motorbuses could be substituted for trolleybuses during alerts to avoid the risk of electrical flashes that might be seen from enemy aircraft from a distance. Understandably the RTC refused to grant additional fuel to permit additional motorbus mileage over trolleybus routes or substitution during "black-out" alerts. Mr England also felt it was impractical for several reasons, adding that the loss to the Department due to the withdrawal of services during alerts was estimated at £4,610 since the beginning of the financial year. As a palliative, the Overhead Department began fitting asbestos sheeting above breakers, crossings and frogs in the wiring where flashing could be anticipated.

It was decided to paint vehicle's entire staircase area white and introduce separate boarding arrangements for the lower and upper saloons indicated by "ENTER THIS SIDE" lettering above the rear platform.

Issue of steel helmets to all employees began by the end of March 1941. Only motorbus crews had received them and another 600 were ordered for those on trolleybuses, regulators, inspectors and spare men at 5s 6d each.

Having experimented with cellophane and black or green window netting, cream coloured lace netting was fitted to all windows not made of safety glass. At first this was affixed to the interior of the windows but as passengers cut holes in the netting to look out of the vehicles, it was removed to the outside of the windows and stronger glue used. At a later date this was replaced by frames of fine wire netting fitted inside the windows on some vehicles.

As the Department now employed a considerable number of conductresses it was felt that female Inspectors should be appointed, the first being Mrs C. Jones who was promoted in January 1941. They received 90% of the male equivalent wage during the first 6 months of service and thereafter the full male traffic inspector's wage.

On 16 August 1940 N&D asked that the figure of 10.25d per vehicle mile, which they retained for mileage operated within the City, be increased to cover higher wartime costs. Although the request was not considered unreasonable, it proved difficult to reach a consensus. A percentage arrangement was suggested, which would give N&D an additional 11.174%, but they sought 18.028%. It was agreed that whatever solution was finally agreed upon, it would become applicable retroactively from 1 April 1940. Only in June 1941 was agreement reached based on a comparison of N&D's costs per mile for the year ending 31 December 1940 with their average costs during the years 1934-1939, and allowing for any increase or decrease in mileage run during 1940. The changed arrangement was to continue until 6 months notice of termination was given by either party to terminate the agreement on 31 March of any year. In respect of the year ending 31 March 1941 the Company was entitled to £1,122 10s 2d.

It is believed that by 1942, following the reintroduction of NCT trolleybus service 41, N&D were not required to carry local passengers outwards within the city boundaries, at least between 5 pm and 6pm, and that as far as Cinderhill their vehicles only stopped to pick-up passengers.

Until now only motorbus crews had worn a personal identification number, in the form of their RTC licence number badge, but in view of national security, trolleybus crews were issued with white celluloid badges. These displayed the employee's departmental number printed in black and the department's initials (NCT) in red. The 700 badges cost £42.

A number of additional trolleybus turning points were erected to cope with increased traffic, introduce short workings and prepare for possible air raid damage. There was no turning point for vehicles heading into the city on the busy Radford Road and Alfreton Road route at any point between Bulwell and the Old Market Square as originally constructed although this ran through one of the most densely populated parts of the city and thus on 7 February 1941 approval was given to construct two additional turning circles. The first was in the Old Market Square itself and effectively replaced the turn back loop offered by Market Street, which had resulted in trolleybuses inappropriately starting their return journey towards Bulwell on the other side of the road to Queen Victoria's Statue, the normal boarding point for the Radford Road services. A turning circle was strung in March 1941 at a cost of £561 10s between the existing wiring on the east side of the traffic island at the junction of Market Street with Long Row and Beastmarket Hill, and made it possible for trolleybuses coming from Bulwell by way of Chapel Bar and Angel Row to turn back into those thoroughfares and use the customary boarding point. The second new turning circle, built at a cost of £363 16s, was at the junction of Peveril Street with Alfreton Road, Radford, enabling works services heading south from Bulwell to turn back rather than continue to the city centre. This circle was only used by works specials, primarily to the nearby Player's tobacco factory, and was never served by a regular service. It is assumed that both new turning circles came into regular use from 6 March 1941.

In December 1941 an additional city centre turning circle for trolleybuses operating from the east was erected above a new roundabout at Theatre Square in Upper Parliament Street, the terminus being known as the Elite Cinema, which was in fact located on the south side of Upper Parliament Street between King Street and Queen Street. It is assumed that service 38 began to use this turning point in March 1942, coincident with revised terminal arrangements at King Street/Queen Street, but no publicity seems to have been issued as the city boarding point for Carlton Road services remained at King's Walk, Upper Parliament Street.

As Parliament Street Depot's mess room and canteen were overcrowded, it was agreed with Lloyds Bank to use two rooms above their premises, rented from NCT, at 6 Southwell Road subject to a rent reduction of £100 pa. In addition, in March 1941 it was decided to convert the Painters Store in the basement into a kitchen and to alter the existing Mess Room and Recreation Room to provide better facilities. On Monday 15 December 1941 the Transport Committee took lunch with the employees in the new canteen and kitchen. Reportedly the meal was "similar" to that supplied to the employees!

Sufficient fuel was not available for an evening extension of motorbus services during the summer of 1941 but trolleybuses were extended from 10.00 pm to 10.30 pm for the period of double daylight saving time i.e. from 4 May until 10 August 1941. For the sake of clarity, it should be mentioned here that British Summer Time (single daylight saving time) was permanently in force during the Second World War from February 1940 until October 1945. Double summer time (double daylight saving time) was in force each summer from 1941-1947 except for 1946. The timings of early Sunday morning trolleybus journeys, and first and last journeys throughout the week were revised from the same date.

The lightweight traction motors in the 1934 Ransomes, Sims & Jeffries trolleybuses 386-406 had never been satisfactory and it was decided in April 1941 to purchase all ten suitable replacement motors which British Thomson-Houston then had available at £236 10s with the cost being met out of revenue. Two months later a further 11 motors were ordered from BTH at £259 each. As the resistances on these trolleybuses were also life-expired, an offer from the original manufacturers, the Electro Mechanical Brake Co. to supply new sets of the latest design at a price of £22 each was accepted on 4 July 1941 (56 sets at a total cost of £1,232).

The 64 miles of copper trolley wire purchased in May 1940 had been supplied on drums that at this stage of the war were difficult to obtain, the supplier charging either a single purchase fee or weekly rental on the drums. The purchase fee was refundable if the drums were returned in good condition within 12 months and the Department decided on this option.

With the end of the winter timetable a peak hour only service was introduced to the new reversing triangle at Hooton Road on Carlton Hill on 6 April 1941, re-utilising the service number 38:

38 Old Market Square (Queen Street/King Street) – Upper Parliament Street – Central Market – Carlton Road – Carlton (Hooton Road) *(eastbound via Central Market – King Edward Street – Bath Street – Handel Street, westbound via Southwell Road – Lower Parliament Street)*

Although the timetable showed the Elite Cinema as the nominal terminus, journeys ran to King Street and returned from Queen Street until the Theatre Square turning circle came into use. Initially the service operated every 6-minutes Monday – Saturday peak hours. Saturday morning journeys continued to/from Wollaton Park (Fairham Drive) thereby extending the 3-minute morning peak frequency on service 39 until around midday (when a 3-minute service on the 39 between Wollaton Park and Carlton (Post Office Square) commenced). Timetable leaflets show that by January 1945 the Saturday journeys had been truncated to the city centre. Hooton Road was to remain the sole reversing triangle on the Nottingham system.

On the same date service 41 reappeared, operated by NCT trolleybuses on a separate peak hours timetable which gradually expanded by the end of the war to show Monday – Friday morning, lunchtime and evening peak journeys, a Saturday morning peak service and then a 20-minute service all Saturday afternoon and evening, but no Sunday service at all. This was probably prompted by heavy loadings on N&D services with local passengers leaving insufficient space for long distance travellers, and, like the introduction of service 38, the arrival of additional rolling stock which increased the fleet to 132 trolleybuses.

41 Old Market Square (Queen Street/King Street) – Upper Parliament Street – Milton Street – Victoria Station – Mansfield Road – Nottingham Road – Stockhill Lane – Nuthall Road – Cinderhill

The inter-working of services 42, 43 and 44 between Bulwell Hall Estate or Bulwell Market and Colwick Road ceased in 1941; however it has proved impossible to find conclusive evidence of the precise date. It is assumed that this change also occurred on Sunday 6 April 1941, coinciding with the start of the summer timetable, the introduction of service 38 and the reappearance of the 41, although one renowned observer believes that it was later in the year. Henceforth services 42, 43 and 44 followed conventional bi-directional routings, viz:

42 Bulwell Market – Basford – Vernon Road – Radford Road – Hyson Green – Alfreton Road – Derby Road – Old Market Square (Long Row West/Angel Row)

43 Bulwell Market – Basford – Vernon Road – Radford Road – Hyson Green – Alfreton Road – Derby Road – Old Market Square – Carrington Street – Arkwright Street – Trent Bridge

44 Bulwell Hall Estate – Bulwell Market – Basford – Vernon Road – Radford Road – Hyson Green – Alfreton Road – Derby Road – Upper Parliament Street – Bath Street – Manvers Street – Colwick Road *(Northbound journeys operated via Upper Parliament Street, George Street, Carlton Street, Victoria Street, The Poultry, South Parade, Old Market Square, Angel Row and Chapel Bar. Southbound journeys operated along Upper Parliament Street.)*

With the curtailment of the 42 from Trent Bridge to the Old Market Square, only trolleybus services 43 and 46, the latter of course by now on a daily basis, ran along Arkwright Street.

The worst air raid of the war, in which 400 bombs and 60 incendiaries are estimated to have fallen on Nottingham leaving 1,286 people homeless, occurred on 8 – 9 May 1941. There were raids on Derby, Hull, Nottingham and Sheffield that night but compared to other large towns in the area, Nottingham suffered relatively lightly. There were 11 separate attacks on the city but use of the "Starfish" fire decoy system, located in the Vale of Belvoir, and radar jamming led to most of the bombs falling north of

Former Hastings Tramways Co. 1928 Guy BTX/Ransomes 304 is seen in Southwell Road immediately east of the junction with Lower Parliament Street (the Westminster Bank is on the corner). Although the indicator blinds are displaying service number 38, the trolley booms are on the inner kerbside westbound wiring and the vehicle will presumably continue south towards Stanhope Street. *BTS*

Nottingham. Nevertheless Mapperley Park, the Meadows and Sneinton took direct hits, whilst in the city centre part of the University College was destroyed, and the Moot Hall on Friar Lane was badly damaged, as were several railway coaches at the Midland Station. At the Coop bakery on Meadow Lane, 49 employees and members of the Home Guard were killed and another 20 injured.

Although Parliament Street Depot and Head Office was fortunate not to receive a direct hit (the Stadium Hotel opposite was totally destroyed), debris badly damaged the depot roof. Three employees were slightly injured. One trolleybus was slightly damaged and nine others received some damage, primarily broken windows. The motorbus fleet was less fortunate: six motorbuses being extensively damaged and over ninety suffering some damage. Overhead wiring was brought down in Colwick Road, Pennyfoot Street, Station Street, at the northern end of London Road and at four other points on the system although no traction poles were destroyed. At the junction of London Road and Parliament Street new BICC adjustable twin-hanger fittings were strung to be replaced later by non-adjustable fittings which later became the system standard. The estimated cost of repairs was £7,151 11s 8d and trolleybuses circulated for some time with plywood panelling and canvas in place of window panes.

During the next few days trolleybuses ran on all services except the 39, which was unable to traverse the city end of Carlton Road due to unexploded landmines and craters at St. Matthias Road and Burrows Street, less than ½ a mile from Parliament Street Depot. A number of trolleybuses were towed via Sneinton Dale to Carlton and operated a shuttle service from Carlton, Post Office Square to Cardale Road where they turned by stowing the booms and then free-wheeling down the gradient of Carlton Road before turning south-east into Cardale Road, and then reversing out under gravity back into Carlton Road. Others ran from Wollaton Park to the Central Market then via Bath Street, Handel Street and the west end of Carlton Road into Southwell Road and back along Lower Parliament Street to the city centre. During the evenings and at night the trolleybuses isolated at the Carlton end were parked at the top of Carlton Hill facing towards Carlton. The two parts of the route were linked by a motorbus shuttle service that used various roads dependent upon which of them had been cleared of obstructions. Even after the reinstatement of through trolleybus journeys an unexploded bomb was found at St. Matthias Road and the service disrupted again.

The Ministry of War Transport (MoWT) was set up in May 1941 to take over the functions of the Ministry of Transport and the Ministry of Shipping: its role was to organise the provision of transport, to and throughout the country given the shortage of labour and materials which became increasingly evident as the War progressed. The MoWT concentrated on the movement of goods and materials by the railways, the risks to merchant shipping and the damage to ports; the provision of passenger transport, with the exception of providing adequate services to workers, taking second priority. Although it did not formally take over the management of operators, the MoWT was equipped with substantial directive powers. As far as Nottingham's trolleybuses were concerned, the MoWT was involved in the licensing of women conductors and drivers, the use of 8ft wide vehicles, the transfer of redundant vehicles from other operators and the allocation of new utility vehicles, although elsewhere it also expedited approval and the provision of equipment for trolleybus route extensions.

All public transport undertakings, not least the municipal operators including Nottingham, had experienced a major increase in passenger journeys and required additional vehicles. The use of trolleybuses provided a further benefit for the war effort in not requiring imported fuel. Some manufacturers had continued to supply vehicles already on order, using materials already to hand, until late 1940 or even 1941 e.g. London Transport P1 class Leylands 1697-1721 and Manchester Crossleys 1137-76, but thereafter production had slowed dramatically as military requirements took precedence.

In July 1941 the MoWT informed UK trolleybus operators that a limited number of vehicles which had been ordered for overseas customers would be made available to British undertakings, as they could no longer be exported due to the lack of shipping or risk of loss en route. These vehicles used components which had been "frozen" in stock by the MoS and which could be assembled without hampering work on military equipment. A "purchase licensing" system was introduced as demand far exceeded supply. As more trolleybuses would be needed in the coming winter, the Transport Committee was granted authority to purchase 8 vehicles, should they be available quickly, with the cost being met from the Reserve Fund. By the autumn it was clear that the vehicles concerned were Sunbeam MF2s intended for the South African systems of Durban and Johannesburg, and that they would be available either as chassis or as complete bodied vehicles. On 14 November 1941 it was learned that the MoWT was now prepared to let Nottingham have 10 instead of 8 vehicles and the purchase of all 10 was authorised.

During the second half of 1941 standard specifications for austerity motorbus and trolleybus chassis and bodywork were prepared jointly by the MoS, the MoWT and representatives of operators and vehicle manufacturers. In an effort to optimise the use of available materials and reduce the number of hours of skilled labour needed in their construction, only pitch pine could be used for the body longitudinal rails although hardwoods were retained for the framing; exterior panelling including the roof was 20-gauge SWG steel and panels were shaped not beaten. Interior side lining panels were not permitted whilst windowpanes had to be fixed direct to the framing with only one half-drop opening window per side in each saloon. Within these limits bodybuilders could make their own interpretations of the detailed design. The MoWT again used the "purchase licensing" system whereby operators had to apply for a licence to acquire vehicles which were then allocated according to availability and demand. It will be noted that even when an allocation of vehicles had been granted, the quantity could vary significantly, and frequently, between application and final delivery.

With the end of double daylight saving time on Sunday 10 August 1941 last trolleybus departures from the city centre were curtailed to 10.00 pm.

The Department's fleet was now dispersed nightly to minimise air raid damage. The difficulty of finding suitable trolleybus routes sufficiently level for unattended parking meant that some 60 trolleybuses operating from Parliament Street Depot could only be dispersed to within half a

Former Hastings Tramways Co. Guy BTX/Ransomes 306 of 1928 waits at the Wollaton Park boarding point of service 45 at Scalford Drive, Middleton Boulevard before heading south to Derby Road then onwards to London Road and Trent Bridge. *BTS*

mile of the depot. This was considered a vulnerable area and having sought a location farther from the centre, the 3 October 1941 Transport Committee meeting considered a request to erect overhead wiring along Gregory Boulevard between Alfreton Road and Mansfield Road at a cost of £600. It was felt that that it would also provide a valuable extension in peacetime for events such as the Goose Fair or exhibitions on the Forest; however approval was refused. By mid-November 1941 reduced enemy activity encouraged the Emergency Committee to approve an end to nightly dispersal for the winter and all vehicles were housed in their depots. However Mr England again unsuccessfully sought approval for overhead wiring along Gregory Boulevard in May 1942.

No doubt frustrated with Nottingham's stance on not operating trolleybuses through "Alerts" during the hours of darkness, the MoWT arranged to have the city observed from the air. An hour's observation from an altitude of 2,500 ft showed only half a dozen weak and occasional flashes which were visible at up to 3 miles distance. The MoWT accordingly ordered on 9 September 1941 that the Department must "so far as may be reasonably practicable, continue to operate their trolley vehicles during periods when air raid warnings are in force, as though no such warnings have been given". Thereafter trolleybuses continued to operate normally during "Alerts" until danger was imminent. Nottingham's Emergency Committee stated that responsibility for the city's safety in this respect now rested with the Government, although it must be added here that no other British city is known to have held such strong views on the possible dangers of electrical flashes from tram or trolleybus current collectors. One can but ponder if this was anchored in a general anti-trolleybus feeling or, indeed, if certain members of the Transport Committee were also active in the Emergency Committee.

The paucity of trolleybus turning points in the original tramway-replacement overhead wiring layout was again becoming embarrassing, there being no opportunity to turn back vehicles on the Ilkeston Road route between the city and the Wollaton Park terminus at Fairham Drive, Middleton Boulevard. To reduce unnecessary mileage, construction of a turning circle at the junction of Wollaton Road with the northern end of Middleton Boulevard was approved although it was never built. A turning circle at the erstwhile tram terminus at the junction of Ransom Road with St. Anns Well Road, about half a mile short of the Kildare Road trolleybus terminus, was also approved at an estimated cost of £368 10s and erected in early 1942. Trolleybus service 47, a short working of service 40, commenced on Monday 15 June 1942:

47 The Wells Road (Ransom Road) – St Ann's Well Road – King Edward Street – Lower Parliament Street – Old Market Square – Wilford Road – Wilford Bridge *(northbound via Long Row – Queen Street – Upper Parliament Street, southbound via Upper Parliament Street – George Street – Carlton Street – Victoria Street – The Poultry – Old Market Square)*

Services 40 and 47 ran to a combined timetable whilst journeys on the 47 followed exactly the same inner city routings and subsequent deviations as service 40. Contrary to the widely held belief that service 47 only operated in a northbound direction, it was advertised as a bi-directional service throughout its life although it soon became common practice, official or otherwise, to display service number 40 on all southbound journeys to Wilford Bridge, not least as only pre-war deliveries and a limited number of later vehicles had the display "47 Wilford Road" on their combined blinds.

Hastings Tramways Co. had a number of Guy BTX60 three-axle single deck trolleybuses dating from 1928-29 for sale as they were taking delivery of 20 double-deck Weymann bodied AECs ordered before the war. In November 1941 a Nottingham representative examined them and stated that they were in quite good working order. The asking price was £200 per vehicle including tyres. Mr England thought that they might be obtained for £150 and he was granted authority to buy six vehicles and a spare motor at £49 at a price to be mutually agreed. It has proved impossible to establish how much was finally paid. They were immediately brought to Nottingham together with a quantity of spares, overhauled and re-painted, entering service between mid-December 1941 and late February 1942 displaying fleet numbers 304-309, the trolleybus fleet thereby increasing to 138 vehicles. These trolleybuses had centre entrances, the first one to enter service being equipped with perimeter seating, whilst the front and rear destination boxes were enlarged to accommodate standard Nottingham blinds. The ex-Hastings single deckers were initially allocated to service 45 where passengers nicknamed them "Kiddy Cars" but following complaints about the lack of seats they were transferred from Trent Bridge to Parliament Street Depot to work on peak hour service 38. After they had been in service for some six months the MoWT instructed that wireless interference suppression apparatus must be fitted, Metropolitan-Vickers equipment being installed at a cost of £10 5s per vehicle.

On 14 November 1941 the Transport Committee considered ordering 15 replacement trolleybuses to cover post-war vehicle requirements. Apparently uncertain about the future of the trolleybus and perhaps based on Mr England's experiences with AEC Renowns in Leicester, he was authorised to order 5 three-axle motorbuses with 64-seat bodywork instead.

As the trolleybus loading point at South Parade was proving impractical due to congestion and illegally parked vehicles, it was moved east to a site nearer the Council House and a double barrier provided.

In December 1941, 94 second-hand traction poles at £4 each to cover normal needs and possible air raid damage were purchased from Huddersfield Corporation.

The MoWT informed the Department that only five of the Sunbeam MF2 trolleybuses (later 447-451) destined originally for Johannesburg could be allocated to Nottingham but as compensation they would receive four 2-axle double deck Karrier utility vehicles (to become 442-445) for delivery in 1942. A firm quotation of

"The class of 1943". Having successfully completed their trolleybus driver training another class of women driver's pose in front of their utility trolleybus at Colwick Road terminus. The daughter of Driving Instructor Jack Sissons cannot recall all the names but has kindly noted: back row - Joan Holmshaw, Marge ?, not known, Jack Sissons, Dave Martin, Bob Burton, not known, Lily Naylor, not known, not known; and, in the front row - not known, not known, Ivy Whyley, not known, not known, Ivonne Drury, "Pudding" Rice, not known. *Joan Marvin*

£1,795 per chassis excluding War Risk Insurance was received in March 1942 for this first allocation of Karrier W utility chassis, plus £4 each for a low air pressure-warning device. Weymann quoted £1,115 each for the utility bodywork subject to a rise and fall clause against wages and material from 1 July 1942. On 2 January 1942 the Transport Committee decided to pay for the Sunbeam MF2 chassis, estimated to cost £1,450 and bodies, estimated at £1,050, out of revenue rather than reserves. By the end of March 1942 however the increased cost of material and labour had seen the price of the complete trolleybuses rise to £2,650 each, this amount still being subject to future adjustment, chassis completion being expected in May 1942.

On 2 January 1942 changes to the city centre trolleybus terminal arrangements at King Street were agreed. Instead of unloading and boarding in the apex of the junction of Queen Street with King Street, in-bound vehicles on services 36, 37, 41 and the N&D A1 would unload in King Street before pulling into Queen Street where they would load outside the GPO. In practice they continued to wait for time in the apex of the junction, in front of the Prudential Building. This required a new overhead wiring layout, costing £120, to enable trolleybuses on other services to pass vehicles loading in Queen Street, and new passenger queuing barriers costing £15. Due to wartime conditions the precise date of the new terminal arrangements were not recorded but an illustrated newspaper article dated 20 February 1942 shows work on the erection of queue barriers in progress whilst by 10 March 1942 the postal authorities complained about passengers at the new barriers waiting in the GPO doorway in wet weather and hindering access. Soon afterwards it was decided to roof the barriers although this was not carried out during the trolleybus era. It can thus be assumed that the boarding point was moved at the beginning of March 1942 and that the new city terminal arrangements for service 38 came into use at the same time:

38 Theatre Square – Upper Parliament Street – Central Market – Carlton Road – Carlton (Hooton Road)

The 38 set down and terminated at the Elite Cinema before circling the traffic islands outside the Theatre Royal and returning east along Upper Parliament Street to pick up passengers at the Kings Walk stop. Heading east the next stop was the busy loading point at the LNER Bridge above the access tracks to Victoria Station and where there was a side entrance to the station. Trolleybuses often left here full and the conductor would pull out the bamboo trolley retrieval pole from its stowage within the lower-saloon nearside body panels to prevent entrance to the platform while he or she tried to collect as many fares as possible before reaching the next stop at Central Market (a fare stage). This became official practice to indicate a full trolleybus or one not in service, suitable chains being added to all vehicles in the fleet in due course and specified for all post-war deliveries. The usual tactic was to race upstairs and check how many seats were still vacant before returning to the lower saloon and starting to collect fares from the front bulkhead back to the platform.

Both Dunlop and Goodyear gave notice to terminate the tyre mileage contract on 31 March 1942, and offered a new agreement from 1 April 1942: The new rate for trolleybuses was 0.275d per vehicle mile (0.025d more than motorbuses) less 10% maintenance allowance. In addition the new contracts contained a one months' notice of price changes clause instead of the then prevailing 3 months' notice period. In an effort to reduce mechanical wear and tear, and tyre life, the number of stops were reduced e.g. the 4 different stops at the top of Carlton Hill became 3 and the Standhill Road stop was moved closer to the one removed.

Trolleybus services were again extended, as in summer 1941, there being no additional fuel available for motorbuses, from 26 April 1942 until 9 August 1942, from 10 pm to 10.30 pm. The MoWT ordered that, after 12 April 1942, throughout the UK passengers must queue as soon as 6 or more are waiting at a stop. White lines were painted on the pavement to aid queue formation prior to the erection of barriers. It was decided on 1 May 1942 to erect loading barriers at Long Row for service 40 and on Ilkeston Road at Radford Boulevard for service 39. In June 1942 the single passenger queue barriers at Bentinck Road and Alfreton Road were replaced with double barriers to ease trolleybus loading at a cost of £41 10s.

Mr Humpidge, Chief Engineer, resigned in March 1942 to take up the position of General Manager and Engineer to the Rochdale Passenger Transport Department, and he left Nottingham on 3 May 1942. The Assistant Engineer, Mr D.P. Martin, had been offered the post of Chief Assistant Engineer at Portsmouth and his application to the National Services Officer to move from a scheduled position had been granted. To avoid Nottingham losing both Engineering Officers, it was resolved to appoint Mr Martin as Chief Engineer at a salary of £450 (Portsmouth had offered £435) from 1 May 1942, and to promote the Technical Assistant, Mr I.H. Mair (reportedly the last genuine electrical engineer to join the undertaking, pro-trolleybus and previously with Brighton Corporation Transport), to Assistant Engineer at a salary of £315 pa. Mr J. Currie of Manchester was appointed to fill this vacancy.

The commutators of the GEC motors in the 1935 Leyland TTB3 trolleybuses 107-136 needed replacement and to avoid a vehicle being out of service while this was being done a spare GEC motor costing £320 was purchased in June 1942.

A request to reinstate the through service between the Midland (LMS) and Victoria (LNER) railway stations, withdrawn at the start of fuel rationing, was refused due to the impossibility of obtaining more fuel for motorbuses and a lack of crews to extend the 36 trolleybus service. Trent was granted permission to suspend the wartime agreement allowing them to pick-up passengers inside the city boundary on inward journeys at double Corporation fares, due to the small number of passengers carried not warranting the clerical effort.

The General Manager informed the 3 July 1942 Transport Committee Meeting that there was a chance to obtain operating powers to run trolleybuses from Middleton Boulevard along Wollaton Road and Russell Drive as far as the junction of Russell Drive with Trowell Road at Wollaton Village. This area was then served by joint Midland General and Trent motorbus services but together with the villages of Bilborough, Strelley and Wollaton had been absorbed into Nottingham on 1 April 1935. He recommended this solution in preference to motorbuses and following consideration by the full City Council on 27 July 1942 the Town Clerk was authorised to seek parliamentary powers. As the stock of traction poles was now low, eighty poles at £6 7s 6d each were ordered in August 1942 from E.J. Walsh & Co.

The MoWT held public enquiries on 24 and 29 September 1942, and were convinced that there was a need to improve public transport to and from Wollaton. They considered that trolleybuses were the most appropriate solution to economise the use of imported fuel and stated on 4 December 1942 that they were prepared to authorise the Corporation by Order under the Defence (General) Regulations 1939 to operate services on the proposed route subject to Midland General (MGOC) and Trent being given the opportunity to financially participate in the new service and a service coordination agreement being reached. This was initially acceptable to Nottingham. However when the draft Order was sent to the MoWT for review, it showed the projected route as continuing a further 0.96 miles beyond Wollaton Village along Trowell Road to its junction with Bilborough Road and Coventry Lane at Balloon Houses and they accordingly asked for an additional plan and details of the terminal facilities. A conference between MGOC, Trent and the RTC took place on 5 January 1943, the Nottingham Transport Committee having agreed in the meantime that, as an alternative, they should buy out the companies' part financial interest in the new service. This made it impossible to reach agreement and in February 1943 the matter was passed to the MoWT.

A plot of land at the road junction near to Balloon Houses had been identified as a suitable location for a turning circle, however the owner, Home Brewery, was not prepared to sell it at that time although they were prepared to lease a portion. In the meantime, a stock of second-hand traction poles for the proposed extension costing £700, had been purchased.

In July 1942 the cost of electricity rose from 0.80d to 0.875d per unit, an annual increase of £3,800, but against this the Electricity Committee granted a rebate for the year of £4,168.

In an effort to combat heavy loadings, from July 1942 some 400 Voluntary Auxiliary Conductors were recruited to stand on the rear platform on their regular rush hour journeys to and from work to supervise loading and unloading, and to give appropriate bell signals to the driver. They were identifiable by brassards and granted free travel on the journeys concerned. Part-time and weekend traffic employees were also engaged but were provided with full uniform and equipment, or a cap and dustcoat. The employment of full or part time female bus cleaners at 90% of the male adult commencing rate, rising to 100% after completion of six months satisfactory service, started. Also from July 1942 seated children were required to give up their seats to adults when adult fare paying passengers were standing. By the end of August 1942 some 42 discharged forces personnel had been taken back into service.

The MPTA asked their members in July 1942 their needs for new utility two axle single or double deck trolleybuses, for delivery in 1944 and Nottingham requested 8 double-deckers.

Michelin approached the undertaking in May 1942 about a retrospective increase of the tyre mileage rates from 1 April 1942. Although they supplied less than 5% of requirements it was felt important to maintain contact with all manufacturers and 0.275d per vehicle mile, exactly the amount paid to Dunlop and Goodyear, was suggested as appropriate for trolleybuses.

Until wartime legislation was introduced it was permissible for vehicles to have their registration numbers applied in translucent transfers on the rear platform window, it being considered that the platform lighting made these sufficiently visible in darkness. The change required that the rear registration number be displayed close to the ground, illuminated from above. New number plates were built into the rear panel on the offside about one-third of the way up from 1942-43 although the registration number transfers on the rear platform window were retained. The Leyland TTB3s already had a separate illuminated box with a translucent registration number pane whilst the Guy BTXs already had a number plate on the offside illuminated by a red/white bulb. No brake light of any sort was then required. A relaxation of "black-out" regulations allowing more light from vehicle headlamps came into force in July 1942 and a new type of headlamp mask was fitted to the trolleybuses at a total cost of £250.

The forthcoming trolleybus deliveries meant that there would be insufficient space at Parliament Street Depot and the area of land bounded by Pennyfoot Street and Manvers Street, immediately south of Trent's garage, was acquired for open-air parking. It was estimated that the overhead equipment would cost £285 and a concrete floor at the entrance, exit and turning point £250 10s. Traction poles with concrete base reinforcements were planted on the Pennyfoot Street side of the yard and bracket arms supporting one pair of trolley wires were attached to the wall of Trent's garage.

Some 51 motorbuses had been ordered for post-war delivery and at the 31 July 1942 Transport Committee Meeting Mr England recommended an order for 38 three-axle trolleybuses. Aware of the Committee's preference for motorbuses, he added that, he considered it likely that economic and legislative conditions after the war would require the continuing operation of trolleybuses. Nonetheless his recommendation was not approved!

The main and intermediate propeller shafts on the 1931-32 Karrier E6 trolleybuses (325-336) were worn at the joints, causing excessive chassis vibration. As it was impossible to secure replacements from the original American manufacturer, equivalents for £637 7s were ordered from Hardy-Spicer & Co. Ltd., Birmingham in July 1942.

From 10 August 1942, last trolleybuses were again cut back from 10.30 pm to 10 pm and a month later priority travel permits for key workers on these services, together with any special journeys operating in the evening or early on Sunday mornings, were introduced. Until now motorbuses and trolleybuses had stopped for anyone waiting at request stops but effective 10 November 1942 it became compulsory to "hail" a bus to stop whilst virtually all compulsory stops were redefined as request stops in an effort to save fuel and rubber. Some early morning Sunday trolleybuses were introduced, all departing at 9.00 am, on services 36 from Queen Street to Vernon Road, 39 from the Elite to Carlton, 40 from Long Row East to Kildare Road, 43 from the Old Market Square to both Trent Bridge and Bulwell Market, and 44 from the Elite to Colwick Road. The RTC instructed that from 22 November 1942 Sunday services could only operate between 1 pm and 9 pm apart from special workers' buses whilst the last departures from the city (motorbus and trolleybus) were cut back to approx 9pm.

In September 1942 the five two axle Sunbeam MF2 chassis diverted from Johannesburg, equipped with 8ft wide Weymann utility bodywork, were delivered in grey primer paint. The first to arrive, 450, was presented to the press on 2 September 1942. The MoWT granted a dispensation for their operation on designated routes, as they were 6 inches wider than then legally permitted in the UK, due to the wartime shortage of vehicles. They were painted into Nottingham livery at Trent Bridge Works and allocated fleet numbers 447-451, as fleet numbers 442-446 had been reserved for the 5 Karrier W utility vehicles that were, at that time, still expected to arrive shortly. The Sunbeams entered service at the beginning of October 1942, based at Parliament Street Depot, their use being limited to services 38 Theatre Square – Carlton, Hooton Road, and 39 Carlton, Post Office Square – Wollaton Park.

Authority was given to train further women as drivers as needed, female trolleybus drivers soon becoming a common sight in Nottingham, Mr Sisson's own notes record having trained 26 "girls". He commented *"They had a standard and record of accident-free driving that beat the men hollow. They drove their 11-ton vehicles through the blackout, snow, fog, and ice with a skill that has not been excelled since"*. Many of the women drivers stayed on well into the post-war era, one of the last being Mrs Deneve who later became a conductor, like several of her colleagues.

On 4 December 1942 it was learned that the 1944 allocation of 8 new Karrier W trolleybuses might be reduced to 7 (later numbers 452-458). A quotation of £1,737 per chassis, subject to a rise and fall clause on labour and material, was received. In February 1943 the undertaking was informed that the trolleybuses allocated for delivery in 1943 and 1944 would be supplied with regenerative equipment. This was expected to bring considerable power economies and Mr England proposed the installation of automatic sectionalising switches on the overhead line to cope with this form of control at an estimated cost of £1,020.

A sub-station fault reduced the number of trolleybuses that could operate on the Nottingham Road and Wollaton Park sections during the morning and evening peaks on 28 September 1942. Additional capacity was provided by motorbuses, some vehicles being hired from Barton and WBUDC.

The Annual Report for year ending 31 March 1943 saw the lowest outstanding loan debt since 1900, however Mr England commented that considerable sums would be needed for renewal purposes after the war as a large percentage of the fleet required replacement and it was expected that the replacement cost would be far in excess of the cost of the existing vehicles. Over 25½ million more passengers were carried than in the year ending 31 March 1939 although over 1 million fewer miles had been run. A further 40 of the 143 trolleybuses received slider heads; 12 were fitted with new motors and 19 equipped with new resistances.

In June 1943 the Transport Committee made the following proposals for the Wollaton trolleybus extension:

1) The Midland General Omnibus Company will buy out at a figure already agreed, the whole interests of the Trent Motor Traction Co. Ltd., as between Cotmanay, Ilkeston, Trowell and Nottingham.
2) The Midland General Omnibus Company herein referred to as the Company will provide all necessary through services (which shall not be deemed to be part of the shuttle service referred to in 3) below) between Cotmanay, Ilkeston, Trowell and Nottingham either by motor omnibus or trolley vehicles and the company will retain all revenue therefrom, subject to the operation of clause

The first of the six women trolleybus drivers completed their training in July 1942, three being at work by the autumn with the remainder ready to take their tests. One of the first, Joan Hughes, subsequently Mrs Mannington of Radcliffe on Trent, who had been a conductress since 1940 and was by then 22 years old, proudly recalled how well the "girls" coped with the task of manoeuvring their "tracklesses" under a maze of overhead wiring in the "black-out" and at a time when driving in general was not yet an everyday skill. *"As the war situation worsened many of the motorbus drivers had to come over to our 11-ton tracklesses which they didn't like because they weighed three tons more than their motorbuses"*. Her fellow trainee immigrated to Rhodesia but she remembered that others included Marjorie Harrison, Violet Drury and Ivy Whyley. Their unmarried status and smart turn out, inevitably with individual fashionable touches to their uniforms, attracted many admirers and the daughter of Driving Instructor Jack Sisson recalls being invited to many weddings.

Joan had some hair-raising experiences in her time as a trolleybus driver. Once when the footbrake of her trolleybus failed on Radford Road she managed to turn the double-decker broadside across the road and stop it with the handbrake. On another occasion she cowered in the cab when she heard her conductress threaten late night drunken passengers "I'll fetch my driver round". Going to help she found the bus packed to the brim and more people crowding on: The two girls appealed to the more sober men on the bus and eventually the troublemakers got off, leaving the girls to get home as best they could after clocking off an hour late. One morning, having reported for duty at Bulwell Depot at 3.15 am, she fell into an inspection pits in the "black-out" and badly hurt her back and hip.

Joan recalled *"On some routes, if you missed getting your light at certain points, the poles had to be changed over to prevent them flying off the wires. The poles would come off if you notched up too quickly at some junctions, and going uphill the big power switches had a habit of flying off"*. The remedy was to stand up quickly in the cab and knock them on again.

All the girls suffered from the same drawback – they were too short to reach the controls of the buses. To remedy this, the male drivers collected metal caps from bottles, which were stacked under the driving seats to heighten them. The girls thus became 'the bottle top brigade'. *"We had to work very hard during the war in conditions unheard of today"*, she said. *"We often did 10-hour shifts with no break, and splits which lasted all day. We got no pension for our war service, as did the forces, only a promised payment of our post-war credits. When those who survived did get them over 30 years later their original value was lost"*. She left the Transport Department in 1946, ran a radio shop for many years, and died in May 1997.

6) hereunder. If operation is by trolley vehicle the Midland General Omnibus' sister company, the Notts and Derby Traction Co. will operate by agreement.

3) The Company and the Corporation shall each provide one half of all necessary shuttle services either by motor omnibuses or trolley vehicles between Nottingham City Centre and Balloon Houses.
   a) between Nottingham City Centre and any point west of Middleton Boulevard but not beyond Balloon Houses.
   b) between any two points lying between Middleton Boulevard and Balloon Houses and,
   c) between any point lying betwixt Nottingham City Centre and Middleton Boulevard and any point lying west of Middleton Boulevard but not beyond Balloon Houses, and each operator shall retain the revenue taken by that operator's vehicles.
4) Provided that in the event of the Company and the Corporation failing to agree upon the shuttle services to be operated under Clause (3) above then the Corporation shall have the right to operate such shuttle service as it thinks fit and the Company at the said Company's option may or may not participate therein in the proportions laid down in (3) above.
5) The Corporation will provide all necessary vehicles either by motor omnibus or trolley vehicles between Nottingham City Centre and Middleton Boulevard, and will provide any necessary additional services between those points or between any two points lying betwixt Nottingham City Centre and Middleton Boulevard for local traffic arising between those points and will retain all revenue therefrom.
6) The Company shall issue Corporation tickets to passengers who board the Company's vehicles (no matter whether such vehicles are operating on the through service or on the shuttle services mentioned in Clause (3) hereof). After leaving Eton Grove on the inward journey and to passengers who alight at or before the setting-down point immediately preceding Eton Grove on the outward journey and the revenue shall be apportioned in the manner determined by (8) hereof.
7) The Company shall pay to the Corporation:-
   a) an agreed rate per trolley vehicle mile to cover the cost of electricity supplies to the Company's vehicles.
   b) an agreed sum per annum based upon the proportion of users by the Company for the provision of overhead line, shelters, stop signs, and other necessary equipment between Middleton Boulevard and Balloon Houses.
   c) an agreed sum per annum for the repairs, maintenance and upkeep of the overhead line, shelters, stop signs, and other necessary equipment between Balloon Houses and the City Centre.
   d) an agreed sum per annum to cover the cost of local rates on the overhead line between Balloon Houses and the City Centre such sum being based upon the proportion of use by the company.
8) The Corporation shall sell to the Company the necessary Corporation tickets for sale as stated in 6) above and such tickets shall be supplied to the Company at 75% of face value and the Company shall pay in addition 25% of the cost of such tickets.
9) This arrangement to be effective as from the date upon which the Corporation commence to operate a service of trolley vehicles upon the proposed route between Middleton Boulevard and Balloon Houses, and shall continue for 21 years from the date of commencement (21 years is the usual agreed period).
10) Any dispute or failure to agree on any matter connected with this agreement shall be referred to the Regional Transport Commissioner (or Chairman of the Traffic Commissioners) whose decision shall be final and binding upon the parties.

The Committee would not agree to the MGOC and Trent having operating rights over the Nottingham Corporation system for through trolleybus services between Cotmanay and Ilkeston, and Nottingham, presumably to be run by Notts & Derby Traction Co. (N&D), or that they should operate half the shuttle service between Balloon Houses and the City Centre. N&D in the meantime had been allocated 6 vehicles from the 1944-45 utility trolleybus production programme, the order subsequently being transferred to Llanelly District Traction as their 43-48. Clearly "out of touch" with wartime needs and the MoWT's aims, they went on to state that the Corporation was prepared to extend their network and operate the entire trolleybus service whilst MGOC and Trent continued to operate motorbuses on the shuttle service between Balloon Houses and the City Centre, and that they were prepared to pay the Companies compensation for the loss of not being able to provide a service.

The MoWT promptly responded that they did not consider compensation as a satisfactory alternative to offering MGOC and Trent a part financial interest in the new service. Due to the urgent needs and the Corporation's apparent unwillingness to accept the conditions recommended in their letter of 16 November 1942, the Minister was inclined to permit the operation of additional motorbuses pending the obtaining of powers to operate trolley vehicles. Having reviewed the matter on 16 July 1943, the Transport Committee repeated that they were not prepared to extend the Corporation's trolley vehicle system on the terms stipulated by the MoWT. They were surprised that the MoWT should authorise additional motorbus services at a time of continuing fuel shortages when the Corporation was prepared to provide the trolleybus service and to pay compensation to MGOC and Trent for any loss in respect of which the Ministry consider they should be compensated.

Wollaton ratepayers discussed the proposed trolleybus service at a meeting on 29 July 1943 leading to a deputation visiting the MoWT in September. They were informed that there would be an increased MGOC motorbus service from 3 October 1943, the necessary fuel being available due to economies resulting from the diversion of services from the west into the new Mount Street bus station.

Notts & Derby Traction Co., on behalf of Midland General, then applied for an Order to operate trolleybuses from Ilkeston into Nottingham via Wollaton connecting with the Corporation system at Middleton Boulevard and

On 25th May 1944, at about midday, an unidentified Sunbeam MF2 crashed into and demolished a temporary wooden "off-licence", replacing a "blitzed" shop, near the junction of Carlton Road and Davis Street. *NCT*

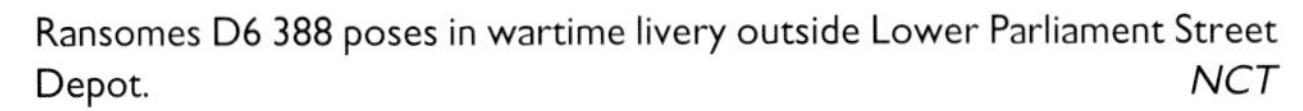
Ransomes D6 388 poses in wartime livery outside Lower Parliament Street Depot. *NCT*

In wartime livery ex-demonstrator Daimler CTM4 stands at Haydn Road, Nottingham Road terminus. *BTS*

with through running powers thence into the city centre. The Minister refused the application based on the improved motorbus services in the Wollaton area. N&D then promoted its own parliamentary Bill to operate trolleybuses in the Borough of Ilkeston, the County of Derby and the Rural District of Basford along the same route, again with running powers into Nottingham. As a result of the combined efforts of Nottingham's MPs in parliament, the City's petitions against the Bill and the MoWT's previous decision, N&D decided to withdraw the Bill in March 1944.

Bearing in mind that trolleybuses would have been using home produced fuel it is, in retrospect, difficult to understand why the MoWT did not use the directive powers at its disposal to enforce an equable decision on both operators with respect to through running powers and protective fare agreements.

By September 1943 the first allocation of 4 Karrier W trolleybus chassis ordered in March 1942 were complete but due to rising costs the price had increased to £1,840 each. In November 1943 Weymann quoted £1,116 net each for utility bodies subject to a rise and fall clause against wages and material. Unlike many utility bodies then being delivered to operators throughout the country, these had a glazed upper deck rear emergency window (rather than a steel panel) and seats upholstered in brown leather (rather than wooden slats). They also had traction batteries beneath the lower saloon seats which soon proved their value in enabling vehicles to move themselves if they had inadvertently stopped beneath a dead insulator section in the overhead wiring in the "black-out". They were delivered between December 1943 and February 1944 and given fleet numbers 442-445, the number 446 being left unused and reflecting the reduced allocation. The first to arrive was demonstrated to the press, it being stressed that battery manoeuvring equipment was not a new invention and that other towns' trolleybuses had had this facility for years. The trolleybus could travel about 4 miles at 4 mph using battery power. The MoWT now asked how many new trolleybuses would be required in the 12 months commencing July 1944 and a further 10 double-deckers were requested although only 7 were initially allocated.

The rejection of an application for a national wage increase led to a strike in Nottingham on 13 May 1943 but soon afterwards the NJIC for the Road Passenger Transport Industry awarded additional war wages of 4s 6d per week to male adults with commensurate increases to women and youths, from 1July 1943. Even the General Manager's salary increased from £1,700 to £1,850, as foreseen in his contract; a healthy figure when compared to that of female junior office staff who received £90 pa.

Carlton UDC had complained of congestion in Main Street and a trolleybuses extension along a 1½ mile circular route by way of Main Street East, Burton Road, Conway Road and Station Road back to Post Office Square was suggested in September 1943. As the UDC supported the idea discussions took place with Nottinghamshire County Council prior to promoting a Parliamentary Bill. Although the NCC had no objections, the MoWT would not agree to the extension unless it could be shown that it was required to support the war effort or in the interests of the maintenance of supplies and services essential to the life of the community, and the proposal was thus deferred until the end of the war. As it was also impossible to extend the Carlton route along Manor Road until after the war Carlton UDC agreed to the construction of a turning circle at the junction of Cemetery Road and Cavendish Road, about 150 yards northwest of the existing terminus in Post Office Square, along a new stretch of road, at a cost of £1,020.

A Barton bus that failed to stop for a red traffic light at the junction of Canal Street with Carrington Street early in the morning of 22 September 1943 collided with a city bound trolleybus. The trolleybus was rammed backwards and extensively damaged.

A member of the Transport Committee queried the necessity for service 44 to run into the city centre along George Street and for intending passengers to use the same queue at Beastmarket Hill as that used by other Alfreton Road routes. He suggested they should run along Upper Parliament Street instead. Following an investigation Mr England recommended no change to the route but agreed that the barriers in Old Market Square be altered so that service 44 passengers could queue separately for service 44 vehicles.

From Sunday 17 October 1943, the inter-working of trolleybus services 39 and 45 commenced. Alternate vehicles on the 39 from Carlton were through-routed around the circular route to or from Wollaton Park provided by Ilkeston Road, Middleton Boulevard and Derby Road, then back to the city and on to Trent Bridge. The remainder turned back at the Wollaton Park, Middleton Boulevard, Fairham Drive turning circle as before. At peak times the frequency between Fairham Drive and Trent Bridge increased from every 7½ minutes to every 6 minutes (the 39 having a 3-minute headway at peaks). Every vehicle on the less frequent 45 ran through to Carlton:

39 Carlton (Post Office Square) – Carlton Road – Southwell Road – Lower Parliament Street – Upper Parliament Street – Derby Road – Ilkeston Road – Wollaton Park (Middleton Boulevard) – Derby Road – Upper Parliament Street – Lower Parliament Street – Bath Street – Pennyfoot Street – London Road – Trent Bridge *(unidirectional)*

45 Trent Bridge – London Road – Pennyfoot Street – Bath Street – Central Market – Upper Parliament Street – Derby Road – Wollaton Park (Middleton Boulevard) – Ilkeston Road – Derby Road – Upper Parliament Street – Central Market – Bath Street – Handel Street – Carlton Road – Carlton (Post Office Square) *(unidirectional)*

Although this pattern continued, from Sunday 13 February 1944 there were some changes to the inter-working schedules possibly including adjustments to the period of peak hour frequencies.

In the morning fog of 18 October 1943 a 44 trolleybus heading towards the city centre collided with a Midland Model Dairies lorry, extensively damaging the lorry and much of its load. The front of the trolleybus was damaged and a child passenger taken to hospital for treatment.

In November 1943 the MoWT informed Nottingham that they would receive 4 Karrier Ws at a cost of £1,645 per chassis, subject to a rise and fall clause, as their 3rd allocation. In fact 10 finally materialised, 459-65 equipped with Roe and 466-468 equipped with Brush bodies.

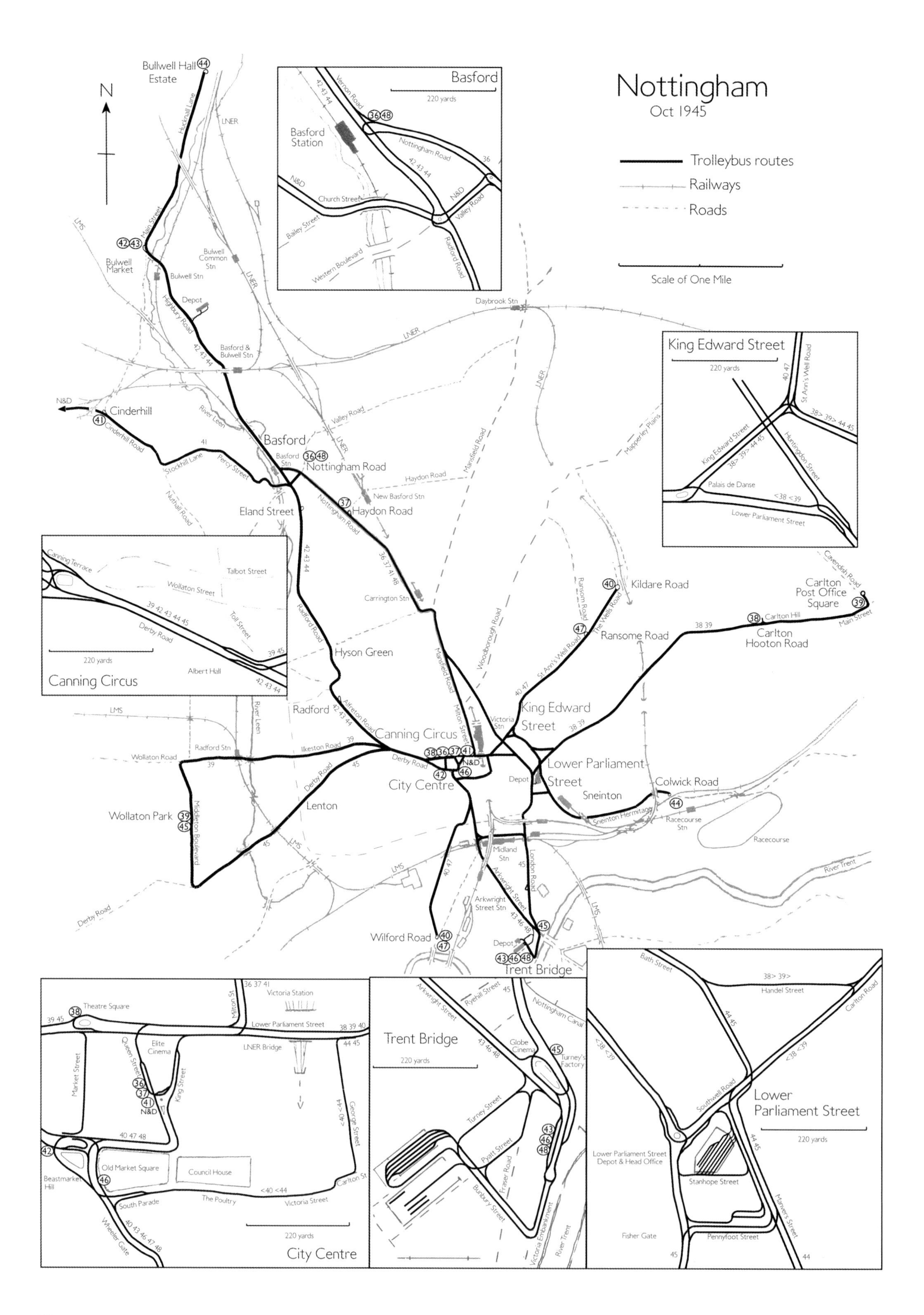

Nottingham
Oct 1945
Trolleybus routes
Railways
Roads
Scale of One Mile
Basford
King Edward Street
Canning Circus
City Centre
Trent Bridge
Lower Parliament Street
Bullwell Hall Estate
Bulwell Market
Cinderhill
Basford
Nottingham Road
Haydon Road
Eland Street
Hyson Green
Radford
Canning Circus
City Centre
Wollaton Park
Lenton
Wilford Road
Trent Bridge
Kildare Road
Ransome Road
Carlton Post Office Square
Carlton Hooton Road
King Edward Street
Lower Parliament Street
Sneinton
Colwick Road
Racecourse

Ex-Cleethorpes AEC 661T 440 climbing Mansfield Road and, despite the destination display, heading out of the city. White stripes have been painted around both traction poles and trees on the pavement to aid drivers in the "black-out". *Roy Marshall*

Seven new Karrier Ws (452-458) making up the 2nd MoWT allocation of utility trolleybuses were delivered between March and May 1944. They were equipped with English Electric 115 hp motors and were, at that time, the most powerful vehicles in the fleet. An order had been placed in January 1944 for three utility bodies with Park Royal at £1,116 each, based on costs applying on 1 November 1943. These were fitted to 452-454 whilst the remainder of the vehicles were fitted with Weymann bodies, all having wooden slatted seats but upper saloon rear windows. In April 1944 it was decided to add an audible and visual dewirement indicator and replace the Bonser trolley wheels with Anti-Attrition carbon slider heads, at an extra charge. Their arrival led to the disposal of English Electric trolleybuses 320, 322, 324 purchased in 1929-30; 1931 Karriers 331, 335; and 305, one of the 1928 ex-Hastings Guy single-deckers for scrap, some of which were no longer in service, after they had been stripped of useful spare parts

All the Council's Committees were instructed to prepare a report on post war planning, works and expenditure for a period of 10 years after end of war and in April 1944 the Transport Committee provided the following estimates with respect to trolleybuses:

Buildings	Estimated cost 1939 prices
1) Improvement and extension No 2 Garage, Parliament Street	£26,500
2) Improvements at Trent Bridge Works	£15,000
3) Improvements at Trent Bridge Depot	£7,000
4) Improvements at No 3 Garage, Parliament Street	£7,500
5) Improvements at Bulwell Depot	£2,000
Sub-total	£58,000
Vehicles	Estimated cost 1939 prices
46 trolleybuses at £2,360 each	£108,560
War Damage	Estimated cost 1939 prices
Repairs to roofs (including motorbuses)	£5,150
Grand Total	£171,710

As there were only 21 traction poles in stock, less than needed for normal replacements, fifty (4 piece) poles were ordered from E.J. Walsh and Co., Edinburgh, at £9 10s each.

In March 1944 the Transport Committee agreed to Mr England's renewed recommendation that double line trolleybus overhead wiring should be installed along Gregory Boulevard from Mansfield Road to Radford Road at an estimated cost £1,750. The General Works and Highways Committee however objected as the Highways and Town Planning Authority, and pointed out that their approval was required. Although there were already Statutory Powers for this route under the Nottingham Corporation Act 1930 making it perfectly legal to proceed, discussions were held with the General Works and Highways Committee. These unfortunately only confirmed their opposition to the extension, as it would require a drastic trimming of an attractive colonnade of trees and road improvements, and the proposals were dropped.

On 5 May 1944 the MoWT allocation of a fourth batch of Karrier W trolleybuses, ten this time, which became 469-478, scheduled for delivery between May 1945 and January 1946, was accepted in order to replace ten English Electric and Ransomes trolleybuses dating from 1930 which were, by now, in poor condition.

Metal clips to hold interior advertisement cards were introduced in May 1944 whilst in addition from autumn 1944 advertisements were also applied to the ceiling cove panels. In June 1944 work started to fit handrails extending the length of the lower saloon ceiling. These were mounted one on each side of the gangway as the positions of the hanging leather straps for standing passengers at the rear of the lower saloon discouraged them from moving forwards towards the front of the vehicle which restricted access to and from the rear platform.

Orders for the utility bodywork to be fitted to the MoWT's 3rd allocation of ten Karrier W trolleybuses were divided in July 1944 between Roe, who had quoted for 7 at £1,245 each, and Brush, who had quoted for 3 at £1,237 each, for delivery in May or June 1945, although Roe bodies for all had originally been specified. These became 459-465 and 466-468 respectively. The three Brush-bodied trolleybuses had upholstered seats, curved rear roof domes, and additional half-drop opening windows to new "relaxed" utility specifications. On 6 October 1944 the 4th allocation of ten more Karrier W chassis, as already mentioned, was accepted at an estimated cost of £1,661 each, plus war risk insurance. These became 469-478.

By July 1944 the undertaking employed 678 women as drivers or conductors, whilst by October 1944 there were 25 female trolleybus drivers. A request for free travel to and from work for depot and works employees was considered on 1 September 1944. At that time only the 1,611 office staff and traffic employees had this privilege out of a complement of 2,164. The facility was estimated to cost £3,450 pa. Following a comparison with other undertakings, in October 1944 all maintenance employees, cleaners and other non-uniformed employees were granted free travelling facilities to and from their places of work.

The five bus stops, including those used by WBUDC motorbuses as a terminus and one served by trolleybus services 40 and 47, in South Parade were designated "No Parking" zones in September 1944.

The undertaking's advertising contract was due to expire on 30 June 1945. Prior to inviting tenders, the General Manager recommended that additional revenue-earning advertising spaces should be created namely, on the back of the rearmost offside seat on the top deck, facing passengers mounting the stairs; a circular "spot" space on the offside rear corner panel of the lower saloon and two spaces on each side of the front destination indicator on the upper saloon. An invitation to tender was sent to 23 contractors and responses received from J.W. Courtenay, Griffiths & Millington, Frank Mason and Henry Squire, that of Mason's for 5 years being accepted. As the position of the fleet number transfers beneath the rear platform window on the Leyland TTB3s made it impossible to carry standard size advertisements on the rear panel, these numbers were moved to the waistband at the advertising contractors' expense in September 1944. The position was changed again from 1949 to the middle (cantrail) cream painted band above the rear platform window to standardise it on all vehicles. In the meantime from May 1945 two identical advertisements started to appear on either side of the destination display on the front upper deck panels.

The war-damaged roof of trolleybus depot 2 at Parliament Street was repaired and 18 windows added.

The short Carlton, Cavendish Road extension opened on 22 October 1944. All journeys were extended to the new terminus at the junction with Cemetery Road (now known as Cavendish Drive), and the turning circle at Post Office Square dismantled. The final destination display remained unchanged as Carlton, Post Office Square. There were discussions with Carlton UDC about a further extension of about two thirds of a mile along Cavendish Road to its junction with Coningswath Road but the proposal was dropped as the road was considered unsuitable for trolleybus operation at that time.

Since 17 October 1943, the 39 and 45 had been operating as a through service, vehicles travelling from Carlton through the city centre, round the Wollaton Park circle, back to the city and then on to Trent Bridge, and vice versa, although only every alternate journey on the 39 had operated through since 13 February 1944. The through service ceased entirely from 4 November 1944, and services 39 and 45 were divided again, using the appropriate Middleton Boulevard turning circle in each case:

39 Carlton (Post Office Square) – Carlton Road – Upper Parliament Street – Derby Road – Ilkeston Road – Wollaton Park (Middleton Boulevard, Fairham Drive) *(eastbound via Central Market – King Edward Street – Bath Street – Handel Street, westbound via Southwell Road – Lower Parliament Street)*

45 Trent Bridge – London Road – Pennyfoot Street – Manvers Street – Bath Street – Lower Parliament Street – Upper Parliament Street – Derby Road – Wollaton Park (Middleton Boulevard, Scalford Drive) *(in both directions)*

The undertaking wanted to build a turning point at the junction of Middleton Boulevard and Wollaton Hall Drive (Wollaton Park Gates) to act as the terminus of both services but the City Engineer and the General Works and Highways Committee would not agree to this and the proposal was deferred until after the war.

As the theatre of war moved increasingly away from Britain's shores lighting restrictions were gradually relaxed whilst Nottingham was fortunately sufficiently far north to be spared from the V1 and V2 flying bombs. From 17 September 1944 "black-out" restrictions were eased and "moonlight" street lighting introduced, the resultant effect gaining the unofficial term of "dim-out". It was announced in mid October 1944 that a later evening service would be introduced as soon as new duty rosters could be arranged, bearing in mind the continuing shortage of labour, and on 5 November 1944, all services were extended from 9pm until 10 pm. The 10.15 pm "permit buses" continued to run and permit holders retained their priority on the 10 pm journeys as had prevailed on the 9 pm ones. Headlamps and some interior lamps were unmasked from 24 December 1944 whilst from 31 December 1944 priority travel for permit holders on journeys departing at 10 pm and on Sunday mornings between 6.30 am and 9 am was withdrawn. Permit holders still retained their priority in boarding at other times. By January 1945 the entire fleet but for those trolleybuses with high-tension lighting (only those with low voltage lighting having been previously equipped) had been fitted with fog lights and it was now decided to equip them with Notek No. 175 fog lamps at a total cost of £320.

On 6 January 1945 a trolleybus collided with a Pool Petrol tanker, both vehicles being badly damaged, and the Petroleum Board claimed £223 19s 2d against the Corporation. By May 1946 this had been negotiated down to £83 10s 9d.

A GEC loudspeaker system was installed in Old Market Square (at a cost of £345) and Queen Street enabling the supervisory staff in the Chief Inspector's office on South Parade to provide traffic information to passengers waiting at the main city centre stops.

It was agreed to fit Lockheed Gates Booster equipment to the braking system of trolleybus 405 at a cost of £54 10s.

In March 1945 Alderman Sir Albert Atkey once again suggested that the trolleybus system should be replaced by motorbuses but consideration was deferred (it will be recalled he had tabled similar proposals in 1938 and supported Mr Gunn's recommendations at that time to this effect).

The Annual Report for the year ending 31 March 1945 saw a transfer of £ 11,333 out of net revenue for the purchase of trolleybuses. Mr England stressed that considerable sums would be required to renew the fleet in the next few years: in 1935 a trolleybus cost £1,860 (motorbus £ 1,527) by 1944 the figures had become £ 2,788 and £ 2,574 respectively. The outstanding loan debt on that date totalled £84,079 made up as follows: buildings £29,140; electrical overhead equipment £18,203; removal of tram track and road reinstatement £36,736. The same mileage had been operated in the year ending 31 March 1945 as in 1936-37 but the number of passengers carried had increased by 42½ million. During the year, five double-deck and one single-deck trolleybus had been withdrawn but there had been four deliveries and thus the trolleybus fleet remained virtually unchanged at 147 double-deckers and 5 single-deckers out of a total fleet of 391 passenger vehicles. The 4 trolleybuses had cost a total of £11,150. An additional trolleybus had been fitted with a new motor, 3 trolleybuses had been fitted with new resistances, 41 trolleybuses had new air operated windscreen wipers and 11 trolleybuses had received new rear springs. The turning circles at Cinderhill, Bulwell Hall and Ransom Road had been rewired whilst automatic sectionalising switches had been installed on the Bulwell and Carlton trolleybus routes.

At the beginning of May 1945 the RTC was asked to remove the restriction allowing only permit holders to be carried on journeys operating from the City at 10.15pm, however they considered that the restriction was still necessary and permission was refused. This was followed on 1 June 1945 by an application to extend all services to 10.30 and simultaneously abolish all travel permits. The RTC granted permission and on Sunday 15 July 1945 all services from the city centre were extended from 10 pm until 10.30 pm, a Sunday morning service between the hours of 9.30 am and 1 pm was reintroduced (representing about 70% of a pre-war Sunday morning service and about 78% of the Sunday morning service operated until November 1942) and all remaining travel permits, introduced on 22 November 1942, giving preferential accommodation to workpeople on certain vehicles, were abolished. At the same time full interior lighting was restored and the "black-out" masks sent for salvage.

Hostilities throughout mainland Europe came to an end at the beginning of May 1945. The British government announced that this would be celebrated with three days of public holidays commencing on 8 May 1945 with "VE" (Victory in Europe) Day. The Council's Emergency Committee considered it essential that services operated throughout and thus it was decided that all employees would receive double pay on the first and third days, and treble pay on the third day, whether on or off duty. On VE Day services commenced at 6.30 am and all works extras were cancelled. On the day following, a Bank Holiday service ran: a reduced headway operated from 7 am until 10 am after which it was increased to approximately a Saturday service for the remainder of the day with as many extras and duplicates as possible. The following Sunday, 13 May 1945, was designated Thanksgiving Day and special 15-30 minutes services operated on most routes from 10 am to 12.30 pm. In all cases this special operation was dependent on the number of crews who reported for duty! Although no vehicles were officially decorated for the occasion, traffic staff made free use of TIM ticket rolls to liberally cover vehicle windows with paper "V"s. From the week after Whitsunday 20 May 1945 work began on repainting trolleybus mudguards all over black commencing with 410 and 402.

On 6 July 1945 the Transport Committee instructed the Town Clerk to apply for a Provisional Order for the construction of the following trolley vehicle route extensions:

1. from Carlton Post Office via Main Street East, Manor Road, and Station Road, thus describing a loop
2. from the turning point in Cavendish Road at Carlton, along Cavendish Road, to the junction of that road with Westdale Lane.
3. from the junction of Middleton Boulevard with Wollaton Road, along Russell Drive and Trowell Road, to the city boundary at Balloon Houses.

Carlton UDC had already indicated their support for the extensions and in preparation 20 heavy and 30 medium steel traction poles were purchased from Stewarts & Lloyds at £22 3s 6d and £17 1s respectively. Alderman Sir Albert Atkey, asked if it was the Transport Committee's policy to retain the trolley bus system or to convert it completely to motorbus operation and it was pointed out that the proposed extensions were simply short extensions of existing services.

The MoWT's 5th allocation of 4 Karrier W chassis, which subsequently received fleet numbers 479-482, was accepted, with chassis delivery scheduled for the last 8 months of 1946 (in fact the completed trolleybuses only arrived in July 1948). As trolleybus 318 needed major repairs and was surplus to requirements it was agreed to sell it at the best price obtainable.

The following trolleybuses had been taken into stock since the outbreak of war:

Fleet No.	Reg No.	Type	Date to NCT	New
437	FW8995	AEC661T/Park Royal	October 1940	1937
438-440	AFU153-155	AEC661T/Park Royal	October 1940	1938
302-303	JN60-61	English Electric E11/EE	December 1940	1930
441	GTO741	Daimler/Weymann	April 1941	1938
304-309	DX5121,5126,5120,5578,5453,5111	Guy BTX/Ransomes	Dec 1941-Feb 1942	1928-29
447-451	GTV47-51	Sunbeam MF2/Weymann	October-December 1942	
442-445	GTV42-45	Karrier W/Weymann	Dec 1943-Feb 1944	
452-454	GTV652-54	Karrier W/Park Royal	March – April 1944	
455-458	GTV655-58	Karrier W/Weymann	March – April 1944	
459-462	GTV659-662	Karrier W/Roe	March 1945	

and the following (5 double deck and 1 single deck) withdrawn:

302 in March 1944 although still extant in December 1945
303 in March 1944 although still extant in December 1945
305 in March 1944 and disposed of in October 1944
313 in February 1945 although still extant in December 1945
331 in January 1944 and disposed of in October 1944
335 in January 1944 and disposed of in October 1944

Before the war motorbus service 26 had operated between the city centre and Elmhurst Avenue (in principle the foreseen terminus, at the junction of Cavendish Road and Westdale Lane, of trolleybus route 2 in the proposed Provisional Order). Mr England feared that trolleybus powers for this extension could not be obtained before July 1946 and he accordingly recommended, with the support of Carlton UDC, that motorbuses be reintroduced along a part of the route of the erstwhile service 26, operating between the junction of Coningswath Road with Cavendish Road, and the vicinity of Netherfield railway crossing, via Cavendish Road and Station Road.

Public holidays were declared on "VJ" (Victory in Japan) Day, 15 August 1945, and the following day, NCT operated special services on all routes to cope with the extra traffic.

Wollaton Park, Fairham Drive boarding point for service 39 to Carlton Post Office Square. Karrier E6/Park Royal 326 has just turned through the central reservation of the dual carriageway Middleton Boulevard to wait at the "railless" stop in the northbound carriageway. The white circle painted on the road surface immediately behind th e trolleybus was a wartime aid to drivers of the trailing frog above so that they could coast and thereby avoid sparks which might give away their location to enemy aircraft during hours of darkness. *BTS*

Chapter 6 Recovery and Booming Traffic 1945-52

The Town Clerk investigated applying for a Provisional Order for the three trolleybus route extensions agreed by the Transport Committee in July 1945. The two Carlton proposals, namely the Manor Road loop and the Cavendish Road extension, were outside the city boundary and within the jurisdiction of Carlton UDC and Nottinghamshire County Council, requiring a Parliamentary Bill to gain the necessary powers. It was felt inadvisable to include them in the 1945 Bill that already contained a large and varied number of topics delayed by six years of war. Although powers for the Middleton Boulevard – Balloon Houses extension, which lay entirely within the city boundary, could be obtained by a Provisional Order, in view of the difficulties experienced in 1943, it was feared that there was not a strong case. On 7 September 1945 the proposal was again deferred to 1946.

There was no longer a need to retain employees past retirement age due to the number of demobbed servicemen returning to "Civvie Street" and the Council instructed that they should be retired from 1 March 1946. Thereafter employees over 65 years old were to be released at the first opportunity with former employees returning from the forces being given priority in filling the resulting vacancies. Until now men and women not required by the forces or in a Reserved Occupation had been allocated work by the Ministry of Labour, normally with a Scheduled Employer such as Nottingham City Transport. There was a rush of resignations, particularly conductresses, for better-paid positions in industry as soon as employees were able to freely leave the undertaking. By October 1945, there was a shortage of 392 platform staff and by January 1946 conductresses were leaving at the rate of 15 a week; indeed by June 1946 there were only 260 left and permission was sought to retain 62 older employees until after 1 March 1946 hoping to fill the positions with returning ex-servicemen.

Karrier quoted £1,684 5s each, for the fifth allocation of W4 utility trolleybus chassis, by now reduced from 10 to 4 units (later 479-482). In the meantime however the MoWT had advised that it might now be possible to provide the other 6 chassis, at a total cost of about £18,000, and that they would agree to finance them with a loan. At the same time Park Royal Vehicles quoted for the fourth allocation of 10 trolleybus bodies, which were to become 469-478, at £1,434 15s each although initially Brush had been expected to provide these bodies.

There was an immediate increase in the number of railway passengers encouraging the reintroduction of a direct link between the city's two mainline stations, the Midland (LMS) about half a mile south of the Old Market Square on Carrington Street, and Victoria (LNER) just off Upper Parliament Street at the southern end of Mansfield Road. This link had been provided by motorbus services 20 (Arnold – Trent Bridge) and 35 (Mapperley – Trent Bridge) until 23 September 1939. An additional trolleybus service, the 48 Nottingham Road (Vernon Road) – Trent Bridge (Victoria Embankment) was introduced on Sunday 14 October 1945 to provide a frequent connection; the Monday-Friday peak hour and all day Saturday service was every 10 minutes with a Monday-Friday off-peak and an all day Sunday 15 minute service. This was achieved by extending certain 36 journeys beyond King Street/Queen Street to and from Trent Bridge, which may have replaced some journeys on service 46.

The immediate post-war trolleybus network thus consisted of the following services:

36 Old Market Square (Queen Street/King Street) – Upper Parliament Street – Milton Street – Victoria Station – Mansfield Road – Nottingham Road (Vernon Road)

37 Old Market Square (Queen Street/King Street) – Upper Parliament Street – Milton Street – Victoria Station – Mansfield Road – Nottingham Road (Haydn Road) *(Monday – Friday peak hours, including lunch time, and all day Saturday)*

Karrier W/Weymann 442 waits outside the Globe Picture House in the apex of the junction between Arkwright Street and London Road, the boarding point of service 45 from Trent Bridge until 1953 and again from 1954 until 1959. *Photobus*

38 Theatre Square – Upper Parliament Street – Carlton Road – Carlton (Hooton Road) (eastbound via Central Market – King Edward Street – Bath Street – Handel Street, westbound via Southwell Road – Lower Parliament Street)

39 Carlton (Post Office Square) – Carlton Road – Central Market – Upper Parliament Street – Ilkeston Road – Wollaton Park (Middleton Boulevard, Fairham Drive) *(eastbound via Central Market – King Edward Street – Bath Street – Handel Street, westbound via Southwell Road – Lower Parliament Street)*

40 The Wells Road (Kildare Road) – St. Anns Well Road – King Edward Street – Upper Parliament Street – Old Market Square – Wilford Road – Wilford Bridge *(northbound via Long Row – Queen Street – Upper Parliament Street, southbound via George Street – Carlton Street – Victoria Street – Poultry – South Parade)*

Sunbeam MF2/Weymann 447 still with its original front destination blind display at the 39 terminus in Middleton Boulevard, Wollaton Park. *GHFA & JMB*

N&D Weymann bodied BUT 9611T 354 of 1949 and NCT Roe bodied BUT 9611T 483 of 1948 wait in the apex of the junction of King Street with Queen Street in January 1951. *GHFA & JMB*

At the Brush works in Loughborough BUT9641T 500 successfully completes the MoT "tilt test". Standing in front of the tilting machinery are (left) Mr F. Rayer, Head of Brush Coachworks Design Office, and (right) Mr D.P. Martin, Chief Engineer NCT. Freddie Rayer had designed the pre-war Metro Cammell all metal bodies and had moved to Brush shortly after the Second World War where he introduced a number of metal bodies based on Metal Section framing. Together with Ian Mair he was instrumental in designing the Brush bodies on Nottingham's BUT9641Ts. *John Lowrie*

41 Old Market Square (Queen Street/King Street) – Upper Parliament Street – Milton Street – Victoria Station – Mansfield Road – Nottingham Road – Stockhill Lane – Nuthall Road – Cinderhill *(Monday to Friday peak operation and daytime Saturday only)*

42 Bulwell Market – Basford – Vernon Road – Radford Road – Hyson Green – Alfreton Road – Derby Road – Old Market Square (Long Row West/Angel Row)

43 Bulwell Market – Basford – Vernon Road – Radford Road – Hyson Green – Alfreton Road – Derby Road – Old Market Square – Carrington Street – Arkwright Street –Trent Bridge

44 Bulwell Hall Estate – Bulwell Market – Basford – Vernon Road – Radford Road – Hyson Green – Alfreton Road – Derby Road – Upper Parliament Street – Bath Street – Manvers Street – Colwick Road *Northbound journeys operated via Upper Parliament Street – George Street – Carlton Street – Victoria Street – The Poultry – South Parade – Old Market Square – Angel Row – Chapel Bar. Southbound journeys operated via Upper Parliament Street.*

45 Trent Bridge (Globe Cinema) – London Road – Pennyfoot Street – Manvers Street – Bath Street – Lower Parliament Street – Upper Parliament Street – Derby Road – Wollaton Park (Middleton Boulevard, Scalford Drive) *(in both directions)*

46 Old Market Square (Processional Way/Beastmarket Hill) – Arkwright Street – Trent Bridge

47 The Wells Road (Ransom Road) – St Ann's Well Road – King Edward Street – Lower Parliament Street – Old Market Square – Wilford Road – Wilford Bridge. *(northbound via Long Row – Queen Street – Upper Parliament Street, southbound via Upper Parliament Street – George Street – Carlton Street – Victoria Street – The Poultry – Old Market Square)*

48 Trent Bridge – Arkwright Street – Carrington Street – Old Market Square – Upper Parliament Street – Victoria Station – Mansfield Road – Nottingham Road (Vernon Road) *(northbound via Queen Street, southbound via King Street)*

In October 1945, 30 new TIM ticket machines and 1,000 metal signs with "FORM QUEUE THIS SIDE" on one side and "FORM QUEUE OTHER SIDE" on the other were ordered. Delivered in 1946 these signs were fixed beneath the green trolleybus stop flags at the busiest boarding points.

In November 1945 the MoWT announced the end of the "purchase licensing" and allocation systems; additional trolleybuses would be available in 1946 and for the first time since the outbreak of the war, orders could be placed direct with manufacturers. Mr England recommended an order for 6 two-axle AEC chassis. The MoWT could not sanction a loan at that time and it was decided to purchase them from reserves. Although vehicles purchased by loan attracted loan charges i.e. interest payments, which included an element equivalent to depreciation, there was no obligation to allow for depreciation when vehicles were bought out of revenue or reserves. The Department had allowed for this in the past but the state of the financial reserves was approaching a stage when this could no longer be afforded. In March 1946 the City Treasurer warned that the purchase would result in the Reserve Fund being £12,000 overdrawn by the end of the financial year. It was decided to amortise some of the fund's investments, specifically an appropriate amount of 2½% National War Bonds as these earned the lowest rate of interest.

Three ex-Hastings Guy BTX (304, 306, 308) and 3 Ransomes Sims & Jeffries trolleybuses (313, 315, 317) dating from 1930, which needed major body overhauls, were sold in January 1946. Towards the end of March 1946 the "Nottingham Evening News" published an article on their new use as bungalows.

The growing fleet led to a lack of space at Parliament Street Depot and vehicles were parked in Stanhope Street. As a solution, land between "No 2 Depot" on the south side of Stanhope Street (the location of Trent's earlier depot) and Trent's Manvers Street Garage was levelled to provide open-air parking equipped with Nottingham-standard "Wembley Lantern" span-wire lighting supported by traction poles (but no trolleybus overhead wiring) and heating pipes for use by motorbuses. The parking area was known as "MX", presumably denoting Manvers or Motorbus Annex, but only trolleybuses out of service were left here. In addition, the air raid shelter at the junction of Pennyfoot Street with Manvers Street, on the other side of Trent's garage to "MX", was removed, the site levelled but left unmetalled, and equipped with overhead wiring to create parking space for trolleybuses at a cost of £750. This second yard could accommodate two rows of parked trolleybuses facing east which entered from Pennyfoot Street and left by Manvers Street. Later, in 1965, it was here that withdrawn trolleybuses were stored pending their collection by scrap dealers, although photographic evidence shows that by autumn 1957, if not earlier, the wiring had been removed.

Other trolleybus-related elements in the Transport Committee's report to the government on its 1946 capital expenditure and maintenance programme, totalling £295,000, were 46 trolleybuses at £147,200 together with £7,500 for painting buildings and traction poles.

It finally proved possible to supply all ten of the Karrier W chassis originally foreseen in Nottingham's fourth allocation and Park Royal supplied "relaxed" utility bodies. Unlike earlier utility deliveries, these featured rear destination indicators and a service number indicator box on the nearside above the rear open platform. Instead of 12-volt electrical equipment, a 24-volt generator and battery were fitted at an additional £127 16s per chassis. They entered service in February – April 1946 numbered 469-478. This enabled the remaining ex-Hastings Guy BTX single-deckers (307, 309) dating from 1929 and 1928 respectively, and the 1930 English Electric (321, 322, 324) and Ransomes (314, 316) trolleybuses to be withdrawn.

Effective 14 January 1946 the RTC instructed that the maximum number of standing passengers permitted on trolleybuses be reduced from 12 to

BUT9611T/Roe 483 crosses Theatre Square on Upper Parliament Street en route to Carlton although the conductor has forgotten to change the side destination indicator screen from the westbound journey. Those ladies' hats were the height of fashion in 1948. *EE/Beilby*

8 whilst on 27 May 1946 it was cut again to 5. In May 1948, heavy loadings and long queues of waiting passengers ensured that this figure was again increased to 8 at peak hours. By the early 1950s up to 8 standing passengers were permitted on trolleybuses at any time and it remained at this level until the closure of the system.

Although petrol rationing remained until June 1950, motor traffic in the city centre increased noticeably and the police requested the rerouting of some services to ease congestion. It was suggested that service 44 (Bulwell Hall Estate – Colwick) should operate northbound along Upper Parliament Street instead of George Street, Victoria Street, South Parade and Old Market Square and that the West Bridgford services should terminate at the Walter Fountain, Greyfriar Gate to reduce congestion in Old Market Square. The Transport Committee rejected this proposal but agreed on 1 February 1946 that the General Manager, together with representatives of the Transport Committee and the Watch Committee, and the Chief Constable should seek alternatives. Mr England complained that on-street parking for long periods of the day promoted congestion and referred to several plots of vacant land suitable for car parks.

As the MoWT had approved use of 8ft wide vehicles nationally on agreed routes, NCT applied for approval of all their routes. The five 8ft wide trolleybuses originally intended for South Africa had operated without inconveniencing other traffic since September 1942 and they offered a more comfortable interior than 7ft 6ins wide vehicles. The Transport Committee agreed to standardise on 8ft wide vehicles as soon as these were permitted and instructed Mr England to obtain alternative tenders for the 7ft 6ins wide vehicles then on order.

In February 1946 it was decided to install a passing loop in the overhead wiring at Cavendish Road, Carlton Post Office Square terminus and another at Colwick terminus, at a cost of £155 10s. The Colwick terminus was close to the entrance to Nottingham Race Course, just over the railway level crossing, whilst the "White City" Greyhound Racing Stadium was nearby in Trent Lane, off Colwick Road. This loop would enable race extras to stand clear of regular trolleybuses on service 44 but no record has survived of the date of its installation and subsequent removal. An additional turning circle was strung at the extreme southern end of the Victoria Embankment overhead wiring at the junction with Bunbury Street (the access to and from Trent Bridge Depot and Works) for turning football extras and later service 41, at a cost of £640. The Bunbury Street turning circle, together with the existing parking loop on the nearside of the northbound through wiring, provided an enlarged passenger waiting area south of the existing Trent Bridge terminus, which enabled the queues to be divided between loading trolleybuses after Nottingham Forest football matches (the ground being on the opposite side of the River Trent). At this time Victoria Embankment was a private road, owned by Nottingham Corporation, equipped with gates just east of Bunbury Street which were shut once each year to legally reinforce the fact that it was not a public highway. Automatic sectionalising switches were fitted at the junction of Carrington Street and Station Street.

Floods on Wilford Road on 10 February 1946 caused the diversion of services 40 and 47 to Trent Bridge; a substitute motorbus service operated along Wilford Road as far as Clyde Street. On 19 February 1946 a motorbus on service 3 heading towards the city centre and a 39 trolleybus bound for Wollaton Park collided at the junction of Radford Boulevard with Ilkeston Road.

Karrier W 476 was experimentally equipped with Metropolitan-Vickers DC fluorescent lighting in both saloons in October 1947. *NCT*

On 30 March 1946 the use of auxiliary conductors, instituted in July 1942, ceased and the 440 volunteer regular travellers so engaged were thanked for their services.

The disused wartime Forces Information Bureau in Old Market Square was offered to the Department in February 1946 for use as a traffic and information office. An alternative to their temporary structure near the Queen Victoria Statue had been sought since before the war and the offer was accepted until something better could be found. In April 1946 the Council decided that all temporary buildings should be removed from the Old Market Square, although, by then, the Department had only identified a room in premises on South Parade. The Queen Victoria Statue was moved to the Victoria Embankment at the end of June 1946 and the traffic and information office demolished.

AEC had received a contract in 1941 for 51 motorbus chassis, including 15 with 3-axles. With the war over trolleybuses were needed more than motorbuses and AEC's alternative quote for 13 2-axle chassis for 56-seater bodies at £2,090 each (£27,170) and15 3-axle chassis for 70-seater bodies at £2,276 each (£34,140) was accepted in March 1946, subject to the MoWT granting a loan. In April 1946 the tenders of Metropolitan-Cammell Weymann at £1,885 each (£24,505) for the former and £2,100 each (£31,500) for the latter, together with a further four 56-seater double-deck trolleybus bodies making up the fifth wartime allocation at £1,885 each (£7,540) were considered. All bodies were given as 7ft 6ins wide. The AEC chassis could be supplied to suit 8ft wide bodies, at an extra cost of about £50 each.

In February 1946 the MoWT confirmed their wartime dispensation by granting formal permission to operate 8ft wide trolleybuses on services 38, 39 and 41. This prompted the City

On learner duties, Karrier W/Weymann 433 stands at Hooton Road reversing triangle. Either the anxious trainee or the instructor relaxes on the nearside of the driver's cab. *Photobus*

En route for Wollaton Park, BUT9611T/Roe 484 is seen in Upper Parliament Street at Theatre Square. Service 39 always benefited from the latest trolleybus deliveries but the stay of these 2-axle vehicles on the hilly Carlton route was to be short-lived and they were moved to the Wells Road – Wilford Road services once the BUT9641Ts arrived. A utility bodied trolleybus is pulling out of Queen Street in the background. *EE/Beilby*

Council on 3 June 1946 to approve the purchase, by 10 year loan, of the 15 three-axle and 13 two-axle trolleybuses as 8ft wide vehicles, if permission could be obtained for their use on all routes, at a total cost of £118,715. Approval to run 8ft wide trolleybuses along George Street was still outstanding in early October 1946 and under the circumstances Mr England recommended an immediate order for thirteen 7ft 6ins wide BUT 9611T two-axle chassis and four 7ft 6ins Metro-Cammell bodies to fit the 4 Karrier W two-axle chassis ordered earlier. Only on 9 September 1950 was permission granted for wider trolleybuses to use George Street, by which time services 40, 44 and 47 had been rerouted to Upper Parliament Street, and even then the regulation stipulated that a regular service of 8ft wide vehicles should not be operated without the Chief Constable's prior consent.

In November 1946 it was decided not to order the other 15 three-axle trolleybus until the width situation had been clarified. As compensation to the manufacturers, 15 motorbuses were ordered instead, although by now it was estimated that a further 6 trolleybuses were needed for increased services and 59 for vehicle replacement. Due to delivery problems at Metro-Cammell the order for four bodies for the Karrier W chassis was passed to Charles Roe in 1947. It will be noted that following the merger of AEC and Leyland's trolleybus interests, the AEC chassis were henceforth referred to as British United Traction (BUT) products.

An experiment with Bell Punch "Ultimate" ticket machines started in March 1946. Their fast operation and the colour coding of tickets according to the value issued impressed conductors, and once delivery was back to normal, the "Ultimate" machine became the undertaking's standard.

On 14 April 1946, having received RTC permission, services were extended back to 11 pm and Sunday morning services were improved. In the meantime the RTC had also made suggestions to combat traffic congestion in the Old Market Square and on Sunday 19 May 1946 service 44 (Bulwell Hall Estate – Colwick) was rerouted northbound, as the police had suggested, to run along Upper Parliament Street instead of George Street, Victoria Street and South Parade. On the same date southbound trolleybus services 40 and 47 (The Wells Road – Wilford Bridge) were diverted to operate along Upper Parliament Street, King Street and Long Row. In July 1946 the Road Safety Council recommended that all bus stops on the north side of Upper Parliament Street between South Sherwood Street and Milton Street be abolished in an effort to reduce traffic congestion.

It was feared that these alterations would create difficulties in handling football traffic when the season opened in August 1946 and it was agreed to reroute trolleybuses proceeding to a match to load in Upper Parliament Street at Victoria Station Bridge (LNER Bridge) and then along Lower Parliament Street instead of via King Edward Street and Bath Street. An overhead wiring passing loop was installed in Upper Parliament Street, between Milton Street and the Palais de Danse, enabling these specials running to stand clear of through trolleybus traffic, at a cost of £105.

At the same time additional overhead equipment was installed at the junction of Pennyfoot Street with Manvers Street to enable trolleybuses to operate outwards Lower Parliament Street – Pennyfoot Street – Colwick Road, serving racing at Colwick Park and the

In early 1950 brand new 8ft wide BUT9641T 509 proceeds gingerly west along Southwell Road at the junction with Manvers Street. A pony and trap waits patiently outside the greengrocers at Sneinton Market. *GHFA & JMB*

"White City", at a cost of £340. There was no equivalent overhead equipment at the junctions of Manvers Street with Pennyfoot Street or Pennyfoot Street with Lower Parliament Street junctions for inbound journeys. Access towards Colwick Road was simplified by hanging a second overhead line, paralleling that of service 45, along the length of Pennyfoot Street eastbound.

Except for a slight increase in fares which had come into operation on 14 April 1940 increasing revenue by just 5.5%, fares were still at pre-war rates although operating costs had risen considerably, with hardly any surplus expected for the year ending 31 March 1946.

The City Council agreed to the new fare levels except those under Clause j., aimed at increasing revenue by £133,600, of which £125,000 would come from trolleybus fares, on 29 July 1946 and they were submitted to the MoT and RTC for approval. Free travel passes were issued to members of the City Council from 1 August 1946.

Increasing traffic demands and a shortage of new vehicles combined with the reduction in the authorised number of standing passengers introduced on 27 May 1946 led to longer queues at bus stops. The shortage of platform staff was by now acute and a recruiting drive commenced. In July 1946 the TGWU was asked to consider giving up vehicle standing time at termini during the peak hours of 7am to 9.15am and 4.30pm to 7.15pm. This would have had the effect of placing 23 more running vehicles on the routes in the morning and 24 in the evening. However the union would not agree, suggesting reduced works services and a transfer of vehicles from the less busy to the overloaded services. An appeal at the end of September 1946 to the traffic employees to consider abolishing standing time faired no better.

A series of overhead equipment breakages left a trail of damage along trolleybus routes in July 1946. On 9 July 1946 a de-wired trolley boom struck an overhead street lamp which fell and smashed the shop window of Isalea Dry Cleaners on Mansfield Road; on 10 July 1946 a trolley boom and its spring unit became detached and fell to the ground from the gantry of a trolleybus going down Nottingham Road towards Haydn Road that morning; and on the next morning a collapsed traction pole near the "Earl of Chesterfield" pub on Main Street, Carlton brought the overhead down causing service 39 to turn at Hooton Road pending repairs.

In July 1946 the Department's Annual Report for the year ending 31 March 1946 was presented to the City Council. The trolleybus network had an outstanding loan debt of £76,421 comprised of buildings £27,005, overhead equipment £15,730 and removal of tram track and road reinstatement £33,686. The cost of electrical energy for trolleybuses increased from 0.84d to 0.903d per unit due to the operation of the Coal Clause and 13¾ million units were consumed at a total cost of £50,000. At 31st March 1946, the trolleybus fleet comprised 157 double deck vehicles, 16 new trolleybuses having been received during the previous twelve months and 11 (6 double deck and 5 single deck) disposed of.

The 16 new trolleybuses had cost £2,980 each but the estimated cost of the vehicles then on order was by now £4,426. During the year slip lines and automatic frogs were installed in Queen Street for service 48 (Trent Bridge – Nottingham Road) whilst six important junctions had been completely reconstructed. Automatic sectionalising switches were fitted at Derby Road and Ilkeston Road. Trolleybuses had been involved in 56.6% of the Department's 1,860 accidents, varying from clothing damage to collisions, including a total of 9 fatalities, 5 being pedestrians, 3 boarding or alighting from vehicles, and 1 person involved in a collision.

As Ransomes D6 398 ran out of Parliament Street Depot on 17 August 1946 to take up service on a 48 journey from Trent Bridge it caught fire just past London Road High Level Station Bridge and suffered roof damage. Driver Anderson could not say exactly what had happened. The dewirement indicator light had apparently only flickered but the trolleybus came to a standstill. *"There was a blinding white light on the roof then the fire turned red as the current was cut off and the flames took hold of the inside of the bus. Windows, shattered by the heat, crashed into the street below, making it uncomfortable for onlookers on the other side of the road".* Another trolleybus crew used their cab fire extinguishers but to no avail and then called for the current to be cut off. The fire brigade were soon on the scene and brought the fire under control but service 45 suffered some delays. Curiously this fire occurred within 50 yards of the location of a similar event involving Karrier 376 on 24 February 1940.

Having studied Mr England's suggestions for fare increases, on 14 June 1946 the Transport Committee submitted them to the City Council:

a. The hours for the issue of workmen's tickets on trolleybuses be standardised with the hours applicable on motorbuses
b. Workmen's return tickets to be available for the return journeys on any day and return tickets issued on a motorbus to be available for return on a trolleybus, and vice versa
c. The wartime condition of issuing and accepting workmen's tickets on Bank Holidays and Sundays be withdrawn
d. Workmen's single tickets be withdrawn leaving workmen's returns in operation.
e. A new scale be adopted to fix the relationship between ordinary and workmen's fares:
   Where ordinary fare is 1d and 1½d workmen's return fare to be 2d
   Where ordinary fare is 2d workmen's return fare to be 3d
   Where ordinary fare is 2½d and 3d workmen's return fare to be 4d
   Where ordinary fare is 3½d and 4d workmen's return fare to be 5d
f. All transfer fares be abolished.
g. Trolleybus fare rates be increased to the same levels as motorbus fares.
h. A minimum ordinary fare of 1½d be introduced on all services, with the result that the fare scale on all services except West Bridgford would be as follows:

Mileage Scale	Ordinary Fare
0.01 to 1.75	1½d
1.76 to 2.25	2d
2.26 to 2.75	2½d
2.76 to 3.25	3d
3.26 to 3.75	3½d
3.76 upward	4d

i. The present maximum fare of 3d on all routes between the City Centre terminus and the City Boundary to remain in operation.
j. Children's ½d fare be increased to 1d.

The fire of Ransomes D6 398 on 17 August 1946. NCT

Apparently not running in passenger service, Karrier Clough E6/Park Royal 350 is seen here beneath the eastbound wires in Colwick Road just past Hermitage Square. Although 350 has had its headlamp masks removed, the aftermath of war is still very evident of the roofless St. Christopher's Church in the background on the corner of Trent Road and the white paint at the base of the front panel and on the mudguards. St. Christopher's was totally rebuilt in the 1950's and is still in use for worship today. *BTS*

Brand new BUT9641Ts wait at the Fairham Drive terminus of service 39 on Middleton Boulevard, Wollaton Park (Selston Drive is the next turn on the left) on 12 March 1950. Both 515 and 504 illustrate the double bumper bar around the offside rear panel with which the Brush bodies were originally fitted. These were removed in the mid-1950s to avoid damage from the Dawson bus washing machine. *Peter Badgery*

Although by the early-mid 1960s the Nottingham network became somewhat of a run-down, dirty system, subject to frequent break-downs of some sort, during the 30s and 40s, it had been comparatively efficient despite a number of accidents, particularly fatal ones, those involving fires on trolleybus roofs and serious dewirements which were, by today's standards, unacceptably high, whether utilising trolleybuses or any other mode of public street transport. Modern trolleybuses running under flexible overhead equipment do not suddenly de-wire at anywhere near the rate found on Britain's post-war systems using rigid overhead designs that had not been changed from before the Second World War. Despite this record, Nottingham's trolleybus system could still impress visitors.

For example, during the morning of 7 September 1946 the trolley poles of two trolleybuses became entangled with the overhead on Vernon Road at Southwark Street breaking the trolley wire and causing delays to services 43 and 44. Many intending passengers walked to Nottingham Road, Vernon Road, to catch a 36 or 48. Later in September 1946 a 12-person delegation from Lyon, France, came to study the trolleybus system. They were presumably suitably impressed and had sufficient foresight to ensure that the Lyon system remains in use today with new vehicles delivered in 2005.

On 4 October 1946 the General Manager reminded the Transport Committee that in 1945 they had deferred a decision on seeking trolleybus powers for the following routes:

1. Commencing at the junction of Middleton Boulevard and Wollaton Road, along Wollaton Road, Russell Drive and Trowell Road to Balloon Houses (8.58 chains west of the City boundary)
2. Main Street East, Manor Road and Station Road, Carlton
3. Along Cavendish Road to its junction with Westdale Lane, Carlton

It was decided to seek powers in the City Council's next Parliamentary Bill but by the end of November 1946 the N&D had also submitted a Bill to operate trolleybuses from the centre of Nottingham to Ilkeston with running powers over the city's system as far as Balloon Houses, as proposed during the war. The Transport Committee resolved to oppose the N&D Bill. In the meantime 100 steel traction poles and 40 ground sleeves in 2 different sizes were purchased from Stewart and Lloyds Ltd. for £2,636, in preparation for these extensions. A public meeting held at Wollaton on 23 December 1946 supported the city's plans and objected to the N&D alternative. The "Nottingham Guardian" noted however that *"the chief objections were that the beauty of the surroundings would be spoiled by the erection of the standards and that radio interference would be caused"* although *"one speaker referred to trolleybuses as 'newly fangled ideas'"*. At the same meeting Mr Owen, the Deputy Town Clerk stated that *"it was not a question of whether they were going to have trolleybuses or petrol buses; it was a question of trolleybuses or nothing"*

The NCC objected to the Corporation's Balloon Houses proposals, which foresaw a turning circle within the County boundary, whilst the MGOC and N&D, lodged a joint petition. The Corporation made technical objections to the Companies' N&D Bill and decided that if these were not upheld a petition would be lodged against it. Both Carlton UDC and the NCC objected to the Main Street East, Manor Road and Station Road, Carlton extension, arguing that the roads were unsuitable for trolleybus operation, as they sought a one-way circular loop rather than the proposed two-way route. The two authorities also claimed that the third planned extension, along Cavendish Road, Carlton, was unsuitable for trolley vehicles. Trent agreed not to oppose the Carlton proposals subject to fares charged by the Company and NCT from common points being standardised. Trent had no objections to the retention of the "Black's Head Inn" protection point, and the Corporation agreed not to seek any new protection should parliamentary approval be granted. The company felt that any trolleybus turning loops or connecting lines should be limited to a maximum length of 150 yards with the exception of any depot or works access sections. As it was Carlton UDC who had requested this extension during the war, it was felt that their objection would result in the defeat of these proposals and they were deleted from the Bill.

It was decided to adopt the Road Safety Council's proposal to remove the eastbound Kings Walk trolleybus stops on the north side of Upper Parliament Street, between South Sherwood Street and Milton Street, in an effort to relieve traffic congestion. As Kings Walk was a fare stage, a fares amendment was necessary. The stops were discontinued on Saturday 4 January 1947 and passengers travelling from west to east who until then had alighted at Kings Walk had to

On a late March day in 1950 with the Council House almost obscured in the misty distance, 8ft wide BUT9641T/Brush 520 reaches the top of the climb up Derby Road from the city centre to Canning Circus. Please note the setting skate or transfer contact in the positive wire for the first westbound Canning Circus auto frog controlling access to the continuation of Derby Road and the pre-war Barton Leyland motorbus behind the trolleybus. *EE/Beilby*

leave the trolleybus at either the Turkish Baths in Milton Street or the Victoria Station (LNER) Bridge, an increased fare i.e. that to the Central Market, being charged if they travelled to Victoria Station Bridge. From the same date the fare stage at the Elite Cinema (in principle the stop opposite Kings Walk), serving services 38, 39, 44 and 45, was moved to the stop at the Derby Road end of Upper Parliament Street heading west and the Turkish Baths heading east. Passengers who had boarded at the Elite Cinema now had to join the trolleybus at either the Turkish Baths or Victoria Station Bridge with no change in fare whereas some passengers who normally boarded at the Turkish Baths benefited from a lower fare. Similarly passengers travelling from east to west to the Derby Road end of Parliament Street were able to travel for the same fare as was previously paid to the Elite whereas passengers who normally boarded at the Elite in some cases had to pay a higher fare i.e. they were charged the fare from the Central Market. Hence from Monday 6 January 1947 the first boarding point for service 38 after turning in Theatre Square was Victoria Station Bridge.

In addition it was suggested that the Old Market Square loading point for services 43 and 46 be moved from the west end of Processional Way to a point opposite the Talbot Hotel, however the police rejected this fearing more congestion in Long Row West.

As winter 1946-47 approached, an ex-army AEC Matador was bought from the MoS for £650 to replace the existing breakdown wagon. It was intended to mount an overhead inspection tower on the chassis of its predecessor. The Matador, fleet number 513, was never used for recovery purposes but retained as a lorry for carrying sand and salt in winter whilst the existing breakdown wagon continued in use for many years. Additional peak hour capacity was provided through the winter by hiring 3-4 coaches from Robin Hood Coaches Ltd. and a further 2 from Skill's Motor Coaches. By January 1947 this had increased to 10 and 4 vehicles respectively, crewed by the operators' drivers and NCT conductors working overtime.

Following their landslide victory in the first post-war general election, held on 26 July 1945, the new Labour Government introduced a series of Bills to bring key industries into public ownership. The country's municipal transport undertakings anticipated that this could lead to their nationalisation and although this did not happen the Transport Bill, introduced into the House of Commons on 27 November 1946, and the Electricity Bill, which followed in early 1947, were to have far-reaching effects on trolleybus operation in and around Nottingham and beyond.

Part IV (Passenger Road Transport) of the Transport Bill proposed that the foreseen British Transport Commission might *"for any area approved by the MoT, prepare and submit to the Minister a scheme as to the road passenger transport services serving the area, being a scheme devised for the purpose of promoting or facilitating the promotion of the co-ordination of the passenger transport services serving the area, whether by road or by rail, and the provision of adequate suitable and efficient passenger road transport services to meet the needs of the area"*. No compensation payments to municipal undertakings were included except for annual sums to cover the sinking fund and interest charges on their outstanding debts. In the past £60,000 pa had been set aside for vehicle replacement which were then bought out of revenue rather than through a central government loan; however in view of these provisions, it was felt appropriate to discontinue this policy. By January 1947 it was calculated that profits for the financial year could be higher than expected making it difficult to justify the application for increased fares approved by the City Council in September 1946, and since submitted to the MoT and RTC. It was decided not to proceed with the application.

The MoT, taking into account the railway companies' weak bridge limits which already restricted the Department's operations, stipulated that the maximum number of 8ft wide trolleybuses which could be used in 1948 was 30 including the 5 already in use. Mr England recommended that a further 66 8ft wide vehicles be included in the next order, to be paid for from the £510,000 loan for which application for sanction to borrow had already been made.

The construction of a turning circle at the junction of Cardale Road with Carlton Road was investigated but found to be inappropriate whilst the gradient made the location unsuitable.

Prior to closing their remaining tram routes, in February 1947 delegates of the Bolton Transport Committee and Transport Department, which owned four trolleybuses operated on their behalf on the interurban South Lancashire Transport network, visited Nottingham to inspect the trolleybus system. The Bolton General Manager, Mr A.A. Jackson, had formerly worked for NCT. However Bolton did not pursue a tram to trolleybus conversion programme.

The first three months of 1947 provided some of the worst winter weather on record, characterised by fog, ice and heavy snowfalls, making road and rail transport difficult. Coal was being exported in great quantities to help the nation's balance of payments difficulties and those coal stocks foreseen for domestic consumption froze solid; the result was coal shortages and wide spread electricity cuts. Railway services suffered generally and by mid-January 1947 the LMS had cancelled some 50 trains locally, including Nottingham suburban services. This all put an increased load on the trolleybuses. It should be remembered that at this time many of the city streets were still paved with granite setts or wooden blocks in the vicinity of churches, hospitals and schools, all being ideal for skidding in frosty or wet weather. Many schools closed temporarily and factories worked modified shift patterns. The crisis deepened when dockers and lorry drivers went on strike, the forces taking over some of their work. By February 1947 heavy snow falls had made the fuel shortage worse,

N&D's Ripley trolleybus service, together with NCT's Nottingham Road services, terminated immediately in front of the Prudential Insurance building at the apex of Queen Street and King Street throughout its existence. Two BUT961 1Ts, the Corporation's Roe-bodied 491 and the Company's Weymann bodied 350 take their lay-over at the beginning of the 1950s. *Nottingham Libraries*

Sunbeam MF2/Weymann 449 is curiously parked in the throat of Hooton Road, Carlton prior to heading back to Theatre Square as a 38 on 17 July 1952. This was the only Sunbeam MF2 to have its front destination indicator box rebuilt and to receive semaphore arm illuminated traffic indicators. *Roy Marshall*

whilst particularly heavy falls on 4 March 1947 led to villages e.g. Cotgrave, within just a few miles of the city being completely cut off by ten foot drifts.

When the thaw began Nottingham suffered the heaviest rain for 58 years and as the level of the River Trent rose Wilford residents had to be evacuated. By 19 March 1947 the Midland Station, over a mile from the river, was inundated by floodwater and the "Evening Post" recommended the LMS railway embankment as the best route by foot between Nottingham and West Bridgford! On 19 and 20 March 1947, trolleybus services 40 and 47 were unable to traverse Wilford Road, motorbuses operating from the Old Market Square as far as the receding waters permitted. On 19 March, service 40 was diverted to operate to Trent Bridge via Arkwright Street, whilst the 47 was curtailed to run between Ransom Road and the Old Market Square. In addition trolleybus service 45 was curtailed at Gregory Street, Lenton, whilst the 44 could not operate north of Bulwell Market. The next day, trolleybus service 40 operated to the Cattle Market turning circle on London Road via Carrington Street and Station Street, this being the sole occasion that Station Street and the Cattle Market turning circle were used on a regular basis. The situation eased over the next few days.

On 3 April 1947 it was decided to sell Ransomes D6 314 and 316, and English Electric 319 and 321, all dating from 1930, which were in bad condition.

As considerable housing development along Trowell Road was expected in the next few years, it was deemed essential to acquire trolley vehicle powers for the Balloon Houses, Wollaton route. There were fears that the MGOC and N&D might seek compensation for loss of business if the powers were granted and the Transport Committee resolved in March 1947 that this would be refused unless recommended by the Parliamentary Committee.

A brand new 8ft wide BUT9641T/Brush 522 is captured in Upper Parliament Street at Theatre Square on a 39 working to Wollaton Park. *EE/Beilby*

The Annual Report for the year ending 31 March 1947 recorded that nearly 14 million units of electricity were used at a cost of £53,000 with a fleet of 157 double-deck trolleybuses:

1947	Trolleybus	Motorbus
Total revenue expenses per vehicle mile	21.944d	19.886d
Total revenue expenses per 100 seat-mile	35.997d	36.754d

Six trolleybus motors had been rewound; 5¼ miles of trolley wire and 16 miles of span wire were renewed. Automatic sectionalising switches were fitted at the junction of Carrington Street with Station Street.

In mid-May 1947 the House of Commons Select Committee rejected the Corporation's Balloon Houses extension plan whereupon the N&D withdrew their petition against the Nottingham Corporation Bill and deleted all references to a similar extension from their own Bill. During the hearing, Alderman Plackett, Chairman of the Transport Committee since 1937, had said that *"a person living at Wollaton who wanted to get to Carlton would have to change at Mount Street under existing conditions, but if the Corporation were successful in their application people could go to Carlton without a change"*, indicating what would have been the likely service pattern. The remaining reference to trolleybuses in the Corporation's Bill, the Carlton proposals, was approved whilst the N&D Bill, containing only administrative and financial powers, was enacted in July 1947. Service number 49 was allocated to the foreseen Carlton, Manor

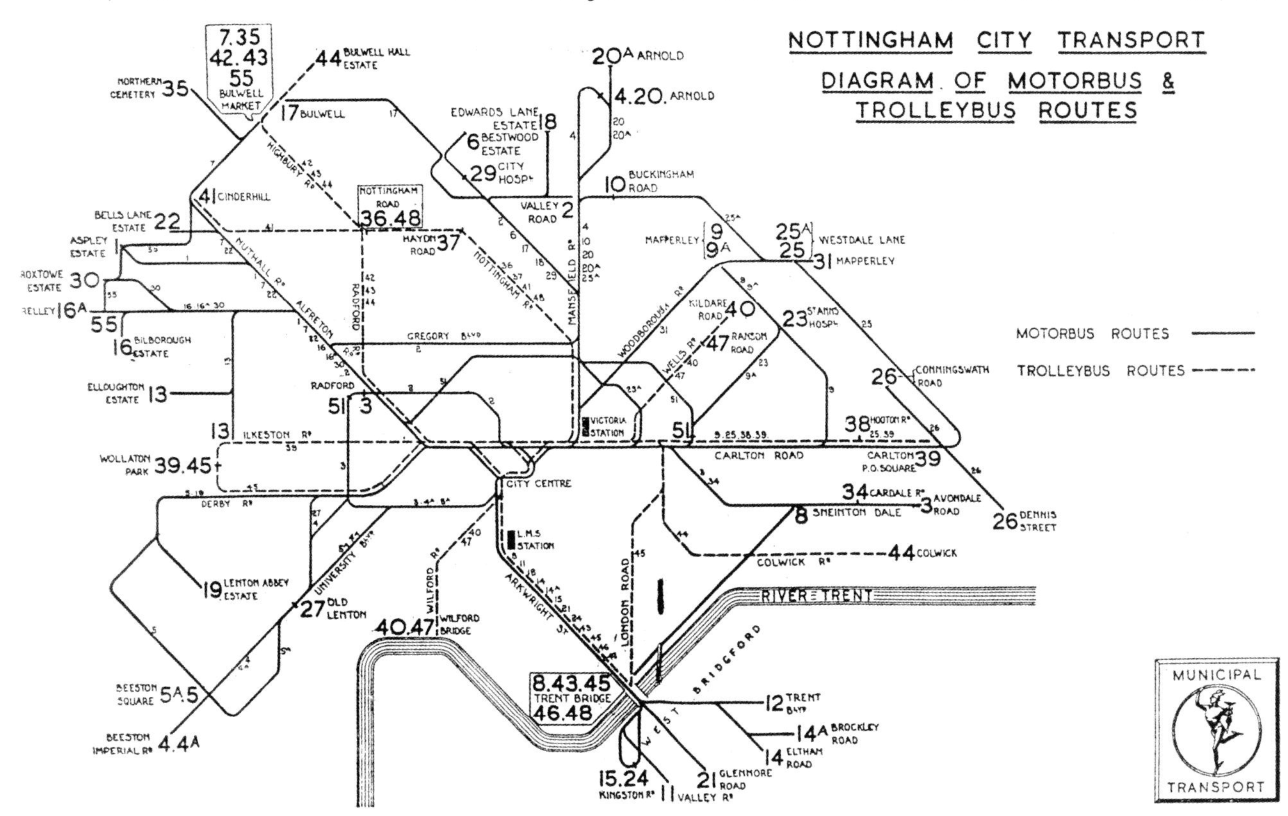

The diagrammatic map of trolleybus and motorbus routes published in July 1947 *NCT*

Karrier W/Roe 459 of 1945 at Processional Walk, Old Market Square prior to heading off south along Wheeler Gate towards Wilford Road. *NTA*

Road extension and certain trolleybuses, including all new deliveries, were fitted with appropriate indicator blinds but it was finally decided that these roads were unsuitable and the service never materialised. This was the final occasion that legislation for trolleybus extensions in and around Nottingham was presented.

On 29 May 1947 the RTC rejected an application by MGOC and N&D for powers to run a service between Mount Street and Strelley Village via Balloon Houses and Bilborough Road. This decision was based on the Corporation's arguments that there was currently no need for a service along Bilborough Road and that the Companies clearly had the Corporation's housing developments for the area in mind. These would be better served by an extension of the NCT services then running through Hollington Road and on Strelley Road. As far as the south side of Trowell Road was concerned, it was proposed to extend Wollaton Vale to Balloon Houses and to develop the back land. When Wollaton Vale was being made up the Corporation intended to apply for an extension of the route from Derby Road along Wollaton Vale to Balloon Houses, necessitating the construction of a new railway bridge (built later). The bus companies had also applied for powers to run from Mount Street, through Wollaton Village to Bramcote Lane End but these were also refused.

In late 1946 BTH automatic acceleration was fitted to Karrier W 476, which had been delivered in February 1946, and following a satisfactory trial, six more sets of equipment were ordered from BTH in December 1947 at a total cost of £336. The additional sets were fitted to 477 and 478 from the same allocation and four for the new Karriers on order (479-482). Subsequently 475 was fitted with Metropolitan Vickers automatic acceleration equipment.

In May 1947 the unused portion of the order with AEC and MCW placed in summer 1942 was formally cancelled, compensating orders having been placed in 1946 for thirteen BUT 9611Ts, some thirty AEC Regent III motorbuses, and bodywork for four Karrier Ws. On 18 July 1947 the Transport Committee approved tenders for:
65 3-axle BUT9641T chassis at £2,549 5s 3d each
40 Brush 70-seater double-deck trolleybus bodies 7ft 6ins wide at £3,108 each
25 Brush 70-seater double-deck trolleybus bodies 8ft wide at £3,108 each
Totalling £367,722 1s 3d, and

The City Council subsequently approved a loan sanction to cover this amount and 58 motorbuses, a grand total of almost £625,000.

Due to the long delivery period for steel traction poles:
100 Class "B" steel traction poles 31ft long at £25 5s 6d – £2,527 10s
50 Class "C" 31ft long at £31 13s each – £1,582 10s
were ordered from Stewarts and Lloyds Ltd.

On 12 October 1947 a more frequent service was introduced on the 40 and 47 daily. The Sunday morning service was improved from every 5 to 4 minutes, and the peak hour service was increased from 3 to every 2½ minutes. From 15 November 1947 the start of the evening peak on services 36, 37 and 48 was brought forward to 4 pm to coordinate better with a change to the N&D A1 timetable. There was a plea to reinstate post boxes on evening journeys to the city but nothing further was heard.

In an effort to negotiate higher payments per vehicle mile for N&D trolleybuses running in Nottingham, 6 months notice expiring on 31 March 1948 was given to terminate the agreement of June 1941.

The Golden Jubilee of the Council's acquisition of the horse tramways fell on 16 October 1947. Trolleybuses did not feature prominently in the celebration although Trent Bridge Works was opened to the public on 15-17 October 1947 and a new BUT 9611T chassis, together with a motorbus chassis and an 1899 horse tram loaned by Chesterfield Corporation, were on display. A Leicester horse bus operated along Castle Boulevard between Greyfriar Gate and Abbey Bridge at a premium fare of 1s, souvenir tickets being issued for the occasion, whilst a motorbus was repainted in a gold livery. A commemorative brochure was published and there was a luncheon at the Council House for the City Council, guests, and representatives of all sections of the Department.

Problems at North Wilford Power Station caused almost an hours' power cut on 21 October 1947 that affected all trolleybus services whilst a transformer breakdown there during the morning peak of 18 November 1947 also brought all trolleybuses to a standstill. Another breakdown at North Wilford on 6 January 1948 stopped all trolleybuses for up to 2 hours during the morning peak.

It was expected that just 17 trolleybus bodies would be delivered in 1948 starting in the middle of the year. In order to maintain services, major overhauls of the Brush bodies on twelve of the 1934 Karrier E6 (361, 373, 378, 380, 381, 383, 384) and 1934 Ransomes D6 (386, 388, 392, 394, 404) trolleybuses were carried out by Nudd Bros & Lockyer at their premises in a hanger at Castle Donington airfield just off the Diseworth to Kegworth road (beneath today's East Midlands Airport), at an estimated cost of £12,000, as Trent Bridge Works did not have sufficient capacity available. Eagle Engineering, presumably sub-contracted by Nudd Bros & Lockyer, carried out some of the overhauls. Interestingly, one of the partners in the firm, Sid Nudd, was son-in-law of Thomas H. Barton, founder of the local independent bus company. Work commenced in 1948, with eleven vehicles complete by early 1949.

The need to "export or die" led to export orders being given priority and in December 1947 it was learned that the 30 motorbuses and 17 trolleybuses on order would probably not be received on time and that, where chassis were available, it might be necessary to select an alternative bodybuilder. Alternative tenders for chassis and/or bodies were invited, subject to acceptance by the Transport Committee Chairman, to MoT agreement to the orders being transferred, and to the previously selected manufacturer(s) agreeing to the cancellation.

Shortly afterwards the MoT informed the undertaking that they could not sanction a loan of £624,897 to cover 123 additional vehicles due to the need to restrict production for the home market so that as many vehicles as possible could be exported. Subject to Treasury consent, they were prepared to grant an amount sufficient for all 65 trolleybuses but only 25 motorbuses as soon as definite delivery dates could be given. The "Nottingham Journal" published *"a salute to Nottingham City Transport trolleybus No 323 – 19 years old and still in service. Her's is an astonishing age for a public service vehicle, and but for the war and its aftermath, No 323, along with many other Nottingham buses and trolleybuses only slightly younger, would have gone into retirement years ago. The normal expectation of life of a trolleybus is 12 years"*.

Delivery of the four Metro-Cammell bodies for the Karrier W chassis was now expected at the end of 1948, whereas delivery of both chassis and bodies of the thirteen BUT 9611Ts had been rescheduled to spring 1949. In an effort to speed up delivery, a number of alternative body builders

In June 1947 it was decided to alter a number of the passenger barriers:
- Extend service 44 and 45 barrier in Lower Parliament Street on the LNER Bridge
- One double barrier at Canning Circus, outwards, in Alfreton Road, to be converted to twin double barriers.
- One double barrier in Bentinck Road to be converted to twin double barrier.
- Removal of the existing double barrier in Alfreton Road at Bentinck Road, inwards, and fixing new twin double barrier for services 43 and 44.

and construct additional new barriers:
- Single barrier in Long Row for services 40 and 47
- Single barrier at Processional Walk for services 40 and 47
- Single barrier in Lower Parliament Street at LNER Bridge for services 38-40 and 47
- Single barrier in Derby Road at Faraday Road, inwards

By October 1947 it was decided to erect a steel shelter at the trolleybus stop at the junction of Derby Road with Middleton Boulevard. There were a total of 35 shelters on the Department's network by January 1948 by which time the purchase of aluminium shelters had become easier and a further 35 shelters from Siddons at £4,878 10s 6d to include erection, glazing and painting by the Corporation were ordered.

Seen on the north side of Canning Circus in "as delivered" condition, 524, numerically the last 8ft wide BUT9641T/Brush, is heading for Carlton Post Office Square. *EE/Beilby*

were contacted and the entire order transferred to Charles H. Roe Ltd., Leeds, the Karrier Ws being delivered in July 1948 numbered 479-482, and the BUT 9611Ts following in October 1948 as 483-495.

The lightweight English Electric traction motors built under wartime conditions and allocated to the undertaking for the 1944 Karrier W trolleybuses 452-458 proved unsatisfactory. Although EE were prepared to repair the motors free of charge, the General Manager preferred to replace them with English Electric Type 410 motors at a total cost of £2,300 and they were fitted at Trent Bridge Works during 1948.

As the shortage of traffic employee continued, pay in lieu of holidays was offered to those volunteering to work their holidays.

Complaints were received from passengers left behind by the last buses on certain routes and an investigation was made to see if the demand warranted later journeys. From May 1948 eight standing passengers were again permitted on trolleybuses at peak hours and after 10.30 pm. A suggestion to the City Council that the time recording clock in Processional Walk, Old Market Square be removed to avoid delaying Wilford Road trolleybuses was refused.

In June 1947 wiring at the junction of Bath Street and King Edward Street was reconstructed around a traffic island whilst during the financial year 108 traction poles were replaced, and 15¼ miles of trolley wire and 14 miles of span wire used throughout the system. Automatic sectionalising switches were fitted in Alfreton Road, near Canning Circus. The sale of 314, 316, 319, 321, which had been out of service for over 12 months, for £200, saw the fleet reduced to 153 trolleybuses but new Karrier Ws and BUT 9611Ts were being delivered.

Saturday traffic patterns changed due to the adoption of the 5-day working week in many industries; the morning peak diminished but there was a considerable increase in mid-morning,

The impressive Nottingham Co-op building at the west end of Upper Parliament Street provides the background to 494, a sparkling Roe bodied BUT9611T just 5 months old, as it pulls into Derby Road at the top of Chapel Bar in April 1949. *GHFA & JMB*

Having just reversed into Hooton Road, the driver of English Electric E11 323 reaches up in his cab to change the destination indicator display before heading back along Carlton Road into the city centre. The absence of headlamp masks suggest that this was towards or after the end of the war in Europe. *BTS*

The Annual Report for the year ending 31 March 1948 showed that working expenses had absorbed 98.84% of income, the highest percentage since the undertaking had been formed. There had been an increase in working expenses of £125,586 of which £92,581 was due to increased wages, salaries and allowances. It was estimated that the working expenses would increase by a further £85,000 during 1948 if the prevailing service frequencies continued. As trolleybus working expenses exceeded their income by £10,106 it was foreseen that future fare increases would be primarily on trolleybus routes, due to the lower fare levels then charged on those vehicles. The average fare per mile still remained at almost pre-war levels of ¾d per mile for trolleybus (1d motorbus) ordinary fares and 0.51d per mile for trolleybus (0.63d motorbus) workmen's fares.

	Trolleybus	Motorbus
Total revenue expenses per vehicle mile	24.086d	20.859d
Total revenue expenses per 100 seat mile	39.380d	38.409d

afternoon and evening traffic. Larger crowds were able to attend sports events and shows, and this accentuated traffic demands, which were increasingly difficult to meet due to continuing delays in the delivery of new vehicles and traffic employee shortages.

On 1 April 1948 the Electricity Act nationalising the power supply industry came into force. Nottingham Corporation Electricity Department became a sub-area within the East Midlands Electricity Board. Balfour Beatty's Midland Counties Electric Supply Co. Ltd. was dissolved, the share capital of its passenger transport subsidiaries, the Mansfield District Traction Co., MGOC and N&D, passed initially to the British Electricity Authority, then to a nominee company and subsequently in January 1949 to the British Transport Commission. On the British Electricity Authority's request, Balfour Beatty continued to provide the management for its former passenger transport investments until January 1949. In the meantime N&D took delivery of 15 new BUT9611T Weymann bodied trolleybuses, replacing the remaining vehicles from the AEC662T English Electric (306-315) and Guy single deckers (316) and 1933 half-cab AEC661T MCCW double deckers (317-331) batches.

It was calculated that by 1951 the Department would have 37 trolleybuses of 16 – 17 years of age requiring replacement, and as deliveries of new vehicles were now running at 3 years from placing the order, on 2 April 1948 the Transport Committee instructed the General Manager to invite tenders for these vehicles. On 30 July 1948 a tender for 37, 7ft 6ins wide, double deck BUT 9641T three-axle trolleybuses was

Ransomes D6 396 approaching on Wheeler Gate towards the end of its life. *NCT*

In the days before package holidays, the banks of the River Trent provided something of a playground for city dwellers. On 28 August 1948 Karrier Clough E6/Brush 301 stands with its trolley booms stowed on Victoria Embankment, Trent Bridge having arrived as a 46 from the Old Market Square. *Roy Marshall*

considered but no decision was taken pending evaluation of the alternative electrical equipment options. English Electric quoted £2,803 19s 6d per chassis, Metropolitan-Vickers £2,817 9s and Crompton Parkinson £2,802 2s 6d whilst Brush offered their bodywork at £3,018. Crossley Motors, starting trolleybus production again after the war, also tendered for both chassis and body, the manufacturer's plans showing conventional rear side windows in both saloons rather than the foreshortened and curvaceous style which typified Crossley post-war bodywork, but the BUT tender was accepted, despite not being the lowest, in the interest of standardisation with those 3-axle trolleybuses and AEC motorbuses (which employed some common parts) already on order.

In June 1948 Mr England presented his estimates as to the undertaking's financial results and deficits for the years ending on 31 March 1949, 31 March 1950 and 31 March 1951 to the Transport Committee. He recommended that the fares increases approved by the City Council on 29 July 1946, which had been recalled from the MoT and RTC in January 1947, now be proceeded with but the Transport Committee made no decision until 2 July 1948. The request for a minimum fare of 1½d on all services, intended to increase revenues by £66,000, was deleted, as a 33% increase would probably have been politically unacceptable.

BUT 9611T 493 was exhibited on the Roe Stand at the 1948 Commercial Motor Show, the first post-war show, held at Earl's Court, London. It was equipped with a number of special features including BTH automatic acceleration, fluorescent lighting supplied with AC current and a chrome windscreen surround (other vehicles in the batch having painted surrounds). "Modern Transport" of 2 October 1948 referred to a press demonstration of the BTH automatic acceleration equipment which had been on trial in a Nottingham Sunbeam (sic) trolleybus i.e. Karrier W 476 which had been built at the Sunbeam factory in Wolverhampton. The press had also been shown their new RP strip type traction resistance, enclosed in a virtually flood-proof casing, designed especially to prevent the ingress of snow and slush. Ben England was clearly preparing for further extreme winter weather!

Mrs Chapman ran a refreshment stall serving primarily trolleybus crews, at Bulwell Hall Estate terminus. As the stall no longer complied with health regulations she wanted to replace it with a brick structure and a 21-year building lease was taken; although this was surrendered in November 1949. Perhaps as a result of this decision, a small canteen, staffed by the employees' Social and Athletic Society, offering midday meals opened at Bulwell Depot.

On 19 September 1948 the timetable of trolleybus services 36 and 48 was again altered to coordinate with changes to N&D's service.

Trolleybus 483, a new BUT 9611T which had only been in service some 10 weeks, skidded in Carlton Road near to Manvers School in the morning peak of 8 December 1948 and collided with a traction pole. It was fully laden at the time, and thirty passengers and the driver, who was thrown from his cab, were injured, one passenger and the driver being detained in hospital. The driver suffered a fractured skull and was subsequently convicted of dangerous driving (excessive speed) and disqualified for one year. Shortly afterwards the Burrows Street stop on Carlton Road was discontinued and a new compulsory stop, intended to slow trolleybuses down, with recorder clock introduced at Alma Road (inwards) probably as a reaction to the accident. It was impossible to determine the extent of the chassis damage without removing the body. As the trolleybus was virtually new and due to the number of body repairs in hand at Trent Bridge Works, it was returned to its manufacturers for repair. The Department towed the damaged vehicle to Roe at Leeds where the body was removed from the chassis, this then being taken south to the AEC Works at Southall. Neither BUT or Roe were able quote for the repairs but based on their labour and material costs, they were estimated as £1,200 – £1,500. No 483 finally re-entered service on 1 August 1949.

A trolleybus ran into a stationary motorbus belonging to Makemson Brothers of Bulwell in Carlton Road in fog on 29 November 1948 causing considerable damage which cost the Department £320. The operational difficulties caused by thick fogs, liberally mixed with fumes and smoke from domestic fires and industry, are difficult to imagine in retrospect. It was

17 years old and still with 2 more years of service to go, Ransomes No 341 in September 1948 is about to pass under a frog into Nottingham Road after turning at Basford Station. The wiring would be removed in 1952. *GHFA & JMB*

occasionally necessary for the conductor to walk in front of the trolleybus as a guide to the driver. The next day a broken trolley wire held up morning peak trolleybus traffic for 30 minutes at the junction of Lower Parliament Street with George Street whilst on 7 December 1948 another breakage at Canning Circus which took almost 2 hours to repair disrupted trolleybus services with some journeys being turned at Theatre Square.

William Kirrage was offered £25 damages plus costs after a trolleybus knocked him down on a pedestrian crossing in Old Market Square on 4 December 1948. The annual report showed that trolleybuses were involved in 53% of the 2,241 accidents in which the Department's vehicles had been involved, varying from clothing damage to collisions. As a whole, the undertaking had been involved in 7 fatalities, 6 being pedestrians and 1 person involved in a collision. The average number of vehicle miles run by trolleybus per accident, excluding clothing damage and miscellaneous accidents, was 5,188 whilst motorbuses ran 9,904 miles per accident. The average number of passengers carried per accident on trolleybuses was 88,409 against 112,583 on motorbuses. These figures reflected the busier traffic conditions of the city streets in which most of the trolleybus routes operated compared to the suburban roads in which the majority of motorbus mileage was run, rather than any inherent increased danger of trolleybuses but commentators interpreted them differently!

The New Year 1949 began with the news that N&D had applied to the Licensing Authority to run a limited stop motorbus service between Ripley Market Place and Mount Street Bus Station. It was feared that the service could attract passengers from the N&D trolleybus route and thus reduce the payments made to the Corporation, and ultimately encourage the company to withdraw its trolleybus service. This would directly affect Corporation revenues and could mean that an alternative service would have to be introduced as far as the city boundary at Cinderhill. As the local authorities to be served by N&D's new service would undoubtedly support the company it was felt unrealistic to object purely on financial grounds.

Increasing congestion in Old Market Square led to a subcommittee recommending in January 1949 that *inter alia* N&D trolleybus services should be diverted via Huntingdon Street and Union Road (which at that time cut through from Huntingdon Street to Mansfield Road immediately north of Victoria Station, being the terminus of an infrequent MGOC service). It is understood that this would have been in the form of a loop whereby trolleybuses would travel inbound along Huntingdon Street and outbound along Mansfield Road, using Union Street as their terminus. Placing their terminus ½ a mile north of the Old Market Square would have put the company at a commercial disadvantage, whilst their infrequent service could hardly have been considered to contribute greatly to the congestion. It was also recommended that NCT trolleybus waiting times at King Street/Queen Street should be generally reduced. On this occasion the TGWU cooperated in a general review of running-time allowances and time spent at termini aimed at reducing the waiting time at Old Market Square. As far as motorbus services were concerned, possible palliatives were seen in the curtailment of all West Bridgford services to

On 18 July 1948 ex-Cleethorpes AEC 661T/Park Royal 438 on a service 48 working boards in the middle of the road at Victoria Embankment, Trent Bridge.
Roy Marshall

Ransomes D6/Brush 387 stands at Wilford Bridge terminus on 2 October 1948. *Roy Marshall*

By early 1949 the 1931 Ransomes D6 were getting run-down and weary. No 347, originally 47 (TV4485) pictured here at Kings Street prior to departure on a 37 to Haydn Road, was apparently still in wartime livery but for white edging to fulfill "black-out" restrictions as evidence by the title CITY TRANSPORT (with Nottingham deleted) and was officially withdrawn in February 1950. *GHFA & JMB*

the Walter Fountain, the diversion of services to Mount Street Bus Station and the construction of a new bus station at the rear of Carrington Street on Broad Marsh.

An earlier decision to convert the single barrier in Long Row into a double barrier rail, as passengers queuing for services 40 and 47 were being crowded off the pavement into the path of oncoming traffic by queues from services 4, 4A, 20 and 20A overlapping on to it, was deferred pending the outcome of the subcommittee's recommendations.

As the sole trolleybus recommendation, the General Manager proposed that southbound services 40 and 47 should once again be routed by way of George Street, Carlton Street, Victoria Street, Poultry, South Parade and Wheeler Gate, instead of via Upper Parliament Street, King Street, Long Row, and past the west end of Processional Walk. However this was rejected in April 1949 and he was asked to negotiate a move of the N&D's Queen Street trolleybus terminus to Union Road. The Chief Constable felt that Mr England's proposals with respect to motorbus services would perpetuate the principle of on-street termini although there was a long-term policy to open off-street bus stations, and that they should thus be considered only as temporary expedients.

By now the 700 hired Bell Punch "Ultimate" ticket machines were in use on trolleybus services run from Bulwell and Trent Bridge Depots and had proved most satisfactory. Each conductor or conductress was issued with a personal machine and as the number of platform employees had increased, a further 150 machines were hired at £4 pa less 10% discount. The TIM ticket machines that they replaced were progressively withdrawn during 1949, dismantled and scrapped but for the last thirty, dating from 1948, which were sold to Middlesbrough Corporation Transport.

On 11 February 1949 the de-wired trolley boom of a passing trolleybus injured a passenger on the upper deck of another trolleybus. He suffered severe concussion and remained in hospital for some time thus in July 1950 the Transport Committee awarded him £250 plus legal costs to settle the claim.

On 18 March 1949 the MoT granted the application for increased fares, bringing trolleybus fares up to the same level as those on motorbuses, and revised conditions for trolleybus services (originally submitted to the City Council on 14 June 1946) effective 3 April 1949 and estimated to bring in an additional £92,000 pa. Approval was given on the understanding that the transport undertaking's profits could not be used for local rate relief without the MoT's prior consent and that any surplus would be retained in a reserve fund for the benefit of the undertaking.

The Annual Report showed that for the first time in the undertaking's history, expenses had exceeded income and there was a deficit of £67,452. In the course of the year the wiring at the junction of Canal Street with London Road was modified to encompass a roundabout there, whilst improved headways were introduced on service 43 Monday-Friday and on the 44 at peak periods.

Probably due to the deteriorating condition of the pre-war vehicles, there were a series of accidents involving electrical equipment. On 2 May 1949 a broken trolley boom fell onto a passing car at the Walter Fountain, and on both 30 May and 15 June 1949 there were cable fires in the roofs of trolleybuses.

During an evening storm on 13 July 1949, trolleybus 398 travelling along London Road to the City was struck by lightning as the driver was pulling into the Station Street stop. Immediately, a fire broke out in the cab, momentarily blinding the driver, and despite his efforts to avoid an accident, the trolleybus mounted the pavement and collided with a traction pole. The vehicle was considerably damaged, whilst 7 passengers and the crew had to be taken to hospital although only one passenger was detained. On 20 August 1949 the driver of Leyland trolleybus 420 travelling along Radford Road, New Basford was distracted by a wasp in his cab. When he took one hand off the steering wheel to wave the wasp away the trolleybus mounted the pavement, hit a traction pole and ran into the wall of Shipstone's brewery. Thirty-two passengers were injured (28 needing hospital treatment), and a further 5 were more seriously hurt, being detained in hospital for several days.

A bill for £1,182 10s 3d, the amount outstanding for the 13 BUT 9611T chassis, was received from BUT in August 1949 resulting in a total purchase price of £59,075 18s 9d as against the £51,675 loan sanction. Similar increases were expected from the body builders, Roe.

Powers had been obtained in the Nottingham Corporation Act 1947 to extend the Carlton trolleybus route although these had not been implemented due to the inadequate power supply and in November 1949 Mr England recommended that the extension should not be constructed for the time being. The powers lapsed, unused, after 5 years.

The first BUT 9641T trolleybuses entered service on 1 December 1949, these being the first three-axle deliveries since the 1935 Leyland TTB3s and with their 70 seats the largest vehicles in the fleet at that time. The bodywork specifications had been prepared by Ian Mair, Assistant Engineer, and the design emanated from Brush Coachworks' Chief Designer, Freddy Raye, who had designed the MCW all metal bodies in the 1930s.

As the Divisional Road Engineer could not agree to the construction of a roundabout at the south end of Market Street while trolleybus services 40 and 47 loaded at the west end of Processional Walk and there was no practical alternative location, it was decided in February 1950 to revert these services to their original route along George Street, Carlton Street, Victoria Street and South Parade on journeys to Wilford

The Annual Report for the year ending 31 March 1949 noted that many vehicles were operating beyond their normal replacement period: 104 trolleybuses, two thirds of the fleet, were 10 or more years old and 69 were 15 or more years old. The motorbus fleet was in a comparable state. This high age profile led to increased maintenance whilst some spare parts and materials were increasingly difficult to obtain.

The trolleybus fleet was made up of:

Built	Type	Fleet Nos.	No. of vehicles
1931	Karrier E6	325-34, 336	11
1930	Karrier E6	350	1
1933	Karrier E6	301	1
1934	Karrier E6	351-85	35
1934	Ransomes D6	386-406	21
1935	Leyland TTB3	407-436	30
1937	AEC661T	437	1
1938	AEC661T	438-440	3
1938	Daimler CTM4	441	1
1942	Sunbeam MF2	447-51	5
1943	Karrier W	442-43	2
1944	Karrier W	444-45	2
1944	Karrier W	452-58	7
1945	Karrier W	459-68	10
1946	Karrier W	469-78	10
1948	Karrier W	479-82	4
1948	BUT9611T	483-95	13
Total			157

There were 3 tower wagons, 1 reel wagon and 1 breakdown wagon in the auxiliary fleet (plus 3 vans, 2 lorries and 3 mobile canteens).

Care-worn 1934 Ransomes D6/Brush 348 on service 41 and sister vehicle 349 on service 37 are seen waiting at King Street terminus on 21 May 1949. Both trolleybuses were withdrawn at the end of February 1950. *Roy Marshall*

The Trent Bridge and Wilford Bridge services separated at the south end of Lister Gate where until 1958 the Walter Fountain monument was situated in the apex of the junction between Carrington Street and Greyfriar Gate. Much of this area now lies beneath the Broad Marsh Shopping Centre although the row of buildings behind Leyland TTB3 428, heading down Carrington Street to Trent Bridge in June 1949, and the Marks & Spencers building in the distance on the corner of Low Pavement remain intact. *GHFA & JMB*

Daimler CTM 4/Weymann 441 at the Kings Street terminus of the Nottingham Road services in June 1949. *GHFA & JMB*

Eight foot wide BUT9641T 524 turning on full right lock at Cavendish Road, Carlton.
Martin Eady

BUT9611T/Roe 494 is seen at the Processional Walk, Old Market Square stop when comparatively new. Unusually for a company photograph, the vehicle is in shown everyday service.
EE/Beilby

Looking down Chapel Bar before it widening towards the Old Market Square with Karrier W/Brush 466 taking on passengers.
NCT

The new and old, posed together in 1949. BUT 9641T 500 and Karrier E6 336, which despite an extra 6 inches of width and eighteen years of age, show subtleties of body styling rather than fundamental differences in design. *NCT*

The upper saloon of 7ft 6ins wide B.U.T. 9641T trolleybus 599. "Upstairs" was the preserve of smokers and white painted ceilings became discoloured nicotine-brown extremely quickly! This view also illustrates the practice of usually removing the interior lamp shades upon overhaul (599 had one of the last trolleybus overhauls and repaints in August 1963). In this instance the actual fittings (metal "square shapes" around the light bulbs) have not been removed but merely painted over. *Neil Lewin*

Bridge thereby reducing trolleybus traffic on Parliament Street, Kings Street, Long Row and New Street (Processional Walk) by 24 vehicles an hour during peaks. This was not introduced until 1953 and, as an interim measure traffic lights rather than a roundabout were installed at the junction of Parliament Street with Milton Street to replace a point duty policeman. They are still there in 2005!

All the 8ft wide BUT 9641T trolleybuses (500-524) but for 523, which was damaged prior to delivery and only arrived in early May 1950, had arrived by the third week of March 1950. They were housed at Parliament Street Depot for use on the Carlton – Wollaton Park services, replacing the remaining 1931 vehicles. In September 1950 the MoT replaced the national 7ft 6ins width restriction for passenger-carrying vehicles with one of 8ft. It proved possible to amend the prevailing motorbus order to this new maximum dimension but work on the body fittings and frame parts for the remaining BUT 9641T trolleybuses (525-601) was too advanced for this to be altered. The first two batches of 7ft 6ins wide vehicles (525-534 and 535–549) were delivered by early December 1950 and allocated to Bulwell. Until the Trent Bridge, Victoria Embankment turning circle, terminus of service 43, had been widened, they were used solely on service 44, and to ease the shortage of new vehicles, some of the utility and post-war two-axle trolleybuses were allocated to Bulwell and Trent Bridge Depots.

By March 1950 there was a shortage of 104 drivers and 70 conductors. The Ministry of Labour and National Service informed the Department that there were suitable applicants on Tyneside and in Northern Ireland, regions suffering unemployment due to cuts in the ship building industry. Applications were already being received from throughout the country, but as applicants were not prepared to pay their own expenses to travel to Nottingham interviews had proved impossible. A £150 budget was set aside to cover applicant's expenses and a series of interviews were scheduled in Newcastle upon Tyne with applicants' local travelling expenses paid by the Department. Even motorbus and trolleybus driver's tests were carried out in Northern Ireland by a Belfast Corporation Transport examiner requiring Nottingham to take out a separate insurance policy as Belfast carried its own risk in the testing of potential drivers. The necessary medical examinations were delegated to a local doctor. Unfortunately the initiative was not a success not least due to the lack of suitable housing in Nottingham. By September 1950 the short fall had reached 200 although this improved slightly to 179 by the end of the year. It was hoped that increased wages would help to retain staff but this had little effect, the deficiency having reached 300 by July 1951 by which time the local armaments industry was expanding due to the outbreak of war in Korea.

The shortage of cleaners led to complaints about vehicle cleanliness although Mr England considered that the fleet's appearance was well above the average of that in the area. It was probably at this stage that Bulwell Depot began to gain its unenviable reputation as turning out the scruffiest looking trolleybuses in the fleet.

Having considered tenders for the advertising contract from J.W.Courtenay, Griffiths & Millington, Frank Mason, W.H. Smith, and Henry Squire it was decided to accept that of Courtenay for a period of 5 years from 1 July 1950.

Today's traffic along Middleton Boulevard would make it almost impossible for a man and a dog to saunter across the road but this is the late summer of 1950. Brand new 7ft 6ins wide BUT 9641T/Brush 535 waits for departure time at the Scalford Drive terminus of service 45. Please observe the semaphore arm illuminated traffic indicator fitted on the side pillar immediately to the rear of the driver's offside sliding cab door. *BTS*

"The old gives way for the new"! On 9 July1950 brand new BUT9641T/ Brush 549, exemplifying Livery 8, and 1934 Ransomes D6/Brush 392 are seen at Bulwell Hall Estate turning circle. It will be noted that 549 has metal panelling over the indicator box above the open rear platform: it was delivered in this form in June 1950 and a conventional indicator brought into use in February 1951). *Roy Marshall*

The City Treasurer recommended application for a reduced rate assessment on the trolleybus system on 14 April 1950. Under normal circumstances a revaluation would not take place for another 2 years but a formal proposal for a change to the Valuation List could bring this forward. Only after some 21 months of negotiations did the Inland Revenue offer to reduce the trolleybus rating assessment, from £26,329 to £18,496. The City Treasurer encouraged the Transport Committee to accept this immediately in order that the amended rateable value would be entered into the Valuation List before 31 March 1952 thus ensuring a reduction for the previous and the current financial year.

The Annual Report for the year ending 31 March 1950 recorded that 24 trolleybuses had been delivered, 12 sold and 15 were unlicensed awaiting sale, resulting in active fleet of 154 vehicles. A new rectifier station and feeder pillars had been built at Chesterfield Street, Carlton Road; the overhead line at the Middleton Boulevard/Western Boulevard roundabouts had been restrung; and work to amend the wiring at the junction of Canal Street with London Road was in progress following the enlargement of the traffic roundabout. Similarly work was in progress to amend the overhead layout at the junction of Valley Road with Nottingham Road where the roundabout was also being enlarged.

Some four months after the public enquiry, approval was given (by the MoT as far as the trolleybuses were concerned) for the 4th fare increase since 1939, effective from 4 June 1950. The inquiry into the next increase was still pending but the recent rise in the cost of fuel oil meant that even if this application was approved and effective from 1 October 1950 there would still be a deficit of over £30,000 at the end of the financial year. This figure was around the level of the remaining reserves and any higher deficit would have to be met from the rates. It must be stressed that these figures related to the Department as a whole, additional fuel taxes in the 1950 budget adding an estimated £ 42,145 to the motorbus operating costs.

It was evident that the approval process between the Council deciding to increase fares and them becoming effective had to be expedited. On 2 June 1950 the Transport Committee resolved that a deputation should meet the MoT in London, the Town Clerk should lobby local MPs and the General Manager should prepare a proposal for further fare increases. The MoT was not impressed and rejected the idea of a meeting although they stated that the public inquiry into the pending increase would be held on 5 July 1950. The Town Clerk suggested a personal discussion with the Minister, which he felt could be arranged through Alderman Wigman, however the Minister of Transport replied that no useful purpose could be served by a personal meeting and that the bureaucratic process required time. It was decided to ask the City's MPs to table a parliamentary question and a local MP, Ian Winterbottom, criticised the MoT's tardy review of applications for increased fares in the House of Commons on 23 July 1951. The MoT responded that, with respect to trolleybus fares, "any Local Authority could promote its own Private Bill seeking authority to raise its fares to the maximum that Parliament sanctioned". Such statutory provision had been made in local Acts prior to the war but the maximum fares referred

Karrier W/Roe 464 takes a breather in Parliament Street Depot. *Fred York*

Despite the missing number plates, the faded fleet number transfers enable this withdrawn Leyland TTB3 standing forlorn at the east end of Stanhope Street to be identified as 421 (ATV184) withdrawn in April 1951 and sold one month later. It has OK chalked on the front panel. *GHFA & JMB*

to therein had by now been partially exceeded. It was therefore decided to include a provision for trolleybus fares in the Parliamentary Bill, which the Corporation planned to promote in November 1951.

On 27 July 1950 the Transport Committee approved a further proposal for increased fares, the 6th since 1939 but referring only to Workmen's return fares and Children's fares, intended to increase revenue by £116,000 pa, the absolute minimum to allow for contingences.

The MoT approved the 5th post-1939 increase and the new fares came into force on 1 October 1950, traffic receipts in the first 4 weeks rising by 4.5% compared to the same period in 1949 or £179,296 pa. During the approval process, specifically on 29 May 1950, petrol rationing had come to an end and although this did not immediately provoke a boom in private motoring it was the catalyst for reduced public transport patronage. In the period June-September 1950 traffic revenue fell by an estimated £17,000 pa. The MoT enquiry into the 6th fares increase was held on 26 February 1951; these increases were also approved and they were introduced on 27 May 1951.

The narrow roadway at the Trent Bridge, Victoria Embankment northern turning circle had led to trolleybuses mounting the pavement over the years whilst the new BUT 9641Ts based at Bulwell Depot were not permitted to operate on service 43 for this reason. The City Engineers Department widened the roadway at this point by 4ft at a cost of £80. At this time this turning circle was used by all services terminating at Trent Bridge but for the 45 (which turned at the Globe Cinema) and football specials (which used the southern, Bunbury Street turning circle). Also during 1950 the overhead wiring at the junction of Greyfriar Gate with Carrington Street was modified to accommodate a new traffic roundabout at that point.

By October 1950 the 46 had been reduced from a daily service to operate only on Sundays (all day) with infrequent late evening journeys Monday – Saturday. The nature of the 46 however meant that it could have continued to operate as un-timetabled extras on cricket or football match days, and bank holidays (the Trent Bridge area was a popular destination for citizens seeking outdoor relaxation) at other times.

Initial discussions as how best to serve the proposed giant Clifton housing estate beyond the city's boundaries south of the River Trent, and seek agreement with the existing operators (WBUDC and the South Notts Bus Co. Ltd., Gotham) took place in September 1950. It was already clear that the services would be motorbus operated primarily due to a railway bridge (removed in September 1974) with 13 ft 6 ins clearance in Wilford Lane which limited motor buses to the low bridge type, and there was never any mention of a trolleybus route extension.

The financial year ending 31 March 1951 showed a departmental loss of £26,782. A request for free off-peak travel for old age pensioners was refused. Losses reached £2,000 per week in April 1951 but a campaign to prevent fare evasion, the revision of children's and workmen's fares together with a few alterations to single fares helped to arrest the decline.

The slate roof and roof glazing at Trent Bridge Works above the fitters, blacksmiths, electricians, welding, turning shops and the stores was repaired in June 1951. It was decided to replace the Department's two Dennis tower wagons by fitting new inspection platforms to two withdrawn motorbus chassis. The cost was reduced to an estimated £1,310 for both vehicles and £990 for labour by carrying out the conversion at Trent Bridge Works however only one conversion was made, by shortening the chassis of 1939 AEC Regent 31 (FTO614) which had been involved in an accident and withdrawn in 1950. It received fleet number 801.

Contributions to the city's central administrative expenses for the financial year ending 31 March 1951 were estimated as £23,000, an unacceptable amount when the undertaking was trading at a loss and which would have to be met from reserves. The withdrawal of loss making services was considered but decided against as such a move would have had to be on a widespread scale to provide any benefit and would attract complaints from the travelling public. The recent fare increases had brought fares to a figure of 45.62% above pre-war levels whilst working expenses per mile during 1950/51 were 95% higher than during 1938/39, and the cost of new vehicle approximately 2¼ times above pre-war figures.

The General Manager felt that fares had to be put on a 1951 basis and reluctantly started to prepare another proposal for increased fares, the 7th since 1939, as the last increase was producing £38,203 pa less than originally calculated. On 13 July 1951 he proposed to:

1. Abolish 2½d and 3½d fare stages, and single fares of 4½d and above to be increased by ½d (estimated additional income £62,253)
2. Introduce a 2d minimum ordinary fare (estimated additional income £21,690)
3. Introduce 1d intervals on children's fares in accordance with the following scale:
4. Introduce the following scale of early morning return fares *in lieu* of the prevailing workmen's return fares:

The package was expected to increase annual revenue by £135,277. The General Manager asked that the City Council be requested for an approval in principle with authorisation for the Transport Committee to implement it wholly or in part. The Transport Committee however felt that further operating economies should be considered first and that any increases should be as small as possible. Verging on a vote of no confidence in Ben England, they decided that the undertaking's affairs should be fully investigated by the Committee and refused to submit the package to the City Council. Mr England added that until now there had been a slight chance that a 1951/52 deficit might be avoided however a further pay award, made effective 22 July 1951 and estimated to cost the undertaking an additional £54,600 pa, now made this impossible.

Even if his proposals were to come into effect, bringing in an estimated £33,800 additional revenue during the 1951/52 financial year, it would be insufficient to meet the additional expenses of the pay award and a pending national increase for craftsmen, whilst costs were still rising.

Perhaps due to his treatment by the Transport Committee, Ben England was taken ill on 8 August 1951. It was learned that he required 6 weeks rest and that when he returned to work (it proved to be November 1951) he would need a quieter office (the General Manager's office being located on the ground floor adjacent to the main entrance at that time). Despite his absence, the Committee decided to proceed with the investigation using an independent consultant. They preferred Mr R.W. Birch, Executive Officer of BET and Chairman of Potteries Motor Traction Co. Ltd. but he was unable to spare the time and commented that it was unlikely that any other General Manager would have time available. He suggested a recently retired official and in December 1951, Mr W.G. Marks, General Manager at Nottingham in the early 1930s, who had retired at Liverpool some 12 months earlier, visited Nottingham to discuss the subject. He stated that most municipal transport undertakings were experiencing exactly the same difficulties and that Nottingham was run on economic lines. In his opinion the City Treasurer, with his intimate knowledge of the undertaking, was the most suitable person to conduct any investigation. However the treasurer saw no need whatsoever, as, in his opinion, increased revenue was the only way out of the undertaking's financial difficulties. The Transport Committee decided to place an examination of the undertaking in abeyance.

By now the undertaking was almost 300 traffic employees short of establishment and saturation point had been reached with respect to employees working overtime and rest days. Over 1,000 miles were being lost each week but this was so arranged that odd journeys were lost on all services rather than any particular service being curtailed.

On 7 September 1951, the proposed new maximum fares on trolleybuses for inclusion in the Parliamentary Bill were approved by the Transport Committee. Ordinary fares would be 2d (instead of 1d) per stage of half-mile, subject to the maximum fare for two or more stages or any part thereof being at the rate of 2d (instead of 1½d) per mile. Workmen's fares would be at a rate not exceeding 1½d (instead of ½d) per mile or fraction of a mile with the right to charge a minimum fare of 2d (instead of 1d).

Prior to his illness, Mr England had suggested an attempt to extend the loan sanction repayment periods for trolleybuses from 10 to 12 years and for motorbuses from 8 to 10 years, saving £20,000 in the prevailing financial year. The MoT indicated that an application would be approved subject to the undertaking having appropriate maintenance facilities however no action was taken.

The Deputy General Manager suggested on 21 September 1951 that the termini of services 39 and 45 on Middleton Boulevard be amended as follows:

39 – trolleybuses to be cut back from Fairham Drive to Orston Drive, at the north end of Middleton Boulevard, economising 0.53 miles per journey or 53,000 miles a year.

45 – trolleybuses to be extended from Scalford Drive to a new turning circle at Hawton Crescent, increasing each journey by 0.42 miles per journey or 20,400 miles a year.

This would save 32,600 miles or £3,568 pa and a trolleybus crew valued at £886 pa. Minimal changes to the overhead wiring, using the same traction poles and equipment would cost £253, however the Transport Committee resolved to rearrange just the 39 to run to Orston Drive instead of Fairham Drive thereby achieving even greater economies.

A meeting on site with the MoT Divisional Road Engineer, the Chief Constable, the City Engineer and the General Manager took place in

A busy scene at The Poultry, led by Leyland TTB4 413 which was to be withdrawn in November 1951.
NCT

December 1951. The City Engineer suggested that both services should terminate at Wollaton Hall Drive offering no economies but additional expenditure of £2,902 pa. The Chief Constable supported this proposal from a road safety perspective but as a compromise he would agree to a turning point at Sutton Passeys Crescent (Wollaton Road end) provided vehicles stood in the lay-by. The Divisional Road Engineer did not support this proposal, and asked the Transport Committee to consider the turning points being in Wollaton Hall Drive. As a result no change took place until 1959.

The Assistant Engineer, Mr Ian H. Mair, an electrical engineer by profession, resigned effective 30 September 1951 to become Chief Engineer at Newcastle upon Tyne, another major trolleybus operator. He was replaced by Mr Donald Machin, Rolling Stock Supervisor.

Metropolitan-Vickers had experimentally fitted DC fluorescent lighting to trolleybus 476 in 1947 at a cost of £182 12s 8d whilst a set of DC fluorescent lighting, costing £585 10s 6d, was installed in 493 upon delivery in 1948. The two sets had given satisfactory service although the fluorescent tubes soon suffered from the power interruptions caused by the trolleybus passing beneath any break in the traction current supply, leaving them flickering or simply "fused". There was no interest in equipping the whole fleet, on the other hand rather than convert the two vehicles back to tungsten lighting it was felt worthwhile to retain the equipment if Metropolitan Vickers reduced their asking price of £537 12s 8d. In November 1951 their reduced offer of £300 was accepted.

As the first of a range of minor economies, MoT approval of the overhead wiring alterations needed to cut back the northern terminus of services 36 and 48 from the junction of Nottingham Road with Vernon Road to the junction of Nottingham Road with Valley Road, reducing operating costs by £721 pa, was sought. Approval was received on 6 February 1952 and the terminus changed on 16 March 1952. The removal of this short section of overhead wiring meant that an alternative route to and from the city centre along Nottingham Road and Mansfield Road was no longer available for trolleybuses on the trunk Bulwell services. It is interesting to note that this first case of overhead equipment removal in Nottingham involved a portion of the initial railless route whilst the remainder survived to become the final trolleybus route in the city!

The City Council suggested that every second trolleybus on service 44 should operate to Trent Bridge instead of Colwick alternating with journeys on the 43. Scheduling difficulties due to the differing running times and congestion at the busy Processional Walk stop meant that this could not be proceeded with.

It proved impossible to reach agreement with the TGWU on reduced time allowances and frequencies for services 43, 44 and 46 on Sundays. The TGWU stated that they could only accept a reduced winter service if the time allowances remained unchanged. By December 1951 the union had approved the proposed Sunday trolleybus running times except those for Trent Bridge and Bulwell Depots, namely services 43-46. By January 1952 the traffic employees had agreed that the proposed Sunday running times on services 43, 44 and 46 were adequate but their representatives refused to accept them. Reduced timings had already been accepted on weekdays and the TGWU felt that traffic employees were thus entitled to easier conditions on Sundays. The Transport Committee sought the utmost economies and the proposed schedules were calculated as saving £766 pa.

The General Manager stressed that the basis of economic operation was a minimum number of vehicles and minimum number of crews. Although he conceded that frequencies and running times for the reduced winter services was purely a managerial matter, the TGWU District Secretary felt that it was unreasonable to ask the employees to accept reduced Sunday running times on services 43, 44 and 46 in addition to a 50% reduction in headway, bearing in mind that these services operated on the undertaking's busiest routes. Delays at Wheeler Gate, Canal Street and Lister Gate traffic signals, and the introduction of "zebra" pedestrian crossings, all made time keeping difficult. He did not consider the standing times excessive in view of the time needed to unload, turn and load the vehicles, and even the prevailing schedules were difficult to maintain. It was finally decided to introduce reduced frequencies but to leave the running times as they were until the consequences were known.

Complaints about irregular running were soon received but these were difficult to avoid on services that operated every 2 minutes and at times every minute. The least delay, accentuated by "zebra" crossings, caused bunching of vehicles. Complaints were also received about long delays at Hyson Green and vehicles arriving full although some of these problems could have been alleviated by use of the short working facilities at Eland Street (outbound) and Peveril Street (inbound).

By now it was estimated that the operating loss for the 1951/52 financial year would be ca. £35,000 and on the same basis that for 1952/53 would be ca. £80,000, based on prevailing costs, but as these were still rising Mr England

Leyland TTB3 411 (ATV174) waits at Processional Walk loading point at the west end of Old Market Square before heading south down Wheeler Gate to Trent Bridge on a service 43 journey. Prominent at the rear in this post-war view is the Griffin and Spalding's department store, still extant as part of the Debenhams Group.
BTS

Shortly after delivery on 1 June 1950, number 549, the first 7ft 6ins wide BUT9641T/Brush bodied trolleybus to reach Nottingham, is posed at the Processional Walk stance, Old Market Square (the loading point for Trent Bridge services) with the Council House in the background. ***EE/Beilby***

recommended a 7th post-1939 fares increase. He proposed the scheme already presented on 3 July 1951, but in January 1952 the Transport Committee again chose to defer a decision.

The police requested that trolleybus parking at Bulwell Market Place should cease to permit construction of a pedestrian refuge and "Keep Left" bollards, to guide traffic around the central island, where Highbury Road entered the Market Place. There were often a number of trolleybuses standing on the Bulwell Market Station railway bridge in Highbury Road, commonly known as Highbury Vale, approaching Bulwell Market where a passing loop in the overhead wiring was provided, and it was suggested that these be moved elsewhere or the number of vehicles standing at the terminus much reduced. One proposal was to move the Bulwell Market terminus ⅜ths of a mile north along Hucknall Lane to a point near the Adelphi Cinema just north of Carey Road. The roadway widened out at this point with a small traffic island already used as the terminal turning circle for motorbus service 17. As it was calculated that the extension of services would entail the operation of 88,499 additional miles annually requiring 4 further crews and 2 more vehicles at a total cost of £7,500 per year together with a new turning circle costing £1,040, it was decided in May 1952 not to follow-up this suggestion although Bulwell's busy Main Street north of the Market Place could potentially have provided compensatory additional revenue.

In early December 1951 it was heard that N&D were promoting a Parliamentary Bill to abandon their trolleybus network and the Corporation, fearing reduced revenues, lodged an objection. The background to this move could be found in the spate of post-war nationalisation whereby Balfour Beatty's electricity supply and passenger transport interests in the Nottinghamshire and Derbyshire coalfields had passed into state control on 1 April 1948. Overnight the commercial benefits from having the interurban trolleybuses as a base load had disappeared. Although they had a modern trolleybus fleet, N&D's overhead equipment needed renewal whilst there were no longer any opportunities for inventive accounting practices with respect to the traction power supply. In addition, the N&D trolleybuses were very much non-standard in the Tilling Group, to which all the Balfour Beatty bus companies had been transferred after electricity nationalisation, the only other electrically-powered activities being at Brighton (where Brighton Hove & District had a commercial arrangement with Brighton Corporation) and Llanelly (another former Balfour Beatty transport undertaking associated to a power supply company operated by the South Wales Electricity Board until sold to South Wales Transport in 1952). In April 1952 the Corporation's Petition against the N&D Trolleybus Abandonment Bill failed before the Select Committee of the House of Lords, and on 1 August 1952 the Nottingham and Derbyshire Traction Bill received the Royal Assent.

N&D were permitted to discontinue trolley vehicle services on any of their routes once they were licensed to provide an alternative service of motorbuses operated by themselves, by other companies within the MGOC group or jointly with other companies within the group. Once a trolley vehicle route was discontinued all overhead equipment had to be removed within two years and all other redundant equipment, upon application to the MoT, within seven years. The above provisos did not apply to those portions of N&D's services within the city boundary for which the Corporation received no financial compensation.

Although up to eight standing passengers could be carried at all times, the TGWU argued that as their employees were being asked to work reduced Sunday services the number of standing passengers on Sunday trolleybuses should be reduced to five. This was accepted and introduced effective Sunday 3 February 1952, except in cases of undue hardship.

The "Nottingham Catenary Suspension System" of overhead wiring and the fading white paint around the base of the telegraph poles exemplify the immediate post-war era. Karrier W/Brush 468, numerically the last utility bodied trolleybus delivered in August 1945, is seen on Carlton Hill opposite Hooton Road on a 39 working to Wollaton Park on 6 July 1948. *Roy Marshall*

Although displaying fleet number 563 and registration number KTV563 this was in fact BUT9641T 565 (KTV565). The error was corrected after the vehicle was displayed on the Brush stand (stand 89) at the 1950 Commercial Vehicle Show at Earls Court, London. The trolleybus is seen here outside the AEC works at Southall, Middlesex. *Peter Badgery*

Seen in its "as delivered" condition, 524, numerically the last 8ft wide BUT9641T/Brush, joins Derby Road at Canning Circus heading for Carlton Post Office Square. *Alstrom/EE*

BUT9641T 539 stands in Stanhope Street immediately opposite the entrance to Parliament Street Depot. *Fred York*

Originally a Bulwell Depot based vehicle, Karrier W/Weymann 444 waits in Stanhope Street outside its second home, Parliament Street Depot, on the Trolleybus Society and DLROS tour of 15 April 1956. *Fred York*

Apparently on an enthusiasts' tour, probably that arranged by the Trolleybus Society and the DLROS on 15 April 1956, 7ft 6ins wide BUT9641T/Brush 587 stands in Hucknall Lane at the northern, Bulwell Hall Estate, terminus of service 44. *Fred York*

Chapter 7 The New Elizabethan Age 1952-60

As Nottingham City Transport department entered the so-called 'New Elizabethan' age, large operating losses was weighing heavily on its management. At the 11 February 1952 Transport Committee Meeting a vote on the General Manager's recommendations for a seventh post-1939 fares increase was not carried. The meeting studied a list of possible economies of little direct relevance to trolleybuses, approving the introduction of shift working for engineering employees at Parliament Street to reduce overtime and better budgetary controls. It was decided to investigate fortnightly payment of wages and the introduction of two-way radios on the overhead tower wagons. The unions objected to wages being paid fortnightly and together with proposals to abolish daily ticket controls and vehicle cleaning on alternate days, these proposals were rejected.

The introduction of two-way radio control was expected to reduce maintenance and emergency requirements by an overhead crew of 3 men representing an annual saving of £917 13s 4d. The redundant personnel could be absorbed into other positions within the Department. Pye Telecommunications Ltd. quoted £608 2s 6d for the equipment and installation, to which had to be added the licence fee of £20, GPO line rental £18, and maintenance contract £69 6s 8d. The proposal was approved on 10 March 1952 however it soon proved impractical, using a transmitter mast on the roof of the Head Office, to get good radio reception throughout the trolleybus system. As the City and County Ambulance services already shared a mast at Mapperley, the General Manager sought and received the approval of the Health Committee to place the Transport Department's aerial on this same mast and to share the mast, buildings and related costs equally between the three parties.

Two roundabouts came into operation on 11 February 1952 at the junctions of Gregory Boulevard with Mansfield Road and with Sherwood Rise, whilst the layout of Eland Street turning circle in Basford was enlarged to accommodate larger trolleybuses.

The introduction of a reduced trolleybus Sunday winter timetable marked the start of the undertaking's economy drive. This took place in two stages: on Sunday 3 February 1952 for all services except 43-46, and on Sunday 24 February 1952 for services 43-46. Henceforth until the end of trolleybus operations, winter services operated each year from the second Sunday in October until the summer timetable commenced on the second Sunday in April. On 16 March 1952 trolleybus services 36 and 48 were curtailed at their northern end to turn at the junction of Nottingham Road and Valley Road near the Futurist Cinema rather than at the junction with Vernon Road. The short section of Nottingham Road between the two junctions was left unserved by trolleybuses and the overhead equipment dismantled:

A surrealistic view of Canning Circus in snow. *Neil Lewin*

36 Old Market Square (Queen Street/King Street) – Upper Parliament Street – Milton Street – Victoria Station – Mansfield Road – Nottingham Road (Valley Road)

48 Trent Bridge – Arkwright Street – Carrington Street – Old Market Square – Upper Parliament Street – Milton Street – Victoria Station – Mansfield Road – Nottingham Road (Valley Road) *(southbound via King Street, northbound via Queen Street)*

The refund of two year's rates reduced the undertaking's deficit for the financial year ending 31 March 1952 to £21,024 but the anticipated loss of £79,870 for the year ending 31 March 1953 had now risen due to fuel tax increases (£31,650), higher National Insurance contributions (£3,609) and a wage award to craftsmen (£1,952) to an estimated £117,081. Allowing for reduced rates on the trolleybus system and loan charges this resulted in a loss of £102,137. Despite this the General Manager and the City Treasurer were unable to motivate the Transport Committee to seek a further fares increase.

The Select Committee of the House of Lords approved the clause in the Nottingham Corporation Bill Section 35, before parliament, relating to the provision by the Corporation,

The northern terminus of service 40 in The Wells Road at Kildare Road. Two BUT9611T/Roe trolleybuses led by 487 take their layover. *Photobus*

Nottingham's first Karrier W, Weymann bodied 442 delivered in December 1943, stands at Wilford Bridge terminus prior to the construction of a roundabout here in 1958. *Photobus*

It must be a hot day as the driver of Karrier W/Roe 480 has opened his windscreen as he pauses in King Edward Street next to the Palais de Danse. *Photobus*

BUT9641T 599 accelerates down the slight gradient away from the Midland Station towards Trent Bridge as 528 approaches. The low bridge carrying the ex-Great Central mainline over Arkwright Street is visible in the background. *Martin Jenkins*

subject to the approval of the MoT, of trolley vehicle services upon any public highway within or outside the City not at present used for such purpose. Although no trolleybus route extensions were in mind this simplification of the legislative procedure would have enabled the undertaking to more expeditiously and flexibly cope with the anticipated introduction of one way systems e.g. Derby Road and Wollaton Street, and the introduction of inner-city re-routings at short notice. Part IV of the 1952 Nottingham Corporation Act granted the Corporation powers to provide, equip, maintain and use trolley vehicles upon any public road within or outside the City not previously authorised, after application to the MoT, who was entitled to issue an Order empowering the Corporation to do so, in place of a special Parliamentary Bill.

So far solely trolleybus service reductions had taken place (the motorbus ones were still pending) yet by 30 May 1952 some members of the Transport Committee felt that the expected economies were purely hypothetical and did not guarantee any real saving. In their opinion the inconvenience to the travelling public was unjustified and it was suggested that those applications still before the Licensing Authority should be withdrawn. It was resolved to discuss future policy in connection with the proposed next fares increase. However by September 1952 it was evident that the curtailment of services 36 and 48 had led to no loss of revenue but economies of £721.

It was now known that the financial year ending 31 March 1952 had closed with a loss of £3,273 5s 5d and that the latest estimated deficit for 1952/53, based on prevailing fares and costs, and considering the latest service economies drive, had fallen to £74,000. The 34 heavy BUT9641Ts delivered during the year had led to 822,000 more units of electricity being used and total power charges had increased by £7,111 to £67,150 although the trolleybus fleet had only risen from 164 to 174 (including unlicensed vehicles awaiting sale). The 1951/52 loss was covered by reducing the Undertaking's contribution to the central administration expenses from £23,000 to £20,000, the rest being covered from the Reserve and Renewals Fund. A wage increase, expected to cost a further £120,000 was pending with the NJIC for the Road Passenger Transport Industry whilst a salaried staff increase of 10% was also in the pipeline. Mr England again asked that there should be an immediate application for increased fares. The City Treasurer added that loan charges were likely to increase by £22,000 and urged an immediate application for the full package with no further discussion or piecemeal increases. On 16 June 1952 the Transport Committee agreed to submit their proposals for a further fare increase, the seventh since 1939, to the City Council and the approved application was passed to the Licensing Authority in September 1952.

At the end of August 1952 the Royal Assent of the Nottingham Corporation Act 1952 granted the City Council statutory powers to deal with future trolley vehicle fare increases themselves (motorbus fare increases still required the approval of the Licensing Authority). It also enabled the Corporation to compulsorily acquire land both within and outside the City for the Transport Department's purposes in the same way that land could be acquired for housing or education. In Part IV, Section 34 increased the maximum fares which could be charged on Corporation trolley vehicles, namely to 2d (instead of 1d) for ordinary fares per stage of half-mile, subject to the maximum fare for two or more stages or any part thereof being at the rate of 2d (instead of 1½d) per mile. Maximum workmen's fares were limited to 1½d (instead of ½d) per mile or fraction of a mile with the right to charge a minimum fare of 2d (instead of 1d). Section 35 provided for a more expeditious procedure for the authorisation of new trolleybus routes whilst Section 36 enabled byelaws to be made as to the conduct of persons using bus stations, shelters, conveniences and other premises forming part of the Transport Undertaking to which the public had access.

Accordingly on 4 September 1952 the Transport Committee asked that the City Council approve new trolleybus fares effective on the same date that the Licensing Authority approved the new motorbus fares. This approval was given on 30 December 1952 and the increased trolleybus and motorbus fares (although a ½d anomaly continued on some works services) were introduced on 11 January 1953 with little reaction from the public. The Chairman of the Licensing Authority commented on the policy of free passes and the Transport Committee asked the Finance and General Purposes Committee to consider whether the cost of blind persons and disabled passes (£5,680 pa) should be met from the rate fund. At the same time the nominal charges made for travel passes issued to blind persons living outside the city were increased from 1s 4d to 2s per week, whilst those for Probation Officers and members of the City Police Force rose from £8 to £9 a year.

Within 3 months it was evident that the fare increase was not bringing in as much additional revenue as had been anticipated but a Transport Committee motion to make a detailed review was not supported. As part of an enquiry into introducing some kind of concessionary travel for OAPs during off-peak periods, a number of other municipal undertakings had been consulted; several stating that there had been no adverse effects on revenues. It was suggested that all OAPs resident within the City be permitted to travel on all services except in the WBUDC area, when boarding between the hours of 09.30 am and 11.30 am and between 2.30 pm and 4.30 pm, Monday – Friday inclusive, at half the adult fare on production of a special travel ticket which could be issued by the department on the production of

On 9 August 1952 Daimler CTM4 441 is seen in Stanhope Street opposite the entrance to Parliament Street Depot following withdrawal on 31 July 1952. Note the non-standard side indicator display and the paint masking to reduce the depth of the rear indicator display aperture. *Peter Badgery*

their pension book. The General Manager pointed out that the Licensing Authority would have to approve an OAP discount applied to motorbus services.

The remainder of the BUT9641Ts were delivered during 1952 and all remaining pre-war trolleybuses were withdrawn. Half-depth top-hinged nearside cab doors were fitted on the later vehicles instead of the sliding doors used on the earlier 7ft 6ins wide vehicles, as it had been found that the location of the contactor cabinet immediately inside the nearside doorway effectively prevented regular use by the driver. The last of Nottingham's pre-war 6 wheelers, Leylands 414, 430 and 436 were withdrawn on the 24th March 1952, followed by the four ex-Cleethorpes AECs in April and May. Last of all the pre-war vehicles to be withdrawn was Daimler 441 on 31st July 1952.

When the City Council had approved the purchase of 37 trolleybuses on 4 October 1948, the loan amount had been based on a purchase price of £215,912 however by the time of their delivery this had risen to £221,907 4 s 9d. As the additional sum of £5,995 4s 9d was covered by the manufacturer's rise and fall clauses it was recommended that the City Council apply to the MoT for sanction to borrow the necessary amount to cover this additional cost.

The Chief Engineer, Mr D.P. Martin, resigned at the end of September 1952 to join Wolverhampton Corporation Transport as Engineer and Deputy General Manager. He was replaced from 2 March 1953 by Frank Thorpe, Technical Engineer of Salford City Transport.

The travelling public were confused as to the number of standing passengers permitted on trolleybuses since the post-war reductions of 1946. This was clarified at the 4 November 1952 City Council Meeting as eight standing passengers except on Sundays when the limit was five (unless undue hardship would result). A year later the local newspapers recorded that the maximum number of standing passengers permitted on trolleybuses was 8 at all times.

Bad weather conditions led to a number of accidents involving trolleybuses in the winter of 1952-53. On 3 December 1952, three trolleybuses were involved in a collision on Radford Road near Boulevard Cinema with 4 people, including a conductor, injured. At lunchtime on 15 December 1952, following a heavy snowstorm, a trolleybus proceeding to the city along Vernon Road, Basford, skidded on the frozen snow as it was pulling up at a stop. The rear of the vehicle swung on to the pavement and hit Mrs Gladys Green who was standing there. She died later that day. On 16 March 1953 a Roe bodied utility trolleybus ran off the road in fog and hit a shop front at the junction of Brierley Street with Wilford Road.

The Depot and Works access wiring in Pyatt Street, Trent Bridge. BUT9641T 526 passes a Singer Gazelle in 1965. *Neil Lewin*

It was decided in December 1952 to reroute service 45 from King Edward Street, Bath Street, Manvers Street, Pennyfoot Street, Lower Parliament Street and then along London Road to Trent Bridge to run from the Palais de Danse via Lower Parliament Street and London Road in both directions, the route originally envisaged in 1935, saving 50-60,000 miles pa or £4,712, and reducing the running time by 6 minutes. The number of passengers using the service on this section of the route was small and with the exception of Pennyfoot Street, the roads were covered by other services. The new routing was introduced on 22 February 1953, provoked no negative reactions and was confirmed on 12 October 1953.

Following the removal of the Queen Victoria Statue the line of the curb on Beastmarket Hill was taken outwards and the 43 trolleybus stop removed to a point near the Odeon Cinema.

In January 1953 the N&D applied to increase fares on their trolleybus services including the A1 service between Ripley and Nottingham without having first agreed their proposals with the Corporation, as was required by the Nottinghamshire and Derbyshire Traction Act 1928. It will be recalled that the N&D paid the Corporation all fares collected by them for journeys within the city boundaries after deduction of working expenses and it was feared that increased fares could be prejudicial to the

On 6 July 1955 HM Queen Elizabeth visited the Royal Show held in Wollaton Park Karrier W/Weymann 445 is seen heading north up Huntingdon Street on this occasion. Note the rebuilt, rubber-mounted front indicator box. *Peter Badgery*

Nothing stops a trolleybus, but the snow prevents indentification of the vehicle and the service number! *Neil Lewin*

After a short break at the Wells Road stop on Long Row East (Old Market Square) the driver of BUT9611T/ Roe 489 climbs back into his seat to take his charge out to Kildare Road. *BTS*

The chassis of Sunbeam MF2 450 was originally destined for Johannesburg. Still displaying its original large indicator box 450 waits at The Wells Road, Kildare Road terminus of service 40. The embankment of the erstwhile Nottingham Suburban Railway features in the background. *BTS*

The rear double bumper bar just visible around the offside corner panel of 525 (numerically the first 7ft 6ins wide BUT9641T) , the retainer above the rearmost upper saloon offside window and the transverse wire to avoid roof damage when stowing the trolley booms and the short "stalk" to the off-side driver's rear view mirror suggest that this photograph was taken in autumn 1950 immediately after the vehicle's delivery. Trolleybus 525 is pictured at the Scalford Drive boarding point of service 45 in the southbound carriageway of Middleton Boulevard. *Photobus*

undertaking's interests in view of the N&D's intention to abandon trolleybus operation in the next few months. The Corporation objected. By early March 1953 withdrawal of the N&D Ripley – Nottingham trolleybus service was considered imminent, much of the company's overhead equipment had suffered from mining subsidence or needed renewal whilst the company's new owner, the British Transport Commission, wanted to integrate the trolleybus routes into existing motorbus services.

Passengers on the main line had to endure the unpopular detour up Nottingham Road due to the lack of a Bobbers Mill Bridge link. The Corporation informed the press that they would provide a service between the City and Cinderhill.

On 8 March 1953 the Omnibus Society and Southern Counties Touring Society organised the only known tour of the N&D trolleybus system using N&D 343, specially equipped with slider trolley heads for the occasion. The tour followed the customary A1 service route along Nottingham Road and Mansfield Road to King Street but, emulating the company's tramcars, then traversed Derby Road, Canning Circus, Alfreton Road and Radford Road. At the junction with Valley Road the trolley booms were transferred to the westbound Church Street wiring.

The surviving N&D trolleybus fleet of 32 vehicles was made up of 17 AEC 661T and 15 BUT 9611Ts, all with Weymann bodies and all were sold to Bradford Corporation for a total of £62,500. Prior to the closure some of these vehicles (including 332, 336, 341 and 342) were repainted at Langley Mill into the lighter blue livery of Bradford, retaining the circular company garter insignia on the lower side panels, although they continued to operate as normal on the N&D system. One vehicle of each type was withdrawn on 28 February 1953 and towed to Bradford during March whilst a further five made their way north during the week preceding closure leaving just 24 trolleybuses available for service on the final day.

Prior to being towed to Bradford, withdrawn trolleybuses were stored on a large open parking area behind the former garage of Williamson's, an early MGO constituent company, in Derby Road, Heanor. Vehicles operated under power as far as Market Street, Heanor (probably Red Lion Square at the junction with Derby Road), and were then towed to the storage area although it is known that at least on the final evening some trolleybuses with poles stowed coasted down the gradient of Derby Road as far as momentum would carry them before being pulled the rest of the way by lorry.

The N&D ceased operating trolleybuses on Saturday 25 April 1953. Souvenir non value tickets, overprinted in red with the single denomination of 1½d and "LAST TROLLEYBUS WEEK" on the front, and with the dates 1913, 1932, 1953 together with outlines of an open-top tram and a trolleybus, on the reverse, were issued to all passengers during the preceding week. BUT 9611T 347 was especially repainted for the occasion and ran in service throughout the system. During the evening as trolleybuses completed their duties instead of returning to the depot they continued to Heanor Market Place and thence to Williamson's garage. The last A1 departure from Nottingham Queen Street 9.55 pm normally operated to Codnor but for the final journey it ran through to Ripley before returning empty to Heanor Market Place. There was no special ceremony although Mr Laing, N&D Traffic

Manager, and Ken Wellman, N&D Traffic Department, were on board the operating trolleybus, 347. The last N&D trolleybus service of all was an A2 which, having reached Hallam Fields at 11.35 pm, was scheduled to return to White Lion Square, Ilkeston, and then run into Ilkeston, Park Road Depot. On this final journey 334, upon reaching Ilkeston, continued empty to Heanor Market Place before being towed into storage.

The company's Nottingham timetable was completely reorganised, all services being licensed jointly to MGOC and N&D. Commencing on 26 April 1953 the main service was provided by a more frequent B1 operating between Nottingham, Mount Street Bus Station and Ripley via Alfreton Road and Nuthall Road. Most journeys on the A1 now ran between Haydn Road, Basford only and Langley Mill or Heanor Market Place although a very limited number of peak hour journeys served Nottingham, Huntingdon Street Bus Station via Mansfield Road and Nottingham Road, or Ripley. Other services into Nottingham were strengthened but none of them continued to King Street or elsewhere in the city centre nor were the replacement motorbuses permitted to pick up or set down passengers within the city boundary.

From Monday 27 April 1953 the withdrawn N&D trolleybuses were towed at the rate of one per day for the first four weeks, followed by a pause before the final one left Heanor on 9 June 1953, to Bradford. By June 1955 they had all re-entered service in Yorkshire. In the meantime the company's overhead wiring equipment was dismantled, the majority being cut down by November 1953 although many traction poles were retained for street lighting purposes.

Until now, the all day service northwest of Valley Road to the city boundary along Nuthall Road, Stockhill Lane, Percy Street and Alpine Street had been provided by N&D trolleybuses. To compensate for their withdrawal, peak hours only NCT service 41 to Cinderhill crossroads (junction of Bells Lane with Nuthall Road) became an all day, daily operation from 26 April 1953 and was extended southwards to Trent Bridge, Victoria Embankment, Bunbury Street via Arkwright Street replacing service 48 entirely. On Nottingham Road the number of journeys between Valley Road and King Street on service 36 was also increased:

41 Trent Bridge – Arkwright Street – Carrington Street – Old Market Square – Upper Parliament Street – Milton Street – Victoria Station – Mansfield Road – Nottingham Road – Stockhill Lane – Nuthall Road – Cinderhill *(southbound via King Street, northbound via Queen Street)*

A request from the Police to remove the busy stop for alighting passengers only in Wheeler Gate on inward journeys to avoid interruptions to the flow of traffic was refused in February 1953. The stop was of operational importance as intending passengers could not board there in an effort to "jump" the queues for services 40, 43 and 47 in the Old Market Square.

In March 1953 a major reconstruction of the overhead equipment began at Old Market Square to accommodate a roundabout.

On 10 May 1953, services 40 and 47 reverted to operating via George Street, Carlton Street, Victoria Street, The Poultry and South Parade in a southbound direction due to the traffic congestion on Upper Parliament Street now being greater than that in George Street and at the end of Processional Walk in the Old Market Square which impaired the efficiency of the traffic lights at Friar Lane! Double barriers replaced the single barriers for northbound services 40 and 47 on Long Row. A proposal to reroute service 44 via George Street, Victoria Street and Old Market Square was put off until Chapel Bar had been widened.

The employment position was again deteriorating and a recruiting campaign started in March 1953 but with little effect. The maximum age for new applicants was raised from 40 to 55 years of age in a further effort to attract traffic staff.

Several municipal operators were experimenting with high capacity single deck vehicles in an effort to maintain services in a period of increasing capital costs and traffic congestion. In addition to operating trials with a Daimler Freeline motorbus in 1953, Nottingham conducted trials with a single deck trolleybus. In February 1953 a two-axle BUT RETB1 with English Electric equipment and East Lancashire 30ft long "standee" bodywork with a rear entrance and centre exit operated on service 48. The vehicle was the prototype of a fleet for Glasgow Corporation Transport, which was converting some of its radial tram routes to trolleybus operation and it later entered service as Glasgow TBS2, registered FYS766. Similar bodies albeit with a different door layout and fitted to Sunbeam MF2B chassis but in a Nottingham style livery were supplied to Colombo Municipal Council in Ceylon (fleet numbers 36-55) in 1956. There proved to be little economy in current consumption due to the small reduction in unladen weight compared to double deck trolleybuses. Not surprisingly, difficulties were experienced in loading and unloading at stops where passenger waiting shelters had been erected due to the non-standard door positions. This was the sole post-war trolleybus demonstrator in Nottingham and was reportedly tested to gauge passenger reactions to standee type vehicles rather than being considered as the prototype for a new trolleybus fleet.

In an effort to reduce the number of trolleybuses standing at Bulwell Market at certain times of the day, it was proposed to reduce standing time at the terminus. The maximum frequency of service 43 was 2 minutes with a scheduled standing time of 6-9 minutes throughout the week. As the service operated through densely populated areas with heavy traffic with various sources of delay, it was accepted that the schedule had been prepared to meet the worst normal conditions on the busiest normal day and no change was made.

On 10 July 1953 the Employees' side of the NJIC for the Road Passenger Transport Industry applied for a substantial wage increase together with a number of expensive changes to the conditions of the national agreement. A similar claim had been submitted for craftsmen. Together these increases would make the higher fares proposed on 29 May 1953 insufficient to cover the rising costs and Mr England suggested that early morning return fares should be discontinued. On 13 July 1953 the Transport Committee recommended this step to the City Council with trolleybus fares to rise on the same dates as the Licensing Authority authorised motorbus fare increases. The City Council approved the proposal

The Department's Annual Report for the year ending 31 March 1953 again recorded a rise in traction power consumption of 449,000 units (+£2,998) whilst the cost of electrical energy rose from 1.030d to 1.046d per unit. In the year to 31st March 1952, there had been 174 trolleybuses in the fleet, of which 7 had been newly delivered and 21 had been sold. 5 were unlicensed and 155 were in active service. In addition there were 3 tower wagons, of which one was in reserve for emergency use, and a reel wagon.

As the last fare increase, the seventh since 1939, was only bringing in £100,000 additional income instead of the intended £135,277, deficits of £77,000 in 1952/1953, £24,000 in 1953/1954 and £40,000 in 1954/1955 were now expected. In order to increase revenues by a further £73,000 pa Mr England recommended that the present early morning return fares should be withdrawn and replaced by an early morning single fare of 3d over the 4d, 5d and 6d fare stages, and one of 4d over the 7d, 8d and 9d ordinary stages. The 29 May 1952 Transport Committee Meeting however deferred the matter.

BUT RETB1/East Lancs Demonstrator TBS2 awaits departure time from the Queen Street stance, boarding point for the Nottingham Road services, immediately outside the Post Office in February 1953. Note the complex overhead wiring layout, to accommodate both waiting and overtaking trolleybuses, above TBS2, and the Council House at the east end of the Old Market Square in the background. *GHFA & JMB*

on 27 July 1953 but also decided to set up a special committee to examine the Department's administration and structure leading to the appointment of consultants in October 1954.

The Licensing Authority agreed that the undertaking required more revenue but considered that the proposal to abolish early morning return fares would cause undue hardship to the travelling public; neither had they ever encouraged the view that cheap morning fares should be abolished in their entirety. They decided to grant solely the 1d increases to the prevailing early morning 3d, 5d and 6d return fares. They estimated that on trolleybuses and motorbuses this would increase revenues by £80,000 pa but the Town Clerk felt that there would be a fall off of passengers reducing the increase to £69,000. Although it would have been legally possible to abolish early morning return fares on trolleybus services alone, it was decided to apply only the approved increase on both motor and trolleybuses effective 26 October 1953.

In September 1953 a trial double barrier was erected at 40 and 47 trolleybus stop in Long Row. By now there were 71 passenger waiting shelters in the city and although it was desirable to construct 15 more the financial state of the undertaking precluded this work. The cost of a 21ft long shelter erected and finished was £144 in steel (the preferred solution) and £118 in pre-cast concrete.

Certain Karrier Ws were taken out of service and put into store pending reconstruction of their timber framed utility bodies which were already beginning to show signs of structural decay and weakness. Properly seasoned wood had been virtually unavailable for MoS allocation at the time of their construction and rot had tended to set in at the base of the pillars, along the waist rail and at the junctions between the two, and along the cantrail. A general policy of internal and external body refurbishment, including fitting an increased number of opening windows, rubber mounted destination boxes and reconditioned upholstered seats had started in 1949, and this was now supplemented by a programme of structural strengthening and re-panelling with aluminium alloy.

A "Februat" vertical brush washing machine, on a sale or return trial, was installed at Bulwell Depot in November 1953, channels being cut into the floor to prevent water from the machine running into the inspection pits. It proved unsatisfactory and was returned to the makers in April 1954. In the meantime the Department's own engineers had designed a washing machine to satisfy local conditions, estimated to cost £350 including installation, and approval was given to install one each at Bulwell, Sherwood and Trent Bridge Depots. Unfortunately the finished article cost more than estimated and solely the one for Bulwell was built.

The Industrial Court granted a 4s per week increase to all adults governed by the NJIC for the Road Passenger Transport Industry effective 7 December 1953 together with an additional national holiday (Good Friday) for which pay at time and a half applied. This increase was expected to cost the Department an additional £25,000 pa and Mr England recommended that those items in the last fares increase application rejected by the Licensing Authority, namely the abolition of 7d, 8d, 10d, 11d and 1s early morning returns, should be reapplied for, resulting in additional revenue of £28,000. Prior to this wage increase the undertaking would probably have broken even in

The BUT RETB1 demonstrator stands at the north end of Victoria Embankment, Trent Bridge in early February 1953 in full Glasgow Corporation livery. *GHFA & JMB*

Trent Bridge bound 526 slows to negotiate the bridge at Arkwright Street Railway Station. The southbound wires were hung above the pavement to allow the greatest possible clearance beneath the bridge whose height was given as 16ft 1 inch (to City) and 16ft 3ins (from City). Note the row of shops on the east side of the road which typified the business premises to be found along most of the main arteries serving older inner suburbs at that time. *Neil Lewin*

On the occasion of the erstwhile Trolleybus Society and DOLRS tour of the system, Sunbeam MF2/ Weymann 451 stands in Cavendish Road, Carlton before using the terminus turning circle. *Photobus*

Bing Crosby stars in "Mississippi" at the Elite Cinema, Upper Parliament Street as 8ft wide BUT9641T 502 pauses on a 39 journey to Wollaton Park. *GHFA & JMB*

Pictured on Nottingham's sole reversing triangle, Hooton Road, Carlton, Roe bodied Karrier 459 awaits departure time for its 38 journey back into the city centre. The short-lived service number box at the top of the lower saloon nearside window bay 5 is clearly visible. Note also the time clock on the traction pole. *GHFA & JMB*

In February 1952 roundabouts were installed at the junctions of Gregory Boulevard with Mansfield Road and Sherwood Rise at the northeast end of the Forest. Here BUT 9611T/Roe 493 prepares to round the latter (the semaphore arm illuminated traffic indicator is just evident by the offside sidelight) en route to Nottingham Road, Valley Road on 25 April 1953, the final day of operation of service 48. *GHFA & JMB*

the financial year although there was still a deficit of £76,000 carried forward from 1952/53. As both the Transport Committee and the full City Council had already approved these proposals he recommended an immediate application to the Licensing Authority. The matter however was left until the next Transport Committee meeting on 11 January 1954 where Mr England, although still recommending abolition of the remaining early morning return fares (increasing fares by up to 6d), presented an alternative proposal introducing early morning single fares limiting the maximum increase for a return journey bought in the early morning to 2d. He estimated this would bring in £21,000 additional revenue as follows but a decision was not taken.

On 8 February 1953 Mr England repeated the 3 alternative proposals:

1. Abolish early morning returns and introduce some lower single fares designed to produce an increase of not more than 4d per return journey.
   Estimated annual revenue increase £25,000
2. Abolish early morning returns and introduce some lower single fares designed to produce an increase of not more than 3d per return journey.
   Estimated annual revenue increase £25,000
3. Abolish early morning returns and introduce special early morning single fares designed to produce an increase of not more than 2d per return journey. Estimated annual revenue increase £21,000

The third alternative was submitted to the Licensing Authority, considered on 10 May 1954 and approved effective 24 May 1954. Early morning return fares were abolished on 24 May 1954 and replaced with early morning single fares.

Under the conditions of the Road Transport Lighting Act 1953 trolleybuses, as well as all other road vehicles, became subject to Road Transport Lighting Regulations from 1 January 1954 requiring the addition of two rear reflectors to vehicles first registered after 1 October 1954. The Department started fixing them to existing vehicles, excluding those approaching withdrawal, during 1954. The post-war Karriers and the BUT9611Ts 479-495 had them positioned under the number plate whereas other vehicles had them level with the rear lights.

There were 3 mobile employee canteens in service, all using second-hand chassis, the oldest being 812 built on a 1928 Daimler chassis and converted in 1945 (the others were 805 (DUC239), a 1937 Morris, and 808 (AWY629) a 1936 Austin). These vehicles had been renumbered from the 500 series upon the delivery of the BUT9641Ts. In May 1956 Trent Bridge Works completed the conversion of 776 (DAU455), a 1937 AEC Regal diesel bus with single deck Cravens body, into a mobile canteen to replace 812 which was by now beyond economic repair. The new canteen was also numbered 812: with its roof-mounted water tank and appetising smells drifting out of the windows it became an integral part of the Victoria Embankment, Trent Bridge trolleybus terminus scene.

In 1935 overhead wiring had been strung in Huntingdon Street between Elm Avenue (Mansfield Road) and King Edward Street as a part of the then planned inner circle route along Canal Street, Castle Boulevard, Lenton Boulevard, Radford Boulevard and Gregory Boulevard. This route was never built and although no regular scheduled trolleybus service ran along Huntingdon Street, use

BUT9641T 526 heading south along Arkwright Street. *Martin Jenkins*

1944 Karrier W/Park Royal 454 waits in the apex of the junction of King Street with Queen Street outside the Prudential Insurance Building, terminus of the Nottingham Road services. *Nottingham Libraries*

being limited to surreptitious late evening runs to Parliament Street Depot, the overhead required regular maintenance, costing ca £200 pa. The Transport Committee, questioned as to whether the equipment should be dismantled or retained for possible emergency use, resolved to retain the link.

On 8 March 1954 it was learned that Clause 2 of the Transport Charges (Miscellaneous Provisions) Bill was intended to give Licensing Authorities the same control over trolleybus fares as for motorbuses. As the City Council had complete freedom in fixing trolleybus fares within the maxima laid down in the Nottingham Corporation Act 1952, this clause was prejudicial to the Corporation's interests. The Town Clerk felt that the Association of Municipal Corporations should seek the deletion of this clause but apparently the MPTA had already agreed to support the Bill and it subsequently became law.

A review into the introduction of night services was carried out in February and March 1954 but indicated that there was no need, no spare traffic staff (the Department was short of 145 drivers and 101 conductors) and that an annual loss of £10,865 could be expected. In November 1955 it was pointed out that the last journeys from the city centre at approx 11pm could be extended to 11.15 pm or 11.30 pm on a limited number of main routes, and this was authorised subject to demand and profitability. The late journeys were introduced on all trolleybus services in 1956.

The police again asked for the removal of the alighting stop at Wheeler Gate as traffic lights had been installed at the junction of Low Pavement with Lister Gate, working in conjunction with those at the junction of Friar Lane with South Parade. A survey taken during the morning peak showed 377 passengers alighting there of whom 181 walked away in a southerly direction. The elimination of this stopping place would result in a long distance between stops heading north, the longest being on service 41 from the stop at Collin's Almshouses on Carrington Street to King Street, a distance of 0.4777 miles. It was decided not to comply with the request, as passengers would be encouraged to get off buses stopped at traffic lights.

The NJIC for Road Passenger Transport Industry increased all adult wages by 3s per week from 5 March 1954, costing £18,000 pa, whilst corresponding awards for the administrative employees increasing annual costs to the undertaking by £4,125. Allowing for these increases and assuming that the Licensing Authority would approve the pending application for higher fares bringing in £18,000 more pa there would still be an estimated accumulated deficit of £158,000 by the end of 1955-56 financial year. The Transport Committee instructed Mr England to develop his proposal of rationalised fare charts based on a ½ mile stage structure with the aim of increasing revenues by £75,000 pa.

The new ½ mile fare structure would be:

2 stages	2d
3	2½d
4	3d
6	4d
8	5d
9 or more	6d

although some special fares would be introduced to ensure that no individual fare was increased by over 1d. It was calculated that if the increased fares were in place for 6 months of the current financial year the cumulated deficit could be removed by 31 March 1955.

The Licensing Authority approved the simplified fare structure, which was introduced on both trolleybus and motorbus services on 10 October 1954. The Authority was impressed by the method proposed to increase revenues and acknowledged that the Department was operating at a loss although if the scheme was successful in removing the deficit and creating a surplus they might wish to review the situation again. A separate yellow notice with black lettering attached to the bottom right hand corner of the bus stop sign marked the new fare stages but these were replaced later with signs having a green background and orange lettering whilst compulsory stop flags were given an orange border. This all contributed towards the undertaking being able to announce an operating profit, for the first occasion since 1948, in the 1954-55 financial year of £54,480, although it should be stressed that the trolleybuses had been profitable throughout but for 1948-49 and 1949-50.

On 22 August 1954 the Trent Bridge-Bulwell services were reorganised as follows:

42 Basford (Northern Baths) – Vernon Road – Radford Road – Hyson Green – Alfreton Road – Derby Road – Old Market Square *(Monday – Saturday peak hours only)*

43 Bulwell Market – Basford – Vernon Road – Radford Road – Hyson Green – Alfreton Road – Derby Road – Old Market Square – Carrington Street – Arkwright Street – Trent Bridge

Having just pulled out of Victoria Embankment onto the Trent Bridge gyratory system, 601 heads north up Arkwright Street. Note the tied-off wiring above the kerb (to the nearside of 601) providing access to Turney Street and thence Trent Bridge Depot and Works. *Martin Jenkins*

Karrier W/Park Royal 471 at the Exchange Walk stop on South Parade, Old Market Square. *BTS*

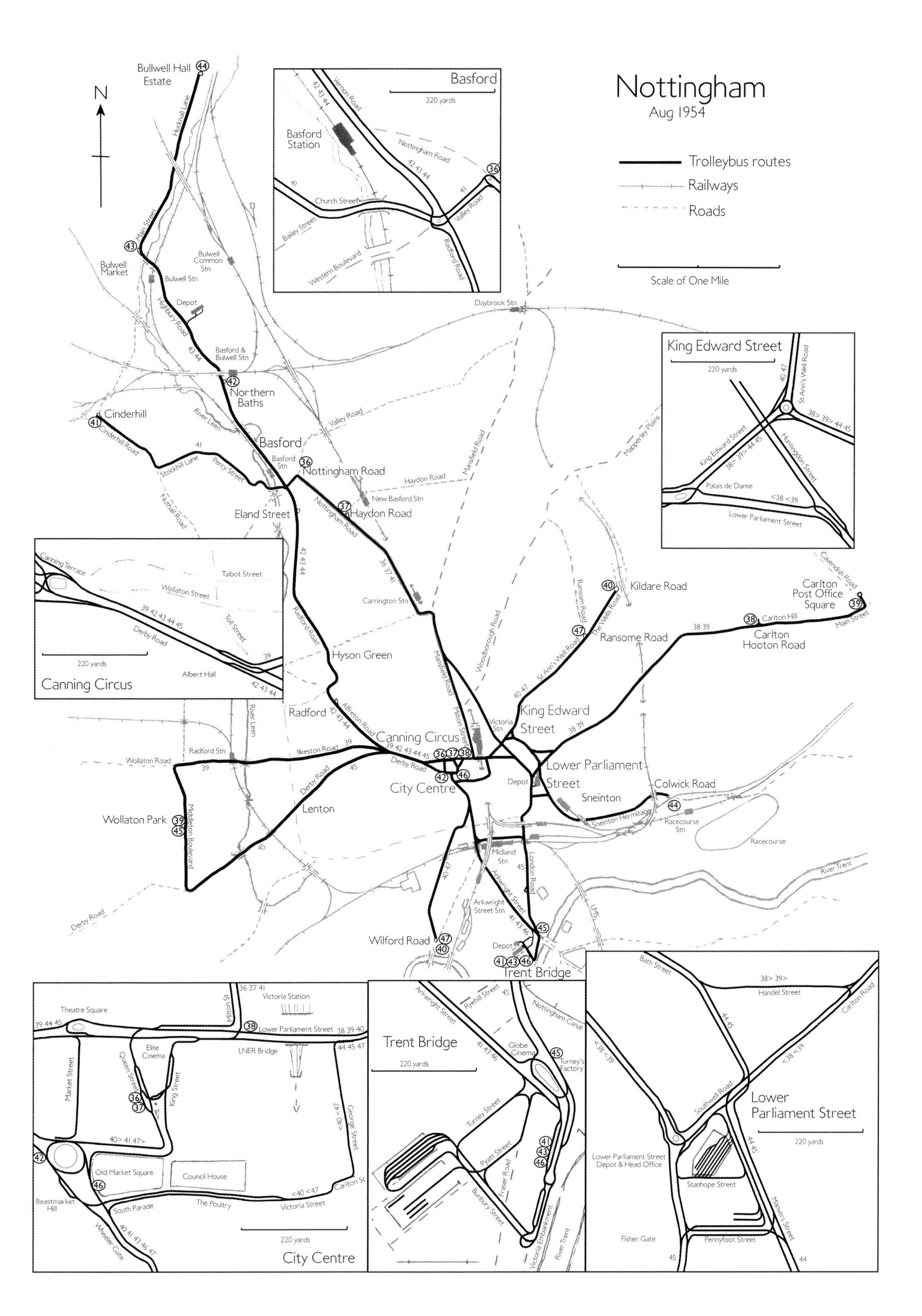

Nottingham
Aug 1954
Trolleybus routes
Railways
Roads
Scale of One Mile
Basford
220 yards
Basford Station
Vernon Road
Nottingham Road
Church Street
Valley Road
Bailey Street
Western Boulevard
Radford Road
King Edward Street
St Ann's Well Road
Huntingdon Street
Palais de Danse
Lower Parliament Street
Canning Circus
Canning Terrace
Talbot Street
Wollaton Street
Derby Road
Toll Street
Albert Hall
Bullwell Hall Estate
Hucknall Lane
Main Street
Bulwell Market
Bulwell Common Stn
Bulwell Stn
Depot
Highbury Road
Basford & Bulwell Stn
Northern Baths
Cinderhill
Cinderhill Road
River Leen
Stockhill Lane
Percy Street
Basford
Basford Stn
Nottingham Road
Valley Road
Haydon Road
New Basford Stn
Eland Street
Nuthall Road
Mansfield Road
Mapperley Plains
Daybrook Stn
Carrington Stn
Kildare Road
Ransom Road
The Wells Road
Carlton Post Office Square
Cavendish Road
Main Street
Carlton Hill
Carlton Hooton Road
Ransome Road
Hyson Green
Woodborough Road
St Ann's Well Road
King Edward Street
Victoria Stn
Radford
Alfreton Road
Milton Street
Radford Stn
Ilkeston Road
Wollaton Road
Lower Parliament Street
Colwick Road
Sneinton
Sneinton Hermitage
Racecourse Stn
Racecourse
City Centre
Lenton
Wollaton Park
Middleton Boulevard
Midland Stn
London Road
River Trent
Arkwright Street
Arkwright Street Stn
LMS
Wilford Road
Trent Bridge
Victoria Station
Theatre Square
Milton St
Lower Parliament Street
Elite Cinema
LNER Bridge
Market Street
Queen Street
King Street
George Street
Old Market Square
Council House
Carlton St
Beastmarket Hill
South Parade
The Poultry
Victoria Street
Wheeler Gate
City Centre
Ryehill Street
Nottingham Canal
Globe Cinema
Turney's Factory
Turney Street
Pyatt Street
Fraser Road
Bunbury Street
Victoria Embankment
Bath Street
Handel Street
Carlton Road
Southwell Road
Lower Parliament Street Depot & Head Office
Stanhope Street
Fisher Gate
Pennyfoot Street
Manvers Street

Karrier W/Weymann 457, complete with flashing trafficators, stands at Wilford Road terminus prior to another journey to Kildare Road. *Photobus*

Roe bodied Karrier W 481 Long Row, Old Market Square. *BTS*

In the early 1950s BUT9641T/Brush 507 is seen climbing Carlton Hill out of Carlton near the Recreation Ground en route to the city centre and Wollaton Park. The catenary overhead suspension is still intact. *Photobus*

46 Old Market Square (Beastmarket Hill) – Carrington Street – Arkwright Street – Trent Bridge *(Occasional peak hour and infrequent late evening journeys Monday – Saturday throughout the year, and summer Sundays only)*

Service 42 was curtailed at its northern end to run to Basford, Northern Baths, a turning circle on Vernon Road that had previously only been used by extras, with operations limited to Monday – Saturday peaks. The number of Saturday journeys on service 43 was reduced, this being compensated in part by service 42 operating most of the day. Service 46 operations were further reduced to summer Sundays only, with occasional peak hour and infrequent late evening journeys Monday – Saturday throughout the year. The position was reversed during the winter timetable period when, from 10 October 1954, the 42 began to operate on Sundays and was extended southwards to operate between Trent Bridge, Victoria Embankment, east end turning circle, and Basford, Northern Baths whilst the 46 winter Sunday operations were discontinued. As there is no evidence of any trolleybus having been equipped with a "42 TRENT BRIDGE" destination display it is presumed that a service 43 display must have been used for these journeys. The last occasion that the 42 operated to and from Trent Bridge on a Winter Sunday was 3 April 1960 although it continued to run north of the Old Market Square on Monday – Friday peak hours until 31 May 1965.

Until now the 43 and 44 had run every 3 minutes but this was now changed to a 6-minute service on the 43 with a 10 minute service on the 44 but complemented by the 42. The newspapers recorded that 50 yard long queues at Angel Row became commonplace. As far as service 46 was concerned the hours of operation and frequency were progressively being reduced until by the summer of 1964 it was confined to an 8-minute headway on Sundays only from the late afternoon until the close of service (which, together with the 43, provided a 4-minute combined headway between the Old Market Square and Trent Bridge). Throughout the 1950s and 1960s there were odd service 46 journeys at the start and end of peak periods (Monday to Friday) and at the end of the evening (Monday to Saturday) but these amounted to no more than three or four departures per day. Trent Bridge was a popular venue for a family afternoon out and it is more than possible that it ran at other times in accordance with operational requirements under the Old Market Square Inspector's instruction offering crews the opportunity of some welcome overtime. In effect the 46, other than its summer Sunday operation, like a number of motorbus services, became something of a "ghost" service with no regular timetabled departures and this situation continued until the conversion of service 43 and the closure of Trent Bridge Depot to trolleybuses on 31 March 1965. Although the 46 was based at Trent Bridge Depot, the other two depots also covered extras on this service; the sole example of a trolleybus service operated by all three depots.

These changes 'saved' 3 trolleybuses, 14 crews and 5,297 miles per week (representing £14,100 pa) and provoked no complaints from the public, but on Friday 3 September 1954 the TGWU called an urgent meeting in which it was complained that the Bulwell service crews were over-worked. It was agreed to jointly investigate the situation yet on Saturday 4 September 1954

Unloading in Milton Street outside the BR(ER) Victoria Station in the winter of 1958-59, the driver of 1944 Karrier W/Park Royal 454 has already changed the destination indicator back to "Nottingham Road", the outer terminus. Note the generously discounted excursion fares to the pleasures of Accrington and Ports-mouth, primarily to watch one of the Nottingham teams play football. *Fred York*

vehicles on services 42-45 commenced running into the depot at 12 noon and ceased entirely for the rest of the day, normal services resuming on the Sunday. The joint investigation was carried out after this unofficial "lightening strike", the TGWU representative pronouncing that there were no weaknesses in the revised schedules.

Flashing trafficators (designed in conjunction with Ericsson the local telephone manufacturing company and using telephone relays) had been introduced on the latest motorbuses in spring 1954. Work now began in replacing the semaphore arm signals fitted to trolleybuses as they became due for replacement, or on adding them to certain utility vehicles which had never been equipped with semaphore arms and that still had a reasonable "life expectancy".

The trolleybus fleet now consisted of 155 vehicles:

Karrier W	442-445	(4)
Sunbeam MF2	447-451	(5)
Karrier W	452-482	(31)
BUT 9611T	483-495	(13)
BUT 9641T	500-601	(102)

The substantial construction of the BUT9641Ts resulted in there being no chassis or chassis extension beyond the rear bulkhead or beneath the open platform to ensure that the unladen weight did not exceed 10 tons. The platform bearers provided little support for the cantilevered platform, which also carried the heavy traction batteries beneath the stairs, and the entire rear structure. After just 3 years in service, the rear ends of these trolleybuses were settling low and 8 vehicles were equipped with an extra leaf on the rear springs. It is assumed that all the other 94 BUT9641Ts were similarly modified.

By now all overhead wiring equipment used on normal service routes except the Basford (Vernon Road – Church Street) to Cinderhill section had been equipped with BICC twin hangars on a single span wire.

On 14 August 1954, a trolley wire had slipped out of its "ramp end" cutting off power to the section from Milton St to Central Market and Southwell Road. Services were suspended 8.15 am – 8.45 am and thereafter trolleybuses used their traction batteries to circumnavigate the breakage, all being back to normal by 9.20 am.

As no serious congestion had been encountered in the rerouting of trolleybus services 40 and 47 along George Street, Carlton Street, Victoria Street and South Parade on 5 May 1953, it was proposed to restore service 44 (Colwick – Bulwell) to its original route via George Street. This would have enabled all the Bulwell services to be regulated from one central point whereas at that time service 44 operated from Parliament Street and joined the other Bulwell services at the top of Chapel Bar. The Police could not agree to this until Chapel Bar had been widened.

When their trolleybus services ended in 1953 the N&D had returned their stocks of unused tickets intended for use in the Corporation area to the Department. A check of the tickets supplied over the years and those reported by the Company as sold led to a £2,645 17s discrepancy. The N&D refused to settle this amount and having investigated the legal position it was decided in March 1955 to take no further action.

On 24 February 1955 the General Works and Highways Committee asked the Transport Committee to accept responsibility for the cost of any alterations to traction poles and overhead equipment necessitated by the increasing number of road improvements. As the trolleybus network extended outside the City it was more advantageous to the Corporation for the expenditure to be borne by the undertaking rather than the General Rate Fund. The MoT were not prepared to make any contributions whilst parliamentary powers invariably included a "common form clause" which required the transport undertaking to bear the cost of altering equipment on such occasions. This situation, atypical of most European countries, was another financial burden which disadvantaged the trolleybus in comparison to other vehicles. Under these circumstances the Transport Committee agreed to the change on 14 March 1955. In the first 3 years such alterations led to expenditure of £2,129 12s 4d.

Trolleybus services on Derby Road and Ilkeston Road were disrupted for some 6 hours from 12.15 pm on Saturday 4 June 1955 by a fault at Broadholme Street substation. The break in supply left ten vehicles stranded on Ilkeston Road. They were towed later to Canning Circus and within 15 minutes a temporary motorbus shuttle service had been instituted between Wollaton Park and Canning Circus.

On 5 July 1955 the Royal Show opened in Wollaton Park with special motorbus services being operated from the Midland Station, Victoria Station and the Old Market Square. HM Queen Elizabeth and the Duke of Edinburgh visited the Show on Wednesday 6 July 1955 necessitating closure of the Old Market Square area from 9.30 am and the curtailment or diversion of a number of motorbus and trolleybus services. Although services 36, 37 continued to operate normally, the 41 was diverted along Huntingdon Street and London Road to/from Trent Bridge. The northern portion of trolleybus services 40, 47 were curtailed to Theatre Square although for a

Although heading west along Upper Parliament Street where the road widens prior to Theatre Square, 7ft 6ins wide BUT9641T 535 incorrectly displays Trent Bridge as its destination. Leyland TTB3 436 (ATV 199) is in hot pursuit approaching the Queen Street crossing. *GHFA & JMB*

Apparently on an enthusiasts' tour, probably that arranged by the Trolleybus Society and the DLROS on 15 April 1956, 8ft wide (identifiable by its white driver's steering wheel) BUT9641T 508 stands at the Wells Road, Kildare Road terminus with the embankment of the erstwhile Nottingham Suburban Railway in the background. *Fred York*

Karrier W/Roe 460 loading on Victoria Station bridge on Lower Parliament Street. This was the location of the post war sports special loop. *NTA*

45 minute period when the Royal Party was in that vicinity vehicles had to turn back at the Central Market. The southern portion was operated by motorbuses running to and from Castle Boulevard. The majority of journeys between 9.05 and 11.15 am to/from Bulwell on trolleybus service 43 were curtailed to Canning Circus with a limited number of vehicles continuing to/from Trent Bridge via Upper Parliament Street and London Road. There was no service at all along Arkwright Street to/from Trent Bridge. Service 44 ran as usual. The departure of the Royal Party from the Show led to widespread traffic congestion disrupting most services.

There were discussions about reinstating trolleybuses to the original terminus of service 36 at the junction of Nottingham Road and Vernon Road on 5 September 1955. This would have required the operation of an additional 12,156 miles pa at a cost of £380 if no extra time allowance were granted whilst replacement of the overhead would cost £1,588. The longer journey times would need two more crews bringing the increased cost to £2,200 pa. Some 3,514 passengers had been lost from service 36 since curtailment although a proportion of these had undoubtedly transferred to services 43 and 44. The minimum fare between Vernon Road and Haydn Road was now 2d instead of 1½d in 1952 and it was doubted that sufficient short distance passengers would be forthcoming at the present minimum fare to offset the cost of reinstating the section. It was decided to retain the northern terminus at Valley Road.

The TGWU showed a preparedness to discuss reduced termini standing time and employment of university students as conductors during their summer vacations. Students were regularly engaged from 1954 to 1957, and thereafter on semi-permanent contracts. They also issued a reminder to their members following complaints about intending passengers who were a short distance from a stop being left behind. Female cleaners were again engaged in August 1955 for the first time since the war and the first West Indian trolleybus drivers went behind the wheel in August 1956, a development that went some way to alleviate the shortage of employees.

The Transport Committee supported plans for a new traffic scheme at Canning Circus at an estimated cost of £5,167 19s 3d having heard Mr England's views. This was the final occasion that any positive developments of the trolleybus system were discussed:

"This scheme would solve the very serious congestion which is encountered at Canning Circus at the present time. Most of the existing stopping places in and around Canning Circus, together with the shelter and barrier at the top of Alfreton Road, would have to be re-sited, but this could be arranged satisfactorily.

The disadvantage of the new layout is that if Talbot Street, Wollaton Street and Derby Road were retained as two-way streets, there would still be a cross-stream of traffic at the junction of Wollaton Street and Derby Road and this would, to a certain extent, reduce the benefit to be derived from the new scheme. Reference has already been made to the possibility of making into one-way streets however and if Talbot Street and Wollaton Street were one-way streets inward and Derby Road a one-way street outward this difficulty would be overcome. Services 39 and 45 could then run via Wollaton Street instead of Derby Road on the inward journey entering Theatre Square near the County Hotel thus relieving considerably the present congestion outside Westminster Buildings, where traffic from Upper Parliament Street to Theatre Square cuts across traffic proceeding from Market Street to Wollaton Street and Goldsmith Street. Service 43 could also run via Wollaton Street to Clarendon Street and then turn right along Toll Street to Chapel Bar. This would entail the widening of Toll Street, but, as this is a long-

On 9 August 1953 BUT9641T/Brush 535 on a 44 to Bulwell hall Estate heads northwestwards beneath the frog for Ilkeston Road at Canning Circus with a N&D Bristol KSW 309 in hot pursuit. It must have been a warm day as the driver has left the nearside sliding cab door open: the manner in which the contactor cabinet blocked access is very evident. *Peter Badgery*

From May 1946 until May 1953, southbound services 40 and 47 operated by way of Upper Parliament Street and King Street to the Old Market Square. Here passengers, caught in mid-flight, alight from BUT9611T/Roe 494 at the Processional Walk, Old Market Square stop before the roundabout was built at the bottom of Market Street. *EE/Beilby*

term policy, it is considered that the cost would be justified and comparatively small, bearing in mind the cost of the scheme as a whole.

If these arrangements are carried out, it would be possible to make considerable alterations to the roundabout at the junction of Parliament Street, Chapel Bar, Park Row and Derby Road to permit several streams of traffic to enter Derby Road at the same time, thus cutting out the bottle-neck at this point which, for some time, has been such a serious source of congestion.

It would be necessary for statutory powers to be obtained for the operation of trolleybuses along Wollaton Street and Toll Street, but this could be incorporated in the general improvement scheme and should not give rise to any difficulty".

Agreement was reached with the TGWU in December 1955 to teach conductors, in their own time, to drive trolleybuses and to select suitable trolleybus driver applicants for motorbus tuition. However the shortage of 147 conductors made it impossible to introduce the scheme for the time being. Since 1 January 1955 the loss of mileage due to personnel shortages had reached 109,780 miles and would have been higher but for the union's agreement to the employment of additional coloured workers and university students.

Trolleybus tyre mileage rates increased from 0.89d to 0.95d per trolleybus vehicle mile from 1 January 1956, a 22% increase since 1 April 1955, and again to 0.96d per from 1 April 1956. It is understood that a proportion of the increases in the 1950s was due to excessive tyre scrub on the rear bogies of the 102 heavy BUT 9641Ts.

Trolleybus drivers had complained about the temperature in their cabs during cold weather and, following an experiment, it was agreed in February 1956 to equip all trolleybuses with tubular electric heaters at the front of the cab by next winter at a cost of £9 8s each and £1,230 for the fleet. Several members of the traffic staff who had originated in the West Indies were well known for wearing their heavy winter overcoats the whole year round!

Plans to install actuated traffic lights at the junction of Parliament Street and Milton Street, necessitating the removal of the Milton's Head request stop, were announced in March 1956. The stop outside Victoria Station would become the last stop before King Street terminus for services 36, 37 and 41, a distance of 368 yards. A survey showed that 1,366 passengers alighted at the Milton's Head between 8.00 and 9.00 am on one day, indicating much passenger inconvenience if no alternative stop was provided. An alternative location at the Welbeck Hotel was felt to be too close to Victoria Station whilst there were fears that passengers would alight at the traffic lights and it was decided to look, without success, for a further alternative.

Work carried out by consultants Urwick, Orr and Partners Ltd. , who had been engaged on 11 October 1954, assumed that trolleybus operation would be retained, deeming it beneficial to segregate motorbus and trolleybus operations at a cost of £75,155. Mr England was of the opinion that, although the City Council would have to decide its future policy in the light of detailed estimates made when trolleybus vehicle replacement became due (in 1963), the then prevailing figures and circumstances would lead him to recommend a move towards the

The road layout at the junction of Greyfriar Gate with Canal Street and Castle Boulevard is being remodelled in this 6 July 1958 view of Roe bodied Karrier W 460 making its way to the city centre and Kildare Road. Since the trolleybuses disappeared from the streets of Nottingham this location has become the southern end of Maid Marian Way. The attractive building on the left still stands, having provided accommodation for a wide range of different tenants including British Midlland Airways at one time. In front of the the Bowling Green Hotel one of Barton's Leyland/BTS1 rebuilds heads east along Canal Street. *Roy Marshall*

In the early 1960's, 513 negotiates the Carlton Post Office Square turning circle at the junction of Cavendish Road with Cemetery Road. This short spur from Main Street was the final extension to the Nottingham trolleybus system, opening on 22 October 1944 albeit merely to accommodate a revised turning arrangement. *Neil Lewin*

The main city centre loading point for trolleybuses to Trent Bridge was at the west end of the Old Market Square on Processional Walk. BUT 9641T 543 and another vehicle load whilst a smart-looking conductress in slacks looks on. *BTS*

Rewiring at Bulwell Hall Estate, BUT9641T 592, rather dented and unwashed. *Martin Eady*

BUT9611T/Roe 495 stands in Stanhope Street opposite the entrance to Parliament Street Depot with double front advertisements. *Fred York*

abandonment of trolleybuses, probably route by route over a number of years. The consultants felt that trolleybuses, with an increased seating capacity, should operate in and around the city centre whilst motorbuses should be used on the outer routes. Mr England felt that this separation would be impractical whilst the Department had already standardised on 70-seat trolleybuses. There was no need in his opinion to segregate the two fleets. He disagreed with many other of the consultant's recommendations as to the undertaking's administration and volunteered a smaller economy scheme involving considerably less capital expenditure.

The Employment Exchange stop on Wilford Street was removed in June 1956 due to peak hour traffic congestion at the junction of Castle Boulevard and Wilford Street. Trolleybuses continued to a new stop at the first traction pole on Greyfriar Gate beyond the junction.

The opening for a Chief Engineer caused by the departure of Frank Thorpe to become General Manager at Bury (where he introduced a similar destination display layout to that employed in Nottingham) had attracted 15 applicants, including Mr Don Machin, Nottingham's Assistant Engineer, and having interviewed a short list of 7 the Transport Committee decided to promote him to the post effective 29 June 1956 at a commencing salary of £1,240 pa. About 9 months later he was nominated to Electric Traction Committee of MPTA. Mr W.H. Herring, Technical Assistant was promoted to the post of Assistant Engineer.

The Transport Committee's annual inspection of the undertaking took place on 30 August 1956, improvements to Bulwell Depot attracting particular attention. It was agreed to widen the entrance, construct a washing bay adjoining the vehicle washing machine to aid the manual finishing of the vehicle exteriors after they had passed through the washing machine, introduce safety precautions for the use of lead-lamps in the inspection pits, and generally improve the canteen facilities.

It was announced on 23 July 1956 that the year ending 31 March 1956 had produced a surplus of £56,281 4s 7d and that after meeting the loss of £11,911 19s 2d for the previous year there remained a profit of £44,369 5s 5d to be carried forward to 1956-57. Earlier a deficit of £20,000 for 1956-57 had been forecast however in view of pending wage increases the City Treasurer recommended an immediate fares review.

By the end of November 1956 it was known that there had been a loss of £39,598 for the half year ending 29 September 1956 and thus a proposal for fare increases was submitted to the City Council where the distances for the 4d and 5d fares be shortened by ½ mile with corresponding changes to children's fares.

On 10 December 1956 it was resolved to apply for increased fares on the basis of Mr Englands latest proposals to bring in £138,000 pa plus a temporary increase to meet the increased fuel tax Bill then before Parliament, relating to the Suez crisis. Purchase tax on fuel increased by 1s, although the suppliers added a further 3d to the price, and motorbus fuel rationing was imposed from 17 December 1956. The Department planned to curtail motorbus services on the edge of the city centre thereby saving 4% of motorbus mileage but it proved possible to maintain all services and carry the additional traffic without inconvenience to the passengers. Diesel fuel stocks were supplemented, in a 20/80 mixture, with a coal derivative. There is no evidence of additional mileage or services being operated by trolleybuses during the emergency. The proposals were approved by the City Council on 7 January 1957. The increases were partially implemented on 20 January 1957 under the Hydrocarbon Oil Duties (Temporary Increase) Act 1956 and, having received the Licensing Authority's approval on 28 February 1957, completely on 17 March 1957.

In March 1957 the Transport Committee considered celebrations of the Undertaking's Diamond Jubilee, which would fall on Wednesday 16 October 1957. The estimated cost of £187 to include a lunch for officials, members of the Transport Committee, representatives of the WBUDC undertaking, the Traffic Commissioners, local Trade Unionists and Departmental Pensioners; dances for employees; and an exhibition at the Central Library was approved. Also included was the production of 500 stickers incorporating a diamond motive with the wording "Diamond Jubilee, 16th October, 1897-1957". By the end of May 1957 it was evident that due to the backlog of work in the body shop only a single deck motorbus could be spared for use as a decorated vehicle. No celebrations were evident on the trolleybus network.

BUT9641T 522, heading down Mansfield Road, collided with the projecting jib of a mobile crane belonging to Frank Berry Ltd. near Huntingdon Street on 27 August 1957. John Cowperthwaite, the undertaking's Claims Superintendent, who was travelling as a passenger on the trolleybus on his way to work, died from his injuries later that same morning. His widow sought damages from Frank Berry Ltd., who issued third party proceedings against the Corporation and John Perkins, the trolleybus driver. Both parties claimed damages against the other for the loss of use of the vehicles. The Town Clerk recommended that the Corporation accept 25% of the claim and indemnify the driver for any damages or costs.

A trolleybus dewired turning from King Street into Queen Street on 15 October 1957. Arcing between the trolleyhead and the positive wire led to the trolley wire being burned and molten metal falling on to a parked car belonging to Hardy's Kimberley Brewery & Hansons Ltd. The undertaking was not insured for this and £30 15s 3d paid in settlement of the claim.

Drivers were given medical examinations upon appointment, every 5 years whilst under 50 years of age, every two years between 50 and 60, and every year over 60 years of age. Under these circumstances and the continuing shortage of traffic staff, the Transport Committee granted the request of Trolleybus Driver A. E. Woodward, 65 years old and with 25½ years service, to continue driving for 12 months commencing 27 December 1957. In October 1958, following a further medical check, he was retained for a further 12 months (when he would be 67 years old).

The Finance Committee asked for a list of proposed capital expenditure with indications as to which items could be postponed for 6 to 12 months. It was acknowledged that the rebuilding of 7 utility trolleybus bodies was urgent and that there was no workshop capacity to do it however delivery of part of a motorbus order was put back one year. The option of placing entirely new bodies on the Karrier W chassis, as was still being undertaken by other trolleybus operators, was not investigated.

By 28 October 1957 tenders for reconstructing the 7 utility bodies had been received from Duple Motor Bodies (Midland) Ltd., Kegworth; Park Royal Vehicle Group, (C.H. Roe) Leeds; G.C. Smith, Long Whatton, Loughborough; Willowbrook Ltd., Loughborough; and W.S. Yeates Ltd., Loughborough. Although the General Manager recommended Park Royal's workmanship, the lowest tender of £786 12s from G.C Smith, Long Whatton (compared to Park Royal's £900-£1,000) was accepted subject to a review of their work on the first 2

BUT9641T 514 waiting in the loop at Carlton, Cavendish Road. Note the chock under the front offside wheel chained to the trolleybus. *BTS*

The north end of Bulwell Market Place. BUT 9641T 562 continues north up Main Street, Bulwell on a 44 working to Bulwell Hall Estate. *BTS*

trolleybuses completed. It was agreed to start the work immediately rather than await loan sanction and if approval was not forthcoming to cover the expenditure from revenue. The reconditioning was carried out during 1958 and 1959, those vehicles with fluorescent internal lighting having this replaced with standard but retrograde tungsten lighting at the same time. This comprised Utility trolleybuses 476 and 478, which had been fitted with fluorescent lighting in 1947 and 1948 respectively, and BUT 493.

Revised calculations presented to the Transport Committee on 17 September 1957 indicated that the loss for the year ending 31 March 1958 would be £37,213 whilst recent wage awards would lead to additional expenditure of £22,700 in 1958/59. Mr England suggested that, to cover this deficit and provide a cushion of working capital, £110,000 additional annual income was required. This could be achieved with a 3d minimum adult fare. The prevailing adult fare of 2d would become 3d and cover up to 4 fare stages (about 2 miles). No change was foreseen for children's fares and the prevailing 1d child's fare for journeys of up to 1 mile would remain. The City Council approved the proposals on 7 October 1957 and they were submitted to the Traffic Commissioners for hearing on 22 November 1957.

On 27 November 1957 it was learned that the Traffic Commissioners were satisfied that the Department needed the additional income but were not satisfied with the proposal to obtain the whole of this from short distance passengers i.e. those travelling up to 1 mile. They felt that the burden should be spread over the passengers as a whole and were concerned at the estimated loss of 10% of the present number of 2d fares and the effect on the elderly and infirm. It was accordingly decided to retain a 2d minimum fare for journeys of one stage and that the fare for journeys of two stages or between one and two stages should be 2½d producing £30,000 pa if applied to trolleybuses and motorbuses. The counter-proposal centred on a reduced distance for the 3d fare from 2 miles to 1½ miles which would bring in £70,000 in addition to the £30,000 suggested by the Traffic Commissioners.

The Traffic Commissioners indicated that they would handle an alternative proposal urgently in view of the undertaking's position and a number of alternatives for raising the additional revenue were presented. The Traffic Commissioners granted the application at a hearing on 30 January 1958 and the increased fares became effective on 16 February 1958, too late to clear the accumulated deficit.

The Annual Report for the year ending 31 March 1958 showed that traction power consumption had decreased by 1.62% in line with a 1.27% decrease in trolleybus mileage, There being 155 vehicles in stock throughout year. The cost of overhead equipment maintenance and repairs rose by £2,579 to £20,919, the costs having doubled over the preceding 5 years primarily due to the change of policy adopted on 14 March 1955 whereby the undertaking bore the cost of all work in connection with alterations of traction poles or wiring arising from road reconstruction. Labour turnover dropped from 33% to 26%, 503 new employees were engaged during the financial year and 511 left.

In June 1958 the traffic improvements for Canning Circus and Trent Bridge, intended for introduction during the financial year, reached the detailed planning stage. The Canning Circus gyratory scheme did not involve rerouting any services but needed a substantial relocation of stops, a re-poling of the area and a complete reconstruction of the overhead line equipment to include St. Helens Street at an estimated total cost £6,647. That at Trent Bridge involved the creation of two one-way streets, namely London Road from Truman's Road to Trent Bridge and Arkwright Street from Trent Bridge to Truman's Road. During the peak periods it was planned to divert trolleybus services 41 and 43 via Arkwright Street, Turney Street, Fraser Road, Bunbury Street and the Victoria Embankment to their existing terminus. This diversion could also be used for football and cricket matches at the discretion of the police. The expected cost of overhead equipment alterations was £6,758.

The Wilford Road terminus was remodelled in conjunction with the extension of Queen's Drive along the north bank of the River Trent past Clifton Colliery and North Wilford Power Station to the new Clifton Bridge. A turning circle was erected above a new roundabout built at the junction of Queen's Drive, Colliery Road and Wilford Road, whilst the boarding point was moved to a lay-by outside the Ernest Purser Health Centre.

In July 1958 the Watch (Road Traffic) (Joint) Subcommittee asked the Transport Committee to consider moving the terminus of trolleybus services 39 and 45 to the roundabout at the Wollaton Road end of Middleton Boulevard. It was acknowledged that the existing terminal arrangements at Fairham Drive and Scalford Drive respectively, were not ideal as in both cases trolleybuses had to turn from the nearside of the carriageway across the fast lane of the dual carriageway ring road, which had no speed limit. It was deemed impractical to link the two services over a circular routing, as there were different service frequencies on the Derby Road and Ilkeston Road portions. Mr England felt that the following arrangements would be possible:

- 39 to turn at the junction of Orston Drive and Middleton Boulevard as the two stopping places adjacent to this point had lay-bys that could be extended if necessary and were situated in a restricted speed area.
- 45 to be extended to a turning point short of Orston Drive to provide facilities along the whole length of Middleton Boulevard

Although the average load on Middleton Boulevard was only 3-5 passengers, it was suggested that both services should turn at Wollaton Hall Drive, involving 33,760 additional miles pa. This was rejected and on 5 September 1958 it was resolved that 39 trolleybuses would turn at the junction of Middleton Boulevard with

595 on a 40 working to Wilford Road pulls out of King Edward Street into Lower Parliament Street. The Central Market is in the background and the Palais de Danse to the right. *Peter Badgery*

On the south side of the Old Market Square, 1946 Karrier W/Park Royal 476 pulls away from the Exchange Walk stop on South Parade en route for Wilford Road. *Fred York*

8ft wide BUT9641T/Brush 515 at the side entrance to Victoria Station on Lower Parliament Street. *BTS*

Heading east along Ilkeston Road towards the city centre and Carlton 8ft wide BUT9641T/Brush 520 crosses the former Midland Railway line at Radford Station. *Neil Lewin*

Harrow Road (opposite Orston Drive) and 45s would be extended to the junction with the north end of Sutton Passeys Crescent. The lay-bys were to be extended or provided and warning signs erected in Middleton Boulevard approaching the new terminals. Although it was agreed that the cantilever steel passenger waiting shelter at the Wollaton Road end of Middleton Boulevard gave inadequate protection against the weather, a decision had been postponed fearing a flood of applications for double-sided concrete shelters which gave more protection. Following the decision to move the service 39 terminus the request was no longer relevant as it was calculated that there would be a trolleybus standing at the stop practically all the time.

However by 23 March 1959 the Watch Subcommittee recommended that both services should turn at the junction with Harrow Road where the road was straight rather than at Sutton Passey's Crescent where a bend in Middleton Boulevard obstructed visibility. This would have the advantage of a single turning point in a length of road where there was a 30 mph speed limit, space for lay-bys and where appropriate warnings signs could be erected. The MoT also supported the scheme. Overhead equipment changes were expected to cost £2,137 and the Department's share of the lay-by construction would be £780. There would be an economy of 30,000 miles. On 11 October 1959 service 39 was foreshortened from Fairham Drive to Harrow Road and the 45 extended from Scalford Drive to Harrow Road. The residents of Wollaton Park presented a petition in November 1959 complained at the inconvenience likely to be caused by the new terminal arrangements but no action was taken. This did much to fuel the rumours that the perambulations of the Middleton Boulevard trolleybus turning point over the years was closely related to the individual preferences of the councillors who chose to live in this residentially-favoured part of the city.

Even in the 1950s not all drivers possessed a watch and it was considered important to leave certain key points on time to ensure that vehicles remained in sequence and crew changes could take place as scheduled. Mechanical clocks for this purpose, adjusted and wound twice weekly, were located around the system. As the TGWU asked for a daily accuracy check, the General Manager recommended their replacement with electric clocks at all termini over a 12 year period indicating 5 or 6 clocks pa. His recommendation to install clocks at the following termini in the financial year at a cost of £179 was approved:

Service 44	Bulwell Hall Estate
Service 44	Bulwell Market (facing the southbound stop on the south side of the market place, almost at the end of Main Street, and immediately before the trailing frog from around the island and the 43 terminus)
Service 43	Bulwell Market (at the terminus on the north side of the market place outside the "Horse & Jockey" public house)
Service 40	Kildare Road
Service 40/47	Wilford Bridge

On 5 January 1959 the City Council asked for an improved frequency for service 45. However having made a one-week analysis it was shown that even the present headways could not be justified on economic grounds. A reduced frequency saving £9,670 pa was approved:

Layover time on Victoria Embankment, Trent Bridge, for BUT9641T/Brush 571 before departing on another 43 working to Bulwell Market. *Neil Lewin*

Day of the week	Headway in Minutes	
Sunday (winter)	Present	Proposed
9.00 am – 4.00pm	15	20
4.00 pm – 11.00 pm	12	20
Monday to Friday		
6.00 am – 9.00 am	6	7-8
9.00 am – 12.30 pm	12	15
12.30 pm – 2.30 pm	7/8	10
2.30 pm – 4.30 pm	10	15
4.30 pm – 6.30 pm	6	7/8
6.30 pm – 11.00 pm	10	15
Saturday		
6.00 am – 7.00 am	10	10
7.00 am – 10.00 pm	6	10
10.00 am – 6.00 pm	6	7/8
6.00 pm – 7.00 pm	6	15
7.00 pm – 11.00 pm	7/8	15

In 1954 the rates of pay for Assistant Linesmen was aligned to that of Tower Wagon Driver. Later in that year the NJIC increased Tower Wagon Driver's wages to those of a Driver but did not consider Assistant Linesmen. These men had been recruited from Drivers in the past but this had involved a wage reduction. This anomaly was corrected in April 1959 when Assistant Linesmen were regraded to Semi-skilled Grade A1. That same month Ben England's salary was increased from £2,450 to £2,700 pa.

By June 1959 the long awaited widening of Chapel Bar was complete and the police agreed to the rerouting of service 44 northbound via King Street, Long Row, Angel Row and Chapel Bar instead of operating along Upper Parliament Street to join the other Bulwell services at the top of Chapel Bar. The overhead wiring alterations necessary to enable trolleybuses to proceed directly from Long Row East onto Beastmarket Hill cost an estimated £522. From

Nottingham's 8 foot wide Utility trolleybuses had been progressively withdrawn over the previous year and the last two, 449 and 451, were de-licensed on 31st October 1958. On 24 November 1958 the Transport Committee approved the following capital expenditure involving trolleybuses for 1959/60 and passed it to the Finance Committee:

Item	Total	Amount in 1959/60
Chassis cleaning plant	£1,750	£1,750
Rebuilding 2 trolleybus bodies	£1,800	£1,800
Replacement of punched card Installation	£27,000	£27,000
Extension of Parliament Street Depot to incorporate Stanhope Street	£18,000	£10,000
Purchase and erection of shelters	£1,963	£1,600 for 5 more shelters.

26 July 1959 service 44 operated northbound by way of the Old Market Square (although it continued to run along Upper Parliament Street southbound), the entire Bulwell service being regulated from a single central point.

44 Bulwell Hall Estate – Bulwell Market – Basford – Vernon Road – Radford Road – Hyson Green – Alfreton Road – Derby Road – Upper Parliament Street – Bath Street – Manvers Street – Sneinton – Colwick Road *(northbound via King Street, Long Row, Beastmarket Hill, Angel Row; southbound via Upper Parliament Street)*

On 22 June 1959 Mr England delivered his annual report to the Transport Committee. In November 1958 he had warned that the July and October 1958 wage awards would lead to a deficit of £41,500 for 1959/60. However he now felt that proposed service economies and reduced licence fees would together probably lead to a break even situation for the year, making it possible to postpone a fare increase by a further 6 months. In the meantime Inspectors had interviewed some 694 passengers who generally felt that to cut costs, off-peak services could be reduced as far as was consistent with an adequate service, there should be no reduction of peak headways, and that the finances should be balanced by means of a fare increase. Following a decline in traffic, in which trolleybus passenger figures fell by 4.65% from 64 to 61 million, a general review had been made of all services. Some headways had already been reduced and when all alterations were completed there would be a saving of 535,103 miles pa without any reductions to Monday-Friday peak headways.

Reports into service frequencies during the slack period of Thursday evening (early closing day) and the confusing destination display "CITY", which gave no specific indication as to where the vehicle was actually travelling to, were requested. These confirmed that there were shorter queues on Thursday evenings and that vehicles suffered little delay from traffic congestion but a revised headway for a single day was not recommended. With respect to destination displays it was noted that the blinds had almost reached their maximum capacity, allowing some space for new destinations. Services operating to termini just outside the city centre had their own separate destination displays e.g. Huntingdon Street, Broad Marsh. The wording "CITY" referred to vehicles genuinely heading to the city centre.

Network route maps were affixed at South Parade, Long Row, Queen Street, Processional Walk, Angel Row and Parliament Street Railway Bridge outwards trolleybus stops.

An order to close Stanhope Street was issued in September 1959 and the City Engineer was requested to invite tenders for roofing over part of the street to provide more covered space at Parliament Street Depot.

By September 1959 a further six utility Karrier W trolleybuses were due for reconditioning at an estimated cost of £1,000 each. During the summer London Transport, which had embarked on a trolleybus replacement programme, sent out a circular to other trolleybus operators seeking to dispose of surplus members of its BUT9641T Q1 class. It was London's intent to retain these vehicles, their only post-war trolleybuses, operating on a group of routes in the south western suburbs, until they had been fully amortised, however only 117 of the 127 strong class were required. Following enquiries, NCT made an offer of £500 each for 5 Q1s, which

Karrier W 477 on a wet day and seen in it's as delivered condition. *NCT*

Learning to drive trolleybuses

"I joined Nottingham Corporation Transport as a conductor, the training being done on trolleybuses due to their heavy loadings. After training I was put on motorbuses based at Bilborough Depot, which was about 6 miles west of the city. My regular driver knew that I wanted to be a driver and when I was 19 years old he gave me a trolleybus driver application form. I pointed out that one had to be 21 years old to drive trolleybuses but he said that there was such a long waiting list for trolleybus training that I would be 21 by the time I got to the top of the list.

He was correct and I was in fact 21 years 2 months old when I was accepted into the Trolleybus Driving School in March 1959.

My Instructor was Nobby Green. He drove Karrier W4 474 from the depot to the junction of Nottingham Road and Haydn Road. I then got behind the wheel and he told me not to accelerate or brake and 474 rolled down the incline, so that he could observe my steering. At the bottom of the incline he was satisfied and my intensive instruction began. The instructor sat on a folding stool on the nearside of the cab next to the learner driver. The Karrier had no back-up battery if the poles came off or if road works forced the trolleybus wide on the wrong side of the road so one had to keep well into the works and hoped the poles were within their maximum stretch.

As a car driver I found it a novelty that the trolleybus accelerator was on the left but soon got used to it. The footbrake was two-fold, halfway down it was an electric brake and full down it was an air brake.

Inspector Wilson, who met the trolleybus at the junction of Bath Street and St. Ann's Well Road, carried out the driving test, which was run on route 40/47 to Wilford Bridge and return. It would seem that this test section covered all sorts of problem turns and junctions with respect to the overhead system so that if a driver could do this correctly then any other route on the Nottingham system could be operated at ease. I passed my test and obtained by Group H Licence – this enabled me to drive without "L" plates – but I still had another test to look forward to before I was allowed on service. This second test with Inspector Wilson replicated my first but with passengers and a conductor on board. So the second part of my training was on service and Nobby and I would start off our duty, go to a relief point and find a driver waiting to take over his trolleybus. Nobby would say that we would do his duty and that driver would then go and sit in the canteen until his next duty or indeed the end of his shift. These relief drivers certainly liked to see Nobby!

My concern was for the conductor as I felt that I would not be able to run on time with being new but Nobby told me to put that out of my mind.

On this training I thoroughly enjoyed being on the 39 with the six wheelers. These were the most modern trolleybuses with a sliding driver's door and were 8 ft wide, this being denoted by a white steering wheel. Some six wheelers at Bulwell Depot on the busy 43/44 Bulwell Trent Bridge services were 7ft 6ins wide and had black steering wheels but the bonus on these for the driver was that acceleration was automatic and on moving off one could press on the accelerator ¼ of the way down, click, click, click and then go flat down to the floor and the electric motor would look after itself – rapid clicks and speed pick up with no risk of blowing the fuses. This did happen on Karriers and the 8ft wide six wheelers if one accelerated too quickly, then Wow! What a bang and flash in the cab and bump, bump, bump, as the bus lost all power and the driver had to pull into the side of the road.

The day of my second test arrived; it was a Friday and Nottingham was busy. After leaving Bath Street the next stop was the Central Market. Many passengers got off and many on, laden with their shopping bags. On again. Right into Parliament Street, operating the junction automatically by applying the handbrake and accelerating through the point. The indicator light on the lamp post ahead of me came on indicating that the points had changed, handbrake off and then a gentle left turn into George Street. Full accelerator up to the George Hotel and throw off the power, indicate right and enter Victoria Street and down into the Old Market Square. Moving off again I could see I was 3 minutes late. I prepared to turn left into Wheeler Gate, a tight turn, gently down by Marks & Spencers to the (Walter) Fountain, indicate right and apply the handbrake as I have to operate the junction light. All OK, and no more major junctions. Round the island to the Astoria Ballroom, right into Castle Boulevard and left into Wilford Road. Just drop off now; 4 stops and I was at the terminus. I changed the destination, signed the defect card and, as we were waiting for "time", I was asked questions on the Highway Code. No problems!

As the trolleybus in front departed I went round the island and awaited my time. The conductor rang the bell twice and off we went again. We were soon back in the Old Market Square and I was now feeling rather pleased. I was on time and there were no adverse comments from Inspector Wilson. On turning left into King Street I knew that this was the "hot potato" of the test as I had to by-pass the 36/41-trolleybus terminus, remember that I was going uphill, and not operate any of the junction change lights. To cap it all there was a "breaker": this was a point of input of electricity into the overhead wires and if you accelerated through the breaker there was a flash on the wire and possible blowing of fuses in the cab, and a definite failure of my test.

Left into King Street, now flat out to the 41-junction light, throw off power (Good! No light!), flat out again and off immediately as I cross beneath the 36 junction, flat out again and off instantly as the 41 wire was now joining my main line wire, perfect. Gentle power indicating right into Parliament Street. A policeman was usually on duty controlling traffic at this point; more often than not it would be PC "Tug" Wilson 6ft 7ins tall with a handlebar moustache. He later told me that he knew when a driver was on test as he recognised Inspector Wilson in the cab and would more often than not give us the right of way by stopping the traffic. So this was a real help! Down Parliament Street, ensure not to operate the 41-junction light, right hand lane and over Parliament Street bridge. Almost done now, move off and cruise down to Central Market. Loaded again and down over the lights to the Victoria Ballroom, handbrake on.

"Thank you Driver Jefford. A nice drive and you are on time. I am pleased to give you a successful pass". Inspector Wilson shook my hand. What a feeling!

I bought Nobby Green 20 Woodbines as a thank you for his patience and duly entered the trolleybus rota at Parliament Street. In later times Nobby would work his rest day on a Saturday driving on service and because he was so careful and correct I would often see him running late with perhaps two trolleybuses behind him on service".

Bernard Jefford, who drove trolleybuses 1960-1963.

On the south side of the Old Market Square, Karrier W/Roe 464 of June 1945 pulls around a WBUDC motorbus at the Exchange Walk stop on South Parade en route to Wilford Road. Note the signs indicating the route for pedestrians between the two main railway stations. *Fred York*

Roe bodied Karrier W 465 of 1945 still in its original livery (note the absence of "Nottingham" in the fleet name transfer application) at the Fairham Drive, Middleton Boulevard, Wollaton Park terminus of service 39. *GHFA & JMB*

A mid-1950s view of 8ft wide BUT9641T/Brush 515 in Parliament Street Depot. Note that 515 still has an external circular driver's rear view mirror on a short stalk beneath the offside front window pillar and semaphore arm illuminated traffic indicators. As an early (1950) delivery, the front access panel has 3 horizontal fluted columns of 6 vanes. *Fred York*

BUT 9641T 526 negotiates the roundabout on Gregory Boulevard at the south end of Sherwood Rise. The cream liveried motorbus in the background is on Mansfield Road. *MJ Russell*

Newly appointed drivers operated spare duties until there was an empty position on the rota (by the early 1960s the waiting time had fallen to about 6 weeks). They were then teamed up with a "driverless" conductor and remained permanently together, a so-called "full bus"; however it was permitted to swap rotas. I was able to persuade my conductor to drop back into spare duties and was then permanently teamed up with my conductress wife. Unlike other undertakings Nottingham did not frown on this practice, which was a human and practical alternative of constantly having to change duties. I used to work a lot of overtime, sometimes a total week would be 85 hours, there were no driver's hours restrictions in those days.

Bernard Jefford, who drove trolleybuses 1960-1963.

would have been technically compatible with their own BUT9641Ts, to replace some of their utility stock but the figure was rejected as derisory. London Transport retained all its Q1s until an offer for the entire class was received from a group of Spanish operators.

Rather than recondition the utility vehicles, the Transport Committee approved the conversion of services 37 and 38, together with some trolleybus "extras", to motorbus operation. It was decided that the 6 trolleybuses requiring reconditioning, along with 2 others scheduled for replacement by the end of 1962, should be replaced with delicensed motorbuses held in reserve. Recertification of the motorbuses was estimated to cost £100 each whilst the proceeds from the sale of the 6 trolleybuses would produce approx £300 resulting in a net expenditure of £500.

In view of the shortage of trolleybus drivers, Driver A.E. Woodward, following a further medical pronouncing him fit, was retained for a further 12 months i.e. to his 68th birthday.

On 1 November 1959, with the completion of the Trent Bridge gyratory scheme, all Arkwright Street services were diverted by Truman's Road on outward journeys from the City whilst on 30 November 1959 the Canning Circus gyratory scheme was brought into use and all services started operating along the newly constructed St. Helen's Street.

At their 28 March 1960 meeting the Transport Committee approved fare increases necessary to meet recently announced national wage settlements estimated to cost £133,350 pa. These became effective on 7 August 1960.

City Councillors seemed to have a recurrent desire to change the Wollaton Park terminal arrangements and on 27 June 1960, Councillor Thomas suggested that the service 39 terminus should be moved from Middleton Boulevard, Harrow Road to the roundabout near the main gates at the junction of Wollaton Hall Drive. Alternately he suggested an additional regular circular service paralleling the 39 and 45 to promote visits to Wollaton Hall itself. In his response Mr England stated that only Harrow Road met the requirements of road safety and economy. An extension of service 39 to Wollaton Hall Drive would require the operation of 86,000 more miles pa, needing 2 more trolleybuses and 4 crews, the cost of which would amount to £13,316 pa plus an initial cost of £2,113 for overhead wiring alterations. If Wollaton Hall Drive was also to be made the terminus of service 45 the annual cost would fall to £8,214 and the overhead wiring changes to £1,915. An additional circular service along Middleton Boulevard would be unrenumerative as a 15-minute service in each direction for 8 hours a day running to the Old Market Square would cost £17,279 pa and bring in little revenue. The proposal was not followed up.

The Annual Report 1959-60 showed that trolleybus revenue fell by £21,283.

	1958-59	1959-60
Trolleybus passengers	61,211,102	59,241,219
Trolleybus mileage	4,398,560	4,053,109

Traction current consumption was 13,844,000 units compared with 14,646,000 units in 1958-59 but the cost fell from 1.203d to 1.198d per unit although consumption increased from 3.330 units per mile to 3.416 reflecting the reduced fleet of 2-axle utility Karrier Ws and perhaps indicating less professional driving. There had been 155 trolleybuses in stock at the beginning of the financial year; 9 vehicles were withdrawn leaving 146 of which 6 were unlicensed awaiting sale. The 9 trolleybuses sold realised £210. The average age of the trolleybus fleet was already 10 years 2 months, 47 vehicles being more than 10 years old.

The southern terminus of service 45 was also moved on several occasions in the 1950s. The alighting stop was at the south end of London Road where it made an end-on junction with Trent Bridge, outside Turney Brothers' leather factory, throughout the trolleybus era. The boarding point was outside the Globe Cinema, in the apex of the junction of Arkwright Street with London Road, from June 1935 until 14 March 1953. It then moved, for no apparent reason, to the Burton's Almshouses, London Road, but had returned to the Globe Cinema by October 1954, which could indicate that this was a temporary move due to road works. On 11 October 1959 the boarding point was moved once again to London Road, utilising a stop at Ryehill Street (in principle the Burton's Almshouses), in preparation for the introduction of the gyratory system on the north side of Trent Bridge. This was clearly not a popular move as on 15 November 1959, the boarding point was relocated to the eastern end of Victoria Embankment in front of the 43/46 stop.

There was a collision between a trolleybus and a car driven by Mr A May at the junction of Derby Road and Upper Parliament Street on 27 June 1960. The next day under similar circumstances the same trolleybus driver collided with Mr May's car at the same place! On 24 March 1961 the County Court found that the first accident, for which £4 damaged had been claimed, had been solely due to the negligence of the trolleybus driver. Damages of £400 were claimed for the second accident but it proved possible to settle the matter out of court for £258 2s including legal costs.

It was decided to replace more mechanical clocks with electric ones, at a cost of £229, on the following trolleybus routes:

Service 36	Nottingham Road, Valley Road
39	Wollaton Park, Harrow Road
39	Carlton, Post Office Square
41	Cinderhill
45	Wollaton Park, Orston Drive
47	Ransom Road

No trolleybus expenditure was foreseen in the capital expenditure programme for 1961/1962 but ominously discussion of the plans for a new depot on Western Boulevard, Basford were postponed pending a decision on the likely trolleybus operation policy.

The precise location of the loop or "slip" wires for sports specials at Victoria Station Bridge in Lower Parliament Street can be seen in this view of Karrier W/Brush 467 en route to Wells Road, Ransom Road on service 47. The gabled roof in front of the trolleybus is the side entrance to the railway station whilst just behind the following vehicle is the Milton's Head Hotel. *BTS*

There were plans to widen Huntingdon Street from Union Road to Howard Street which would require the replanting of 6 traction poles and some adjustments to the span wires. Service trolleybuses did not use the line although vehicles running into Parliament Street Depot off services 40 and 47 used the section further south from the junction of King Edward Street to Parliament Street. On 24 October 1960 the Transport Committee decided that the overhead wiring in Huntingdon Street, exception for the section used for depot journeys referred to above, should be dismantled. Apart from a short length, one way from King Edward Street to Lower Parliament Street this was cut down between January and May 1961 and 61 surplus traction poles were sold to the Lighting Department.

Driver A.E. Woodward, who had been retained as a trolleybus driver since he had attained the age of 65 on 22 December 1957, was retained for a further year (making him 69) and a new application from Driver J.H. Morris, who would be 65 on 11 February 1961, was granted. Both drivers satisfied the Departmental Doctor that they were fit to drive whilst there was a continuing shortage of drivers.

On 28 November 1960 Ben England presented a report to the Transport Committee setting out the advantages and disadvantages of motorbuses and trolleybuses. In view of his more recent comments it must have been a damning indictment of trolleybuses. Unfortunately, no copy of the report appears to have survived. The Committee deferred any consideration for 2 months.

The northernmost boarding point on Victoria Embankment, Trent Bridge, was that for London Road service 45. In conjunction with the introduction of the Trent Bridge gyratory system in 1959, wiring was erected enabling Arkwright Street services to overtake service 45 trolleybuses waiting here. BUT9641T 531 is displaying an advertisement for Carter Gate Motor Co. formerly owned by Alderman Sir Albert Atkey. The Globe Cinema is visible in the background. *Fred York*

Latterly Karrier W/Park Royal 470 featured rubber-mounted destination indicator boxes, a different layout of half-drop saloon windows and rubber mounted fixed panes at the front of the upper deck. 470 is seen here at the crossroads of King Edward Street with Huntingdon Street, by now bereft of trolleybus overhead wiring, with the awnings of Central Market visible to the nearside. *NTA*

The southern turning circle on Victoria Embankment, Trent Bridge at Bunbury Street with a backdrop of the River Trent. *MJ Russell*

On Wednesday 6 July 1955 HM Queen and the Duke of Edinburgh visited the Royal Show in Wollaton Park necessitating the curtailment or diversion of several trolleybus services. A limited number of 43s reached Trent Bridge along London Road, BUT9641T/Brush 571 being seen in the resultant heavy traffic at London Road High Level Station. *Peter Badgery*

The few passengers in the upper saloon of 8ft wide BUT9641T 515 are just about to experience a rumbling above them as the trolley booms pass beneath the right hand frog at the top of Norfolk Place providing access to the Theatre Square turning circle. Please note the advertisements each side of the front indicator box destination, the original lamp glass of the headlights but the latterday triangular Hella flashing trafficator on the side panels. *BTS*

A rare view of a trolleybus beneath the eastbound wiring in Southwell Road, not used by any regular services. It can be assumed that BUT9641T 538, a Bulwell Depot based vehicle, is operating a short working on service 44 and that it will turn back towards the city centre, by way of King Edward Street, at Bath Street. On the other side of the road sister vehicle 514 waits outside the Department's Head Office with its trolley booms stowed. *Neil Lewin*

Numerically the last BUT9641T, 601 pulls back on to The Wells Road having negotiated the Kildare Road turning circle. The former Nottingham Suburban Railway bridge has been demolished. *Martin Eady*

Trams never operated along the west end of Stockhill Lane indeed they cut off diagonally on their own private track (known as Dark Lane) across the recreation ground to Nuthall Road. The right of way can still be identified today. Here 7ft 6ins wide BUT9641T/Brush 577 cruises along Stockhill Lane towards Basford. The crossroads at Nuthall Road is visible in the background. Albion lorries, like their parent company Leyland, are now a thing of the past, just like Saxby's carriers. *MJ Russell*

At the summit of the Carlton route BUT 9641T/Brush 516 is seen opposite Hooton Road reversing triangle heading west to Wollaton Park via Ilkeston Road. Carlton Hill drops steeply away in the background. *MJ Russell*

Chapter 8 Rundown and Closure 1961-66

The "sea change" which was to spell the end of electric street traction in Nottingham until the reappearance of trams in 2004 had its formal origins in the Transport Committee Meeting of 23 January 1961 although it had been evident since before the War that there was no real enthusiasm for retaining trolleybuses despite their significance to the nearby coal-mining communities and their independence of imported fuel. In the late 1930s Mr Gunn's proposals to abandon the system had been inopportune with a considerable loan debt outstanding and a fleet of relatively new vehicles. Immediately after the war, replacement trolleybuses had been easier to acquire than building up a large fleet of additional motorbuses but by 1961 the utility vehicles were starting to show their age and their successors needed to be ordered soon. The Transport Committee was unlikely to be enthusiastic about electric traction with the owner of Shipsides Garage, Councillor Dyer, as its Vice Chairman.

Mr England asked that the Committee decide whether the trolleybus system should be abandoned or retained before deciding on a vehicle replacement policy and determining the design of the proposed Western Boulevard Depot in Basford. Accommodation for motorbuses alone required a cheaper, simpler design than two vehicle allocations. If it were decided to abandon the trolleybuses he would submit suggestions for an economical abandonment programme at a later meeting. In a momentous decision the Transport Committee agreed in principle to abandonment and decided that any new depot on Western Boulevard should be built solely for motorbuses. Although it weighed heavily against trolleybus retention, this depot was never built. No decision was made as to the phasing of the gradual abandonment, but it was proposed to take a first step by buying motorbuses to replace 11 trolleybuses scheduled for withdrawal in 1962-63.

Many observers consider that by 1961 the fate of the trolleybus in the UK was already sealed, not least by the spiralling cost of DC traction power supplied by the nationalised electricity industry, falling passenger loads and increasing urban road congestion. The influence of London Transport's 1954 decision to abandon the world's largest trolleybus system of some 1,800 vehicles, many of which were becoming due for replacement, and 256 route miles, on both manufacturers and operators should not be underestimated although the continuing development of the trolleybus abroad clearly shows that this mode of transport is well able to cope with twenty-first century conditions if there is an appropriate political will. Nonetheless, Nottingham was one of the first large provincial operators to announce a total abandonment, curiously only weeks after new trolleybuses entered service in nearby Derby.

The abandonment decision was only made public on 1 March 1961 when the first reports appeared in the local newspapers. The "Nottingham Evening Post" considered the news worthy of front-page headlines that proclaimed *"Nottingham To Scrap It's Trolleybuses"* whilst the "Nottingham Evening News" graphically announced *"Nottingham's Trolleybuses To Get The Axe"*. This provoked several critical readers' letters.

Both the "Nottingham Evening Post" and the "Nottingham Evening News", in identical reports in their 7 March 1961 editions, trumpeted that there would be *"No hasty scrapping of trolleybuses"*. They noted that *"Nottingham's trolleybuses, which are to be taken out of service gradually by the City Transport Committee, will be a familiar sight in the city streets for another six or eight years, it was stated at yesterday's council meeting. Ald. Sydney Hill, Chairman of the Transport Committee, answering questions from Mr David Jackson, said that the replacing of trolleybuses with motorbuses would take a considerable number of years. 'It would be quite easy to build up an argument for their retention', he said, 'but their disadvantages, we have reckoned, outweigh their advantages'. Answering a question on the problem of fumes emitted by motorbuses, Ald. Hill said that recent* (sic) *medical evidence had proved that this problem had been greatly exaggerated. 'Fumes from motorcars are much more dangerous', he said"*. Interestingly, a year later the "Nottingham Evening Post" published an article on air pollution in Nottingham, criticising the plumes of oily smoke from motorbuses, and which showed *"that the biggest dirt contributor was diesel oil"*. By 1964 the newspaper's readers were writing *"It is a sad day for us now that the clean trolleybus is playing out its last few months. There will be still more muck for the main road residents"*.

At this time the fleet consisted of 138 trolleybuses, 8 vehicles having been sold:

Karrier W	444, 454, 457, 459-465, 466, 469-471, 473, 475-478	(utility bodies)	19
Karrier W	479-482	Roe	4
BUT9611T	483-495	Roe	13
BUT 9641T	500-524	Brush 8ft	25
BUT 9641T	525-601	Brush 7ft 6ins	77

In an effort to retain trolleybus expertise without training a new generation of specialists as the fleet shrunk in size, Foreman Electrician J.R.C. Bailey was allowed to carry on working beyond his 65th birthday. Some time later it was decided that the Overhead Line Foreman no longer needed a departmental telephone line in his home.

Mr H.G. Morley, Deputy General Manager and Traffic Manager, who had joined the undertaking in 1910, at 14 years of age, retired on 6 May 1961. He had succeeded his father as Traffic Superintendent in 1930 and had been appointed Deputy General Manager in 1939. The vacancy attracted 27 applications and Mr Leonard Harrison, General Manager at West Bridgford, was selected. Due to a misunderstanding the position's responsibility for the Traffic Section passed to Mr L.A. Ward, Traffic Officer. It was clarified later that the intention had been to retain the two responsibilities in a single post and Mr Ward was compensated for the 9-month period he had carried out these duties.

In late March 1961 the EMEB advised that their traction current tariff would increase effective 1 April 1961 and the Department sought to negotiate a cheaper rate, without success. The new tariff included an adjustment clause based on the fuel cost per ton used by the CEGB whereas the fuel adjustment clause, which had been applicable since April 1942, related to the fuel cost at North Wilford Power Station. In drawn out discussions the Board showed no flexibility and by the end of June 1962 the Department had no alternative but to accept the new tariff, likely to cost £11,000 more pa, backdated to 1 April 1961 subject to agreement that there would be no further increases for at least 5 years, but the Board was not even prepared to give this assurance. In fact in the financial year ending 31 March 1962 the cost of traction current increased by £10,584, from £68,933 to £79,517.

The NJIC for Craftsmen in Municipal Passenger Transport Undertakings increased wages by 3d per hour from 2 April 1961 costing the undertaking £5,800 pa. The employees' side

Roe-bodied Karrier W 460 pauses in Bulwell Depot during an NTA tour of the system on 24 May 1964. Although the two-axle utility trolleybuses had performed regularly at peak hours on service 43 until November 1962 when Trent Bridge Depot's allocation was transferred to Parliament Street Depot coincident with the conversion of service 45, it was thereafter rare to see any two-axle trolleybus on the Bulwell services. To find such a vehicle within the confines of Bulwell Depot was rarer still. *Neil Lewin*

On 2 May 1965 1949 8ft wide BUT9641T/Brush 500 turns out of George Street into Carlton Street on a Nottingham Trolleybus Group tour, the cardboard sign on the front dash indicating that this was "The last trolleybus to Cinderhill and Trent Bridge" although trolleybuses had ceased to operate service 41 on the previous Friday night 30 April 1965. It was rare to see an 8ft wide BUT9641T in George Street as, apart from the final week of trolleybus operation of services 40 and 47, they did not run on The Wells Road – Wilford Road services. *Neil Lewin*

of the NJIC for the Road Passenger Transport Industry appealed to the Board of Arbitration for a wage increase and improved conditions, and were granted 11s per week, effective 16 April 1961. This would increase the undertaking's annual costs by £70,000. Taking into account the salary awards amounting to £8,000 granted in 1960, the pending increased current charges of £11,000 and the Craftsmens award it was estimated that the Department's expenditure for 1961/62 would equal its income. The additional income from the fare increase of 7 August 1960 would accrue during the 1961-62 financial year rather than in 1960-61, and it was immediately apparent that a further fare increase would be needed. The latest proposals were anchored in increases to the fares for 3 stages from 3d to 4d, 4 stages from 4d to 5d, 5 stages from 5d to 6d, 8 stages from 6d to 7d and 10-14 stages from 7d to 8d which all together would bring in an estimated £203,980 more revenue.

Trolleybuses were once again brought to a standstill on 8 June 1961 by flooding in Radford Road near its junction with Isandula Road, Basford, after heavy rainfall as the River Leen was unable to accept greater volumes of surface water. Services 42-44 were rerouted along Chelmsford Road and Nottingham Road using battery power.

In June 1961 it was noted that as trolleybuses circled the roundabout in the Old Market Square to proceed along Chapel Bar, the underneath of their rear platforms and the tube retaining their bamboo trolley retrieval poles scraped along the road surface. This was due to the road foundations having settled and major repairs were necessary to correct the problem: it was not caused by the dropped rear platforms of the BUT9641Ts!

At about 4.45 pm on 14 August 1961, as peak hour traffic began to build up, the dewirement of a 47 trolleybus at the junction of St. Peters Gate and Wheeler Gate, wrenched one of the trolley wires out of its hanger. A 43 trolleybus immediately behind tried to manoeuvre around the stranded vehicle but this resulted in the two trolley wires touching and the positive wire snapped. It fell, flailing wildly, to the ground and power was immediately cut off, leaving those trolleybuses in the Carrington Street section stranded. Emergency repairs were quickly carried out and the trolleybus service reinstated by 5.50 pm but not before traffic jams had built up between Castle Boulevard and the Old Market Square, and along Canal Street as far as the Ice Stadium on Lower Parliament Street.

In conjunction with the trolleybus abandonment a new single style of bus stop flag replaced the separate green and red colour coded versions. Following earlier debate about improved visibility, it was decided on 23 October 1961 to replace motorbus stop flags as they became due for replacement with yellow flags having black lettering and showing the numbers of the services using the stop in a grid. These yellow flags replaced their green trolleybus equivalents as each route was converted to motorbus operation, their appearance often providing advance notice of an impending change before it was announced in the press.

The "Nottingham Evening Post" of 9 October 1961 announced the formation of the Nottingham Trolleybus Group (NTG) whose declared aim was to campaign against the trolleybus

"On a Saturday the service timing on the 39 Wollaton Park – Carlton was a trolleybus every 3 minutes. This was a 77-seater with 8 standing and they were busy. After 9.30 am the driver would stay in his cab at the terminus so that he could depart "on the dot" knowing that a delay of 2 minutes would put you 5 minutes behind the service in front of you and only one minute in front of the trolleybus behind. Because you were running late you not only got your own passengers but possibly those of the trolleybus behind you. I do believe that the Nottingham trolleybuses operated the fastest service in Britain.
Imagine leaving Wollaton Park on a 39 at 5.30pm, the next stop is the Raleigh Cycle factory and 50 workers get on. The next stop was also for Raleigh and a further 30 get on. Almost full and the trolleybus, made up of its 10 ton unladen weight together with its load, is now feeling rather heavy for the driver. The following stop Faraday Road is also a Raleigh boarding point, the driver can now see the 39 in front similarly laden and in his mirror the one behind, also full!"

Bernard Jefford, who drove trolleybuses 1960-1963.

Although not strictly a low bridge, the deeply curved arches of the bridge carrying the erstwhile Great Northern Railway's Derby line across Vernon Road at Basford North Station has caused the driver of BUT9641T 526 to move to the centre of the road as he heads south on 2 May 1964. Trolleybuses were not permitted to pass each other beneath this bridge. *Peter Badgery*

BUT 9611T/Roe 484 having just crossed Friar Lane traffic lights heading south into Wheeler Gate. Home Ales like the trolleybuses is a thing of the past but the magnficent brewery building complete with reliefs of the beer making process still stands at on Mansfield Road at Daybrook. *NTA*

The trolleybus route between Nottingham Road, Basford and Bells Lane, Cinderhill was originally constructed by NCT at the behest of N&D. BUT9641T/Brush 500 is seen at the junction of Alpine Street with High Street, Basford, a location unchanged today, heading for the city centre and Trent Bridge. *MJ Russell*

abandonment policy but also, increasingly, as their campaigning bore no fruit, to try to preserve representative members of the fleet for posterity.

As a result of the continuing shortage of trolleybus drivers, Drivers Morris and Woodward (by now 69 years old) were retained for a further 12 months. By the early 1960s, it was normally the 41 Cinderhill service from which inspectors first took off vehicles as it was paralleled throughout, except between Nottingham Road and Bells Lane terminus, by other trolleybus services. On one occasion there was solely a single vehicle running on the service!

Rather than replace the eleven 56-seater utility trolleybuses due for withdrawal in 1962 by motorbuses on a one-for-one basis, it had been decided in March 1961 to order motorbuses of a higher capacity which would also be suitable for serving the new Bestwood housing estates. Daimler "Fleetlines" were ordered for delivery in spring 1962. Work to widen London Road between the entrance to Eastcroft and Canal Street, necessitating realignment of the overhead equipment at a cost of £2,000 – £3,000, was expected to start about the same time. This was felt to be the opportunity to carry out the first stage of the abandonment programme and on 17 November 1961 the Transport Committee resolved that either from the start of road works or the arrival of the new motorbuses, whichever was earlier, trolleybus service 45 should be permanently replaced.

Cries to alleviate peak hour traffic congestion on the city side of Trent Bridge by making parts of Arkwright Street and London Road one-way streets were supported by the Transport Committee in February 1962 even if it might lead to the abandonment of trolleybus services in this area earlier than expected.

The first quarter of 1962 was plagued with difficulties involving the overhead equipment. A broken trolley wire at Canning Circus at 5.30 pm on 31 January 1962 delayed peak hour services whilst a snapped span wire at the junction of Milton Street with Upper Parliament Street caused delays on 7 February 1962. On 19 March 1962 a high load brought down the wiring at the junction of Arkwright Street with Waterway Street causing short delays to trolleybus services 41 and 43. The last item in this run of bad luck was on 25 April 1962 when a 41 trolleybus dewired at the Nuthall Road end of end of Stockhill Lane damaging the Rediffusion cables.

Until March 1962 the size of the trolleybus fleet remained constant with 138 vehicles in stock, indeed the last withdrawal had been in 1959 prior to any abandonment decision. In April 1962 Karrier W 466, the last utility trolleybus with a Brush body, was withdrawn. It was seen at Parliament Street Depot on 17 March 1962 having received accident damage to its platform and rear panelling. Clearly there was some debate as to its future, not least as 466 had received attention to its rear panelling at Trent Bridge Works during May 1961, but on 29 April 1962 it was in Manvers Street Yard awaiting disposal. The vehicle immediately became a candidate for preservation by the Nottingham Trolleybus Group but initial enquiries revealed a scrap value of around £100 and thus out of the Group's financial reach. However, Mr. England kindly suggested that he would place the matter before the Transport Committee if a reasonable figure was proposed and £60 was offered.

Mr England was due to retire on 14 December 1962 having reached 65 years of age and in March 1962 the forthcoming vacancy was advertised at £3,695 pa rising by three annual increments of £125 to £4,070 pa, the appointment including responsibility for the fleet of the Ambulance Service. Yet the General Manager was still busily shaping the future with suggestions for a cheaper simplified vehicle colour scheme using more cream which, but for minimal modifications, was to become the fleet livery for the next 30 years. His spray-painted livery proposals were adopted but, although trolleybus overhauls and repainting continued, it was never applied to a trolleybus. The only concession to

The Annual Report for 1961-62 recorded that the average age of trolleybus fleet was now 12 years 1 month (motorbuses 8 years 4 months), with 119 of them being more than 10 years old. Although the Transport Committee had agreed to trolleybus abandonment over a period of years, it was becoming evident that the programme would have to be accelerated by phasing it with the introduction of one-way streets in the city centre. This would avoid heavy expenditure on overhead line alterations which would only be used for a short period of time.

BUT9641T 574 approaching Gregory Boulevard roundabout on Mansfield Road en route for Nottingham Road, Valley Road. *MJ Russell*

The illuminated globe on top of the Palais de Danse and the uncompromising Coombes building on Lower Parliament Street provide the background to Karrier W/Roe 479 at the crossroads of Huntingdon Street with King Edward Street as it heads northeastwards to Ransom Road on a 47. *BTS*

Karrier W/Park Royal 469 leaves Canning Circus citywards along Derby Road on one of the eastbound peak hour journeys on service 38 which originated at Wollaton Park rather than the customary Elite Cinema. From at least 1960, no 469 operated with hardboard in one of its front upper deck louvre windows! In the background two cream liveried rear engine motorbuses weave into the right hand lane whilst the Sir John Borlace Warren public house at the top of the isolated portion of Ilkeston Road advertises the wares of Shipstones New Basford "Star" Brewery (which finally closed in 1991). *Neil Lewin*

the change was the revised application of the undertaking's title in two lines rather than one, 520 being the first to appear so treated during May 1962.

By 5 July 1962 a short list of candidates had been prepared consisting of R.F. Bennett, General Manager and Engineer, Bolton; L.C. Harrison, Deputy General Manager and Traffic Manager, Nottingham; E. Haughton, Chief Engineer, Liverpool; J. Rostron, General Manager and Engineer, Grimsby and Cleethorpes; L.H. Smith, Deputy General Manager, Leicester; and J.C. Wake, General Manager, Bradford.

John Wake was appointed. Although coming from the trolleybus stronghold of Bradford it is understood that he had just been successful in persuading that city's Transport Committee to adopt a policy of conversion to motorbus operation. Whatever the trolleybus enthusiasts of the period may have thought, Mr Wake proved a humane and shrewd administrator who implemented the Transport Committee's trolleybus abandonment decision in line with financial principles and good business practice. Hopes that a change of management might provoke a change of direction were adolescent pipe dreams. Upon retirement, 11 years later, he was interviewed by the "Nottingham Evening Post": in their 27 November 1973 edition he reflected upon his career and stated *"I began to think that my mission in life was to get rid of trolley buses. I'd done it at St. Helens and in Bradford. Now, it was my first job on arriving in Nottingham"*. He went on to admit that, "In terms of pollution you can't beat the trolleybus".

Effective 8 April 1962, the headway of service 45 was reduced from 15 to 20 minutes between 9.00 am and 2.00 pm and from 10 to 12 minutes from 2 pm onwards on Sundays. The service 39 headway was also reduced from 6 to 7½ minutes between 9 am and 2 pm and from 5 to 6 minutes from 2 pm onwards on Sundays.

In November 1961 the tender of William Appleby & Son Ltd for roofing over part of Stanhope Street was accepted, all overhead equipment in Stanhope Street between bay 5 of Parliament Street Depot and the junction with Manvers Street having been removed in the first 8 months of the year. By coincidence in May 1962, A.R. Atkey & Co., trading as Carter Gate Motor Co., offered to give up the leasehold of their property at the corner of Stanhope Street with Lower Parliament Street. It was estimated that the acquisition of the leasehold, which still had 57 years to run, would cost £100,000 plus ground rents. This would enable Bulwell Depot, by now classified as life-expired and unsuitable for modernisation, to be closed but it was feared that the combined costs of demolition and rebuilding of the site, roofing over Stanhope Street and the "annex" would be more expensive than the alternative of a new depot at Western Boulevard, Basford, and it was decided not to take up the offer.

The NJIC for the Road Passenger Transport Industry awarded 6s 6d per week to traffic employees, semi-skilled and un-skilled depot employees, plus an addition of £2 to the two weeks annual holiday pay from 20 May 1962. Although this award cost the undertaking £46,000 pa it was decided not to seek a fares increase but to meet the cost from the expected operating surplus. In fact the net revenue account for the year ending 31 March 1962 showed a surplus of £92,018 plus an amount of £3,865 brought forward from 1961. This was the highest surplus since the undertaking's inception (the record surplus recorded in 1942-43 of £124,000 had been reduced to £69,400 after payment of £54,600 income tax). As a result £65,898 was invested in capital expenditure, for example roofing over Stanhope Street, filling in pits, chassis cleaning plant, 18 motorbus chassis, stores van and passenger shelters; with £29,985 being carried forward to the following year.

The fleet was further reduced in May 1962 by the withdrawal of 457, the last of the 1944 Karrier Ws with Weymann utility bodies (batch 455-458). This trolleybus operated all day on service 36 on 30 May 1962 before being parked in Stanhope Street and by 8 June 1962 in Manvers Street Yard. During June 1962 it was taken to Trent Bridge Works where salvageable electrical equipment, including trolley booms, was removed. Thence it was towed to Sherwood motorbus depot where it became a temporary staff canteen during garage renovation work and probably the sole trolleybus to enter this former tram depot.

The Transport Committee of 17 September 1962 approved the purchase of 2 miles of unused trolley wire from Doncaster at £749 (it would have cost £836 new). They also agreed to a capital expenditure programme covering the next 5 years, which included 60 motorbuses in 1964/65

Brush bodied Karrier W 466, subsequently preserved, climbs Queen Street past the Nottingham Road services stop, showing its shiny new rear dome, fitted in May 1961 and contrasting with the rest of the vehicle which had not received a full repaint since 12/55. By this date work on utility trolley-buses, other than routine maintenance, was minimal thus the re-panelling on 466 was rather unusual. It was unfortunate that 466 would be the next withdrawal, following an accident in March 1962, when its rear end was damaged! *Rod Bramley*

The well known double bracket arm traction pole at the junction of Queen Street with King Street. *MJ Russell*

(£408,000) and a further 67 in 1965/66 (£455,600) to replace trolleybuses.

An article in the "Guardian Journal" of 4 September 1962 stated that trolleybuses would continue to run until they were life-expired or changes to their routes, for example one-way systems, were needed. Trolleybus maintenance in 1961-62 cost £9,346 (a reduction of £1,974). The surplus on trolleybus operation was £57,000 whilst that on the motorbuses was £35,000.

On 22 October 1962 a member of the Transport Committee tabled a question on *"the life of certain trolleybuses and their routes in the city"* and suggested that the decision to gradually abandon the fleet should be reviewed, as the principal trolleybus routes were most profitable. Although the power to run the trolleybus system was generated from locally mined coal and there was an influential miner's lobby, the Committee did not reconsider their decision. A request that service 43 be extended to Bulwell Hall Estate was refused after a passenger census. At the same meeting they agreed to sell withdrawn trolleybus 466 to the Nottingham Trolleybus Group for £60. The NTG, having no idea of the Committee's proceedings, were beginning to fear the worst having heard nothing for some time but now received a delightful reply from Mr England stating that the bid had been accepted and *"can you please move your vehicle from our depot!"* The Group intimated that they might wish to purchase a second trolleybus later and that they would preserve them in a "working museum".

It was deemed necessary to withdraw trolleybus service 45 on 3 November 1962 in order that road works on London Road could start. On 23 October 1962 a handbill, printed in red as used in motorbus announcements as opposed to the green used for trolleybus information, appeared, headed:

Service 45
Commencing on Sunday November 4th this service will be operated by motorbuses and there will be a slight revision of the timetable.

This was the sole occasion in Nottingham where such a handbill was published in connection with a trolleybus route abandonment. The timetable revision was due to the transfer of service 45 operations from Trent Bridge Depot to Parliament Street Depot ensuring that Trent Bridge retained its status as a trolleybus-only depot.

This was also the only abandonment under the stewardship of Ben England and followed established practice whereby the last trolleybus operated on a Saturday evening to coincide with the Sunday to Saturday duty roster and enabling crews of the replacement motorbuses to get used to the changes during the more relaxed Sunday schedules. Financial and licensing convenience ensured that most subsequent abandonments coincided with the last day of a month whether a weekend or not.

Side bracket traction poles of the tramway era retaining their ornamental scrollwork and complete with cast iron bases featuring the Corporation coat of arms could be found in Wilford Road until this route closed on 9 October 1965. BUT 9611T 486 is seen near Kirkwhite Street en route to Wilford Bridge on 27 March 1965 some 4 days before the operation of two axle trolleybuses in Nottingham ceased. The Council House dome is evident in the background. *Neil Lewin*

In June 1966 BUT9641T 507 ascends Nottingham Road on its way back to the City. Service 37, the peak hours only service to Haydn Road, terminated where the road widens out in the distance. *Neil Lewin*

No. 575 has stopped in Carrington Street at the Nottingham Midland Station northbound stop hence the destination details shown on the board attached to traction pole. As no wiring leading into Station Street, on the opposite side of the road with the pub on the corner, is evident, this photograph must have been taken at sometime between May 1963 and 31 March 1965 when trolleybus service 43 was withdrawn. *Neil Lewin*

Overhead crews were out during the last week of service 45 replacing the green trolleybus stops flags with red motorbus ones, the only occasion during the abandonment programme that the established red type rather than the new yellow flags were used.

As anticipated, some of the oldest trolleybuses in the fleet, Parliament Street's utility vehicles were withdrawn, and in compensation Trent Bridge Depot transferred utilities 459 and 460 together with some of their BUT9641Ts (ultimately nos. 594-601). Rather than make empty journeys, as each BUT9641T-operated 45 passed Parliament Street Depot after 10.00 pm, it was run into the depot and replaced by one of the condemned utility vehicles thereby ensuring a maximum of economy. Karrier Ws 462, 465, 473, 475 and 476 all operated on the 45 during its final hours, completing their duties at Trent Bridge Depot. Indeed 475 performed the last through journey from Trent Bridge to Wollaton Park via London Road, Upper Parliament Street and Derby Road, and returned, as usual for the last service 45 departure on Saturday evenings, from Wollaton Park via Derby Road but then as a non-scheduled 43 journey through the Old Market Square and along Arkwright Street to Trent Bridge. It reached Trent Bridge Depot shortly after midnight on Sunday 4 November 1962.

Despite the lack of prior notice of the closure, the NTG asked the Department if they could hire a trolleybus to tour the service 45 wiring and were surprised when Sunday 4 November 1962, the day following conversion, was suggested. Unaware of the Department's plans to transfer utility vehicles in service on the final night, 464, which under ordinary circumstances would have been an unusual sight on the 45, was chosen. The rarely used Cattle Market and Gregory Street turning circles were utilised but it was not possible to energise the Station Street wiring for a last trip although 464 did run as far as the section breaker and thus the start of the "dead" wiring before reversing out into London Road. Power to London Road was switched off immediately after the tour, and on 14 November 1962 a start was made on cutting down the overhead wiring although much still remained in January 1963.

In the ensuing days the press published a number of comments to the conversion from the public: some professed not to have noticed the difference whilst others were critical and said that they preferred the trolleybuses. The overhead layout at Canning Circus was simplified (this being the final "big job" that the overhead crews were to undertake other than routine maintenance and, of course, removal of disused wiring) and other re-alignments were carried out in November/December 1962 following the 45 withdrawal.

The removal of the direct link between Parliament Street and Trent Bridge Depots meant that maintenance staff henceforth often followed George Street, Victoria Street and South Parade, when moving vehicles south, reintroducing 3-axle trolleybuses to these streets for the first time in some 15 years albeit infrequently and not in passenger service. Use of 2-axle trolleybuses was increasingly restricted to services 40 and 47, whilst their use on peak hour 41 duties became virtually unknown, with a greater number of 3-axle vehicles sharing duties on services 36, 37 and 38.

As an immediate consequence of the 45 conversion trolleybuses 444, 454, 462, 465, 473, 475, 476 and 477 were withdrawn and ultimately stripped at Trent Bridge Works for spares. Amongst them were certain vehicles of interest: 444 was the last survivor of a quartet of 1943/4 Karrier W utility vehicles (442-445) with Weymann bodies and the final Weymann trolleybus in the fleet, and had been taken out of service on 31 October 1962; 454 was the last member of a trio of 1944 Karrier Ws (452-454) with Park Royal bodies and was last used on 30 October 1962 although some similar vehicles of a later series remained in stock; in 1946 476 had been the first trolleybus in the UK to be equipped with automatic acceleration and had also been an early user of fluorescent lighting (1947-1958/9). Shortly thereafter, following "learner" duties on 28 November 1962, trolleybus 463 was withdrawn too.

With this first service withdrawal the Nottingham trolleybus network appeared as follows:

36 Old Market Square (Queen Street/King Street) – Upper Parliament Street – Milton Street – Victoria Station – Mansfield Road – Nottingham Road (Valley Road)

Karrier W 480 Turney Street Trent Bridge on an enthusiasts tour 7 March 1965. *Martin Eady*

A proud father balances precariously with his baby child on the rear open platform of BUT9641T 527 as it swings out of Bentinck Road over the setts into Alfreton Road on 19 July 1964. *Peter Badgery*

37 Old Market Square (Queen Street/King Street) – Upper Parliament Street – Milton Street – Victoria Station – Mansfield Road – Nottingham Road (Haydn Road) *(Monday – Friday peak hours only)*

38 Theatre Square – Upper Parliament Street – Carlton Road – Carlton (Hooton Road) (eastbound via Central Market – King Edward Street – Bath Street – Handel Street, westbound via Southwell Road – Lower Parliament Street) *(Monday – Friday peak hours only)*

39 Carlton (Post Office Square) – Carlton Road – Central Market – Upper Parliament Street – Ilkeston Road – Wollaton Park (Middleton Boulevard, Harrow Road) *(eastbound via Central Market – King Edward Street – Bath Street – Handel Street, westbound via Southwell Road – Lower Parliament Street)*

40 The Wells Road (Kildare Road) – St. Ann's Wells Road – King Edward Street – Upper Parliament Street – Old Market Square – Wilford Road – Wilford Bridge *(northbound via Long Row – Queen Street – Upper Parliament Street, southbound via George Street – Carlton Street – Victoria Street – Poultry – South Parade)*

41 Trent Bridge – Arkwright Street – Carrington Street – Old Market Square – Upper Parliament Street – Milton Street – Victoria Station – Mansfield Road – Nottingham Road – Stockhill Lane – Nuthall Road – Cinderhill *(northbound via Queen Street, southbound via King Street)*

42 Basford (Northern Baths) – Vernon Road – Radford Road – Hyson Green – Alfreton Road – Derby Road – Old Market Square *(Monday – Friday peak hours only)*

43 Bulwell Market – Basford – Vernon Road – Radford Road – Hyson Green – Alfreton Road – Derby Road – Old Market Square – Carrington Street – Arkwright Street – Trent Bridge

44 Bulwell Hall Estate – Bulwell Market – Basford – Vernon Road – Radford Road – Hyson Green – Alfreton Road – Derby Road – Upper Parliament Street – Bath Street – Manvers Street – Sneinton – Colwick Road *(northbound via King Street, Long Row, Beastmarket Hill, Angel Row; southbound via Upper Parliament Street)*

46 Old Market Square (Processional Way) – Carrington Street – Arkwright Street – Trent Bridge *(Summer Sundays only, with occasional peak hour and infrequent late evening journeys Monday – Saturday throughout the year)*

47 The Wells Road (Ransom Road) – St Ann's Well Road – King Edward Street – Lower Parliament Street – Old Market Square – Wilford Road – Wilford Bridge *(northbound via Long Row – Queen Street – Upper Parliament Street, southbound via Upper Parliament Street – George Street – Carlton Street – Victoria Street – The Poultry – Old Market Square)*

In November 1962 Norman's offered a trial shelter which, if the proposed advertising matter proved unacceptable, could be returned or offered to the Department for purchase, and it was decided to erect it in King Edward Street at the inwards stop of services 40 and 47. By now however few trolleybuses were left in service having "47 Wilford Road" printed on their blinds, most southbound vehicles from either Kildare Road or Ransom Road displaying "40 WILFORD ROAD".

The presence of barrow boys was obstructing the bus stops in Long Row whilst at the alighting stop outside Pearson Brothers store trolleybuses frequently had to stop some distance from the kerb due to double parking by other vehicles at this point. The Chief Constable supported the proposal to prohibit parking at a number of city centre bus stops where drivers were frequently hindered from pulling into the kerb by parked vehicles and in addition "Bus Stop" was to be painted on the road surface. Those involving trolleybuses were:

40/47	Outward	Long Row
40/47	Outward	Bath Street
40/47	Inward	Bath Street
40, 44, 47	Inward	King Edward Street
All	Inward	Pearson's, Long Row
36	Outward	Mansfield Road/Shakespeare Street
All	Inward	Lower Parliament Street (Star Stores), opposite the Palais de Danse
All	Inward	Derby Road (Roughton's shop), between Canning Circus and the Cathedral, opposite Upper College Street
40/47	Outward	South Parade
All	Inward	Derby Road (Albert Hotel), prior to the junction with Upper Parliament Street

Already planning ahead, Mr Wake reported to the 31 December 1962 Transport Committee Meeting that preparatory work to build an inner ring road would necessitate the replacement of a considerable number of trolley vehicles in 1964/65. It proved a complex situation but following discussions with the City Engineer and the City Treasurer, on 25 February 1963 he received approval for a purchasing programme, aimed at maintaining services with a minimum of new overhead wiring or realignments of existing equipment.

The southern (Trent Bridge) end of Arkwright Street with 7ft 6ins wide BUT9641T 575 on service 43 being followed by 8ft 0ins wide BUT9641T 520 on service 41. The white arrow painted on the road indicates the turn into Truman's Road, starting point of the gyratory system introduced on 1 November 1959. *Neil Lewin*

With the withdrawal of Roe bodied utility 464 during March 1963, there were 126 trolleybuses recorded as being available for service:

Karrier W	459-461	Roe utility bodies	3
Karrier W	469-471, 478	Park Royal utility bodies	4
Karrier W	479-482	Roe	4
BUT 9611T	483-495	Roe	13
BUT 9641T	500-524	Brush 8ft	25
BUT 9641T	525-601	Brush 7ft 6ins	77

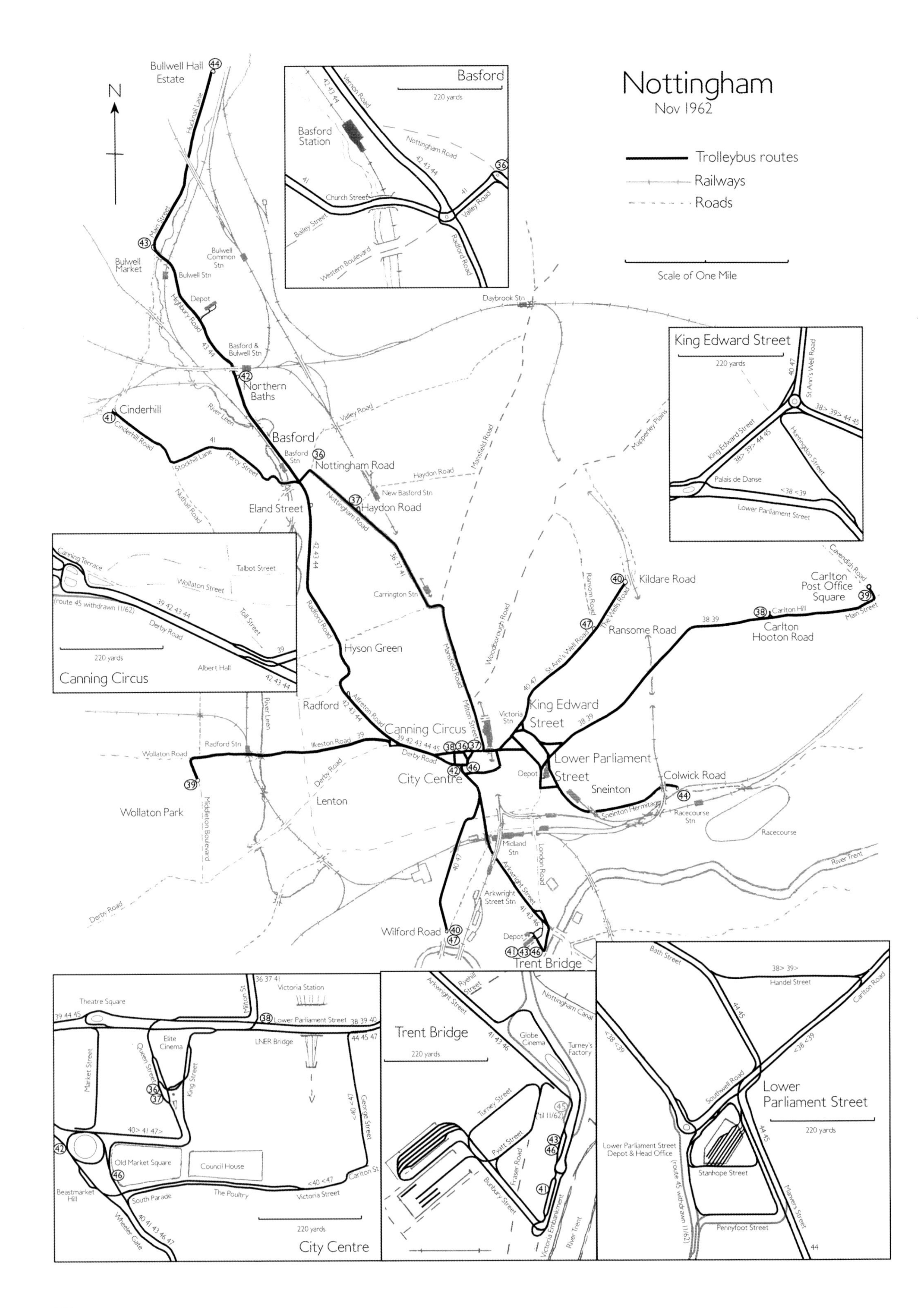
Nottingham
Nov 1962
Trolleybus routes
Railways
Roads
Scale of One Mile
N
Basford
220 yards
Basford Station
Vernon Road
Nottingham Road
Church Street
Bailey Street
Western Boulevard
Valley Road
Radford Road
King Edward Street
St Ann's Well Road
Huntingdon Street
Palais de Danse
Lower Parliament Street
Canning Circus
Canning Terrace
Talbot Street
Wollaton Street
(route 45 withdrawn 11/62)
Derby Road
Toll Street
Albert Hall
Bullwell Hall Estate
Hucknall Lane
Main Street
Bulwell Market
Bulwell Common Stn
Bulwell Stn
Depot
Highbury Road
Basford & Bulwell Stn
Northern Baths
Cinderhill
Cinderhill Road
River Leen
Stockhill Lane
Percy Street
Basford Stn
Nottingham Road
Haydon Road
New Basford Stn
Eland Street
Nuthall Road
Valley Road
Daybrook Stn
Mansfield Road
Mapperley Plains
Carrington Stn
Hyson Green
Radford
Alfreton Road
Woodborough Road
Kildare Road
Ransom Road
The Wells Road
Ransome Road
Carlton Post Office Square
Cavendish Road
Carlton Hill
Main Street
Carlton Hooton Road
Victoria Stn
Milton Street
Radford Stn
Wollaton Road
Ilkeston Road
Wollaton Park
Middleton Boulevard
Lenton
City Centre
Depot
Sneinton
Colwick Road
Sneinton Hermitage
Racecourse Stn
Racecourse
Midland Stn
London Road
Arkwright Street
Arkwright Street Stn
River Trent
Wilford Road
Trent Bridge
City Centre
Theatre Square
Milton St
Victoria Station
Lower Parliament Street
Elite Cinema
LNER Bridge
Market Street
Queen Street
King Street
George Street
Old Market Square
Council House
Carlton St
Beastmarket Hill
South Parade
The Poultry
Victoria Street
Wheeler Gate
Trent Bridge
Ryehill Street
Nottingham Canal
Globe Cinema
Turney's Factory
Turney Street
Pyatt Street
Fraser Road
Bunbury Street
Victoria Embankment
'til 11/62
Lower Parliament Street
Bath Street
Handel Street
Carlton Road
Southwell Road
Lower Parliament Street Depot & Head Office
Stanhope Street
Pennyfoot Street
Manvers Street
(route 45 withdrawn 11/62)

The long climb up Derby Road presented no challenge to the trolleybuses. Here 7ft 6ins wide B.U.T.9641T 542 leads 8ft wide counterpart 516 past Upper College Street. Visible is the blackened spire of St. Barnabas' Roman Catholic Cathedral, since cleaned, with the tower of St. Mary's Church, sometimes called the "Mother Church of Nottingham", on the horizon. *Neil Lewin*

Eight foot wide BUT9641T 509 negotiates Bells Lane roundabout Cinderhill, northern terminus of service 41. *MJ Russell*

1964/65		
41	9 vehicles	
42	4 vehicles	
43	30 vehicles	Total 43
1965/66		
40, 47	18 vehicles	
44	19 vehicles	Total 37
1966/67		

The remaining 47 trolley vehicles would be replaced.

These figures reflected minimum requirements, indicating orders for 44, 40 and 43 motorbuses respectively although Mr Wake considered that the final figure might be 4-5 units less to allow for the advantages of a unified fleet. By the time these figures were approved by the City Council on 29 July 1963 the number of replacement motorbuses required had been finalised as 44 in 1964, 40 in 1965-66 and 37 in 1966-67.

The trolleybus fleet appeared increasingly run-down and shabby; in particular Bulwell Depot's vehicles illustrated a lack of attention and cleanliness. The rear panels and windows suffered from carbon and grease deposits from the trolleyheads above but were infrequently washed. The lower deck side panel inspection hatches were often left unsecured, merrily banging open and shut as vehicles travelled along! Inside, the half-drop wind down windows remained jammed open at curious angles in the worst of weathers whilst the green leathercloth on the stairwell interior panelling suffered tears or was ripped off completely. Depressingly little was done to correct these superficial signs of wear and tear. Driver training continued with Karrier Ws straying somewhat from their usual territories, the routes of services 36-38, 40 and 47. The almost reckless driving standards of newer recruits, particularly in disregarding the speed limits for passing beneath special overhead work, resulting in dewirements and delays to other road traffic, did nothing to improve the trolleybuses' reputation although it must be stressed that the vehicles remained mechanically sound.

It became policy not to repair accident damaged trolleybuses rather than withdraw the oldest first, the remaining utility vehicles having all benefited from a substantial post-war rebuilding. On 10 May 1963 BUT9611T 484 was seen in Manvers Street Yard in poor condition with some damage to the front paneling and at the end of the month became the first post-war vehicle to be officially withdrawn. Curiously 493 returned to service a few days later following an overhaul and repaint precipitated by a serious accident in St. Anns Well Road on 15 February 1963. This was the last occasion that a BUT9611T benefited from such treatment. Utility trolleybuses were by now increasingly rare on Britain's streets. In June 1963 utility trolleybuses 459 and 470 were withdrawn whilst 457 was towed to Trent Bridge Depot for disposal following use as a temporary canteen at Sherwood motorbus depot.

There were a number of complaints about gaps in the peak hour service along Radford Road and Nottingham Road. The General Manager replied that the high frequencies combined with traffic congestion leading to delays at peak periods, made it impossible for the services to operate strictly to schedule and some bunching of vehicles was inevitable. There might be some improvements when the planned "No Parking" measures on certain main routes at peak periods had been introduced. By June 1965 he was reporting that the bunching of vehicles on service 43 had been much reduced by the withdrawal of trolleybuses.

The 27 May 1963 Transport Committee Meeting accepted Mr Wake's recommendation that for motorbus replacement 70-seater forward entrance, front engine vehicles should be used whereas for trolleybus replacement 77-seater front entrance rear-engine vehicles should be employed. The 44 motorbuses required for trolleybus replacement would be needed by 1 January 1965 to avoid any conflict with the construction of the southern end of the inner ring (today's Maid Marian Way) although at this stage it was anticipated a new roundabout at its northern end near Chapel Bar would require new overhead wiring. He doubted whether Northern Counties Motor and Engineering Co. Ltd., who had submitted the lowest tender, could build all the bodies in time as the first of their 31 bodies due for completion by 31 May 1963 had yet to be delivered. The order was accordingly split as follows: 44 Leyland "Atlantean" chassis at £3,082 11s per chassis, together with 22 Northern Counties bodies at £3,723 19s 3d and 22 Metropolitan-Cammell-Weymann (MCW) bodies at £4,002 10s each.

The financial year 1962/63 ended with a £98,490 surplus, which with a £29,985 balance from the previous year, made a total of £128,475.

"Dusty" Miller was not over-keen on work. When running on a 40 or 47 he would deliberately misjudge the frog setter at the southern end of Queen Street resulting in his trolley booms taking the Post Office 36, 37, 41 loop, forcing the vehicle behind to overtake him and thus pick up the passengers en route to St. Anne's Well Road whilst he followed almost empty!"

"Some of the later recruits gave scant attention to speed limits! One day a hanger was pulled out on Carlton Road bringing a trolley wire almost down to the road surface. A passer-by had witnessed the previous trolleybus doing a terrific speed. It was necessary to de-pole and battery around the damaged overhead equipment whilst the trolleybus behind was asked to wait there and warn the next trolleybus and so on. When I reached Carlton terminus I telephoned the overhead crew to come and make emergency repairs".

One morning Bernard and his wife travelled in to Parliament Street on their motor scooter for an early shift. Understandably he assisted his wife with some of her duties such as "dressing" the vehicle i.e. correctly setting the indicator boxes. Suddenly she screamed and a man came running down the stairs. He had fallen asleep on the upper deck and had spent the night in the trolleybus! On another occasion they reached the depot when his wife, who was not a great enthusiast for getting up early, realised that, despite being in full uniform, she had sleepily not remembered to change her footwear. The shift was worked in carpet slippers, which no doubt added to the homely welcome on the trolleybus!

Happy memories of operating 39s on hot summer days with both cab sliding doors open and the windscreen panels pushed forward. From Hooton Road to Carlton vehicles frequently reached 50 mph. In the winters despite a two bar electric heater, the cabs were still cold and drivers wore heavy greatcoats.

Inbound Carlton Road trolleybuses would wait in the lay-by outside the Manvers School to ensure that the time clock there was punched at the correct time. The conductor would wait until the correct moment with the card in the recording machine.

Basford Northern Baths to the junction with Nottingham Road (the city ring road) was known as the "mad mile" as trolleybuses travelled so fast on this stretch.

Bernard Jefford, who drove trolleybuses 1960-1963.

On 24 May 1964 the NTA hired 1945 Karrier W/Roe 460 and BUT9641T 562 for a tour of the system. Here 460 turns from Turney Street into Frazer Road, part of the access and test wiring for the Trent Bridge Depot and Works. Although many undertakings either rebodied or substantially rebuilt their utility vehicles, Nottingham continued to operate them in substantially original condition but for a few improvements until final withdrawal from service. 460 has had its half-drop opening windows replaced by sliding windows and a rear destination indicator box fitted. *Neil Lewin*

The City Treasurer suggested £83,365 contributions towards capital expenditure and that after adjustments £46,972 should be carried forward.

A proposal for increased fares, estimated to increase income by £110,944, was insufficient to cover the undertaking's capital expenditure programme for the next 3 years and 3 further alternatives were discussed, together with a 1d increase on all workmen's fares. The General Manager showed that a £100,000 revenue increase would only cover additional expenditure for 1 year, £200,000 2 years and £250,000 3 years. The Transport Committee recommended Proposal A to the City Council, which approved it on 29 July 1963. The Traffic Commissioners however felt that the existing 2d adult minimum fare should only be increased to 2½d and not 3d with the exception of two stages jointly operated with WBUDC. The new fares were introduced on Sunday 13 October 1963 and on 28 October 1963 it was decided to increase the price of passes for blind persons living outside the city to 4s per week, and those for Police and Probationary Officers from £19 to £21 pa.

A newspaper article on 12 June 1963 headed *"Move to put up city bus fares on way"* also contained the first public intimation of the pending trolleybus abandonment programme, stating that services 41, 42 and 43 would be converted to motorbus operation in January 1965 followed by services 40, 44 and 47 around 1 June 1965 and finally the 36, 37 and 39 in mid-1966.

On Sunday 6 October 1963 the disused Nottingham Suburban Railway bridge over Colwick Road, immediately to the west of Roughill Woods, was demolished and the road was closed to all traffic between the bridge and Colwick Road Railway Crossing. Several spans of overhead wiring were temporarily removed to carry out this work and service 44 trolleybuses terminated just short of the bridge by reversing into a side road using their traction batteries, the route east thereof being left un-served.

At the end of September 1963 the first BUT9641T, 536, together with BUT9611T 483, was withdrawn; in October 1963 BUT 9611Ts 490, 494 and BUT9641Ts 534, 543 and 544 followed; whilst 554 went in November 1963. The loss of 12 trolleybuses from the operating fleet during the course of 1963 with no service abandoned and a lack of trolleybus drivers meant that motorbuses began to appear on service 38 and 42 trolleybus schedules, almost half of the 38 being motorbus operated. Motorbuses had always been used to alleviate temporary shortages of trolleybus drivers or trolleybuses, although their destination blinds had an incomplete coverage of trolleybus services, and, in particular, for extra journeys to sporting or other special events. However as far as service 42 was concerned these appearances became more frequent. During the course of 1963 the use of motorbuses on the 42 increased from once every couple of weeks to, by 5 November 1963, a daily journey. Thereafter usage increased until it became rare to see a trolleybus operating on this service. During the last two months of its electric operation (April – May 1965) however the 42 was operated entirely by trolleybuses due to the availability of vehicles still in good repair and a shortage of motorbus drivers. By now 71 years old, Driver Woodward was retained as a trolleybus driver for a further year but on a sadder note *ex gratia* payments were introduced for crews incapacitated by assault on duty whilst sick pay was made up to normal pay.

Saturday frequencies on services 39, 40 and 47 between 9.30 am and 5 pm were reduced from 3 to 4 minutes on 19 October 1963. As the 2-axle fleet reduced in size 7ft 6ins wide BUT9641Ts began to appear regularly on services 40 and 47 starting on 30 October 1963 when 596 operated throughout the evening, whilst 601 appeared the following evening. Exceptionally even the 8ft wide model appeared, 508 being seen on 11 November 1963.

On 21 January 1964 a power failure at the Hooton Road rectifier brought service 39 to a halt. There was no service at all for some 45 minutes after which motorbuses were substituted for trolleybuses. On 9 March 1964 workmen using an excavator severed an underground feeder cable leaving the section between the Northern Baths (Dob Park, Vernon Road) feeder and the Piccadilly division point at Piccadilly without power. The trolleybuses were replaced by a temporary motorbus shuttle service until repairs were completed.

The Annual Report noted that on 31 March 1964 there were 123 trolleybuses in stock of which 9 were unlicensed awaiting sale, giving an active fleet of 114 vehicles.

An article in the "Nottingham Evening Post and News" of 30 July 1963 reported that *"a belated effort to win a reprieve for Nottingham's condemned trolleybus service made no impression on the Council. Mr Watkinson defended the service but Alderman Hill told him 'It's a policy of this Council that the trolleybus service should be abolished. We have our instructions to abolish them and that's the end of it'".*

The 29 August 1963 edition of the "Guardian Journal" recorded that *"The "running down" programme for trolley buses in Nottingham will cost an estimated £1.5 million over the next four years, Nottingham City Council will be told on Monday. The alternative would be heavy expenditure on overhead line alterations, which would not be economical unless trolleybus operation were to continue for many year, states the annual report of the Transport Committee. Trolley bus abandonment will be completed by 1966-67 to co-ordinate with one-way street planning for the city centre".*

Heading south along Vernon Road at Basford Northern Baths turning circle with the Brough Superior motorcycle factory on the opposite side of the road, 7ft 6ins wide BUT9641T/Brush 547 is en route for Trent Bridge. *MJ Russell*

Trolleybus enthusiast Paul Creswell checks the itinerary of the tour with the driver of Karrier W 480 at the rarely-used Peveril Street turning circle. *Martin Eady*

BUT9611T/Roe 489 at the north end of Wheeler Gate opposite Boots 24 hour chemists. *BTS*

With yellow motorbus stop flags already in place indicating the pending trolleybus route abandonment, BUT9641T 510 has crested Sherwood Rise and passes Alexandra Street, City bound to King Street. *Neil Lewin*

Trolleybus repaints continued, numbers 482, 514, 518 and 576 benefiting in late 1963/early 1964, thereafter, in March 1964, routine overhauls and repaints ceased entirely with the out-shopping of 521 from Trent Bridge Works.

Three month's experience showed that "Bus Stop" markings on the road had had no effect in reducing parking at city centre stops and a Traffic Regulation Order prohibiting parking 08.20-09.10 am and 5.15-6.15 pm was ordered on 23 March 1964 for 15 trolleybus stops.

The series of fares increases that had been implemented, had the desired effect, there being a surplus of £227,518 for the financial year 1963/64, the highest figure since the undertaking's inception, with a balance of £46,972 brought forward. Contributions of £200,854 to capital expenditure (roofing over Stanhope Street, 31 motorbuses and Sherwood Depot canteen and office block) were made and £73,636 carried forward.

The departmental telephone link between Parliament Street Depot and Trent Bridge Works, using life-expired 20-year old cables, was strung from the redundant traction poles along London Road. As these would be replaced by concrete lighting standards when the road widening was complete GPO tie-lines were rented with Ericsson equipment at each end at a cost of £935 6s plus an additional £37 12s rental pa.

By June 1964 use of 2-axle vehicles on Sundays or during the evenings had ceased.

On 22 June 1964 fixed price tenders were accepted for 40 rear-engine Leyland "Atlantean" chassis for trolleybus replacement at £3,093 18s 7d each for delivery in 1965/66. MCW 77-seat front entrance bodies were ordered at £4,006 5s each as Northern Counties were unable to quote for the delivery date stipulated and Park Royal could only offer extended deliveries. In addition the Transport Committee approved further capital expenditure for the trolleybus conversion programme on 31 July 1964 comprising 30 motorbuses with the costs divided as £95,850 in 1965/66 for the chassis and £123,974 in 1966/67 for their bodies.

Throughout the tramway and trolleybus era there were a considerable number of passengers transferring between the two main line stations, Nottingham Midland and Nottingham Victoria, situated on opposite sides of the city centre. The busy narrow streets or passageways made this an impractical ¾ mile walk for many and NCT benefited from the short stage cross-city traffic conveniently joining inbound vehicles as they progressively emptied. By the mid-1960s British Railways were pursuing a national policy of withdrawing duplicate services and running down the Great Central route between Yorkshire and London. As far as Nottingham Victoria was concerned, many local services including those to Basford, Chesterfield, Daybrook, Mansfield and Sheffield, had already been completely withdrawn or diverted to the Midland Station, whilst expresses were operated to slower schedules. On 2 January 1964 express services from both Bradford and Manchester to London Marylebone were withdrawn, followed by the local trains to Derby on 7 September 1964 and the remaining semi-fast through trains to London on 3 September 1966. Finally on 4 September 1967 this impressive 12-platform station closed completely with the diversion of Grantham trains into the Midland Station, and the curtailment of the remaining Rugby local trains to Nottingham Arkwright Street.

Although he would be 72 years old on 22 December 1964, Mr Woodward was again

Basford Northern Baths turning circle, northern terminus of peak hour service 42 from 1954, was located above the junction of Bulwell Lane with Vernon Road. Behind BUT9641T 549, portraying Livery 8 and with one oif its offside access doors swinging open, the railway bridge at Basford North Station on the former Great Northern line to Derby (Friargate) can be seen. *MJ Russell*

The latterday Wollaton Park terminus of service 39 at Harrow Road, Middleton Boulevard on 7 March 1965. By this date the interlaced turning circle and all trolleybus wiring south thereof had been dismantled. *Martin Eady*

The crossover for the exit wiring from the Hooton Road reversing triangle on Carlton Hill apparently provoked the dewirement of 516 on an outbound service 39 working on 7 March 1965. *Martin Eady*

pronounced fit to drive trolleybuses and his employment was again extended until July 1965.

In October 1964 it was decided that the second phase of the trolleybus conversion programme would take place in July 1965.

Just after 9 pm on Saturday evening 28 November 1964 one of the southbound trolley wires in Wheeler Gate broke, resulting in traction power in the city centre being cut off disrupting services to all points south of Chapel Bar and along Upper Parliament Street. Until power could be restored and the broken wire circumnavigated by use of traction batteries, a queue of 18 trolleybuses had built up between Wheeler Gate and the city centre, 12 on Chapel Bar and another dozen in the Old Market Square. The situation was back to normal within two hours but some motorbuses ran on trolleybus routes to cope with the backlog of passengers.

On Saturday 12 December 1964, due to the lack of progress in negotiating an improved Attendance/Merit Pay Scheme, some 431 out of 1,050 employees went on strike following a withdrawal of labour from voluntary overtime and rest-day working during the preceding fortnight. An interim payment was sought until the national award had been agreed upon. As it became clear that the national bonus scheme proposals were related to the seating capacity of vehicles and not attendance/merit, the General Manager and the Trade Unions negotiated a complex scheme based on the earlier proposals.

The trolleybuses began to receive some bad press culminating in two articles in the "Guardian Journal". The headlines of 16 January 1965 read, *"The trolleys really will have to go"* and highlighted "falling trolleybus wires – failures becoming all too frequent in Nottingham these days." This was in response to a statement in the previous night's "Nottingham Evening Post and News" by an NCT spokesman who admitted that *"trolley failures are human"*. An article on 8 March 1965 was headed *"City in a hurry to oust trolley buses"*. The grounds for these articles were easily found: excessive speed beneath overhead wiring special work leading to dewirements, damaged overhead equipment and traffic hold-ups.

The EMEB notified an increased traction current tariff from 1 April 1965, expected to cost the undertaking £2,550 in the 1965/66 financial year. This was exacerbated by the rescheduled trolleybus conversion programme, caused by delivery delays for the replacement motorbuses, and which, by end-February 1965, appeared as:

1st phase – March/April 1965 reducing vehicle operating hours by 35.35%

2nd phase – June/July 1965 reducing vehicle operating hours by 34.60%

3rd phase – July 1966 reducing vehicle operating hours by 30.05%

The increased cost of electricity would therefore only start to reduce significantly in the 1966/67 financial year but would disappear completely in the following year.

The last fares revision had been on 13 October 1963 since when there had been a number of increases in operating costs and more were pending. At that time the General Manager had estimated that there would be a net surplus of £260,000 for 1964/65, which together with the balance of £73,636 brought forward from the preceding year would enable the undertaking to meet more than half of its capital expenditure from revenue, but result in a deficit of £25,276 for 1965/66. These estimates had been based on the

The sole photograph found by the author of a trolleybus turning north out of Station Street into Carrington Street. Karrier W/Park Royal 478 included the Station Street wiring, especially energized for the occasion, on the itinerary of a Nottingham Trolleybus Group's enthusiasts' tour on 24 June 1962. *Rod Bramley*

Having just pulled out of Parliament Street Depot, 8 ft wide BUT9641T 511 turns west out of Manvers Street into Southwell Road heading for Queen Street where it will take up service on a 37 working to Haydn Road. *MJ Russell*

Withdrawals continued at a reduced pace in 1964: BUT9641Ts 573, 586 and 505 (the first 8ft wide vehicle, following slight accident damage), and BUT9611T 491 being taken out of service in January, May, July and December 1964 respectively. At the beginning of 1965 there remained 111 trolleybuses in stock, together with 2 tower wagons and a reel wagon, giving Nottingham once again, as other systems reduced in size, and only for a short period, the second largest trolleybus fleet in the UK exceeded only by Glasgow.

Karrier W 460-461	Roe utility bodies	2
Karrier W 469, 471, 478	Park Royal utility bodies	3
Karrier W 479-482	Roe	4
BUT 9611T 485-489, 492, 493, 495	Roe	8
BUT 9641T 500-504, 506-524	Brush 8ft	24
BUT 9641T 525-533, 535, 537-542, 545-553, 555-572, 574-585, 587-601	Brush 7ft 6ins	70

The continued survival of the 5 utility-bodied trolleybuses was remarkable: despite the well-known longevity of trolleybus chassis and their post-war bodywork and seating improvements these were still austerity vehicles. By 1965 only Derby, Nottingham and Walsall were still operating utility-bodied trolleybuses although the Walsall examples, whilst retaining their original bodies, had been heavily rebuilt including having their windows mounted in rubber.

Huntingdon Street Bus Station and St. Ann' power station are visible in the background as BUT9641T/Brush 550 ascends Bath Street from the roundabout at the junction with King Edward Street and St. Ann's Well Road on Sunday 30 May 1965 the penultimate day of trolleybus operation on service 44. The new yellow motorbus stop flag is already in place at the stop immediately behind 550. *Neil Lewin*

correct assumption that a 40-hour week would be introduced from 1 January 1966 but did not take into account any other possible increases. Although capital expenditure was likely to fall once the trolleybus conversion programme was complete, Mr Wake suggested on 22 February 1965 that a further fares increase be considered, an increase of the minimum fare from 2½d to 3d plus a 1d increase on all other fares would bring in about £279,000 more revenue. By the time of the next Transport Committee Meeting, Mr Wake had revised his calculations, which now showed 1964/65, £274,687 surplus; 1965/66, £28,649 surplus; and 1966/67, £94,451 deficit. He was instructed to prepare detailed proposals and these were submitted to City Council for approval.

The Traffic Commissioners approved another fare increase on 17 September 1965 and it came into operation on Sunday 3 October 1965.

Despite the delayed delivery of replacement motorbuses it was eventually announced in the "Nottingham Evening Post and News" for Monday 29 March 1965 that "Trolleybuses give way to progress". This gave news of the service 43 conversion on 31 March 1965 and said that the 42 and 41 would be converted "later in the month!" The short notice made the planning of any commemorative activity extremely difficult. During the next few days a limited number of yellow motorbus stop flags appeared along the route of services 43 and 46, however, as the 41 would continue to serve Trent Bridge via Arkwright Street and the Bulwell section would still be covered by the 44, in most locations the green trolleybus stops remained in place.

There were a number of interesting movements during the evening peak of 31 March 1965, as all trolleybuses being withdrawn that evening were required to finish with a revenue-earning duty before being taken out of service. As an illustration, some of the 2-axle fleet ran on services 39 and 41, 493 being the last Nottingham 2-axle trolleybus in passenger service leaving Queen Street at 6.15 pm on a service 41 duty. The final trolleybus to operate on service 46 from the Old Market Square to Trent Bridge was BUT9641T 533 at 8.30 pm whilst later in the evening 527 was the last through service trolleybus on the 43 from Bulwell Market to

The following 24 trolleybuses were taken out of service, reducing the fleet to 87:

Karrier W	460-461	Roe utility bodies	2
Karrier W	469, 471, 478	Park Royal utility bodies	3
Karrier W	479-482	Roe	4
BUT 9611T	485-489, 492, 493, 495	Roe	8
BUT 9641T	530, 532, 533, 540, 545, 555, 560	Brush 7ft 6ins	7

Of these, 488 is thought to have been out of service for some months and was parked in Trent Bridge Depot, whilst 530, although operational, had not been used for several weeks.

Less advanced tyre technology, rear bogie scrub on 3-axle vehicles and indifferent road surfaces made punctures more common in the trolleybus era than today. BUT9641T 556 en route to Bulwell Hall Estate displays a very flat offside leading bogie tyre as it waits, with trolley booms hooked down, for rescue in Alfreton Road near Canning Circus. By 1963-64 many trolleybuses were decidedly down at heel in appearance but mechanically sound and a half-hearted attempt was made to smarten up the fleet. The green panels beneath the lower deck window line and the three cream bands have been repainted on 556. Alas, on other trolleybuses this "touch up" was limited to just the cream bands! *Neil Lewin*

Trent Bridge. As they ran in out of service the five remaining utility-bodied vehicles and the post-war Karrier Ws 479-482 were moved into Manvers Street Yard, and the remaining BUT9611Ts, together with those BUT9641Ts taken out of service as a result of this conversion, were taken to Pennyfoot Street Yard.

Trunk service 43 had been operated jointly from Bulwell and Trent Bridge Depots; the latter now ceased to be a trolleybus running depot whilst the motorbus allocation at Bulwell was increased. Additionally, following the withdrawal of the entire 2-axle trolleybus fleet, Parliament Street Depot's vehicle allocation was replenished by 16 of Trent Bridge's BUT9641Ts.

New rear-engine Leyland "Atlantean" motorbuses took over services 43 and 46 the next morning, the public being initially impressed with the front entrance platform doors, fluorescent lighting and heaters. The contrast between the clean appearance of the new motorbuses in their lighter livery and the jaded look of the trolleybuses with their nicotine-stained upper deck ceilings and generally neglected appearance was stark. However before long complaints about vibration when the engines were idling, engine noise and squealing brakes were received, and within a few days of the conversion it was not unusual to see passengers letting a 43 motorbus go by to catch the 44 trolleybus behind. One elderly lady was heard to say *"I'll just wait for the 44, it'll probably get there before the 43 anyway. Besides, I prefer to go on by trackless – they are just so much quieter"*. "Trackless" being a term for the trolleybuses often used by older Nottinghamians.

The enthusiast fraternity had not expected the withdrawal of the post-war two-axle vehicles at this juncture believing that the continued operation of services 40 and 47 would ensure their survival. Eager to preserve an example of both designs of the utility-bodied vehicles, a Roe-bodied BUT9611T and, sooner or later, a BUT9641T, their limited finances presented them with a difficult decision to be made under time pressure. The NTG could only afford to make a single bid, namely £50, for BUT9611T 493 which had been exhibited on the Roe stand at the 1948 Commercial Vehicle Show.

Since November 1963 service 42 had been almost entirely worked by motorbuses, indeed most observers considered that its conversion had already taken place, but as a result of the 43 and 46 conversion more trolleybus rolling stock was available and from 1 April 1965 it reverted entirely to electric operation. This meant that the only portions of overhead wiring abandoned with the 31 March 1965 conversion were the turning circles at each end plus the few feet above the southeast portion of the roundabout at the foot of Market Street between the junction frog where the service 43 wiring continued to the Processional Walk stop and Wheeler Gate, and the trailing frog with the westbound wiring from Long Row East.

Unexpectedly utility-bodied Karrier W 461 reappeared on driver training duties on Monday 5 April 1965. It was parked in Stanhope Street on 7 April 1965 and returned to Manvers Street Yard a few days later having become the last utility-bodied trolleybus to move under power in Nottingham.

There was a serious accident at the Five Ways "Shoulder of Mutton" roundabout at the junction of Valley Road and Radford Road on Saturday 24 April 1965 when trolleybus 582 heading towards Cinderhill on a service 41 working was struck violently on the nearside by a heavy lorry laden with steel girders. The leading rear axle, offering lateral strength, took much of the impact but nine people were taken to hospital including the conductor and two from the lorry, only the lorry driver being detained. The "Nottingham Evening Post and News" rightly reported that it was a *"miracle that nobody died"*. Both 582 and 601, which had sustained rear end damage in an unconnected collision, were withdrawn in April 1965.

As the sole remaining trolleybus service serving Trent Bridge, it was obvious that the 41 would not survive long once more motorbuses were available and towards the end of April 1965 yellow motorbus stop flags began to appear along Arkwright Street and north-westwards towards Cinderhill. On Friday 30 April 1965 the last through run, final service trolleybus and last electrically operated service 41 left Trent Bridge 10.50 pm operated by 502. The final departure to Cinderhill was however the 11.30 pm from Queen Street, operated by 519, arriving back at Parliament Street Depot shortly before 12.20 am on 1 May 1965. This was the first conversion of a trolleybus service operated by Parliament Street Depot. Such was the lack of information that several enthusiasts had concentrated on service 42 that evening, believing, erroneously, that it too would be withdrawn. Half-

BUT9611T/Roe 491 waits at the Exchange Walk stop on South Parade, Old Market Square with a Karrier W/Roe immediately behind. Exchange Walk provides a short-cut between the Old Market Square and the north end of Albert Street. *BTS*

cab AEC Renown motorbuses equipped with front entrances took over the 41 next morning.

The NTG was again successful in gaining permission to tour the abandoned routes after their closure to scheduled services and on Sunday 2 May 1965, displaying signs on its front dash "The Last Trolleybus To Cinderhill and Trent Bridge", BUT9641T 500 traversed the Nottingham Road (Valley Road) – Cinderhill section for the final time, became the last 8ft wide trolleybus to visit Bulwell Market and covered all available wiring at Trent Bridge. Until the end of April 1965 the majority of the erstwhile service 43 wiring had been required for operational purposes, indeed up to that time it would still have been technically possible to have operated both services 43 and 46 with electric traction, and thus the Overhead Department had decided to concentrate on removing only the redundant and rarely used circuit in Frazer Road, Pyatt Street and Turney Street in the vicinity of Trent Bridge. The tour participants had to be content with battery operation along Turney Street before reaching live wiring at Bunbury Street although 500 was able to negotiate the former service 43 turning loop on the Victoria Embankment.

In addition to accident victims 582 and 601, eight more trolleybuses were taken out of service, 525-529, 531, 559, and 598, reducing the active fleet to 77 vehicles.

From 1 May 1965 the following trolleybus services remained:

36 Old Market Square (Queen Street/King Street) – Upper Parliament Street – Milton Street – Victoria Station – Mansfield Road – Nottingham Road (Valley Road)

37 Old Market Square (Queen Street/King Street) – Upper Parliament Street – Milton Street – Victoria Station – Mansfield Road – Nottingham Road (Haydn Road) *(Monday – Friday peak hours only)*

38 Theatre Square – Upper Parliament Street – Carlton Road – Carlton (Hooton Road) (eastbound via Central Market – King Edward Street – Bath Street – Handel Street, westbound via Southwell Road – Lower Parliament Street) *(Monday – Friday peak hours only)*

39 Carlton (Post Office Square) – Carlton Road – Central Market – Upper Parliament Street – Ilkeston Road – Wollaton Park (Middleton Boulevard, Harrow Road) *(eastbound via Central Market – King Edward Street – Bath Street – Handel Street, westbound via Southwell Road – Lower Parliament Street)*

40 The Wells Road (Kildare Road) – King Edward Street – Upper Parliament Street – Old Market Square – Wilford Road – Wilford Bridge *(northbound via Long Row – Queen Street – Upper Parliament Street, southbound via George Street – Carlton Street – Victoria Street – Poultry – South Parade)*

42 Basford (Northern Baths) – Vernon Road – Radford Road – Hyson Green – Alfreton Road – Derby Road – Old Market Square *(Monday – Friday peak hours only)*

44 Bulwell Hall Estate – Bulwell Market – Basford – Vernon Road – Radford Road – Hyson Green – Alfreton Road – Derby Road – Upper Parliament Street – Bath Street – Manvers Street – Sneinton – Colwick Road *(northbound via King Street – Long Row – Beastmarket Hill – Angel Row; southbound via Upper Parliament Street)*

47 The Wells Road (Ransom Road) – St Ann's Well Road – King Edward Street – Lower Parliament Street – Old Market Square – Wilford Road – Wilford Bridge *(northbound via Long Row – Queen Street – Upper Parliament Street, southbound via Upper Parliament Street – George Street – Carlton Street – Victoria Street – The Poultry – Old Market Square)*

Service 42's new lease of life did not last long however as towards the end of May 1965 the forbidding yellow motorbus stop flags began to appear along the route of service 44, the undertaking's longest trolleybus route with an end-to-end running time of 37 minutes, and as both the 42 and 44 operated out of Bulwell Depot it could be logically assumed that both services would be converted together at the end of May 1965.

Both services operated normally on Monday 31 May 1965, no motorbus substitution, to ensure a minimum of empty mileage, taking place in the evening, and all trolleybus duties terminated at Bulwell Depot as usual. Thereafter a sad convoy of empty trolleybuses made their way towards Parliament Street Depot passing 537 operating the final duty on service 42. It too ran into Bulwell Depot before chasing the procession back to the City and oblivion.

The very last 44 to Colwick Road was operated by 563 which then returned towards Bulwell Hall Estate at 11.18 pm. Due to the conversion, there was an extra northbound working from the city to Bulwell Hall Estate some minutes later run by 538. The two vehicles passed each other heading in opposite directions in Hucknall Lane, Bulwell. Following a delay for photography at Bulwell Hall Estate terminus, 538 made its way back towards the city shortly after midnight, to find 563 with trolley poles stowed down and a flat tyre at Main Street, Bulwell. Continuing to complete its duty at the Piccadilly stop on Vernon Road, the maintenance crew taking over to transfer 538 to Parliament Street Depot kindly allowed the enthusiasts to stay on board. When Parliament Street Depot was reached at 12.50 am, it was considered that the Bulwell routes had witnessed their last trolleybus and that the immobile 563 would be recovered by towing. Bulwell Depot was now devoid of trolleybuses and became a wholly motorbus operating depot.

As the enthusiasts prepared to go home, they were offered the opportunity to be on the very last trolleybus from Bulwell. It emerged that 563's puncture had already been fixed and that it would therefore be transferred under power! They were ferried out by motorbus to the Piccadilly stop on Vernon Road where 563 was waiting and shortly after 1.15 am it departed towards the city at speed. Just past the Peveril Street turning circle on Alfreton Road, the dewirement buzzer was heard and the trolleybus ground to a halt as the traction power had been cut off. The changeman thought that there would be live overhead at Canning Circus and the journey continued on battery power but the slight uphill grade in the vicinity of Forest Road proved too demanding for this source of supply.

Breakdown tender 809 arrived to tow 563 to Parliament Street Depot as by now it was felt that time switches would have cut off the traction power supply throughout the system for the night. Rising to the occasion, the breakdown crew acknowledged that this was the last Bulwell trolleybus and that it was important that 563 reach the depot "under its own steam". The tow was interrupted at the top of Wollaton Street just beyond the junction with Talbot Street and with its trolleybooms stowed 563 set off by gravity down Wollaton Street with 809 in front making certain

The retaining wall of the erstwhile London & North Western Railway Goods Station above Manvers Street in Sneinton Hermitage does not provide the ideal setting for an afternoon walk with the pram. BUT9641T/Brush 557 on a 44 to Colwick passes by on 26 September 1964. *Peter Badgery*

Roe bodied Karrier W 480 ascending Market Street on an enthusiast's tour 7 March 1965. Both trolleyheads are arching. *Martin Eady*

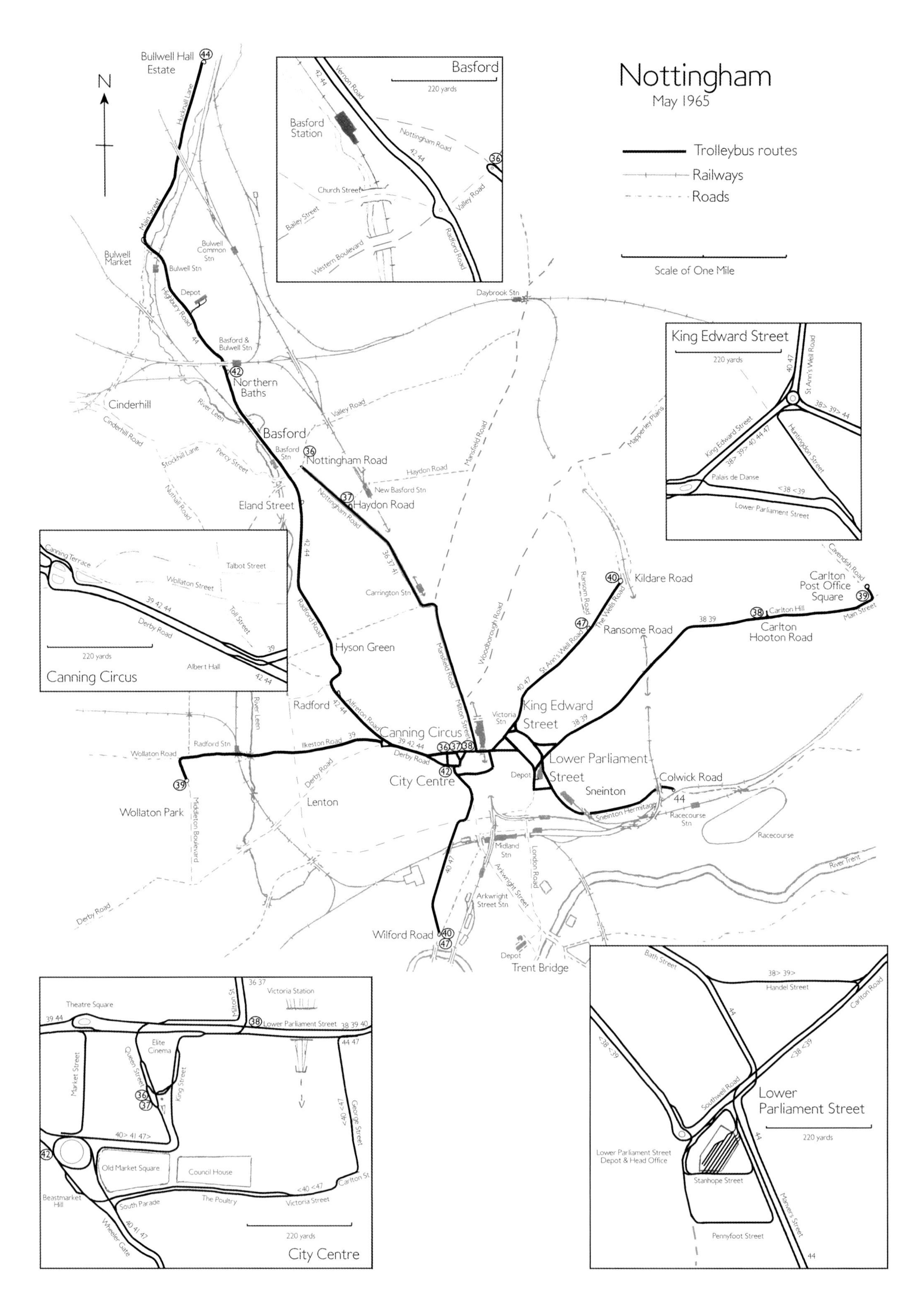
Nottingham
May 1965
Trolleybus routes
Railways
Roads
Scale of One Mile
N
Basford
220 yards
Basford Station
Vernon Road
Nottingham Road
Church Street
Bailey Street
Western Boulevard
Valley Road
Radford Road
King Edward Street
220 yards
St Ann's Well Road
Huntingdon Street
Palais de Danse
Lower Parliament Street
Canning Circus
Canning Terrace
Talbot Street
Wollaton Street
Toll Street
Derby Road
Albert Hall
City Centre
Theatre Square
Victoria Station
Lower Parliament Street
Milton St
Elite Cinema
Market Street
Queen Street
King Street
George Street
Old Market Square
Council House
Beastmarket Hill
South Parade
The Poultry
Victoria Street
Carlton St
Wheeler Gate
Lower Parliament Street
Bath Street
Handel Street
Carlton Road
Southwell Road
Lower Parliament Street Depot & Head Office
Stanhope Street
Pennyfoot Street
Manvers Street
Bullwell Hall Estate
Hucknall Lane
Main Street
Bulwell Market
Bulwell Stn
Bulwell Common Stn
Depot
Highbury Road
Basford & Bulwell Stn
Northern Baths
Cinderhill
Cinderhill Road
River Leen
Basford
Basford Stn
Nottingham Road
Haydon Road
New Basford Stn
Valley Road
Mansfield Road
Mapperley Plains
Daybrook Stn
Stockhill Lane
Percy Street
Nuthall Road
Eland Street
Carrington Stn
Hyson Green
Radford Road
Woodborough Road
Ransom Road
Kildare Road
The Wells Road
Ransome Road
St Ann's Well Road
Carlton Post Office Square
Cavendish Road
Carlton Hill
Main Street
Carlton Hooton Road
Radford
Alfreton Road
Canning Circus
Milton Street
Victoria Stn
King Edward Street
Lower Parliament Street
Depot
Sneinton
Sneinton Hermitage
Colwick Road
Racecourse Stn
Racecourse
River Trent
Radford Stn
Wollaton Road
Ilkeston Road
Derby Road
City Centre
Wollaton Park
Middleton Boulevard
Lenton
Midland Stn
London Road
Arkwright Street
Arkwright Street Stn
Wilford Road
Depot
Trent Bridge
Derby Road

These withdrawals reduced the fleet to 57 trolleybuses:

BUT 9641T 500-504, 506-524	Brush 8ft	24
BUT 9641T 535, 538-539, 550, 561-564, 572, 574-581, 583-585, 587-597, 599-600	Brush 7ft 6ins	33

that the roads were clear. Judicious use of the gradient and the remaining power in the traction batteries brought 563 as far as Shipside's Garage just past the junction of Lower Parliament Street and Huntingdon Street but the final ½ mile had to be completed on tow, reaching Parliament Street Depot just before 3.00 am on Tuesday 1 June 1965.

As a consequence of the 42 and 44 conversions 20 more trolleybuses were withdrawn: 537, 541-542, 546-549, 551, 553, 556-558, 565, 567-571, together with 552, which had been previously taken out of service, and 566, which had suffered rear end accident damage. This spelt the end for the remaining vehicles with Crompton Parkinson motors, including 565, which had been an exhibit at the 1950 Commercial Motor Show.

The initial phase of the trolleybus abandonment programme was now complete, six of the former 12 services having been converted to motorbus operation. There were now 30 withdrawn trolleybuses for disposal. The NTA had offered a nominal sum of £10 for 460 whilst the NTG had offered £50 for 493 excluding tyres. The scrap merchants' highest tender for these vehicles was £100 each but the NTG's offer for 493 was accepted although the remainder were sold to the highest bidder. On 11 June 1965 it was decided to accept Daimler's tender for 30 "Fleetline" chassis at £3,435 2s each for the final phase of the trolleybus conversion programme.

At this stage, to the casual observer little had changed. No overhead wiring in the central area had been removed, there were still plenty of trolleybuses in Upper Parliament Street and they still circumnavigated Old Market Square. No announcements were made about services 40 and 47, the next candidates for conversion, for the time being. Nonetheless the fleet strength continued to fall with 503, 523, 587 and 592 withdrawn by the end of July 1965, leaving just 53 vehicles in stock.

Looking ahead to the final trolleybus abandonment, six of the older trolleybus drivers who were due to retire in the next few years and who had been found unsuitable for training as motorbus drivers needed to be transferred to other work. The TGWU asked that the four due for retirement after August 1966 be permitted to continue their pension contributions at the drivers' rate should they be required to take up conducting duties. On 31 December 1965 it was decided that all trolleybus drivers transferred to a lower paid job must accept reduced wages but that these four drivers approaching retirement would be permitted to continue to make driver's payments into the pension scheme. Any other employee suffering as the result of the trolleybus abandonment wishing to retain higher pension rights would be considered on their merits. In April 1967 a number of Overhead Department employees who, having completed the dismantlement of the overhead equipment, had transferred to lower paid duties were also granted permission to continue their pension payments at the higher level.

Karrier W/Roe 461 No. 461 on a 37 working to Haydn Road passes beneath the Bluecoat Street feeder on the long climb up Mansfield Road. The presence of a parked "B" suffix (1964) registration Austin Cambridge and green foliage on the trees suggest that this photo was taken in the summer of 1964 as both sister vehicle 460 and 461, the last remaining Roe bodied utility vehicles in the Nottingham fleet, were withdrawn in March/April 1965. *Neil Lewin*

An inbound 36 operated by BUT9641T 516, its destination blind already prepared for the return journey, pulls out of Milton Street into Upper Parliament Street. *MJ Russell*

On 24 May 1964 an NTA enthusiast's tour used two vehicles on different sections of the system where they would not normally be seen in service. Two-axle Karrier W 460 was hired to traverse the Bulwell routes and Bulwell Depot based BUT9641T 562 was used to travel on routes normally operated by Parliament Street Depot's vehicles. Here 562 is seen beneath the rarely-used Market Street wiring at the junction with Upper Parliament Street. Corrosion and dirt on the trolley wires explains the wisp of smoke discernable near the trolley heads. *Neil Lewin*

On 27 March 1965 BUT9611T/Roe 493 circumnavigates the Wilford Bridge terminus roundabout with Queen's Walk in the background. This trolleybus was withdrawn at the end of the month and is now preserved at the Sandtoft Transport Centre. *Neil Lewin*

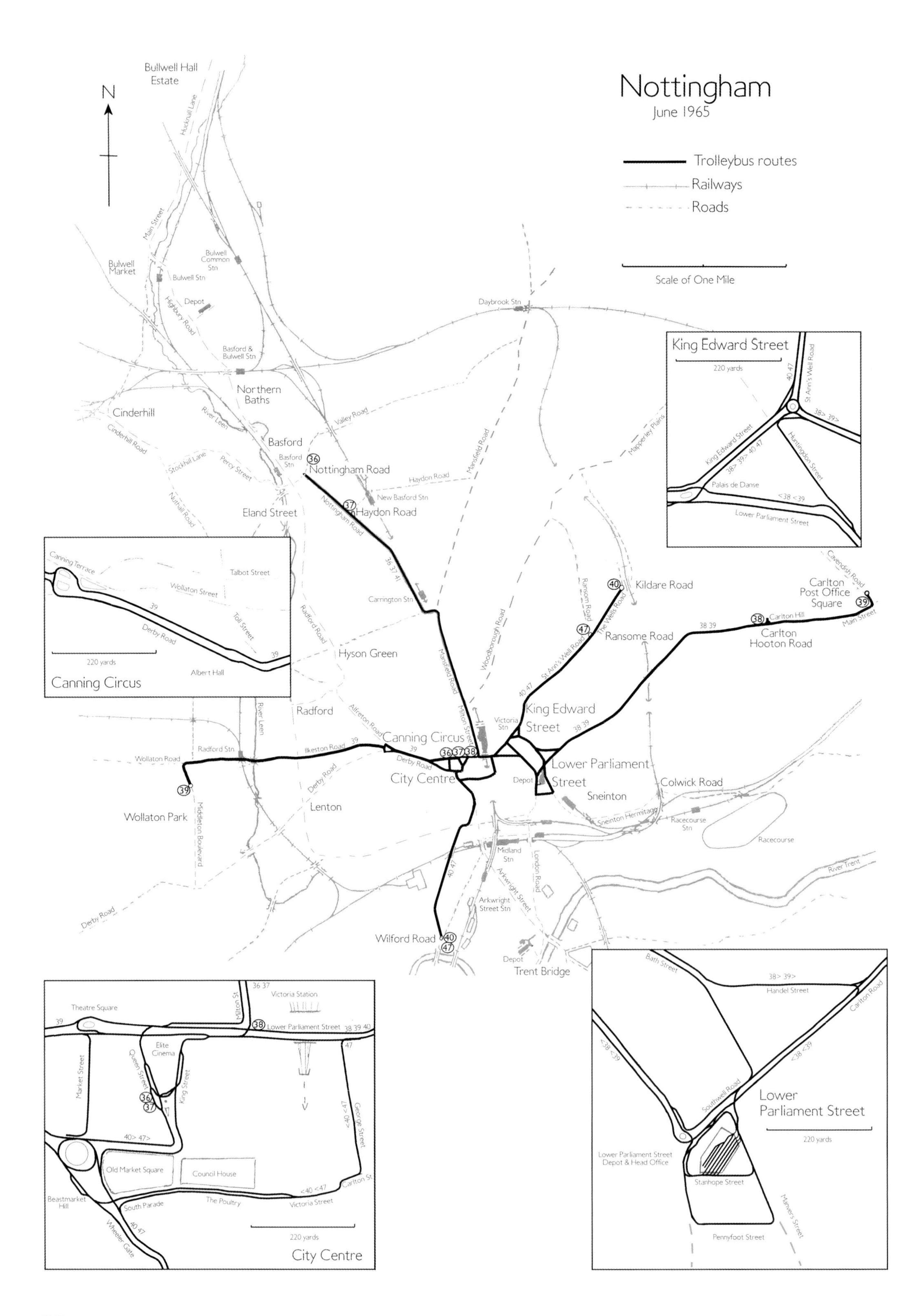
Nottingham
June 1965
Trolleybus routes
Railways
Roads
Scale of One Mile
N
Bullwell Hall Estate
Bulwell Market
Bulwell Stn
Bulwell Common Stn
Depot
Basford & Bulwell Stn
Northern Baths
Cinderhill
Basford
Basford Stn
Nottingham Road
Haydon Road
Eland Street
Daybrook Stn
Carrington Stn
Hyson Green
Radford
Radford Stn
Wollaton Park
Lenton
Canning Circus
City Centre
Victoria Stn
King Edward Street
Lower Parliament Street
Depot
Sneinton
Colwick Road
Kildare Road
Ransome Road
Carlton Post Office Square
Carlton Hooton Road
Racecourse Stn
Racecourse
Midland Stn
Arkwright Street Stn
Wilford Road
Depot
Trent Bridge
River Trent
Canning Circus
220 yards
City Centre
Victoria Station
Theatre Square
Elite Cinema
Old Market Square
Council House
Beastmarket Hill
South Parade
The Poultry
Victoria Street
Lower Parliament Street
King Edward Street
Palais de Danse
Lower Parliament Street
Lower Parliament Street Depot & Head Office
Stanhope Street
Pennyfoot Street
Handel Street

The postwar Carlton Post Office Square terminus of service 39 was located at the junction of Cavendish Road and Cemetery Road. Here 8ft wide BUT9641Ts 517 and 513 negotiate the turning circle *Neil Lewin*

During the last week of trolleybus operation of services 40 and 47 in October 1965, BUT9641T 578 passes Ransom Road turning circle (the northern terminus of service 47) en route to Kildare Road. On Sunday 10 October 1965, no. 578 would become the last 7ft 6ins wide BUT9641T to operate on a "farewell" tour of several services, including the Wells Road section. This vehicle was subsequently preserved. *Neil Lewin*

Unexpectedly towards the end of September 1965 yellow motorbus stop flags started to appear along the route of service 39, which had been expected to be Nottingham's final trolleybus route. Equally surprising was the proposed conversion of services 40 and 47 on the same date. Due to increased vehicle requirements during the annual Goose Fair (first Thursday to Saturday in October) the latter conversion was subsequently postponed until after the Fair. Until now it had been hoped that the trolleybus system might survive until 1966/67 but it now seemed possible that the final closure could be later in 1965. A lead article in the 22 September 1965 issue of the "Guardian Journal", headed *"Time has run out for city trolleybuses"*, seemed to confirm the system's imminent demise.

The evening of Thursday 30 September 1965 was an unpleasantly wet evening, the first such inclement weather on a conversion day. The final through service trolleybus from Wollaton Park, Harrow Road to Carlton Post Office Square departed at 11.17 pm operated by 514; this formed the last departure on service 39 leaving Carlton at 11.51 pm for Parliament Street Depot which was reached at 12.16 am.

Once again, Leyland "Atlantean" rear engine motorbuses replaced the trolleybuses but they got off to an unhappy start on the Carlton route with its fast schedule and long, arduous hills. The "Guardian Journal" wrote on 2 October 1965 of the *"Uphill struggle for buses"* and featured delays and poor time-keeping. Mr Wake responded that *"all drivers on the route were trained motorbus men"* and emphasised that the new vehicles were not being "run in"!

By now it was practise to show the trolleybuses in the worst possible light and the 6 October 1965 edition of the "Evening Post" quoted Mr Wake speaking at the annual safety award presentation *"Nottingham Corporation's trolleybuses have an accident record worse than the national average. The trolleys were involved in one accident for something like every 4,100 miles last year – a total of 827 accidents. And this figure was 12 accidents more than the 1963 total – despite a cut in the number of trolleys in use. But city motorbus accidents were down and the year's figure was far better than the average authority's which was about one accident involving motorbuses every 8,500 miles, while the national average was one in every 7,000 miles"*. It is important to add here that the undertaking's accident statistics referred to all types of incidents, including such minor things as clothing being torn on a handrail, and was not limited to serious traffic accidents. The trolleybus replacement motorbuses were all equipped with platform doors which contributed significantly to reducing the number of recorded accidents for that type of vehicle.

The loss of the 39 trolleybuses was lamented more than any other conversion and letters in the newspapers asking for their return appeared for a long time.

A further 20 trolleybuses were withdrawn: 512, 538-539, 550, 561-562, 564, 581, 588-591, 593-597, 599-600, together with 563 which had been taken out of service earlier following loss of a front wheel in Carlton on 15 September 1965. The ranks of operational trolleybuses were thus reduced to 33.

It had been assumed that service 38, a short-working of the 39 by now operating Monday-Friday peak hours only between Theatre Square (Elite Cinema) and Carlton (Hooton Road), would be withdrawn at the same time but on Friday 1 October 1965 a full peak hour trolleybus service reappeared, including those few duties originating from Wollaton Park which had, of late, been motorbus operated. It is recorded that three trolleybuses operating on the 38 ran from

At Bulwell Hall Estate terminus trolleybuses turned into a layby on the east side of Hucknall Lane which, together with Sidcars Garage (the brick building behind BUT 9641T 563), was squeezed into a narrow parcel of land between the main road and the former Midland Railway line to Sheffield. The garage was built on some 19⅓ sq yards of land leased to Messrs Sidcars in early 1946 at £1 pa for 21 years. Presumably they sold motorcycle sidecars, a mode of transport very much in vogue at the time. *BTS*

BUT9641T 517 at the much photographed junction of King Street and Queen Street. *MJ Russell*

The Roe bodied BUT9611Ts and Karrier Ws were the standard post-war trolleybus on services 40 and 47 until the end of two-axle trolleybus operations in Nottingham on 31 March 1965. Here 1948 Karrier W 482 passes the Westminster Abbey Hotel in St. Ann's Well Road at the junction with Ransom Road and The Wells Road. The turning circle and "slip" wires of service 47's northern terminus are clearly visible.

Neil Lewin

About to turn at Haydn Road turning circle, BUT 9641T 518 in Nottingham Road with the blind ready for the return to the City. *MJ Russell*

Wollaton Park that day: 516 and 517 operated the initial workings to Wollaton Park at the start of evening peak, followed some time later by 517 making its second through journey and then 518. Despite rumours that some journeys continued erroneously to Post Office Square they all terminated at Hooton Road, the last through journey of all being operated by 518. From Monday 4 October 1965 the western terminus of all service 38 trolley duties was cut back to Theatre Square.

Three axle 8ft wide BUT9641Ts now appeared operating regular duties on services 40 and 47 for the first time in their careers. On 6 October 1965 the "Nottingham Evening Post and News" confirmed that the Wilford Bridge – St. Ann's Well Road services would be converted to motorbus operation on Saturday 9 October 1965 (rather than the end of the month). The report went on to state that services 36, 37 and 38 would remain, confounding those who had understandably predicted that trolleybus operation of service 38 would only survive for the duration of Goose Fair. The article added, *"Electricity would be kept on during Sunday, as the Nottingham Trolleybus Group had asked for a run around the services which are being withdrawn".* By now it had been gleaned that the fleet would be standardised on 8ft wide trolleybuses and that the remaining 7ft 6ins wide models would be withdrawn from this date. The NTG therefore requested a tour on Sunday 10 October 1965 using a 7ft 6ins wide BUT9641T to follow the routes of erstwhile services 39, 40 and 47.

The last through service 47 trolleybus was 509 and the final through service journey of all on the 40 was operated by 511, both 8ft wide BUT9641Ts previously precluded from operating along the narrow and busy George Street and Victoria Street. Leaving Wilford Bridge at 11.15 pm, 511 reached Kildare Road at 11.41 pm, departed again at 11.45 pm and used the depot access link from King Edward Street along the remaining section of Huntingdon Street wiring to reach Parliament Street Depot at midnight. Passengers would hardly have considered this a step forward as 1953/4 AEC Regent III Park Royal bodied motorbuses, with half cabs and open rear platforms replaced the trolleybuses.

The Transport Department ensured that the enthusiasts had a day to remember on Sunday 10 October 1965 for it unexpectedly proved possible to travel along Arkwright Street to Trent Bridge, in addition to the newly converted routes. The selected vehicle, 578, was not only the last 7ft 6ins wide trolleybus to run in Nottingham but also the final trolleybus to operate beyond Hooton Road to Carlton Post Office Square; along St. Ann's Well Road and Wilford Road; along Ilkeston Road to Wollaton Park, and along Arkwright Street to Trent Bridge. The tour finished in Manvers Street with the intent of stowing 578's trolley booms and reversing it into Pennyfoot Street Yard with other withdrawn trolleybuses to await collection by the scrap merchants. However an impromptu "whip round" ultimately contributed to saving the vehicle for preservation. This was also the final occasion that a trolleybus would run through the Old Market Square and other inner city streets, indeed shortly afterwards the overhead equipment between Canning Circus and Market Street was removed to facilitate the inner ring road construction. Elsewhere, however, much redundant overhead wiring remained intact.

There is a good queue at the passenger waiting shelter for BUT9641T/Brush 518 once it can pull across the road and use the Haydn Road, Nottingham Road turning circle. Sister vehicle 516 endeavours to overtake and continue its journey to Valley Road. *MJ Russell*

BUT9611T 493 negotiates the Ransom Road turning circle. This trolleybus had been exhibited on the Roe stand at the 1948 Commercial Motor Show and was originally equipped with a number of non-standard features. Although photographed less than 9 months prior to its withdrawal, 493 is in excellent condition having received an overhaul and further repaint. *Neil Lewin*

A further 15 trolleybuses were withdrawn: 513, 517, 519, 535, 572, 574-580, 583-585, and 518, 520 and 524 were placed in store, leaving a mere 18 trolleybuses in stock of which only 15 were in service. The two accident victims, 505 and 582, which had been held at Trent Bridge Depot as a source of spares, were disposed of, 582 being the last trolleybus to leave.

Trolleybus operation continued on service 38, indeed it reverted to more or less 100% electric operation, although the Winter Timetable, which came into effect from 10 October 1965, containing no further references to trolleybuses.

In a little over six months Nottingham's system had contracted to just three services:

36 Old Market Square (Queen Street/King Street) – Upper Parliament Street – Milton Street – Victoria Station – Mansfield Road – Nottingham Road (Valley Road)

37 Old Market Square (Queen Street/King Street) – Upper Parliament Street – Milton Street – Victoria Station – Mansfield Road – Nottingham Road (Haydn Road) *(Monday – Friday peak hours only)*

38 Theatre Square – Upper Parliament Street – Carlton Road – Carlton (Hooton Road) *(eastbound via Central Market – King Edward Street – Bath Street – Handel Street, westbound via Southwell Road – Lower Parliament Street) (Monday – Friday peak hours only)*

On 4 November 1962, having turned at the Cattle Market turning circle, Karrier W/Roe 464 on an enthusiasts' tour waits in the elongated "slip wire" in London Road facing north. Behind the motorbus, a wall and row of trees marks the boundary between London Road and the Nottingham Canal. *Rod Bramley*

Despite newspaper articles stating that trolleybuses were to be kept operating until mid-1966, it was by now widely anticipated that the system would close at the end of October or November 1965. The last quarter of 1965 would see more than 30 new motorbuses entering service and it was difficult to believe that some of these would not replace the remaining handful of trolleybuses. Evening and Sunday rosters required only three trolleybuses to maintain the full service. As if to confirm the risk of an imminent closure trolleybuses 502 and 508 were withdrawn by the end of October 1965.

By the end of October 1965 it was evident that the last fares increase was not bringing in the level of additional revenues expected, primarily and not surprisingly due to the introduction of free travel for OAPs. By the end of February 1966 the expected surplus at the end of the financial year had fallen to £130,000, the loss of revenue from elderly person's fares being estimated as around £100,000 to which the Finance Committee made a contribution of just £25,000, which they were not prepared to increase. The Transport Committee decided to use the net surplus towards meeting the capital expenditure on new vehicles. The General Manager warned that the trade unions were seeking pay parity with London rates, which could increase wages by around £3 per week and lead to additional costs of £398,000 pa. He added that labour costs already represented 14s 4½d of every £1 spent!

The curious survival of service 38 for some three months after the main Carlton service is believed to have come to an end on 31 December 1965, as far as official notices were concerned, but there is evidence that BUT9641Ts 506 and 507 were still running on the 38 during the first few days of 1966. There were two enthusiasts' tours in January 1966 which reached the Hooton Road reversing triangle, the second of these, on 16 January 1966, is thought to have been the last occasion that passengers were carried by trolleybus along Carlton Road. However it is understood that one evening in early February 1966 trolleybus 506 was commandeered for a non-scheduled journey with a spare wheel on its rear platform to a motorbus which had developed a puncture outside Standhill Garage on Carlton Hill. The trolleybus continued to Hooton Road before reversing and returning to Parliament Street Depot.

The 38 conversion made another four trolleybuses surplus to requirements and 501, 509, 514 and 515 were withdrawn from 31 January 1966 leaving only 12 vehicles in stock of which only nine were needed to maintain a full service. Solely the Nottingham Road services, the first trolleybus route in the city, remained. The city centre turning circle at Theatre Square was left intact for emergency use and depot workings, many drivers preferring to use this circle when running in to Parliament Street Depot rather than King Street, the official inbound terminus of the Nottingham Road services. This established practice continued until final closure.

In fact the financial year ending 31 March 1966 closed with a net surplus of £145,067and this was used entirely for capital expenditure including the filling in of pits at Parliament Street Depot and new motorbuses. The undertaking's rateable value fell by £3,995 due to the ongoing trolleybus route abandonments. The Annual Report recorded that 103 trolleybuses had been sold during the course of the financial year.

It was calculated that upon completion of the trolleybus abandonment programme there would be about 1,950 redundant traction poles supporting street lighting. Although the Lighting Department had agreed to purchase these at £2 each, the Finance Committee felt that they should be transferred free of charge. This was accepted subject to the Lighting Department taking over all such poles rather than just selected ones and that the Transport Department retained the right to use them to support their internal telephone system cables.

At the end of April 1966 trolleybuses 500, 504 and 506 were withdrawn, the latter being, curiously, parked under the covered portion of Stanhope Street; in their place 518, 520 and 521, which had been stored since the conversion of services 40 and 47 in October 1965, were reinstated. Certainly 518 was still in smart condition, having been the penultimate trolleybus to receive an overhaul and repaint in February 1964, in contrast to the generally shabby appearance of the remainder of the fleet. Following these withdrawals and changes only the following ten 8ft wide BUT 9641T trolleybuses remained available for operation: 506, 507, 510, 511, 516, 518, 520, 521, 522 and 524.

It became evident that this one route system, operated by the same number of vehicles as in 1927, would survive until summer 1966. It is rumoured that this occurred in order that some of the older drivers could be retained until attaining their retirement age. There was an

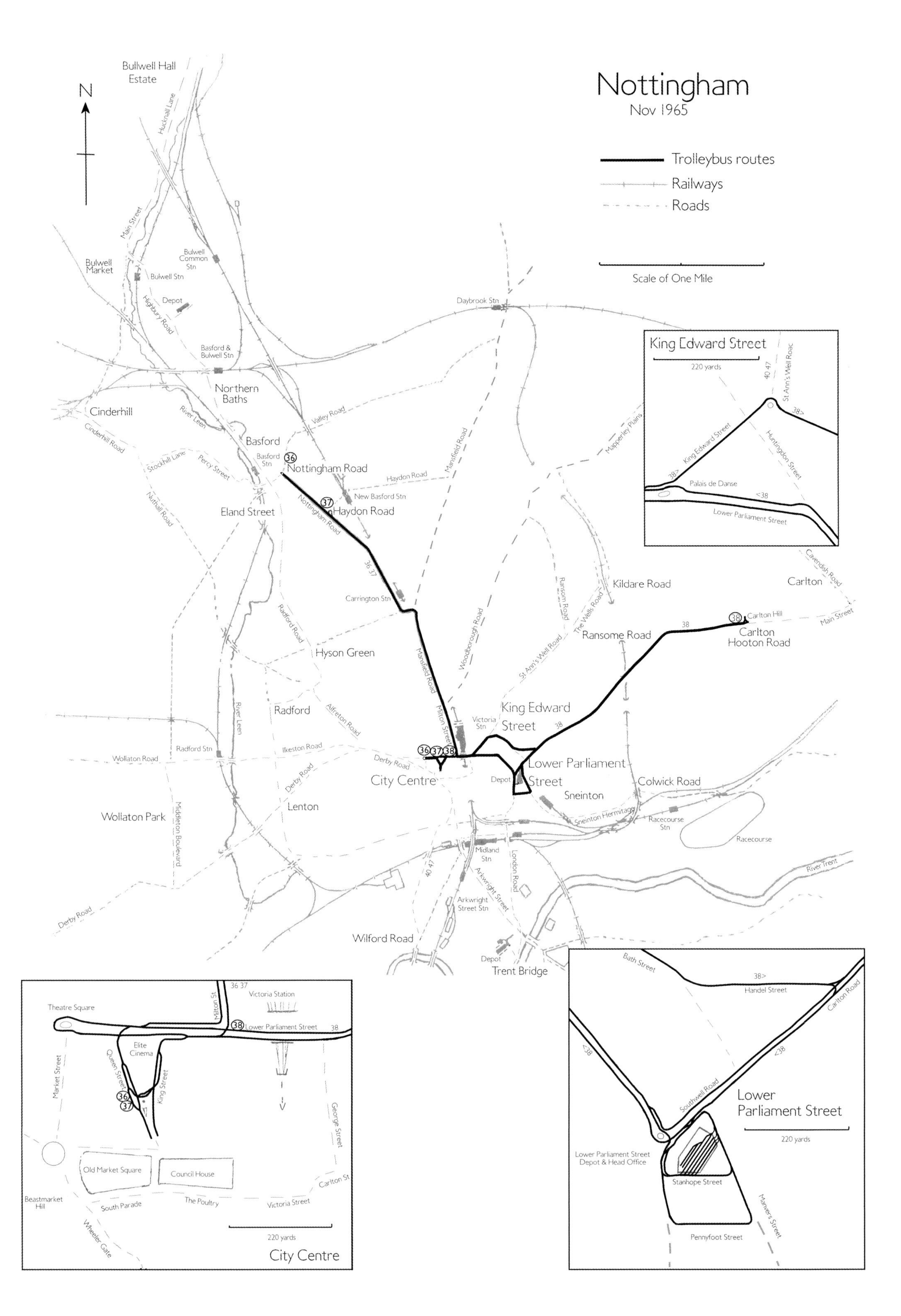
Nottingham
Nov 1965
Trolleybus routes
Railways
Roads
Scale of One Mile
N
Bullwell Hall Estate
Bulwell Market
Bulwell Common Stn
Bulwell Stn
Depot
Basford & Bulwell Stn
Northern Baths
Cinderhill
Basford
Basford Stn
Nottingham Road
Haydon Road
New Basford Stn
Eland Street
Carrington Stn
Hyson Green
Radford
Radford Stn
Wollaton Road
Wollaton Park
Lenton
City Centre
Victoria Stn
King Edward Street
Lower Parliament Street
Depot
Sneinton
Colwick Road
Racecourse Stn
Racecourse
Midland Stn
Arkwright Street Stn
Wilford Road
Depot
Trent Bridge
Daybrook Stn
Kildare Road
Ransome Road
Carlton
Carlton Hooton Road
Carlton Hill
Mansfield Road
Milton Street
Woodborough Road
Mapperley Plains
River Leen
River Trent
Derby Road
Ilkeston Road
Alfreton Road
Middleton Boulevard
London Road
Arkwright Street
Sneinton Hermitage
St Ann's Well Road
Main Street
Cavendish Road
King Edward Street
220 yards
Palais de Danse
Lower Parliament Street
Huntingdon Street
St Ann's Well Road
City Centre
Theatre Square
Victoria Station
Lower Parliament Street
Elite Cinema
Queen Street
King Street
Market Street
Old Market Square
Council House
George Street
Beastmarket Hill
South Parade
The Poultry
Victoria Street
Carlton St
Wheeler Gate
Lower Parliament Street
Bath Street
Handel Street
Carlton Road
Southwell Road
Lower Parliament Street Depot & Head Office
Stanhope Street
Pennyfoot Street
Manvers Street

Trolleybus operation of service 41 ceased on Friday 30 April 1965. The last through journey to Cinderhill left Trent Bridge at 10.50 pm with an intermediate stop at Queen Street at 11.00 pm and was operated by 502 however the final working on the northern section to Cinderhill originated and terminated in the city centre. Here BUT9641T 519 waits at Queen Street for departure time of the final journey at 11.30 pm. *Neil Lewin*

Having deposited the passengers at the Cinderhill terminal stop, BUT9641T 594 negotiates the tight turning circle around the small traffic island in Nuthall Road prior to returning to Trent Bridge. Until 25 April 1953 the blue and cream N&D trolleybuses continued northwestwards along Nottingham Road (the road being taken by the red Mini) on their service A1 to Ripley. *Neil Lewin*

adequate stock of spares and the overhead crews were also available although their duties by now were mainly concentrated on removing the miles of redundant wiring hanging all over the city.

On 25 April 1966 Mr Wake informed the Transport Committee that despite continuing delays in the delivery of replacement motorbuses, the undertaking would be in the position to finally abandon trolleybus operation on Thursday 30 June 1966. This was reported in the press the next day. By now only 6 trolley vehicles were in operation off-peak and 7 during peak hours. He suggested that the occasion should be marked by an official last trolleybus journey from Queen Street to Valley Road on Friday 1 July 1966 which could be conveniently combined with the Transport Committee's annual inspection of the undertaking. Lunch would be offered at the Council House with the usual guests normally invited to the annual inspection and, in addition, union officials and the crew of the last trolleybus. A small trolleybus display would be staged in the Central Lending Library in the city centre. During May 1966, 506 was towed from Stanhope Street to Trent Bridge Works for a spruce-up as Nottingham's last trolleybus.

Haydn Road, the last departure being run by 511 leaving Queen Street at 5.57 pm. On returning to the city it dropped its passengers at the Elite stop, turned on the Theatre Square circle and headed off to Parliament Street Depot.

The final 36 departure, operated by 522 crewed by Driver George Wykes and his conductress Pauline left Queen Street with a full load on schedule at 11.15 pm but there was no sign of the enthusiast's special. Few passengers alighted at Nottingham Road and the majority were allowed to stay on as 522 turned around the roundabout in Valley Road that formed the terminal loop. A crowd of over 150 people had congregated at the terminus to see the last two trolleybuses. Scheduled to depart at 11.36 pm, Driver Wykes waited for the arrival, a few minutes later, of 510 with a full load of enthusiasts travelling on the last private hire duty ever undertaken by a trolleybus in Nottingham. The trolleybuses waited on the opposite sides of Nottingham Road in order that photographers could record the event but then at 11.45 pm, 522 departed for the city and Parliament Street Depot.

Driver Wykes concluded the inbound journey correctly at King Street, rather than Theatre

On 17 June 1966 notices were stuck on the windows of the remaining trolleybuses:

<u>TROLLEY BUS ABANDONMENT</u>
THIS IS THE FINAL FORTNIGHT OF TROLLEY BUS
SERVICES IN NOTTINGHAM. SOUVENIR TICKETS AT
3d EACH CAN BE BOUGHT FROM CONDUCTORS
OF TROLLEYBUSES OR FROM INSPECTORS IN THE
CITY CENTRE

The souvenir tickets were not valid for transportation and had to be purchased in addition to the normal fare payable.

An NTA enthusiasts' tour on Sunday 26 June 1966, operated by 518, traversed Nottingham Road twice and the depot access wiring including, for the final time, that along Carter Gate, Pennyfoot Street and Manvers Street. By now Pennyfoot Street Yard was devoid of withdrawn trolleybuses and was used as a staff car park. During its perambulations 518 parked on the inner loop between King Street and Queen Streets to be overtaken by 510; this being the last occasion that the outer loop was used.

A full trolleybus service was turned out on Thursday 30 June 1966, the final day of normal trolleybus operations, with every available vehicle, except 506, being used. The "Nottingham Evening Post and News" carried an article warning of the *"Last chance tonight for trolley ride"* and added that the final enthusiast's tour was scheduled to leave Parliament Street Depot at 11.10 pm and follow the last service trolleybus. The evening peak service saw 511, 518 and 524 on the 37 to

Square, as he *"wanted the journey to last as long as possible!"* Again, nobody alighted and the trolleybus set off once more for the short trip to the depot. As the trolleybus turned into Stanhope Street to enter Parliament Street Depot the passengers, who, until now had been wrapped in animated conversation, fell into a curious silence. The depot foreman could distinctly be heard to shout "five – right" this being the depot "road" into which 522 had been designated. The rumble from above indicated passage beneath depot entrance frogs and the last Nottingham service trolleybus was parked behind all the others that had finished earlier. The passengers alighted and awaited the arrival of 510 which appeared some 5 minutes later at approximately 12.15 am and joined the back of the line of trolleybuses behind 522. Spontaneously depot night staff, crews, enthusiasts and well wishers, linked arms and sang "Auld Lang Syne" in a wide arc around the rear of the line up of trolleybuses. Later that morning, the "Guardian Journal" newspaper wrote, *"A little bit of Nottingham disappears"*.

In preparation for the official last trolleybus journey BUT9641T 506 had been given a full external repaint at Trent Bridge Works featuring the following text on its upper deck side panels, in standard cream paint:

1927 CITY OF NOTTINGHAM 1966
LAST TROLLEYBUS

The driver's cab front panel showed "1927/1966" also in cream, whilst each destination box displayed "LAST TROLLEYBUS" in red painted on the glass.

Early in the morning of Friday 1 July 1966, 506 was towed to Parliament Street Depot leaving there under its own power to reach King Street at 11.30 am to collect the Mayor, Alderman Percy Holland, and the official party. The crew was Driver Albert Parish, a favourite with enthusiasts and due to retire the following month, and Conductor Fred Cooper who, although a motorbus conductor based at Sherwood, was the conductor with the longest service having worked with the Department since 1918. Amidst a considerable number of bystanders, bearing in mind that this was a normal working day, the trolleybus left King Street/Queen Street at 11.45 am and travelled at a gentle pace to Nottingham Road. It was unfortunate that the commemorative last journey could not have taken place the following day, a Saturday, when more members of the public could have viewed this historic occasion. People came out of shops to look as 506 passed by followed by a small convoy of other vehicles. At Nottingham Road there was a short break with civic dignitaries shaking hands with each other and Driver Parish. Thereafter 506 returned to King Street, followed by its vehicular entourage, from whence the passengers and crew made their way over to the nearby Council House for lunch. Eric Saxby, Depot Superintendent, with a changeman standing guard on the rear platform, then took 506 back empty to Parliament Street Depot where it dewired entering Stanhope Street. The trolley booms were hooked down and, using battery power, 506 took its place at the back of the line up of trolleybuses, which had run in the previous evening.

The "Evening Post" interviewed Bernard Parker. *"He was engaged in putting the first trolley bus wires up in Nottingham Road 39 years ago. Now he is the charge hand on the overhead tower wagon which maintains and repairs the trolley wires. He retires in 16 months time-just after trolley wires will have been taken down"*.

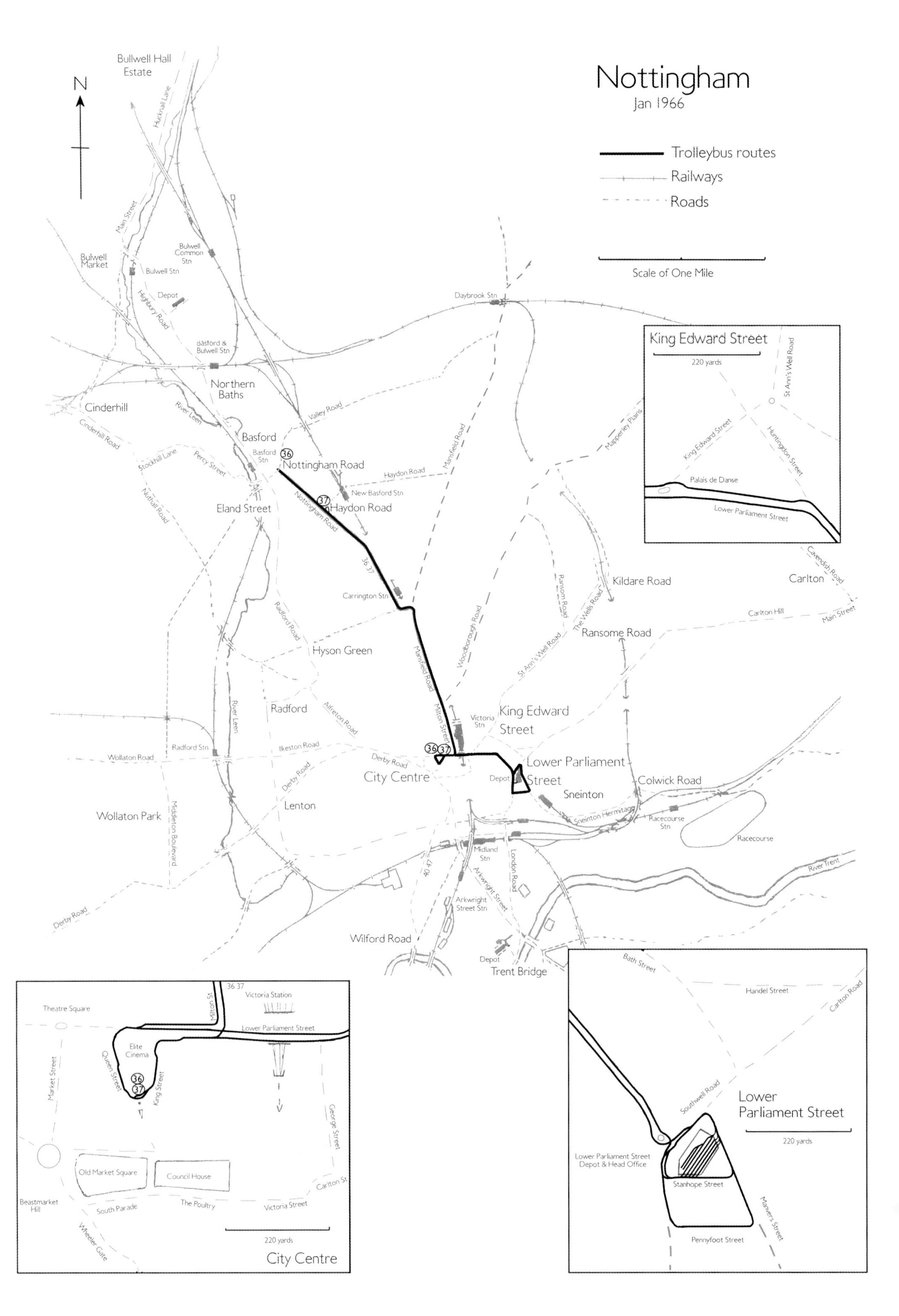
Nottingham
Jan 1966
Trolleybus routes
Railways
Roads
Scale of One Mile
N
Bullwell Hall Estate
Hucknall Lane
Main Street
Bulwell Market
Bulwell Common Stn
Bulwell Stn
Depot
Highbury Road
Basford & Bulwell Stn
Northern Baths
Cinderhill
Cinderhill Road
River Leen
Basford
Basford Stn
Stockhill Lane
Percy Street
Nuthall Road
Valley Road
Nottingham Road
Haydon Road
New Basford Stn
Eland Street
Nottingham Road
Mansfield Road
Daybrook Stn
Mapperley Plains
Carrington Stn
Radford Road
Hyson Green
Woodborough Road
Mansfield Road
Ransom Road
The Wells Road
Kildare Road
St Ann's Well Road
Ransome Road
Carlton
Cavendish Road
Carlton Hill
Main Street
Radford
Alfreton Road
River Leen
Milton Street
Victoria Stn
King Edward Street
Radford Stn
Wollaton Road
Ilkeston Road
Derby Road
City Centre
Derby Road
Depot
Lower Parliament Street
Colwick Road
Sneinton
Lenton
Wollaton Park
Middleton Boulevard
Sneinton Hermitage
Racecourse Stn
Racecourse
Midland Stn
London Road
River Trent
Arkwright Street
Arkwright Street Stn
Derby Road
Wilford Road
Depot
Trent Bridge
King Edward Street
220 yards
St Ann's Well Road
King Edward Street
Huntingdon Street
Palais de Danse
Lower Parliament Street
36 37
Victoria Station
Theatre Square
Milton St
Lower Parliament Street
Elite Cinema
Queen Street
King Street
Market Street
George Street
Old Market Square
Council House
Carlton St
Beastmarket Hill
South Parade
The Poultry
Victoria Street
Wheeler Gate
220 yards
City Centre
Bath Street
Handel Street
Carlton Road
Southwell Road
Lower Parliament Street
220 yards
Lower Parliament Street Depot & Head Office
Stanhope Street
Manvers Street
Pennyfoot Street

Consecutively numbered trolleybuses 566 and 567 in Radford Road at Beaconsfield Street, Hyson Green in March 1965. Conversion of this route to motorbus operation was imminent as evidenced by the new yellow motorbus stop flag already in place on the traction pole against which 567 will deposit the passengers already congregating on the platform and stairwell. Please note the end of the bamboo trolley retrieval pole protruding out of its stowage beneath the rear platform of 567.

Neil Lewin

Another journey to Carlton for BUT9641T 524 heading west along Handel Street on 1 August 1965.

Peter Badgery

On 30 March 1965 BUT9611T/Roe 495 was, as usual, in operation on the Wells Road – Wilford Bridge group of services. Here 495 is seen turning out of George Street into Carlton Street.

Peter Badgery

With the closure of service 36 just hours away 516 ascends Mansfield Road on 30 June 1966 the final day of scheduled trolleybus operations. In the background, opposite the motorbus, Huntingdon Street branches off to the left whilst in the distance can be seen the red brick frontage of the Nottingham Victoria Station Hotel. Although the railway station has long since gone this scene has little changed in 2005. *Neil Lewin*

No doubt attracted by the Transport Department's mobile canteen on the other side of the road, 570's crew have left their charge unattended "high and dry" in the middle of the road at the north end of Victoria Embankment, Trent Bridge (no doubt 570 had been left "double parked" next to another trolleybus at the kerbside but this vehicle had since departed!). Clearly visible are two distinguishing features of the 7ft 6ins wide version of the BUT9641T/Brush trolleybuses; the separate rear mudguards and black driver's steering wheel whereas their 8ft wide equivalents had a one-piece "fairing" over the mudguards and white steering wheels. *Neil Lewin*

With its destination screen display already prepared for the return journey to Wilford Road albeit as a "40" rather than a "47", BUT 9641T 597 uses the turning circle in the throat of Ransom Road. 597, together with other late-delivery 7ft 6ins wide BUT 9641Ts, did not feature a nearside sliding driver's cab door. Instead these vehicles were equipped with a hinged window that could be used as an exit in an emergency and consequently there was no need for a nearside access step and "kicking plate" immediately behind the front wheel. *Neil Lewin*

Nottingham's last trolleybus, especially prepared BUT9641T 506, carrying a civil party, positively sparkles as it turns from Gregory Boulevard into Mansfield Road on 1 July 1966. The last service journeys had run the night before making 506 the sole trolleybus to operate on 1 July 1966 and the final Nottingham trolleybus of all. This vehicle was preserved and can now be seen at the Sandtoft Transport Centre. *Neil Lewin*

In his lunchtime speech Alderman Sir Sydney P. Hill, Chairman of the Transport Committee said *"I don't know if I feel nostalgic or not. I feel that while one era has passed we are moving into another. In 20 years time we might be talking about monorails or moving causeways or pavements"*. Little could he know that electric passenger transport would return to the streets of Nottingham in the early years of the next century albeit in the form of tramcars rather than trolleybuses.

There was one last chance for farewells! The Transport Department had arranged one of its Open Days at Parliament Street Depot for Saturday 2 July 1966 and the line up of trolleybuses remained parked just as they had entered the depot from their various duties. That day 506 was reversed out into Stanhope Street, again using battery power, for Driver Parish to be presented with a mounted trolley head by enthusiasts. There was a steady stream of visitors throughout the day; many sitting in the trolleybuses to reflect on a past youthful encounter in which the trolleybuses had played a part. An elderly couple from the Meadows reflected on their courting days. On summer weekends, they would catch a 48 "trackless" through to Nottingham Road where they would change to the Blue A1 and go to Ripley. From here they would go hiking into the Derbyshire countryside nearby. Returning on the A1 to Fiveways in Basford, they would catch a 43 to Hyson Green and have a fish and chips supper before catching another 43 back to Waterway Street! *"Wish we could do it today"* said the old gentleman *"but we had to sit on the trackless for the last time"*.

At 4 pm it was all over. The remaining trolleybuses were taken to Manvers Street Yard to await the scrap merchant whilst 506 remained under cover at Parliament Street Depot and became the final trolleybus to leave the Department's premises on 29 March 1967, for preservation. The last 12 trolleybuses realised £1,725 from the scrap merchant.

The overhead wiring team continued their painful task of removing all evidence of trolleybuses from the streets of Nottingham, the last piece of trolleybus wiring being officially removed from St. Peters Gate in the city centre on 18 March 1967. The sale of scrap overhead line equipment, after having met the cost of dismantling, realised £24,000, which was invested in new motorbuses. The 2 tower wagons and 1 reel wagon were retained, and the ten remaining Overhead Department employees were transferred to other duties within the undertaking.

Having just turned at Ransom Road BUT9641T 527 waits beneath the kerbside "slip" wires in St. Ann's Well Road before departure on a 40 to Wilford Road. Note the folding-flap waiting limit road sign of the period *Martin Eady*

On a wintery Sunday afternoon 572 turns on the northern Victoria Embankment turning circle immediately outside of the gates. Nottinghamshire County Hall can be seen on the south bank of the River Trent in neighbouring West Bridgford.
Martin Eady

BUT9641T 541 circles the roundabout at the bottom of Market Street, Old Market Square before returning up Chapel Bar and Derby Road to Bulwell whilst a BUT9611T 494 scoots past behind along Long Row on a service 40 working to The Wells Road, Kildare Road. *BTS*

Another view of Karrier W/Roe 460 on an NTA tour stands at Peveril Street turning circle, Alfreton Road, on 24 May 1964. Peveril Street turning circle, erected in 1941, provided an unusual opportunity for trolleybuses to short work on an inward bound journey and was primarily intended for works "specials" serving the nearby Players cigarette factory. Skills Coaches' Alfreton Road premises were adjacent as evidenced by the coach behind 460. *Neil Lewin*

Stanhope Street with the tram tracks still visible, as BUT 9641T 506 turns into Lower Parliament Street Depot on the final run. *MJ Russell*

Karrier W 460 standing at Lower Parliament Street Depot on 28th March 1964. *Geoff Lumb*

Karrier W 478 with its offside front wheel chocked, as its booms are de-poled at Ransome Road loop, to allow Karrier W 481 to pass en route for Wilford Road along St. Ann's Well Road. 28th March 1964. *Geoff Lumb*

Sisters BUT 9641T 528 and 530 vie for the off on the passing loop for service 43 at Victoria Embankment, Trent Bridge. Mobile canteen AEC Regal 812 is to the left and an excited toddler to the right. 28th March 1964. *Geoff Lumb*

BUT 9641T 596 heads south along King Street, under the ornate double bracket arm pole inherited from tram days. Karrier W/Park Royal 478, with relaxed austerity specification bodywork, heads into Queen Street. 28th March 1964. *Geoff Lumb*

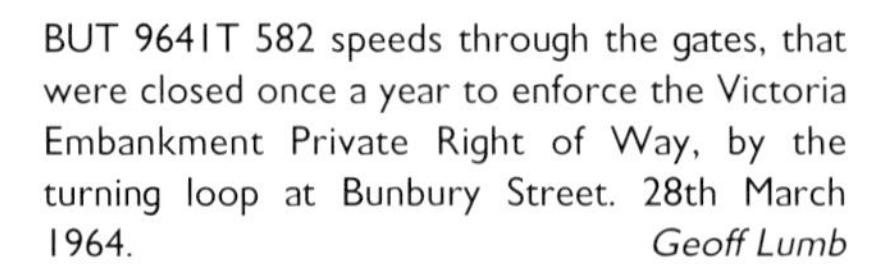
BUT 9641T 582 speeds through the gates, that were closed once a year to enforce the Victoria Embankment Private Right of Way, by the turning loop at Bunbury Street. 28th March 1964. *Geoff Lumb*

BUT 9641T 546 enters the Five Ways "Shoulder of Mutton" roundabout from Vernon Road as BUT 9641T 521, behind, enters from Church Street on 19th June 1962. *Geoff Lumb*

BUT 9641T 529 draws into service 43 layby at Victoria Embankment, Trent Bridge. Mobile canteen AEC Regal 812 is to the right and behind, BUT 9641T 562 is heading towards Arkwright Street. 28th March 1964. *Geoff Lumb*

In the evening sun, BUT 9641T 513 waits on the slip wires at Carlton terminus, with blinds already turned for the return journey to Wollaton Park and a chock under the front offside wheel. Sister vehicle 549 pulls in behind. 19th June 1962. *Geoff Lumb*

Appendix A Trolleybus Fleet Details

1-10 Railless

A posed photograph of 1927 Railless LF 4 (TO5005), still in its original livery but carrying the scars of several year's service. Ropes retain the trolleypoles at their usual operating height but no trolleybus overhead wiring is in place. The housing in the background and the tram track in the road way suggest that this photograph was taken on the west side of Victoria Embankment in the vicinity of Bunbury Street and thus close to Trent Bridge Depot where Nottingham's early trackless trolleys were housed. *EE/Beilby*

Chassis: Two axle type Railless LF marketed by Railless Ltd., 29-30 Charing Cross, London SW1 but designed and built by Shorts Bros (Rochester and Bedford) Ltd. at their Rochester, Kent, works.

Motor: English Electric DK 99A (2 x 35 hp at 500 volts) roller armature bearings.

Electrical equipment: English Electric, Preston, Lancashire
W1/A Foot-operated controller for series parallel control with hand reverser in a separate case and without mechanical interlock. Line contactor with control resistance.

Dewirement indicator: Low voltage bulbs behind the trolley boom deviation indicator.

Brakes: Mechanical foot and hand brakes.

Body: Shorts H26/26ROS.

Length: 25ft

Width 7ft 6ins

Height: 14ft 6ins

Wheelbase: 15ft

Unladen weight: 6tons 15cwts 1qtr

Turning Circle: Believed to have been 59ft (although 10 is shown as having a 51ft turning circle.)

1-10 Railless LF

No.	New No.	Registration	Chassis	Chassis No.	Body	Body No.	Delivered	Registered	Into Service	Withdrawn	Sold
1	-	TO5002	Railless LF		Short		02.03.1927		10.04.1927	12.04.1932	Broken up
2	-	TO5003	Railless LF		Short		07.01.1927		10.04.1927	31.05.1935	
3	-	TO5004	Railless LF		Short		10.01.1927		10.04.1927	10.05.1934	
4	-	TO5005	Railless LF		Short		13.01.1927		10.04.1927	31.05.1935	
5	-	TO5006	Railless LF		Short		15.01.1927		10.04.1927	1934	
6	-	TO5007	Railless LF		Short		19.01.1927		10.04.1927	1934	
7	-	TO5008	Railless LF		Short		25.01.1927		10.04.1927	29.06.1934	
8	-	TO5009	Railless LF		Short		03.02.1927		10/04/1927	31.05.1935	
9	-	TO5010	Railless LF		Short		22.02.1927		10.04.1927	14.05.1932	Broken up
10	-	TO5011	Railless LF		Short		02.03.1927		10.04.1927	1934	

Chassis:

The straight frame was constructed from standard high grade 3% nickel steel channel with a minimum number of cross members, bracketed to the side frame. The Railless LF (low floor) design, with a lower saloon floor level only 2ft 4ins above the ground, was considered a major development when first proposed in 1924. It was made possible by fitting a Kirkstall Forge Ltd., Leeds, rear axle equipped with under slung long laminated springs having auxiliary rubber cones, worm gears, shaft and pinion drive to internal gear rings bolted to the brake drums. The drive from the motors was transmitted through a sectioned propeller shaft, equipped with Spicer universal joints, to a David Brown overhead worm gear contained in the Kirkstall double-reduction rear axle. The front axle was of the Kirkstall one-piece heavy type. The eight spoke aluminium alloy road wheels were fitted with Dunlop 881 X 140 mm solid rubber tyres on the front and "twin air-cushion" solids at the rear giving an outside diameter of 1,050 mm.

Electrics:

The left foot pedal of the "push-to-on" type operated an English Electric horizontal rotary drum controller and thus the two 35 hp motors in tandem. English Electric reversing gear, line contactor and circuit breakers. The EMB starting and shunting resistances were placed in a dust and water proof box immediately behind the front destination box on the roof of the driver's cab to avoid using an exposed, chassis location or inside the cab. The motor suspension was designed to simplify the removal of the motors and all necessary cabling was carried in a trough beneath the offside of the chassis. The trolley booms were mounted on trolley masts, similar to those used on open-top tramcars, at the front of the upper saloon enclosed in a panelled wooden box which on vehicles 1-9 projected about 8 ins in front of the upper saloon and about 7 ins into the saloon. The trolley booms were 20ft 5ins long and equipped with lightweight trolley wheels.

The dashboard of the driver's cab was equipped with a trolley boom deviation indicator in the form of an elongated box on the face of which was marked: "L.15.12.9.6.3.0.3.6.9.12.15.R" showing the position of the trolley vehicle in feet in relation to the overhead wire. Low voltage bulbs behind each number activated by finger contacts on the trolley booms lit up as required.

Initially the trolley vehicles operated out of Trent Bridge tram depot, travelling in and out of service along Arkwright Street and collecting current from the single overhead tram wire with the positive, off-side trolley boom. A skate, in fact a series of cast iron links trailing in the groove of the tram rail, carried on the offside rear and connected to the vehicle by flexible cable completed the return current circuit. The vehicles were equipped with a socket on the offside rear of the chassis into which the flexible cable was plugged. A large changeover switch in the driver's cab marked "TROLLEY" and "SKATE" controlled this electrically.

Brakes:

Mechanical brakes made in aluminium alloy to a semi-cruciform section were applied to all four wheels. The foot and hand brakes were reportedly interlinked. The brakes were applied by pressing the right foot pedal and/or by pulling the hand lever to the driver's right (either independently or by combined effort) as the vehicles were relatively heavy for the equipment of that period. A second set of brakes for use in emergency operated on the rear wheels only using separate drums. All brakes were of the internal expanding type, the shoes being equipped with Ferodo linings.

Bodywork:

Composite five-bay highbridge double-deck construction with curved forwards-ascending half-turn (90°) open staircase and open platform at the rear, built by Short Bros. Ltd., Rochester, Kent. Cost £ 2,382 7s 0d complete. There were a number of detail differences between 10 and the rest of the batch; it had been apparently advertised at Olympia at a price of £ 1,450 (chassis) or £ 2,400 (body and chassis).

The tramcar-like body featured waist and concave rocker panels to the lower saloon, a domed upper-deck roof, open rear platform and curved staircase rather similar to the London NS type motor bus of the period. Lower deck ventilation was by green-tinted opaque inward opening top lights above the main saloon side windows in bays 1-5 on both sides and by three "hit and miss" type wickets in the front bulkhead. The upper deck had drop light windows in bays 2-4 on both sides, which were moved up and down by two metal Laycock finger grips in the upper third of each pane. A protruding central panelled wooden box containing the trolley masts, extending from the roof of the driver's cab to the upper saloon roof, with two small windows on either side, disfigured the front of the upper-saloon. The outer front window on each corner used flat glass although the panels beneath were curved. The rear of the upper saloon had two almost square windows, a small window above the curved nearside panel matching those at the front and an arched entrance. Neither the entrance in the centre of the rear bulkhead to the lower saloon nor the offside entrance at the rear of the upper saloon was equipped with doors. There was one step beneath the rear platform and a further step into the lower saloon.

A gutter ran around the base of the roof with drains descending both sides of the vehicle towards the front of bay 1.

The driver's cab was equipped with an offside opening windscreen and a single front-hinged access door with a brass circular "door knocker" handle on the nearside. The offside driver's cab window was divided into three sections: a fixed top light, a fixed middle pane and a lower section equipped with horizontally sliding panes for "signalling" purposes. The nearside driver's cab door and the small window to the rear thereof were both equipped with fixed top lights. There were 3 glazed

The spartan ceiling and open staircase but deep antique leather seats of the upper saloon of 1927 Shorts Brothers bodied Railless LF number 10.
Roy Marshall

panels in the bulkhead behind the driver, that in the centre being smaller than the other two. A small rectangular driver's rear view mirror was mounted externally half way up the offside pillar of the cab. A bulb warning hooter extended through the centre of the base of the off-side driver's windscreen. The cab interior was finished in natural grain and white enamel. A bamboo trolley retrieval pole was carried on supporting hooks mounted at the base of the window pillars (waist rail) to bays 1 (front) and 4 beneath the nearside lower saloon windows. The front registration number plate was attached to the front bumper. It is believed that the rear registration number was transferred to the top of the nearside lower saloon rear window.

Inside the lower saloon was a transfer stating "Designed and built by Short Bros. Rochester for Railless Ltd.". There were five life guard rails of varying depths on each side, extending between the front and rear axles, although there was no protection beneath the high-mounted, bulbous front panel which was equipped with a substantial, curved bumper.

Lighting:

External lighting comprised a single central headlight mounted on the bulbous front panel and two "pilot lights" (side lights) mounted somewhat higher on each side of the curved coping to the front panel. At the rear a single taillight was mounted on the offside of the rear open platform at the height of divide between the waist and rocker panels. There were 5 lights inside the lower saloon and 4 in the upper saloon, all enclosed in frosted glass shades set in oxidised bronze fittings. It is assumed that the rear platform was illuminated by a single light fixed to the underside of the canopy which extended over the forwards portion of the rear platform at lower deck ceiling height. The lighting arrangement consisted of four circuits each of four 125-volt traction lamps.

Seating:

The lower saloon was equipped with a single rearwards-facing seat attached to the driver's cab rear bulkhead capable of seating 4 passengers, two longitudinal seats on each side above the rear axle each accommodating 3 passengers and four rows of double transverse seats. The upper saloon was equipped with six rows of double transverse seats on the offside and seven rows of double transverse seats on the nearside, the rearmost row being opposite the open entrance to the staircase. Those seats not having stanchions attached on the gangway side were fitted with chromed, hooped hand holds. All seats were upholstered in quilted green antique leather. All other grips, handrails and stanchions were covered with black Doverite.

Destination equipment:

A free-standing destination box capable of displaying a single line of information was mounted centrally on the roof of the driver's cab. Prior to entering service, a taller, separate square service number indicator box, displaying linen blinds with translucent lettering on a black background, was mounted to the nearside of the destination box. This could also accommodate metal service letter stencils, as used on the tramcars, presumably with the blind behind set to a blank white display.

Internal Livery:

The woodwork of the lower saloon was finished in natural grain, the ceiling being painted with white enamel. Natural light grain alone was used in the upper saloon. Floors grey.

External Livery:

Delivered in Livery 1 (see Appendix C).

Notes:

10 was originally a Railless demonstrator and appeared at the International Commercial Motor Exhibition held at Olympia, 29 October – 7 November 1925, in Birmingham Corporation Tramways livery. As it had been equipped with a W1/A foot controller instead of a hand controller (at this time Birmingham's trolley vehicles were fitted with a tramcar-style controller, which the driver worked with his left hand while steering with his right), the vehicle was unacceptable to Birmingham and in 1926 it was sold to Nottingham. The trunking in the centre of the upper-deck front panel did not protrude over the driver's cab but was built into the upper saloon making access to the front pair of double seats awkward. The front dome was cut away to ease access to the trolley bases.

As originally built and exhibited, 10 had a centrally mounted single-line destination box but no number indicator box mounted on the driver's cab roof, and an offside cab door with a single window, surmounted by a fixed top light, on the nearside. Prior to, or shortly after, entering service the offside cab door was replaced by one on the nearside as fitted to 1-9 but with a simpler handle.

These were the first rubber tyred vehicles in Nottingham with four-wheel brakes.

These were the last trolley vehicles to be built by Railless as in 1926 Short Bros decided to withdraw from the market and concentrate on more lucrative branches of their business.

Subsequent alterations:

An equipment box behind the front destination box on the driver's cab roof and an access step beneath the cab door were added.

The curved bumper beneath the bulbous front panel was removed at an early date and the registration number plate was thereafter attached beneath the front panel

The trolley wheels were replaced with Wilkinson metal slipper heads to reduce sparking on the overhead wires. These caused excessive wear to the overhead equipment whilst in wet weather greenish drops fell from the trolley heads on to passengers using the open rear staircase or platform. As the stains on passenger's clothing were difficult to remove, collecting scoops beneath the trolley heads and drainage piping down the trolley booms was fitted but to no avail as the drainage pipes emptied on to the vehicle's roof, which also developed a green stain.

Disposal:

1 was broken up for spares.

9 was withdrawn early due to an accident on 14 May 1932 and broken up for spares.

3, 5-7, 10 sold to J. Abbott, Ashover, Derbyshire in February 1935 for dismantling although some are believed to have become caravans.

2, 4, 8 sold to an unknown dealer in June 1935.

A pre-delivery view of the Railless LF/Shorts demonstrator which became Nottingham 10. No fleet number or other insignia are evident. It will be noted that, unlike on numbers 1-9, the trunking in the centre of the upper-deck front panel did not protrude over the driver's cab but was built into the upper saloon whilst the front dome was cut away to ease access to the trolley bases. *BTS*

11-12 Ransomes D4

Ransomes No 12 waiting at the Haydon Road terminus of route 37 during September 1933. Very similar to the Railless vehicles, including the fitting of vertical Munro patent cam-controlled trolley bases. *GHFA & JMB*

Chassis: Two axle type Ransomes D4 manufactured by Ransomes, Sims & Jefferies Ltd., Orwell Works, Ipswich, Suffolk.
Motor: Ransomes Sims & Jefferies T23 (65 hp at 500 volts) twin armature. Series parallel control.
Electrical equipment: British Thomson-Houston Co. Ltd., Rugby.
Foot-operated controller
Dewirement indicator: low voltage bulbs behind the trolley boom deviation indicator.
Brakes: mechanical and hand brakes.
Body: Ransomes, Sims & Jefferies H25/27ROS.
Length: 25 ft
Width: 7 ft 6 ins
Wheelbase: not known
Unladen weight: 6tons 9cwt 0qtr

11 - 12 Ransomes D4;

No.	New No.	Registration	Chassis	Chassis No.	Body	Body No.	Delivered	Registered	Into Service	Withdrawn	Sold
11	-	TO8621	Ransomes	D41893	Ransomes	702	04.09.1929		18.09.1929	05.1936	05.1936
12	-	TO8622	Ransomes	D41892	Ransomes	701	04.09.1929		18.09.1929	05.1936	05.1936

Chassis:

Pneumatic tyres.

Electrics:

The trolley booms were mounted on trolley masts, similar to those used on open-top tramcars, at the front of the upper saloon enclosed in a panelled wooden box projecting about 8ins in front of the upper saloon and about 7ins into the saloon. The trolley booms were equipped with lightweight trolley wheels.

The dashboard of the driver's cab was equipped with a trolley boom deviation indicator in the form of an elongated box on the face of which was marked: "L.15.12.9.6.3.0.3.6.9.12.15.R" showing the position of the trolley vehicle in feet in relation to the overhead wire. Low voltage bulbs behind each number activated by finger contacts on the trolley booms lit up as required.

Initially the trolley vehicles operated out of Trent Bridge tram depot, travelling in and out of service along Arkwright Street and collecting current from the single overhead tram wire with the positive, off-side trolley boom. A skate, in fact a series of cast iron links trailing in the groove of the tram rail, carried on the offside rear and connected to the vehicle by flexible cable completed the return current circuit. The vehicles were equipped with a socket on the offside rear of the chassis into which the flexible cable was plugged. A large changeover switch in the driver's cab marked "TROLLEY" and "SKATE" controlled this electrically.

Brakes:

Mechanical on rear wheels and hand brakes. No "power brakes" i.e. no rheostatic or vacuum brakes.

It has been suggested that these vehicles had an electric or rheostatic brake controlled by a separate vertical tramcar type controller standing to the nearside of the driver and worked by his left hand however no documentary or photographic evidence has been found.

Bodywork:

Composite six-bay highbridge double-deck construction with forwards-ascending curved half-turn (90°) open staircase and open platform at the rear, built by Ransomes, Sims & Jefferies Ltd., Orwell Works, Ipswich, Suffolk. Cost £ 1,751 10s 0d complete.

The tramcar-like body featured waist and rocker panels to the lower saloon, a domed upper-deck roof, open rear platform and staircase was almost identical to the Shorts Bros body on Railless trolley vehicles 1-10. However the main body had six bays instead of five on 1-10. Lower deck ventilation was by inward opening top lights above the main saloon side windows in bays 1-5 (both sides). The upper deck had drop light windows in bays 2-4 on both sides.

A protruding central panelled wooden box containing the trolley masts, extending from the roof of the driver's cab to the upper saloon roof, with two small windows on either side, disfigured the front of the upper-deck. The outer front window on each corner used flat glass although the panels beneath were curved. The rear of the upper saloon had two almost square windows, a small window above the curved nearside panel matching those at the front and an arched entrance. Neither the entrance in the centre of the rear bulkhead to the lower saloon nor the off-side entrance at the rear of the upper saloon was equipped with doors.

There was a single step up to the open rear platform which was at the same height as the lower saloon floor. The upper deck floor extended towards the rear as far as the vertical handrail dividing the rear platform providing the conductor with limited protection from the elements. The staircase to the upper deck had eight steps with unpainted kicking plates and lightweight panels attached to two vertical metal rails and the hand rail extending from the rear of the upper saloon to the platform floor. At the top of the staircase a safety rail gave an additional handhold above the main hand rail. The lightweight wrap around rear platform panel was attached to the base of the staircase and the rear of the offside lower saloon.

A gutter ran around the base of the roof with drains descending down the rear pillar of bay 6 on both sides of the vehicle.

All windows of the driver's cab were equipped with fixed half-lights. The main panes of both the offside and nearside windscreen were divided horizontally and the upper part opened outwards. The offside lower pane was equipped with a horizontally sliding "signalling" window. There was a one-piece nearside cab window and half-light in the front hinged door which provided the only access to the cab. There were 3 glazed panels in the bulkhead behind the driver, that in the centre being smaller than the other two. There was a considerable ground clearance beneath the base of the bulbous front panel, which descended to about 6ins above the level of the front axle, and carried a rounded bumper bar. A small rectangular driver's rear view mirror was mounted externally half way up the offside pillar of the cab. Raked steering wheel. A bulb warning hooter extended through the offside front windscreen pillar.

A bamboo trolley retrieval pole was carried on supporting hooks mounted immediately at the base of rear window pillars to bays 3 and 5 along the offside waist rail. A further hook placed at the base of the driver's cab bulkhead pillar restrained the pole. Two trolley restraining hooks at the extreme rear of the roof held down the trolley booms when out of use but these extended some 8 ins beyond the rear of the platform below. There were five life guard rails on each side of varying thickness, extending between the front and rear axles, although there was no protection beneath the high-mounted, bulbous front panel which was equipped with a substantial, curved bumper. A current collection skate was carried on the offside rear.

Lighting:

External lighting comprised a single central headlight mounted on the bulbous front panel and side lights on the curved coping to the front panel. At the rear a single light was mounted on the offside of the rear open platform at the height of divide between the waist and rocker panels. It is assumed that the rear platform was illuminated by a single light attached to the underside of the canopy which extended over the forwards portion of the rear platform at lower deck ceiling height.

Seating:

The lower saloon was equipped with a single rearwards-facing seat attached to the driver's cab rear bulkhead capable of seating 5 passengers, two longitudinal seats on each side above the rear axle each accommodating 3 passengers and four rows of double transverse seats. The upper saloon was equipped with five rows of double transverse seats on the offside and six rows on the nearside, together with a seventh nearside row opposite the open entrance to the staircase for 3 passengers.

Destination equipment:

A free-standing destination box capable of displaying a single line of information was mounted off-centre towards the off-side on the roof of the driver's cab. A taller, separate square service number indicator box, displaying linen blinds with translucent numbering on a black background, and showing no evidence of being able to display route letter stencils was mounted to the nearside of the destination box.

Internal Livery:

Woodwork was finished in natural grain. Ceilings were painted with white enamel. The ceiling of the driver's cab and the upper portions of the bulkheads were also painted white. Floors grey. All internal transfers were gold with two-tone blue shading.

External Livery:

Delivered in Livery I (see Appendix C).

Notes:

These were the first Ransomes, Sims and Jefferies D-type vehicles built for use with a double-deck body.

A month after the inauguration of trackless trolley system in Nottingham, it was realised that more vehicles would be needed but Railless would not quote a price or delivery date and the order was therefore placed with Ransomes, Sims and Jefferies for basically similar vehicles to 1-10 but with pneumatic tyres.

These vehicles were not popular with the drivers and were officially recommended for withdrawal in 1936 although they had already been stored out of use beforehand due to the lack of a "power brake".

Disposal:

As the last open-staircase trolley vehicles in the fleet, 11 -12 were stored out of service in the tower wagon garage for a period, possibly several years. They were officially withdrawn at the end of May 1936 and sold for scrap but their subsequent disposal is not known.

13-18 Ransomes D6

Ransomes D6 13 believed to have been photographed at Ransomes, Sims & Jefferies' Ipswich factory prior to delivery. *MERL*

Chassis: Three axle type Ransomes D6 manufactured by Ransomes, Sims & Jefferies, Ltd., Orwell Works, Ipswich, Suffolk. RSJ drawing OV3496 dated 24 July 1929. NCT drawing 7/1.

Motor: Ransomes, Sims & Jefferies, Ltd., Orwell Works, Ipswich, Suffolk, Type T37 (2 x 40 hp at 500 volts).
The traction motor casing housed two separate armatures thus facilitating series-parallel control.

Electrical equipment: British Thomson-Houston contactor controller.

Dewirement indicator: Assumed to have been line-lights.

Brakes: Westinghouse pneumatic, hand and rheostatic brakes.

Body: Ransomes, Sims & Jeffries H32/28R. RSJ drawing OV3498 dated 22 August 1929. NCT drawing 11/1.

Length: 26ft

Width 7ft 6ins

Height: 15ft 3ins to the top of the trolley bases.

Wheelbase: 15ft 7ins

Wheel track: front 6ft 5¾ins, rear 6ft 6½ins

Bogie wheelbase: 4ft

Unladen weight: 8tons 2cwt 0qtrs

Pneumatic tyres: 36 X 8ins

Together with English Electric 19-24 these were Nottingham's first three axle trolley vehicles, ordered after inspecting similar Ransomes vehicles at Maidstone, and one example, probably 14, was displayed at the 1929 Commercial Motor Show.

13 -18 Ransomes D6

No.	New No.	Registration	Chassis	Chassis No.	Body	Body No.	Delivered	Registered	Into Service	Withdrawn	Sold
13	313	TV743	Ransomes D6	2018	Ransomes	1059	17.02.1930	01.02.1930	23.02.1930	24.02.1945	04.01.1946
14	314	TV744	Ransomes D6	2016	Ransomes	1057	01.02.1930	01.02.1930	24.02.1930	31.01.1946	30.05.1947
15	315	TV745	Ransomes D6	2021	Ransomes	1062	07.02.1930	01.02.1930	24.02.1930	01.10.1945	21.01.1946
16	316	TV746	Ransomes D6	2019	Ransomes	1060	13.02.1930	01.02.1930	24.02.1930	31.01.1946	30.05.1947
17	317	TV747	Ransomes D6	2017	Ransomes	1058	25.02.1930	01.02.1930	01.03.1930	31.08.1945	21.01.1946
18	318	TV748	Ransomes D6	2020	Ransomes	1061	28.02.1930	01.02.1930	03.03.1930	30.06.1945	09.08.1945

Chassis:

The front axle was equipped with Marles steering. The Thornycroft patent rear bogie, number 259327, was equipped with double-pivoted springs on each side intended to balance the torque reactions in the bogie itself and thereby avoid the necessity of torque rods. The load on the bogie wheels under all conditions of acceleration and braking was thus equally distributed. The spring ends were articulated to the axles by trunnion brackets, preventing the lateral displacement of the spring leaves one to another. There was a differential in the centre of each rear axle. The chassis cost £1,142.

Chassis length:

26ft.

Chassis frame width:

front 3ft 3ins, rear 3ft 9ins

Electrics:

The motor was placed towards the front of the chassis.

Foot-operated BTH contactor controller with series parallel control incorporating rheostatic braking mounted transversely in the cab, partially under the driver's seat. Although some photographs give the impression that there was a hand-operated controller on the offside of the driver's cab between the steering column and side panel, it is believed that this equipment was probably the reverser. By 1930 it would have been a retrograde step to fit a hand-operated controller, bearing in mind that foot-operated controllers had been stipulated for all previous deliveries, and there is no evidence of one on official drawings.

Brackets were fixed to the roof rail immediately above the upper-deck body pillars between bays 1 and 2, and bays 3 and 4 to support the two diagonal girders of the Ransomes patent exposed trolley gantry, which was not in direct contact with the roof, and equipped with Brecknell Willis & Co. Ltd. trolleybases.

Brakes:

Rheostatic brake, Westinghouse air brakes on all wheels, hand brake operating on the rear wheels.

The air brake compressor and reservoir were fixed to the chassis nearside. There was one air-brake cylinder each side of the chassis behind the front axle and one brake cylinder on the offside of the chassis in front of the leading rear axle.

The handbrake lever was to the nearside of the driver's steering column.

Bodywork:

Composite six-bay highbridge double-deck construction, enclosed forwards-ascending half-turn (90°) staircase with conventional semi-vestibuled open platform entrance and exit at the rear, built by Ransomes, Sims & Jeffries, Ltd., Ipswich, Suffolk. The body cost £917.

The high mounted and upright body still possessed many tramcar features including divided body side panels but was more noticeably a road rather than rail vehicle than the Railless and Ransomes, Sims and Jefferies predecessors. The domed roof overhung the front of the upper-deck, the trolley poles were fitted in a conventional manner on an exposed roof-mounted gantry above bays 2 and 3 enabling the entire front of the upper saloon to be glazed. A gutter ran around the base of the roof but no drains are evident on photographs. These were Nottingham's first trolley vehicles in which the staircase and rear platform did not appear as an "after thought" attached to the rear of the body. The main transverse chassis girders were visible at the front beneath the headlamps and at the rear beneath the rear platform panel.

All windows on the lower-deck, including the nearside driver's windscreen and rear platform window were surmounted with tramcar style top lights typical of the period. The top light in bay 1 immediately behind the driver's cab on both sides of the lower deck was equipped with a sliding ventilator however there is no photographic evidence that any other lower deck saloon top lights opened. The NCT drawings show drop lights fitted in the main panes of the windows in bays 1 and 3 of the nearside of the lower saloon and bays 1, 3 and 5 of the offside.

The upper saloon side windows in bays 2, 3, 5 and 6 on both sides were equipped with drop light panes. There were three almost square, non-opening front upper-deck windows and a narrow glazed panel in the nearside and offside corners instead of body pillars. At the rear there were two almost square windows with radiused external corners which made up the upper-saloon emergency exit, the pane on the nearside sliding transversely behind the fixed offside pane to provide ventilation and access to the trolley gantry.

The main power cables ran from the trolleybase down the central front upper-deck window pillars to reach the driver's cab. The offside of the staircase was glazed with a single pane and half-light. At the rear of the upper-saloon there were two large oblong windows separated by a dividing bar. The nearside pane slid transversely to the offside outside the offside pane providing access to the trolley gantry and offering an upper-deck emergency exit. The rear platform window comprised two almost square lower panes surmounted by a transverse pane, somewhat deeper than the half-lights above the side windows, and an integral service number indicator box on the nearside. The rear registration number was transferred onto the transverse pane (positions varied).

The driver's cab was equipped with a single opening windscreen, the pane of glass having a "V"-shaped lower edge, on the offside. The nearside windscreen had a separate panel at the top, divided in half, one side being glazed and that nearest to the body pillar having louvres for ventilator through a duct to the lower saloon. There was a rear-hinged door, incorporating a half-light, on the nearside which provided the only access to the cab. To allow for the sloping front projection of the cab a narrow quarter light was provided between the nearside cab door and the cab front pillar. The lower pane of the offside cab window was provided with a horizontally sliding "signalling" window. The front nearside wheel hub was equipped with a driver's step ring.

A small rectangular driver's rear view mirror was mounted externally half way up the offside front cab pillar. A bulb warning-hooter with a bugle-like loop extended through the base of the offside front windscreen whilst a circular road fund licence holder was mounted externally at the base of the driver's cab nearside pillar. There was a used ticket box below the nearside vestibule window on the rear open platform.

It is believed that at least some, if not all, vehicles were delivered with a stowage tube beneath the chassis for a bamboo trolley retrieval pole. Thereafter the trolley retrieval pole was carried on supporting hooks mounted at the base of the rear window pillars to bays

Although already equipped with its registration number plate TV748, Ransomes D6 18 is also equipped with trade plates and is believed to have been photographed on test in Ipswich. *MERL*

1, 3 and 5 along the nearside waist rail. It was restrained by a further hook placed at the base of the nearside driver's cab bulkhead pillar with a metal plate beneath to reduce paintwork damage. This feature is not evident in photographs of 18 on test in Ipswich, although there does appear to be a stowage tube beneath the chassis, on 14, immediately upon arrival in Nottingham, and it is assumed that the supporting hooks were added before the vehicles entered service. A current collection skate was carried on the offside rear.

There was step on the rear platform and a further step up into the lower saloon. The staircase had three steps from the platform to the half-landing and then three steps to the upper deck. There were three life guard rails on each extending between the front and second axles, although there was no protection beneath the high-mounted, still slightly bulbous front panel.

Lighting:

External lighting was 2 headlights or spotlights mounted beneath the flat front panel, and at the rear a single red "bulls eye" light at the top of the cream-painted offside rear platform corner panel. The rear registration number was transferred onto the top of the transverse rear platform half-light window. A red reflector triangle was fitted at the base of the rear platform offside panel.

Seating:

Semi-bucket type upholstered in quilted green leather. The tops of most seats on the gangway side were equipped with semi-circular grab handles covered in black Doverite.

The lower saloon had a 4-person inwards-facing bench seat on each side over the rear axles and 5 rows of forwards-facing double seats. The upper saloon had 7 rows of double seats on the offside and 9 rows on the nearside.

Destination equipment:

A free-standing destination box capable of displaying a single line of information was mounted off-centre on the roof of the driver's cab. A taller, separate square service number indicator box was mounted to the nearside of the destination box. A destination indicator box was also mounted in the half-light of bay 5 on the nearside. A further rectangular service number indicator box was mounted on the nearside of the transverse lower deck rear platform window.

Internal Livery:

All mouldings and panel work were finished in a rich mahogany shade. The ceilings and coves of both saloons were painted with white enamel with varnished/polished wood frames. The ceiling of the driver's cab was painted cream and the upper portions of the bulkheads were painted white. The windows were all surrounded internally by varnished wood frames. Saloon floors brown, platform floor grey. All internal transfers were gold with two-tone blue shading.

External Livery:

Delivered in Livery 2 (see Appendix C).

Subsequent alterations:

A rear view mirror was mounted externally half way up the nearside front cab pillar, probably during the war.

Small front sidelights were added to the top corners of the front panel pre-war.

A red power brakes triangle plate was added to the offside lower corner of the rear panel.

The top lights of 315, possibly 316 and potentially other vehicles in this batch, were painted over green post-1932.

In late 1939, 13-18 were renumbered in sequence as 313-318.

Additional front side lights complying with wartime lighting measures were fitted to the base of the front mudguards, in addition to brackets for emergency paraffin lamps which were attached when the trolleybuses were parked at the roadside with their trolley booms down or when there was any disruption to the power supply. A rear registration number plate, inset to the lower part of the rear platform panel on the offside and illuminated from the top, was added progressively to vehicles of this class in the early part of the war.

Notes:

13-18, together with English Electric 19-24, entered service on the Wilford Road – Wells Road service.

Disposal:

313, 315, 317 sold to Cardale Service Garage (Rhodes), Carlton Road, Nottingham, dealers, in January 1946. 313 was used later as a caravan.

314, 316 sold to Acks Motors, 61A Sandon Street Basford, Nottingham, in May 1947.

318 sold to H. Tempest Ltd., Mundella Works, Felton Road, Nottingham, photographers, in August 1945.

Ransomes D6 15 in Stanhope Street, at Lower Parliament Street Depot, with the small current collector skate connected at the rear of the vehicle but not in the tram rails. This view dates from after 1932, when livery changes to the roof, upper and lower window surrounds were implemented. *NCT*

19 – 24 English Electric E11

A manufacturer's photograph of 1930 English Electric E11 prior to delivery. *EE/Beilby*

Chassis: Three axle type English Electric E11 manufactured by the English Electric Co. Ltd. at the Dick, Kerr works in Preston, Lancashire. EE drawing P2800/016 dated 20 November 1929. NCT drawing 7/3.

Motor: English Electric, Type DK 122A (B) (2 X 40 hp at 500 volts) twin armature with roller armature bearings arranged to give series-parallel control.

Electrical equipment: English Electric manufactured by English Electric Co. Ltd. at their Phoenix Works, Bradford, Yorkshire. WD1-B foot-operated controller (DK 45123-28). Chassis-mounted Type S resistances. Type D, form A circuit breakers. Four series notches, three parallel notches and a weak-field notch, with pump action notch regulator.

Dewirement indicator: Buzzer.

Brakes: Westinghouse compressed air, 4-stage rheostatic and hand brakes.

Body: English Electric H30/30R. EE drawing 28657A dated 1 August 1929. NCT drawing 11/3.

Length: 28ft 0¼ins

Width: 7ft 6ins over mudguards (7ft 2ins over pillars)

Height: 14ft 9⅛ins to top of trolley plank.

Wheelbase: 16ft 6ins giving a turning circle on either lock of 54ft.

Wheel track: front 6ft 5¼ins, rear 6ft 5¼ins

Bogie wheelbase: 4ft

Unladen weight: 8tons 2cwt 3qtrs although it is known that later most erroneously displayed 8tons 2cwt0 qtrs (as 13-18)

Tyres: High pressure pneumatic 36 X 8 on all wheels.

19 - 24 English Electric

No.	New No.	Registration	Chassis	Chassis No.	Body	Body No.	Delivered	Registered	Into Service	Withdrawn	Sold
19	319	TV749	English Electric	122	Eng. Electric		28.12.1929	19.02.1930	24.02.1930	31.07.1946	30.05.1947
20	320	TV750	English Electric	121	Eng. Electric		28.12.1929	19.02.1930	24.02.1930	31.10.1944	03.10.1944
21	321	TV751	English Electric	124	Eng. Electric		30.01.1930	19.02.1930	24.02.1930	31.01.1946	02.06.1947
22	322	TV752	English Electric	123	Eng. Electric		30.01.1930	19.02.1930	24.02.1930	21.03.1944	03.10.1944
23	323	TV753	English Electric	126	Eng. Electric		18.02.1930	01.03.1930	01.03.1930	01.10.1948	04.08.1949
24	324	TV754	English Electric	125	Eng. Electric		21.02.1930	01.03.1930	03.03.1930	31.05.1944	03.10.1944

Chassis:

The rear bogie had a swivelling suspension intended to overcome any tendency to tilting during braking and to prevent torsional stresses in the springs. Each rear axle had its own differential.

These vehicles were constructed between two batches of Bradford English Electric E11s, namely 572-583 (1929-30) and 584-595 (1931), and it is likely that they, like their Bradford counterparts, had their chassis construction sub-contracted to Rubery Owen, a specialist manufacturer.

Chassis length:

27ft 4¼ins.

Chassis frame width:

front 3ft 1½ins, rear 3ft 5½ins

Overall width

(over front hubs): 7ft 5¾ins

Electrics:

Series parallel control was obtained by using 2 X 40 hp motors with twin armatures located amidships. These vehicles proved quite slow when compared to 13-18. The motor drive was transmitted to the rear axles by a differential in the centre of each axle. The foot pedal operated camshaft contactor type controller was placed in the nearside of the driver's cab. The driver had to contend with three foot pedals, two of which were related to the controller and one to the foot brake, namely:

Offside of the steering column – footbrake (FB on drawing)

"Inner" nearside of the steering column – controller (C on drawing)

"Outer" nearside of the steering column – rheostatic brake (BP on drawing)

Notching-up was commenced by depressing the controller pedal until the camshaft was held by a pawl. By partially releasing the pedal and again depressing it, the second notch was obtained. Releasing the pedal entirely also released the pawl and the camshaft sprang back to the zero position. When fully notched-up the camshaft was held by a comparatively light pedal pressure in order to minimise driver fatigue.

The brake switch was on the nearside of the driver's seat against the bulkhead and adjacent to the controller.

Two banks of resistances were mounted on the offside and one bank on the nearside of the chassis.

The trolley base was supported by an exposed gantry with supports immediately above the upper-deck body pillars between bays 1 and 2, and bays 3 and 4, and further supports each side of the body pillar between bays 2 and 3. The Brecknell Munro and Rogers trolley poles, unlike contemporary English Electric deliveries which employed the Estler Bros. system and had both poles superimposed on a single pivot, for example Maidstone and Southend-on-Sea, were mounted side by side and could deviate up to 16ft on either side of the overhead wiring. Each trolley pole was equipped with a short chain and loop for rewiring purposes at its extremity. Brecknell Munro and Rogers trolley head. The vehicle was equipped with a trailing skate and appropriate Type 34A changeover switch.

Brakes:

Four notch foot-operated rheostatic brakes, a Westinghouse Brake & Saxby Signal Co. compensating air brake working independently on each of the six wheels and a hand brake on the rear bogie wheels.

The air brake compressor was fixed to the chassis nearside with the reservoir between the chassis frame. There was one air-brake cylinder each side of the chassis forward of the front axle and two brake cylinders fitted to each rear axle.

The handbrake lever was to the offside of the driver's steering column.

Bodywork:

Composite six-bay highbridge double-deck construction, enclosed forwards-ascending half-turn (90°) staircase with conventional semi-vestibuled open platform entrance and exit at the rear built by English Electric Co. Ltd. at Preston. Cost £2,098 10s complete.

Although delivered concurrently with 13-18 built by Ransomes, Sims and Jefferies, these trolley vehicles had a much more modern appearance with no evidence of a tramcar ancestry. The domed roof overhung the front of the upper-deck with a central service number indicator box at the top of a panel between the two front windows, the trolley poles were fitted side by side on an exposed roof-mounted gantry above bays 2 and 3. A gutter ran around the base of the roof but no drains are evident on photographs. The staircase and rear platform were integrated into the bodywork. The main transverse chassis girders were visible beneath the front panel to the driver's cab and at the rear beneath the rear platform panel.

The cantrail vent panel area above the lower-deck windows, which had featured top lights on earlier deliveries, was panelled, ventilation to the lower saloon being entirely by means of sliding windows. Glass louvres were fitted above the lower deck saloon side windows in bay 1, 3, and 4. The lower saloon side windows in bays 1, 3, 4 and the upper saloon side windows in bays 2, 3, 5, 6 were equipped with drop light panes. The entire front of the upper-deck was gently curved with wide side body pillars and two large front windows separated by central panel which was surmounted by a square service number indicator box. At the rear of the upper-saloon there were two large windows with radiused extremities. The nearside pane slid transversely to the offside (behind the offside pane) providing access to the trolley gantry and offered an upper-deck emergency exit. The upper saloon was equipped with two roof mounted ventilators (one on each side) towards the rear of bay 6. There were two windows at the rear of the platform with radiused upper extremities, the rear registration number being transferred onto the top of the offside platform window and also applied to a number plate attached to the offside bottom of the rear platform.

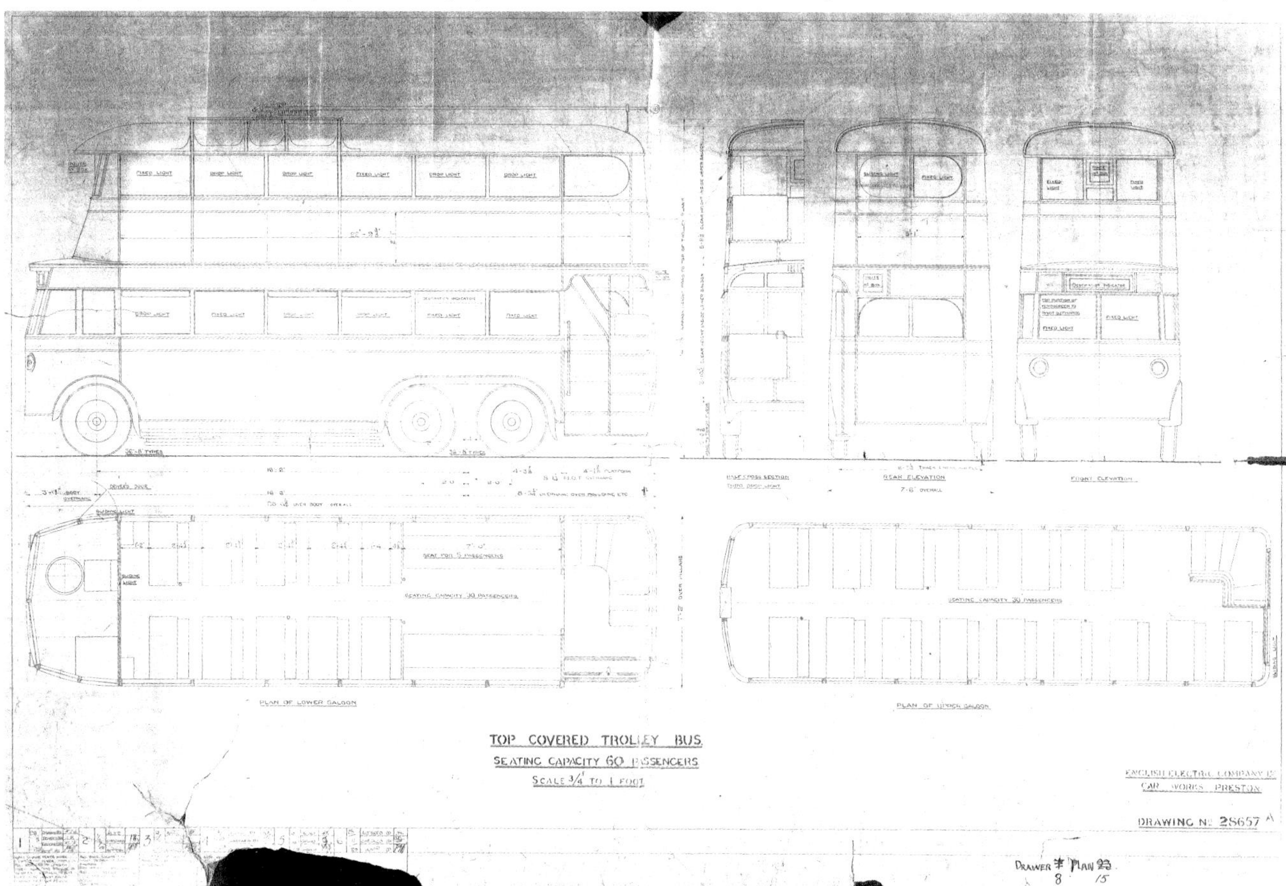

English Electric Company Ltd. general arrangement drawing for a 60 seat trolleybus. Drawing No.28657A, which was revised 6 times between 29th May and 25th November 1929, was used to produce 19-24. *NCT*

Above the open rear platform, a curved coping matched the side and rear cantrail panels.

The lower saloon floor was covered in linoleum whilst the upper saloon floor was fitted with English oak hardwood slats. The vehicle was equipped with Numa air bells.

The driver's cab, which protruded well forward of the upper deck, was equipped with a single opening windscreen on the offside and a front hinged door on the offside. The window in the offside cab door was provided with a sliding "signalling" window. Fixed quarter lights preceded the offside cab door and its matching counterpart. A small rectangular driver's rear view mirror was mounted externally half way up the offside pillar of the cab.

A bamboo trolley retrieval pole was carried in a tube mounted centrally under the chassis. A current collection skate was carried on the offside rear.

There was step on the rear platform and a further step up into the lower saloon. The staircase had three steps from the platform to the half-landing and then three steps to the upper deck. There were three lifeguard rails on each extending between the front and second axles, although there was no protection beneath the high-mounted, slight curved front panel to the driver's cab. The front axle wheel hubs were equipped with a driver's step ring.

Lighting:

External lighting was 2 headlights mounted two thirds of the way up on the extreme nearside and offside of the front panel beneath the driver's windscreen and at the rear a single red light to the offside of the registration number plate at the base of the rear panels. The rear registration number was also transferred onto the top of the transverse rear platform half-light window.

Seating:

Although the type and style of seating has not been positively identified it is known that it was similar to that employed in 13 –18, that is of the semi-bucket type, appears to have had quilted leather seat covers and that it was manufactured by Lace Web, Sandiacre, Derbyshire. The tops of most seats on the gangway side were equipped with semi-circular grab handles covered in black Doverite.

The lower saloon had a 5-person inwards-facing bench seat on each side over the rear axles and 5 rows of forwards-facing double seats. The upper saloon had 6 rows of double seats on the offside and 9 rows on the nearside.

Destination equipment:

A destination box capable of displaying a single line of information was mounted centrally in the cream painted panelling immediately above the driver's windscreen and also at the top of the nearside lower saloon window bay 6. A square service number indicator box was fitted at the top of the cream painted central panel between the two windows at the front of the upper deck and immediately above the nearside rear platform window towards the nearside.

Internal Livery:

Ceilings white. The lower saloon was covered with linoleum and the upper saloon with English oak hardwood slats. Saloon floors brown, platform floor grey.

External Livery:

Delivered in Livery 2 (see Appendix C).

Subsequent alterations:

Operating experience showed that stones and other street detritus thrown up by the wheels on the second axle were damaging the bodywork and causing punctures to the tyres of the third axle. A mud flap hanging between the second and third axle was added at an early date.

It is believed that the red rear light was moved to the top of the cream-painted rear platform offside corner panel, possibly concurrent with the removal of the low mounted registration number plate. A red reflector triangle was fitted at the base of the rear platform offside panel.

Stowage of the bamboo trolley retrieval pole in a tube beneath the chassis ceased and it was carried on supporting hooks mounted at the base of the rear window pillars to bays 1, 3 and 5 along the nearside waist rail.

A nearside driver's rear view mirror was added, mounted at the top of the pillar between the main nearside cab window and the triangular quarter light.

In 1937, 24 was decorated for the Coronation of King George VI.

In late 1939, 19-24 were renumbered in sequence as 319-324.

There are discrepancies in respect of the seating capacity between NCT's drawings, dating from the batches' delivery, and record cards, which date from the late 1939 renumbering. It is thus possible that these vehicles were re-seated from H30/30R to H32/28R at some stage in the 1930s.

Additional front side lights complying with wartime lighting measures were fitted at the top of the front panel beneath the driver's windscreen, on the waistband, on the extreme nearside and offside, in addition to brackets at the base of the front mudguards for emergency paraffin lamps which were attached when the trolleybuses were parked at the roadside with their trolley booms down or when there was any disruption to the power supply. At the same time the headlamps were moved downwards some 8 ins from their original position on the front panel and the red rear light lowered to a more conventional position. A rear registration number plate, inset to the lower part of the rear platform panel on the offside and illuminated from the top, was again added progressively to vehicles of this class in the early part of the war.

Notes:

19-24, together with Ransomes, Sims & Jefferies 13-18, entered service on the Wilford Road – Wells Road service.

Disposal:

319 sold to Acks Motors, 61A Sandon Street, Basford, Nottingham, breakers, in May 1947.

320, 322, 324 sold to H. Lane, 35 Tadema Road, off Lots Road, Chelsea, London, dealers, in October 1944.

321 sold to G.A. Jennings, 84 Chilwell Road, Beeston, Nottingham, in June 1947.

323 sold to A. Devey, Lynn Lane, House Farm, Lichfield, Staffordshire, breakers, in August 1949.

English Electric E11 19 at Wheeler Gate, en route for Wilford Bridge, in it's orginal livery. A foggy but busy scene of the early 30's. *NCT*

25 – 36 Karrier E6

The 1931 Karrier E6 deliveries with Park Royal composite bodywork are exemplified by no. 26 pictured at Kings Street in September 1933. *GHFA & JMB*

Chassis: Three axle type Karrier E6 marketed by Karrier-Clough and manufactured by Karrier Motors, Huddersfield, Yorkshire. Karrier drawing 2926 dated 27 November 1930. NCT drawing 7/4.
Motor: British Thomson-Houston Co. Ltd., Rugby, Warwickshire. Type BTH 110D (80hp) series wound 136 armature amps at 1,650 rpm at 500 volts.
Electrical equipment: British Thomson-Houston Co. Ltd., Rugby, Warwickshire.
Brakes: Westinghouse pneumatic and hand brakes.
Body: Park Royal H30/30R.
Length: ca. 26ft
Width: 7ft 6ins
Height: 15ft 5ins to the top of the trolley bases (laden).
Wheelbase: 15ft 11ins
Wheel track: front 6ft 6¾ins, rear 6ft 6ins
Bogie wheelbase: 4ft
Unladen weight: 8tons 2cwt 0qtrs
Tyres: 36 X 8

One of these vehicles, probably 25 which features in Park Royal publicity photographs, was exhibited at the 1931 Commercial Motor Show.

25 - 36 Karrier E6

No.	New No.	Registration	Chassis	Chassis No.	Body	Body No.	Delivered	Registered	Into Service	Withdrawn	Sold
25	325	TV4463	Karrier E6	54037	Park Royal	B3141	15/10/1931		01.12.1931	01.10.1948	04.08.1949
26	326	TV4464	Karrier E6	54033	Park Royal	B3142	22/10/1931		01.12.1931	01.10.1948	04.08.1949
27	327	TV4465	Karrier E6	54035	Park Royal	B3143	27/10/1931		29.11.1931	01.10.1948	11.1948
28	328	TV4466	Karrier E6	54039	Park Royal	B3144	29/10/1931		29.11.1931	01.10.1948	31.03.1949
29	329	TV4467	Karrier E6	54034	Park Royal	B3145	02/11/1931		29.11.1931	30.09.1948	04.08.1949
30	330	TV4468	Karrier E6	54036	Park Royal	B3146	09/11/1931		01.12.1931	01.10.1948	11.1948
31	331	TV4469	Karrier E6	54032	Park Royal	B3147	19/11/1931		19.12.1931	31.07.1944	10.1944
32	332	TV4470	Karrier E6	54040	Park Royal	B3148	12/11/1931		05.12.1931	01.10.1948	09.04.1949
33	333	TV4471	Karrier E6	54041	Park Royal	B3149	16/11/1931		05.12.1931	01.10.1948	31.03.1949
34	334	TV4472	Karrier E6	54042	Park Royal	B3150	24/11/1931		19.12.1931	09.1948	17.06.1949
35	335	TV4473	Karrier E6	54038	Park Royal	B3151	04/12/1931		12.01.1932	31.01.1944	10.1944
36	336	TV4474	Karrier E6	54043	Park Royal	B3152	30/12/1931		08.01.1932	31.01.1950	20.02.1950

Chassis:

Spectacle frame and Karrier rear axle. The chassis cost £ 1,189 15s. "Flush" wheels, attached conventionally.

Chassis length:

26ft.

Chassis frame width:

front 3ft, rear 4ft 3½ins

Overall width

(over hubs): front 7ft 4¾ins, rear 7ft 2 13/16ins

Electrics:

The motor was placed towards the front of, and along the centreline of, the chassis with one very short propeller shaft which engaged end-on with a second long propeller shaft to the rear axles.

BTH type RQ Form G resistances and BTH MR502 circuit breakers.

There were 2 contactor cabinets: one on the nearside beneath the driver's cab windscreen whilst the other is believed to have been against the cab rear bulkhead. The BTH controller was mounted beneath the cab floor to the nearside of the driver's steering column.

Brecknell Willis & Co. Ltd. trolleybases and poles.

All lighting was supplied from the traction power.

Brakes:

Westinghouse air and hand brakes.

The Bull air brake compressor was fixed to the inner face of the chassis nearside with the air reservoir on the inner face of the chassis offside. There was one air-brake cylinder each side of each rear axle.

The handbrake lever was to the offside of the driver's steering column.

Bodywork:

Composite seven-bay highbridge double-deck construction, enclosed forwards-ascending half-turn (90°) staircase with conventional semi-vestibuled open platform rear entrance and exit at the rear, built by Park Royal Coachworks Ltd., Abbey Road, Park Royal, Willesden, London NW10. The body cost £ 712 6s.

The front of the upper-saloon was equipped with a central service number indicator box at the top of a panel between the two front windows. Steel bands fastened to the lower-deck body pillars, cantrail and upper-deck body pillars between bays 1 and 2, bays 2 and 3, bays 3 and 4, bays 4 and 5 continued over the rounded edges of the roof to support the 4 girders of the exposed trolley gantry above bays 2, 3 and 4. Platform handrails and stanchions were covered with black Doverite. Pneumatic bells.

Metal louvres were fitted above the upper and lower deck saloon side windows. The rearmost side window on both sides of the upper-saloon was radiused towards the rear at both top and bottom in the shape of a "D". Typhoon half-drop openers were fitted to the side windows in bays 1, 3, 5, 7 of the upper deck and bays 2, 4, 6 of the lower-deck saloons. Square ventilators were mounted immediately above the lower deck side windows in bays 2, 4, 6. At the rear there were two almost square windows with radiused external corners which made up the upper-saloon emergency exit, the pane on the nearside sliding transversely behind the fixed offside pane to provide ventilation and access to the trolley gantry. The upper corners of the single rear platform window were radiused, the rear registration number being transferred centrally on to the top of the pane. A gutter ran around the base of the roof with drains descending down the front pillar of bay 1 and the rear pillar of bay 7 on both sides.

The slightly bulbous front panel of the driver's cab featured an outline "radiator" position with the front registration number plate at its base. The top two thirds of the offside driver's windscreen opened outwards and carried a windscreen wiper. There was a front-hinged door on the offside, curved at the top, with a sliding "signalling" window in the lower portion of the pane. A matching sliding window on the nearside provided additional cab ventilation although the window itself was noteworthy in having a square top. There were fixed quarter lights between the offside cab door and its matching nearside counterpart, and the cab front pillars. Four small louvre style inlet ventilator vanes were installed in the cream-painted band immediately above the windscreen, two on each side of the central pillar. Three similar ventilators were installed in the front upper-deck panel above the destination indicator. A wheel nut cover, which was used as a step into the driver's cab, was fitted to both front wheels. An access step was inset into the base of the offside bay 1 side panel, immediately behind the front axle, at the same height as the wheel hub.

There were 3 glazed panels, which were not as deep as the saloon windows, in the bulkhead behind the driver. A rectangular driver's rear view mirror was mounted externally at the top of the offside cab door front pillar.

There was a single step on the rear platform, that is two from street level, on the nearside of the rear platform, the riser of which carried a "Karrier-Clough" maker's plate and a further step up into the lower saloon. It is believed that the half-turn (90°) staircase had four steps from the platform to the half-landing and then two steps to the upper deck, all fitted with aluminium "kicking plates" to the risers. Both decks had high density cork tiles on the floors. There was a single lifeguard rail on each side extending between the front and second axles. A bamboo trolley retrieval pole was carried within the lower-saloon nearside body panels at waist rail height with a tube access from the rear platform vestibule.

Lighting:

External lighting was 2 headlights mounted half way up the slightly bulbous front panel however that on the nearside was a fog light with an orange lens, and large sidelights at the extremities immediately above the driver's cab windscreen. At the rear there was a single red light at the top of the cream-painted offside rear platform corner panel.

A bracket for a square emergency paraffin lamp with a clear lens at the front and red lens at the rear was fitted to the offside front pillar and in the base of the rear light fitting for use when the trolleybuses were parked at the roadside with their trolley booms down or when there was any disruption to the power supply as the vehicles carried no batteries.

Seating:

The lower saloon had a 3-person inwards-facing bench seat on each side over the rear axles and 6 rows of forwards-facing double seats. The upper saloon had 7 rows of double seats on the offside and 8 rows on the nearside.

Green leather seat covers. Black Doverite covered grab handles and stanchions.

Destination equipment:

A single-line destination box was located centrally in the upper deck panels above the driver's windscreen. A square (9 ins x 10 ins) service number indicator box was mounted at the top of a wide central panel separating the front upper-saloon windows and at the rear centrally on the upper deck panels above the rear platform window. There was a single-line destination box in the cream-painted vent panel above the rearmost nearside lower saloon window (bay 7).

Internal Livery:

Ceilings and coves were covered with white painted panels with varnished/polished wood frames. The ceiling of the driver's cab and the upper portions of the bulkheads were painted cream. The internal window frames were varnished wood. Saloon floors brown, platform floor grey. All internal transfers were gold with two-tone blue shading. A thin rail protected the rear platform window at shoulder height.

External Livery:

Delivered in Livery 3 (see Appendix C).

Subsequent alterations:

In late 1939, 25-36 were renumbered in sequence as 325-336.

The large sidelights above the driver's windscreen were removed. On some vehicles they were moved to the waistband beneath the side windows to the driver's cab whilst on others they were replaced by small sidelights also on the waistband.

Some vehicles including 26-28 and 36, received a protruding sun visor above the driver's cab windscreen and the outline "radiator" on the front panel was removed.

The internal varnished wood window frames were painted white by the early wartime period.

A rectangular driver's rear view mirror was fitted at cantrail height on the nearside.

All vehicles except 335 were fitted with a spot light beneath the front panel somewhat more towards the centre of the vehicle than the nearside headlight in December 1943 – January 1944. The orange lens was removed from the nearside fog light, the fitting becoming a headlight.

Additional brackets for emergency paraffin lamps were fitted to the base of the front mudguards to comply with wartime lighting measures.

A rear registration number plate, inset to the lower part of the rear platform panel on the offside and illuminated from the top, was added progressively to vehicles of this class in the early part of the war and the red rear light lowered to a more conventional position.

Notes:

25-36, together with Ransomes D6 37-49, entered service on the Carlton-Wollaton Park services. 335 was withdrawn in January 1944 due to fire damage.

Disposal:

325, 326, 329 sold to A. Devey, Lynn Lane, House Farm, Lichfield, Staffordshire, dealers, in August 1949.

327 sold to T. Mitchell, 7 Bentinck Road, Nottingham, in November 1948.

328 sold to H. Hallam, 35 Ashfield Avenue, Beeston, Nottingham, in March 1949.

330 sold to Mrs R. Morgan, 183 Standhill Road, Carlton, Nottingham, in November 1948.

331, 335 sold to H. Lane, 35 Tadema Road, off Lots Road, Chelsea, London, in October 1944.

332 sold to M.H. Pope, Hungerton, Grantham, Lincolnshire, in April 1949.

333 sold to Mrs Bradbury, 30 Kingswood Road, Wollaton, Nottingham, in March 1949.

334 sold to M.J. Staines, Severns Yard, High Street, Alfreton, Derbyshire, in June 1949.

336 sold to Mr Clarke, The Sawmill, Long Sutton, Spalding, Lincolnshire, dealer, in February 1950. Later used as a caravan (September 1956)

Initially 325, 326, 328, 329, 332-334, 336 were sold to R. Blair, Ceniarth Hall, Machynlleth, Montgomeryshire in November 1948 but subsequently resold as above.

1 Karrier E6

Chassis: Three axle type Karrier E6 manufactured by Karrier Motors, Huddersfield, Yorkshire. Karrier drawing 3094 dated 1 October 1931
Motor: British Thomson-Houston Co. Ltd., Rugby, Warwickshire. Type BTH 201DK (80hp)
Electrical equipment: British Thomson-Houston Co. Ltd., Rugby, Warwickshire.
Brakes: Westinghouse air and hand brakes.
Body: Brush H32/28R.
Length: 27ft quoted but 26ft when scaled from the manufacturer's drawings
Width: 7ft 6ins
Height: 14ft 7½ins to roof panels.
Wheelbase: 16ft 3½ins
Wheel track: front 6ft 7⅝ins, rear 6ft 7⅜ins
Bogie wheelbase: 4ft
Unladen weight: 8tons 5cwt 1qtr
Tyres: 36ins X 8ins all round.

The composite body of this vehicle was formerly mounted on the chassis of Brush Thornycroft 1931 demonstrator 28 (TV3460), which was hired to Nottingham between November 1930 and June 1931.

1 Karrier E6

No.	New No.	Registration	Chassis	Chassis No.	Body	Body No.	Delivered	Registered	Into Service	Withdrawn	Sold
1	301	TV8473	Karrier E6	54045	Brush		1933		06/05/1933	01/10/1948	04/08/1949

Chassis:

Although earlier publications have described this vehicle as having an E6A chassis, the Karrier Motors' drawing 3094, and thus the NCT chassis data sheet 7/5 and drawing 11/5, are entitled "Arrangement of Chassis Type E6". There are clear differences between this chassis and the E6As supplied later to Newcastle upon Tyne and Belfast.

Pressed steel spectacle frame of deep section.

Chassis frame width:

front 3ft, rear 3ft 10ins

Overall width (over hubs):

front 7ft 5⅝ins, rear 7ft 5¾ins

Electrics:

The motor was placed towards the front of, and along the centreline of, the chassis with a propeller shaft to the rear axles.

BTH type RQ Form G resistances and BTH MR506 Form B circuit breakers. NCT drawings show the controller as being mounted in front of the steering column.

Brakes:

The air brake compressor was fixed to the inner face of the chassis nearside with the air reservoir on the inner face of the chassis offside. There was one air-brake cylinder each side of the chassis ahead of the front axle and one brake cylinder each side of each rear axle.

The handbrake lever was to the nearside of the driver's steering column.

Bodywork:

Composite six-bay highbridge double-deck construction, enclosed forwards-ascending half-turn (90°) staircase with conventional semi-vestibuled open platform entrance and exit at the rear, built by Brush Electrical Engineering Co. Ltd., Loughborough, Leicestershire. The body was formerly mounted on Thornycroft demonstrator 28 and acquired at a cost of £ 712.60.

A number of modifications to the body were necessary to fit the new chassis. The rear wheel arch area was remodelled to fit the Karrier 4ft wheelbase rear bogie (the Thornycroft had a 4ft 6in wheelbase). The Thorneycroft's front mudguards were part of the chassis and presumably went with the chassis when the body was removed. The Karrier's front axle was set further back and this resulted in an "amateurish" cut away look to the front of the body in the cab area.

The sun visor above the driver's cab windscreen was removed.

See Demonstrator 28 for further details.

Lighting:

See 28.

The nearside headlight was equipped with an orange lens to serve as a fog light.

Seating: See 28.

Destination Equipment:

See 28.

Internal Livery:

See 28.

External Livery:

See 28.

Rear fleet number transferred centrally beneath lower saloon rear window.

The cream-painted cheat line on the lower deck panels continued beneath the platform vestibule window and across the width of the trolleybus.

The seating capacity details were applied with gold, blue shaded, transfers at cantrail height immediately above the rear bulkhead window on the platform.

Subsequent alterations:

In late 1939, 1 was renumbered as 301.

A solid panel replaced the rearmost lower deck offside window, behind the staircase.

The front panel beneath the driver's cab windscreen was divided into two parts, separated by horizontal beading. The lower part accommodated the front registration number plate, mounted centrally, whilst there was no longer a small "D"-shaped gap at its base. The base of the offside and nearside side panels between the front panel and the mudguards of the front axle, together with parts of the front panel itself, were cut away (perhaps to improve air flow to the front brakes). The headlights were moved from their positions half way down the front mudguards to the front panel at wheel arch height and the large sidelights above the windscreen were moved to the waistband beneath the cab side windows.

Additional front side lights complying with wartime lighting measures were fitted to the base of the front mudguards, in addition to brackets for emergency paraffin lamps which were attached when the trolleybuses were parked at the roadside with their trolley booms down or when there was any disruption to the power supply. A rear registration number plate, inset to the lower part of the rear platform panel on the offside and illuminated from the top, was added in the early part of the war and the red rear light lowered to a more conventional position.

Disposal:

301 was initially sold to R. Blair, Ceniarth Hall, Machynlleth, Montgomeryshire in November 1948 but not collected. In August 1949 it was resold to A. Devey, dealers, Lichfield, Staffordshire.

37- 49 Ransomes D6

On a beautiful summer's day in 1932 one of the latest examples of modern railless electric traction Ransomes D6/Brush 44, just some six months old, stands in the sunshine in the northbound carriageway of Middleton Boulevard at Fairham Drive. Note the driver's white-topped cap and summer dustcoat. *BTS*

Chassis: Three axle type Ransomes D6 manufactured by Ransomes, Sims & Jeffries, Ltd., Orwell Works, Ipswich, Suffolk. RSJ drawing OV3496 dated 24 July 1929. NCT drawing 7/1.

Motor: Ransomes, Sims & Jeffries, Ltd., Orwell Works, Ipswich, Suffolk, Type T50 (80 hp).

Electrical equipment: British Thomson-Houston Company Ltd., Rugby, Warwickshire.
BTH Type RQ, form G resistances; BTH MR502 circuit breakers.

Dewirement indicator: Two neon lamps together with a buzzer operated through a relay in series.

Brakes: Westinghouse air, hand and rheostatic brakes.

Body: Brush H32/28R. Brush drawing 62031N dated 17 April 1931. NCT drawing 11/6.

Length: 26ft 7ins

Width: 7ft 6ins

Wheelbase: 15ft 7ins

Unladen weight: 8tons 0cwt 2qtrs

Tyres: 36 X 8

37 - 49 Ransomes D6

No.	New No.	Registration	Chassis	Chassis No.	Body	Body No.	Delivered	Registered	Into Service	Withdrawn	Sold
37	337	TV4475	Ransomes D6	2132	Brush		21.10.1931		29.11.1931	31.01.1950	15.02.1950
38	338	TV4476	Ransomes D6	2131	Brush		22.10.1931		29.11.1931	28.02.1950	30.03.1950
39	339	TV4477	Ransomes D6	2134	Brush		23.10.1931		29.11.1931	07.04.1949	26.05.1949
40	340	TV4478	Ransomes D6	2130	Brush		23.10.1931		30.11.1931	31.01.1950	23.02.1950
41	341	TV4479	Ransomes D6	2137	Brush		27.10.1931		29.11.1931	28.02.1950	28.06.1950
42	342	TV4480	Ransomes D6	2135	Brush		27.10.1931		29.11.1931	01.10.1948	04.08.1949
43	343	TV4481	Ransomes D6	2136	Brush		02.11.1931		29.11.1931	01.10.1948	30.03.1949
44	344	TV4482	Ransomes D6	2139	Brush		02.11.1931		29.11.1931	28.02.1950	20.06.1950
45	345	TV4483	Ransomes D6	2138	Brush		08.12.1931		11.12.1931	28.02.1950	17.06.1950
46	346	TV4484	Ransomes D6	2140	Brush		08.12.1931		10.11.1931	28.02.1950	27.05.1950
47	347	TV4485	Ransomes D6	2141	Brush				19.11.1931	28.02.1950	28.06.1950
48	348	TV4486	Ransomes D6	2142	Brush				19.11.1931	28.02.1950	27.05.1950
49	349	TV4487	Ransomes D6	2133	Brush		31.12.1931		16.01.1932	28.02.1950	15.06.1950

Interior of the upper deck of Ransomes D6 37.
NCT

Chassis:

The vehicles were equipped with a patent flexible rear bogie incorporating a third differential to equalise the drive between all four wheels and Ransome-Garrett propeller shaft. Kirkstall front axle and Thornycroft patent rear bogie. The construction was so arranged that midway between the 2 driving axles were 2 transverse shafts carried by steel brackets fastened to the longitudinal frame members. On these shafts were mounted rotary spring clamping brackets, the spring ends being secured to the twin axles by pins of large diameter that passed through bushed eyes. These pins connected the spring ends to gimbal brackets, which were so pivoted to the axles that any canting of one or other of the axles could not cause torsional displacement of the springs, and the tendency for the leaves to get out of position relative to one another. The chassis cost £1,236.

Electrics:

BTH controller.

The contactor cabinet appears to have been on the nearside of the driver's cab against the cab rear bulkhead.

The driver was provided with an ampere hour meter, electric automatic windscreen wiper, and (in addition to a bulb horn) an electric horn.

Brakes:

Westinghouse air (Ransomes compressor) and hand brake.

Internal expanding brakes, fitted to the rear wheels

Bodywork:

Highbridge double-deck composite six bay construction, enclosed forwards-ascending half-turn (90°) staircase with conventional semi-vestibuled open platform entrance and exit at the rear, built by Brush Electrical Engineering Co., Loughborough, Leicestershire. The body cost £897.

The upright rear and the overhanging roof to the front of the upper-saloon gave these trolley vehicles a rather dated look despite the then fashionable "torpedo" panelling to the front panels beneath the driver's cab windscreen in a style reminiscent of the London United AEC "Diddlers".

Brackets were bolted to the roof rail immediately above the upper-deck body pillars between bays 1 and 2, bays 2 and 3, bays 3 and 4 to support the three diagonal girders of the exposed trolley gantry above bays 2 and 3 and the Brecknell Willis trolley base, which was not in direct contact with the roof.

Conductor's mirror on staircase. Platform handrails and stanchions were covered with black Doverite. Pneumatic bells. There were two steps on the rear platform but no further step up into the lower saloon.

The front upper deck corner pillars were noticeably wide for the period, the front upper deck and forward-most side windows having radiused corners. Shallow metal louvres were fitted above the upper and lower deck saloon side windows, bays 1-6 and above the rearmost upper-deck side window, with a protruding sun visor above the driver's cab windscreen. "Typhoon" half-drop light openers were fitted to the side windows in bays 1, 3, 5 of both decks on both the nearside and offside. There were two windows at the rear of the upper-saloon, the pane on the nearside sliding transversely behind the fixed offside pane to provide access to the trolley gantry and offer an emergency exit, and two rear platform windows, the nearside and offside corners being heavily radiused. The rear registration number was transferred onto the nearside rear platform windowpane. Elongated extractor ventilators were fitted in the cream-painted vent panel above the body pillars between bays 1 and 2, bays 3 and 4, and bays 5 and 6. Inside the lower saloon, small wooden Brush patent panels were pulled inwards on a concertina to control the ventilation. Further ventilation to the lower saloon was by means of a Brush patent panel ventilator in the

Interior of the lower deck of Ransomes D6 37.
NCT

front bulkhead, air entering through slots at the top of the driver's windscreen and through a duct in the cab roof. Similar ventilation was provided in the upper-saloon by two vertical panel ventilators fitted in the front corners of the roof, air entering through cowls in the front panels of the lower saloon. Four Ashanco hopper ventilators were fitted towards the rear of the roof on each side.

A gutter ran around the base of the roof with drains descending down the front pillar of bay 1 on both sides and the rear pillar of bay 6 on the offside.

The curvaceous nose to the front panel of the driver's cab featured an outline "radiator" position. The top half of the offside driver's windscreen opened outwards, the nearside windscreen was fixed. There was a front-hinged driver's cab door on the offside, the window therein was provided with a sliding square "signalling" window in the lower portion of the pane. There were fixed quarter lights between the offside cab door and its matching nearside counterpart, and the cab front pillars.

There were 3 glazed panels rising from waist height in the bulkhead behind the driver that in the middle not being as deep as the other two. A circular driver's rear view mirror was mounted externally at the top of the offside cab door front pillar. There were 2 fire extinguishers on board.

There was a single step, that is two from street level, on the nearside of the rear platform and a further step up into the lower saloon. There was a used ticket box immediately below the nearside vestibule window. The staircase had three steps from the platform to the half-landing and then three steps to the upper deck. There were two lifeguard rails on each side extending between the front and second axles. All wheel hubs were equipped with a chromed wheel trims. There were separate mudguards to the rear wheels and a mud flap hung between the second and third axle. A bamboo trolley retrieval pole was carried within the lower-saloon nearside body panels at waist rail height with a tube access from the rear platform vestibule.

Lighting:

External lighting was 2 headlights mounted on the curved panel each side of the outline "radiator" however that on the nearside was a fog light with an orange lens which could be dipped (presumably the headlamp body dipped). On the cream-painted panels above the driver's windscreen, at the top of the nearside and offside front pillars, a large sidelight was affixed. There was a single red light at the rear mounted above waist height on the cream-painted offside rear platform corner panel.

A bracket for a square emergency paraffin lamp with a clear lens at the front and red lens at the rear was fitted to the offside front pillar, adjacent to the rear view mirror, and in the base of the rear light fitting for use when the trolleybus was parked at the roadside with its trolley booms down or when there was any disruption to the power supply as the vehicles carried no batteries.

There were 8 lamps in the ceiling of the lower saloon and 10 in the upper saloon, equipped with opal bulbs and having white enamelled flush-fitting backings.

Seating:

The seats were manufactured by the Lace Web Spring Co., Sandiacre, Derbyshire and upholstered in green leather.

The lower saloon had a 6-person inwards-facing bench seat on each side over the rear axles and 4 rows of forwards-facing double seats. The upper saloon had 7 rows of double seats on the offside and 8 rows on the nearside.

Four stanchions covered in black "Doverite" were provided in the lower saloon adjacent to the transverse seats, with ten hand-grips above the longitudinal seats. Grab handles were fixed to the ceiling adjacent to the lower saloon longitudinal seats.

Destination equipment:

The front upper deck panels above the driver's windscreen accommodated a combined square service number indicator and single-line destination box in one, located centrally in the lower third of the panel. There was a destination box on the nearside at the top of the window bay 6 and a square service number indicator at the base of the upper deck rear panels above the rear nearside platform window, towards the nearside.

Internal Livery:

Walnut was used for the interior woodwork. Ceilings and coves were painted with white enamel. The ceiling of the driver's cab and the upper portions of the bulkheads were also painted white. The panels were covered with green scratch-proof leather cloth to match the seating upholstery. Brown floors. All internal transfers were gold with two-tone blue shading.

External Livery:

Delivered in Livery 3 (see Appendix C).

Subsequent alterations:

The large sidelights above the driver's windscreen were removed and on some vehicles they were moved to the waistband beneath the side windows to the driver's cab.

The wheel trims were discarded.

The outline "radiator" on the front panel was removed from at least 37 and 41.

In late 1939 37- 49 were renumbered as 337-349.

The internal varnished woodwork was painted white by the early wartime period.

A spot light was fitted beneath the front panel somewhat more towards the centre of the vehicle than the nearside headlight, 337, 342, 344-349 being dealt with in December 1943 and 343 in March 1944. The orange lens was removed from the nearside fog light, the fitting becoming a headlight.

By the post-war period, the nearside destination box had been removed.

Additional brackets for emergency paraffin lamps were fitted to the base of the front mudguards to comply with wartime lighting measures. A rear registration number plate, inset to the lower part of the rear platform panel on the offside and illuminated from the top, was added progressively to vehicles of this class in the early part of the war and the red rear light lowered to a more conventional position.

343 was fitted with long ceiling-mounted hand rails in the lower saloon 11 March 1944.

337 equipped with BTH 110D motor (probably from 331 or 335) and Hardy Spicer transmission shaft in March 1945.

Notes:

37-49, together with Karrier E6 25-36, entered service on the Carlton-Wollaton Park services.

By the early 1940s the Brush bodywork had deteriorated, it being no longer possible to restrain the internal flaps behind the destination boxes.

The collapsed remains of 46 (346) were auctioned at Home Farm, Faldingworth near Market Rasen, Lincolnshire, in October 1999 and purchased by Brian Maguire and Tom Bowden on behalf of the Sandtoft Transport Centre for £ 24. Parts of the upper deck, aluminium panelling, drip mouldings and guttering sections, light fittings, windows and the chassis (less the front axle) were moved to Sandtoft on 8 December 1999. It is intended to restore the Ransomes, Sims and Jefferies chassis for display as time and finances permit. The body parts will be used in the restoration of Brush-bodied Karrier E6, 67 (367) in due course.

Disposal:

337 sold to A.E. Bromley, 32 Thorneywood Rise, Nottingham, in February 1950.

338 sold to Mr Clarke, The Sawmill, Long Sutton, Spalding, Lincolnshire, dealers, in March 1950.

339 sold to J. Stapleton (NCT Foreman), 7 Belton Street, Hyson Green, Nottingham, in May 1949.

340 sold to Mr Clarke, The Sawmill, Long Sutton, Spalding, Lincolnshire, dealers, in February 1950

341, 344, 345, 347, 349 sold to Mrs A.P. Clarke, Westmoor Lane, Kettlethorpe, Lincolnshire, dealers, in June 1950.

342 sold to A. Devey, Lynn Lane, House Farm, Lichfield, Staffordshire breaker, in August 1949.

343 sold to Mr Marchant, The Caravan, Cossington, Leicestershire, in March 1949.

346, 348 sold to Mrs A.P. Clarke, The Gravel Pits, Doddington, Lincolnshire, dealers, in May 1950.

Initially 348 was sold to R. Blair, Machynlleth, Montgomery but subsequently resold as above.

50 Karrier E6

Chassis: Three axle type Karrier E6 marketed by Karrier-Clough and manufactured by Karrier Motors, Huddersfield, Yorkshire.

Motor: Manufacturer's publicity literature indicates that this vehicle was supplied to Nottingham as a demonstrator with a series wound BTH508 (75 hp) motor manufactured by British Thomson-Houston Co. Ltd., Rugby, Warwickshire. Further sources indicate that by the time it was purchased in January 1932, it had been re-equipped with a Type BTH 110D (80hp) motor series wound 136 armature amps at 1,650 rpm at 500 volts. The NCT fleet list of 1947 and the history card of this vehicle however still refer to a BTH508 (75hp) motor equipped with BTH MR506 Form B circuit breakers.

Electrical equipment: British Thomson-Houston Co. Ltd., Rugby, Warwickshire.

Brakes: Westinghouse pneumatic and hand brakes.
At least during the period this vehicle was a demonstrator it also had eddy current brakes.

Body: Park Royal H30/30R. Design number 2027 dated 21 April 1931. NCT drawing 11/4.

Length: 28ft 6ins

Width: 7ft 6ins over mudguards

Height: 15ft 2½ins to the top of the trolley bases.

Wheelbase: 17ft 6ins

Unladen weight: 8tons 1cwt 3qtrs

Tyres: 36 X 8

This vehicle was originally a Karrier-Clough demonstrator which came to Nottingham in October 1930 and was originally numbered 27. It was purchased in January 1932 for £1,555 13s 1d having been renumbered 50 in late 1931.

50 Karrier E6

No.	New No.	Registration	Chassis	Chassis No.	Body	Body No.	Delivered	Registered	Into Service	Withdrawn	Sold
50	350	VH3305	Karrier E6	54023	Park Royal		01/11/1930	14/10/1930	11.1930	30/09/1948	04/08/1949

The Delivery, Registered and Into Service dates refers the period it was a Demonstrator.

Chassis:
See Demonstrator 27.

Electrics:
See Demonstrator 27.

Brakes:
See Demonstrator 27.

Bodywork:
See Demonstrator 27.

Lighting:
See Demonstrator 27.

Seating:
See Demonstrator 27.

Destination equipment:
See Demonstrator 27.

Internal Livery:
See Demonstrator 27.

External Livery:
Delivered in Livery 3 (see Appendix C).

Subsequent alterations:

By May 1933 the imitation "radiator" was removed from the front panel of the driver's cab but the curvaceous nose and ledge immediately beneath the windscreen were retained. The front was now made up of the two metal panels previous hidden by the imitation "radiator" with a bumper across its lower edge. The front registration number plate hung beneath the front panel.

The offside circular driver's rear view mirror was replaced by a small rectangular mirror and a matching rear view mirror was added on the nearside.

In late 1931, 27 was renumbered as 50 to avoid confusion with the new Karrier E6, registration number TV4465, delivered at the end of October 1931. In 1939, 50 was renumbered as 350.

The sidelights above the driver's windscreen were removed and replaced by smaller sidelights mounted on the lower cream-painted at waistband height and beneath the side windows to the driver's cab.

Additional front side lights complying with wartime lighting measures were fitted to the base of the front mudguards, in addition to brackets for emergency paraffin lamps which were attached when the trolleybuses were parked at the roadside with their trolley booms down or when there was any disruption to the power supply as the vehicle carried no batteries. A rear registration number plate, inset to the lower part of the rear platform panel on the offside and illuminated from the top, was added in the early part of the war and the red rear light lowered to a more conventional position.

Notes:

Just before the war, 50 was equipped with a single trolleypole having twin heads, possibly based on a Fischer tramcar bow collector frame, termed a "sledge collector" by NCT, and used for an experiment in the streets around Trent Bridge Depot and Works. NCT drawing RS-8D-167 of May 1938 refers to 337 yards of overhead wiring on the circuit Pyatt Street, Fraser Street and Turney Street where the distance between the positive and negative wires had been narrowed to 12 ins centres.

The trolleybus did reappear with conventional trolleypoles later in the war but seems to have been restricted to peak hour and football special use only.

Disposal:

350 sold to A. Devey, Lynn Lane, House Farm, Lichfield, Staffordshire, dealers, in August 1949.

Initially 350 was sold to R. Blair, Ceniarth Hall, Machynlleth, Montgomeryshire in November 1948 but subsequently resold as above.

51 – 60 Karrier E6

An official offside photograph of Karrier E6 54. *NCT*

Chassis: Three axle type E6 manufactured by Karrier Motors, Huddersfield, Yorkshire. Karrier drawing 3523 dated 24 October 1933 and issued to NCT on 28 February 1934. NCT drawing 7/7.
Motor: English Electric. Type EE 405/5B (80hp).
Electrical equipment: English Electric augmented field contactor controller.
Brakes: G.D. Peters air and hand brakes.
Body: Metro-Cammell H34/30R. Metro-Cammell-Weymann Motor Bodies Ltd. drawing D1099 dated 27 June 1933. NCT drawing 11/9.
Length: 28ft 0¼ins
Width: 7ft 6ins over mudguards (7ft 4ins over panels)
Height: 14ft 6ins to roof panels.
Wheelbase: 16ft 4ins
Wheel track: front 6ft 6ins, rear 6ft 5¼ins
Bogie wheelbase: 4ft
Unladen weight: 8tons 15cwts 3qtrs
Tyres: low pressure 10.50 × 20 all round.

These vehicles were not registered in fleet number sequence.

51 - 60 Karrier E6

No.	New No.	Registration	Chassis	Chassis No.	Body	Body No.	Delivered	Registered	Into Service	Withdrawn	Sold
51	351	TV9313	Karrier E6	54083	MCCW & F	51	14.03.1934	10.05.1934	11.05.1934	29.02.1952	30/06/1952
52	352	TV9315	Karrier E6	54082	MCCW & F	52	10.03.1934	10.05.1934	12.05.1934	24.03.1952	10/07/1952
53	353	TV9316	Karrier E6	54084	MCCW & F	53	19.03.1934	10.05.1934	14.05.1934	01.11.1950	03.01.1951
54	354	TV9310	Karrier E6	54081	MCCW & F	54	10.03.1934	10.05.1934	11/05/1934	31.01.1952	28.04.1952
55	355	TV9311	Karrier E6	54080	MCCW & F	55	09.03.1934	10.05.1934	12.05.1934	29.02.1952	21.04.1952
56	356	TV9312	Karrier E6	54079	MCCW & F	56	13.03.1934	10.05.1934	14.05.1934	30.06.1951	01.09.1951
57	357	TV9307	Karrier E6	54075	MCCW & F	57	08.02.1934	13.02.1934	24.04.1934	31.01.1951	09/08/1951
58	358	TV9314	Karrier E6	54076	MCCW & F	58	15.03.1934	10.05.1934	10.05.1934	24.03.1952	07.07.1952
59	359	TV9308	Karrier E6	54077	MCCW & F	59	06.03.1934	10.05.1934	13.05.1934	29.02.1952	02.07.1952
60	360	TV9309	Karrier E6	54078	MCCW & F	60	07.03.1934	10.05.1934	10.05.1934	29.02.1952	22.05.1952

Chassis:

Conventional cranked chassis frame over rear bogie with special insulation points for all-metal bodies. Karrier rear axles.

Chassis length:

27ft 6ins

Chassis frame width:

front 2ft 11ins (3ft 5ins at the rear of the front wheels), rear 4ft 7¼ins

Overall width

(over hubs): front 7ft 5¾ins, rear 7ft 5½ins

Electrics:

The traction motor was centrally mounted, that is about halfway along the chassis, offset to the nearside with one propeller shaft to the rear axles which had matching offset differentials.

There were 2 contactor cabinets in the cab, both mounted on ebonite panels: one on the nearside beneath the driver's windscreen and the other over the nearside wheel arch. The controller was mounted in front of the driver's steering column with the reversing switch against the cab rear bulkhead.

The resistances were placed between the chassis frame to the rear of the front axle. A motor generator set for lighting purposes was fitted on the external face of the chassis nearside.

The exposed trolley gantry was constructed of pressed steel Welsh hat and channel sections framed together and mounted on the upper deck cantrail structure. The Brecknell Willis lightweight trolley base was mounted as follows: a steel plate, to both sides of which insulating rubber was moulded through holes in the plate, was mounted between the channel members

Karrier E6 51 upper deck interior, looking toward the rear. *NCT*

Karrier E6 51 lower deck, looking forward. *NCT*

An official nearside front photograph of Karrier E6 54. *NCT*

An official nearside rear photograph of Karrier E6 54. *NCT*

In wartime garb complete with white-painted mudguards and lifeguards, and canister saloon lighting covers, Karrier E6/MCCW & F 352 waits at Middleton Boulevard at Fairham Drive, Middleton Boulevard. *BTS*

The ubiquitous tilt test of Karier E6 51. It is doubtful that the vehicle is being held by the gentleman in the coat! The tilt indicator is reading 25 degrees. *NCT*

of the gantry. The moulded rubber and plate were of similar construction to that then used for railway carriage buffers and draw-gear springs by Messrs Spencer Moulton. The bolts securing the trolley base passed entirely through the rubber and could not come into contact with any portion of the steel structure providing a resilient mounting, insulated electrically from the vehicles' body and reducing the transmission of trolley noises to the interior. A rubber covered plate with its front and rear edges bent upwards to ensure that rain water ran off at the sides, provided dry-spot insulation between the trolley base and its rubber mounting.

Brakes:

G.D. Peters air and hand brakes. It is not known if rheostatic brakes were also fitted.

The English Electric air brake compressor and reservoir were fixed to the external face of the chassis offside. There was one air-brake cylinder each side of the chassis ahead of the front axle and one cylinder each side of each rear axle.

The handbrake lever was to the nearside of the driver's steering column.

Bodywork:

All metal (patented) six-bay highbridge double-deck construction, forwards-ascending half-turn (90°) staircase with conventional semi-vestibuled open platform entrance and exit at the rear, built by the Metropolitan-Cammell Carriage, Wagon and Finance Company Ltd., Saltley, Birmingham. There were several discrepancies between the body builders drawing and the finished article.

These were the first trolleybuses with all metal bodies in the fleet. In profile, the front of the body featured a "swept-back" styling between the vertical front panel of the driver's cab and the upper deck roof, the upper deck front corner panel being in line with the front of the driver's cab door but fractionally in front of the front axle. The curved rear profile had similarities with Metro-Cammell's later deliveries to London Transport. The front of the upper-deck was equipped with a central service number indicator box at the top of a panel between the two fixed front windows, the trolley poles were fitted on an exposed roof-mounted gantry above bay 2. Platform handrails and stanchions were covered with black Doverite. Numa air bells.

Brackets were bolted to the roof rail immediately above the upper-deck body pillars between bays 1 and 2, and bays 2 and 3, to support the two girders of the exposed trolley gantry which was mounted above bay 2, and not in direct contact with the roof.

Metal louvres were fitted above the upper and lower deck saloon side windows, and above the front service number panel. Chromium plated half-drop openers with central gripper at the top of the upper pane were fitted to the side windows in bays 1, 3, 5 of both sides of the upper deck, bays 1, 2, 3 of the lower-deck nearside and bays 1, 3, 5 of the lower-deck offside. The upper pane dropped outside the fixed lower pane. Immediately above the lower deck side windows in bays 1, 3 and 5, square Colt extractor ventilators were mounted. There were two Colt roof ventilators, one on each side above bay 5 on the nearside and above bay 1 on the offside. At the rear of the upper-saloon there were two oblong window panes without a dividing bar, the pane on the nearside sliding transversely behind the fixed offside pane to provide access to the trolley gantry and offer an emergency exit. There was rail across the window aperture. The floors on both decks were 3/8 ins thick tiling.

The driver's steering wheel was noticeably raked back. The top two thirds of the offside driver's windscreen was chromium plated and opened outwards. It carried a top-mounted windscreen wiper. There was a front-hinged door on the offside provided with a square sliding "signalling" window in lower one-third of the pane and an inset, opening handle. There was a matching panel and window on the nearside. There were large fixed quarter lights between the offside cab door and its matching nearside counterpart, and the cab front pillars. The base of the cab door was curved over the wheel arch. Two small horizontal hooded inlet ducts were installed on each side above the driver's cab door, above the side window to the front of the door and in equivalent positions on the nearside. An access step was let into the base of the bay 1 side panel, but without any form of protection to the bodywork, immediately behind the front axle, on the offside slightly above the height of the wheel hub. A wheel nut guard ring, which on the offside was used as a step into the driver's cab, was fitted to both front wheels.

There were 3 glazed panels in the bulkhead behind the driver. A circular driver's rear view mirror was mounted externally towards the top of the offside front cab pillar.

There was step on the rear platform and a further step up into the lower saloon. The staircase had three steps from the platform to the half-landing and then three steps to the upper deck. There was a single lifeguard rail on each side extending between the flared rear of the front wheel mudguard to the leading rear axle. There were separate mudguards to the rear wheels, the front of that around the leading rear axle and the rear of that around the third axle flared to match that around the front wheels. A mud flap hung between the second and third axle.

There were hinged valance panels on the nearside in bays 1 (part) and 2 to access the motor generator set, and on the offside in bay 3 to access the air brake compressor.

The flat front panel incorporated a single fluted column of 3 louvred vanes placed centrally at the level of the headlamps with the fleet number transferred above. There was no removable front panel for towing purposes. The registration number plate was affixed at the base of the front panel. A bamboo trolley retrieval pole was carried within the lower-saloon nearside body panels at waist rail height with a tube access from the rear platform vestibule.

Lighting:

External lighting was 2 headlights mounted half-way up the front panel however that on the nearside was a fog light with an orange lens, 2 circular front side lights on the lower cream band and a single red "bulls-eye" light at the rear mounted above waist height on the rear platform corner panel, at approximately half the depth of the platform window. The rear light mounting incorporated a bracket for an emergency paraffin lamp which could be attached when the trolleybus was parked at the roadside with its trolley booms down or when there was any disruption to the power supply.

Beneath certain internal light fittings the wording "emergency light" could be found. Under normal circumstances a low-tension power supply for normal lighting purposes was provided by the motor generator set thus batteries for limited emergency lighting must have been carried but the details are not known.

Seating:

Based on green painted G.D. Peters concealed interior frames with exposed steel supports and "torpedo" grab handles adjacent to the aisle. Grab handles hanging from leather straps were fixed to the ceiling adjacent to the lower saloon longitudinal seats. Some of the seats in the upper saloon were equipped with stanchions. Spring cushion seats upholstered in best quality hand-buffed hide.

The lower saloon had a 5-person inwards-facing bench seat on each side over the rear axles and 5 rows of forwards-facing double seats. The upper saloon had 7 rows of double seats on the offside and 10 rows on the nearside.

Destination equipment:

The front upper deck panels above the driver's windscreen accommodated a rectangular single line destination box, located centrally in the lower third of the panel. A square (9 ins x 10 ins) service number indicator box was mounted at the top of a wide central panel separating the front upper-saloon windows and at the rear centrally in the lower third of the upper deck rear panel immediately above the cream-painted middle band above the rear platform window. A similar single line destination box was built into the middle cream-painted band above the rearmost nearside lower saloon window (bay 6).

Internal Livery:

Ceilings and coves were covered with white enamelled panels with varnished/polished wood frames. The ceiling of the driver's cab and the upper portions of the bulkheads were painted cream. The window surrounds and saloon front bulkhead above the windows were varnished wood. Brown floors. All internal transfers were gold with two-tone blue shading.

External Livery:

Delivered in Livery 4 (see Appendix C).

Subsequent alterations:

In late 1939, 51-60 were renumbered in sequence as 351-360.

A spot light was fitted beneath the flat front panel somewhat more towards the centre of the vehicle than the nearside headlight. The orange lens was removed from the nearside fog light, the fitting becoming a headlight. It is believed that these changes took place very early in the war, the headlamp being fitted with appropriate shields.

A rear view mirror was mounted externally to the front nearside cab pillar at an early date.

Some vehicles, including 358, received shallower nearside driver's cab windscreens with a bottom-mounted windscreen wiper.

The original internal transfers were replaced with gold transfers having green edges.

The nearside wheel nut protector was removed whilst that on the offside had holes drilled in it for access to the wheel nuts.

Numbers 354, 359 were equipped with 10.3:1 worm drive at a later date.

The varnished wood internal window surrounds and front bulkhead above the windows were painted white at some time in the early stages of the war.

Additional front sidelights and brackets for emergency paraffin lamps were fitted to the base of the front mudguards to comply with wartime lighting measures. A nearside windscreen wiper was mounted at the base of the nearside windscreen ca. 1940. A rear registration number plate, inset to the lower part of the rear platform panel on the offside and illuminated from the top, was added progressively to vehicles of this class in the early part of the war.

Long white handrails to assist the increased number of standing passengers in wartime blackout conditions were fitted to 353, 354, 355, 357 in 1944, and the original ceiling grab handles were removed.

External advertising began to be displayed on the offside rear platform panel (circular "spot") from May 1945. Also post-war advertisements were added on either side of the front destination box.

Notes:

354 was delicensed July 1949 – December 1949.

357 was withdrawn after an accident on 17 January 1951.

359 was rebuilt at Trent Bridge Works in June 1949 following an accident.

352 was the last pre-war trolleybus to leave Trent Bridge Works (30 April 1952).

The Metro-Cammell all metal bodies, which were still something of an innovation when they entered service, proved to be far superior to the contemporary Brush composite bodies. These vehicles were never based at Lower Parliament Street Depot.

Disposal:

351 sold to Mrs A.P. Clarke, Brownwood, Thorney, Lincolnshire, dealer, in June 1952.

352 sold to Mrs A.P. Clarke, Brownwood, Thorney, Lincolnshire, dealer, in July 1952.

353 sold to Mrs A.P. Clarke, Westmoor Lane, Kettlethorpe, Lincolnshire, dealer, in January 1951.

354 sold to Mrs A.P. Clarke, Brownwood, Thorney, Lincolnshire, dealer, in April 1952.

355 sold to Thomas Bow, 45 Lamartine Street, Nottingham, builders, in April 1952.

356 sold to W. Beardow, Larklands House, Ilkeston, Derbyshire, in September 1951.

357 sold to T. Grimer, West View, Billingborough, Lincolnshire, in August 1951.

358 sold to Mrs A.P. Clarke, Brownwood, Thorney, Lincolnshire, dealer, in July 1952.

359 sold to Hayes & Cox, North Street, Ilkeston, Derbyshire, in July 1952.

360 sold to Mrs A.P. Clarke, Brownwood, Thorney, Lincolnshire, dealer, in May 1952.

61 – 85 Karrier E6

In wartime garb complete with white-painted base to the front panel, mudguards and lifeguards, emergency paraffin lamps and anti-blast window netting, Karrier E6/Brush 370 waits at Middleton Boulevard at Fairham Drive. *BTS*

Chassis: Three axle type E6 manufactured by Karrier Motors, Huddersfield, Yorkshire. Karrier drawing 3453 dated 14 March 1933 and issued to NCT on 12 October 1933. NCT drawing 7/6.
Motor: British Thomson-Houston Co. Ltd., Rugby. Type BTH 201 Form DX (80hp at 500 volts) regulated field.
Electrical equipment: British Thomson-Houston Co. Ltd., Rugby, Warwickshire.
Dewirement indicator: Assumed to have been equipped with line-lights and buzzer.
Brakes: G.D. Peters air and hand brakes.
Body: Brush H34/30R.
Length: 28ft 2ins
Width: 7ft 6 ins
Wheelbase: 16ft 4ins
Wheel track: front 6ft 6ins, rear 6ft 5¼ins
Bogie wheelbase: 4ft
Unladen weight: 8tons 13cwt 0qtrs
Tyres: 10.50 X 20

These vehicles were not registered in numerical sequence.

61 - 85 Karrier E6

No.	New No.	Registration	Chassis	Chassis No.	Body	Body No.	Delivered	Registered	Into Service	Withdrawn	Sold
61	361	TV9327	Karrier E6	54071	Brush		15.06.1934	16.06.1934	16.06.1934	31.01.1952	10.04.1956
62	362	TV9328	Karrier E6	54067	Brush		21.06.1934	01.08.1934	01.08.1934	01.09.1950	26.10.1950
63	363	TV9319	Karrier E6	54068	Brush		05.03.1934	02.05.1934	02.05.1934	01.10.1950	23.10.1950
64	364	TV9320	Karrier E6	54065	Brush		20.03.1934	02.05.1934	03.05.1934	30.12.1950	12.07.1951
65	365	TV9331	Karrier E6	54073	Brush		29.06.1934	01.09.1934	01.09.1934	01.10.1950	04.11.1950
66	366	TV9332	Karrier E6	54070	Brush			29.09.1934	02.10.1934	30.11.1950	01.02.1951
67	367	TV9333	Karrier E6	54072	Brush			01.08.1934	01.08.1934	25.03.1950	29.04.1950
68	368	TV9334	Karrier E6	54074	Brush			01.09.1934	01.09.1934	01.11.1950	10.01.1951
69	369	TV9336	Karrier E6	54069	Brush			01.08.1934	01.08.1934	30.11.1950	13.03.1951
70	370	TV9340	Karrier E6	54066	Brush			01.09.1934	01.09.1934	01.09.1950	31.10.1950
71	371	TV9317	Karrier E6	54055	Brush		11.02.1934		31.03.1934	25.03.1950	08.05.1950
72	372	TV9318	Karrier E6	54052	Brush			10.05.1934	11.05.1934	01.03.1951	14.04.1951
73	373	TV9329	Karrier E6	54050	Brush		16.06.1934	16.06.1934	16.06.1934	01.03.1951	22.04.1951
74	374	TV9330	Karrier E6	54063	Brush		22.06.1934	01.09.1934	01.09.1934	01.10.1950	02.11.1950
75	375	TV9321	Karrier E6	54058	Brush		20.04.1934	02.05.1934	03.05.1934	30.12.1950	21.08.1951
76	376	TV9322	Karrier E6	54064	Brush		20.04.1934	10.05.1934	12.05.1934	30.11.1950	18.04.1951
77	377	TV9323	Karrier E6	54053	Brush		10.03.1934	02.05.1934	03.05.1934	30.11.1950	23.01.1951
78	378	TV9324	Karrier E6	54054	Brush		23.03.1934	02.05.1934	03.05.1934	31.01.1952	03.04.1952
79	379	TV9325	Karrier E6	54051	Brush		25.04.1934	10.05.1934	14.05.1934	01.09.1950	24.11.1950

No.	New No.	Registration	Chassis	Chassis No.	Body	Body No.	Delivered	Registered	Into Service	Withdrawn	Sold
80	380	TV9326	Karrier E6	54061	Brush		25.04.1934	10.05.1934	11.05.1934	31.01.1952	13.03.1952
81	381	TV9337	Karrier E6	54059	Brush		25.06.1934	01.08.1934	01.08.1934	31.01.1952	04.04.1952
82	382	TV9338	Karrier E6	54056	Brush			29.09.1934	02.10.1934	01.10.1950	27.10.1950
83	383	TV9335	Karrier E6	54060	Brush			01.09.1934	01.09.1934	31.01.1952	27.03.1952
84	384	TV9341	Karrier E6	54057	Brush			01.09.1934	01.09.1934	30.12.1950	08.05.1951
85	385	TV9342	Karrier E6	54062	Brush		19.06.1934		02.07.1934	31.10.1948	05.07.1949

Chassis:

Cranked chassis frame over rear bogie. The differentials were offset to the nearside of the Karrier rear axles.

Chassis length:

27ft 6ins

Chassis frame width:

front 2ft 11ins (3ft 5ins at the rear of the front wheels), rear 4ft 7¼ins

Overall width

(over hubs): front 7ft 5¾ins, rear 7ft 5½ins

Electrics:

The motor was centrally mounted, that is about halfway along the chassis, off set to the nearside with one propeller shaft to the rear axles which had matching offset differentials.

The BTH controller was mounted in front of the driver's steering column with the main switches and fuses above and to the rear of the driver's head.

The resistances were placed between the chassis frame to the rear of the front axle.

The contactor cabinet was in the driver's cab.

Brakes:

G.D. Peters air and hand brakes.

The air brake compressor (Ransomes compressor motor) and reservoir were fixed to the external face of the chassis offside. There was one air-brake cylinder each side of the chassis ahead of the front axle and two cylinders fitted to each rear axle.

The handbrake lever was to the nearside of the driver's steering column.

Bodywork:

Composite six-bay highbridge double-deck construction, forwards-ascending half-turn (90°) staircase with conventional semi-vestibuled open platform entrance and exit at the rear, built by Brush Electrical Engineering Co. Ltd., Loughborough, Leicestershire.

The bodywork was basically identical to that fitted to 1934 Ransomes D6 86-106. In profile, the front of the body featured a "swept-back" styling between the upright but bulbous front panel of the driver's cab and the upper deck roof, the upper-saloon front corner panel being in line with the front of the driver's cab door but fractionally in front of the front axle. The curved rear profile had similarities with Brush's subsequent deliveries to London Transport, for example 1935 Leylands 94-131, 1937 AECs 554-603).

Extensions were bolted to the roof rail immediately above the upper-deck body pillars between bays 1 and 2, bays 2 and 3, and bays 3 and 4 to support the three girders of the exposed trolley gantry which was mounted above bays 2 and 3, and the Brecknell Willis lightweight special trolleybases which were not in direct contact with the roof.

Metal louvres were fitted above the upper and lower deck saloon side windows, including the radiused rear side window to the upper-saloon. There was a deep protruding sun visor above the driver's cab windscreen. The front of the upper-deck was equipped with a central service number indicator box at the top of a panel between the two fixed front windows. Half-drop openers with a clip-operated grippers attached centrally to the top of the upper pane were fitted to the side windows in bays 1, 3, 5 of the upper deck and bays 2, 4, 6 of the lower-deck. Oblong extractor ventilators were mounted immediately above the lower deck side windows in bays 1, 3 and 5. At the rear of the upper-saloon there were two almost square windows, although the outer top corners of the window spaces in the bodywork were curved, without a dividing bar which, when the nearside pane was slid transversely behind the offside pane, provided access to the trolley gantry and offered an emergency exit

There were two almost square rear windows to the platform, separated by a narrow dividing bar, the rear registration number being transferred on to the top of the nearside pane. There was a used ticket box immediately below the nearside vestibule window on the rear open platform and a conductor's locker beneath the staircase. Platform handrails and stanchions were black.

The layout of the rear platform steps differed somewhat from 86-106 as the rear part of the Karrier chassis was wider that that on the Ransomes D6.

The column of the high-mounted driver's steering wheel was noticeably raked back (whereas that on the Ransomes D6 86-106 was upright). The top two thirds of the chromium plated offside driver's windscreen opened outwards and carried a top-mounted windscreen wiper. There was a front-hinged door on the offside, the window thereof being provided with a square sliding "signalling" window in the lower one-third of the pane and an inset opening handle. There was a matching panel on the nearside. There were large fixed quarter lights between the offside cab door and its matching nearside counterpart, and the cab front pillars. The base of the cab door was curved over the wheel arch to a position about 4 ins from the rear of the door thereafter the base, beneath the cab door handle, was horizontal, parallel to the cream-painted and about 6 ins below it. An access step was let into the base of the bay 1 offside panel, but without any form of protection to the bodywork, immediately behind the front axle, at the height of the wheel hub.

Karrier E6 61 is tilt tested to 24 degrees in 1934. *NCT*

There were 3 glazed panels in the bulkhead behind the driver. A circular driver's rear view mirror was mounted externally towards the top of the offside front cab pillar. There was step on the rear platform and a further step up into the lower saloon.

There were two lifeguard rails on each side extending between the flared rear of the front wheel mudguard to the leading rear axle. There were separate mudguards to the rear wheels, the front of that around the leading rear axle and the rear of that around the third axle flared to match that around the front wheels. A mud flap hung between the second and third axle. Both front wheel hubs were equipped with chromed wheel nut guard rings that on the offside being used as a step into the driver's cab whilst the rear wheel hubs had cosmetic differences to those employed ion the Ransomes D6 86-106. There was a valence panel on the offside bay 3 providing access to the air brake compressor,

The bulbous front panel of the driver's cab featured beading which encroached into the position of what would have been the lower band cream-painted band beneath the windscreen and which appeared as an outline "radiator". There was no removable front panel for towing purposes. The registration number plate was affixed to the front panel at the base of the outline "radiator".

A bamboo trolley retrieval pole was carried within the lower-saloon nearside body panels at waist rail height with a tube access from the rear platform vestibule.

Lighting:

External lighting was 2 headlights mounted half-way up the rounded extremities of the front panel on protruding plinths however that on the nearside was a fog light with an orange lens, 2 large circular front side lights mounted on the lower cream band at the base of the front cab side pillars and extending beyond the width of the body and a single red light, incorporated a bracket for an emergency paraffin lamp, at the rear mounted immediately beneath the cream-painted cantrail or vent panel, level with the top of the rear platform windows, on the offside corner panel.

A bracket for a square emergency paraffin lamp with a clear lens at the front and a red lens at the rear was also fitted to the offside front pillar, beneath the driver's rear view mirror, for use when the trolleybus was parked at the roadside with its trolley booms down or when there was any disruption to the power supply.

Internal lighting was provided by exposed tungsten bulbs in circular porcelain mountings positioned in the ceiling cove panels; in the lower saloon the lights were positioned forward of the oblong pull-in ventilators in bay 3, to the rear of the ventilators in bay 1 and centrally in bays 4 and 6. In the upper saloon lights were placed above the windows towards the front of bay 1, centrally in bays 2 and 5, and in bay 4 immediately to the rear of the pillar between bays 3 and 4 on both sides. There was also a lamp in the upper deck rear dome above the head of the staircase and a further light above the rear platform.

Seating:

Based on green painted G.D. Peters tubular steel frames with black torpedo-shaped grab handles curving gently upwards on the top of the seat adjacent to the aisle. Green leather cushions and backs, the latter quilted at each side and the middle. The third and sixth row of nearside and offside double seats, and the rearmost offside seat in the upper saloon were equipped with black stanchions. The lower saloon was equipped with long 5-person inwards-facing bench seats above the rear bogie on both sides and 5 rows of forwards-facing double seats. The upper saloon had 8 rows of double seats on the offside and 9 rows on the nearside, the ninth bench seat at the rear of the upper saloon above the open platform also accommodating just 2 passengers.

The third and sixth row of nearside and offside double seats, and the rearmost offside seat in the upper saloon were equipped with black stanchions.

Destination equipment:

The front upper deck panels above the driver's windscreen accommodated a rectangular single line destination box, located centrally in the lower third of the panel. A similar single line destination box was built into the middle cream-painted band above the rearmost nearside lower saloon window (bay 6). A square (9 ins x 10 ins) service number indicator box was mounted at the top of a wide central panel separating the front upper-saloon windows and at the rear centrally in the upper deck rear panel.

Internal Livery:

Ceilings and coves were covered with white coloured panels with varnished/polished wood frames. The ceiling of the driver's cab and the upper portions of the bulkheads were painted cream. The window surrounds and saloon front bulkhead above the windows were varnished wood. Brown floors. All internal transfers were gold with two-tone blue shading.

External Livery:

Delivered in Livery 4 (see Appendix C).

Subsequent alterations:

In late 1939, 61-85 were renumbered in sequence as 361-85.

A spot light was fitted beneath the flat front panel somewhat more towards the centre of the vehicle than the nearside headlight. The orange lens was removed from the nearside fog light, the fitting becoming a headlight. It is believed that these changes took place ca. 1944, the headlamp being fitted with appropriate shields.

The original internal transfers were replaced with gold transfers having green edges.

The nearside wheel nut guard ring was removed.

Additional front sidelights and brackets for emergency paraffin lamps were fitted to the base of the front mudguards to comply with wartime lighting measures.

A rear registration number plate, inset to the lower part of the rear platform panel on the offside and illuminated from the top, was added progressively to vehicles of this class in the early part of the war and the red rear light lowered to a more conventional position.

362 was fitted with cellophane anti-blast window covers ca. 1942. This vehicle also had the half-drop openers in the upper saloon replaced by top lights equipped with sliders in the windows in bays 1, 3, 5 during the war.

New headlamps complying with changed wartime lighting restrictions were fitted to 371 and 378 in December 1943 and to 363, 365, 367 and 377 in January 1944.

Karrier E6 70 standing at Victoria Embankment. *NCT*

To cope with higher wartime loadings, the existing ceiling grab handles above the longitudinal seats at the rear of the lower saloon were replaced by white handrails extending the entire length of the ceiling in 1944.

It appears that the upper saloon rear window of some vehicles may have been equipped with two diagonal strengthening bars running from the base to the top of the pane.

In the post-war period the outline "radiator" ribbing was removed on some vehicles from the front panel of the driver's cab and the lower cream-painted band extended across the front of the vehicle beneath the windscreen. At least the following vehicles underwent this change:

363, 364, 367, 369, 375, 377-380, 382, 383.

Also post-war, possibly in the same process, a circular driver's rear view mirror was mounted externally at the base of the middle cream-painted band immediately above the first nearside cab side pillar and the two life guard rails on each side were replaced by a single rail.

Some vehicles were equipped with 10.3:1 worm drive at a later date.

External advertising began to be displayed on the offside rear platform panel (circular "spot") from May 1945. Also post-war advertisements were added on either side of the front destination box.

Trent Bridge Works substantially rebuilt the body of 373 in July 1947.

Nudd Bros & Lockyer carried out bodywork overhauls to 361 (March 1948), 378 (July 1948), 380 (October 1948), 381 (January 1949), 383 (July 1948), 384 (September 1948), the work on 381 and perhaps 383 (at least) being sub-contracted to Eagle Engineering, Bulwell.

61 (361) was equipped with a rheostatic brake at some time.

370 ran with special BICC trolleyheads 31 October 1945 – 18 February 1946.

Notes:

369 was withdrawn after an accident on 2 November 1950.

The remains of 367 were purchased in 1974 by Brian Maguire and Tom Bowden for preservation. Parts from 346, including sections of the upper deck, aluminium panelling, drip mouldings and guttering sections, light fittings, windows, acquired in 1999, will be used to restore the Brush body. Work, at the Sandtoft Transport Centre, started in 2004.

It is understood that this batch of vehicles were originally intended to have had their fleet numbers and registration numbers in ascending numerical sequence, that is fleet numbers 61-85, registration numbers TV9317-9338, TV9340-9342, however some were renumbered before entering service to ensure that those vehicles with the same tyre suppliers were in fleet number sequence.

TV9339 was issued elsewhere.

Disposal:

361 sold to Mrs A.P. Clarke, Brownwood, Thorney, Lincolnshire, in April 1952.

362, 363, 370, 382 sold to Mrs A.P. Clarke, Westmoor Lane, Kettlethorpe, Lincolnshire, in October 1950.

364 sold to G. Boddy, Canal Farm, Hickling, Leicestershire, in July 1951.

365, 374, 379 sold to Mrs A.P. Clarke, Westmoor Lane, Kettlethorpe, Lincolnshire, in November 1950.

366 sold to Mrs A.P. Clarke, Westmoor Lane, Kettlethorpe, Lincolnshire, in February 1951.

367 sold to Mr Clarke, The Sawmill, Long Sutton, Spalding, Lincolnshire, in April 1950 (subsequently used as a shed by Leverton, Quadring).

368, 377 sold to Mrs A.P. Clarke, Westmoor Lane, Kettlethorpe, Lincolnshire, in January 1951.

369 sold to Mrs A.P. Clarke, Westmoor Lane, Kettlethorpe, Lincolnshire, in March 1951.

371 sold to Mr Clarke, The Sawmill, Long Sutton, Spalding, Lincolnshire, in May 1950. (subsequently used as a store-room near Spilsby until at least June 1960).

372 sold to Sharman, Little Dale Cottage Farm, Hallam, Southwell, Nottinghamshire, in April 1951.

373, 376 sold to G. Boddy, Canal Farm, Hickling, Leicestershire, in April 1951.

375 sold to Wheldon & Briggs, 28 Andrew Avenue, Ilkeston, Derbyshire, in August 1951.

378, 381 sold to Mrs A.P. Clarke, Brownwood, Thorney, Lincolnshire, in April 1952.

380, 383 sold to Mrs A.P. Clarke, Brownwood, Thorney, Lincolnshire, in March 1952 (380 is known to have been used subsequently as a store-room at Dunham-on-Trent).

384 sold to Mr Moult, Stapleford, Nottinghamshire, in May 1951.

385 sold to Mr Clarke, The Sawmill, Long Sutton, Spalding, Lincolnshire, in July 1949.

86 – 106 Ransomes D6

Shortly after delivery Ransomes D6/Brush 90 stands in the northbound carriageway of Middleton Boulevard, Wollaton Park at Scalford Drive prior to returning to Carlton via Ilkeston Road on a service 39. *GHFA & JMB*

Chassis:	Three axle type D6 manufactured by Ransomes, Sims & Jeffries Ltd., Orwell Works, Ipswich, Suffolk. RSJ drawing OV5243 dated 18 January 1934. NCT drawing 7/2.
Motor:	Lightweight, field-regulated RSJ T69 (80 hp). Ransomes winding specification referred to 65 hp at an hourly rating of 500 volts.
Electrical equipment:	British Thomson-Houston Co. Ltd., Rugby, Warwickshire.
Dewirement indicator:	Assumed to have been equipped with line-lights and buzzer.
Brakes:	G.D. Peters compressed air and hand brakes.
Body:	Brush H34/30R.
Length:	8ft 0ins
Width:	7ft 6ins
Wheelbase:	16ft 6ins
Wheel track:	front 6ft 5ins, rear 6ft 4½ins
Bogie wheelbase:	4ft
Unladen weight:	8tons 9cwt 2qtrs
Tyres:	10.50 x 20 all round.

These vehicles were not registered in numerical sequence.

86 - 106 Ransomes D6

No.	New No.	Registration	Chassis	Chassis No.	Body	Body No.	Delivered	Registered	Into Service	Withdrawn	Sold
86	386	TV9343	Ransomes D6	2170	Brush		01.02.1934	10.05.1934	11.05.1934	01.02.1951	03.07.1951
87	387	TV9344	Ransomes D6	2172	Brush		05.02.1934	10.05.1934	11.05.1934	25.03.1950	20.06.1950
88	388	TV9345	Ransomes D6	2171	Brush		07.02.1934	10.05.1934	10.05.1934	30.11.1951	15.04.1952
89	389	TV9346	Ransomes D6	2169	Brush		07.02.1934	10.05.1934	14.05.1934	25.04.1950	27.05.1950
90	390	TV9347	Ransomes D6	2173	Brush		08.02.1934	2.34	22.02.1934	01.10.1950	21.11.1950
91	391	TV9353	Ransomes D6	2180	Brush		18.04.1934	02.05.1934	03.05.1934	28.02.1950	12.05.1950
92	392	TV9354	Ransomes D6	2179	Brush		18.04.1934	10.05.1934	10.05.1934	30.11.1951	22.04.1952
93	393	TV9350	Ransomes D6	2178	Brush		01.03.1934	10.05.1934	14.05.1934	30.12.1950	30.04.1951
94	394	TV9351	Ransomes D6	2177	Brush		20.03.1934	10.05.1934	13.05.1934	01.11.1950	17.01.1951
95	395	TV9355	Ransomes D6	2181	Brush		26.04.1934	02.05.1934	02.05.1934	01.02.1951	09.05.1951
96	396	TV9363	Ransomes D6	2189	Brush		02.06.1934	04.06.1934	03.06.1934	25.03.1950	17.06.1950
97	397	TV9357	Ransomes D6	2188	Brush		20.03.1934	12.05.1934	15.05.1934	30.11.1950	29.01.1951
98	398	TV9362	Ransomes D6	2184	Brush		14.05.1934	10.05.1934	14.05.1934	10.08.1950	18.09.1950
99	399	TV9356	Ransomes D6	2183	Brush		26.04.1934	02.05.1934	02.05.1934	25.03.1950	16.06.1950
100	400	TV9358	Ransomes D6	2182	Brush		26.04.1934	02.05.1934	03.05.1934	31.10.1948	05.12.1949
101	401	TV9348	Ransomes D6	2174	Brush		26.02.1934	10.05.1934	11.05.1934	25.03.1950	27.03.1950

No.	New No.	Registration	Chassis	Chassis No.	Body	Body No.	Delivered	Registered	Into Service	Withdrawn	Sold
102	402	TV9349	Ransomes D6	2175	Brush		01.03.1934	10.05.1934	14.05.1934	31.10.1948	17.06.1949
103	403	TV9359	Ransomes D6	2187	Brush		27.04.1934	02.05.1934	02.05.1934	01.02.1951	17.02.1951
104	404	TV9361	Ransomes D6	2185	Brush		19.05.1934	19.05.1934	16.05.1934	31.10.1951	24.03.1952
105	405	TV9352	Ransomes D6	2176	Brush		26.03.1934	04.06.1934	11.05.1934	01.08.1950	14.11.1950
106	406	TV9360	Ransomes D6	2186	Brush		02.06.1934	04.06.1934	02.06.1934	30.12.1950	08.01.1951

Chassis:

Cranked chassis frame over rear bogie. The differentials were at the centre of the rear axles. Thornycroft patent rear bogie.

Chassis

length: 27ft

Chassis frame width:

front 3ft 1ins, rear 3ft 9ins

Overall width (over hubs):

7ft 5⅝ins

Electrics:

The motor was placed amidships. BTH controller. EMB resistances.

The circuit breakers, main switches and fuses were located on the cab rear bulkhead above and to the rear of the driver's seat.

Brakes:

G.D. Peters air and hand brakes.

The Ransomes air brake compressor was fixed to the nearside of the chassis frame and the reservoir to the chassis offside. There was one air-brake cylinder each side of the chassis ahead of the front axle, one cylinder each side on the rear face of the leading rear axle casing and one cylinder each side on the leading face of the rearmost rear axle casting.

The handbrake lever was to the nearside of the driver's steering column.

Bodywork:

The bodywork was basically identical to that fitted to 1934 Karrier E6 61-85. The detail differences were: an upright driver's steering column (that on 61-85 being raked at an angle), a valence panel on the nearside bay 3 providing access to the air brake compressor, variations in the layout of the rear platform steps (as the rear part of the chassis was narrower that that on 61-85) and cosmetic differences between the rear wheel hubs.

Lighting:

See 61-85.

Seating:

See 61-85.

Destination equipment:

See 61-85.

Internal Livery:

See 61-85.

External Livery:

Delivered in Livery 4 (see Appendix C).

Subsequent alterations:

In late 1939, 86-106 were renumbered in sequence as 386-406.

In addition to those shown under Karrier E6 61-85 the following alterations were made:

All wheel nut guard rings were removed but a small step ring was fitted to the offside front wheel.

All vehicles were re-motored in 1941-1943 with new series wound BTH201 B4 motors for regulated series control due to unsatisfactory performance of the original RSJ lightweight motors n.b. B4 and C1 armatures were identical. These gave an hourly rating of 85 hp (138 armature amps, 72 series amps) at 1,150 RPM and 550 volts. Later 386, 387 and 402 received BTH207 C1 motors. New resistances were fitted to some or all at the same time.

New headlamps complying with changed wartime lighting restrictions were fitted to 387, 389-397, 403–406 in September 1943 – February 1944.

In the post-war period the outline "radiator" ribbing was removed from at least the following vehicles: 386, 388, 396, 398, 405.

Nudd Bros & Lockyer carried out bodywork overhauls to 386 (September 1948), 388 (September 1948), 392 (July 1948), 394 (March 1948), 404 (January 1948), the work on 386 and 394 being sub-contracted to Eagle Engineering, Bulwell.

Trent Bridge Works carried out bodywork overhauls to 395 (May 1947), 398 (August 1947), 401 (November 1946), 403 (1946), 406 (September 1947).

Notes:

It is understood that this batch of vehicles were originally intended to have had their fleet numbers and registration numbers in ascending numerical sequence, that is fleet numbers 86-106, registration numbers TV9343-9363, however some were renumbered before entering service to ensure that those vehicles with the same tyre suppliers were in fleet number sequence.

386 was withdrawn after an accident on 28 January 1951.

392 was the last Ransomes vehicle to leave Trent Bridge Works on 14 December 1951.

Disposal:

386 sold to Mr French, 246 Derby Road, Stapleford, Nottinghamshire, in July 1951.

387, 396, 399 sold to Mrs A.P. Clarke, Westmoor Lane, Kettlethorpe, Lincolnshire, breakers, in June 1950.

388, 392 sold to Mrs A.P. Clarke, Brownwood, Thorney, Lincolnshire, breakers, in April 1952.

389, 391 sold to Mrs A.P. Clarke, The Gravel Pit, Doddington, Lincolnshire, breakers, in May 1950.

390, 405 sold to Mrs A.P. Clarke, Westmoor Lane, Kettlethorpe, breakers, in November 1950.

393 sold to G. Boddy, Canal Farm, Hickling, in April 1951.

394, 397, 406 sold to Mrs A.P. Clarke, Westmoor Lane, Kettlethorpe, breakers, in January 1951.

395 sold to G. Boddy, Canal Farm, Hickling, in May 1951.

Ransomes D6 86 is tilt tested to 26 degrees NCT.

The upper deck of Ransomes 87, photographed prior to entering service in 1934. *NCT*

The lower deck of Ransomes 87, photographed prior to entering service in 1934. *NCT*

The lower saloon of Ransomes D6/Brush 402 showing wartime "black-out" light canisters. *NCT*

398 sold to W.M. McGrath, 6 Stoneygate Road, Leicester, in September 1950.

400 sold to Mr Clarke, The Sawmills, Long Sutton, Spalding, Lincolnshire, in December 1949.

401 sold to Mrs A.P. Clarke, The Gravel Pit, Doddington, Lincolnshire, breakers, in March 1950.

402 sold to M.J. Staines, Severns Yard, High Street, Alfreton, Derbyshire, in June 1949.

403 sold to H. Mitchell, Laughterton, Lincolnshire, in February 1951.

404 sold to Mrs A.P. Clarke, Brownwood, Thorney, Lincolnshire, breakers, in March 1952.

107 – 136 Leyland TTB3

Leyland TTB3 132 somewhat strangely posed at Old Market Square in a heavily retouched publicity image. *NCT*

Chassis:	Three axle type Leyland TTB3 manufactured by Leyland Motors Ltd., Leyland, Lancashire. Leyland drawing 14336 dated 29 October 1934. NCT drawing 7/9.
Motor:	GEC WT2511E (80 hp at 500 volts). Series-wound, regulated field.
Electrical equipment:	Gen eral Electric Co. Ltd., Witton, Birmingham.
Dewirement indicator:	Assumed to have been equipped with line-lights and buzzer.
Brakes:	G.D. Peters compressed air; hand and rheostatic brakes.
Body:	Metro-Cammell H34/30R. Metropolitan-Cammell Carriage & Wagon drawing 577-1 dated 23 November 1934. NCT drawing 11/10.
Length:	28ft 2¾ins
Width:	7ft 6ins over mudguards (7ft 4ins over panels)
Height:	14ft 4$\frac{7}{16}$ins over roof panels.
Wheelbase:	16ft 6ins
Wheel track:	front 6ft 5⅝ins, rear 6ft 4½ins
Bogie wheelbase:	4ft
Unladen weight:	8tons 17cwt 1qtrs
Tyres:	10.50 × 20 all round.

107-136 Leyland TTB3

No.	New No.	Registration	Chassis	Chassis No.	Body	Body No.	Delivered	Registered	Into Service	Withdrawn	Sold
107	407	ATV170	Leyland TTB3	5825	MCCW & F			31.05.1935	02.06.1935	01.10.1950	21.12.1950
108	408	ATV171	Leyland TTB3	5822	MCCW & F			31.05.1935	02.06.1935	24.04.1950	16.06.1950
109	409	ATV172	Leyland TTB3	5819	MCCW & F			31.05.1935	02.06.1935	01.08.1950	07.11.1950
110	410	ATV173	Leyland TTB3	5823	MCCW & F			31.05.1935	02.06.1935	29.02.1952	17.07.1952
111	411	ATV174	Leyland TTB3	5818	MCCW & F			31.05.1935	03.06.1935	31.10.1951	14.11.1951
112	412	ATV175	Leyland TTB3	5827	MCCW & F			31.05.1935	03.06.1935	30.11.1950	23.01.1951
113	413	ATV176	Leyland TTB3	5821	MCCW & F			31.05.1935	02.06.1935	30.11.1951	04.03.1952
114	414	ATV177	Leyland TTB3	5820	MCCW & F			31.05.1935	02.06.1935	24.03.1952	22.05.1952
115	415	ATV178	Leyland TTB3	5831	MCCW & F			31.05.1935	02.06.1935	30.11.1951	08.04.1952
116	416	ATV179	Leyland TTB3	5830	MCCW & F			31.05.1935	02.06.1935	30.11.1951	21.02.1952
117	417	ATV180	Leyland TTB3	5833	MCCW & F			31.05.1935	02.06.1935	31.07.1951	23.08.1951
118	418	ATV181	Leyland TTB3	5826	MCCW & F			31.05.1935	02.06.1935	25.03.1950	08.05.1950
119	419	ATV182	Leyland TTB3	5828	MCCW & F			31.05.1935	02.06.1935	31.08.1949	02.12.1949
120	420	ATV183	Leyland TTB3	5834	MCCW & F			31.05.1935	03.06.1935	30.06.1949	02.12.1949
121	421	ATV184	Leyland TTB3	5824	MCCW & F			01.07.1935	10.07.1935	30.04.1951	28.05.1951
122	422	ATV185	Leyland TTB3	5841	MCCW & F			01.07.1935	03.07.1935	31.10.1951	18.03.1952
123	423	ATV186	Leyland TTB3	5832	MCCW & F			01.07.1935	03.07.1935	01.11.1950	18.01.1951
124	424	ATV187	Leyland TTB3	5829	MCCW & F			01.07.1935	04.07.1935	30.06.1951	14.07.1951
125	425	ATV188	Leyland TTB3	5840	MCCW & F			01.07.1935	04.07.1935	30.06.1951	16.08.1951
126	426	ATV189	Leyland TTB3	5836	MCCW & F			01.07.1935	05.07.1935	30.06.1950	21.07.1950
127	427	ATV190	Leyland TTB3	5835	MCCW & F			01.07.1935	04.07.1935	01.06.1951	21.08.1951
128	428	ATV191	Leyland TTB3	5838	MCCW & F			01.07.1935	03.07.1935	30.11.1951	12.05.1952
129	429	ATV192	Leyland TTB3	5839	MCCW & F			01.07.1935	09.07.1935	01.08.1950	09.11.1950
130	430	ATV193	Leyland TTB3	5842	MCCW & F			01.07.1935	02.07.1935	24.03.1952	29.07.1952
131	431	ATV194	Leyland TTB3	5837	MCCW & F			01.07.1935	04.07.1935	07.01.1900	02.12.1949
132	432	ATV195	Leyland TTB3	5814	MCCW & F			31.05.1935	01.06.1935	29.02.1952	28.08.1952
133	433	ATV196	Leyland TTB3	5813	MCCW & F			31.05.1935	01.06.1935	31.10.1951	11.03.1952
134	434	ATV197	Leyland TTB3	5815	MCCW & F			31.05.1935	01.06.1935	30.11.1951	07.05.1952
135	435	ATV198	Leyland TTB3	5816	MCCW & F			31.05.1935	01.06.1935	30.11.1951	05.04.1952
136	436	ATV199	Leyland TTB3	5817	MCCW & F			01.07.1935	04.07.193,5	24.03.1952	05.08.1952

Leyland TTB3 420 upper deck. *NCT*

Leyland TTB3 420 lower deck. *NCT*

Chassis:

Although earlier publications have described these trolleybuses as having Leyland TTB4 chassis, the NCT history cards record them as TTB3 whilst the official Metro-Cammell photograph of 132 on its tilt test at their works on 24 April 1935 is endorsed as referring to Leyland chassis number TTB3 5814 and signed by the Company Secretary. The successful tilting test, by the way, was to 25.5°.

Cranked chassis frame over rear bogie.

Chassis length:

26ft 10¾ins

Chassis frame width:

front 3ft, rear 5ft 1½ins

Overall width (over hubs):

front 7ft 5½ins, rear 7ft 5½ins

Brakes:

The air brake compressor was fixed to the external face of the chassis offside with the reservoir located between the chassis frame adjacent to the traction motor. There was one air-brake cylinder each side on top of the king pin (steering joint) and one cylinder each side of each rear axle.

The handbrake lever was located to the nearside of the driver's steering column.

A red "power brake triangle" which illuminated when the foot-operated brakes were applied was mounted on the offside of the lower deck rear panel midway between the registration number plate and the cream-painted waist rail band.

Electrics:

The motor was mounted towards the front of the chassis and offset to the nearside, approximately under bays 2 and 3, with a single propeller shaft to the rear axles. The resistances were placed between the chassis frame beneath the driver's cab in front of the traction motor. A motor generator set was fitted on the external face of the chassis offside adjacent to the air brake compressor.

Bodywork:

Metal framed six-bay highbridge double-deck construction, forwards-ascending half-turn (90°) staircase with conventional semi-vestibuled open platform entrance and exits at the rear built by the Metropolitan-Cammell Carriage, Wagon and Finance Company Ltd., Saltley, Birmingham.

The front of the upper-saloon was equipped with a central service number indicator box at the top of a panel between the two fixed front windows, the trolley poles were fitted on an exposed roof-mounted gantry above bay 3. Platform handrails and stanchions were covered with black Doverite.

Brackets or extensions were bolted to the roof rail immediately above the upper-deck body pillars between bays 1 and 2, and bays 2 and 3, to support the two girders of the exposed trolley gantry, which was mounted above bay 2, and the Brecknell Willis lightweight special trolleybases which were not in direct contact with the roof.

Metal louvres were fitted above the upper and lower deck saloon side windows, and above the upper deck front widows and service number panel. Chromium plated half-drop openers with clip-operated grippers fixed centrally to the top of the upper pane were fitted to the side windows in bays 1, 3, 5 of the upper deck and bays 1, 2, 3 of the lower-deck (both sides). Immediately above the lower saloon side windows in bays 1, 3 and 5, square Colt extractor ventilators were mounted. Colt ventilators were also fitted to the roof, one each side on the nearside above bay 5 and on the offside above bay 1. At the rear of the upper-saloon there was a was an emergency door having three hinges at its base and a grab handle at the top with two almost square fixed windows having rounded corners at the upper extremities, rather than the previous sliding window arrangement found on other pre-war Nottingham trolleybuses, which also provided access to the roof catwalk. The handle to open the emergency door was located immediately above the central window pillar beneath a step at the end of the catwalk.

432 was fitted with Super Ashanco lower saloon ventilators, in the same positions as the standard Colt design on the central cream-painted band immediately above the lower saloon side windows, and one roof mounted ventilator each side above bay 5.

The driver's cab featured a noticeably low, set-back seat. The offside driver's windscreen was chromium plated and the top two thirds opened outwards. It carried a windscreen wiper. There were front-hinged doors on both sides with inset opening handles; the window in the offside cab door was provided with a sliding "signalling" window in lower portion of the pane. There were large fixed side windows between the cab door and the front pillars. Two small hooded inlet ducts were installed on each side above the driver's cab door and above the side window to the front of the door. An access step was let into the base of the bay 1 side panel, immediately behind the front axle, on both the nearside and offside at the same height as the wheel hub.

There were 3 glazed panels having the same depth as the lower saloon side windows in the bulkhead behind the driver. Rectangular driver's rear view mirrors were mounted externally towards the top of the front cab pillars.

The driver also benefited from a "turn indicator" in the form an illuminated arrow at the base of the offside windscreen to the offside of the driver's steering wheel; this normally stood upright but could be turned either to the left or right to indicate the driver's turning intentions to other traffic and traffic duty policemen.

There was step on the rear platform and a further step up into the lower saloon. The staircase had three steps from the platform to the half-landing and then three steps to the upper deck.

There was a used ticket box immediately below the nearside vestibule window and in the rear panel at the

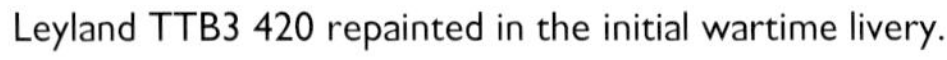

Leyland TTB3 420 repainted in the initial wartime livery. *NCT*

base of the stairs on the rear open platform. There was a single lifeguard rail on each side extending between the flared rear of the front wheel mudguard to the second axle. The front panel beneath the driver's cab windscreen was particularly close to the road surface. A mud flap hung between the second and third axle whilst the rear wheel mudguard flared towards the rear to match that around the front wheels.

There was a top hinged valance panel on the offside at the base of bays 1 and 2 to access the motor generator set and air brake compressor.

The front panel incorporated 2 horizontal fluted columns of 5 louvre type vanes placed centrally below the level of the headlamps and above the registration number plate. The base of the rear panel and part of the offside corner panel had 3 Pyrene bumper bars. An Almet registration number box, which displayed the necessary marks on a translucent square pane of glass having curved corners, was fitted to the offside rear corner panel immediately above the bumper bars. A bamboo trolley retrieval pole was carried within the lower-saloon nearside body panels at waist rail height with a tube access from the rear platform vestibule.

Lighting:

External lighting was 2 headlights low-set on slightly protruding plinths on the front panel, 2 circular front sidelights on the lower cream-painted band and at the rear a single red "bulls-eye" light mounted on the rear platform corner panel, at approximately half the depth of the platform window. The rear light mounting incorporated a bracket for an emergency paraffin lamp which could be attached when the trolleybus was parked at the roadside with its trolley booms down or when there was any disruption to the power supply.

Internal lighting was provided by exposed tungsten bulbs in circular porcelain mountings positioned in the ceiling cove panels; in the lower saloon the lights were positioned just forward of the pillar between bays 1 and 2, centrally in bay 3, above the pillar between bays 4 and 5, and just to the rear of the pillar between bays 5 and 6. In the upper saloon lights were placed above the forward pillar of bay 1, centrally in bay 2, immediately above the pillar between bays 3 and 4, and just to the rear of the pillar between bays 4 and 5. There was also a lamp in the upper deck rear dome above the head of the staircase and a further light above the rear platform.

Under normal circumstances a low tension power supply for normal lighting purposes was provided by the motor generator set thus batteries for limited emergency lighting must have been carried but the details are not known.

Seating:

Based on green painted G.D. Peters concealed frames with pressed steel bases and curved grab handles adjacent to the aisle. Green leather covers. Four grab handles on short leather straps were fixed to the lower saloon ceiling each side adjacent to the longitudinal seats. There was a cigarette stubber mounted centrally on the back of each forwards-facing seat. The third and sixth double seat on the nearside, and the first and fifth double seat on the offside in the upper saloon were equipped with black Doverite covered stanchions.

The lower saloon had a 5-person inwards-facing bench seat on each side over the rear axles and 5 rows of forwards-facing double seats. The upper saloon had 7 rows of double seats on the offside and 10 rows on the nearside.

Destination equipment:

Rectangular indicator boxes capable of displaying a single blind with the final destination, a small "via" and up to 3 lines of information (en route points) were fitted centrally on the green-painted upper deck panels above the drivers' cab windows and at the rear, protruding slightly, above the rear platform window. A square (9 ins x 10 ins) service number indicator box was mounted at the top of a wide central panel separating the front upper deck windows and on the nearside immediately above the rear open platform entrance (mounted towards the front of the trolleybus).

Internal Livery:

Ceilings and coves were covered with white enamelled panels with varnished/polished wood frames. The lower saloon front bulkhead above the windows was varnished wood. The ceiling and sides of the driver's cab, and the upper portions of the cab rear bulkhead were painted cream. Brown floors. All internal transfers were gold with two-tone blue shading.

External Livery:

Delivered in Livery 4 (see Appendix C).

Subsequent alterations:

Pre-war 122, 125, 128-30 were fitted with Westinghouse brakes.

In late 1939, 107-136 were renumbered in sequence as 407-436.

As delivered the front axle wheel hubs were equipped with wheel trims but these were removed before the vehicles entered service and replaced by a large hub, similar to those used at the rear and capable of use as drivers step.

The lower saloon front bulkhead above the windows was painted white at some time during the war. To cope with higher wartime loadings, the existing ceiling grab handles above the longitudinal seats at the rear of the lower saloon in 424, 425, 427, 429, were replaced by white handrails extending the entire length of the ceiling in May – September 1944.

External advertising began to be displayed on the rear panels beneath the platform window from November 1944 and on the offside rear platform panel (circular "spot") from May 1945.

Notes:

These vehicles were noted for their poor steering characteristics and a violently juddering steering wheel when braking.

Following the collapse of the upper saloon floor on 25 September 1950, 407 was immediately taken out of service.

408 suffered a broken chassis on 24 April 1950.

411 was withdrawn after an accident on 16 October 1951.

436 was the last Leyland vehicle to leave Trent Bridge Works on 2 April 1952.

Disposal:

407 sold to Mrs A.P. Clarke, Westmoor Lane, Kettlethorpe, Lincolnshire, breakers, in December 1950.

408 sold to Mrs A.P. Clarke, Westmoor Lane, Kettlethorpe, Lincolnshire, breakers, in June 1950.

409, 429 sold to Mrs A.P. Clarke, Westmoor Lane, Kettlethorpe, Lincolnshire, breakers, in November 1950.

410, 430 sold to Mrs A.P. Clarke, Brownwood, Thorney, Lincolnshire, breakers, in July 1952.

411 sold to G. Littlewood, 66 Austin Street, Bulwell, Nottingham, in November 1951 for use as a caravan.

412, 423 sold to Mrs A.P. Clarke, Westmoor Lane, Kettlethorpe, Lincolnshire, breakers, in January 1951.

413, 433 sold to Mrs A.P. Clarke, Brownwood, Thorney, Lincolnshire, breakers, in March 1952.

414 sold to F. Grocock, 50 Beacon Hill Road, Newark, Nottinghamshire, in May 1952 for use as a caravan.

415, 435 sold to Mrs A.P. Clarke, Brownwood, Thorney, Lincolnshire, breakers, in April 1952.

416 sold to Mr Gent, Redfern Farm, Walesby, Nottinghamshire, in February 1952 for use as a shed.

417 sold to W. Beardon, Larklands House, Ilkeston, Derbyshire, in August 1951.

418 sold to Mr Clarke, The Saw Mills, Long Sutton, Spalding, Lincolnshire, in May 1950.

419-420, 431 sold to Mr Clarke, The Saw Mills, Long Sutton, Spalding, Lincolnshire, in December 1949.

421 sold to G. Boddy, Canal Farm, Hickling, Nottinghamshire, in May 1951 for use as a shed.

422 sold to Mrs A.P. Clarke, Brownwood, Thorney, Lincolnshire, breakers, in March 1952.

424 sold to G. Boddy, Canal Farm, Hickling, Leicestershire, in July 1951 for use as a shed.

425 sold to Mr H. Whitmore, 8 East Estate, RAF Folkingham, Lincolnshire in August 1951 for use as a caravan or shed.

426 sold to H.S. Holt, Hooley's Garage, Nottingham, in July 1950 for use as a caravan or shed.

427 sold to Wheldon & Briggs, 28 Andrew Avenue, Ilkeston, Derbyshire in August 1951.

428, 434 sold to Mrs A.P. Clarke, Brownwood, Thorney, Lincolnshire, breakers, in May 1952.

432, 436 sold to Mrs A.P. Clarke, Brownwood, Thorney, Lincolnshire, breakers, in August 1952.

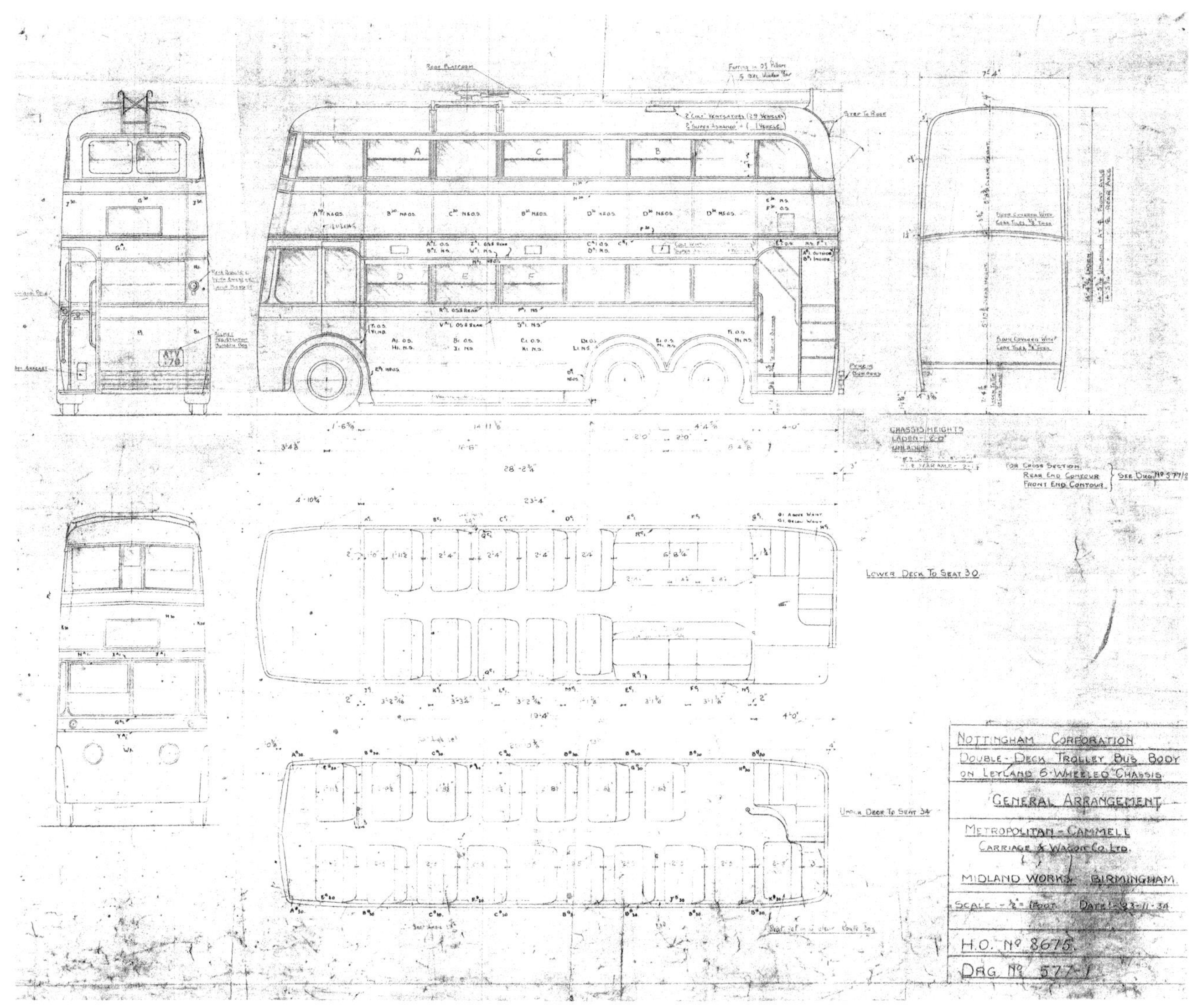

Metropolitan-Cammell Carriage & Wagon Co Ltd general arrangement drawing for Nottingham Corporation Leyland 6 wheel chassis. HO No.8675 DRG No.577-1 is dated 23rd November 1934 and was used to produce 107-136. *NCT*

Leyland TTB3 132 tilted to 25 degrees. *NCT*

302 - 303 English Electric E11

The original layout of these two trolleybuses, Southend-on-Sea 110 and 111, included a front exit. The two vehicles are seen here together, it is believed, just after delivery to Southend-on-Sea in 1930. *Richard Delahoy*

Chassis: Three axle type English Electric E11 manufactured by the English Electric Co. Ltd. at the Dick, Kerr works in Preston, Lancashire. It is assumed that the chassis were identical with those beneath 19-24 and that NCT drawing 7/3 was applicable.
Motor: English Electric DK 122D C637P (2 X 50 hp at 500 volts) twin armature with roller armature bearings arranged to give series-parallel control.
Electrical equipment: English Electric manufactured by English Electric Co. Ltd. at their Phoenix Works, Bradford, Yorkshire.
Dewirement indicator: Buzzer
Brakes: Westinghouse compressed air, 4-stage rheostatic and hand brakes.
Body: English Electric H30/26R
Length: 28ft 0¼ins
Width: 7ft 6ins over mudguards (7ft 2ins over pillars)
Height: 14ft 9⅛ins to top of trolley plank.
Wheelbase: 16ft 6ins giving a turning circle on either lock of 54ft.
Wheel track: front 6ft 5¼ins, rear 6ft 5¼ins
Bogie wheelbase: 4ft
Unladen weight: 8tons 7cwt 2qtrs
Tyres: 36 X 8 on all wheels.

Southend-on-Sea Corporation Transport took delivery of 110 and 111 in July 1930. They were originally fitted with a front exit, in addition to the open platform entrance and exit at the rear, for use of lower deck passengers only, resulting in an H33/26D layout, but this was removed in November 1937. Similar dual doorway layouts were specified by Southend for both motorbus and trolleybus deliveries in the late 1920's and early 1930's. Southend 110 and 111 were withdrawn in 1939 and were sold to Nottingham in November 1940 where they remained in service until March 1945.

Mechanically these vehicles were very similar to Nottingham's own English Electric E11 trolleybuses 319-24.

302 - 303 English Electric ex-Southend-on-Sea

No.	Old No.	Registration	Chassis	Chassis No.	Body	Body No.	Delivered	Registered	Into Service	Withdrawn	Sold
302	110	JN60	English Electric		Eng. Electric			07.1930	11.1940	23/03/1945	01.1946
303	111	JN61	English Electric		Eng. Electric			07.1930	11.1940	14/03/1945	01.1946

Registered dates refer to first registration at Southend-on-Sea. Original Nottingham numbers were transposed.

Chassis:

The rear bogie had a swivelling suspension intended to overcome any tendency to tilting during braking and to prevent torsional stresses in the springs. Each rear axle had its own differential. It is likely that they had their chassis construction sub-contracted to Rubery Owen, a specialist manufacturer.

Chassis length:

27ft 4¾ins.

Chassis frame width:

front 3ft 1½ins, rear 3ft 5¼ins

Overall width

(over front hubs): 7ft 5¾ins

Electrics:

English Electric "twin" motors. Rheostatic Brake Co. resistances.

Although the vehicles had been supplied to Southend with both trolley poles mounted on a common pivot (the Estler system), by the time they were purchased by Nottingham they had been equipped with Brecknell Willis lightweight trolleybases with the trolley poles mounted side by side.

Brackets or extensions were bolted to the roof rail immediately above the upper-deck body pillars to the front of bay 1 and to the rear of bay 2, and above bays 1 and 2, to support the four girders of the exposed trolley gantry which was mounted above bays 1 and 2, and not in direct contact with the roof.

Brakes:

Four notch foot-operated rheostatic brakes, a Westinghouse Brake & Saxby Signal Co. compensating air brake working independently on each of the six wheels and a hand brake on the rear bogie wheels.

Bodywork:

Metal framed composite highbridge double-deck construction, enclosed forwards-ascending half-turn (90°) staircase with semi-vestibuled open platform entrance and exit at the rear, built by English Electric Co. Ltd. at Preston. The upper-deck had 6-bays but the

English Electric E11 302 newly repainted and running as a Special. *NCT*

lower-deck employed a 6½ bay construction with a half-bay immediately behind the front axle and cab rear bulkhead related to the former front exit.

The domed roof overhung the front of the upper-deck. The main transverse chassis girders and front axle were visible beneath the front panel to the driver's cab. The upper deck floor line was "hipped" upwards towards the centre line of the vehicle for drainage purposes, this being clearly apparent at the front and rear. The rear platform featured a single low-step with a further step up to the inclined floor of the lower-saloon which rose towards the front of the vehicle.

At the front of the lower saloon, between the front bulkhead and the position of the former front exit, there was a half-bay with fixed glazing to match the other lower saloon windows. The panes of glass in the lower deck saloon side windows in bays 2, 3 and in the upper deck saloon side windows in bays 1, 3, 5 could slide down. Glass louvres were fitted above all the sliding windows. The top of the lower saloon bay 4 windows on both sides of the vehicle resembled half-lights due to the removal of a destination indicator box used in Southend.

The two large front upper-deck windows were fixed with wide corner pillars and a vertical strengthening between the panes which was probably a duct for the traction power cables running from the trolley poles to the control equipment. At the rear of the upper saloon there were two almost square windows with radiused corners and a narrow dividing bar. The nearside pane slid transversely to the offside (behind the offside pane) providing to the trolley gantry, ventilation and an emergency exit. The rear platform window was divided into two large panes the upper extremities of which were deeply radiused to match those above and 3 transverse protective rails. The registration number was applied with transfers to the top of the nearside pane of glass.

The driver's cab, which slightly protruded forward of the upper deck, was equipped with a single opening windscreen on the offside and a front hinged door on the offside which provided the only access to the cab. The window in the offside cab door was provided with a sliding "signalling" window. Ventilation was provided by 3 horizontal fluted columns of 3 louvred vanes immediately above the windscreen centre pillar. Small rectangular driver's rear view mirrors were mounted towards the top of the cab corner pillars and a windscreen wiper was mounted at the top of the of-side windscreen.

There was a single life guard rail on each side extending between the front and second axles, although there was no protection beneath the high-mounted, slight curved front panel to the driver's cab. There was a one piece "fairing" incorporating both mudguards over the rear wheels and a mud flap hung between the second and third axle.

A bamboo trolley retrieval pole was carried on three hooks fixed at the base of the window pillars between bays 1 and 2, 3 and 4, and 5 and 6 on the nearside lower deck waist rail.

Lighting:

These trolleybuses entered service in Nottingham at the time of wartime lighting restrictions. External lighting was 2 headlights mounted two thirds of the way up on the front panel beneath the driver's windscreen at the top of the green-painted portion and 2 sidelights on the lower deck waistband. There was a single rear light mounted at the top of the offside corner panel.

Brackets were fitted at the front base of the front mudguards for emergency oil or paraffin lights for use when the trolleybuses were parked at the roadside with their trolley booms down.

Seating:

Wrap round seats with pleated backs in the lower saloon. Straight backs to the seats in the upper saloon. Green leather seat covers (the Southend livery having been green at the time of these vehicle's delivery). Green painted stanchions.

Destination equipment:

The "piano" front of the upper-deck incorporated a single line destination box above the nearside front windscreen of the driver's cab and a square service number indicator box above and to the offside of the central pillar. A destination box capable of displaying a single line of information was mounted in the cream-painted panel immediately above the nearside rear platform window.

Internal Livery:

Varnished wood window frames and green panels.

External Livery:

Entered service in Nottingham in Livery 6 (see Appendix C).

Subsequent alterations: An illuminated registration number plate was built into the offside rear panel during the war.

Notes:

The Nottingham fleet numbers were originally transposed on these vehicles but the error was corrected before they entered service.

Disposal:

302, 303 sold to Cardale Service Garage (Rhodes), Carlton Road, Nottingham, dealer, in January 1946.

304 – 309 Guy BTX

Guy BTX 305 (ex-Hastings Tramways 25) depicted immediately after its overhaul and repaint into Nottingham's wartime livery in January 1942 turning into Bunbury Street from Victoria Embankment, Trent Bridge. The frog and parallel loop wiring heading north up Victoria Embankment are clearly visible. *NCT*

Chassis: Three axle type BTX60 manufactured by Guy Motors Ltd., Fallings Park, Wolverhampton.
Motor: Front-mounted Rees-Stevens (60 hp at 500 volts) compound wound manufactured by Rees-Roturbo Co. Ltd., Wednesfield Road Works, Wolverhampton.
Electrical equipment: Rees-Stevens
Dewirement indicator: Buzzer
Brakes: pneumatic (believed to be Westinghouse), Rees-Stevens regenerative, hand and rheostatic brakes.
Body: Ransomes, Sims and Jefferies B32C.
Length: 27ft
Width: 7ft 6ins
Wheelbase: 14ft 5ins
Bogie wheelbase: 3ft 9ins
Unladen weight: 6tons 5cwt 0qtrs
Tyres: 36 X 8

Ex- Hastings Tramways Co. in November 1941. These were individual vehicles from two identical batches delivered to Hastings in 1928 and 1929. 305 and 309 (Hastings 24 and 9) had been withdrawn from service there in 1940, the remainder sold to Nottingham were withdrawn during the course of 1941.

Known as "kiddy cars" these were Nottingham's sole class of single-deck trolleybuses.

304 - 309 Guy BTX ex-Hastings

No.	Old No.	Registration	Chassis	Chassis No.	Body	Body No.	Delivered	Registered	Into Service	Withdrawn	Sold
304	35	DY5121	Guy BTX60	22885 266/5	Ransomes	740		07.1928	18.12.1941	31.08.1945	01.1946
305	24	DY5126	Guy BTX60	22894 267/4	Ransomes	729		07.1928	31.01.1942	21.03.1944	10.1944
306	34	DY5120	Guy BTX60	22846 262/6	Ransomes	739		07.1928	16.01.1942	31.10.1945	01.1946
307	51	DY5578	Guy BTX60	23359	Ransomes	963		05.1929	31.01.1942	31.01.1946	04.1946
308	40	DY5453	Guy BTX60	23158	Ransomes	847		01.1929	14.02.1942	31.05.1945	01.1946
309	9	DY5111	Guy BTX60	22843 262/3	Ransomes	712		05.1928	28.02.1942	31.01.1946	04.1946

Chassis:

The rear bogie had two inverted leaf springs each side and 3ft 9ins centres. Conventional leaf springs were employed on the front axle.

Electrics:

Rees-Stevens controllers and regenerative control.

The traction motor was mounted over the front axle.

Brakes:

Rheostatic brake, air brakes (believed to be Westinghouse manufacture), hand brake operating on the leading rear axle only.

There were separate air brake and hand brake shoes, of the same style but operating independently within each drum. The front brake shoes were of a different design comprising 3 aluminium alloy shoes mounted on an aluminium alloy back plate.

Metropolitan-Vickers compressor motors potentially with replacement machined bronze front cylinders made by Hastings Tramways at Silverhill.

Bodywork:

Composite seven-bay single-deck construction

including a wider central fourth bay and centre entrance and exit, and integral trolley gantry (beneath a second roof or fairing) built by Ransomes, Sims and Jefferies Ltd., Orwell Works, Ipswich, Suffolk.

The trolley bases were fitted above bay 2 to a second roof or fairing which extended above bays 1-5. Platform handrails and stanchions were covered with black Doverite.

The main side body panels were divided horizontally, tramcar style, into upper and lower sections, however the cab front, cab sides and rear panels were not divided. Glass louvres were fitted above the drop light windows in bays 1-3 and 5-7 on both sides of the vehicle. The rearmost side windows featured a radiused bottom corner and abutted wide rear corner pillars. There were two windows at the rear surmounted by destination and service number boxes. The wide central combined entrance and exit was vestibuled but had no doors: there were two steps, that is three from street level. The rear saloon floor line rose above the rear bogie and was about 8½ins above the level of that in the front saloon and central platform.

Four roof-mounted extractor ventilators were placed towards the centre-line of the roof (two on each side) towards the front of bay 2 and towards the rear of bay 7, those in bay 2 encroaching beneath the trolley gantry fairing.

The slightly bulbous front panel of the driver's cab was extremely shallow and did not even extend down to the height of the front axle. Arched beading gave the impression of a wide outline "radiator" position. A warning hooter horn extended through the offside front pillar. The front registration number plate was mounted beneath the front panel. The top two-thirds of the nearside and offside driver's windscreen opened outwards, with a wiper being affixed to the upper portion of the offside windscreen. There was a front hinged driver's cab door on the offside, the upper three-quarters of the window therein having a sliding "signalling" window. There were 2 glazed panels in the bulkhead behind the driver. Rectangular driver's rear view mirrors were mounted externally towards the top of the front cab pillars with an additional one above the other on the offside to permit the driver to view the trolleybooms.

There were three lifeguard rails on each side, the lowest being more substantial than the two above, extending between the front and second axles that on the nearside continuing behind the combined entrance and exit steps. The rear of the front mudguards, and the front and rear of the second and third wheel mudguards extended below the side body panels. The offside front wheel was equipped with a step ring. Separate rear mudguards. A mud flap hung between the second and third axle. A bamboo trolley retrieval pole was carried at the side of the roof on the nearside with retaining hooks above the roof gutter at the top of the pillars between bays 1 and 2, bays 4 (the centre entrance and exit) and 5, and to the rear of bay 7.

There were used ticket boxes in the nearside front and rear vestibules of the central entrance/exit, immediately below the nearside bulkhead windows.

Lighting:

These trolleybuses entered service in Nottingham at the time of wartime lighting restrictions. External lighting was 2 headlights mounted on the extremities of the front panel and 2 small circular front sidelights mounted at the base of the driver's windscreen corner pillars. The internal lights in the rear saloon shone through a red glass lens and a translucent number plate, both mounted at the top of the offside corner panel, to provide the single rear light and an illuminated rear registration number. Deep, peaked headlamp masks and a partial blanking-of to the sidelights were fitted before the vehicles entered service to comply with wartime "black-out" requirements.

Internal illumination was provided by 4 ceiling-mounted exposed tungsten bulbs in the front saloon (bays 1 and 3 on each side), a single light on the offside platform ceiling and 5 in the rear saloon (bays 5 and 7 on each side and a single light in the nearside ceiling bay 8). Again these were subject to wartime lighting restrictions.

Destination equipment:

The roof above the driver's cab windscreen accommodated a square service number indicator on the offside combined with a shallower single-line destination box on the nearside. At the rear a similar display was built into the top of the rear windows with the square service number indicator on the offside and the shallower single-line destination box on the nearside. There was no side destination display.

Seating:

The double seats had separate squabs and backs attached to painted tubular steel frames with grab-handles at the side of the gangway. Squabs and backs were upholstered in leather (pleated backs and plain squabs) with wooden seat backs. Immediately behind the driver's cab rear bulkhead there was a rearwards facing transverse seat extending across the width of the vehicle, seating 5 passengers. In the front saloon there was a single forwards-facing double seat and one single inwards facing seat on the nearside and two rows of forwards-facing double seats on the offside. Opposite the open centre entrance/exit, there was an inwards facing longitudinal bench seat for 3 persons. In the rear saloon there were three rows of forwards-facing double seats on the nearside and on the offside an inwards facing longitudinal bench seat accommodating 2 passengers and two rows of forwards-facing double seats with a transverse seat for 5 passengers at the rear.

Internal Livery:

The tongue and groove ceiling planking and window pillars were white. Two ceiling mounted longitudinal hand-rails extended the whole length of the vehicle with leather strap hangers. A conductor's bell-signalling rope hung parallel to the offside handrail above the gangway with a connected extension towards the central entrance and exit. The central entrance floor area and the foot space in front of each forwards or rearwards facing seat was covered with transverse wooden slats. The gangway floor was covered with longitudinal wooden slats.

Unpainted brass rods protected the drop light window panes in bays 5-7 and the rearmost windows on both sides of the rear saloon.

External Livery:

Entered service in Nottingham in single-deck version of Livery 6 (see Appendix C).

Notes:

304 was fitted with perimeter seating to accommodate more standing passengers but without a loss of seating capacity.

Initially these vehicles were allocated to Trent Bridge Depot and, in view of their low capacity invariably relegated to the quieter London Road service 45. Thereafter they were moved to Lower Parliament Street Depot and used at peak hours only.

Disposal:

304, 306 sold to Cardale Service Garage (Rhodes), Carlton Road, Nottingham, dealer, in January 1946.

305 sold to G. King, 16 Daybrook Avenue, Sherwood, Nottingham, in October 1944 for use as a caravan or shed.

307, 309 sold to A. Devey, Lynn Lane, House Farm, Lichfield, Staffordshire, dealer, in April 1946.

308 sold to B.E. Whitehouse, St. Ives, Highbury Road, Keyworth, Nottinghamshire, in January 1946, for conversion into a caravan and resale.

437 – 440 AEC 661T

A post-war view of ex-Cleethorpes AEC661T/Park Royal 437 at the junction of Queen Street with King Street. Note the masked indicator apertures. *GHFA & JMB*

Chassis:	Two axle type AEC 661T manufactured by the Associated Equipment Company Ltd. at the AEC works, Windmill Lane, Southall, Middlesex.
Motor:	Metropolitan-Vickers, Type 201DV (80 hp) mounted amidships within the chassis frame.
	Regulated field equipment with a 1 hour rating of 80 hp at 500 volts.
Electrical equipment:	Metropolitan-Vickers. Rheostatic Brake Co. resistances.
Dewirement indicator:	single Urcol line-lights.
Brakes:	Westinghouse compressed air and hand brakes. No evidence of electric braking in the circuit diagrams, etc.
Body:	Park Royal H30/26R.
Length:	26ft
Width:	7ft 6ins
Wheelbase:	16ft 3ins
Unladen weight:	437 6tons 13cwt 1qtrs
	438-440 6tons 13cwt 0qtrs
Tyres:	36 X 8 on all wheels.

Ex-Cleethorpes Corporation in October 1940. 437 (Cleethorpes 59, registration number FW8995) was one of the ten vehicles with which Cleethorpes Corporation started trolleybus operations on 18 July 1937. 438-440 (Cleethorpes 60-62, registration numbers AFU153-AFU155) were of identical design and delivered in July 1938.

437 - 440 AEC 661T ex-Cleethorpes

No.	Old No.	Registration	Chassis	Chassis No.	Body	Body No.	Delivered	Registered	Into Service	Withdrawn	Sold
437	59	FW8995	AEC 661T	661T195	Park Royal			18.07.1937	10.1940	31.05.52	09.04.53
438	60	AFU153	AEC 661T	661T265	Park Royal			01.07.1938	10.1940	30.04.52	15.04.53
439	61	AFU154	AEC 661T	661T266	Park Royal			01.07.1938	10.1940	30.04.52	11.08.53
440	62	AFU155	AEC 661T	661T267	Park Royal			01.07.1938	10.1940	31.05.52	15.04.53

Chassis:

based on the AEC Regent 661 motorbus chassis and axles.

Electrics:

All electrical equipment, including the contactor panel, was mounted in an insulated unit on the nearside chassis frame member. There were four main cable runs carried within the frame channel sheathed in rubber ply tubing. The controller was mounted beneath the driver's seat. The vehicles in Cleethorpes first batch of trolleybuses had a front-end fitted 12-volt Metropolitan-Vickers motor generator set to provide power for supplying exterior and emergency lighting, and auxiliary equipment. The second batch is understood to have been similarly equipped; nonetheless NCT's own records refer to a CAV 12-volt dynamo. Metropolitan-Vickers tuned radio interference coils were mounted on the roof.

The upper-deck body pillars slotted into the wooden rail of the framework above the upper saloon windows, that is the cantrail. There were steel brackets bolted to the metal roof (inside the roof there was a steel strengthening plate on each side) and each end of the two girders, between bays 1 and 2, and bays 2 and 3, supporting the exposed trolley gantry, which was not in direct contact with the roof, rested on these brackets, each foot being secured by four metal bolts.

The main power cable entered the offside bay 2 roof panelling between the girders of the trolley gantry. The vehicles were equipped with Brecknell Willis lightweight trolley equipment and trolley bases. A radio interference suppressor was mounted centrally in front of the trolley gantry. The access catwalk on the roof had two steps above the rear dome beneath the utilitarian trolley boom retaining hooks.

Brakes:

Cleethorpes had chosen to employ the most utilitarian equipment, no rheostatic or regenerative braking being installed, not least as the system, and that of neighbouring Grimsby, was flat with but two slight gradients. The compressed air brakes, incorporating AEC patents, used a compressor unit with 5 cubic ft capacity attached to the chassis with Silentbloc bushings to eliminate vibration and provide secondary insulation. The patented arrangement of combined reservoir unit and check-valve, silencer and governor, reduced piping and facilitated maintenance. The compressor unit was located behind the offside inspection hatch.

Bodywork:

Highbridge double-deck composite five bay construction with conventional, enclosed forwards-ascending half-turn (90°) staircase with semi-vestibuled open platform entrance and exit at the rear, and roof ribbing built by Park Royal Coachworks Ltd., Abbey Road, Park Royal, Willesden, London NW10.

The composite body was of a lightweight type based on a selected seasoned ash frame with oak underframe. The front elevation curved gently rearwards. The rounded roof was deeper than usual with the upper saloon side windows 2 ins shallower than those in the lower saloon, giving a stronger roof and reducing the weight of the top deck. The upper saloon was equipped with four Colt roof-mounted extractor ventilators (two on each side) located towards the front of bay 1 and the rear of bay 4 on each side. A double fold at the base of the upper-deck side panels bays 1 – 5 provided a gutter. Oblong extractor ventilators were mounted immediately above the lower deck side windows in bays 2 and 4. The trolley poles were fitted on an exposed roof-mounted gantry above bays 2.

Metal louvres were fitted above the upper and lower saloon side windows, and above the upper saloon front windows. Widney Stuart "Aero" half-drop windows were fitted to the side windows in bays 2-4 on both sides of the lower deck, bays 1, 2, 4, 5 on the nearside of the upper deck, and bays 1-4 on the offside of the upper deck. The front upper-deck windows had "push-out" opening-top ventilators. Top hinged access doors were fitted at the base of the lower-deck off-side panel bay 2 providing access to the air brake compressor unit and on the nearside in bay 2 and part of bay 3 providing access to the contactors in an insulated unit mounted on the nearside chassis member.

The upper corners of the rear platform window and the upper deck emergency exit window were radiused, the gutter around the edge of the roof curving down the upper deck rear corner panel to end beneath the emergency exit window, all in the mid-late 1930s Park Royal style. The rear upper deck emergency door had three hinges at its base and an opening handle on the offside above; it could be retained open by leather-covered chains on each side to provide access to the trolley gantry. The emergency door lock involved a bar across the inside of the door with prongs which located into three hooks above, mounted on the framework of the dome. Small rubber bumpers on the nearside and offside of the emergency exit window aligned with similar bumpers on the panel beneath, to the nearside and offside of the rear indicator boxes. Handrails were covered in blue Doverite (to match the Cleethorpes colour scheme).

Bell pushes were mounted in the ceiling of the lower saloon towards the front of bay 2, towards the rear of bay 3; in the upper saloon on the nearside of bay 2, the offside of bay 5 and on the rear platform beneath the staircase.

The driver's cab was equipped with a single chromium plated opening windscreen on the off-side equipped with a top-mounted windscreen wiper whilst the nearside windscreen was fitted with a bottom-mounted wiper after arrival in Nottingham. The frame of the opening pane had radiused upper corners. Above the windscreen, two 3-vane louvred ventilators were mounted centrally on the cream-painted central band. There was a front hinged cab door on the offside only equipped with a sliding "signalling" window in the lower half of the pane and an inset opening handle. There was a matching panel and sliding window on the nearside. The base of the cab door was curved over the wheel arch to a position about 4 ins from the rear of the door thereafter the base, beneath the cab door handle, was horizontal, parallel to the cream-painted and about 1ft 3ins below it.

A step was let into the base of the bay 1 side panel, but without any form of protection to the bodywork, immediately behind the front axle, on the offside. The front wheels were equipped with wheel trims although those on the nearside were removed from all vehicles at a later date as they were not required for access to the cab. Individual mud flaps hung behind each wheel.

There were 2 glazed panels in the bulkhead behind the driver with a wide central pillar. The panel behind the driver had two panes of glass, one pane sliding to allow the driver to communicate with the conductor. Small rectangular driver's rear view mirrors were mounted externally towards the top of the front cab pillars. An inverted triangular AEC maker's badge was fitted centrally beneath the driver's windscreen on the waistband. The driver's windscreen was of Triplex toughened safety glass.

A large removable panel with four columns of six louvred ventilation vanes extended across the base of the front panel from beneath the offside to beneath the nearside headlamp with the front registration number plate centred at the bottom. The rear registration number plate was at the base of the rear platform panel, beneath the advertisement position on the offside with a single rear light immediately above.

A single lifeguard, in the form of a round-section steel tube, ran beneath the side panels between the front and rear axles. A bamboo trolley retrieval pole was carried in a tube mounted offset to the offside under the chassis.

Lighting:

These trolleybuses entered service in Nottingham at the time of wartime lighting restrictions. External lighting was 2 headlights halfway up the front panel with 2 front side lights immediately above but mounted slight more towards the extremity of the panel. A spotlight was mounted behind a hole in the front panel below the nearside headlight.

At the rear there was a single rear light mounted immediately above the square offside registration number plate and a brake light, the lens displaying the word STOP on the lower cream-painted band to the off-side of the rear platform window.

Interior lighting was provided by an installation of 40-volt, 40-watt traction type pearl bulbs: 5 lights were mounted in shell-shaped indents of the ceiling cove panels on each side of the lower and upper saloons and one above the rear upper deck emergency window, making 21 in all. These were wired in series with the lights in the destination indicator boxes (two lights in each box) and service number indicator boxes (one each) making a grand total of 30. They were wired in two series of 15, the nearside bulbs being in one series and the offside in the other.

Internal emergency lighting was provided by means of a separate low voltage lights on each deck. One was mounted in the ceiling above the rear upper deck emergency window and thus above the staircase and another was located on the front bulkhead of the lower saloon, centrally placed above the windows.

Seating:

The sprung squabs on 437 and the Dunlopillo cushioned squabs on 438-440 were fitted to tubular metal frames. Those in the upper saloon were covered in blue leather; those in the lower saloon were covered with dark and light blue and cream moquette with blue leather edges.

The seat backs consisted of two moquette panels, vertical dark blue leather strips each side and in the middle, and also across the top of each moquette panel.

The lower saloon had a 3-person inwards-facing bench seat on each side over the rear axle and 5 rows of forwards-facing double seats. The upper saloon had 6 rows of double seats on the off-side and 9 rows on the nearside, that is the bench seat at the rear of the upper saloon above the open platform also accommodated 2 passengers. Stanchions rose up behind the first and fourth seat on the nearside and the second and fifth seat on the offside of the lower saloon, and behind the second seat on the nearside and fourth seat on the offside (together with one at the head of the stairs) in the upper saloon. The driver's seat was in blue leather.

Destination equipment:

Rectangular indicator boxes were mounted centrally at the front on the upper-deck panels above the driver's cab windscreen and at the rear above the platform window. The apertures were reduced in both depth and width with paint masking from the Cleethorpes standard size to 27ins X 5½ins in order to accept the Nottingham standard pre-war blinds. These two boxes were surmounted by a square service number indicator, which in the Nottingham livery encroached into the upper cream-painted waistband beneath the upper saloon windows. In addition a slightly deeper indicator box was fitted immediately above the rear open platform entrance. The boxes had noticeably square corners to match the design of the windows.

Internal Livery:

The interior panels were lined with scratchproof dark blue Rexine with window mouldings and finishings in French-polished walnut.

External Livery:

Entered service in Nottingham in Livery 6 (see Appendix C).

Notes:

437, 440 (at least) were reconditioned by NCT in November 1950 and December 1950 respectively.

438 de-licensed 31.12.1950 and reinstated 01.02.1951, possibly having been reconditioned.

Disposal:

437, 438, 440 sold to Thomas Bow, Contractor, 43 Lamartine Street, Nottingham, in April 1953 for use as site caravans.

439 sold to Mrs A.P. Clarke, Brownwood, Thorney, Lincolnshire, in August 1953.

Initially all were sold to Thomas Bow but 439 was not collected and subsequently resold to Mrs Clark.

441 Daimler CTM4

The Daimler CTM4 as originally completed in June 1938. Although illustrated in a grey primer finish, the body beading to suit Kingston-upon-Hull Corporation's streamlined livery of the period is most evident. *Roy Marshall*

Chassis: Two axle type Daimler CTM4 built by Transport Vehicles (Daimler) Ltd., Coventry, Warwickshire.
Motor: Metropolitan-Vickers Ltd., Type MV 201 EV (85 hp at 550 volts) regulated field.
Electrical equipment: Metropolitan-Vickers Co. Ltd., Trafford Park, Manchester. Rheostatic Brake Co. resistances.
Dewirement indicator: Assumed to have been equipped with line-lights.
Brakes: Westinghouse compressed air and hand brakes.
Body: Weymann H28/26R.
Length: 26ft
Width 7ft 6ins
Wheelbase: 16ft 3ins
Unladen weight: 6tons 18cwt 0qtrs
Tyres: 36 X 8 on all wheels.

Daimler built this demonstrator in June 1938 targeted at obtaining a major order from Kingston-upon-Hull Corporation and the vehicle closely followed that undertaking's specifications of the period including a regulated field motor (as used on Hull's Leyland TB4 trolleybuses 1-25) and suitable body beading for their streamlined livery. In the event Hull turned down the offer of a free trial of the demonstrator probably because they had decided to standardise on compound wound motors for full regenerative braking in all subsequent pre-war trolleybus orders.

The designation CTM4 indicated Commercial, Trolleybus, Metropolitan-Vickers electrical equipment, 4 wheels. Nottingham acquired the vehicle direct from Daimler in January 1941.

441 Daimler CTM4 ex-Daimler Motors

No.	Registration	Chassis	Chassis No.	Body	Body No.	Delivered	Registered	Into Service	Withdrawn	Sold
441 -	GTO471	Daimler CTM4	20002	Weymann	C5225		01.02.1941	01.02.1941	31.07.1952	15.04.53

Chassis:

Believed to have been based on that of the contemporary Daimler CO motorbus chassis. Rear axle ratio 9⅓ to 1

Electrics:

Brecknell Willis & Co. Ltd. trolley collector gear with BICC Edinburgh type slipper heads using renewable carbon inserts. The original 18ft 9ins long trolley booms, when restrained by the retaining hooks, extended 3ft beyond the rear-most part of the bodywork, but there is no photographic evidence that these survived long in Nottingham if they were even still in place when the vehicle was purchased.

The main control gear was of unit construction and featured the assembly of all electrical control items on one insulating base, mounted in a rounded-top cabinet to the nearside of the driver's seat, on the cab bulkhead. Metropolitan-Vickers controller.

A radio interference suppressor, to meet Ministry of Transport requirements, was mounted centrally on the roof immediately in front of the trolley bases.

Brakes:

Rheostatic braking was used down to 4 mph, further pressure on the brake pedal at this speed bringing the compressed air brake into use. A ¾ hp compressor of 5 cubic ft capacity controlled by an automatic governor supplied the Westinghouse air brakes.

The handbrake lever was to the nearside of the driver's steering column.

Bodywork:

Composite five-bay highbridge double-deck construction, enclosed forwards-ascending half-turn (90°) staircase with conventional semi-vestibuled open platform entrance and exit at the rear, and integral trolley gantry built by Weymann Motor Bodies Ltd, Addlestone, Surrey (marketed by Metropolitan Cammell-Weymann Motor Bodies Ltd).

Beclawat "Typhoon" half-drop openers having "pinch fasteners" mounted centrally at the top of each pane were fitted to the tops of the side windows in bays 1, 3 and 5 (both sides) of the upper-deck and bays 2-4 (both sides) of the lower deck. The front upper-deck windows were fixed. The side windows of the upper and lower deck saloon windows had radiused bottom

Former demonstrator Daimler CTM4/Weymann 441 at rest in Parliament Street Depot on 15 July 1952. Note that front destination screen aperture has been masked in depth to enable a standard sized blind to be fitted. *Roy Marshall*

corners and were surmounted by metal louvres. Above the lower saloon windows in bays 1, 3, 5 on both sides in the middle cream-painted band there were a series of 10 ventilation vents slanting rearwards somewhat from the vertical at the top. A gutter moulding ran along the top of the middle cream-painted band on both sides from above the foremost driver's cab side window to the rear of bay 5 shielding the gap along the edge of the top deck floor which provided a drain for water from wet clothing and footwear. The front upper-saloon windows were surmounted by two horizontal ventilator slats, a Weymann feature of the period, positioned towards the centre line of the vehicle and surrounded by a curved moulding. The rear upper-deck emergency exit was bottom hinged and divided vertically into two almost square windows having radiused corners, the radii at the top being greater than those at the bottom.

The roof was fitted with a gutter moulding across the top of the upper saloon front and side windows at cantrail level, following the curve of the rearmost side windows to pass beneath the rear upper saloon emergency exit at upper-deck waistrail level. To prevent water-ingress there was a second gutter moulding across the rear dome above the rear emergency exit. There were four extractor ventilators in the roof mounted towards the rear of the panelling above bays 3 and 5.

The driver's cab had a single, offside opening windscreen equipped with a top-mounted windscreen wiper affixed centrally above the pane. The wiper on the nearside was bottom-mounted, centrally beneath the fixed pane. There was an offside front-hinged door equipped with a sliding "signalling" window in the lower half of the pane. The waist rail beneath the cab side windows and windscreens was at the same height as the lower-saloon waist rail but the windows were deeper, the top of the rearmost side pane of the cab curving upwards to meet the top of the foremost side pane which itself gradually deepened slightly towards the front of the trolleybus.

An access step was let into the base of the bay 1 side panel, with a sheet of protective aluminium reaching from the lintel of the driver's cab door to approximately the height of the front axle, immediately behind the front axle on the offside. There were 2 glazed panels, separated by a solid panel about 1ft wide, in the bulkhead behind the driver. Rear view mirrors were mounted externally above the driver's cab nearside and offside side window immediately to the rear of the front pillar.

A large top-hinged removable panel which carried the registration plate extended across the front of the cab from beneath the offside to beneath the nearside headlamp. There is no evidence that the ventilator vanes with which the vehicle had been equipped as a demonstrator, remained by the time of its arrival in Nottingham. The bodywork closely reproduced the characteristics of the Weymann-bodied Leyland TB4s supplied to Kingston-upon-Hull Corporation Transport in 1937 but all beading for the streamlined livery had been replaced by conventional waistband beading.

The rear platform window had all four corners radiused, the top being of greater radius than those at the bottom in the Weymann style of the period. There was a used ticket box immediately below the nearside vestibule window on the rear open platform. The rear registration number plate was mounted at the rear offside of the lower deck rear panel.

A single lifeguard ran beneath the side panels between the front and rear axles. A bamboo trolley retrieval pole was carried in a tube mounted centrally under the chassis.

Lighting:

This trolleybus entered service in Nottingham at the time of wartime lighting restrictions. External lighting was 2 protruding chromium-plated headlights with dishings behind on the front panel, 2 front side lights (resembling the front light of a bicycle) on stems at the side of the vehicle on the lower cream-painted band in line with the front corner pillars of the driver's cab. A spotlight was recessed into the front panel below the nearside headlight but somewhat closer to the centre line of the vehicle. A single rear light and brake light were fitted above the square registration number plate at the base of the offside rear panel, the rear light being to the offside of the brake light.

Interior lights were equipped with rectangular diffused glass covers and chromium-plated frames, and were fitted in the cove panels on each side in each bay of both the upper and lower saloons (10 lamps on each deck), with a single fitting on the offside of the upper-deck above the staircase. In addition there was a single exposed light in the ceiling of the open rear platform above the nearside bulkhead. Again these were subject to wartime lighting restrictions.

Seating:

Based on painted tubular steel frames with chromium-plated top shaped to a "butterfly" pattern. Squabs and backs in the lower-saloon were upholstered in red patterned moquette trimmed in black leather whilst those in the upper-saloon were upholstered with brown leather. The lower-saloon had a 3-person bench seat over the rear axle on both sides and 5 rows of forwards-facing double seats. The upper saloon had 7 rows of double seats on the nearside with a further double seat somewhat inset towards the centre line of the vehicle above the open rear platform, and 6 rows of double seat on the offside. The seats on the upper deck were staggered to provide more space on the offside at the top of the staircase. The driver's seat was in quilted brown hide.

Glass-fronted notice cases were fitted to the front of both decks and electric heating elements, later disconnected, were contained in tubes running the length of the saloon just above floor level on both decks.

Destination equipment:

Single large (36ins X 24ins) rectangular indicator boxes with square corners capable of displaying a service number and up to 4 lines of information, in a larger format than usual, were mounted centrally at the front on the upper deck panels above the driver's cab windscreen and at the rear above the rear platform window. A further rectangular indicator box of the same size and equipped with a gutter above was fitted on the nearside immediately above the open rear platform entrance.

Internal Livery:

Ceilings and coves were painted white with polished walnut used for all window frames and wooden ceiling mouldings. Side panels below the waist rail were covered with brown Rexine. Handrails and stanchions were covered in black Doverite. The saloon floors were covered in brown linoleum.

Internal advertisement frames were mounted above the glazed panels in the bulkhead at the rear of the driver's cab and above the front windows in the upper saloon.

External Livery:

Entered service in Nottingham in Livery 6 (see Appendix C).

Subsequent alterations:

The original large front destination screen aperture was reduced in depth with paint masking, in the same manner as on the Sunbeam MF2s, to enable what became a standard sized blind to be fitted.

Notes:

There is some uncertainty as to whether the vehicle had been previously registered before its purchase by Nottingham; it has been suggested that it was first registered in Coventry in June 1938 but no indications as to why the registration was surrendered.

The ex-Cleethorpes Corporation AEC 661Ts and the Daimler CTM4 were the first Nottingham trolleybuses with Metropolitan-Vickers electrical equipment and traction motors. In 1928 Metropolitan-Vickers (Metrovick) merged with British Thomson-Houston (BTH) and in January 1929 both companies were amalgamated into Associated Electrical Industries Limited (AEI). This resulted in a history of commercial rivalry between the two firms which Sir Felix J.C. Pole, formerly the successful General Manager of the Great Western Railway and AEI Chairman from 1931, failed to bring under control.

Nottingham trolleybus drivers were required to have a knowledge of the idiosyncrasies of each type of vehicle and thus in later years 441 seemed to spend a disproportionate amount of time on driver training duties.

Disposal:

441 sold to Mrs A.P. Clarke, Brownwood, Thorney, Lincolnshire, in April 1953.

442 – 445, 452 - 468 Karrier W

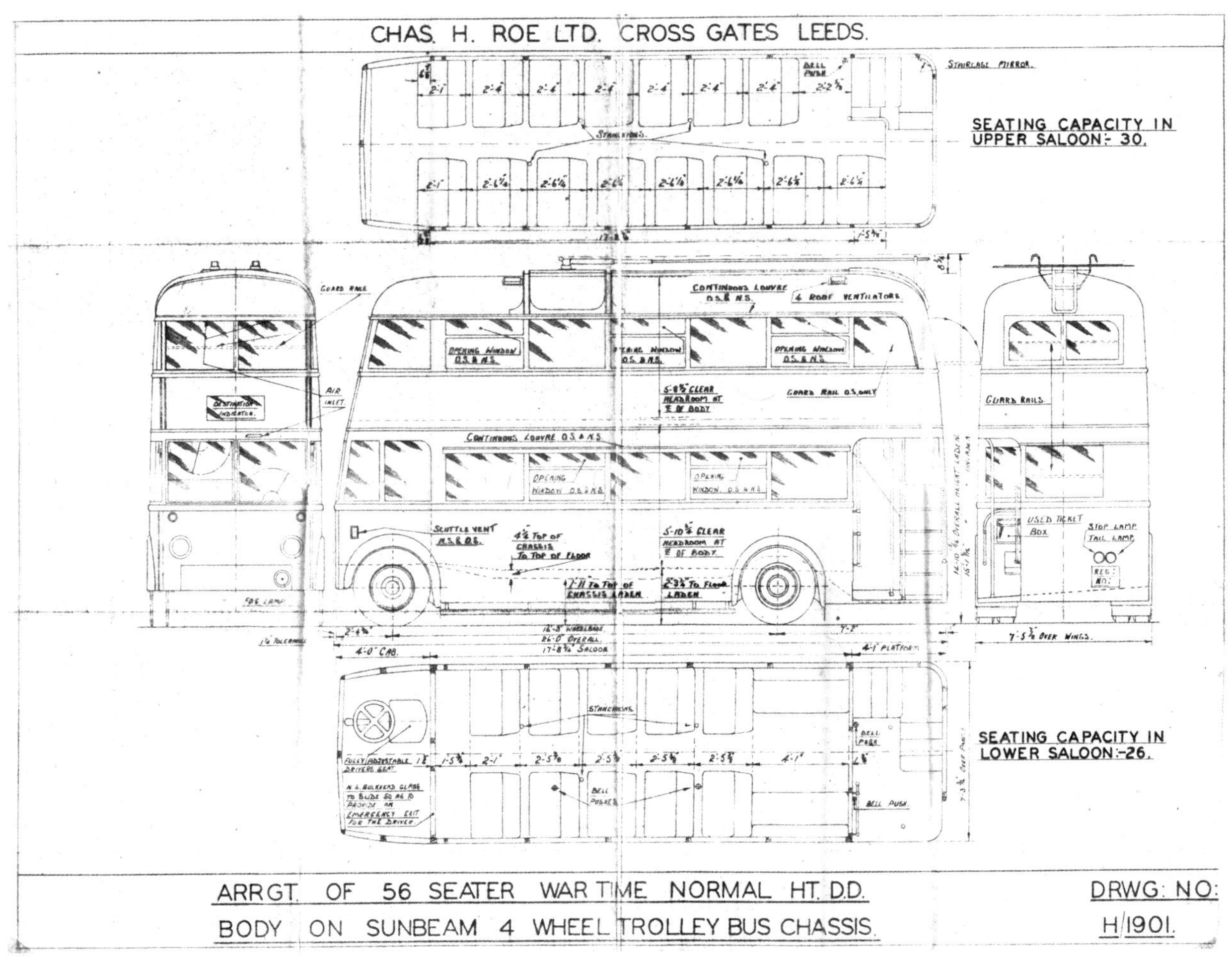

A Roe general layout drawing of a 'Wartime' body for a Sunbeam W chassis.

Chassis: Two axle wartime utility type Karrier W marketed by Commer-Karrier, Biscot Road, Luton, Bedfordshire and manufactured by Karrier Motors Ltd. at the Sunbeam trolleybus factory, Moorfield Road, Wolverhampton.
442-445 Karrier drawing KB151 dated 30 October 1941. NCT drawing 7/12.
452-454, 455-458 drawing details not known.
459-468 Karrier drawing CB219 dated 13 March 1944. NCT drawing 7/15.

Motor: 442-445 British Thomson-Houston Co. Ltd., Rugby, Type 207 C1 (85 hp at 550 volts)
452-454 English Electric Ltd., Bradford, Type EE 408C (115 hp at 550 volts)
455-458 English Electric Ltd., Bradford, Type EE 408C (115 hp at 550 volts)
459-468 British Thomson-Houston Co. Ltd., Rugby, Type 207 A3 (85 hp at 550 volts)

Electrical equipment: 442-445 British Thomson-Houston Co. Ltd., Rugby, Warwickshire.
452-454 English Electric Ltd., Preston, Lancashire.
455-458 English Electric Ltd., Preston, Lancashire.
459-468 British Thomson-Houston Co. Ltd., Rugby, Warwickshire.

Dewirement indicator: Urcol line-lights and buzzer (assumed fitted from new).

Brakes: 442-445 G.D. Peters compressed air, hand and rheostatic brakes.
452-454 Westinghouse compressed air, hand, regenerative and rheostatic brakes
455-458 Westinghouse compressed air, hand, regenerative and rheostatic brakes
459-468 Westinghouse compressed air, hand and rheostatic brakes
all with Ransomes Type A500 compressor motors.

Body: 442-445 Weymann Motor Bodies Ltd, Addlestone, Surrey drawing V2276 dated 10 August 1942. NCT drawing 11/12.
452-454 Park Royal Coachworks Ltd., Abbey Road, Park Royal, Willesden, London NW10 drawing NHT1/A. NCT drawing 11/14.
455-458 Weymann Motor Bodies Ltd, Addlestone, Surrey drawing V2280 (undated). NCT drawing 11/13.
459-465 Charles H. Roe Ltd., Crossgates, Leeds, Yorkshire drawing H/1802 dated 10 May 1944. NCT drawing 11/15.
466-468 Brush Coachworks Ltd., Loughborough, Leicestershire drawing 32/FA/101 dated 5 July 1944. NCT drawing 11/16.
all UH30/26R.

Length: 25ft 11ins (except 459-465 26ft, 466-468 25ft 10½ins)

Width: 7ft 6ins

Wheelbase: 16ft 3ins

Wheel track: front 6ft 6ins, rear 5ft 9¼ins

Unladen weight: 442-445 8tons 4cwts 1qtr
452-454 7tons 18cwt 1qtrs
455-458 8tons 1cwt 0qtrs
459-465 7tons 8cwts 2qtrs
466-468 7tons 6cwts 3qtrs

Tyres: front wheels 36 X 8ins; rear wheels 9.00 X 20ins. Later 9.00 x 20ins all round.

The Ministry of War Transport allocated the vehicles and their component parts.

442 - 445 Karrier W4

No.	Registration	Chassis	Chassis No.	Body	Body No.	Delivered	Registered	Into Service	Withdrawn	Sold
442	GTV42	Karrier W4	50040	Weymann	7404		06.12.1943	09.12.1943	31.10.1959	04.05.1960
443	GTV43	Karrier W4	50041	Weymann	7405		15.12.1943	19.12.1943	12.01.1955	01.12.1959
444	GTV44	Karrier W4	50042	Weymann	7406		31.01.1944	01.02.1944	31.10.1962	05.1963
445	GTV45	Karrier W4	50043	Weymann	7407		09.02.1944	12.02.1944	28.02.1959	06.05.1960

452 - 468 Karrier W4

No.	Registration	Chassis	Chassis No.	Body	Body No.	Delivered	Registered	Into Service	Withdrawn	Sold
452	GTV652	Karrier W4	50056	Park Royal	26402		24.03.1944	25.03.1944	1957	02.12.1959
453	GTV653	Karrier W4	50057	Park Royal	26403		06.04.1944	07.04.1944	1957	25.05.1959
454	GTV654	Karrier W4	50058	Park Royal	26401		11.03.1944	11.03.1944	31.10.1962	06.05.1963
455	GTV655	Karrier W4	50059	Weymann	8005		11.03.1944	11.03.1944	1957	30.11.1959
456	GTV656	Karrier W4	50060	Weymann	8007		11.03.1944	21.03.1944	1957	29.11.1959
457	GTV657	Karrier W4	50061	Weymann	8008		06.04.1944	07.04.1944	31.05.1962	22.05.1963
458	GTV658	Karrier W4	50062	Weymann	8009		03.05.1944	05.05.1944	31.10.1959	03.05.1960
459	GTV659	Karrier W4	50137	Roe	GO1983		07.03.1945	14.03.1945	30.06.1963	04.09.1963
460	GTV660	Karrier W4	50138	Roe	GO1984		22.03.1945	26.03.1945	31.03.1965	18.08.1965
461	GTV661	Karrier W4	50139	Roe	GO1985		07.03.1945	13.03.1945	31.03.1965	18.08.1965
462	GTV662	Karrier W4	50140	Roe	GO1986		22.03.1945	30.03.1945	30.11.1962	15.05.1963
463	GTV663	Karrier W4	50185	Roe	GO2000		29.06.1945	11.07.1945	30.11.1962	02.09.1963
464	GTV664	Karrier W4	50186	Roe	GO1999		14.06.1945	16.06.1945	31.07.1963	15.05.1963
465	GTV665	Karrier W4	50187	Roe	GO2001		29.06.1945	16.07.1945	30.11.1962	15.05.1963
466	GTV666	Karrier W4	50188	Brush			30.07.1945	23.07.1945	31.03.1962	28.11.1962
467	GTV667	Karrier W4	50189	Brush			01.08.1945	04.08.1945	31.01.1958	25.11.1959
468	GTV668	Karrier W4	50190	Brush			01.08.1945	04.08.1945	31.01.1958	27.05.1959

Chassis:

Standard basic wartime chassis for use beneath double deck or (with a longer wheelbase) single deck bodies incorporating salient features of the pre-war Sunbeam MF2 and Karrier E4 chassis. There is some evidence to suggest that these chassis were designated W4, that is Wartime 4-wheel, to differentiate from a three axle standard wartime chassis once under consideration however both Karrier's drawings and the chassis plates in the driver's cab clearly showed Nottingham's examples to be designated as Karrier W. The chassis frame employed deep channel section side-members braced with large diameter tubular cross members. Full depth channel section members across the centre of the frame ensured torsional rigidity. The whole of the frame structure was bolted together with high tensile steel bolts fitted in reamed holes.

Conventional front axle with forged steel hubs mounted on taper roller bearings, similar bearings being used to take the thrust of the king pins. Double roller cam and roller steering unit of robust dimensions for heavy-duty use.

Chassis length:

25ft 7ins

Chassis frame width:

front 3ft 3⅞ins, rear 3ft 8ins

Overall width (over tyres):

7ft 5⅝ins

The under slung worm type rear axle had fully floating shafts, the main axle casing being a nickel steel drop-forging. The differential was housed in a drop-forged steel casing on which the phosphor-bronze worm wheel which meshed with a hardened steel worm was also mounted. The differential casing was offset towards the near side of the chassis to permit a low and unobstructed centre gangway. The steel hubs were mounted on roller bearings. The driving shafts were machined from heat treated nickel chrome molybdenum steel, the hub driving flanges being forged solid with the shafts removing the necessity for splining the hub end of each shaft.

The axle gear ratio was 9.7 to 1.

The short transmission shaft was equipped with a needle roller universal joint at each end. The slide, due to axle movement, was taken through a large diameter splined sleeve at the forward end of the shaft, and end thrust through a ball thrust bearing mounted in the end case of the motor thus relieving the armature of any load. The driving torque reaction is taken through the rear road springs.

The laminated road springs were 3½ins wide, the front springs were 44ins in length and the rear springs 59¼ins, these dimensions being between the spring eyes. The eyes of the main plates were forged solid, and on the rear springs the main plates were of the divided type, having inner eyes to provide a positive location for the axle. The spring shackle pins were protected on the wearing surfaces with a deposit of hard chrome to reduce wear.

The motor-driven compressor unit for the air brakes was mounted on an insulated base on the off side main frame side member. The compressor had a displacement of 5 cubic ft per minute. The compressor motor was totally enclosed and operated direct from the line voltage. An electric governor, also mounted on an insulated base, controlled the operation of the motor and automatically cut out when the pressure in the air reservoir reached 80 lb per sq. in., and cut in again when the pressure fell to 65 lb per sq.in.

Electrics:

Compound-wound traction motor with rheostatic braking operating in conjunction with the mechanical braking system. The traction motor was mounted between the chassis frames towards the rear and just ahead of the rear axle, enabling it to be carried lower in the frame than was then normal practice so that low-height double-deck bodies could be fitted, and offset to the nearside. The contactor switchgear was mounted on a single panel in a cabinet on the rear wall of the driver's cab, with the master controller under the driver's seat. Those vehicles with BTH equipment (442-445, 459-468) had a removable panel in the nearside of the front bulkhead to give access to the rear of the contactor cabinet.

There was a dynamo on the commutator end of the traction motor. A speedometer of the electrical "tachometer" type was fitted, the generator portion being mounted on and driven from the forward end of the traction motor.

All equipped with Rheostatic Brake Co. resistances and Brecknell Willis lightweight trolleybases.

442-445 there was one main bank of resistances between the chassis frames ahead of the motor. The shunt resistance was mounted on the external face of the chassis nearside (approximately beneath bay 3 of the body). These trolleybuses were delivered with traction battery manoeuvring equipment and 60 volt batteries, the first Nottingham vehicles so equipped and the only wartime deliveries with this feature.

452-458 were delivered with English Electric traction motor whose serial numbers were intermingled with those of the London Transport SA3 class AEC 664T vehicles originally intended for South African systems. Until re-equipped with English Electric EE410 motors in 1949, they had regenerative control and were the most powerful trolleybuses on the Nottingham system.

459-468 there were two resistance banks between the chassis frames ahead of the motor. The shunt resistance was located beneath the cab.

An 'official' photograph of the Sunbeam/Karrier utility "W" chassis that appeared in the trade press during 1942. *Transport World*

Karrier W chassis photographed at Sunbeam's Wolverhampton works to show the typical layout of the electrical equipment, in this case of BTH manufacture. ("Modern Transport" 27 June 1941)

Brakes:

Compressed air, hand and rheostatic brakes. In addition the English Electric equipped vehicles 452-458 were provided with regenerative braking.

The compressor and air reservoir, complete with a safety valve and drain cock, were bolted directly to the offside external face of the mainframe member. There was one air-brake cylinder on top of each king pin and one cylinder attached to each side of the chassis cross-member ahead of the rear axle. An anti-freezing unit was fitted on the suction side of the compressor. Seamless steel tubing incorporating drainage was used for the pipeline. There were insulators in the pipeline between the motor-driven compressor and reservoir. The dash panel of the driver's cab was equipped with two gauges to indicate reservoir and brake cylinder pressure. There was an air brake governor in the cab.

The brake drums on both front and rear wheels were 17ins in diameter, the front shoes being 3ins and the rear shoes 6ins wide. The hand brake was of the "pull on" type and operated on the same set of shoes in the rear axle as the foot brakes and through the same cam gear.

Electrical rheostatic braking was operated from the same pedal as the air brake and was effective all speeds down to 3 or 4 mph. Approximately the first 1½ins of pedal travel was used to obtain rheostatic braking whilst further pedal travel brought in the air-operated mechanical brakes.

The handbrake lever was to the offside of the driver's steering column.

Bodywork:

Composite five-bay highbridge double-deck utility construction, enclosed forwards-ascending half-turn (90°) staircase with conventional semi-vestibuled open platform entrance and exit at the rear, designed to Ministry of Supply specifications. In order to optimise the use of available materials and reduce the amount of labour required, hardwoods were only used for the main body framing, the longitudinal rails being of pitch pine. Exterior panelling, including the roof, was of 20-gauge SWG steel whilst panels were shaped rather than beaten resulting in noticeably angular roof domes. The Brush bodies had conventional curved roof domes.

Metal louvres were fitted above the upper and lower deck saloon side windows, and above the upper-saloon front windows. Half-drop openers with central gripper at the top of the upper pane were fitted to the side windows in bay 3 of the upper deck and bay 3 of the lower deck but there were variations between batches and body builder. The upper pane dropped outside the fixed lower pane. All window glass was fixed direct to the framing.

Brackets or extensions were bolted to the roof rail immediately above the upper-deck body pillars between bays 1 and 2, and bays 2 and 3 to support the two girders of the exposed trolley gantry which was mounted above bay 2, and not in direct contact with the roof. All platform handrails and stanchions were white although those inside the saloons and on the staircase were black.

There were pull-in ventilators at the top of the upper saloon front windows with top-mounted central clip catch. At the rear of the upper saloon there was a bottom-hinged emergency exit door incorporating two square windows which also provided access to the trolley gantry and could be retained open by leather covered chains on each side. Exceptionally the Brush bodied-vehicles had a single rear window. Ventilators were also fitted to the roof, above bays 3 and 5 (466-468 bays 1 and 5). The Brush, Park Royal and Roe bodied vehicles had noticeably wider body pillars between the front side windows and bay 1 which on the offside accommodated the main traction power cable from the roof.

The driver's cab was equipped with a single opening windscreen on the offside equipped with a top-mounted windscreen wiper whilst the nearside windscreen had a bottom-mounted wiper. The frame of the opening pane had radiused upper corners. There was a front hinged cab door on the offside only equipped with a sliding "signalling" window in the lower half of the pane and an inset opening handle. An outwards opening vertical vent was positioned on both sides of the cab immediately beneath the waistline. The base of the cab door was curved over the wheel arch on the Park Royal and Weymann bodies. There were 2 glazed panels in the bulkhead behind the driver, that on the nearside incorporating a sliding pane, with a wide central pillar. Circular driver's rear view mirrors were mounted externally towards the top of the front cab pillars. A large removable panel extended across the front of the cab from beneath the offside to beneath the nearside headlamp but had no ventilation vanes. A Karrier maker's badge was fitted centrally beneath the driver's windscreen, its position in relation to the lower cream-painted band varying between the batches and body builder.

A step was let into the base of the bay 1 side panel, but without any form of protection to the bodywork, immediately behind the front axle, on the offside. The offside front wheel was equipped with a large step ring which served as a wheel nut protector.

The staircase had 3 steps from the platform to the landing and then 3 steps to the upper deck.

Ceiling-mounted handrails extended above the longitudinal seats at the rear of the lower saloon. There were also upright stanchions in both saloons the positions varying:

442-445, 455-458
Lower saloon: seats 2, 4 nearside; seats 1, 3 offside
Upper saloon: seats 3, 6 nearside; seats 2, 5 offside.

452-454
Lower saloon: seats 1, 3, 5 offside
Upper saloon: seats 3, 6 nearside; seats 2, 5 offside.

459-465
Lower saloon: seats 2 nearside; 1, 5 offside
Upper saloon: seats 3, 6 nearside; seats 2, 5 offside.

466-468
Lower saloon: seats 2 nearside; 1, 4 offside
Upper saloon: seats 3, 6 nearside; seats 2, 5 offside.

In the lower saloon there were 2 bell pushes in the ceiling located in bay 1 on the nearside and bay 3 on the offside. There were also 2 bell pushes in the upper saloon located on the nearside cantrail in bay 1 and on the offside in bay 5 at the top of the stairs. On the rear platform there was a further bell push on the offside of the rear bulkhead adjacent to staircase.

There was a used ticket box below the nearside vestibule window on the rear platform. A bamboo trolley retrieval pole was carried within the lower-saloon nearside body panels at waist rail height with a tube access from the rear platform vestibule. The conductor had a locker on the rear platform under the stairs. The rear registration number was transferred on the top left hand corner or centre of the rear platform window in the earlier deliveries but from ca. 1943 this was progressively supplemented by a rear registration number plate fitted on the offside of the rear platform panel although some vehicles, for example 457, never received one. A circular conductor's mirror was fixed in the upper deck rear offside dome at the head of the stairs.

There was a single lifeguard rail on each side extending between the front and rear axles.

There were detail differences to the bodywork between batches and body builder as follows:

442 – 445 Weymann

Half-drop openers with central gripper at the top of the upper pane were fitted to the side windows in bay 2 of the upper saloon, and bay 2 nearside, bay 3 offside of the lower saloon.

A gutter moulding ran along the base of the upper-deck side panels bays 1 – 5 at the joint of the upper and lower deck structure and gave covered drainage from the floor of the upper saloon.

The main traction power cable descended the front nearside pillar of bay 1.

There was a small outlet drain above the cab pillar on both sides.

The nearside fixed windscreen was slightly less deep than that on the offside.

Top hinged access doors were fitted at the base of the lower-deck nearside panel in bay 3, giving access to the shunt field resistance, and on the offside panels in bay 3 and part of bay 4 (immediately in front of the rear axle), giving access to the air compressor and reservoir.

The front registration number plate was mounted centrally on the front panel of the driver's cab immediately above the removable towing hatch.

Karrier W4 445, the forth W delivered, photographed by the Transport Department in 1944. *NCT*

Karrier W4 445, the forth W delivered, photographed by the Transport Department in 1944. *NCT*

452 – 454 Park Royal

There were 2 louvred vane ventilators on each side of the front indicator box, mounted two-thirds of the distance between the outer edge of the box and the extremity of the panel, immediately above the driver's cab windscreen, and one each side above the lower deck saloon side window in bay 1.

A gutter moulding ran along the base of the upper-deck side panels bays 1 – 5 at the joint of the upper and lower deck structure and gave covered drainage from the floor of the upper saloon. There was a small outlet drain above the cab pillar on both sides

The driver's cab windscreen was noticeably deeper than those on the other utility bodies: the lower cream band swept down from the side pillars of the cab some 3 ins at full depth across the front of the vehicle. As compensation the cream band above the lower deck windows was progressively thinner towards the front of the vehicle and there was no middle cream band at all above the windscreen. The outwards opening vent on both sides of the cab immediately beneath the waistline was mounted horizontally.

Top hinged access doors were fitted at the base of the lower-deck nearside panels in bays 1 and 2, giving access to the battery cradle and shunt field resistance respectively, and on the offside panels in bay 2, giving access to the air compressor.

The front registration number plate was mounted centrally almost two-thirds of the way up the removable towing hatch.

455 – 458 Weymann

Half-drop openers with central gripper fixed to the top rail of the upper pane were fitted to the side windows in bay 2 of the upper deck and bay 3 of the lower-deck offside, and bay 2 of the upper and lower deck nearside.

The main traction power cable descended the front nearside pillar of bay 1.

Top hinged access doors were fitted at the base of the lower-deck nearside panels in bays 1 and 2, giving access to the battery cradle and shunt field resistance respectively, and on the offside panels in bay 2, giving access to the air compressor.

The front registration number plate was mounted centrally almost at the base of the removable towing hatch.

459 – 465 Roe

The bodywork featured a deeply domed roof and deep lower deck waistrail built on a teak frame.

Half-drop openers with central gripper fixed to the top rail of the upper pane were fitted to the side windows in bay 2 on the nearside of both decks and bay 3 on the offside of both decks.

There were 6 horizontal ducts at the base of the upper-deck side panels fitted centrally in bays 1 – 5 and towards the rear of the panel above the driver's cab for drainage and ventilation purposes.

Top hinged access doors were fitted at the base of the lower-deck nearside panels in bay 3, giving access to the battery cradle, and on the offside panels in bay 2, giving access to the air compressor.

The base of the cab door was horizontal, parallel to the lower deck waistband about 1ins below it.

There was a sliding window in the driver's cab rear bulkhead from lower saloon to cab.

The front registration number plate was mounted centrally almost at the base of the removable towing hatch.

466 – 468 Brush

Half-drop openers with central gripper fixed to the top rail of the upper pane were fitted to the side windows in bays 1, 3, 5 nearside and bays 1, 3, 4 offside of the upper deck and bays 2, 4 of both sides of the lower-deck. Single rear window to the upper saloon which provided the emergency exit. Curved roof domes.

Roe bodied Karrier W 466 in Stanhope Street, which had gained a rubber mounted destination window in 1954. The vehicle was sold to the Nottingham Trolleybus Group in 1962 and is now at Sandtoft Transport Centre. *BTS*

Roof-mounted trunking, which protected the main power cables, was visible leading to the wide offside front pillar to bay 1.

In the cantrail above the lower saloon windows in bays 1, 3, 5 on both sides there were a series of 6 louvred ventilation vents slanting rearwards somewhat from the vertical at the top. Four small louvred ventilator vents were fitted in the cream-painted middle band above the top of the driver's cab windscreen.

Top hinged access doors were fitted at the base of the lower-deck nearside panel in bay 3, giving access to the battery cradle, and on the offside panels in bay 2, giving access to the air compressor.

The base of the cab door descended rearwards at an angle from the lower cream-painted band to a position about 4ins from the rear of the door thereafter the base, beneath the cab door handle, was horizontal, parallel to the lower deck waistband and about 5ins below it.

The front registration number plate was mounted centrally halfway up the removable towing hatch.

Lighting:

External lighting was 2 headlights towards the top of the front panel, surmounted by 2 front side lights on the lower cream-painted band for all body designs except 455-458 which had a narrower cream-painted band beneath the driver's windscreen and thus the side lights were on the main panel although essentially in the same position.

At the rear there was a single rear light and a brake light mounted towards the bottom of the rear offside lower-deck panel or fitted behind a small access panel, immediately above the square offside registration number plate (where fitted), which also illuminated the rear registration number plate immediately beneath.

A spotlight was recessed into the front panel below the nearside headlight; again there were differences between batches, 455-458 and 459-465 having the spotlight placed somewhat towards the centre line of the vehicle, that on 459-465 being recessed into the removable towing hatch.

Internal lighting was provided by exposed tungsten bulbs fed from the traction current supply except for traction battery equipped 442-445 which used entirely battery power for their lighting circuits. In the lower saloon one light was mounted in the ceiling cove panels of each bay on both the nearside and the offside. In the upper saloon there were also lights in each bay on both sides with additional lights each side over the front seats, that is over the cab, over the rearmost seat and above the staircase, totalling 7 lights each side. There was an additional lamp on the platform.

Internal emergency lighting was provided by means of 2 separate lights on each deck fed from 12-volt batteries stored in a box beneath one of the lower saloon seats. Their location varied:

442-445 No emergency lighting.

452-454 In the lower saloon an emergency light was fitted centrally in the front bulkhead with the other in the offside rear bulkhead. Upstairs an emergency light was provided centrally in the front dome and over the stairwell.

455-458, 459-465, 466-468 In the lower saloon an emergency light was fitted on the nearside in either bay 1 or 2 with the other on the offside in bay 4. Upstairs an emergency light was provided on the nearside in either bay 1 or 2 and on the offside over the stairwell.

All pre-1945 deliveries, that is 442-445, 452-458, were fitted with brackets at the base of the front mudguards for emergency oil or paraffin lights for use when the trolleybuses were parked at the roadside with their trolley booms down.

Seating:

Wooden slatted seats on both decks with green painted pressed steel frames (each body builder having

Sporting upholstered seating and a rubber mounted front indicator box but retaining the original window arrangement 1945 Karrier W/Roe 459 stands at Wilford Bridge terminus on 12 July 1952. *Roy Marshall*

Complete with advertisements on either side of the front indicator box, Karrier W/Roe 459 waits outside the National Laundry at Wilford Bridge terminus. *BTS*

The conductresses chat as two sucessive 40s wait at Wilford Road terminus opposite Colliery Road prior to using the turning circle. An early Vespa motor scooter rushes past. The roads in this area were completely remodelled in 1957-58 for the construction of the Queen's Drive extension along the side of the River Trent and past Clifton Colliery (named after Sir Robert Clifton, the local landowner, who had it 'sunk' circa 1867) and North Wilford Power Station in conjunction with the opening of Clifton Bridge in March 1958. Until the mid 1950s the former Great Central Railway branch from the Queen's Walk goods yard to Clifton Colliery crossed the road on a level crossing just a few yards in front of 466. *Photobus*

Karrier W 468 was experimentally equipped with Metropolitan-Vickers DC fluorescent lighting in both saloons in September 1948. *NCT*

its own design) with the exception of 442-445 which were delivered with brown leathercloth seats and 466-468 which had upholstered green leathercloth seats.

The lower saloon had a 3-person inwards-facing bench seat on each side over the rear axle and 5 rows of forwards-facing double seats. The upper saloon had 7 rows of double seats on the offside and 8 rows on the nearside, the eighth seat at the rear of the upper saloon above the open platform also accommodating 2 passengers.

The driver's seat had pleated squab and backs in green hide leather.

Destination equipment:

A single rectangular indicator box capable of displaying a service number and up to 2 lines of information was mounted centrally at the front on the green-painted panels above the driver's cab windscreen. The vehicles had no indicator boxes at the rear or above the platform. The box had noticeably square corners to match the design of the windows. The indicator blinds were printed with the service number to the left of the information, the number being as deep as the two lines of information.

There were differences in the positioning of the front indicator box on the green-painted front panels above the driver's cab windscreen between batches and body builder:

442-445 Weymann fitted a large rectangular indicator box 36½ins x 20ins capable of displaying a service number and up to 4 lines of information (2in large lettering, 2in smaller lettering) centrally on the panel, as used in Weymann-bodied Sunbeam MF2s 447-451. These were masked off to conform to the standard wartime blind before entering service.

452-454 Park Royal placed the box at the base of the panel

455-458 Weymann placed the box towards the top of the front panel

459-465 Roe mounted the box halfway up the front panel

466-468 Brush placed the box towards the top of the front panel

Internal Livery:

White ceilings and cove panels. The windows were surrounded by varnished wood frames with green panels below. Cork tiling floors. Grey platform.

External Livery:

Delivered in Livery 6 (see Appendix C).

As the war in Europe was over and lighting restrictions had come to an end at the time of their delivery, 466-468 never received white painted mudguards, lifeguard rail or front and rear panels.

Subsequent alterations:

Red reflectors were fitted at the same height as the rear light about halfway up the rear panel beneath the platform window, at the outer extremities of the panel, in 1954.

Leather upholstered seats on tubular frames, mainly with chrome plated top rails although some had "torpedo-shaped" grabs towards the aisle from withdrawn 1936/37 motorbuses, replaced the original wooden slatted seats on both decks of the following vehicles:

452 May 1950, 453 date unknown, 454 January 1950, 455 August 1949, 456 July 1949, 457 June 1949, 458 November 1949, 459 June 1949, 460 February 1958 , 461 February 1958, 462 November 1953, 463 October 1952, 464 August 1949 and 465 October 1949

It is recorded that the fitting of upholstered seats to 452-454, 457 increased their unladen weight to 8 tons 1 cwt 1 qtr and 459 increased to 7 tons 9 cwts 2 qtrs. As 453 was the first wartime trolleybus to be withdrawn from service it is possible that it was never re-seated.

The Roe bodied vehicles (459-465) except 459 and 461 were fitted with additional half-drop windows in both upper and lower deck saloons before entering service in 1945, the layout being as follows:

Original configuration

	Nearside (bay)	Offside (bay)
Upper deck	2. 3.	
Lower deck	2. 3.	

Fleet No: .	Nearside (bay)	Offside (bay)
459 Upper deck	2.	3.
459 Lower deck	2.	3.
Note: Retained original configuration until withdrawal.		
460 Upper deck	2. 4.	1. 3.
460 Lower deck	2. 4.	1. 3.
Note: Sliding windows, not half-drop, fitted.		
461 Upper deck	2. 4.	1. 3.
461 Lower deck	2. 4.	1. 3.
Note: Retained original configuration until refurbished 02.1958		
462 Upper deck	2. 4.	1. 3.
462 Lower deck	2. 4.	2. 4.
463 Upper deck	2. 4.	1. 3.
463 Lower deck	2. 4.	1. 3.
464 Upper deck	2. 4.	1. 3.
464 Lower deck	2. 4.	1. 3.
465 Upper deck	2. 4.	1. 3.
465 Lower deck	2. 4.	1. 3.

Brown linoleum replaced the cork tiling floors in the gangways in both saloons, cork being retained between the forwards facing seats.

By 1947, 467, and by 1948, 459, had been equipped with a small wooden service number box at the top of the lower saloon nearside window bay 5 but these were removed at an early date.

To conform with the rest of the trolleybus fleet and to combat water-ingress from the original indicator boxes, the following vehicles had their front destination indicator boxes rebuilt and rear ones fitted in the upper deck panels above the rear platform window, both being rubber-mounted, on the dates shown:

Fleet No.	Front	Rear
442	07/1950	07/1950
444	10/1950	10/1950
445	06/1951	06/1951
454	date unknown	06/1952
Note. Louvres over windscreen removed		
457	date unknown	04/1953
458	02/1952	02/1952
459	date unknown	06/1952
460	date unknown	1952
461	original style	date unknown
462	date unknown	11/1953
463	date unknown	09/1952
464	original style	date unknown
465	date unknown	date unknown
466	date unknown	02/1954

The final, post-1960 destination box layout on individual vehicles (2 line displays with service number on the left-hand side) was:

Fleet No:		
444	Front	Rubber-mounted ⅔rds up panel
	Rear	Rubber-mounted ⅔rds up panel
454	Front	Rubber-mounted bottom of panel. Vents each side removed.
	Rear	Rubber-mounted at top of panel.
457	Front	Rubber-mounted in middle of panel
	Rear	Rubber-mounted ⅓rd up panel
459	Front	Rubber-mounted in middle of panel
	Rear	Rubber-mounted at top of panel
460	Front	Rubber-mounted in middle of panel
	Rear	Rubber-mounted in middle
461	Front	Original style (square in middle of panel)
	Rear	Rubber-mounted ⅔rds up panel
462	Front	Rubber-mounted in middle of panel
	Rear	Rubber-mounted in middle
463	Front	Rubber-mounted in middle of panel
	Rear	Rubber-mounted in middle
464	Front	Original style (square in middle of panel)
	Rear	Rubber-mounted in middle
465	Front	Rubber-mounted in middle of panel
	Rear	Rubber-mounted in middle
466	Front	Rubber-mounted in middle of panel
	Rear	Rubber-mounted in middle

It is understood that the vehicles were never equipped with semaphore arm illuminated traffic indicators. Later flashing trafficators were mounted on the lower deck waistband immediately behind the driver's cab doors on the cream band below the lower deck side windows from 1954

Two types were used the Klaxon "Edinburgh" plain rectangular type made from transparent orange plastic material with rounded top and bottom mouldings, 2 bulbs and a pressed steel base plate with a lip into which the cover slid, and, more frequently the Ericsson type made from a thicker orange plastic material with rounded ends, 3 protrusions on the side of the moulded body to accommodate the 3 bulbs and two visible fixing screws (between the protrusions) securing it to a cast metal base. The Klaxon "Edinburgh" type fitted neatly between the lower and upper beading of the cream band but the Ericsson type were longer necessitating the removal of part of the lower beading to accommodate the additional length.

Due to early withdrawals, not all these trolleybuses received flashing trafficators, however at least the following vehicles were so equipped: 444, 454, 457-466

442 was fitted with a B4 armature, removed from 393, on 3 May 1945.

444 was fitted with a B4 armature on 10 November 1945.

452-458 were fitted with English Electric EE410 120 hp motors and had their regenerative control removed in 1949.

Interior view of the upper saloon of Karrier W 466, showing the newly fitted rear dome. *Rod Bramley*

455 was fitted with trolley poles having special PCV insulation in September 1949.

457 received vertically-mounted rectangular front sidelights, as used on the BUT9641Ts, prior to 1960.

459 received BIC trolley heads in October 1945.

466 received a new rear dome and upper saloon single rear window (emergency exit) as late as May 1961. The upper deck rear panels and rubber-mounted rear destination box which had been fitted in the 1950s were replaced at the same time and the whole rear area repainted.

Notes:

In 1934 Karrier Motors Ltd. had been rescued from receivership by Humber Ltd. and had thus become part of the Rootes Group, as was Sunbeam Commercial Vehicles Ltd. When the Ministry of War Transport authorised the construction of a limited number of utility trolleybuses orders were placed either with Karrier at Luton or Sunbeam at Wolverhampton. The resultant W vehicles were however identical, incorporating features of the pre-war Karrier E4 and Sunbeam MF2 two axle trolleybus.

The term "utility" was not an official description as applied to vehicles and bodies built in the war, both "utility" and "austerity" being terms then in general use to describe any article, from furniture through to railway engines, made in this period that were not to peace time standards. The specification for "utility bodywork" was drawn up by the National Federation of Vehicle Trades (NFVT) in conjunction with operators, the MoS and the MoWT, and was titled "General Works Specification for Standard Double Deck Bodywork (or Standard Single Deck Bodywork) of Wartime Design and Construction as approved by the Ministries of Supply and War Transport". There were written specifications, general arrangement drawings and more specific drawings, for example covering the "wooden slatted seat", issued at varying times during the period 1942 to 1945 by the NFVT. Nottingham's Park Royal utility trolleybus bodies fitted to 452-454 most closely resembled the NFVT general arrangement drawings.

When referring to utility bodies, post-war enthusiasts have on occasion added supplementary terms such as "relaxed specification" or Mark II for those bodies having with rounded domes and upholstered seats but there is no supporting evidence that these terms were ever in official use.

There was never a trolleybus numbered 446 (the registration number GTV46 being used for a Fordson agricultural tractor). Five Weymann bodied utility trolleybuses had been allocated for delivery in 1943 but the allocation was subsequently reduced to four.

The utility bodywork suffered considerably from the use of unseasoned wood, several vehicles being de-licensed early although not regarded as withdrawn:

443 de-licensed 31.10.1953

452 de-licensed 22.02.1954

453 de-licensed 31.03.1952

455 de-licensed 26.10.1955

456 de-licensed 09.05.1954

460 de-licensed 31.10.1953; refurbished, fitted with upholstered seats and reinstated 02.1958

461 de-licensed 31.10.1953; refurbished, fitted with upholstered seats and reinstated 02.1958

465 de-licensed 31.08.1954 but reinstated later (probably after overhaul in 10.1956)

466 de-licensed 29.08.1953 but reinstated later (probably after gaining rubber-mounted rear destination box in 02.1954)

467 de-licensed 31.10.1955

468 de-licensed 04.01.1955

The following de-licensed trolleybuses were stored at Bilborough (motorbus) Garage in the 1950s: 443, 452, 453, 460, 461, 467 with 455, 456, 465 being noted in open storage in the MX yard at Lower Parliament Street in 1954.

Disposal:

442, 445, 458 sold to Mrs J. Lyman, Barnsley, Yorkshire, in May 1960.

443, 452 sold to Black Bank Salvage Co., Doncaster, Yorkshire, in December 1959.

444 sold to R.W. Dunsmore, 32 Albert Drive, Larkhall, Lanarkshire, in April 1963.

453, 468 sold to Mrs J. Lyman, Barnsley, Yorkshire, in May 1959.

454, 457, 462, 464, 465 sold to R.W. Dunsmore, 32 Albert Drive, Larkhall, Lanarkshire, in May 1963.

455, 456 sold to Black Bank Salvage Co., Doncaster, Yorkshire, in November 1959.

459, 463 sold to C. Hoyle, Wombwell, Yorkshire, in September 1963.

460, 461 sold to Nottingham Scrap Metal Co., Plimsole Street, Nottingham, in August 1965 (broken up by Star Car Dismantlers, Dunkirk, Nottingham).

466 sold to the Nottingham Trolleybus Group for preservation in October 1962. It was initially stored at Gunthorpe, Nottinghamshire.

467 sold to Black Bank Salvage Co., Doncaster, Yorkshire, in November 1959.

469 - 478 Karrier W

1946 Karrier W/Park Royal 474 stands in Stanhope Street opposite the entrance to Parliament Street Depot with the service number indicator above the open rear platform and the double front advertisement panels above the driver's cab. *Fred York*

Chassis:	Two axle wartime utility type Karrier W marketed by Commer-Karrier, Biscot Road, Luton, Bedfordshire and manufactured by Karrier Motors Ltd. at the Sunbeam trolleybus factory, Moorfield Road, Wolverhampton. Karrier drawing CB219 dated 13 March 1944. NCT drawing 7/15.
Motor:	British Thomson-Houston BTH 207 A3 (85 hp at 550 volts)
Electrical equipment:	British Thomson-Houston Co. Ltd., Rugby, Warwickshire.
Dewirement indicator:	Single Urcol line-lights and buzzer (assumed fitted from new).
Brakes:	Westinghouse compressed air, hand and rheostatic brakes Ransomes Type A500 compressor motors.
Body:	Park Royal UH30/26R
Length:	26ft
Width:	7ft 6ins
Wheelbase:	16ft 3ins
Wheel track:	front 6ft 6ins, rear 5ft 9¼ins
Unladen weight:	7tons 10cwts 1qtr
Tyres:	front wheels 36 X 8ins; rear wheels 9.00 X 20ins: later 9.00 x 20ins all round.

The Ministry of War Transport allocated the vehicles and their component parts.

469 - 478 Karrier W4

No.	Registration	Chassis	Chassis No.	Body	Body No.	Registered	Into Service	Withdrawn	Sold
469	HAU169	Karrier W4	50267	Park Royal	B31672	30.01.1946	01.02.1946	31.03.1965	17.07.1965
470	HAU170	Karrier W4	50268	Park Royal	B31673	30.01.1946	01.02.1946	30.06.1963	04.09.1963
471	HAU171	Karrier W4	50269	Park Royal	B31674	30.01.1946	11.02.1946	31.03.1965	17.07.1965
472	HAU172	Karrier W4	50270	Park Royal	B31675	30.01.1946	01.02.1946	10.1959	29.12.1960
473	HAU173	Karrier W4	50271	Park Royal	B31676	30.01.1946	02.02.1946	30.11.1962	15.05.1963
474	HAU174	Karrier W4	50272	Park Royal	B31677	30.01.1946	02.02.1946	10.1959	29.12.1960
475	HAU175	Karrier W4	50273	Park Royal	B31678	28.02.1946	02.03.1946	30.11.1962	09.05.1963
476	HAU176	Karrier W4	50274	Park Royal	B31679	28.02.1946	09.03.1946	30.11.1962	17.05.1963
477	HAU177	Karrier W4	50275	Park Royal	B31680	22.03.1946	20.04.1946	30.11.1962	06.05.1963
478	HAU178	Karrier W4	50276	Park Royal	B31681	22.03.1946	26.03.1946	31.03.1965	17.07.1965

Chassis:

Standard basic wartime chassis.

See 459-468.

Chassis length:

25ft 7ins

Chassis frame width:

front 3ft 3⅞ins, rear 3ft 8ins

Overall width (over tyres):

7ft 5⅝ins

These chassis made up the 4th MoWT allocation.

Electrics:

BTH controller, Rheostatic Brake Co. resistances and CAV dynamo.

No traction battery manoeuvring equipment.

Brecknell Willis lightweight trolleybases.

See 459-468.

Brakes: Westinghouse compressed air, hand and rheostatic brakes.

See 459-468.

Bodywork:

Composite five-bay highbridge utility construction,

enclosed forwards-ascending half-turn (90°) staircase with conventional semi-vestibuled open platform entrance and exit at the rear, and exposed trolley gantry, designed to a relaxed Ministry of Supply wartime specification and built by Park Royal Coachworks Ltd., Abbey Road, Park Royal, Willesden, London NW10 (although Brush had originally been the authorised builder). Conventional curved roof domes.

Metal louvres were fitted above the upper and lower deck saloon side windows, and above the upper deck front windows. Half-drop openers with grippers at the centre of the top rail of the upper pane or drop light were fitted to the side windows in bays 1, 3 and 5 of the nearside and bays 1, 3 and 4 of the offside of the upper deck, and bays 2 and 3 on both sides of the lower deck. The drop light dropped outside the fixed lower pane.

Top hinged access doors were fitted at the base of the lower-deck nearside panel in bay 3, giving access to the battery cradle, and on the offside panels in bay 2, giving access to the air compressor.

Brackets or extensions were bolted to the roof rail immediately above the upper-deck body pillars between bays 1 and 2, and bays 2 and 3 to support the two girders of the exposed trolley gantry which was mounted above bay 2, and not in direct contact with the roof. All platform, saloon (except for the lower saloon ceiling-mounted longitudinal handrails which were black) and staircase handrails and stanchions were white although it is believed that some were finished in black in the early 1950s.

There were pull-in ventilators at the top of the upper saloon front windows. Immediately above the lower deck side windows in bay 1, rearwards sloping louvred ventilators were positioned in the ventilator panel or cantrail on both sides of the trolleybus. Roof mounted ventilators on both sides above bays 3 and 5. At the rear of the upper saloon there was a bottom hinged emergency exit door incorporating two square windows which also provided access to the trolley gantry and could be retained open by leather covered chains on each side.

The windows were all surrounded internally by varnished wood frames. The driver's cab was equipped with a single opening windscreen on the offside equipped with a top-mounted windscreen wiper whilst the nearside windscreen had a bottom-mounted wiper. The frame of the opening pane had radiused upper corners. There was a front hinged cab door on the offside only equipped with a sliding "signalling" window in the lower half of the pane and an inset opening handle. Above the driver's cab windscreen at the same height as the base of the indicator box, a metal plate with two small horizontal louvred ventilator vents was fitted each side at the extremities of the front upper deck panel.

The driver's cab windscreen, like that in Park Royal bodied 452-454 was noticeably deeper than those on other manufacturer's utility bodies. The lower cream band swept down from the side pillars of the cab about 1½ins at full depth across the front of the vehicle. As compensation the middle cream-painted band above the door and side windows to the driver's cab was progressively thinner towards the front of the vehicle and there was no middle cream band at all above the windscreen. The base of the cab door curved over the front wheel arch to a position about 4ins from the rear of the door thereafter the base, beneath the cab door handle, was horizontal, parallel to the cream-painted and about 5ins below it. There was a large green-painted wooden contactor cabinet on the nearside of the driver's cab with a removable panel in the nearside of the front bulkhead to give access to the rear.

The front registration number plate was mounted centrally in the lower half of the removable towing hatch. There were 2 glazed panels in the bulkhead behind the driver with a wide central pillar. Circular driver's rear view mirrors were mounted externally towards the top of the front cab pillars. A removable panel extended across the front of the cab slightly narrower than the distance between the two headlamps but it had no ventilation vanes.

A high-mounted step was let into the base of the bay 1 side panel, but without any form of protection to the bodywork, immediately behind the front axle, on the offside. The offside front wheel was equipped with a large step ring which served as a wheel nut protector.

There was a used ticket box below the nearside vestibule window on the rear platform. A bamboo trolley retrieval pole was carried within the lower-saloon nearside body panels at waist rail height with a tube access from the rear platform vestibule. The conductor had a locker on the rear platform under the stairs.

There was a single lifeguard rail on each side extending between the front and rear axles.

Lighting:

External lighting was 2 headlights towards the top of the front panel, surmounted by 2 large front side lights on the lower cream-painted band and encroaching onto the main green-painted front panel.

At the rear there was a single rear light fitted behind a small access panel towards the bottom of the rear offside lower-deck panel, immediately above the square offside registration number plate, which also illuminated the rear registration number plate immediately beneath. A single brake light was fitted above the rear light.

A spotlight was recessed into the front panel below the nearside headlight but about 2ins closer to the centre line of the vehicle.

Internal lighting was provided by exposed tungsten bulbs fed from the traction current supply. In the lower saloon one light was mounted in the ceiling cove panels evenly distributed in bays 1, 2, 3, 5 on both the nearside and the offside (4 fittings each side) with an additional light on the platform. In the upper saloon there were lights in each bay on both sides (5 fittings each side) with an additional light over the stairwell.

Internal emergency lighting was provided by means of 2 separate lights on each deck fed from the chassis-mounted batteries. In the lower saloon an emergency light was fitted centrally in the front bulkhead with the other in the offside rear bulkhead. Upstairs an emergency light was provided centrally in the front dome and over the stairwell.

Seating:

Based on green painted tubular steel frames with chromium-plated top and integrated grab handles (on each side of the seat back). Squabs and backs were upholstered in green leathercloth with pleated squabs and plain backs, each seat back being individually "framed", in the upper saloon, and pleated squabs and backs on the forwards-facing seats in the lower saloon. The backs of the bench seats were in one piece (each seat back being individually "framed"). The seat backs were covered with scratchproof patterned Rexine and there was a cigarette stubber mounted centrally on the back of each forwards-facing seat.

The lower saloon had a 3-person inwards-facing bench seat on each side over the rear axle and 5 rows of forwards-facing double seats. The upper saloon had 7 rows of double seats on the offside and 8 rows on the nearside, the eighth seat at the rear of the upper saloon above the open platform also accommodating 2 passengers. The driver's seat had pleated squab and backs in green hide leather.

Destination equipment:

A single rectangular indicator box capable of displaying a service number and up to 2 lines of information was mounted centrally towards the base of the upper deck front panels above the driver's cab windscreen and above the rear platform window. A square service number box was mounted on the nearside immediately above the rear open platform entrance, towards the rear of the central stanchion. The boxes had noticeably square corners to match the design of the windows. The indicator blinds were printed with the service number to the left of the information, the number being as deep as the two lines of information.

Internal Livery:

White ceilings and cove panels. The windows were surrounded by varnished wood frames with green panels below. Cork tiling floors. Grey platform floor.

External Livery:

In Livery 6 but without white edging (see Appendix C).

Subsequent alterations:

Red reflectors were fitted at the same height as the rear light about halfway up the rear panel beneath the platform window, at the outer extremities of the panel, in 1954.

To combat water-ingress from the original indicator boxes, at an unknown date in the early 1950s 470, 473, 474 had their front destination indicator boxes rebuilt and rubber-mounted. The indicator box was moved slightly higher on the front upper-deck panel, mounted in rubber with rounded corners. The two small horizontal ventilator vents were not replaced. 472, 477 also had their front destination indicator boxes rebuilt and rubber-mounted but retained the two small horizontal ventilator vents. All others retained their original indicator boxes and vents.

At withdrawal, the destination indicator box situation of each vehicle was thus:

Fleet No.	Front	Rear
469	Original style	Original style
Retained front vents		
470	Rubber-mounted	Rubber-mounted
Vents removed		
471	Original style	Original style
Retained front vents		
472	Rubber-mounted	Not known
Retained front vents		
473	Rubber-mounted	Not Known
Vents removed		
474	Rubber mounted	Not known
Vents removed		
475	Original style	Original style
Retained front vents		
476	Original style	Original style
Retained front vents		
477	Rubber-mounted	Rubber-mounted
Retained front vents		
478	Original style	Original style
Retained front vents		

The Park Royal utility bodywork suffered considerably from the use of unseasoned wood, several vehicles being de-licensed early although not regarded as withdrawn:

472 de-licensed by 31.12.1958
474 de-licensed by 30.04.1959
475 date not known
476 de-licensed 31.08.1954
478 de-licensed 31.08.1954

NCT gave 477 a thorough body overhaul at Trent Bridge Works in 1957 but contracted G.C. Smith, Long Whatton, Loughborough to carry out similar overhauls on 469-471 and 478 in 1958, and 473, 475, 476 in 1959.

During these body overhauls the layout of the half-drop windows in many of the vehicles was rebuilt as follows:

Original configuration

	Nearside (bay)	Offside (bay)
Upper deck	1. 3. 5.	1.3..4.
Lower deck	2.3.	2.3.
Fleet No:	Nearside (bay)	Offside (bay)
469 Upper deck	1. 3. 5.	1. 3.4.
469 Lower deck	1. 3.	2. 4.

470 Upper deck	1. 3. 5.	1. 3.4.
470 Lower deck	1. 3.	2. 4.

Notes: Front upper deck windows rubber mounted with no ventilators.

471 Upper deck	1. 3. 5.	1. 3.4.
471 Lower deck	2.3.	2.3.

Notes: Only one of series to retain original window configuration.

472 Upper deck	1. 3. 5.	Not known
472 Lower deck	2.3.	Not known

Notes: Last operated in 1958 and officially withdrawn in 1959.

473 Upper deck	Not known.	1. 3.4.
473 Lower deck	Not known	2. 4.

Notes: Front upper deck windows rubber mounted with no ventilators.

474 Upper deck	1. 3. 5.	Not known
474 Lower deck	2.3.	Not known

Notes: Withdrawn 1959.

475 Upper deck	Not known	1. 3.4.
475 Lower deck	Not known	2. 4.
476 Upper deck	1. 3. 5.	1. 3.4.
476 Lower deck	1. 3.	2. 4.
477 Upper deck	1. 3. 5.	1. 3.4.
477 Lower deck	1. 3.	2. 4.
478 Upper deck	1. 3. 5.	1. 3.4.
478 Lower deck	1. 3.	2. 4.

Nos. 472, 474 were not reconstructed and withdrawn early.

The rearwards sloping louvred ventilators above the lower deck side windows in bay 1 were replaced later with square hooded ventilators on those vehicles rebuilt by G.C. Smith.

The front upper-deck windows in 470 and 473 were replaced with rubber mounted fixed panes excluding an opening ventilator. It is assumed that this was carried out during their body reconstruction at Smith's.

Flashing trafficators were mounted on the lower cream-painted band immediately behind the driver's cab doors on the cream band below the lower deck side windows from 1954 (the vehicles were never equipped with semaphore arm illuminated traffic indicators). All these trolleybuses eventually received flashing indicators. See 442-445, 452-468 for details on the types of trafficators used.

475 was equipped with Metropolitan-Vickers automatic acceleration equipment in late 1947

476 was equipped in October 1946 with the first all-electric automatic acceleration equipment to be fitted in the United Kingdom, manufactured by British Thomson-Houston, and in October 1947 with Metropolitan-Vickers DC fluorescent lighting.

477 was equipped with BTH automatic acceleration equipment in July 1948.

478 was equipped with BTH automatic acceleration equipment and Metropolitan-Vickers fluorescent lighting in September 1948.

During refurbishment, the fluorescent lighting in 476 and 478 was replaced by standard tungsten lighting.

Brown linoleum replaced the cork tiling floors in the gangways in both saloons, cork being retained between the forwards facing seats.

Only one vehicle in this batch, 478, received the revised undertaking title transfers introduced with Livery 8 when it received a partial lower panel repaint in spring 1964 incorporating the two-line fleet title.

478 was fitted with convex lamp glasses with an adaptor ring to permit fitment into the original headlamp mounting during overhaul and repaint in December 1961.

Disposal:

469, 471, 478 sold to Nottingham Scrap Metal Co., Plimsole Street, Nottingham, in July 1965 (broken up by Star Car Dismantlers, Dunkirk, Nottingham).

470 sold to C. Hoyle, Wombwell, Yorkshire, in September 1963.

472, 474 sold to A. Smith, Nottingham, in December 1960.

473, 475-477 sold to R.W. Dunsmore, 32 Albert Drive, Larkhall, Lanarkshire, in May 1963.

447 – 451 Sunbeam MF2

Sunbeam MF2 450, the first of the batch to be delivered, posed when brand new and demonstrating the initial wartime livery. *NCT*

Chassis: Two axle type Sunbeam MF2 manufactured by Sunbeam Commercial Vehicles Ltd. (part of the Rootes Group), Moorfield Road, Wolverhampton, built as part of an export order for 25 vehicles for Johannesburg Municipal Tramways placed in 1939. Sunbeam drawing CB194 dated 7 October 1939. NCT drawing 7/75.
Motor: British Thomson-Houston Co. Ltd., Rugby, Warwickshire. Type BTH 206 E1 (103 hp at 550 volts) compound-wound for regenerative control.
Electrical equipment: British Thomson-Houston Co. Ltd., Rugby, Warwickshire.
Dewirement indicator: Assumed to have been equipped with buzzer and line-lights.
Brakes: Regenerative and hand brakes.
Body: Weymann UH30/26R. Weymann drawing V2272 (undated). NCT drawing 11/10.
Length: 25ft 10¾ins
Width: 7ft 10ins
Height: 15ft 3ins to the top of the trolley bases.
Wheelbase: 16ft 3ins
Wheel track: front 6ft 11½ins, rear 5ft 10½ins
Unladen weight: 8tons 1cwt 3qtrs
Tyres: front wheels 10.50 X 22ins; rear wheels 9.75 X 22ins.

447 - 451 Sunbeam MF2

No.	Registration	Chassis	Chassis No.	Body	Body No.	Registered	Into Service	Withdrawn	Sold
447	GTV47	Sunbeam MF2	13082	Weymann	7728	01.10.1942	03.10.1942	31.01.1958	26.11.1959
448	GTV48	Sunbeam MF2	13083	Weymann	7729	01.10.1942	04.10.1942	16.07.1958	05.05.1960
449	GTV49	Sunbeam MF2	13084	Weymann	7730	01.10.1942	05.10.1942	31.10.1958	05.05.1960
450	GTV50	Sunbeam MF2	13085	Weymann	7731	05.09.1942	01.10.1942	11.1957	27.05.1959

Chassis:

Constructed for export to accommodate an 8ft wide body. There is a note on the Sunbeam drawing that the chassis length was to be "cut off to suit body".

Chassis length:

26ft 1ins

Chassis frame width:

front 3ft 3⅞ins, rear 3ft 8ins

Overall width (over front tyres):

front 7ft 11⅜ins

The differential was offset to the nearside of the rear axle.

Electrics:

The traction motor was centrally mounted, that is about halfway along the chassis, between the chassis frame offset to the nearside matching the offset differential. BTH controller. The contactor switchgear was mounted on a single panel in a cabinet on the rear wall of the driver's cab, with the braking contactor at the front of the cab. The master controller was under the driver's seat. There were three banks of resistances on the offside external face of the chassis frame. The shunt field resistance was mounted transversally between the chassis frames ahead of the motor.

Brecknell Willis lightweight trolleybases.

There was a dynamo on the commutator end of the traction motor.

Brakes:

The air brake compressor and reservoir were fixed to the external face of the chassis nearside. There was one air-brake cylinder each side on top of the king pin (steering joint) and one cylinder attached to each side of the chassis cross member ahead of the rear axle. Air brake governor in the driver's cab.

The handbrake lever was located to the offside of the driver's steering column.

Bodywork:

Composite five-bay highbridge double-deck utility construction, enclosed forwards-ascending half-turn (90°) staircase with conventional semi-vestibuled open platform entrance and exit at the rear, designed to Ministry of Supply specifications and built by Weymann Motor Bodies Ltd., Addlestone, Surrey. In order to optimise the use of available materials and reduce the amount of labour required, hardwoods were only used for the main body framing, the longitudinal rails being of pitch pine. Exterior panelling, including the roof, was of 20-gauge SWG steel whilst panels were shaped rather than beaten resulting in noticeably angular roof domes.

Brackets or extensions were bolted to the roof rail immediately above the upper-deck body pillars between bays 1 and 2, and bays 2 and 3 to support the two girders of the exposed trolley gantry which was mounted above bay 2, and not in direct contact with the roof. Platform handrails and stanchions, and horizontal handrails in the saloons were white.

Metal louvres were fitted above the upper and lower deck saloon side windows, and above the upper deck front widows. Sliding openers were fitted to the side windows in bay 2 of the upper deck and lower deck on the nearside, and bay 4 of the upper and lower deck on the offside. There were pull-in ventilators at the top of the upper saloon front windows. The cantrail or vent panel featured a row of 12 almost vertical louvres, sloping slightly to the rear at the top, above the lower deck windows in bays 1, 3 and 5 on both sides. A row of 3 similar louvres was placed in the cantrail above the nearside driver's cab window towards the rear. There were roof-mounted ventilators above bays 1 and 5. The main traction power cable descended the front nearside pillar of bay 1.

An unglazed rear panel provided the bottom-hinged emergency exit to the upper saloon. Top hinged access doors were fitted at the base of the lower-deck nearside panels in bays 1, probably giving access to the battery cradle, and 3, giving access to the air compressor; and on the offside panels in bays 1 – 3, giving access to the resistance banks.

The driver's cab was equipped with a single opening windscreen on the offside equipped with a top-mounted windscreen wiper whilst the nearside windscreen had a bottom-mounted wiper. The frame of the opening pane had radiused corners. Three small ventilator vents were fitted at the base of the cream-painted middle band mounted centrally above the top of each pane of the driver's cab windscreen.

There was a front hinged cab door on the offside only equipped with a sliding "signalling" window in the lower half of the pane and an inset opening handle. The base of the cab door was curved over the wheel arch to a position about 4ins from the rear of the door thereafter the base, beneath the cab door handle, was horizontal, parallel to the waistband and about 1ft below it.

The upper edge of the driver's cab side windows was inclined from the rear to align with the top of the windscreen whilst the upper edge of the moulding edging the cream band beneath the side windows curved downwards again to align with the base of the windscreen. There were 2 glazed panels in the bulkhead behind the driver with a wide central pillar. Circular driver's rear view mirrors were mounted externally towards the top of the front cab pillars. A large and deep removable panel, without ventilation vanes, extended across the front of the cab from a position just inboard of the headlamps about one-third of the way up the headlamps. A triangular Sunbeam maker's badge was fitted centrally on and slightly below the lower cream-painted beneath the driver's windscreen. The front registration number plate was mounted centrally at the base of the removable towing hatch on the front panel of the driver's cab.

Sunbeam MF2/Weymann 451 pulled up hard against the kerb, at Southwell Road outside Parliament Street Depot with one of the Avenues of Sneinton Market visible in the background. *NCT*

A step was let into the base of the bay 1 side panel, but without any form of protection to the bodywork, immediately behind the front axle, on the offside. The offside front wheel was equipped with a step ring and it is believed that a mileometer was mounted on the nearside front hub (but not used) of some vehicles.

Ceiling-mounted handrails extended above the longitudinal seats at the rear of the lower saloon. There were also upright stanchions in both saloons, those in the lower saloon being attached to seat 3 nearside and seats 1, 5 offside.

In the lower saloon there were 2 bell pushes in the ceiling located in bay 2 and bay 4 on the offside. There were also 2 bell pushes in the upper saloon located on the offside cantrail in bay 3 and bay 5, that is at the top of the stairs. On the rear platform there was a further bell push on the offside of the rear bulkhead adjacent to staircase.

There was a used ticket box below the nearside vestibule window on the rear platform. A bamboo trolley retrieval pole was carried within the lower-saloon nearside body panels at waist rail height with a tube access from the rear platform vestibule. The conductor had a locker on the rear platform under the stairs.

There was a single lifeguard rail on each side extending between the front and rear axles, and a double bumper at the base of the rounded offside rear panel.

Lighting:

These trolleybuses entered service in Nottingham at the time of wartime lighting restrictions. External lighting was 2 headlights half way up the front panel, surmounted by 2 front side lights intruding into the lower narrow cream-painted band beneath the driver's windscreen, with a spotlight recessed into the front panel immediately below the nearside headlight.

At the rear there was a single rear light fitted behind a small access panel, immediately above the square offside registration number plate, which also illuminated the number plate. A single brake light was fitted half way up the rear panel above the rear light.

Brackets were fitted to the base of the front mudguards for emergency oil or paraffin lights for use when the trolleybuses were parked at the roadside with their trolley booms down.

Internal lighting was provided by exposed tungsten bulbs fed from the traction current supply.

In the lower saloon one light was mounted in the ceiling cove panels of each bay on both the nearside and the offside. In the upper saloon there were also lights in each bay on both sides with additional lights each side over the front seats, that is over the cab, over the rearmost seat and above the staircase, totalling 7 lights each side. There was an additional lamp on the platform.

It is assumed that internal emergency lighting was provided by means of 2 separate lights on each deck, one at the front and one at the back, fed from 12-volt batteries stored in a box beneath one of the lower saloon seats.

Seating:

Green leather covered seats on both decks with green painted pressed steel frames.

The lower saloon had a 3-person inwards-facing bench seat on each side over the rear axle and 5 rows of forwards-facing double seats. The upper saloon had 7 rows of double seats on the offside and 8 rows on the nearside, the eighth seat at the rear of the upper saloon above the open platform also accommodating 2 passengers.

The driver's seat had pleated squab and backs in green hide leather.

Destination equipment:

A large rectangular indicator box 36½ins x 20ins capable of displaying a service number and up to 4 lines of information (2 in large lettering, 2 in smaller lettering) was mounted centrally at the front on the upper deck panels above the driver's cab windscreen. There were no other indicator boxes. The box had noticeably square corners to match the design of the windows. The indicator blinds were printed with the service number to the left of the information, the number being half the depth of the box.

Internal Livery:

White ceilings and cove panels. Brown floors.

The windows were all surrounded internally by varnished wood frames

External Livery:

It is believed that these vehicles were delivered in grey primer and finished in Livery 6 (see Appendix C) at Trent Bridge Works.

Subsequent alterations:

The regenerative braking and control system was removed in November 1942, due to high tension light bulbs being "burnt out" on adjacent trolleybuses in rectifier-fed section and reportedly due to an incident on the Wollaton Park section where a current surge damaged traction supply equipment.

The unglazed rear panel making up the emergency exit to the upper saloon was fitted with two square windows.

Red reflectors were fitted at the same height as the rear light about halfway up the panel beneath the rear platform window, at the outer extremities of the panel, in 1954

The original large destination screen apertures of 447-451 were reduced in depth with paint masking to enable what became a standard sized blind to be fitted. To conform with the rest of the trolleybus fleet and to combat water-ingress from the original indicator boxes, 449 had its front destination indicator box rebuilt and a rear one fitted in the upper deck panels above the rear platform window, in January 1951.The boxes were placed towards the top of the front and rear panels and were rubber-mounted. The number of ventilator vents above the driver's cab windscreen was reduced from three to two.

In the early 1950s and possibly during its January 1951 reconstruction, 449 was fitted with semaphore arm illuminated traffic indicators beneath the cab side windows adjacent to the ventilator. There is no evidence that further vehicles received semaphore arm indicators or that any received flashing trafficators. The side lights on 449 were also moved beneath the lower narrow cream-painted band beneath the driver's cab windscreen.

Notes:

The 5 Sunbeam MF2s 447-451 were part of an order of 25 chassis placed in October 1939 by Johannesburg Municipal Transport, South Africa, but which it was felt unwise to export in view of the wartime risks to merchant shipping. Other chassis from this order were diverted to Bradford (10) and St. Helens (10). The chassis were constructed for 8ft wide bodies, six inches wider than legally permitted in the UK at that time and for which the MoT granted a special dispensation for their operation on the Carlton – Wollaton Park service in view of the shortage of vehicles due to the war.

As early examples of utility bodied trolleybuses, the full specification was not closely adhered to by Weymann; indeed, there are a number of discrepancies between the body builders drawing and the finished product, for example sliding instead of half-drop openers fitted in different bays than specified. Certain of these discrepancies could be explained by the unavailability of items due to wartime conditions.

These were the only utility bodied trolleybuses supplied to Nottingham with an unglazed emergency exit to the upper saloon.

The utility bodywork suffered considerably from the use of unseasoned wood, two vehicles being de-licensed early although not regarded as withdrawn:

447 last day in service 03.05.1957

450 last day in service 12.01.1955

Disposal:

447 sold to Black Bank Salvage Co., Doncaster, Yorkshire, in November 1959.

448-451 sold to Mrs J. Lyman, Barnsley, Yorkshire, in May 1960.

Sunbeam MF2 450, posed in an almost pefect offside view, when brand new in September 1942. *NCT*

479 - 482 Karrier W

A brand new Karrier W/Roe 480 poses for the City Transport photographer in 1948. *NCT*

Chassis: Two axle type Karrier W marketed by Commer-Karrier, Biscot Road, Luton, Bedfordshire and manufactured by Karrier Motors Ltd. at the Sunbeam trolleybus factory, Moorfield Road, Wolverhampton. Karrier drawing CB242 dated 13 March 1946. NCT drawing 7/58.

Motor: British Thomson-Houston Co. Ltd., Rugby, Warwickshire. BTH 209 AYG3 (95 hp).
NCT records quoted 103 hp but BTH descriptions were based on 600 volt traction current rather than 550 volts as used in Nottingham.

Electrical equipment: BTH equipped for automatic acceleration.

Dewirement indicator: single Urcol line-lights and buzzer.

Brakes: Westinghouse compressed air, hand and rheostatic brakes

Body: Roe H31/25R.

Length: 26ft

Width: 7ft 6ins

Wheelbase: 16ft 3ins

Wheel track: front 6ft 6ins, rear 5ft 9¼ins

Unladen weight: 7tons 14cwts 0qtrs

Tyres: front wheels 10.50 X 20ins; rear wheels 9.00 X 20ins.

The Ministry of War Transport allocated the chassis.

479 - 482 Karrier W4

No.	Registration	Chassis	Chassis No.	Body	Body No.	Registered	Into Service	Withdrawn	Sold
479	KTV479	Karrier W4	50428	Roe	GO2756	14.07.1948	19.07.1948	31.03.1965	04.08.1965
480	KTV480	Karrier W4	50429	Roe	GO2757	14.07.1948	15.07.1948	31.03.1965	04.08.1965
481	KTV481	Karrier W4	50430	Roe	GO2758	14.07.1948	19.07.1948	31.03.1965	18.08.1965
482	KTV482	Karrier W4	50431	Roe	GO2755	14.07.1948	19.07.1948	31.03.1965	04.08.1965

Chassis:

Standard basic wartime chassis.

See 459-478.

Chassislength:

25ft 7ins

Chassis frame width:

front 3ft 3⅞ins, rear 3ft 8ins

Overall width (over tyres):

7ft 5⅝ins

These chassis made up the 5th and final MoWT allocation (the drawings being marked as applicable for 4 Sunbeams) and were originally expected to have been delivered with MCW metal framed bodies.

Electrics:

See 459-478.

Compound-wound traction motor with rheostatic braking operating in conjunction with the mechanical braking system. The traction motor was mounted between the chassis frames offset to the nearside towards the rear and just ahead of the rear axle. The contactor switchgear was mounted on a single panel on the rear wall of the cab to the nearside of the driver's seat, with the master controller under the driver's seat. There was a removable panel in the nearside of the front bulkhead to give access to the rear of the contactor cabinet.

There was a BTH dynamo on the commutator end of the traction motor. A speedometer of the electrical "tachometer" type was fitted, the generator portion being mounted on and driven from the forward end of the traction motor.

There were two resistance banks between the chassis frames ahead of the motor. The shunt resistance was located beneath the cab. 24-volt batteries for lighting purposes.

BTH controller, Rheostatic Brake Co. resistances and Brecknell Willis lightweight trolleybases.

Automatic acceleration. No battery manoeuvring equipment.

Brakes:

See 459-478.

Westinghouse compressed air, hand and rheostatic brakes. Ransomes Type A500 compressor motors.

The compressor and air reservoir were bolted directly to the offside external face of the chassis frame. There was one air-brake cylinder on top of each king pin and one cylinder attached to each side of the chassis cross-member ahead of the rear axle. Brake valve between chassis frames offset to the offside ahead of the main resistance banks. There was an air brake governor in the cab.

The handbrake lever was to the offside of the driver's steering column.

Bodywork:

Teak framed composite five-bay highbridge double-deck construction, enclosed forwards-ascending half-turn (90°) Roe "safety" staircase with conventional semi-vestibuled open platform entrance and exit at the rear built by Charles H. Roe Ltd., Crossgates, Leeds, Yorkshire. The design was very similar to that used on the BUT 9611Ts 483-495, notable differences being the styling and depth of the cab side windows and the manner in which the profile above the rear platform matched that above the nearside cab windows.

Brackets or extensions were bolted to the roof rail immediately above the upper-deck body pillars between bays 1 and 2, and bays 2 and 3 to support the two girders of the exposed trolley gantry which was mounted above bay 2, and not in direct contact with the roof. Immediately above the rearmost upper-deck window on each side, at the rear end of the roof-mounted catwalk, a roof-mounted bracket secured a transverse rod which extended across much of the width of the vehicle to avoid roof damage when pulling down the trolley poles and stowing them beneath the restraining hooks.

Sliding top light openers were fitted to the side windows in bays 1, 3 and 5 (both sides) of the upper-deck and bays 2-4 (both sides) of the lower-deck. The front upper-deck windows were fixed. The front and side windows of the upper-saloon, and the lower-deck saloon windows were all surmounted by metal louvres. The lower-deck offside rear window was narrower than the others to better accommodate the standard Roe "safety" staircase (which featured a longer flight of 4 steps along the offside of the vehicle, a landing and a short flight of 2 steps to the platform) and a large "orange segment" shaped staircase window behind. There were 7 horizontal ducts at the top of the cantrail for drainage purposes. Top hinged access doors were fitted at the base of the lower-deck nearside panel in bay 3, giving access to the battery cradle, and on the offside panels in bay 2, giving access to the air compressor.

The rear upper deck emergency door had three hinges at its base and a handle at the top offside with two windows. It could be retained open by leather-covered chains on each side. Although all other windows had almost square corners, two panes in the rear upper deck window/emergency exit decreased in depth towards their extremities with heavily radiused outer corners whilst the top of the rear platform window also featured radiused corners. The base of the rear panel was finished with a steel bumper bar whilst there was a double chromium-plated bumper bar around the offside corner panel. The rear registration number plate was about halfway up the rear offside panel. A circular conductor's mirror was fixed in the upper deck rear offside dome at the head of the stairs. All internal, platform and staircase handrails and stanchions were coated in black. There were white ceiling mounted handrails above the lower saloon gangway.

Unlike the BUT9611Ts the base of all glazing in the driver's cab area was aligned with the base of the windows in the lower saloon and middle cream-painted band became narrower at the position of the cab rear bulkhead to accommodate the deeper side windows and windscreen which rose up some 6ins into this band. The upper and lower deck front pillar in line with the driver's cab rear bulkhead was noticeably broader than that on the BUT9611Ts, as, on the offside, it carried the main power cables from the trolley gear. The driver's cab had an offside front-hinged square topped door equipped with a sliding "signalling" window, the upper part of window having a rectangular pane. The nearside driver's cab windows were fixed, the upper rear corner of the larger second pane and the middle cream band above being curved.

There was a single, full-depth offside opening windscreen which had a top-mounted wiper whilst that on the nearside was mounted at the base of the windscreen. An outwards opening vertical vent was positioned on both sides of the cab forward of the door immediately beneath the waistline. A step was let into the base of the off-side bay 1 side panel, a sheet of protective aluminium reaching from this step to the lintel of the driver's cab door, immediately behind the front axle and there was a large step ring on the front offside (only) wheel. There was a large green-painted wooden contactor cabinet on the nearside of the driver's cab.

The upper portion of the wide central panel between the two windows in the driver's cab bulkhead opened into the lower saloon to provide access to the control equipment wiring. Circular driver's rear view mirrors were mounted externally towards the top of the front cab pillars.

A large removable panel which carried the registration plate extended across the front of the cab from beneath the offside to beneath the nearside headlamp but had no ventilation vanes. The Karrier maker's symbol was fitted centrally beneath the driver's windscreen at the top of the lower cream-painted band.

Karrier W/Roe 480 stands just inside the Manvers Street exit on the northernmost road of Parliament Street Depot. Note the bus washer to the left of the second trolleybus.. *MJ Russell*

Karrier W/Roe 480 poses for the City Transport photographer at Middleton Boulevard in 1948. *NCT*

The bodywork featured Roe characteristics of the period such as the swept back front profile, rounded lower window corners but square upper corners to the windows, a rounded front roof dome and offside "orange segment" window to the staircase. The nearside panel and cream-painted middle band rose in a curve from the vestibule above the open rear platform to match the shape of the rear top corner of the nearside driver's cab window.

A single lifeguard ran beneath the side panels between the front and rear axles. A bamboo trolley retrieval pole was carried within the lower-saloon nearside body panels at waist rail height with a tube access from the rear platform vestibule. The conductor had a locker on the rear platform under the stairs.

Lighting:

External lighting was 2 low-set headlights and 2 front side lights on the front panel, the side lights being immediately beneath the lower cream-painted band but slightly more to the extremities of the front panel than the headlights, and a single rear light immediately above the rear registration number plate which also illuminated this plate. A spot light was fitted in the front panel immediately beneath the nearside headlight but marginally closer to the extremity of the front panel. At the rear, on the lower cream-painted band immediately beneath the rear platform window, there was a single inverted triangular panel containing (at the top) trafficators, the fretwork word "STOP" and a single brake light. Semaphore arm illuminated traffic indicators accommodated in a black moulding were fitted to the lower side panels beneath the driver's cab corner pillars immediately above the front mudguards and forwards of the vent, the upper third of the housing encroaching into the lower deck cream-painted waistband.

Internal lighting was provided by tungsten bulbs, provided by tungsten bulbs, behind oblong fluted glass shades 5½ins long and 6¼ins high having a small central inset metal base at the bottom of the glass through which passed a single retaining screw, fed from the 24 volt batteries. In the lower saloon one light was mounted in the ceiling cove panels of each bay on both the nearside and the offside. In the upper saloon there were also lights in each bay on both sides. There was an additional lamp on the platform.

No internal emergency lighting was fitted.

Seating:

Based on painted tubular steel frames with chromium-plated top and integrated grab handles (on each side of the seat back). Squabs and backs were upholstered in green leather (pleated backs and plain squabs).

The lower saloon had a 2-person inwards-facing bench seat on the off-side (due to the intrusion of the straight staircase) and one for 3 persons on the nearside over the rear axle and 5 rows of forwards-facing double seats. The upper saloon had 8 rows of double seats on the off-side and 6 rows on the nearside, with a bench seat at the rear of the upper saloon above the open platform accommodating 3 passengers. The driver's seat was in green leather.

Destination equipment:

Single rectangular indicator boxes 34ins X 10ins capable of displaying a service number and up to 2 lines of information were mounted centrally at the front on the upper-deck front panel above the driver's cab windscreen and at the rear above the rear platform window. A further rectangular indicator box of the same dimensions also displaying a service number and up to 2 lines of information was fitted immediately above the rear open platform entrance, encroaching somewhat forward of the rear pillar bay 5. The front indicator box was mounted half-way up the panel whereas those at the rear and above the platform were mounted in the lower portion of the panel. The boxes had noticeably square corners to match the design of the windows. The indicator blinds were printed with the service number to the left of the information, the number being as deep as the two lines of information.

Internal Livery:

White ceilings, cove panels and bulkheads above the glazing. The windows were surrounded by varnished wood frames with green panels below. Cork tiling floors. Grey platform floor.

Cab area painted medium green with white ceiling.

External Livery:

Delivered in Livery 7 (see Appendix C)

Subsequent alterations:

Red reflectors were fitted on the nearside and offside at the base of the rear panel from 1954.

The semaphore arm illuminated traffic indicators were replaced from 1954 onwards by flashing trafficators mounted on the lower deck cream-painted band immediately behind the driver's cab doors beneath the wide body pillar in line with the cab rear bulkhead. It is believe that the cab side outwards opening vertical vents were removed at this time. See 442-445, 452-468 as to the types of flashing trafficators employed.

One unidentified post-war Roe bodied 2-axle trolleybus was fitted with a double bumper bar across the width of the rear panel. This was removed later together with the rear double bumper bar carried by other vehicles of this batch around the offside corner panel as these snagged the bus washing machines.

Disposal:

479-482 sold to Nottingham Scrap Metal Co., Plimsole Street, Nottingham, breakers, in August 1965 (broken up by Star Car Dismantlers, Dunkirk, Nottingham).

483 – 495 BUT 9611T

Demonstrating the Department's immediate post war Livery style 7 in which it was exhibited at the 1948 Commercial Motor Show, BUT9611T/Roe 493 stands facing north at the Wilford Bridge terminus of service 47. In the backgound, through the ornate gates to Wilford Bridge, can be seen the ex-Great Central Railway girder bridge across the River Trent. *BTS*

Chassis: Two axle type BUT 9611T manufactured by the British United Traction Ltd., Hanover House, 14 Hanover Square, London W1 at Leyland Motor's Ham Works, Kingston upon Thames, Surrey using AEC components. BUT drawing SK10-1416 dated 1 January 1948. NCT drawing 7/60.
Motor: English Electric Ltd., Bradford, Yorkshire Type EE 410/3B (120hp at 550 volts).
Electrical equipment: English Electric.
Dewirement indicator: single Urcol line-light and buzzer.
Brakes: Westinghouse compressed air, hand and rheostatic brakes.
Body: Roe H31/25R.
Length: 26ft
Width 7ft 6ins
Wheelbase: 16ft 4ins
Wheel track: front 6ft 5½ins, rear 5ft 9 3/16ins
Unladen weight: 8tons 5cwt 0qtrs
Tyres: front wheels 11.00 X 20ins; rear wheels 9.00 X 20ins.

483 - 495 BUT 9611T

No.	Registration	Chassis	Chassis No.	Body	Body No.	Registered	Into Service	Withdrawn	Sold
483	KTV483	BUT9611T	050	Roe	GO2784	01/10/1948	01/10/1948	30/09/1963	23/04/1964
484	KTV484	BUT9611T	051	Roe	GO2785	01/10/1948	01/10/1948	31/05/1963	02/09/1963
485	KTV485	BUT9611T	052	Roe	GO2783	01/10/1948	01/10/1948	31/03/1965	02/06/1965
486	KTV486	BUT9611T	053	Roe	GO2786	01/10/1948	01/10/1948	31/03/1965	01/06/1965
487	KTV487	BUT9611T	054	Roe	GO2792	01/10/1948	01/10/1948	31/03/1965	03/06/1965
488	KTV488	BUT9611T	055	Roe	GO2782	01/10/1948	01/10/1948	31/03/1965	29/06/1965
489	KTV489	BUT9611T	056	Roe	GO2790	01/11/1948	01/11/1948	31/03/1965	17/06/1965
490	KTV490	BUT9611T	057	Roe	GO2791	01/11/1948	01/11/1948	31/10/1963	16/04/1964
491	KTV491	BUT9611T	058	Roe	GO2787	01/10/1948	01/10/1948	30/11/1964	15/06/1965
492	KTV492	BUT9611T	059	Roe	GO2788	01/11/1948	01/11/1948	31/03/1965	29/06/1965
493	KTV493	BUT9611T	060	Roe	GO2794	01/11/1948	01/11/1948	31/03/1965	09/07/1965
494	KTV494	BUT9611T	061	Roe	GO2789	01/11/1948	01/11/1948	31/10/1963	20/04/1964
495	KTV495	BUT9611T	062	Roe	GO2793	01/11/1948	01/11/1948	31/03/1965	30/05/1965

Chassis:

The BUT9611T chassis was based on AEC Regent 3 motorbus chassis.

Chassis length:

26ft

Chassis frame width:

front 3ft 3⅞ins, rear 3ft 9 11/32ins

Overall width (over tyres):

7ft 5⅝ins

The BUT drawing was marked with the remark "Coachbuilders to cut rear end of chassis to suit body. The overall length of the vehicle not to exceed length prescribed by statutory requirements current at the date of official order".

Electrics:

The motor was mounted between the chassis frames offset to the nearside, just ahead of the rear axle. The resistances were placed between the chassis frame in front of the traction motor with the shunt field resistance located under the cab. The master controller was underneath the driver's seat. The contactor cabinet was mounted on the rear wall of the cab to the nearside of the driver's seat.

There was a CAV dynamo on the commutator end of the traction motor.

English Electric controller, Rheostatic Brake Co. resistances and Brecknell Willis lightweight trolleybases.

Traction battery manoeuvring equipment. The vehicles were supplied with the traction battery (64 volt) stowage on the rear platform beneath the staircase. 24 volt batteries for lighting purposes.

Brakes:

Westinghouse air brakes, hand and rheostatic brakes. Two stages of rheostatic braking was used (down to 4 mph), further pressure on the brake pedal at this speed bringing the compressed air brake into use.

The compressor and air reservoir were bolted directly to the offside external face of the chassis frame. There was one air-brake cylinder on top of each king pin and one cylinder attached to each side of the chassis cross-member ahead of the rear axle. There was an air brake governor in the cab.

The handbrake lever was to the offside of the driver's steering column.

Bodywork:

Teak framed composite five-bay highbridge double-deck construction, enclosed forwards-ascending half-turn (90°) Roe "safety" staircase with conventional semi-vestibuled open platform entrance and exit at the rear built by Charles H. Roe Ltd., Crossgates, Leeds, Yorkshire.

The design was very similar to that used on the Karrier W4s 479-482, notable differences being the styling and depth of the cab side windows and the manner in which the profile above the rear platform matched that above the nearside cab windows. It is possible that this was due to a styling change on Roe's part during the 4-month period between the delivery of 479-482 and 483-495 rather than something that was NCT inspired, cf. the Roe bodied Karriers supplied to Grimsby, Nottingham and Hull with the Roe bodied BUTs supplied to Bradford and Nottingham or the Crossleys supplied to Cleethorpes.

Unlike the Karrier W4s 479-482 the glazing in the driver's cab area deepened progressively from the position of the cab rear bulkhead towards the front of the trolleybus although the base of the glazing in the offside cab door was aligned with the base of the windows in the lower saloon, the base of the equivalent nearside window curving fractionally downwards. The lower cream-painted band curved downwards fractionally from the position of the cab rear bulkhead and more noticeably from the position of the leading pillar of the driver's cab door and its nearside equivalent to pass beneath the windscreen. The middle cream-painted band became progressively narrower, above the side glazing of the driver's cab, towards the front of the trolleybus. The upper and lower deck front pillar in line with the driver's cab rear bulkhead was noticeably narrower than that on the Karrier W4s. The driver's cab had an offside front-hinged square topped door, which encroached into the middle cream-painted band, equipped with a sliding "signalling" window, the upper part of window rising towards the front of the trolleybus. The nearside driver's cab windows were fixed, the larger second pane also rose towards the front.

The nearside panel and cream-painted middle band narrowed towards the rear of the trolleybus from the vestibule above the open rear platform to match the shape of the top of the nearside driver's cab window.

Lighting:

External lighting was 2 low-set headlights on the front panel, 2 front side lights on the lower cream-painted band and a single rear light immediately above the rear registration number plate which also illuminated this plate. A spot light was fitted below the front panel somewhat closer to the centre line of the vehicle than the nearside headlight. At the rear, on the lower cream-painted band immediately beneath the rear platform window, there was a single inverted triangular panel containing (at the top) trafficators, the fretwork word "STOP" and a single brake light. Semaphore arm illuminated traffic indicators accommodated in a black moulding were fitted to the lower side panels beneath the driver's cab corner pillars immediately above the front mudguards and forwards of the vertical cab side ventilator, the upper third of the housing encroaching into the lower deck cream-painted band.

Internal lighting, except 493 which was delivered with fluorescent lighting (see Notes), was provided by tungsten bulbs, behind oblong fluted glass shades 5½ins long and 6¼ins high having a small central inset metal base at the bottom of the glass through which passed a single retaining screw, fed at 35 volts from the traction batteries.

In the lower saloon one light was mounted in the ceiling cove panels of each bay on both the nearside and the offside. In the upper saloon there were also lights in each bay on both sides. There was an additional lamp on the platform.

No internal emergency lighting was fitted however 493 had a front bulkhead light with glass cover and a similar fitting at the top of the staircase which was presumably necessary during the period that it was equipped with fluorescent lighting.

Seating:

See 479-482.

Destination equipment:

See 479-482.

Internal Livery:

See 479-482.

493 differed slightly from the other vehicles in that its lower deck bulkheads were covered in green leather cloth above the glazing apart from a central rectangular section at the front (similar to the Brush bodied 7ft 6ins wide BUT9641Ts).

External Livery:

Delivered in Livery 7 (see Appendix C).

Subsequent alterations:

The traction battery stowage was moved from the rear platform beneath the staircase to beneath the lower saloon seats at an early date, for example 483 in August 1949.

Red reflectors were fitted on the nearside and offside at the base of the rear panel from 1954.

The semaphore arm illuminated traffic indicators were replaced from 1954 onwards by flashing trafficators mounted on the lower deck cream-painted band immediately behind the driver's cab doors beneath the body pillar in line with the cab rear bulkhead. It is believe that the cab side outwards opening vertical vents were removed at this time. See 442-445, 452-468 as to the types of flashing trafficators employed.

493 was fitted with a double bumper bar across the width of the rear panel. This was removed later together with the rear double bumper bar carried by other vehicles of this batch around the offside corner panel as these snagged the bus washing machines.

485 and 492 received rubber-mounted rear destination indicator boxes as a result of accident damage sustained in May 1962 and August 1963 respectively.

Notes:

493 was exhibited on the Roe stand at the 1948 Commercial Motor Show and was equipped with a number of special features including BTH automatic acceleration and fluorescent lighting, and a chrome windscreen surround (other vehicles in the batch having painted surrounds). The BTH fluorescent lighting was installed under almost clear glass fittings supplied with DC current which required ballast lamps, which were used to illuminate the front, side and rear destination indicators. A polarity change over switch was necessary, to reverse the polarity on each occasion that the lights were switched on. The transformer equipment was carried beneath the staircase. Normal lighting was fitted in March 1955 although it retained the long light fittings and lamp glasses, adapted for tungsten light bulbs, and the mounting bolts for the under stairs equipment, until withdrawal in March 1965. 493 was subsequently preserved and is now on display at the Sandtoft Transport Centre near Doncaster.

483 suffered serious damage in an accident on 8 December 1948 and was returned to Roe where the body was removed from the chassis which was then taken to the AEC Works for reconstruction. It re-entered service on 1 August 1949.

Disposal:

483, 490, 494 sold to G. Harris, Saffron Walden, Essex, in April 1964.

484 sold to C. Hoyle, Wombwell, Yorkshire, in September 1963.

485-487, 489, 491 sold to Autospares (Bingley) Ltd., Hill Top Works, Bingley, Yorkshire, breakers, in June 1965.

488, 492 sold to Nottingham Scrap Metal Co., Plimsole Street, Nottingham, in June 1965 (broken up by Star Car Dismantlers, Dunkirk, Nottingham).

493 sold to the Nottingham Trolleybus Group for preservation in July 1965.

495 sold to Autospares (Bingley) Ltd., Hill Top Works, Bingley, Yorkshire, breakers, in May 1965.

500 - 601 BUT9641T

Pre-delivery photograph of 8ft wide BUT9641T 501 (KTV501) at Brush Coachworks Ltd. in Loughborough (November 1949). *John Lowrie*

Chassis: Three axle type BUT 9641T manufactured by the British United Traction Ltd., Hanover House, 14 Hanover Square, London W1 at the AEC works, Windmill Lane, Southall, Middlesex.
500-524 BUT drawing SK10 1495 (English Electric equipment) dated 16 March 1949. NCT drawing 7/64.
525-534, 565-571 BUT drawing SK10 1582 dated 3 April 1950, 1496 dated 17 March 1949 (all with Crompton Parkinson equipment). NCT drawing 7/63, 7/69.
535-564, 587-601 BUT drawing SK10 1497 undated but issued 5 October 1949, 1497 dated 9 May 1949, 1581 dated 22 March 1950 (all with Metropolitan-Vickers equipment). NCT drawing 7/62, 7/66, 7/68.
572-586 BUT drawing SK10 1580 (English Electric equipment) dated 28 February 1950. NCT drawing 7/67.

Motor: 500-524 English Electric 410/3B (120 hp)
525-534 Crompton Parkinson C422E3 (120 hp)
535-540, 542-546, 548-562, 564 Metropolitan Vickers 210 EYG (115 hp)
541, 547, 563, Metropolitan-Vickers 210 AYG3 (115 hp)
565-571 Crompton Parkinson C422E3 (120 hp)
572-586 English Electric 410B/4B (120 hp)
587-601 Metropolitan-Vickers 210 EYG (115 hp)
(all quoted with a one-hour rating at 550 volts)

Electrical equipment: 500-524 English Electric Ltd., Bradford, Yorkshire
525-534 Allen West Co. Ltd., Brighton, Sussex
535-564 Metropolitan-Vickers Ltd., Rugby, Warwickshire.
565-571 Allen West Co. Ltd., Brighton, Sussex
572-586 English Electric Ltd., Bradford, Yorkshire
587-601 Metropolitan-Vickers Ltd., Rugby, Warwickshire.

Dewirement indicator: Single Urcol line-lights and buzzer.

Brakes: 500-511 Westinghouse compressed air,
512-601 G.D. Peters compressed air; hand and rheostatic brakes.

Body: Brush H38/32R.

Length: 30ft

Width: 500-524 8ft (7ft 10½ins actual)
525-601 7ft 6 ins (7ft 4½ins actual)

Height: 15ft 2½ins to the top of the trolley bases.

Wheelbase: 18ft 5ins (to centre of rear bogie) with a rear bogic wheelbase of 4ft giving a turning circle on either lock of 63ft.

Wheel track: 500-524 front 6ft 8 15/16ins, rear 6ft 8 15/16ins,
525-601 front 6ft 5½ins, rear 6ft 5ins

Unladen weight: 9tons 19cwt 3qtrs

Tyres: 11.00 X 20ins all round.

500-601 BUT9641T

No.	Registration	Chassis	Chassis No.	Body	Body No.	Delivered	Registered	Into Service	Withdrawn	Sold
500	KTV500	BUT9641T	339	Brush		10.11.1949	01.12.1949	01.12.1949	30/04/1966	23/06/1966
501	KTV501	BUT9641T	340	Brush		02.11.1949	01.12.1949	01.12.1949	31/01/1966	26/03/1966
502	KTV502	BUT9641T	341	Brush		31.01.1950	01.02.1950	01.02.1950	31/10/1965	25/04/1966
503	KTV503	BUT9641T	342	Brush		27.01.1950	01.02.1950	01.02.1950	31/05/1965	13/10/1965
504	KTV504	BUT9641T	343	Brush		10.02.1950	01.02.1950	12.02.1950	30/04/1966	01/08/1966
505	KTV505	BUT9641T	344	Brush		10.02.1950	01.02.1950	17.02.1950	31/07/1964	22/10/1965
506	KTV506	BUT9641T	345	Brush		17.02.1950	01.02.1950	21.02.1950	01/07/1966	29/03/1967
507	KTV507	BUT9641T	346	Brush		02.02.1950	01.02.1950	03.02.1950	30/06/1966	06/09/1966
508	KTV508	BUT9641T	347	Brush		09.02.1950	01.02.1950	17.02.1950	31/10/1965	25/03/1966
509	KTV509	BUT9641T	348	Brush		20.02.1950	01.03.1950	01.03.1950	31/01/1966	30/03/1966
510	KTV510	BUT9641T	349	Brush		21.02.1950	01.03.1950	02.03.1950	30/06/1966	30/07/1966
511	KTV511	BUT9641T	350	Brush		24.02.1950	01.03.1950	01.03.1950	30/06/1966	07/09/1966
512	KTV512	BUT9641T	351	Brush		27.02.1950	01.03.1950	01.03.1950	30/09/1965	21/10/1965
513	KTV513	BUT9641T	352	Brush		24.02.1950	01.03.1950	01.03.1950	09/10/1965	30/03/1966
514	KTV514	BUT9641T	353	Brush		02.03.1950	01.03.1950	03.03.1950	31/01/1966	31/03/1966
515	KTV515	BUT9641T	354	Brush		02.03.1950	01.03.1950	05.03.1950	31/01/1966	28/03/1966
516	KTV516	BUT9641T	355	Brush		13.03.1950	01.03.1950	16.03.1950	30/06/1966	05/09/1966
517	KTV517	BUT9641T	356	Brush		23.02.1950	01.03.1950	01.03.1950	09/10/1965	23/03/1966
518	KTV518	BUT9641T	357	Brush		14.03.1950	25.03.1950	25.03.1950	30/06/1966	18/08/1966
519	KTV519	BUT9641T	358	Brush		23.03.1950	25.03.1950	26.03.1950	09/10/1965	29/03/1966
520	KTV520	BUT9641T	359	Brush		17.03.1950	25.03.1950	25.03.1950	30/06/1966	11/08/1966
521	KTV521	BUT9641T	360	Brush		15.03.1950	25.03.1950	25.03.1950	30/06/1966	05/08/1966
522	KTV522	BUT9641T	361	Brush		24.03.1950	25.03.1950	28.03.1950	30/06/1966	08/08/1966
523	KTV523	BUT9641T	362	Brush		09.05.1950	03.05.1950	10.05.1950	31/07/1965	29/10/1965
524	KTV524	BUT9641T	363	Brush		29.03.1950	25.03.1950	31.03.1950	30/06/1966	08/08/1966
525	KTV525	BUT9641T	376	Brush		26.09.1950	30.09.1950	01.10.1950	30/04/1965	28/05/1965
526	KTV526	BUT9641T	377	Brush		05.09.1950	06.09.1950	11.09.1950	30/04/1965	19/07/1965
527	KTV527	BUT9641T	378	Brush		13.09.1950	06.09.1950	20.09.1950	30/04/1965	30/05/1965
528	KTV528	BUT9641T	379	Brush		27.09.1950	30.09.1950	01.10.1950	30/04/1965	28/05/1965
529	KTV529	BUT9641T	380	Brush		05.10.1950	30.09.1950	06.10.1950	30/04/1965	27/05/1965
530	KTV530	BUT9641T	381	Brush		06.10.1950	30.09.1950	07.10.1950	31.03.1965	12/08/1965
531	KTV531	BUT9641T	382	Brush		15.11.1950	01.11.1950	18.11.1950	30/04/1965	27/05/1965
532	KTV532	BUT9641T	383	Brush		30.10.1950	01.11.1950	01.11.1950	31.03.1965	29/05/1965
533	KTV533	BUT9641T	384	Brush		17.11.1950	01.11.1950	20.11.1950	31.03.1965	29/05/1965
534	KTV534	BUT9641T	385	Brush		29.11.1950	01.12.1950	02.12.1950	31.10.1963	27/04/1964
535	KTV535	BUT9641T	386	Brush		14.08.1950	01.08.1950	18.08.1950	09.10.1965	26/10/1965
536	KTV536	BUT9641T	387	Brush		15.08.1950	01.08.1950	19.08.1950	30/09/1963	16/04/1964
537	KTV537	BUT9641T	388	Brush		18.08.1950	09.09.1950	10.09.1950	31/05/1965	26/08/1965
538	KTV538	BUT9641T	389	Brush		08.09.1950	06.09.1950	13.09.1950	30/09/1965	23/10/1965
539	KTV539	BUT9641T	390	Brush		22.09.1950	30.09.1950	01.10.1950	30/09/1965	22/11/1965
540	KTV540	BUT9641T	391	Brush		27.07.1950	01.08.1950	01.08.1950	31.03.1965	15/07/1965
541	KTV541	BUT9641T	392	Brush		29.11.1950	01.12.1950	01.12.1950	31/05/1965	23/08/1965
542	KTV542	BUT9641T	393	Brush		31.10.1950	01.11.1950	01.11.1950	31/05/1965	04/10/1965
543	KTV543	BUT9641T	394	Brush		17.10.1950	02.11.1950	02.11.1950	31/10/1963	27/04/1964
544	KTV544	BUT9641T	395	Brush		21.11.1950	17.11.1950	23.11.1950	31/10/1963	20/04/1964
545	KTV545	BUT9641T	396	Brush		28.11.1950	17.11.1950	30.11.1950	31.03.1965	14/07/1965
546	KTV546	BUT9641T	397	Brush		08.12.1950	03.01.1951	05.01.1951	31/05/1965	29/07/1965
547	KTV547	BUT9641T	398	Brush		07.12.1950	30.11.1950	12.12.1950	31/05/1965	09/09/1965
548	KTV548	BUT9641T	399	Brush		28.07.1950	01.08.1950	03.08.1950	31/05/1965	26/08/1965
549	KTV549	BUT9641T	400	Brush		01.06.1950	01/07/1950	01.07.1950	31/05/1965	14/09/1965
550	KTV550	BUT9641T	401	Brush		22.12.1950	01.01.1951	03.01.1951	30/09/1965	20/10/1965
551	KTV551	BUT9641T	402	Brush		20.12.1950	01.01.1951	01.01.1951	31/05/1965	13/08/1965
552	KTV552	BUT9641T	403	Brush		20.12.1950	01.01.1951	01.01.1951	31/05/1965	28/07/1965
553	KTV553	BUT9641T	404	Brush		28.12.1950	01.01.1951	03.01.1951	31/05/1965	25/08/1965
554	KTV554	BUT9641T	405	Brush		22.12.1950	01.01.1951	01.01.1951	30/11/1963	04/05/1964
555	KTV555	BUT9641T	406	Brush		06.01.1951	01.01.1951	09.01.1951	31.03.1965	29/06/1965
556	KTV556	BUT9641T	407	Brush		08.01.1951	12.01.1951	13.01.1951	31/05/1965	04/10/1965
557	KTV557	BUT9641T	408	Brush		10.01.1951	01.01.1951	10.01.1951	31/05/1965	16/08/1965
558	KTV558	BUT9641T	409	Brush		01.06.1951	07.06.1951	08.06.1951	31/05/1965	17/08/1965
559	KTV559	BUT9641T	410	Brush		01.06.1951	07.06.1951	08.06.1951	30/04/1965	24/07/1965
560	KTV560	BUT9641T	411	Brush		20.06.1951	29.06.1951	02.07.1951	31.03.1965	16/07/1965
561	KTV561	BUT9641T	412	Brush		02.02.1951	07.02.1951	08.02.1951	30/09/1965	02/11/1965
562	KTV562	BUT9641T	413	Brush		06.02.1951	07.02.1951	10.02.1951	30/09/1965	21/10/1965
563	KTV563	BUT9641T	414	Brush		28.06.1951	29.06.1951	06.07.1951	30/09/1965	29/10/1965
564	KTV564	BUT9641T	415	Brush		27.02.1952	01.03.1951	08.03.1952	30/09/1965	27/10/1965
565	KTV565	BUT9641T	530	Brush		21.11.1950	01.12.1950	01.12.1950	31/05/1965	28/07/1965
566	KTV566	BUT9641T	531	Brush		17.01.1952	01.02.1952	01.02.1952	31/05/1965	19/07/1965
567	KTV567	BUT9641T	532	Brush		13.02.1952	01.03.1952	01.03.1952	31/05/1965	25/07/1965
568	KTV568	BUT9641T	533	Brush		07.02.1952	01.03.1952	01.03.1952	31/05/1965	12/07/1965
569	KTV569	BUT9641T	534	Brush		24.01.1952	01.02.1952	01.02.1952	31/05/1965	24/07/1965

No.	Registration	Chassis	Chassis No.	Body	Body No.	Delivered	Registered	Into Service	Withdrawn	Sold
570	KTV570	BUT9641T	535	Brush		25.01.1952	01.02.1952	01.02.1952	31/05/1965	28/07/1965
571	KTV571	BUT9641T	536	Brush		10.03.1952	25.03.1952	26.03.1952	31/05/1965	11/08/1965
572	KTV572	BUT9641T	500	Brush		08.11.1951	01.12.1951	01.12.1951	09.10.1965	20/12/1965
573	KTV573	BUT9641T	501	Brush		05.11.1951	01.12.1951	01.12.1951	31/01/1964	14/06/1965
574	KTV574	BUT9641T	502	Brush		29.10.1951	01.11.1951	01.12.1951	09.10.1965	20/12/1965
575	KTV575	BUT9641T	503	Brush		27.11.1951	01.12.1951	01.12.1951	09.10.1965	18/11/1965
576	KTV576	BUT9641T	504	Brush		22.11.1951	01.12.1951	01.12.1951	09.10.1965	19/11/1965
577	KTV577	BUT9641T	505	Brush		26.10.1951	01.11.1951	01.11.1951	09.10.1965	17/11/1965
578	KTV578	BUT9641T	506	Brush		21.11.1951	01.12.1951	01.12.1951	10.10.1965	09/01/1966
579	KTV579	BUT9641T	507	Brush		16.11.1951	01.12.1951	01.12.1951	09.10.1965	21/12/1965
580	KTV580	BUT9641T	508	Brush		12.11.1951	01.12.1951	01.12.1951	09.10.1965	13/11/1965
581	KTV581	BUT9641T	509	Brush		25.10.1951	01.11.1951	01.11.1951	30/09/1965	22/10/1965
582	KTV582	BUT9641T	510	Brush		05.12.1951	01.12.1951	10.12.1951	30/04/1965	02/02/1966
583	KTV583	BUT9641T	511	Brush		18.01.1952	01.02.1952	01.02.1952	09.10.1965	12/11/1965
584	KTV584	BUT9641T	512	Brush		22.10.1951	01.11.1951	01.11.1951	09.10.1965	21/12/1965
585	KTV585	BUT9641T	513	Brush		16.01.1952	01.02.1952	01.02.1952	09.10.1965	24/12/1965
586	KTV586	BUT9641T	514	Brush		18.12.1951	01.02.1952	01.02.1952	31/05/1964	09/06/1965
587	KTV587	BUT9641T	515	Brush		25.02.1952	01.03.1952	01.03.1952	31.05.1965	13/07/1965
588	KTV588	BUT9641T	516	Brush		21.02.1952	01.03.1952	01.03.1952	30/09/1965	09/10/1965
589	KTV589	BUT9641T	517	Brush		07.03.1952	25.03.1952	25.03.1952	30/09/1965	06/10/1965
590	KTV590	BUT9641T	518	Brush		18.03.1952	25.03.1952	25.03.1952	30/09/1965	13/10/1965
591	KTV591	BUT9641T	519	Brush		18.02.1952	01.03.1952	01.03.1952	30/09/1965	14/10/1965
592	KTV592	BUT9641T	520	Brush		19.03.1952	25.03.1952	25.03.1952	31/07/1965	30/09/1965
593	KTV593	BUT9641T	521	Brush		02.04.1952	01.05.1952	01.05.1952	30/09/1965	08/10/1965
594	KTV594	BUT9641T	522	Brush		25.03.1952	25.03.1952	28.03.1952	30/09/1965	30/09/1965
595	KTV595	BUT9641T	523	Brush		21.03.1952	25.03.1952	25.03.1952	30/09/1965	12/10/1965
596	KTV596	BUT9641T	524	Brush		07.04.1952	01.05.1952	01.05.1952	30/09/1965	14/10/1965
597	KTV597	BUT9641T	525	Brush		28.04.1952	01.05.1952	02.05.1952	30/09/1965	08/10/1965
598	KTV598	BUT9641T	526	Brush		15.05.1952	01.06.1952	05.06.1952	30/04/1965	12/07/1965
599	KTV599	BUT9641T	527	Brush		17.04.1952	01.05.1952	01.05.1952	30/09/1965	13/10/1965
600	KTV600	BUT9641T	528	Brush		18.07.1952	01.08.1952	07.08.1952	30/09/1965	06/10/1965
601	KTV601	BUT9641T	529	Brush		19.06.1952	01.07.1952	01.07.1952	30/04/1965	13/07/1965

Pre-delivery photograph of 8ft wide BUT9641T 501 (KTV501) at Brush Coachworks Ltd. in Loughborough (November 1949). *John Lowrie*

Chassis:

The BUT9641T used a number of components from the AEC Regent III motorbus chassis such as front axle and steering gear. The rear bogie was, in fact, an improved version of the one used on the pre-war AEC664T.

Channel section shallow steel frame, braced by tubular cross members. Front axle beam of alloy steel stamping with taper fit swivel pins and taper-roller thrust bearings to take vertical loads. Underslung worm, two-axle drive, incorporating a third differential; ratio 10 1/3 to 1; fully-floating axle shafts. Reverse camber, semi-elliptic front springs and reverse camber semi-elliptic inverted rear springs with torque reaction linkage inside the right-hand frame member. Worm and nut steering.

Chassis length:

29ft 11½ins

500 – 524

Chassis frame width:

front 3ft 3 13/16ins, rear 5ft 4 1/16ins

Overall width (over hubs):

front 7ft 9 5/16ins, rear 7ft 9 1/16ins

525 – 601

Chassis frame width:

front 3ft 3 13/16ins, rear 5ft 0 1/8ins

Overall width (over hubs):

front 7ft 5½ins, rear 7ft 5 3/8ins

Underslung worm drive to the differentials, offset to the nearside, of the two fully-floating rear axles.

To absorb vibration, the traction motor and the air compressor were mounted on rubber supports. The rear bogie design incorporated radius arms to transmit the axle torque reaction directly to the frame thus equalizing the axle loading and providing greater acceleration without wheelspin and smoother and more efficient braking. A mileage-operated mechanical pump provided automatic lubrication to 40 points on the chassis; it was belt driven from the drive end of the traction motor with the oil tank being located in the driver's cab

In an effort to ensure that the completed vehicles' unladen weight did not exceed 10 tons there was no chassis or chassis extension beyond the position of the rear bulkhead. This difficulty was only identified after chassis delivery commenced and there was evidence that the chassis beneath the open platform had been cut away. This move resulted in an absence of support beneath the cantilevered platform and the entire rear structure, leading to major structural problems after some years in service.

Electrics:

The flood proof traction motor was mounted between the chassis frames immediately ahead of the leading rear axle offset to the nearside and with a short propeller shaft to the leading differential.

There were two banks of resistances between the chassis frames ahead of the motor. On the Crompton Parkinson and English Electric equipped vehicles the shunt field resistance was mounted on the external face of the chassis nearside (approximately beneath bay 2 of the body). The Metropolitan-Vickers equipped vehicles had the shunt field resistance located in the contactor cabinet.

All the BUT9641Ts had battery manoeuvring equipment and traction batteries (64 volt) which were carried on the rear open platform beneath the staircase. This same set of batteries supplied power, at 35 volts, for lighting purposes. An additional small power pedal for use when operating on batteries was located to the nearside of the main power pedal. The eight 8-volt batteries were charged by a dynamo fixed to the commutator end of the traction motor.

The master controller was beneath the driver's seat and the control equipment was mounted on the nearside alongside the driver's seat. The English Electric contactor cabinet was taller than its Crompton and Metropolitan-Vickers equivalents and stood above the lower edge of the nearside bulkhead window with a separate controller under the driver's seat. The Metropolitan-Vickers equipped vehicles had a combined contactor cabinet and master controller unit.

563, 565-601 were equipped with automatic acceleration.

Those vehicles equipped with Crompton Parkinson or English Electric traction motors had Expanded Metal Co. resistances whereas those with Metropolitan-Vickers motors used their own make of resistances.

Brecknell Willis lightweight trolley bases.

Brakes:

Two stages of rheostatic braking was used (down to 4 mph), further pressure on the brake pedal at this speed bringing the compressed air brake into use.

The two-cylinder compressor and air reservoir were bolted directly to the offside external face of the chassis frame. There was a brake control valve carried on the air reservoir. The G.D. Peters or Westinghouse compressed-air brakes operated on all wheels with a separate cylinder to each wheel, one being on top of each king pin with four cylinders on the rear bogie. The compressor governor was mounted on the front nearside of the driver's cab.

The handbrake operated on all rear wheels; the handbrake lever was to the offside of the driver's steering column.

Bodywork:

Metal framed six-bay highbridge double-deck construction with timber fillets for panel fixing purposes, forwards-ascending half-turn (90°) staircase and semi-vestibuled open platform at the rear built by Brush Coachworks Ltd., Loughborough, Leicestershire. A Brush makers' Falcon emblem was affixed to the stair case stringers.

Brackets or extensions were bolted to the upper-deck body pillars (roof sticks) between bays 1 and 2, and bays 2 and 3 which protruded through the rounded edges of the roof to support the two girders of the exposed trolley gantry which was not in direct contact with the roof. Immediately above the rearmost upper-deck window on each side a roof-mounted bracket secured a transverse rod which extended across much of the width of the vehicle to avoid roof damage when pulling down the trolley booms and stowing them beneath the restraining hooks.

All six wheels were equipped with chromed hubs and wheel nut protector rings

The platform itself sloped noticeably to the nearside and was finished with a rubber edge. The base of the rear panel was finished with a chromed sprung steel bumper bar whilst there was a double bumper bar around the offside corner panel. The staircase had 3 steps from the platform to a landing and then 3 steps to the upper deck. All platform and staircase handrails and stanchions were coated with white Doverite; others, for example upper saloon offside rear bay 6 and "D" window at the head of the stairs, were black.

Wind down half-drop openers were fitted to the tops of the side windows in bays 1, 3, 5 of the upper and lower-deck, the winding handle in the top rail of the fixed lower pane being placed variously at one third or halfway along the top rail. Turning the handle actuated a mechanism that caused the upper pane to move up or down. The upper pane dropped outside the fixed lower pane. These mechanisms wore with time leaving the upper pane out of lateral alignment or the winding handle disconnected from the mechanism. The front upper-deck windows were fixed. The lower and upper deck side windows and the upper deck front windows were surmounted by metal louvres. Square ventilators were mounted immediately above the lower deck side windows in bays 1 and 6.

The rear upper deck emergency door had three hinges at its base and a handle at the top with two windows. Retained open by leather covered chains on each side, a separate wooden platform normally stowed behind the upper saloon rear nearside seat fitted into retaining slits in the door to provide access to the roof catwalk. There were roof-mounted vents on the nearside and offside mounted centrally above bays 1, 4 and 6. Above the front offside pillar of bay 1 a roof-mounted metal hood gave added protection to the main cables which were led down the pillar to the control equipment in the driver's cab.

Small inlet ducts were installed above the driver's cab windscreens, immediately to the left and right of the divider, disguised by the black painted beading. The rear upper-deck window/ emergency exit had two almost square panes. The windows were all surrounded internally by strip mouldings. The driver's cab was equipped with a single opening windscreen on the offside, both windscreens having chromium-plated frames. The offside windscreen had a top-mounted wiper whilst that on the nearside was mounted at the base of the windscreen. There was a large green-painted metal contactor cabinet with plunger catches on the nearside of the driver's cab.

Forward-sliding cab doors were fitted on the nearside and the offside of the 8ft wide vehicles with internally-mounted grab handles to each side of the doorway that towards the rear being covered in cream coloured plastic. The offside sliding door was equipped with sliding "signalling" windows. All the 7ft 6ins wide vehicles had sliding cab doors on the offside however on the nearside some had a sliding door whereas others had a half-depth top hinged door encompassing only the nearside cab window above the cream band. This served as an access to the contactor cabinet and the driver's emergency exit. There was a latch mechanism operated by a handle in the lower front corner of the window; on the exterior this was mounted by the black beading at the top of the lower cream band.

Photographic evidence suggests that the English Electric equipped vehicles 572-586 delivered between November 1951 and February 1952 had nearside sliding cab doors; the Metropolitan-Vickers and Crompton equipped vehicles 561, delivered in February 1951 and presumed to have been rebuilt after accident damage early in its life, together with 564, 566-571 and 587-601 delivered between February and August 1952 had hinged nearside cab windows although 565 had a sliding near side cab door. Both the 8ft wide and the 7ft 6ins wide vehicles were delivered with black steering wheels.

Top hinged access doors were fitted at the base of the lower-deck offside panel bays 1 and 2, giving access to the air compressor, and at the rear providing access to the batteries beneath the stairs. The Crompton Parkinson and English Electric equipped vehicles had top hinged access doors on the nearside in bay 2 giving access to the shunt field resistance. A step was let into the base of the bay 1 side panel, a sheet of protective stainless steel reaching from this step to the lintel of the driver's cab sliding door, immediately behind the front axle, on both the nearside and offside. Vehicles equipped with nearside cab windows had no nearside step or protective "kicking plate". The green-painted contactor cabinet on the nearside of the driver's cab made access through the nearside sliding door difficult. The cab floor had a square raised portion of a mortar-like substance, brick red in colour, through which the pedals protruded and where the driver could rest his feet, in the middle of which was a BUT maker's emblem. Interestingly on 518, 544, 548, 555, 557, 559-562 and 564 this was an AEC emblem.

There were 2 glazed panels in the bulkhead behind the driver, separated by a wide central panel, with a wooden hatch above the offside glazed panel to allow the driver to talk to the conductor.

Lower saloon. Note the advertisement panels centred above each body pillar between the fluted glass light fittings. *John Lowrie*

Lower saloon looking towards the rear of the vehicle. *John Lowrie*

Upper saloon. *John Lowrie*

An external circular driver's rear view mirror on a short "stalk" was mounted on the cream-painted lower band beneath the offside front window pillar, its nearside counterpart was mounted traditionally at the top of the front cab pillar. Before all deliveries were completed the offside rear view mirror was also moved towards the top of the front cab pillars, probably to avoid light reflecting from the semaphore arm illuminated traffic indicator.

A glass-fronted panel at the rear of the longitudinal offside seat in the lower saloon was used to display timetable information. In the lower saloon there were 2 ceiling mounted bell pushes on the nearside above the gangway. There were 3 ceiling mounted bell pushes in the upper saloon just to the offside of the gangway, one of which was at the top of the stairs. On the rear platform there was a further bell push on the offside of the rear bulkhead adjacent to staircase/rear bulkhead.

There was a used ticket box immediately below the nearside vestibule window and in the rear panel at the base of the stairs on the rear open platform. Internal advertisement frames were mounted on the curved ceiling cove panels above the side windows in both saloons whilst paper notifications of timetable changes or fares revisions were stuck on the lower saloon window nearest the platform facing outwards. A circular conductor's mirror was fixed in the upper deck rear offside dome at the head of the stairs.

The front registration number plate was mounted immediately above the removable access panel, which incorporated 3 horizontal fluted columns of 6 vanes, on all deliveries up to about 534 however due to towing bar damage the access panel was deepened by some 4-5ins and henceforth also accommodated the number plate. This modification was incorporated into all subsequent deliveries. A single lifeguard ran beneath the side panels between the first and second axle. A bamboo trolley retrieval pole was carried in a tube mounted centrally under the chassis. The conductor had a locker on the rear platform under the stairs.

The 8ft wide vehicles had a one piece "fairing" incorporating both mudguards over the rear wheels whereas the 7ft 6ins wide vehicles had separate rear mudguards.

The final Brush bodies were completed by Willowbrook, some partially finished bodies were towed to Willowbrook elsewhere in Loughborough for completion, 593, 596, 597, 599 were ready in May 1952, 598 in June 1952, and 600 and 601 in July (600 being the last on 18 July 1952). The final body completed by Brush and thus the last Brush trolleybus body built, is believed to be 594 which was delivered to NCT on 25 March 1952 (albeit only recorded as entering NCT stock the following day).

Lighting:

External lighting was 2 headlights on the front panel, 2 vertically-mounted rectangular front side lights on the lower deck waistband and a single rear light, fitted behind a small access panel, to the offside of the rear lower panel which also illuminated the rear registration number plate immediately beneath. There was also a single rubber mounted panel containing brake lights and trafficators built into the lower deck waistband below the rear platform window.

A spotlight was recessed into the front panel below the nearside headlight and slightly more towards the centre of the vehicle. Semaphore arm illuminated traffic indicators were fitted on the side pillars immediately to the rear of the driver's cab doors.

Internal lighting was provided by tungsten bulbs, behind oblong fluted glass shades 5½ins long and 6¼ins high having a small central inset metal base at the bottom of the glass through which passed a single retaining screw, fed at 35 volts from the traction batteries. There were 6 lamps each side in the lower saloon and 8 each side in the upper saloon mounted in the ceiling cove panels centrally in each bay, and 2 further lamps above the rear platform. In addition there was a cleaner's light switch fixed in the rear bulkhead under the stairs.

There was no internal emergency lighting.

Seating:

Based on green painted Peters tubular steel frames with stainless steel handrails across the backs. Squabs and backs were upholstered in green leather (pleated squabs and plain backs, each seat back being individually "framed") and Dunlopillo cushions with scratchproof patterned Rexine seat backs. The lower saloon had a 6-person inwards-facing bench seat on each side over the rear bogie and 5 rows of forwards-facing double seats. The backs of the bench seats were in one piece (each seat back being individually "framed") and on the 8ft wide vehicles rose above the lower edge of the windows, whereas the top of the seat back was flush with the lower edge of the windows on their 7ft 6ins wide equivalents. The upper saloon had 8 rows of double seats on the offside and 11 rows (including that at the rear fastened to a frame above the platform ceiling panel) on the nearside. There was a cigarette stubber mounted centrally on the back of each forwards-facing seat. An advertisement was affixed to the back of the rear offside seat in the upper saloon at the head of the stairs. The driver's seat was in green leather.

Destination equipment:

Rectangular indicator boxes 36ins X 10ins with rounded corners capable of displaying a single blind with the service number and up to 2 lines of information (en route points and the final destination) were fitted approximately one third up on the upper-deck front panel above the drivers' cab windows, the rear platform window and on the nearside immediately above the rear open platform entrance. The front and nearside boxes were flush with the body panelling however the box above the rear platform window protruded a few inches beyond the panel in order not to encroach onto the staircase area.

Prior to the construction of a roundabout at the south end of Market Street in early 1953, 1950 BUT9641T 565 is seen, in a damaged photograph, at the loading point for services 42 and 43 in front of the Queen Victoria Statue at the junction of Angel Row and Beastmarket Hill on a northbound service 43 duty. *Fred York*

Internal Livery:

Both saloons featured stained and varnished hardwood window mouldings, advertisement panels (5 each side in the lower saloon and 6 in the upper) and strips along the ceiling, all of which had to be removed for internal repainting. The advertisement panels were centred above each body pillar between the saloon light fittings. There was a further advertisement panel mounted centrally on the lower saloon front bulkhead. Green Rexine panels beneath the windows except at the front of each saloon which was covered with fluted green rubber.

The bulkheads on the 8ft wide vehicles were painted cream above the windows whereas the 7ft 6ins wide equivalents had green leather cloth apart from a rectangular section in the centre over the middle of the bulkhead glazing. The rear panel and back to the destination box were covered in green leather cloth.

The floor was covered in brown linoleum with 7 rubber strips (although 600-601 reportedly had 8 strips) along the gangway in the lower saloon and 6 strips in the upper saloon. Between the seats there were 4 short strips. The metal window pans were painted a dark brown. White enamelled ceiling and cove panels. The cab area was painted medium green with white ceiling.

External Livery:

Delivered in Livery 8 (see Appendix C)

Subsequent alterations:

532 was fitted with Anti-Attrition trolley heads in November 1950.

Commencing in July 1951 the 8ft wide vehicles had their black steering wheels replaced with white ones as an identifying feature to drivers.

In an effort to reduce the weight of the substantial Brush bodywork, there was no chassis extension to the rear of the third axle, weaker platform bearers being used instead. After a few years use the platform and the entire rear portion of the bodywork began to sag, producing splits around the rear emergency window. An extra leaf was added to the rear springs in an effort to prevent the rear end settling too low.

Another especially posed photograph of 549, the first 7ft 6ins wide BUT9641T/Brush bodied trolleybus to reach Nottingham, in Colwick Road at the terminus with a background of Roughill (Colwick) Wood. The happy "passengers" are no doubt Transport Department employees able to sample a trip in the latest trolleybus. *EE/Beilby*

BUT9641T/Brush 507 looking new, at Middleton Boulevard, Wollaton Park. The window stickers advertise a gymnasium. *EE/Beilby*

535 was sent to Willowbrook in mid-1953 for repairs to the rear dome.

At some stage after delivery 508 was equipped with automatic acceleration.

The rear double bumper bar around the offside corner panel was removed in the mid-1950s to avoid damage from the Dawson bus washing machine.

Red reflectors were fitted half way down the offside and nearside of the rear panel beneath the advertisement panel from 1954 that on the offside being fitted to the small access panel protecting the single rear light and above the rear registration number plate, to the offside of the rear light lens.

The semaphore arm illuminated traffic indicators fitted on the side pillars immediately to the rear of the driver's cab doors were replaced by flashing trafficators from 1954. Two types were used, the Klaxon "Edinburgh" plain rectangular type made from transparent orange plastic material with rounded top and bottom mouldings, 2 bulbs and a pressed steel base plate with a lip into which the cover slid, and, more frequently the Ericsson type made from a thicker orange plastic material with rounded ends, 3 protrusions on the side of the moulded body to accommodate the 3 bulbs and two visible fixing screws (between the protrusions) securing it to a cast metal base. The Klaxon "Edinburgh" type fitted neatly between the lower and upper beading of the cream band but the Ericsson type were longer necessitating the removal of part of the lower beading to accommodate the additional length.

Lastly triangular Hella units with 2 bulbs at the front and one at the rear were fitted. Reportedly, the Hella units, which were first fitted in April 1962, were preferred as the other types tended to get damaged or removed by the bus washing machines! No other type of trolleybus was ever fitted with Hella trafficators. Towards the end of trolleybus operations, following repaints, Ericsson units, out of stock, were again employed.

583 was experimentally fitted with thin tubular flashing indicators obtained from Rotherham Corporation, covering the former trafficator fittings, in February 1957.

539 had a painted rear number plate for most of its life (all others had: raised letters and numbers).

549 ran without a rear side indicator box for a period immediately after delivery (believed to be at some time between June 1950 and February 1951).

From the late 1950s the fluted glass lamp covers used inside the BUT9641Ts were progressively removed during overhaul or repaint (although the same style of covers used in the post war Roe bodied 2 axle trolleybuses were retained until final withdrawal). The metal plates which had secured the covers were also removed leaving 4 small rivet holes which once painted over were quite unobtrusive, however latterly these metal plates were left in situ and merely painted over leaving a somewhat unfinished look. By the end of trolleybus operations most vehicles had lost their lamp covers.

In the early 1960s the original style of headlights, which featured a flat lens with ribbing on the inside of the lamp glass and a bulb mounted in a triangular fitting, was replaced by normal convex lamp glasses with an adaptor ring to permit fitment into the original mounting. This style of headlight appeared to have a slightly larger chrome surround than on the original fittings. The main recipients appear to have been the 8ft wide vehicles but 539 and 581 were also so equipped.

Non-standard front upper deck windows were fitted to 522 as a result of accident damage incurred on 27 August 1957 when a projecting crane jib killed a passenger on the top deck.

Following an accident in Arkwright Street on 18 July 1962 when a mobile crane jib collided with the offside of the upper deck going through 2 windows, 558 was repaired with just 2 standard wind-down windows on the offside of the upper saloon (bays 1 and 4 only).

567 re-entered service in November 1961 with a removable front panel lacking any form of ventilation vanes. This was corrected within a fortnight.

Latterly plain instead of pleated seat squabs were used as replacements. When the fluted green rubber at the front of each saloon was replaced a black coloured replacement was used.

Latterly 516 was equipped with a white steering wheel of thinner section.

Notes:

It is known that Brush had considerable difficulties in producing the bodywork for these vehicles within the maximum permitted weight, indeed there are suggestions that although the vehicle(s) supplied for weighing were within the permitted figure the other members of the class exceeded that figure. Brush files record several exchanges of correspondence in guarded terms about Construction, Dimensions and Weight of Trolley vehicles and their equipment in the latter part of 1949, and possible fines for non-compliance. Until 1935 the maximum permitted laden weight of Nottingham's trolleybuses had been limited by a clause in each Act of Parliament (as was) thereafter this was aligned to the national standard which by 1949 was 14½ tons and 8 tons per axle for 3-axle vehicles.

565 was exhibited on the Brush stand at the 1950 Commercial Vehicle Show erroneously displaying fleet number 563. This was corrected prior to delivery.

Disposal:

500 sold to Whitaker, Goldthorpe, Yorkshire, breakers, in June 1966.

501, 508, 509, 513-515, 517, 519 sold to Autospares (Bingley) Ltd., Hill Top Works, Bingley, Yorkshire, breakers, in March 1966.

502 sold to Tom Bowden on behalf of the Nottingham Trolleybus Group for preservation in April 1966. After some years at Plumtree and Sandtoft, although it has never operated since withdrawal, it is currently stored at Boughton, Nottinghamshire in an un-restored state.

503, 505, sold to Autospares (Bingley) Ltd., Hill Top Works, Bingley, Yorkshire, breakers, in October 1965.

504, 518, 520-522, 524 sold to Whitaker, Goldthorpe, Yorkshire, breakers, in August 1966.

506 sold to J.B. Ayrey, Huddersfield in March 1967 on behalf of the Huddersfield Trolleybus Preservation Society and Bradford Model Railway Centre for preservation in May 1967. Subsequently passed to David & Bernice Needham, Carterton and now on display at the Sandtoft Transport Centre.

507, 511, 516 sold to Whitaker, Goldthorpe, Yorkshire, breakers, in September 1966.

510 sold to Whitaker, Goldthorpe, Yorkshire, breakers, in July 1966.

512, 523, 535, 538, 542, 550, 556, 562-564, 588-591, 593, 595-597, 599, 600 sold to Colbro, Rothwell, Yorkshire, breakers, in October 1965.

525, 527-529, 531-533 sold to Autospares (Bingley) Ltd., Hill Top Works, Bingley, Yorkshire, breakers, in May 1965.

526, 540, 545, 546, 559, 560, 565-570, 587, 598, 601 sold to Autospares (Bingley) Ltd., Hill Top Works, Bingley, Yorkshire, breakers, in July 1965.

530, 537, 541, 548, 551, 557-558, 571 sold to Autospares (Bingley) Ltd., Hill Top Works, Bingley, Yorkshire, breakers, in August 1965.

534, 536, 543, 544 sold to G. Harris, Saffron Walden, Essex, in April 1964.

539 sold to Mellors, Bulwell, Nottingham, showmen, in November 1965.

547, 549 sold to Autospares (Bingley) Ltd., Hill Top Works, Bingley, Yorkshire, breakers, in September 1965.

552 sold to Colbro, Rothwell, Yorkshire, breakers, in July 1965.

553 sold to Autospares (Bingley) Ltd., Hill Top Works, Bingley, Yorkshire, breakers, in August 1965.

554 sold to G. Harris, Saffron Walden, Essex, in May 1964.

555 sold to Nottingham Scrap Metal Co., Plimsole Street, Nottingham, in June 1965.

561 sold to Colbro, Rothwell, Yorkshire, breakers, in November 1965.

572, 574, 577, 579, 584, 585 sold to Autospares (Bingley) Ltd., Hill Top Works, Bingley, Yorkshire, breakers, in December 1965.

573, 586 sold to Autospares (Bingley) Ltd., Hill Top Works, Bingley, Yorkshire, breakers, in June 1965.

575, 576, 577, 580, 583 sold to Autospares (Bingley) Ltd., Hill Top Works, Bingley, Yorkshire, breakers, in November 1965.

578 sold to Autospares (Bingley) Ltd., Hill Top Works, Bingley, Yorkshire, breakers, in January 1966 and purchased shortly afterwards by R. Alan Calderbank for preservation. By the early 1980s the vehicle had been acquired by Phillip Howard who carried out restoration work to operable condition and put it on display at the Sandtoft Transport Centre. It subsequently returned to Nottingham for an event in Wollaton Park and operated at the Black Country Museum in 1992. Since the early 1990s the vehicle has been in store at Boughton, Nottinghamshire.

581 sold to Mellors, Bulwell, Nottingham, showmen, in October 1965.

582 sold to Autospares (Bingley) Ltd., Hill Top Works, Bingley, Yorkshire, breakers, in February 1966.

592, 594 sold to Colbro, Rothwell, Yorkshire, breakers, in September 1965.

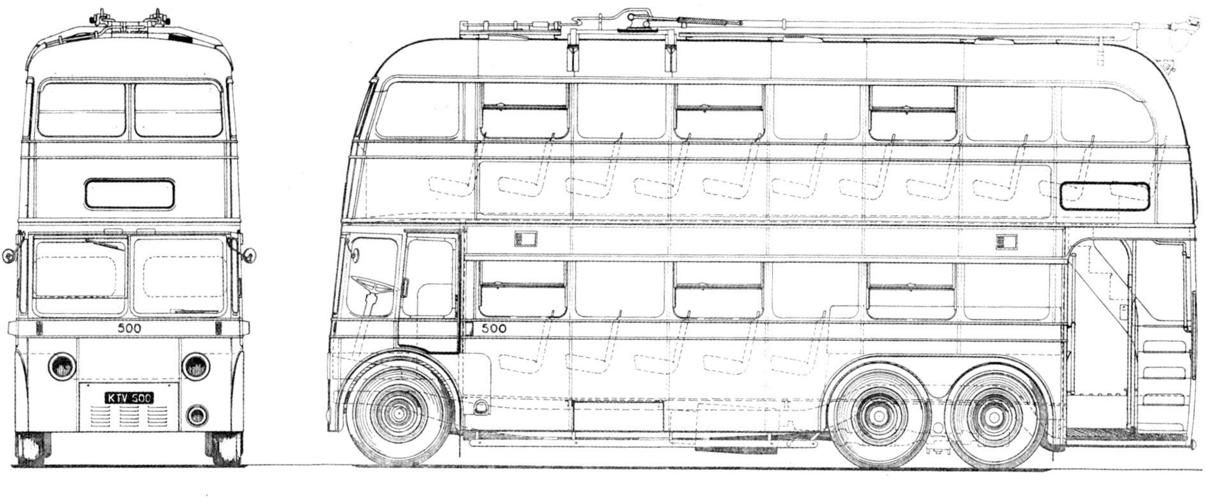

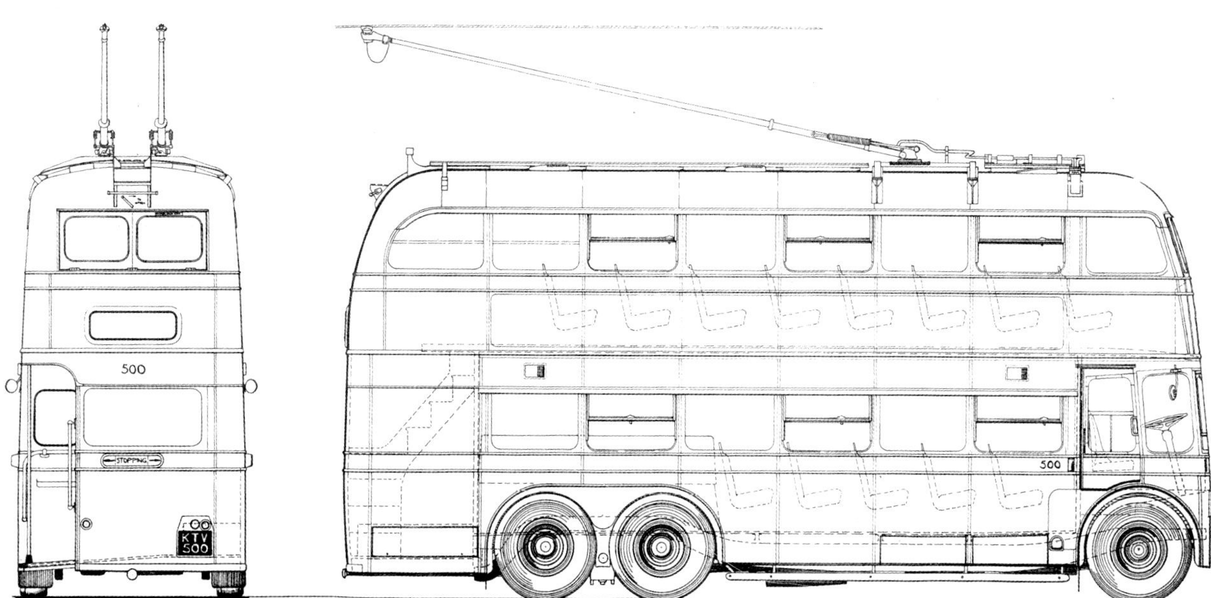

Detailed drawings of BUT9641T/Brush 500

John Lowrie

59 Guy BTX

Guy Motors supplied Wolverhampton Corporation Transport 59 to Nottingham for demonstration purposes 6 - 24 May 1929. It is seen here at the city centre terminus of the Nottingham Road services in the apex of the junction between Queen Street and King Street. *GHFA & JMB*

Chassis: Three-axle type Guy BTX manufactured by Guy Motors Ltd., Fallings Park, Wolverhampton.
Motor: Front-mounted Rees-Stevens (60 hp at 500 volts) built by Rees Roturbo Co. Ltd., Wednesfield Road, Wolverhampton.
Electrical equipment: Rees-Stevens patent employing controllers built by British Thomson-Houston Co. Ltd., Rugby, Warwickshire.
Dewirement indicator: Assumed to have been equipped with line lights.
Brakes: Pneumatic (believed to be Westinghouse), Rees-Stevens regenerative, hand and rheostatic brakes. Other sources suggest vacuum brakes to all wheels instead of pneumatic brakes.
Body: Christopher Dodson H33/28R
Length: 26ft
Width: 7ft 6ins
Wheelbase: 16ft 4¾ins
Unladen weight: 6tons 10cwt 1qtr

It is believed that the BTX demonstrated in Nottingham was completed at the beginning of May 1929 and delivered direct from the manufacturers prior to entering service in Wolverhampton. It is understood that 59 was used to test the suitability of three axle vehicles for use on the then planned St. Ann's Well Road – Wilford Bridge service and that it was in Nottingham until 25 May 1929.

Chassis:

Based on the Guy BX 3-axle motorbus chassis.

Chassis number BTX 23247 this being the last chassis of the Wolverhampton batch (57-61).

Electrics:

The traction motor was mounted between the chassis frame, over the front axle, resulting in a particularly long propeller shaft to the leading rear axle.

Much of the electrical equipment was built by Electrical Construction Co., Wolverhampton.

Brakes:

No further details have been found.

Bodywork:

Composite seven-bay highbridge double-deck construction, enclosed forwards-ascending half-turn (90°) staircase with conventional semi-vestibuled open platform entrance and exit at the rear, built by Christopher Dodson Ltd., Cobbold Road, Willesden, London NW10.

The high mounted and upright body still possessed many tramcar features and although the lower deck body sides were not divided into waist and rocker panels there was a horizontal line of beading aligned with the top of the wheel arches. The front of the upper saloon was set back, lying approximately mid-way between the front panels and the rear bulkhead of the driver's cab. The roof of the driver's cab and the upper-deck floor were cambered for drainage purposes. There was a slightly domed roof but no overhang at the front of the upper-deck. The trolley poles were fitted on a concealed roof-mounted gantry above bays 3 and 4; photographs of the upper saloon of other examples from the same batch of Wolverhampton vehicles show that the gantry was visible from inside, beneath the outer roof skin. The main transverse chassis girders were visible at the front beneath the headlamps and at the rear beneath the rear platform panel.

Lower deck ventilation was by inward opening top lights above the main saloon side windows in bays 1-5 (both sides). The position of the top lights was taken by a destination box in bay 6 whilst bay 7 was panelled over, again on both sides. Half drop panes were fitted in the lower saloon in bays 2 and 4 on both sides and in the upper saloon in bays 2, 4 and 6 on both sides.

The outer front window on each corner of the upper saloon used flat glass although the panels beneath were curved. The upper deck rear corner panels and the window at the top of the staircase gave evidence of window framing although panelled over.

The rear offside profile was almost semi-circular and reminiscent of a tramcar platform vestibule. There

Wolverhampton Corporation Guy BTX/Dodson 59 in service at Gregory Boulevard between Sherwood Rise and Mansfield Road heading towards the city centre. Note the spare wheel stowed beneath the open rear platform. *GHFA & JMB*

were three matching windows at the rear of the lower and upper decks, that towards the nearside being almost square and the remainder oblong in shape, whilst the window position on the offside of the upper deck was panelled over. The base of the rear platform panelling was aligned with that of the side panels, providing access to a cradle suitable for stowing a spare wheel. There were two steps up to the rear platform, which was at the same height as the lower saloon floor. The rear registration number was displayed above the nearside bulkhead window on the rear platform.

The front of the driver's cab had a deep vertical flat panel with rounded edges beneath the shallow windscreens (which were about 10ins shorter than the lower saloon side window area) descended to about 12ins above the level of the front axle with a considerable ground clearance beneath. The offside windscreen was divided horizontally; the upper two-thirds opened outwards and was equipped with a windscreen wiper.

The offside of the drivers cab featured a front-hinged door with a noticeably high handle, which provided the only access to the cab, towards the front of the vehicle with a second narrow panel between the door and the bulkhead. There was a single fixed panel and window on the nearside. The side windows and windscreen extended to the cab roofline, the base of the side windows being aligned with the base of the windscreen to better accommodate the high driving position. The driver's cab door was equipped with a sliding "signalling" window and there was a small rectangular driver's rear view mirror mounted externally half way up the cab offside front pillar. The panelling immediately beneath the cab side windows was painted cream to align better with the lower saloon windows. There were 3 glazed panels in the bulkhead behind the driver, that in the centre being smaller than the other two.

There was a large step ring on the front offside wheel.

A bamboo trolley retrieval pole was carried on supporting hooks mounted at the base of the offside lower saloon panels between bays 1-7. Two trolley-restraining hooks towards the front of the rear roof dome held down the trolley booms when out of use but these extended over 1ft beyond the rear of the platform below. There were four life guard rails on each side, the lower rail being somewhat thicker than those above, extending between the front and rear axles and lengthening progressively at the rear to reach in front of the second axle, although there was no protection beneath the high-mounted, flat front panel. The one-piece mudguard over the rear axles descended in a gentle concave curve beneath the offside of the rear platform. A mud flap hung between the second and third axle.

A gutter ran around the base of the roof with drains running down the rear pillar of bay 7 on both sides.

The upper saloon had a ribbed ceiling.

Lighting:

External lighting comprised two headlights mounted at the top of deep, vertical front panel and a single rear light on the extreme offside of the rear platform at the height of the lower saloon half-lights.

Internal lighting was from the traction supply and is believed to have used 130 volt lamps in series.

Seating:

Full seating details have not been found however it is known that the lower saloon had a full width rear facing seat against the cab bulkhead and long inwards-facing bench seats on each side over the rear axles. The seats were covered in brown leathercloth.

Destination equipment:

A single line destination box was built into the half-light windows above the lower saloon side windows in bay 6 on both the near and offside.

There was a freestanding square service number indicator box placed towards the front of the cab roof mounted centrally above the driver's windscreen with a metal restraint to the front of the upper saloon. The nearside upper saloon rear window included a matching square number indicator box behind the pane of glass.

Internal Livery:

Brown stained wood with cream or off-white ceilings.

External Livery:

Delivered in full Wolverhampton Corporation apple green and primrose yellow livery of the period. The lower deck panels beneath the waistband and the front of the driver's cab beneath the high-mounted windscreen were painted apple green; everything above was painted primrose but for a narrow band of green immediately beneath the upper deck windows. The roof was finished in light grey.

The Wolverhampton coat of arms, with that undertaking's title and legal lettering beneath, was displayed on both sides of the lower deck waist panels, beneath bays 1-3 and centred beneath bay 2. The coat of arms and fleet number were repeated on the front panel beneath the driver's cab windscreen. Fleet numbers were also transferred on the lower side panels, that on the nearside being immediately above the front axle and that on the offside being centred on the driver's cab door.

Notes:

Wolverhampton fleet number 59 (registration number UK6359) was one of a batch of five Guy BTX vehicles (57-61, registration numbers UK6357-61) that entered service there between 4 – 27 May 1929. As number 59 was the last to go into service in Wolverhampton (27 May 1929) by some 12 days, its sojourn in Nottingham can be narrowed down to the period 6-24 May 1929. After demonstration Guy Motors took the vehicle to Wolverhampton

Disposal:

The entire batch were delicensed on 31 October 1940 and sold for scrap to John Cashmore Ltd., Great Bridge, Staffordshire, on 17 August 1943.

Here demonstrator 59 climbs the slight gradient at the east end of Gregory Boulevard up to Mansfield Road in May 1929. *GHFA & JMB*

8 Karrier-Clough E6

The retouched picture of Doncaster's Karrier Clough 8, DT1146, seemingly without fleet number, appeared in December 18 1930 issue of Tramway and Railway World trade magazine. *Tramway and Railway World*

Chassis: Three axle type Karrier E6 marketed by Clough, Smith & Co. Ltd. and manufactured by Karrier Motors Ltd., Huddersfield, Yorkshire.
Motor: BTH 508D 66hp series wound.
Electrical equipment: BTH controller
Dewirement indicator: Assumed to have been equipped with line lights.
Brakes: Westinghouse compressed air and hand brakes.
Body: Roe H32/28R
Length: 28ft
Width: 7ft 6ins
Wheelbase: 1 ft 6ins
Unladen weight: 7tons 0cwt 0qtrs

The original design of the Karrier-Clough E6 vehicle was developed from the three axle Karrier WL6/2 motorbus chassis and originally designated as the LL (low loading) type. The E6 was demonstrated in Nottingham in the summer of 1929 although the precise dates are not known.

Chassis:

Chassis number 54006.

Chassis length:

26ft 11ins

No third differential.

Electrics:

BTH controller. Elongated, roof-mounted trolley gantry. The trolley springs were mounted to the rear of the trolley base.

The trolleypole restraining hooks were affixed to the upper deck rear window surrounds above the destination box and were bent towards the centre line of the vehicle rather than outwards, requiring a non-standard stowage procedure, that is from the centre and then outwards.

Brakes:

No further details have been found.

Bodywork:

Composite six-bay highbridge double-deck construction, forwards-ascending half-turn (90°) staircase with conventional semi-vestibuled open platform entrance and exit at the rear, built by Charles H. Roe Ltd., Crossgates, Leeds, Yorkshire. Roe body number GO 1029.

The domed roof overhung the front of the upper-deck with a central service number indicator box in the top half of the middle of the three front windows. An elongated roof-mounted trolley gantry was fitted running from immediately behind the front dome above bay 1 to the rear of bay 3. A gutter ran around the base of the roof and at upper deck floor level with drains descending the pillars at the front of bay 1 and at the rear of bay 6. The staircase and rear platform were integrated into the bodywork.

The front panels to the upper saloon were set back some distance from the front of the driver's cab beneath and were approximately aligned with the rear of the front axle. They featured gentle external curves and wide panelled corner pillars. The roof of the driver's cab was gently curved with lips above the side panels and a pronounced peak at the front.

It is assumed that half-drop openers were fitted to some of the lower saloon side windows as glass louvres surmounted the windows in bays 2, 4 and 5 on the nearside and bays 2-5 on the offside but photographic evidence is lacking. The upper saloon side windows in bays 2 and 6 appear to have been fitted with horizontally sliding panes with a protecting bar inside. Particularly long "torpedo" ventilators were fitted in the cream-painted vent panel above both the lower and upper deck windows bays 1-6 and above the upper deck rearmost side "D" window. The foremost corners of the upper saloon windows in bay 1 on both sides of the vehicle were radiused to match the rear side "D" windows. There were three fixed windows at the front of the upper saloon, those on the nearside and offside having radiused external corners. At the rear of the upper saloon there were two rectangular windows again with radiused external corners having half-light windows above mounted towards the wide external pillars and separated by a centrally mounted rear destination box. The window to the rear of the platform was divided into 2 panes by a central pillar, the whole again with radiused external corners, with half-lights above, matching the upper saloon rear window.

The driver's cab protruded well forward of the upper deck, both windscreens being surmounted by an opening half-light window, which tilted centrally on its vertical axis for ventilation purposes. The half-lights were mounted towards the corner pillars and separated by a centrally mounted front destination box. The top half of the offside driver's windscreen opened outwards and was equipped with a windscreen wiper. There was an upright bulbous front panel to the driver's cab equipped with beading in the shape of a radiator with deeply curved front mudguards. The front registration number plate was affixed along the base of the front panel. There were front-hinged doors on both sides of the cab equipped with horizontally sliding "signalling" window as deep as the pane and exposed door handles towards the rear of each door. There were fixed quarter lights between the cab doors and the cab front pillars. A bulb warning hooter extended through the base of the offside front windscreen just inboard of the offside pillar.

There was a single step, that is two from street level, on the nearside of the rear platform, the riser of which carried a "Karrier-Clough" maker's plate and centrally-mounted handrail, and a further shallow step up into the lower saloon. Three lifeguard rails on each side extended between the front and second axles. A mud flap hung between the second and third axle.

Destination equipment:

A single line destination box was built into the half-light windows at the front centrally above the driver's windscreen and in the upper portion of the nearside lower saloon window in bay 3. At the rear a single line destination box was built into the half-light windows centrally at the rear of the upper deck saloon. There was a central service number indicator box in the upper half of the central front upper deck window.

Seating:

The lower saloon had a 4-person inwards-facing bench seat on each side over the rear axles and 5 rows of forwards-facing double seats. The upper saloon had 7 rows of double seats on the offside and 9 rows on the nearside.

External Livery:

Delivered in the tramcar-style Doncaster Corporation Transport livery of the period. The lower portions of the lower deck and upper deck side and rear panels, the lower portion of the upper deck front panel, the lower deck and upper deck window surrounds, and the roof were cream. The deep lower deck waistband, an equivalent band around the upper deck panels, the driver's cab beneath the windows and a narrow band at upper deck floor level were painted maroon. The main panels and curved upper deck corner panels were lined in tramcar style single lining with ornate corner designs.

The Doncaster coat of arms was displayed on both sides of the lower deck waist panels, beneath the window pillar between bays 3 and 4, and centred between the headlights within the "radiator" beading on the front panel of the driver's cab.

Lighting:

External lighting was 2 headlights mounted half way down and standing proud of the curved external edges to the bulbous front panel. There were no sidelights. It is assumed that there was a single rear light at the top of the offside lower deck corner panel but no supporting photographic evidence has been found.

Notes:

Doncaster E6 fleet number 8 (registration number DT1146) was one of a batch of six Karrier Clough LL Type three axle trolley omnibuses (Doncaster 5-10, chassis numbers 54001-6) built in July-September 1928. Upon delivery, understood to be in the period August-October 1928, they had been re-designated by Karrier-Clough as model type E6.

Disposal:

After demonstration at Nottingham, 8 returned to Doncaster. It was subsequently withdrawn from service on 30 April 1939 and sold to Buxton (dealer) on 25 May 1939.

25 Guy BTX 60

Guy BTX60 25 (UK8948) arrives at King Street in October 1930. *GHFA & JMB*

Chassis: Three axle type Guy BTX 60 manufactured by Guy Motors Ltd., Fallings Park, Wolverhampton.
Motor: Front-mounted Rees-Stevens (60 hp at 500 volts) built by Rees Roturbo Co. Ltd., Wednesfield Road, Wolverhampton.
Electrical equipment: Rees-Stevens patent employing controllers built by British Thomson-Houston Co. Ltd., Rugby, Warwickshire.
Dewirement indicator: Assumed to have been equipped with line lights.
Brakes: Westinghouse pneumatic, Rees-Stevens regenerative, hand and rheostatic brakes.
Body: Guy H31/28R
Length: NCT records quote 26ft other sources show 25ft 9ins
Width: 7ft 6ins
Wheelbase: NCT records quote 16ft 7ins other sources show 16ft 4½ins
Unladen weight: Not known

The BTX60 (the suffixed digits indicating the nominal seating capacity of an appropriate body although other examples had 57 or 58 seats), was completed in January 1930 and demonstrated in Nottingham from June 1930 until at least October 1930.

Chassis:

Based on the low frame Guy BX three axle motorbus chassis with an offset transmission having the differential and worm cases on the nearside to permit a lower floor to the lower saloon. There was no third differential between the two rear driving axles. Chassis number 23447.

Electrics:

The traction motor was mounted between the chassis frame, over the front axle, in order that the commutator brushes could be inspected without using a pit, resulting in a high front lower saloon floor line which sloped towards the rear of the bus and a high-mounted driver's cab. It also resulted in a particularly long propeller shaft to the leading rear axle. The motor was built with aluminium end covers to reduce weight to a minimum.

The motor shunt circuit was never broken whilst the windings were designed to give a smooth and effective retarding effect when the vehicle was slowing down from high speeds on the level or when going down hills at normal speeds.

As the motor field was excited by shunt as well as series windings, the series resistances, operated by way of the contactors by the foot pedal, had a greater effect on the speed control than in earlier vehicles. A resistance was automatically brought into circuit with the shunt winding during regenerative braking to prevent the voltage of the generator rising above line voltage when the vehicle was coasting with the power pedal in the "off" position and with the outside current supply cut off. A further resistance in the lighting circuits prevented the lamps being burned out when regenerative braking took place.

The control gear consisted of a patent combined drum type controller and shunt regulator mounted on an aluminium case. The power pedal control was mechanically interlocked with the reversing switch: the reversing switch hand lever could not be moved until current was cut off from the motor whilst the power pedal could not be depressed until the reversing switch was in the correct position.

Radio interference choke coils were mounted in the master controller case.

Brakes:

No further details have been found.

Bodywork:

Composite six bay highbridge double-deck construction, enclosed forwards-ascending half-turn (90°) staircase with conventional semi-vestibuled open platform entrance and exit at the rear, built by Guy Motors, Fallings Park, Wolverhampton.

The domed roof somewhat overhung the front of the upper-saloon which had two windows with radiused outer corners and particularly wide front corner panels. The trolley base and poles were fitted in a conventional manner on a concealed roof-mounted gantry above bay 2. A gutter ran around the base of the roof but no drains are evident on photographs. The staircase and rear platform were integrated into the bodywork. The main transverse chassis girders were partially visible beneath the front panel to the driver's cab.

Half-drop openers were fitted to the lower saloon side windows in bays 1, 2, 3 and upper deck bays 2, 4 and 6. Shallow glass louvres were fitted above the opening side windows on both decks. The rearmost side windows to the upper saloon (offside and nearside) and lower deck offside diffused glass window behind the staircase had large-radius corners to match those at the front and rear of the upper saloon and in the rear platform window. The upright rear elevation incorporated two large windows (the pane on the nearside presumably sliding transversely behind the fixed offside pane) to the upper saloon, which provided access to the trolley gantry and the upper-deck emergency exit, and two matching windows to the lower-deck open rear platform.

There was a single step from the rear platform into the lower saloon whilst the offside and rear panelling to the platform was noticeably deeper than earlier vehicles.

The "piano front" of the upper-deck curved forwards above the driver's cab, the vertical front elevation being equipped with a single-line destination box built into the panelling. This also resulted in an overhang above the driver's cab windscreen. The driver's cab, which protruded well forward of the upper-deck, was equipped with shallow opening windscreens on the off and nearside and a front hinged door on the offside. The door was equipped with an old-fashioned brass circular "door knocker" handle. The equally shallow window (about 6ins shorter than the lower saloon side windows) in the offside cab door and its counterpart on the nearside was provided with a sliding "signalling" window. There were fixed quarter lights between the offside cab door and its matching nearside counterpart, and the cab front pillars. A small rectangular driver's rear view mirror was mounted externally half way up the offside front pillar of the cab. There were 3 glazed panels in the bulkhead behind the driver.

The high-mounted, flat front panel beneath the driver's cab windscreen was upright with rounded edges, its base being almost 1ft above the base of the lower saloon side panels. The front registration number plate was affixed to a protective shield that hung beneath the front panel between the dumb irons, level with the spotlight, and featuring a Guy maker's plate on the nearside, whilst that at the rear was applied with transfers at the top of the offside rear platform window.

The low body panels required solely a single lifeguard rail on each side, extending between the front and second axles. All wheels were equipped with chrome hubcap covers. The vehicle operated with chrome-plated hub cabs to all wheels and with a one piece "fairing" over the rear wheels which left the bogie trunnion exposed to view. A mud flap hung between the second and third axle.

Lighting:

External lighting was 2 headlights mounted half way up the flat front panel beneath the driver's windscreen on the extreme nearside and offside. Old-fashioned "carriage lamps", for emergency use, were affixed to the top of the front panel at the base of the front side pillars. A spot light hung beneath the front panel on the nearside but seems to have been covered up, out of use, during the demonstrator's stay. There was a single rear light at the top of the offside lower deck corner panel and a red triangular reflector at the nearside base of the rear panel.

It is believed that the interior lamps were fitted with circular chromed surrounds and opaque glass diffusers mounted along the ceiling on each side.

The manufacturer's literature states: "Should the poles leave the wires the lighting system of the bus (interior and exterior) does not fail", indicating that the vehicle was equipped with some form of emergency or standby battery lighting.

Seating:

No details of the seating layout have come to light however based on what is known about similar Guy BTX demonstrators of the period used in Birmingham and Llanelly, and limited photographic evidence, it is possible that in the lower saloon there was a longitudinal bench seat for 6 passengers on the rear nearside and one for 5 passengers on the offside. Guy favoured a rearwards facing bench seat for 5 passengers behind the driver's cab bulkhead and thus there would have been 3 rows of forwards facing double transverse seats. In the upper saloon there were 8 double transverse seats on the nearside, six on the offside and a transverse seat for 3 passengers at the rear above the open rear platform.

Moquette covered seats with curved backs.

Destination equipment:

A destination box capable of displaying a single-line of information was mounted centrally in the upright panelling at the front of the driver's cab roof and at the rear in the cream-painted panel immediately above the rear platform window.

Internal Livery:

The ceilings were white probably with stained and varnished window surrounds.

Floors grey.

External Livery:

The demonstrator was supplied in a basic Nottingham Livery 3 (see Appendix C). with a cream cheat line applied to the lower saloon side panels some 3ins below the base of the lower cream window surrounds, vertically towards the front and around the lower edge.

No Nottingham coat of arms was displayed.

A gold fleet number, shaded blue, 25 was affixed centrally on the front panel aligned with the base of the headlamps and beneath the oval Guy "Indian Chief" maker's plate, and on the rear panel beneath the rear platform window.

Minimal legal lettering was painted at the base of the nearside lower panels, including "Speed 20 mph" immediately behind the front axle. On the offside, the manager's name and title, and the name and address of the undertaking was sign-written at the base of the lower panels, bay 2. Further information appeared on the rear offside corner of the lower deck panelling but this is illegible on photographs.

Notes:

Registration number UK8948.

Disposal:

The vehicle was returned to Guy Motors in October or November 1930, being supplied to Pontypridd UDC as a demonstrator in December 1930. It remained there on loan until March 1932 when it was purchased and given fleet number 8. Pontypridd withdrew the vehicle in 1946.

26 AEC 663T

Following registration as HX1460, the AEC663T demonstrator entered passenger carrying service in Nottingham displaying the fleet number 26. It is seen here at The Wells Road, Kildare Road terminus in October 1930. *GHFA & JMB*

Chassis:	Three axle type AEC 663T manufactured by the Associated Equipment Company Ltd. at the AEC works, Windmill Lane, Southall, Middlesex.
Motor:	English Electric, Type DK130A (80 hp at 500 volts) twin armature with roller armature bearings, series-wound, forward mounted manufactured by English Electric Co. Ltd. at the Dick, Kerr Works, Strand Road, Preston, Lancashire.
Electrical equipment:	English Electric foot-operated contactor master controller, probably type D701B, and reverser equipped for semi-automatic acceleration. Notch regulator switch.
Dewirement indicator:	Assumed to have been linelights.
Brakes:	Compressed air, 2-stage rheostatic and hand brakes.
Body:	English Electric H33/27R.
Length:	26ft 11ins
Width:	7ft 6ins
Height:	13ft 8$\frac{9}{16}$ins to top of roof, 14ft 0$\frac{9}{16}$ins to top of trolley base
Wheelbase:	16ft 6ins giving a turning circle on either lock of 59ft.
Wheel track:	front 6ft 5$\frac{3}{8}$ins, rear 6ft 2$\frac{3}{4}$ins
Bogie wheelbase:	4ft
Unladen weight::	Not known
Laden weight:	12tons
Tyres:	36 X 8

Three 663T demonstrators were built, equipped with flimsy-looking highbridge but low-height double deck bodies. Except for subtle detail differences, for examplethe position of the driver's cab door handle in relation to the side beading, the bodies were identical. One was finished in AEC demonstration colours of grey with blue bands and displayed at the Tramways, Light Railways and Transport Association Annual Congress in Hastings 11-13 June 1930. It did not operate on the local system. Another was painted in a red livery with the fleet number 11, all in the style of South Lancashire Transport, perhaps in anticipation of being demonstrated to that company which started trolleybus operations with just ten lowbridge vehicles in August 1930. It is not known if this demonstrator actually ran on the company's fledgling network but it was a static exhibit at the Royal Agricultural Society's Show in Manchester in July 1930. This same vehicle was demonstrated to senior staff of the London United Tramways from 1 October 1930 running on trade plates between Fulwell and Teddington. The third, which can be identified as having chassis number 001, was finished in a green and cream livery of the NCT style but without the undertaking's title, coat of arms or fleet numbers, and reached Nottingham, unregistered, it is believed, in July 1930. One of the three demonstrators may have run on test at Ashton-under-Lyne. It must be stressed that no conclusive records have been found to show which chassis number was carried by the other two demonstrators, as they were not registered until after they had been re-bodied.

The Nottingham demonstrator was registered HX1460 by the Middlesex licensing authority, who recorded the chassis number as 663T001, on 23 September 1930. It entered passenger carrying service on service 10, carrying fleet number 26, and remained on trial in Nottingham until early 1931. Its registration number was surrendered on 23 March 1931. Revised Conditions of Fitness Regulations, which came into force on 1 February 1931, stipulated minimum headroom of 5ft 10ins in the lower saloon and 5ft 8ins in the upper saloon, in both new and existing vehicles. The 11ft 8ins overall height of the English Electric bodies could not comply with these requirements. There were other conflicts with the new regulations, including the opening windows, whilst daily use in passenger service had shown the bodies to be structurally weak and there had been difficulties in accessing the motor for maintenance. There was no alternative but to re-body all three vehicles before they could be used again.

Prototype chassis 663T001 was equipped with a new English Electric highbridge body featuring a half cab and dummy radiator, a front exit equipped with folding door (in addition to the rear open platform) and twin staircases, whilst the two front windows of the upper saloon opened as one unit to offer an unconventional emergency exit. It is believed to have then gone on trial to Bradford before being exhibited at the Commercial Motor Show of November 1931. In May 1932 it went to Southend-on-Sea where it was given fleet number 116 and purchased in November 1932 receiving local registration number JN2086. The undertaking rebuilt it later with a full front, minus "radiator", and the front stairs and doorway were removed. After withdrawal in 1950 it was converted into mobile ladies toilet being finally sold to a breaker in 1967.

Chassis:

Based on the AEC Renown motorbus chassis. Chassis number 663T001.

Chassis length:

26ft 9ins

Chassis frame width:

front 3ft 0¼ins, rear 5ft

Overall width (over hubs):

front 7ft 5½ins, rear 7ft 4½ins

Electrics:

The forward mounted traction motor, inclining towards the rear of the vehicle, and air compressor projected into the floor area of the driver's cab. The motor drove both rear axles through a cardan propeller shaft with a differential on each. The contactor cabinet was mounted in the nearside of the cab and the drum type master controller on the nearside dash. The manufacturers placed great store on the convenient location of all electrical equipment, including the motor, in a single place (the driver' cab).

Inside the contactor cabinet was a current-limit relay intended to offer an early form of automatic acceleration whereby the first and second notches were under the driver's full control but all further notches were subject to the value set on the relay however the power pedal was depressed. It is understood that this was not entirely successful.

Brecknell Willis supplied their low-mounted 10½ins square trolley bases equipped with Timken bearings, trolley heads and trolley wheels, to fit 18ft long trolley poles. The vehicle was equipped with an insulated trailing skate and appropriate changeover switch.

Brakes:

Compressed air, hand and electric rheostatic brakes. The service brake was the rheostatic supplemented by compressed air, both operated by the same foot pedal. Initial pressure on the foot pedal applied successively the two notches of the rheostatic brake, further movement at a comparatively low speed actuating the air brake control valve and applying the compressed air brake whilst still retaining rheostatic braking. The rheostatic brake was also used to hold the vehicle at speed downhill; on a grade of 1 in 18 the second brake notch could hold the vehicle at 10-12 mph whilst the first brake notch could hold it at ca. 15 mph.

The air brakes operated on all wheels. The motor-driven air-compressor was mounted on the top of the traction motor and thus projected well into the driver's cab. One air-brake cylinder actuated the brake drums on the front axle and a second actuated those on the rear axle.

The handbrake operated on the rear bogie wheels only. The handbrake lever was to the offside of the driver's steering column.

Bodywork:

Highbridge double-deck composite five bay construction, enclosed forwards-ascending half-turn (90°) staircase with conventional rear, semi-vestibuled open platform entrance and exit, and roof ribbing built by English Electric Co. Ltd., Dick, Kerr Works, Strand Road, Preston, Lancashire. The low overall height was achieved by restricted saloon headroom.

The lightweight composite body was one of three built by English Electric with the upper and lower decks as separate units. The front elevation featured almost upright panels with rearwards inclined driver's cab windscreen and upper-saloon windows, resulting in the upper deck front panelling being some 6ins set back in relation to the front of lower deck. There was a small "lip" immediately below the driver's cab windscreen and the upper-saloon front windows giving something of a reduced "piano" front. The slightly domed roof, with a prominent central rib overhung the front of the upper-saloon, which had two almost square windows and particularly narrow front pillars which, together with five bay construction, did nothing to add strength to the body. The roof was particularly shallow for the period, reducing the weight of the top deck but increasing the separation between the roof line and the trolley gantry.

A gutter ran around the base of the roof with drains descending both sides of the vehicle down the front pillar of bay 1 and the rear pillar of bay 5.

Extensions were bolted to the roof rail immediately above the upper-deck body pillars between bays 1 and 2, and bays 2 and 3 to support the two diagonal girders of the exposed gantry above bays 1-3, which was not in direct contact with the roof. Additional gantry supports fore and aft were mounted centrally above bay 1 and 3.

Half-drop windows with glass louvres above were fitted to the side windows in bays 1 and 3 of the lower deck and 1, 3 and 5 of the upper deck. The front upper-deck windows were fixed and featured transverse protective rails inside. At the rear of the upper-saloon there were two large almost square windows, the pane on the nearside sliding transversely behind the fixed offside pane to provide access to the trolley gantry and offer an emergency exit. There were two matching rear platform windows whilst the rearmost offside panel behind the staircase was also glazed. There is no evidence of additional ventilation.

The upper-deck front panels slightly overhung the front of the driver's cab, which was equipped with a single opening windscreen on the offside and a top-mounted windscreen wiper. There was a deep front-hinged cab door on the offside only equipped with a vertical sliding "signalling" window involving the entire pane and an inset opening handle. There were large fixed quarter lights between the offside cab door and its matching nearside counterpart, and the cab front pillars. The rearmost top corner of the driver's cab door side window was radiused. Matching panels and window layout were found on the nearside of the driver's cab. The base of the cab door was curved over the wheel arch to a position about 4ins from the rear of the door thereafter the base, beneath the cab door handle, was horizontal, parallel to the base of the side window and about 2ft below it.

There were 2 glazed panels in the bulkhead behind the driver with a narrow central pillar. A small circular driver's rear view mirror was mounted externally towards the top of the offside front cab pillar. The English Electric winged symbol with a triangular AEC badge beneath was fitted centrally beneath the driver's windscreen towards the top of the outline "radiator" and between the ventilation vanes. The cab was equipped with a bulb horn and a fire extinguisher.

The slightly bulbous front beneath the driver's windscreen had a large, deep removable panel with a curved top, appearing as an outline "radiator", designed to ease access to and removal of the traction motor, and equipped with two columns of fourteen louvre type ventilation vanes. The extremities of the front panel were curved and accommodated protruding headlights which also acted as sidelights. The front registration number plate hung centrally beneath the front panel.

There was no step on the rear platform and a single step up into the lower saloon. The vehicle was equipped with Numa air bells.

A single lifeguard ran beneath the side panels between the front and leading rear axle. A bamboo trolley retrieval pole was carried centrally under the chassis. All wheels were equipped with wheel nut protector rings.

Lighting:

External lighting was 2 headlights mounted on the extremities of the curved panel each side of the outline "radiator". There were no separate front sidelights. There was a single rear light mounted at the top of the cream-painted offside rear platform corner panel. .

Internal diffused lighting with white enamel fittings mounted in the cove panels were supplied at line voltage. Solely the platform light was of the exposed type.

Seating:

The lower saloon had a 5-person inwards-facing bench seat on the offside over the rear axle, a bench seat for 6 persons on the nearside, and 4 rows of forwards-facing double seats. The upper saloon had 7 rows of double seats on each side and a single bench seat at the rear above the open platform accommodating 5 passengers. The driver's seat was upholstered in quilted leather.

The spring cushion seats featured arched or hipped backs, those in the lower saloon were upholstered in moquette and those in the upper saloon in hand-buffed leather.

Destination equipment: Rectangular indicator boxes were mounted centrally in the lower two-thirds of the front upper-deck panels above the driver's cab windscreen, the screen being partially masked off to show a single line of destination information, and towards the base of upper-deck panels at the rear. The rear screen was substantially smaller than that at the front.

Internal Livery:

The interior woodwork was mahogany faced below the windows with black "Doverite" and nickel-plated fittings. The floors were covered in linoleum.

External Livery:

The demonstrator was supplied in a basic version of Nottingham's Livery 3 (see Appendix C). A cream cheat line was applied to the lower saloon side panels some 3ins below the base of the lower cream window surrounds and arched over the outline "radiator".

No Nottingham coat of arms was displayed.

The gold shaded fleet number 26 was affixed on the cream-painted panel centrally above the driver's cab windscreen. No photograph of the rear elevation of this vehicle at Nottingham has been found but it is likely that a fleet number was carried at the rear beneath the platform window.

Minimal legal lettering and ownership details were painted at the base of the nearside lower panels whilst further information appeared on the rear offside corner of the lower deck panelling but this is illegible on photographs.

Disposal:

26 was returned to AEC in early 1931.

Karrier-Clough E6

Karrier Clough E6/Park Royal demonstrator 27 pulled up outside Lower Parliament Street Depot before being renumbered 50 in 1931. *NCT*

Chassis: Three axle type Karrier E6 marketed by Clough, Smith and manufactured by Karrier Motors Ltd., Huddersfield, Yorkshire.

Motor: British Thomson-Houston Co. Ltd., Rugby, Warwickshire. Type BTH 508 (75hp) series wound motor equipped with BTH MR506 Form B circuit breakers.
This specification is based on the manufacturer's publicity literature, the NCT fleet list of 1947 and the history card of this vehicle, although other sources indicate that by the time the demonstrator was purchased, it had been re-equipped with a BTH 110D (80hp) motor series wound 136 armature amps at 1,650 rpm at 500 volts.

Electrical equipment: British Thomson-Houston Co. Ltd., Rugby, Warwickshire.

Brakes: Westinghouse pneumatic and hand brakes.
As a demonstrator this vehicle also had eddy current brakes.

Body: Park Royal H30/30R. Design number 2027 dated 21 April 1931. NCT drawing 11/4.

Length: 28ft 6ins

Width: 7ft 6ins over mudguards

Height: 15ft 2½ins to the top of the trolley bases.

Wheelbase: 17ft 6ins

Unladen weight: 8tons 1cwt 3qtrs

Tyres: 36 X 8

First licensed on 14 October 1930 as VH3305, this vehicle arrived in Nottingham on 1 November 1930 as a Karrier-Clough demonstrator and was given fleet number 27. Following comparative trials against AEC-English Electric, Brush Thornycroft and Guy vehicles, it was purchased in January 1932 and renumbered 50.

Chassis:

Pressed steel spectacle frame of deep section, carried 2ft 1in above the ground except at the rear which was 1ft 0¼ins above the ground (laden). Chassis number 54023.

The front axle was a high tensile drop forging of "H" section, thrust on swivel pins being taken by taper roller bearings. The hubs were mounted on adjustable taper roller bearings. Fully-enclosed worm and segment steering.

The final drive was taken to the rear axles by a tubular driving shaft fitted with two Mechanics universal joints and a splined plunger joint protected by a sliding muff. The rear axle incorporated twin axles of bogie construction. They were of the inverted worm-driven type; the gearing of each axle was mounted as a self-contained unit, removable from the main casing. The wheels were mounted on taper roller bearings. The rear bogie was fitted with two pairs of semi-elliptical springs, free to swivel on a central fulcrum attached to the frame, made of silico-manganese steel. Alcyl automatic chassis lubrication.

"Dished" front and rear wheels. The chassis, less equipment, cost £466 17s 1d.

Electrics: The motor was placed towards the front of, and along the centreline of, the chassis. It was of the self-ventilating type using the parallel flow method, a double-sided fan being mounted at the pinion end. The air-flow entered at the commutator end and left at the pinion end in two directions, one passing over the armature and field coils and the other through the armature core by means of longitudinal ducts.

Foot-operated contactor controller with eight accelerating notches and a shunted field notch. The equipment consisted of a master controller, contactors and a reverser all housed beneath a weatherproof cover.

Extensions, continuing over the rounded edges of the roof, were bolted to the roof rail immediately above the upper-deck body pillars between bays 1 and 2, bays 2 and 3, bays 3 and 4, bays 4 and 5 to support the exposed trolley gantry above bays 2, 3 and 4, the Brecknell Willis & Co. Ltd. trolleybases not being in direct contact with the roof. The vehicle could deviate up to 13 feet either side of the overhead line. Dish type trolleywheels.

The traction power cable looped over the front nearside roof overhand and made its way down the front pillar to enter the driver's cab at ventilator panel height immediately above the forward nearside cab window.

Brakes:

Westinghouse air pressure brakes of the internal expanding type were fitted to all rear wheels, utilising a Bull compressor. BTH eddy-current brakes.

Bodywork:

Composite seven-bay highbridge double-deck construction, enclosed forwards-ascending half-turn (90°) staircase with conventional semi-vestibuled open platform entrance and exit at the rear, built by Park Royal Coachworks Ltd., Abbey Road, Park Royal, Willesden, London NW10. The body cost £1,595 18s 1d, and as constructed included several discrepancies with the manufacturer's drawing.

The body framing was of English ash, strengthened where necessary with Duralumin and mild steel plates. The longitudinal side framing was diagonally strutted in an effort to conduct all stresses from the trolley gantry ultimately to the chassis frame. The body panels and roof were 18 gauge aluminium sheets, the upper roof being joined laterally, covered with moleskin canvas, bedded with footings and suspended from angle iron hoops.

The upright rear, overhanging roof to the front of the upper-saloon and overhanging upper deck front panel above the driver's cab windscreen gave this vehicles a heavy look despite the then fashionable "torpedo" panelling to the front panels featuring a broad imitation radiator beneath the driver's cab windscreen. The "radiator" was wider at the top than the base, somewhat similar to the AEC motorbus style of the period but with diagonal vanes.

The front of the upper-saloon was equipped with a small central service number indicator box at the top of a panel between the two front windows. The main traction power cable ran down the nearside front pillar and panel from the roof into the cab at ceiling height.

The stairs were fitted with aluminium "kicking plates" to the risers and Ferodo treads. Platform handrails and stanchions were black Doverite, other handrails and stanchions were chromium plated aluminium alloy.

Narrow front upper deck corner pillars. Shallow metal louvres were fitted above all the upper and lower deck saloon side windows, bays 1-7 and above the rearmost upper-deck side window, whilst the protruding front upper-deck panel provided something of a sun visor above the driver's cab windscreen. The side windows in bay 7 on the upper and lower decks were around ⅙th broader than those in bays 1-6. The rearmost side window on both sides of the upper-saloon was radiused towards the rear at both top and bottom in the shape of a "D". Half-drop Quickthro NS openers were fitted to the upper saloon side windows in bays 1, 3, 5 and 7, and to the lower saloon side windows in bays 2, 4, 6 on both the nearside and offside. At the rear of the upper saloon there were two almost square windows with radiused external corners, the pane on the nearside sliding transversely towards the offside to provide ventilation and access to the trolley gantry. The corners of the almost square rear platform window were radiused to match.

Square shaped Ashanco extractor ventilators were fitted in the cream-painted ventilator panel (cantrail) above the lower saloon windows in bays 1, 4 and 7. Four Ashanco extractors were built into the roof above bays 4 and 7. A ventilator grill was fitted centrally in the lower cream-painted portion of the front upper-deck panel above the driver's windscreen providing additional ventilation to the lower saloon through a duct in the cab roof. Smaller three-section ventilators were fitted beneath the overhanging roof immediately in front of the upper-saloon front windows.

The curvaceous nose to the front panel of the driver's cab featured an imitation, chrome edged "radiator" with the registration number plate at its base. The top half of the offside driver's windscreen opened outwards and was equipped with a windscreen wiper, the nearside windscreen was fixed. Bulb warning horn. There was a front hinged driver's cab door arched over the front axle with inset opening handle on the nearside with a sliding "signalling" window extending vertically from the top to the bottom of the pane. There was a small step with kicking plate in the side panel immediately beneath the door's deepest part. There appears to have been an "outline" door on the offside but without hinges or handle. There were fixed quarter lights between the offside cab door and its matching nearside counterpart, and the cab front pillars. A small circular driver's rear view mirror was mounted externally two thirds of the way up the offside cab front pillar.

There was a single step on the nearside of the rear platform, the riser of which carried a Karrier-Clough maker's plate, and a further step up into the lower saloon. The staircase had four steps from the platform to the half-landing and then two steps to the upper deck. There was a single life guard rail on each side extending between the front and second axles, although there was no protection beneath the high-mounted, slight curved front panel to the driver's cab. There was a one piece "fairing" incorporating both mudguards over the rear wheels and a mud flap hung between the second and third axle. A bamboo trolley retrieval pole was carried within the lower-saloon nearside body panels with a tube access from the rear platform vestibule.

Lighting:

External lighting was 2 headlights mounted on the curved panel each side of the imitation "radiator". Round sidelights were fitted on the cream-painted panels overhanging the driver's windscreen, at the top of the nearside and offside front pillars. There was a single rear red "bulls eye" light mounted at the top of the offside corner panel.

Seating:

Park Royal Type X, using spring case cushions covered in buffed green hide and scratchproof Rexine seat backs.

The lower saloon had a 3-person inwards-facing bench seat on each side over the rear axles and 6 rows of forwards-facing double seats. The upper saloon had 7 rows of double seats on the offside and 8 rows on the nearside.

Destination equipment:

A single-line destination box was located centrally halfway up the green-painted upper deck panels above the drivers' cab windscreen. A small square service number indicator box was mounted at the top of a wide central panel separating the front upper saloon windows and centrally at the rear towards the top of the upper deck panels above the rear platform window. There was a single-line destination box in the cream-painted ventilator panel above the nearside lower saloon window bay 6.

Internal Livery:

Ceilings and coves were covered with white painted panels with varnished/polished wood frames. The centre of the lower saloon ceiling was covered in scratchproof Rexine, matching the seat backs in colour. The ceiling of the driver's cab was cream and the upper portions of the bulkheads were painted white. Varnished wood frames surrounded all the windows. All internal transfers were gold with two-tone blue shading.

External Livery:

Delivered in Livery 3 (see Appendix C) complete with lower deck waistband in a darker shade of green and cream cheat line beneath. A large Karrier symbol was attached beneath the front destination-box.

Particularly large gold numerals, shaded blue, were mounted above the front destination box on the upper deck front panels centrally underneath the front upper saloon windows and at the rear centrally beneath the rear platform window.

Subsequent alterations:

In late 1931, 27 was renumbered as 50 to avoid confusion with the new Karrier E6, registration number TV4465, delivered at the end of October 1931. In late 1939, 50 was renumbered as 350.

Notes:

Prior to reaching Nottingham, the Karrier-Clough demonstrator was tested in the second half of October 1930, in Nottingham livery, by London United Tramways. It was based at their Fulwell Depot and ran on their experimental line (which had been built by Clough, Smith) between Fulwell and Teddington.

Disposal:

350 sold to A. Devey, Lynn Lane House Farm, Lichfield, dealers, in August 1949.

Former demonstrator 27, renumbered 50 in late 1932 and with its imitation "radiator" removed, in Gregory Boulevard just prior to the turn on to Sherwood Rise en route for Nottingham Road, Vernon Road. *GHFA & JMB*

28 Brush Thornycroft

The nearside view of 1930 Brush-bodied Thornycroft HD demonstrator 28 as advertised in the company's 1931 catalogue. *John Bath*

Chassis: Three axle type HD manufactured by John I. Thornycroft & Co., Ltd., Basingstoke, Hampshire. Chassis number 22422. Brush drawing originating from Thornycroft drawing X2525, dated 9 January 1931. NCT drawing 7/8.
The complete vehicle was marketed by the Brush Electrical Engineering Co., Ltd., of Loughborough, Leicestershire.

Motor: Brush four pole lightweight motor.

Electrical equipment: Nine notch controller made by British Thomson-Houston Co. Ltd., Rugby, Warwickshire. Seven resistance notches, one full field running position and a weak-field notch.

Dewirement indicator: A relay working in series with two Neon lamps and buzzer.

Brakes: Westinghouse compressed air, hand and rheostatic (8 notches) brakes.

Body: Brush H32/28R. NCT drawing 11/5.

Length: 27ft quoted but 26ft when scaled from the manufacturer's drawings.

Width: 7ft 6ins

Height: 14ft 7½ins to roof panels.

Wheelbase: Conflicting information from Brush and Thornycroft drawings give the wheelbase as either 17ft or 18ft with a rear bogie wheelbase of 4ft 6ins.

Unladen weight: 7tons 10cwts

Tyres: 36 × 8

Turning circle: 62ft fully laden.

Chassis:

The three-axle chassis was one of just three trolleybus chassis ever built by Thornycroft and incorporated their patented rear suspension intended to give an even weight distribution to all four wheels of the rear bogie and freedom from spring distortion under all conditions of driving and braking. The chassis frame comprised channel-section pressed steel side members cranked over the rear bogie and reinforced at the raised portions by channel type cross members bolted in position. The chassis was fitted with front wings. Trolleybus chassis HD22422 originated as single deck motorbus chassis FC20808. Four inverted semi-elliptic springs formed the only connection between the axles and the frame. The suspension permitted 6ins difference in the levels of the driving axles and allowed either axle to tilt to an angle of 8 degrees without causing any distortion of the springs. Grease-gun lubrication was provided for all working parts; those which were not readily accessible were fed by brass tubes from lubricators grouped below the floor traps.

The two rear axles had nickel steel casings with fully floating differential shafts driven by under-type worms. The differentials were situated in the centre of the rear axles.

The road springs were designed to be almost flat under normal loading conditions causing minimum movement of the pins in their bushes. The front springs were secured to the axle by a patented relieving plate which enabled the holding-down bolts to effectively withstand the stresses due to the flexing of the springs without suffering undue elongation. Friction-type shock absorbers connected the front axle to the chassis frame, in order to damp out excessive oscillation of the springs.

Electrics:

The four-pole lightweight Brush motor had commutating pole windings and a roller bearing armature. The motor was placed towards the front of the chassis and coupled through a universal joint to a cardan propeller shaft that continued as far as a chassis cross member where it engaged end-on to a second longer propeller shaft leading to a differential drive on the leading rear axle. The motor was designed for scheduled service speeds of 9¼, 11 and 13¼ mph, with eight, six and four stops per mile respectively.

British Thomson-Houston foot pedal operated controller master controller, a number of panel-mounted magnetic contactors and a reverser. The resistances appear to have been placed beneath the driver's cab at the front of the chassis with the controller immediately behind.

At that stage of trolley vehicle development, the advantages claimed for this method of operation were:

(1) Pedal operation left the driver's hands free for steering and applying the handbrake.
(2) There was a complete absence of burning at the contacts of the foot-operated controller as it dealt only with control currents; no ratchet notching device was required.
(3) The effort required from the driver was reduced to a minimum due to the small contacts in the master controller and the comparatively light return spring.
4) Both controller and contactors required the minimum of maintenance care.

The accelerating master controller was a small drum controller provided with a geared operating sector to which it was secured by a suitable pedal-plate and lever. By depressing the pedal against the operating spring, the controller was moved towards the "on" position, and returned by the spring when pressure was removed to the "off" position. The controller had seven resistance notches, an eighth full-field running notch and a ninth or weak-field notch. The driver could not move from the eighth to the ninth notch without a small but definite backward movement of the pedal towards the "off" position, which released a stop and enabled the pedal to be further depressed to reach the weak-field notch.

A second master controller, electrically interlocked to the accelerating controller and connected to the air-brake mechanism by levers, offered eight rheostatic braking notches.

The contactors were mounted on two panels of lightweight insulating compound. Each had its own individual blow out coil, arc chute, and 500-volt operating coil. On one panel five 150-amp contactors were mounted. Two had their contacts connected in series, their function being to open and close the line circuit on the first accelerating notch, the double break ensuring that this function was adequately performed even in exceptional circumstances. These contactors, in conjunction with two further contactors, were also used for reversing the motor field during braking, the line and braking contactor being mechanically interlocked so that they could not be closed simultaneously.

The fifth contactor was a resistance contactor used only on the braking notches. On the second panel eight (seven 80 amp, one 150 amp) contactors were mounted; seven were used for short-circuiting sections of the starting resistance, while the eighth connected the diverter resistance across the motor field on the last control notch.

The contactor control circuit was made through a segment of the master controller on the first resistance notch only and subsequently by means of an interlock on one of the two line contactors. This ensured that the power circuit could not be remade after interruption without returning the master controller to the first notch, and re-inserting the whole of the starting resistance.

The reverser was a small hand-operated drum controller provided with three positions: "off", "forward" and "reverse". This controller reversed the connections to the motor armature and was provided with auxiliary contacts so arranged that it was impossible to close, or retain closed, any of the contactors, except when the reverse was in one of the two running positions.

The operation of the controls was as follows:

On depressing the power pedal the line contactors closed, connecting the motor across the line with the whole accelerating resistance in series. Further movement of the pedal closed the resistance contactors one by one, cutting out resistances from the two lines of resistance alternately, until on the eighth notch the large resistance contactor closed, short-circuiting the whole accelerating resistance, and connecting the motor directly across the line with full field. After passing the stop, the field-shunting contactor was closed, connecting a diverter resistance across the motor field, and increasing the speed of the vehicle. Movement of the braking pedal to the first notch reversed the motor field and established the braking connections with all resistance in circuit. On the second braking notch the additional resistance was cut out. On the remaining notches the same contactors as were used in acceleration were closed successively, leaving only one section in circuit on the last point to limit the load during emergency stops. This permitted adequate electric braking from the vehicle's maximum speed down to approximately 3 mph, after which the handbrake was sufficient. At the end of its travel the brake pedal engaged with a mechanism connected to the operating valve of the air brakes. The braking action of the electric brake was comparable with that of the air brake, either being capable of bringing the vehicle to a stop from a speed of 20 mph in just over its own length.

Extensions were bolted to the roof rail immediately above the upper-deck body pillars between bays 1 and 2, bays 2 and 3, and bays 3 and 4 to support the three girders of the exposed trolley gantry which was not in direct contact with the roof. The trolley booms were mounted on Timken roller bearing trolley bases and featured rearwards facing springs; they were stepped at suitable intervals to ensure minimum deflection when loaded and made of steel having a tensile strength of 35-40 tons per sq. ins. Lubrication was carried out by Tecalemit nipples to fit a standard Tecalemit grease gun. The trolley heads were manufactured from gunmetal and mounted on rubber sleeves to insulate the heads from the booms. Metal loops hung beneath the heads to facilitate adjustment with a bamboo trolley retrieval pole. The trolley wheels had hollow spindles to provide adequate lubrication to the bearing surfaces. The trolley retaining hooks were mounted at the extreme rear of the roof immediately above the upper saloon rear windows.

Brakes:

Westinghouse compressed air, hand and electric rheostatic brakes. The service brake was the rheostatic supplemented by compressed air, both operated by the same foot pedal. Initial pressure on the foot pedal applied the rheostatic brake in successive degrees up to its maximum, further movement actuating the air brake control valve and applying the compressed air brake. Thus, for service braking, the pedal was operated through its rheostatic braking notches until the vehicle speed was very low, at which stage the air-brake was lightly applied to bring the vehicle to a stop and, if necessary, to hold it on a grade. The rheostatic brake was also used to hold the vehicle at speed downhill. This form of operation reduced the wear of brake linings and in case of emergency or failure of the electric braking, a small further movement of the pedal brought the air-brake into operation. The air-pressure brake operated on the front wheels as well as the rear, and although cylinders were only applied to the rearmost axle of the rear wheels, braking action was transmitted to the other two wheels by the transmission gear. There was one air-brake cylinder each side of the chassis well to the rear of the front axle and one brake cylinder each side of the third axle.

The air brake compressor was fixed to the inner face of the chassis nearside with the air reservoir on the inner face of the chassis offside. In order to eliminate rigging and to equalise the braking action on each side of the vehicle, the cylinders were carried on brackets fitted directly to the brackets of the rear axle. A small motor-driven air-compressor provided compressed air for the brakes through a check valve into the reservoir until it reached a pre-determined maximum, when the air compressor governor came into action and cut the electric circuit to the motor, thus preventing overloading of the reservoir. As a further precaution, a safety valve was fitted to the reservoir, and the latter was of sufficient capacity to provide for several successive applications of the brake should the air compressor cease to operate, for exampledue to a power failure.

The handbrake was applied to the foremost drums of the rear wheels but braking was also obtained on the rear wheels by the transmission gear. The lever to operate the handbrake was to the offside of the steering column.

Bodywork:

Composite six-bay highbridge double-deck construction, forwards-ascending half-turn (90°) staircase with conventional semi-vestibuled open platform entrance and exit at the rear, built by Brush Electrical Engineering Co., Ltd., of Loughborough, Leicestershire. Indeed the first "modern" Brush trolleybus body.

The exterior panels were of aluminium with a waterproof birch plywood roof aimed at weight reduction with maximum strength. The front of the body featured a particularly "swept-back" styling between the upright bulbous front panel of the driver's cab and the upper deck roof, the upper deck front corner panel being in line with the front of the driver's cab door and somewhat behind the front axle.

Half-drop openers were fitted to the tops of the side windows in bays 1, 3, 5 on the offside and nearside of both decks, the upper pane sliding down outside the fixed lower pane. Elongated louvre ventilators were fitted in the cream-painted vent panel above the lower deck body pillars between bays 1 and 2, bays 3 and 4, and bays 5 and 6. These fed air into the cove panels then into the saloon though varnished wood Brush patent ventilators which were opened by pulling inwards by hand. There were three fixed windows at the front of the upper saloon, those on the nearside and offside having radiused external corners. At the rear of the upper saloon there were two almost square windows with radiused upper external corners which made up the upper-deck emergency exit. The upper saloon was equipped with four roof mounted ventilators (two on each side) towards the rear of bay 1 and towards the front of bay 6, in addition to a Brush patent ventilator in the front of the upper deck panel immediately above destination and indicator number box. There was a single step on the nearside of the rear platform, that is two from street level, and a further small step up from the platform to the level of the lower saloon floor. Half way up the staircase was an enlarged step to enable passengers to pass, there being three steps from the platform to the half landing and three steps to the upper deck. The window to the rear of the platform was divided into 2 panes by a central pillar, the whole again with radiused upper external corners matching the upper saloon rear window, the rear registration number being painted at the top of the nearside pane. The rearmost offside panel to the lower deck, behind the staircase, was glazed with radiused rear corners. A gutter ran around the base of the roof with drains down the front pillar of bay 1 on both sides and at the rear on both sides of the rear windows.

The top half of the offside driver's windscreen opened outwards. There was a front-hinged door on the offside of the cab with a sliding "signalling" window in the lower one-third of the pane and an inset, opening handle. There was a matching panel on the nearside equipped with a horizontally sliding window as deep as the pane. There were large fixed quarter lights between the offside cab door and its matching nearside counterpart, and the cab front pillars. There was a single ventilator inlet vane installed beneath the sun visor immediately above the centre of the windscreen. An access step was set into the base of the offside side panel, underneath the driver's cab door and immediately behind the front axle, just above the height of the wheel hub. The base of the front panel had a small "D"-shaped gap on the offside for access to a towing eye.

Two lifeguard rails on each side extended between the front and second axles. A mud flap hung between the second and third axle which had separate rear mudguards. The front registration number plate was affixed along the base of the front panel.

Destination equipment:

The front upper deck panel above the driver's windscreen accommodated a combined square service number indicator and single line destination box in one, the service number being displayed on the offside, located centrally in the lower third of the panel. The base of the box was set back deeply into the pronounced rearwards slope of the upper deck panel. The metal louvres were not continued above the nearside lower saloon window in bay 6 in which a single line destination box was mounted. At the rear a square service number indicator box was located at the bottom of the rear upper deck panel above the nearside rear platform window, towards the nearside.

Seating:

Sprung cushions and semi-bucket-type back, with spring fillings, covered in hand-buffed green leather of antique pattern on both decks.

The lower saloon had a 6-person inwards-facing bench seat on each side over the rear bogie and 4 rows of forwards-facing double seats. The upper saloon had 7 rows of double seats on the offside and 8 rows on the nearside.

Lighting:

External lighting was 2 headlights mounted half way down the front mudguards and 2 large side lights affixed to the cream-painted panels above the driver's windscreen, at the top of the nearside and off-side front pillars. There was a single rear light at the top of the offside lower deck corner panel.

Internal lighting in the upper saloon comprised pairs of ceiling-mounted lamps in circular porcelain bases in bays 1, 2, 4, 5 and in the rear dome. The lighting layout in the lower saloon is not known.

Internal Livery:

Natural grain woodwork, leather interior panels and white enamel ceilings.

The space below the seat rails was panelled with scratchproof leather material suitably moulded, the lower portions being provided with panels of corrugated aluminium.

External Livery:

Delivered in Livery 3 (see Appendix C) complete with lower deck waistband in a darker shade of green and cream cheat line beneath.

At a later date the roof was repainted grey.

External advertising was only applied when the body had been absorbed into the permanent fleet.

Notes:

Following initial testing in Nottingham in November 1930, the vehicle was registered TV3460 and returned to Nottingham for 6 months trial in passenger service until June 1931. It is believed that the Brush traction motor was less than successful.

Disposal:

In June 1931; the chassis was returned to Thornycroft. In 1933 the Brush body was mounted on a new Karrier E6 chassis which entered service as 1 (TV8473) in May 1933.

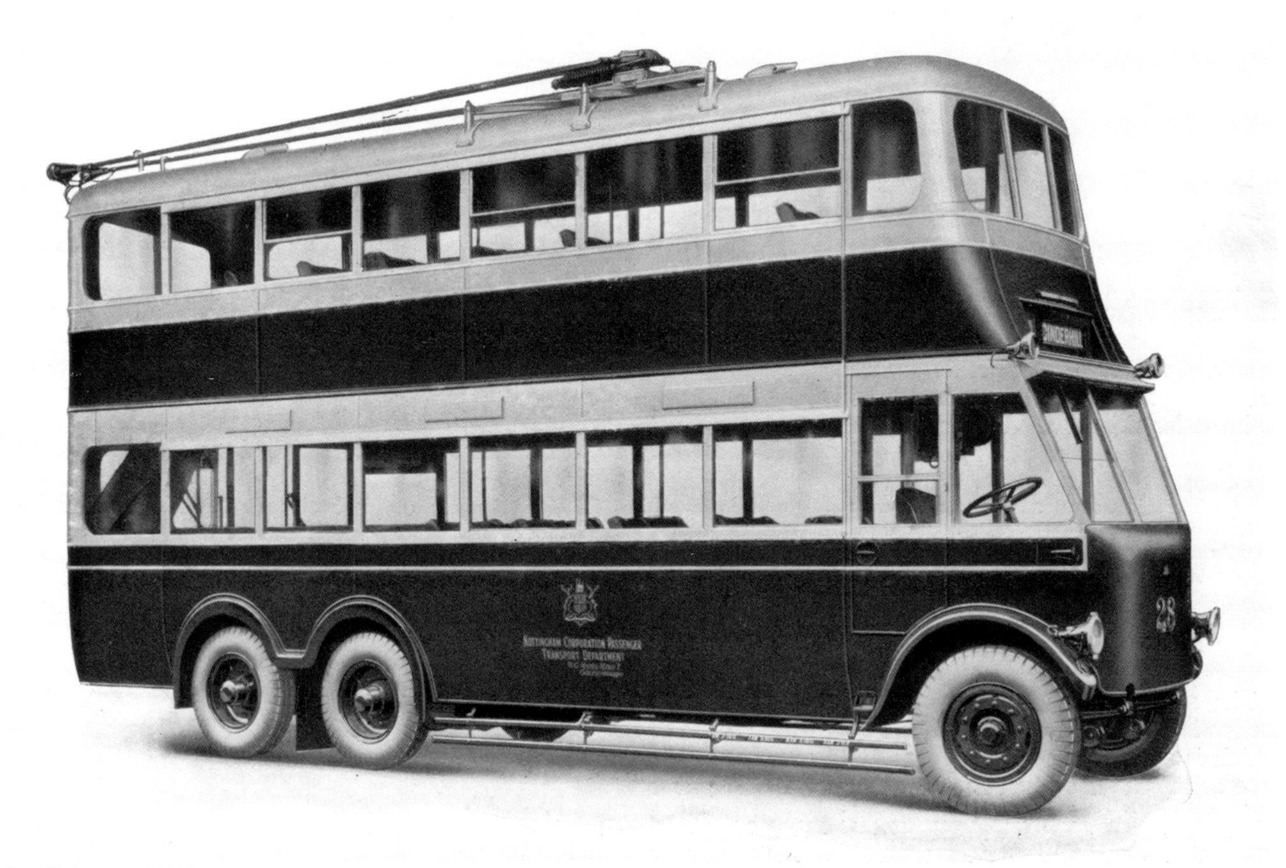

The offside view of 1930 Brush-bodied Thornycroft HD demonstrator 28 as advertised in the company's 1931 catalogue. *John Bath*

17 Leyland TTBD1

Leylands official picture of prototype TTDB1, 1932. *John Aldridge*

Chassis: Three axle type Leyland TTBD1 manufactured by Leyland Motors Ltd., Leyland, Lancashire.
Motor: GEC WT257, 65 hp, series wound (some sources state WT252A, 80 hp) manufactured by General Electric Co. Ltd., Witton, Birmingham.
Electrical equipment: FA3A controller made by General Electric Co. Ltd., Witton, Birmingham.
Dewirement indicator: Assumed to have been line-lights.
Brakes: Vacuum and hand brakes.
Body: Leyland H34/26R
Length: 27ft
Width: 7ft 6ins
Wheelbase: Understood to have been 16ft 6ins
Unladen weight: Not known

This vehicle, completed in January 1933 and registered TJ939, was Leyland's first three axle trolleybus chassis and body. It was tested on the South Lancashire Transport system before being demonstrated at Chesterfield in early 1933. Following trials and use as a driver trainer with Birmingham Corporation Transport from 11 March to 31 July 1933, the demonstrator, displaying fleet number 17 in the Birmingham style, was used in passenger service at Nottingham from 5 to 9 September 1933. The vehicle then returned to Leyland and although not used for demonstration purposes for more than two years, it was involved in the chassis design work for London Transport's B1 and B2 classes. It was fitted with a GEC WT254C motor before being despatched to Birmingham again in May 1936 where it entered service with the fleet number 68 on 9 July 1936, finally returning to Leyland in October 1937.

The sole TTBD1 to be built, it is rumoured that TJ939, was jointly funded by GEC, Leyland and Birmingham Corporation Transport. The latter's involvement emanated from the need to support local industry, in the form of GEC, whilst the demonstrator was seen as a test bed for the GEC motor and electrical equipment prior to placing a substantial order.

Chassis:

Chassis number 1654. F.A. Garrett, formerly with Ransomes, designed the chassis.

Brakes:

Vacuum brake (pedal operated) and mechanical hand brake.

The handbrake lever was to the offside of the driver's steering column.

Electrics:

The series wound traction motor, number 69657, was mounted towards the front of the chassis with the aim of reducing the floor height.

Brecknell Willis "Bradford" or low type trolleybases.

Bodywork:

Composite six-bay highbridge double-deck construction, forwards-ascending half-turn (90°) staircase with conventional semi-vestibuled open platform entrance and exits at the rear built by Leyland. The body was very similar to that employed on the 1932 metal framed Leyland Titan motor bus.

Substantial girder-like extensions, continuing over the rounded edges of the roof, were bolted to the outer face of the upper-deck body pillars (at about two-thirds depth of the window pane) between bays 2 and 3, bays 4 and 5 to support the exposed trolley gantry above bays 3 and 4, and the Brecknell Willis lightweight special trolleybases which were not in direct contact with the roof. These body pillars were more than double the breadth of the other upper-deck body pillars. The trolley boom retaining hooks were mounted on tubular frames each side of the trolley plank towards the rear of bay 5.

Half drop openers were fitted to the tops of the side windows in bays 1, 3, 5 of the upper deck and bays 2, 4 of the lower-deck, with "V" shaped glass louvres above. Ventilation flutes were fitted above all the lower deck side windows. There was a large single window at the rear of the upper-deck which provided the emergency exit.

The driver's cab featured a noticeably low, set-back seat and raked steering column. The shallow driver's cab windscreen was equipped with a metal rain shield curving gently to the front pillars on the offside and nearside. The top half of the driver's windscreens opened outwards that on the offside being equipped with a windscreen wiper. There was a rear-hinged door on the offside with an inset opening handle towards the front of the vehicle; the window in the offside cab door was divided horizontally into two panes, the lower pane sliding upwards behind the fixed upper pane to provide a "signalling" window. A protruding access step was placed at the base of the panel beneath the cab door, immediately behind the front axle, on the offside at the same height as the wheel nut protector ring. The front panel carried a large rectangular "Leyland" maker's-plate beneath the windscreen centre pillar.

A small rectangular driver's rear view mirror was mounted externally towards the top of the offside front cab pillar.

There were two lifeguard rails or tubes on each side, the lower one being more substantial, extending between the rear of the front wheel mudguard to the second axle. The front panel beneath the driver's cab windscreen descended to the same height above the road surface as the main side panels. The front axle wheel hubs featured chromed discs and were equipped with a wheel nut protector ring. A mud flap hung between the second and third axle. A bamboo trolley retrieval pole was carried towards the offside under the chassis.

Platform handrails and stanchions were covered in black Doverite.

Lighting:

External lighting was 2 headlights mounted halfway down the front panel, 2 circular front "bicycle style" side lights on the lower cream band at the base of cab side pillars and at the rear a single red "bulls-eye" light mounted above the offside of the rear platform window.

Seating:

Curved top seats throughout, those in the upper saloon being covered in moquette and those in the upper saloon with leathercloth.

The lower saloon was equipped with 5-person inwards-facing bench seats above the rear bogie on both sides and 4 rows of forwards-facing double seats. The upper saloon had 8 rows of double seats on the offside and 9 rows on the nearside, the ninth bench seat at the rear of the upper saloon above the open platform also accommodating just 2 passengers.

Destination equipment:

A single-line destination box was located centrally in the lower half of the upper deck panels, which had a gentle "piano front", above the driver's windscreen and at the rear on a protruding plinth above the rear platform window.

Internal Livery:

Ceilings and coves were covered with white enamelled panels with dark varnished/ polished wood window and ceiling frames. Standard Birmingham fittings and fixtures were used.

External Livery:

Leyland supplied the demonstrator in the Birmingham Corporation style cobalt blue and cream livery used until ca. 1929. The lower deck panels and waistband were blue with single gold lining; everything above the waistband was painted cream with wide blue lining to accentuate the gentle "piano front" to the upper deck front panel, and thinner single blue lining elsewhere.

The Birmingham coat of arms was displayed on both sides of the lower deck waist panels, centred in bay 3, with that undertaking's title and legal lettering at the base of the bay 1 and 2 side panels.

Notes:

It is possible that solely the chassis was tested on the South Lancashire Transport system. This was the closest trolleybus system to the manufacturer and it later became usual practice for Leyland trolleybuses to be tested there. It is unclear if the Leyland TTBD1 was demonstrated there too. Following a visit to the one route Chesterfield system it was used on Birmingham's Nechells route for driver training, evaluation of the GEC motor and equipment, and, new evidence suggests, limited passenger service. It was sufficiently successful to warrant an order for 50 TTBD2 trolleybuses with 58-seat Metropolitan-Cammell Carriage and Wagon Co. bodies being placed in May 1933.

Disposal:

After the vehicle's second period in Birmingham it was returned to Leyland in October 1937 and scrapped.

TBS2 BUT RETB1

Prior to departure for Nottingham Road, Glasgow TBS2 awaits passengers at the 48 stance on Victoria Embankment, Trent Bridge. *Nottingham Libraries (LSL5)*

Chassis: Two axle type BUT RETB1 manufactured by the British United Traction Ltd., Hanover House, 14 Hanover Square, London W1 at Leyland Motors', Leyland, Lancashire factory.
Motor: English Electric EE410/10C (120 hp).
Electrical equipment: English Electric
Dewirement indicator: Assumed to have been line-lights and buzzer.
Brakes: Lockheed electric hydraulic, hand and rheostatic brakes.
Body: East Lancashire Coachbuilders, Blackburn B27D
Length: 30ft
Width: 8ft
Height: 10ft 6ins laden, excluding trolley base and booms.
Wheelbase: 15ft 7ins
Wheel track: front 6ft 6¾ins, rear 5ft 11½ins
Unladen weight: 8tons 4cwts 0qtrs
Tyres: India 10.00 X 20 – 14 P.R.

Glasgow TBS2 was delivered to Nottingham on trade plates direct from the coachbuilders on Tuesday 27 January 1953, and was first licensed (registration number FYS766) on 1 February 1953. It operated in normal passenger service on the Nottingham Road group of services 2-18 February 1953 and was noteworthy for delays in boarding and payment, congestion of passengers towards the rear of the vehicle and poor time keeping. TBS2 then moved on to Walsall for further demonstration, being towed away by the Nottingham Leyland depot (Derby Road) on 19 February 1953, and only reaching Glasgow on 23 March 1953.

Chassis:

The ETB1 chassis was designed for overseas use, the type prefix designating the position of the controls, that is R for right-hand drive. The low-level frame was constructed of alloy steel side members of channel section, braced by one channel section and eight tubular cross members. The frame was upswept over the axles with an overhang at front and rear, and capable of carrying "transit" type bodies up to 33ft long with front, centre or double entrances. Although the contactor gear was normally carried at the rear end of the frame, the Glasgow RETB1s had their electrical equipment at the side to leave sufficient space for a rear drop frame and entrance.

The front axle was an "I" section beam with stub axles swivelling in phosphor bronze bushes, vertical loading being taken between hardened steel buttons with spherical faces at the base of the swivel pin, the whole assembly being totally enclosed and filled with lubricant. The wheel hubs were mounted on taper roller bearings, packed with grease, having oil seals and oil throwers to prevent grease or oil reaching the braking surfaces.

Marles cam and double roller steering gear was incorporated in a malleable iron casting mounted on top of the frame side member at the front end, motion being transmitted by an intermediate drag link inside the frame to a relay shaft mounted adjacent to the front spring mounting and from there by a second drag link outside the frame to the front axle swivel.

Fully floating rear axle with a 5ins offset underslung worm drive running at 9ins centres. The casing was formed by a one-piece forging, the spring seats and brake anchorages being pressed on. Drive was taken at the outer ends of the axle shafts through large diameter upset flanges that were secured by eight studs to the hubs. Each hub had oil seals and oil throwers.

Suspension was provided by 4 semi-elliptic road springs, 4ins wide, and 5f long at the front and 5ft 2ins at the rear. Rubber-bonded bushes requiring no lubrication were used at the spring mountings, the rotary oscillation between the eyes and the spring and shackle pins being wholly absorbed in the rubber bushes. Luvax-Girling hydraulic dampers controlled the spring action at front and rear.

Glasgow TBS2 had a Leyland built chassis number 521590.

Chassis length:

Not known

Chassis frame width:

front 3ft 3½ins, rear 3ft 8ins

Overall width (rear axle):

7ft 10¼ins

Electrics:

Automatic acceleration. The master controller and reverser were located beneath the driver's seat. Other control equipment, the battery manoeuvring gear and lead acid traction batteries were carried on the offside of the chassis between the front and rear axles.

Four resilient mountings on the chassis nearside side member and a longitudinal tubular member supported the English Electric traction motor which was offset 5ins to the nearside of the chassis centre line to better accommodate an air filter. The drive was taken through a tubular propeller shaft with Hardy-Spicer all metal universal joints fitted with needle roller bearings.

Brakes:

Lockheed electric hydraulic, hand and rheostatic brakes.

Foot brake actuation was by hydraulic pressure cylinders mounted directly on the front stub axles and the rear axles. The power valve was mounted beneath the footplate of the driver's compartment and pedal operated. It was equipped with a servo system requiring a light brake pedal pressure and providing similar characteristics to traditional trolleybus braking systems. The fluid pump was driven by a double "V"-belt from the transmission. The combined needle-type power and cut-out valve controlled operating brake line pressure and reservoir charging. A supplementary reservoir, protected by a non-return valve to ensure that there was no loss of pressure in the brake reservoir, was used to operate the folding entrance and exit doors. There was a low-pressure alarm mounted in front of the driver to give visual and audible warning if the pressure fell enough to affect braking performance.

The pull-on handbrake was mounted on the offside of the driver's compartment and operated on the rear wheels only through a mechanical linkage. The ratchet mechanism was completely enclosed and operated in an oil bath.

Bodywork:

Metal framed five-bay single-deck construction with a noticeably deep roof to accommodate small standee windows (intended to give standing passengers a view out of the side of the trolleybus) above the main saloon and foremost nearside windows, fully-enclosed rear platform entrance and centre exit equipped with folding doors and a driver's cab area integral with the passenger compartment built by East Lancashire Coachbuilders Ltd., Blackburn, Lancashire.

Horizontally sliding half-width openers were fitted to the tops of the side windows in bays 1-5 of the offside, and bays 1, 3, 5, together with the foremost window opposite the driver's position on the nearside. The standee windows could not be opened. There was a single large "orange segment" shaped rear window built into a larger opening panel, which provided a bottom-hinged emergency exit. There was an opening skylight immediately to the rear of the trolley boom restraining hooks. The four-leaf, air operated folding Glider doors at the centre and rear were half-glazed to match the saloon side windows. In place of standee windows the area immediately above these doors were equipped with matching but narrower cream-painted translucent glass signs lettered "ENTRANCE" and "EXIT" as appropriate. There was a single step up from the street to the rear platform, which, equipped with a queuing barrier, provided a waiting area prior to obtaining a ticket, and then a second step up to the saloon with bulkheads on each side. To the offside of this second step, immediately forward of the bulkhead, was the conductor's desk and seat. There were two steps down from the centre exit to the street.

Top hinged access doors were fitted at the base of the offside panel bays 2, 3 and 4.

Unusually for a British trolleybus of the early 1950s, the driver's position was forward of the front axle and did not extend across the entire width of the vehicle. The driver's seat and controls were accessed through a waist height door from inside the passenger compartment (there being no external door). There was a single opening windscreen on the offside, both windscreens having chromium-plated frames. The offside windscreen had a top-mounted wiper whilst that on the nearside was mounted at the base of the windscreen. The offside of the driver's cab had a full-depth semi-triangular quarter light window immediately to the rear of the corner pillar and then a sliding "signalling" window surmounted by a small pane to match the sliders in the saloon side windows.

There was a white, 4-spoke, steering wheel; the colour drawing the driver's attention to the fact that this was an 8ft wide vehicle in a period when this was not yet the norm. Small rectangular driver's rear view mirrors were mounted externally towards the top of both front cab pillars.

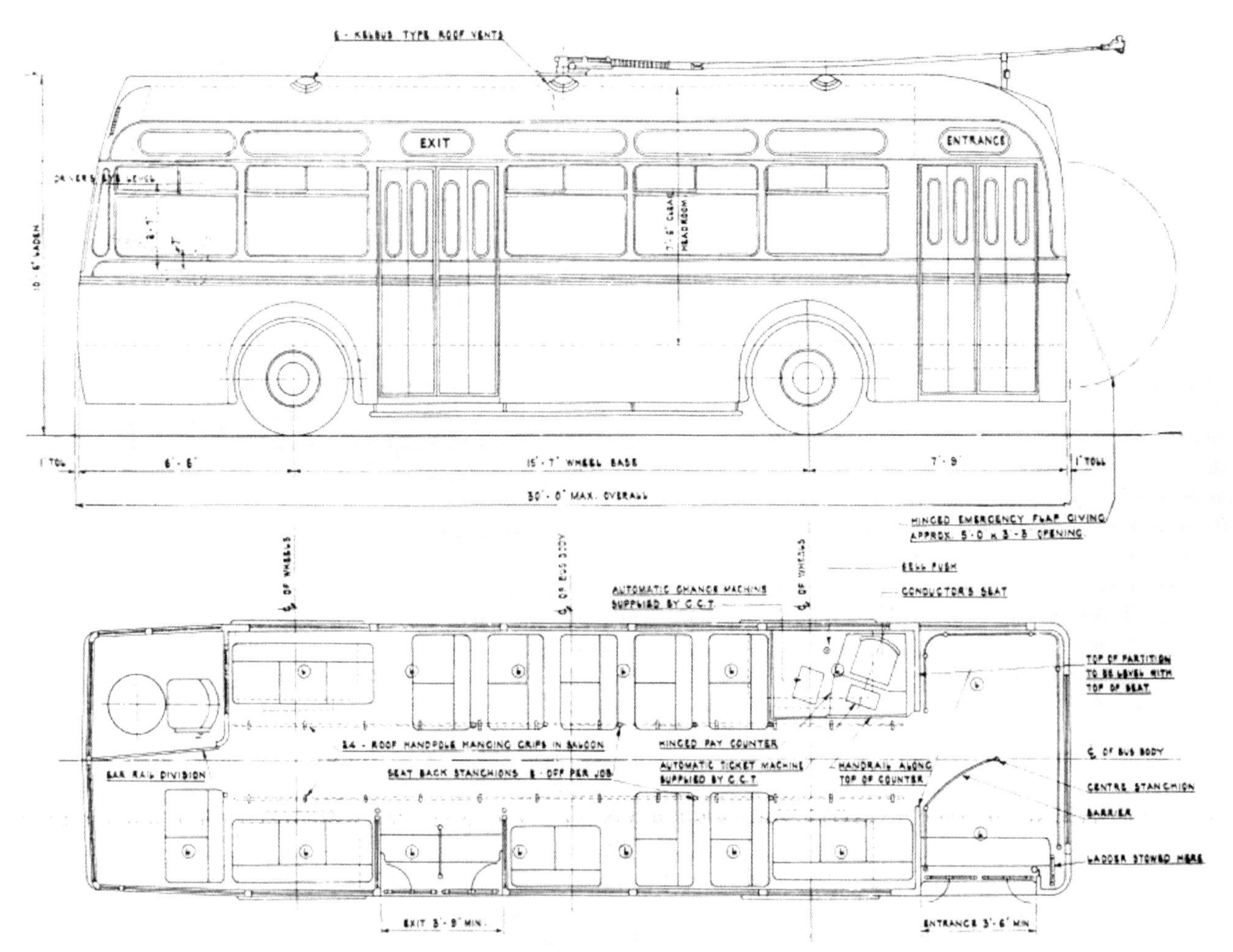

The leading dimensions and seating layout of Glasgow's new B.U.T. single-deck trolleybus. This vehicle, which seats 27 passengers and has exceptionally large standing capacity, has bodywork by East Lancashire Coach Builders, Ltd.

The plans of the East Lancashire Coach Builders bodywork that appeared in Passenger Transport magazine 1953. *Passenger Transport*

The front wheels were equipped with chromed wheel nut protector rings.

The "passenger flow" design encompassed a seated conductor equipped with a desk and change machine, just inside the rear offside bulkhead, a centre exit positioned immediately to the rear of the front axle, 27 seats and an MoT permitted capacity for a further 40 (reduced to 30 in 1955) standing passengers.

There was a removable panel approximately as wide as the space between the two headlights, incorporating, centred at the top, the registration number plate, at the base of the front panel beneath the windscreen. A single lifeguard ran beneath the side panels between the front and rear axle. A bamboo trolley retrieval pole was carried in a tube mounted centrally under the chassis.

Lighting:

External lighting was 2 headlights half way down the front panel, 2 circular front sidelights mounted towards the extremities of the front panel above the level of the top of the headlights and a single rear light, fitted behind a small access panel, to the offside of the rear lower panel which also illuminated the rear registration number plate immediately beneath.

A spotlight was recessed into the front panel below the nearside headlight, centred slightly more towards the nearside of the vehicle and thus aligned with the nearside of the headlight.

CAV D13 TB-1 dynamo and CAV 210/17 control box.

Seating:

Moving towards the front of the trolleybus, on the offside, after the conductor's position over the rear axle, there were 5 forwards-facing double seats and then an inwards-facing bench seat (over the front axle) for 3-persons. On the nearside there was an inwards-facing bench seat for 3-persons opposite the conductor's position, followed by 2 forwards-facing double seats and an inward-facing bench seat for 2-persons, before the exit was reached. Then came an inwards-facing bench seat for 3-persons over the front axle and one forwards-facing double seat opposite the driver. The rails above the backs of the seats were attached to the ceiling by handhold stanchions. The seat cushions and backs were covered in green leatherette.

Destination equipment:

A large indicator box capable of displaying three different blinds showing the final destination, en route points and service number was built into the front dome, centred immediately above the driver's windscreen. At the top of the box on the offside was an aperture for the final destination with a rectangular box for the en route points beneath. The service number indicator was on the nearside, the aperture being as deep as the final destination and en route points indicator combined. All the apertures had rounded corners.

There was no rear or side display.

Whilst in Nottingham, NCT blinds were displayed in the suitably masked en route points and service number boxes.

Internal Livery:

The wood faced window surrounds and ceilings were painted white. Green leathercloth was applied to the lower body panels.

External Livery:

Delivered in full Glasgow Corporation Transport orange, cream and green livery of the period. The side panels beneath the waistband were orange. Everything above the waistband was cream except for the waistband and the side panels around the standee windows, which were painted pale green.

The Glasgow city arms were carried on side panels centred in bay 3. The undertaking's title and other legal lettering were transferred in black at the base of side panels immediately in front of the nearside front axle. Fleet numbers were applied with aluminium, black edged transfers to the front panel at the level of the sidelights, centrally beneath the driver's windscreen, and centrally on the rear panels beneath the emergency exit window. Mudguards and lifeguard rails were black and wheels maroon.

Notes:

The idea of using high capacity "crush loader" or "standee" type trolleybuses, so typical of urban passenger-carrying vehicles in continental Europe, emanated from a visit by the Glasgow Manager, E.R.L. Fitzpayne to a transport conference in Stockholm in 1949.

On 28 May 1951 Glasgow's Transport Committee awarded BUT an order for 35 trolleybus chassis, 25 of which were to be equipped with double-deck and the remaining 10 with single-deck bodywork, all with Lockheed electric hydraulic brakes, at a cost of £88,000. As a result of further information from BUT, in September 1951 the double-deck chassis order was reduced to 20 and awarded to Sunbeam. The single-deck chassis order remained with BUT and East Lancashire Coachbuilders' tender for the bodywork at £21,500 was accepted in November 1951.

The batch of vehicles from which this demonstrator was an example was based on Glasgow's experiences with TB35, itself a modified version of the export BUT ETB1 trolleybus built by Leyland and fitted with a Weymann body. TB35, with its rear entrance equipped with a large platform and pay-desk with seated conductor, and a front exit opposite the driver, had attracted much interest and had been demonstrated at Edinburgh, running with a skate along the tram track and to South Lancashire Transport at Atherton, operating into Bolton.

Glasgow considered that a "standee" trolleybus had many of the advantages of a conventional three-axle double-decker but cost £750 less. Maintenance and running costs were less, the problem of uncollected fares particularly at peak hours was theoretically eliminated and from the point of view of safety the absence of a stairway coupled with the use of power operated doors interlocked to the driver's controls reduced the risk of platform accidents.

In 1952 TB35 was renumbered TBS1 (Trolleybus BUT Single deck) in preparation for the delivery of ten further single deckers TBS2-11 to the same basic design but with a widened exit door positioned immediately to the rear of the front axle. Initially the batch was mainly used on service 104 but following the MoT-imposed reduction in their standing capacity in March 1955 they were employed on any peak-hour working along High Street, Glasgow, that is services 101-104, as well as Shawfield greyhound racing specials. From November 1958 they also appeared on peak-hour service 108 journeys to Linthouse and Shieldhall. In the period 1959-1961 all vehicles were rebuilt as conventional 36-seaters by removing the rear door and introducing a roving conductor.

Disposal:

TBS2 was withdrawn from service on 12 November 1964 and sold to J.Kelly, Carmyle, breakers, in March 1965.

Appendix C Livery

The railless cars, trolley vehicles and trolleybuses, as they were officially referred to variously during the 39 year life of the system, never carried the tramcar livery of maroon and cream but introduced a new colour scheme of green and cream to the streets of Nottingham. The hues of paint were referred to as "Nottingham Green" and "Nottingham Cream". During the trolleybus era there were basically two styles of application, the earlier employing larger areas of cream paint and two shades of green, which can be divided into nine variations. The differences were relatively minor, relating primarily to the location of transferred lettering, etc. Wheel hubs were painted "Post Office Red" and beadings, lining, mouldings, mudguards and wings were stock black.

It is important to note that the vehicles circulating on the streets did not necessarily all appear in the then current livery application: several variations could be seen at the same time.

Until the decision was taken to abandon trolleybus operation there was a scheduled overhaul and repainting programme. This was a thorough and time-consuming process, including for example the replacement of dented panels, taking several months.

The nine variations of application were:

1) 1927 – 1929

Applied to the following vehicles upon delivery:

1-10 Railless

11-12 Ransomes

The lower deck and upper deck window surrounds, and the roof were cream. The main upper and lower deck body panels were painted in two shades of green; light green being used for the upper deck waistband, that is the deep band immediately below the upper-deck windows. The darker green panels were lined in tramcar style gold double lining or outer gold and inner white lining, with ornate corner designs. Mudguards and lifeguard rails were black and wheels red (some sources state that the wheels were originally black). The centre area of the roof was grey.

The Nottingham coat of arms was displayed on both sides of the lower deck waist panels, centred between the axles, that is beneath the rear window pillar of bay 2 on 1-10 and centred in bay 3 on 11-12, with the undertaking's title NOTTINGHAM CORPORATION TRAMWAYS in large gold block capital lettering edged in black transferred in a single line, the first letter of each word being slightly larger than the other lettering. The General Manager's name and title beneath in small gold script lettering edged in black, running from below the coat of arms towards the front of the vehicle.

The seating capacity was indicated on the rocker panel immediately behind the rear axle on the offside and nearside.

Large gold numerals, shaded blue, were mounted on the bulbous front panel centrally beneath the driver's cab windscreen and above the headlamp, and at lower deck waistrail height on the open rear staircase panelling at the rear.

External banner advertising, normally in the form of stove-enamelled metal plates, was carried on the upper deck side panel, bays 1-5

Detail differences by vehicle type:

Railless 1-10: By 1930, at least 4 displayed the title NOTTINGHAM CORPORATION TRAMWAYS and the General Manager's name and title moved forward with CORPORATION centred on bay 2.

Ransomes 11– 12: The upper deck body panels and the gutter immediately above the upper saloon windows were dark green (no light green waistband). The lower deck body panels were painted in two shades of green; light green being applied beneath the deep lower deck waistband, that is the concave rocker panels at the base of the lower-deck sides. The darker green lower deck waist panels were lined in tramcar style gold single lining with restrained corner designs.

The front fleet numbers were mounted centrally between the headlamp and the registration number plate.

External banner advertising, normally in the form of stove-enamelled metal plates, was carried on the upper deck side panel bays 1-6, the top being immediately beneath the upper deck windows.

2) 1930

Applied to the following vehicles upon delivery and earlier vehicles in the fleet upon repaint:

13-18 Ransomes

19-24 English Electric

The lower deck and upper deck window surrounds, a deep waistband below the upper-deck windows and the roof were painted cream. The main upper and lower deck body panels were painted medium green although the lower deck waistband was a darker shade of green. Mudguards and lifeguard rails were black and wheels bright red. The centre area of the roof was grey.

The Nottingham coat of arms was displayed on both sides of the lower deck, centred in bay 3, with the undertaking's title NOTTINGHAM CORPORATION PASSENGER TRANSPORT DEPARTMENT transferred in two lines, NOTTINGHAM CORPORATION PASSENGER being displayed above TRANSPORT DEPARTMENT, in gold block capital lettering edged in black beneath and with the General Manager's name and title centred below in gold block lettering edged in black.

The seating capacity was indicated on the platform side of the nearside rear bulkhead above the lower saloon rear window.

Large gold numerals, shaded blue, were mounted on the front panel centrally beneath the driver's cab windscreen and centrally mounted below the rear platform window.

External banner advertising, normally in the form of stove-enamelled metal plates, was carried on the upper deck side panel bays 1-5 and on the upper deck rear panel.

Detail differences by vehicle type:

1-10 Railless, 11-12 Ransomes: Roofs were repainted grey. The unladen weight and, it is assumed, the individual axle weights, were transferred on the offside lower panels behind the rear axle.

13-18 Ransomes: The undertaking's title was displayed in three lines, NOTTINGHAM being displayed above CORPORATION PASSENGER with TRANSPORT DEPARTMENT below.

19-24 English Electric: The cantrail or vent panel area above the lower-deck windows was also painted cream. The lower deck waistband beadings were picked out in cream. At least one vehicle including 20, had the darker green lower deck waistband and cream beading across the front of the driver's cab.

The General Manager's name and title in gold script lettering edged in black was affixed in the lower half of the bay 2 side panels.

External banner advertising was carried on the upper deck side panel bays 1-6 (banners), across the curved front to the upper deck and on the upper deck rear panels.

3) 1930 1932

Applied to the following vehicles upon delivery and earlier vehicles in the fleet upon repaint:

25-36 Karrier E6

37-49 Ransomes D6

50 Karrier E6

1 Karrier E6

25 Guy BTX60 demonstrator

26 AEC663T demonstrator

27 Karrier E6 demonstrator

28 Thornycroft demonstrator

The lower deck and upper deck window surrounds, a deep upper deck waistband and the roof were cream. The main upper and lower deck body panels were medium green. A cream cheat line was painted on the lower deck, lower waistband beading some 6 ins below the lower edge of the cream lower deck window surrounds at the side, front (except 1) and rear. The lower deck waistband was a darker shade of green. Mudguards and lifeguard rails were black, wheels red. The centre area of the roof was battleship grey, applied with water sealant paint.

The Nottingham coat of arms was displayed on both sides of the lower deck, centred in bay 3. The operator's name, and title NOTTINGHAM CORPORATION PASSENGER TRANSPORT DEPARTMENT appeared in gold block capital lettering edged in black the first letter of each word being slightly larger than the other lettering, with the General Manager's name and title beneath in gold script lettering edged in black at the bottom of bay 3 on both sides.

The seating capacity was indicated on the platform side of the nearside rear bulkhead above the lower saloon rear window. The maximum permitted speed was transferred in white lettering onto the base of the lower deck side panel forward of the leading offside rear mudguard.

Large gold numerals, shaded blue, were mounted within the outline "radiator" on the front panel beneath the driver's cab windscreen and centrally mounted below the rear platform window.

External banner advertising, normally in the form of stove-enamelled metal plates due to the long duration of the contracts, was carried on the upper deck side panels bays 1-7.

Detail differences by vehicle type:

25-36 Karrier E6: The fleet numbers were originally plain gold without edging or shading.

25-36 Karrier E6, 37-49 Ransomes D6, 50 Karrier E6: The cream cheat line followed the upper beading of the outline "radiator" on the front panel beneath the driver's cab windscreen.

1 Karrier E6, 37-49 Ransomes D6: The coat of arms was displayed beneath the body pillar between bays 2 and 3. The operator's name, and the General Manager's name and title were affixed at the base of bays 1 and 2 on both sides.

External banner advertising was carried on the upper deck side panel bays 1-6.

4) 1932 – 1936

Applied to the following vehicles upon delivery and earlier vehicles in the fleet upon repaint:

51-60 Karrier E6

61-85 Karrier E6

86-106 Ransomes D6

107-136 Leyland TTB4

All over medium green, with three cream bands painted at the lower deck waistband, that is below the lower deck windows; at the cantrail or centre vent panel, that is above the lower deck windows, and the upper deck waistband, that is below the upper deck windows. The beadings edging the cream bands were black. Mudguards and lifeguard rails were black. Wheels red.

The Nottingham coat of arms was displayed on both sides of the lower deck, centred in bay 3. The undertaking's title NOTTINGHAM CORPORATION PASSENGER TRANSPORT DEPARTMENT was transferred in two lines, NOTTINGHAM CORPORATION PASSENGER being displayed above TRANSPORT DEPARTMENT, in medium sized gold block capital lettering edged in black, the first letter of each word being slightly larger than the other lettering, at the base of bay 2 on both sides. The General Manager's name and title were shown beneath in one line in gold script lettering.

The seating capacity was indicated at the nearside base of the rear platform panel. The unladen weight was transferred immediately in front of the leading rear axle, and the maximum permitted speed immediately to the rear of the third axle, in small white block capital letters and numbers at the base of the offside lower deck side.

Large gold numerals, shaded blue, were mounted at the front slightly above the level of the top of the headlights centrally within the outline "radiator" beneath the driver's cab windscreen, and centrally mounted on the lower panels below the rear platform window.

A small white "T" was painted centrally on the rear platform panel beneath the fleet number indicating that this was a trolley vehicle (to avoid one overtaking another). This became a standard feature of the fleet until the 1939 renumbering.

External advertising, often in the form of stove-enamelled metal plates due to the long duration of the contracts, was carried on the upper deck side panel bays (banners).

Detail differences by vehicle type:

Karrier E6 25-36, Karrier E6 50, Karrier E6 61-85, Ransomes D6 86-106: The revised livery saw these vehicles repainted in all over medium green with three cream bands however the lower deck cream-painted waistband did not extend across the top of the front panel beneath the driver's windscreen.

Ransomes D6 37-49: The revised livery saw these vehicles repainted in all over green with three cream bands however the cream-painted cantrail band did not extend across the sun visor at the top of the driver's windscreen and the lower deck waistband did not extend across the top of the front panel beneath the driver's windscreen.

Leyland TTB4 107-36: The unladen weight appeared in small white lettering at the base of the bay 4 offside panel immediately in front of the second axle whilst the maximum permitted speed was also displayed in white at the base of the panel behind the rear axle. Due to the position of the rear bumpers, the seating capacity was indicated in gold transfers, shaded blue, on the nearside to the rear of the third axle adjacent to the open rear platform immediately beneath the lower deck cream-painted waistband.

Gold numerals, shaded blue, were mounted in the centre of the front panel beneath the driver's cab windscreen and centrally mounted on the lower panels below the rear platform window.

5) 1937 – 1939

Applied to all vehicles in the fleet upon repaint.

All over medium green, with three cream bands painted at the lower deck waistband, that is below the lower deck windows; at the cantrail or centre vent panel, that is above the lower deck windows, and the upper deck waistband, that is below the upper deck windows. The beadings edging the cream bands were black. Mudguards and lifeguard rails were black. Wheels red.

The Nottingham coat of arms was displayed on both sides of the lower deck, centred in bay 3. The undertaking's revised title NOTTINGHAM CITY TRANSPORT in black edged large gold block capital lettering, the first letter of each word being slightly larger than the other lettering, appeared in a single line at the base of bay 2 on both sides. The General Manager's name and title were shown beneath in one line in small gold script lettering.

The seating capacity was indicated on the platform side of the nearside rear bulkhead above the lower saloon rear window and on the nearside to the rear of third axle adjacent to the open rear platform immediately beneath the lower deck cream-painted waistband in gold shaded with two hues of blue. The unladen weight with the maximum permitted speed above, was transferred in white lettering to the base of the lower deck side panel in front of the leading rear axle on the nearside.

Gold numerals, somewhat smaller than previously, edged in black, were mounted centrally on the front panel beneath the driver's cab windscreen and on the lower panels below the rear platform window.

A small white "T" was painted centrally on the rear platform panel beneath the fleet number indicating that this was a trolley vehicle (to avoid one overtaking another).

External advertising was carried on the upper deck side panel bays (banners).

Detail differences by vehicle type:

319-324 English Electric E11: Advertisements were also carried on the upper deck front panel above the driver's cab.

6) 1939 – 1945

Applied to the following vehicles upon delivery and earlier vehicles in the fleet upon repaint:

437-440 AEC661T
441 Daimler CTM
442-445 Karrier W4
447-451 Sunbeam MF2
452-468 Karrier W4
469-478 Karrier W4
302-303 English Electric
304-309 Guy BTX

All over medium green, with three cream bands painted at the lower deck waistband, that is below the lower deck windows; at the cantrail or centre vent panel, that is above the lower deck windows, and the upper deck waistband, that is below the upper deck windows. The beadings edging the cream bands were black. Bumpers (where fitted), the base of the front and rear panels, all mudguards and the side life guard rails were painted white to fulfil wartime "blackout" restrictions. To further aid the driver, the outline of cab access step in the offside lower deck panels and the cab door handle were also painted white on some vehicles. Wheels red. Some vehicles had the centre area of the roof painted grey, perhaps to conserve paint supplies.

The application of the cream band(s) on the front of trolleybuses varied: 301, 337-349 had solely a single band underneath the upper saloon front windows; 313-336, 350, 361-406 had a band beneath the upper saloon front windows and above the windscreen whilst 320, 351-360, 407-436 had all three bands.

The Nottingham coat of arms was displayed on both sides of the lower deck, centred in bay 3. The wartime title CITY TRANSPORT (with Nottingham deleted) in black edged large gold block capital lettering appeared in a single line at the base of bay 2 on both sides, with the General Manager's name and title beneath in small plain gold block capital lettering edged in black.

The seating capacity was indicated on the nearside to the rear of the rear axle adjacent to the open rear platform immediately beneath the lower deck cream-painted waistband in small gold block lettering and numerals. The unladen weight with the maximum permitted speed beneath was transferred in small plain block capital white lettering and numerals at the base of the nearside lower panel immediately in front of the (leading) rear axle.

From ca. 1940 "ENTER THIS SIDE LOWER SALOON" and "ENTER THIS SIDE UPPER SALOON" was shown in black letters in the nearside cream-painted cantrail band above the open rear platform either side of the entrance stanchion, appearing in one or two lines, according to the depth of the band at this point.

Plain black edged gold numerals were mounted at the base of the bay 1 lower deck side panels on the near and offside immediately to the rear of the driver's cab access step; at the same level as the headlights centrally beneath the driver's cab windscreen and centrally on the rear panel beneath the platform window. Some vehicles carried the General Manager's name and title immediately to the rear of low-mounted side fleet number. By late 1943 the position of the side fleet numbers was changed to beneath the cream-painted lower deck waistband on the near and offside adjacent to the front bulkhead, that is immediately to the rear of the driver's cab.

From late 1940 the Department specified green edged gold transfers where black edged equivalents had previously been used, resulting in a much bolder appearance although the use of green edging on a green background gave the impression that there was no edging at all. It is understood that wartime shortages led to the continued use of black edged gold transfers whilst for the same reason during the period 1942 to about November 1944 straw-coloured transfers replaced gold.

Use of a small white "T" on the rear platform panel was discontinued.

From 1942 many trolleybuses in the 361-406 series had the lowest cream band painted across the front of the driver's cab beneath the windscreen. The Nottingham coat-of-arms was added to the front panels beneath the windscreen.

External paper poster or painted advertising was carried on the upper deck side panel bays ("banners") and on the lower panels beneath the rear platform window. Utility trolleybuses without a rear destination display carried a rectangular advertisement on the rear upper deck panels. From May 1945 on either side of the front destination box and on the offside rear platform panel (circular "spot").

Once hostilities came to an end, the white panel edging and mudguards was discontinued and the title reverted to NOTTINGHAM CITY TRANSPORT positioned as before.

Detail differences by vehicle type:

304-309 Guy BTX: All over medium green, with a single narrow cream band painted on a raised waistband, below the side and rear windows, and rising above the bulbous front panel. As the waistband had no beading, the cream bands were not edged in black paint.

The Nottingham coat of arms was displayed centrally on the front panel and on both sides, centred in the wider bay 4 on the offside and bay 2 on the nearside. The undertaking's title, and the General Manager's name and title were transferred on to the base of bay 3 on the offside and bay 2 on the nearside. The unladen weight was shown in small plain block capital white lettering and numerals at the base of nearside bay 8, behind the rear axle.

Plain gold or straw numerals, edged in green, were mounted beneath the cream band in bay 1 behind the driver's cab door on the offside, above the coat of arms on the front panel and beneath the foremost triangular cab side window on the nearside.

No external advertising was carried.

319-324 English Electric E11: Advertisements were also carried on the upper deck front panel above the driver's cab.

351-360 Karrier E6: The wartime title CITY TRANSPORT in black edged large gold block capital lettering appeared in a single line at the base of bay 1 on both sides, immediately to the rear of the front axle, with the General Manager's name and title beneath in small black edged plain gold block capital lettering.

447-451 Sunbeam MF2: battleship grey rooftop, not visible from street level (this may have applied to other wartime deliveries).

7) 1945 – 1949

Applied to the following vehicles upon delivery and earlier vehicles in the fleet upon repaint:

479-482 Karrier W4

483-495 BUT 9611T

All over medium green, with three cream bands painted at the lower deck waistband, that is below the lower deck windows; at the cantrail or centre vent panel, that is above the lower deck windows, and the upper deck waistband, that is below the upper deck windows. The beadings edging the cream bands were black, that separating the upper and lower decks being noticeably wider than the others. Mudguards and lifeguard rails were black and wheels red.

The Nottingham coat of arms was displayed on both sides of the lower deck, centred in bay 2 on three axle vehicles or bay 3 on two axle vehicles. The undertaking's title NOTTINGHAM CITY TRANSPORT in green edged large (3 ins high) gold block capital lettering appeared in a single line at the base of bays 1 and 2 on the nearside, and the base of bays 2 and 3 on the offside, with the head office address, and the General Manager's name and title beneath in green edged (1 ins high) gold block capital lettering.

The seating capacity was indicated on the nearside to the rear of the rear axle adjacent to the open rear platform immediately beneath the lower deck cream-painted waistband in small green edged gold block lettering and numerals. The maximum permitted speed and unladen weight was transferred in small green edged gold block lettering and numerals at the base of the nearside lower panel immediately in front of the (leading) rear axle.

Small upper-case white lettering appeared above the two window panes of the upper-deck rear emergency exit, that on the nearside reading "EMERGENCY EXIT" and that on the offside (the door opening handle was mounted on the top offside of the door) reading "TO OPEN".

"ENTER THIS SIDE LOWER SALOON" and "ENTER THIS SIDE UPPER SALOON" was show in black letters in the cream-painted cantrail band on the nearside above the open rear platform, appearing in one or two lines, according to the depth of the band at this point.

Plain (4 ins high) green edged gold numerals were mounted beneath the cream-painted lower deck waistband on the near and offside adjacent to the front bulkhead, that is immediately to the rear of the driver's cab; aligned with the top of the headlights centrally beneath the driver's cab windscreen and centrally on the rear panel beneath the platform window.

External paper poster banner advertising, together with a limited number of painted advertisements initially, was carried on the upper deck side panel bays 1-5 (2 axle vehicles) and 1-6 (3 axle vehicles), irregularly on the front panels above the driver's cab windscreen on either side of the indicator box and on the offside rear platform staircase panel (circular "spot").

Detail differences by vehicle type:

None known.

8) 1949 – 1962

Applied to the following vehicles upon delivery and earlier vehicles in the fleet upon repaint:

500-601 BUT9641T

All over medium green, with three cream bands painted at the lower deck waistband, that is below the lower deck windows; at the cantrail or centre vent panel, that is above the lower deck windows, and the upper deck waistband, that is below the upper deck windows. The beadings edging the cream bands were black, that separating the upper and lower decks being noticeably wider than the others. Mudguards and lifeguard rails were black and wheels red.

The Nottingham coat of arms was displayed on both sides of the lower deck, centred in bay 2 of both two and three axle vehicles, surmounted by the undertaking's title NOTTINGHAM CITY TRANSPORT in green edged large (3 ins high) gold block capital lettering transferred in a single line. Beneath the coat of arms at the base of bay 2, the head office address was introduced, followed by the General Manager's name and title, all appearing in small (1 ins high) green edged gold block capital lettering.

In 1956 large gold block capital lettering with a white outline was introduced for the undertaking's title transfers whilst small white edged gold block capital lettering was introduced for the head office address, and the General Manager's name and title. The first trolleybus appearing in this style was 537, during the week ending 24 March 1956, followed the week thereafter by 489. The practice of extending the cream lower deck waistband around the rear platform became standard.

The seating capacity was indicated on the nearside to the rear of the rear axle adjacent to the open rear platform immediately beneath the lower deck cream-painted waistband in small white edged gold block lettering and numerals. The unladen weight with the maximum permitted speed beneath was transferred in small white edged gold capital lettering and numerals at the base of the nearside lower panel immediately in front of the (leading) rear axle. The unladen weight was also shown in the same position on the offside until about 1958-59 and on the nearside was applied above the maximum permitted speed.

Small upper-case white-edged gold lettering appeared above the two window panes of the upper-deck rear emergency exit, that on the nearside reading "EMERGENCY EXIT" and that on the offside (the door opening handle was mounted on the top offside of the door) reading "TO OPEN". Cast metal plates reading "EMERGENCY EXIT" in polished lettering on a red background were specified for the BUT9641Ts and affixed above the offside window of the emergency exit. The plates were accompanied by either a sign "TO OPEN" in red lettering on a white background with a directional arrow above the nearside window or white-edged gold lettered operating instructions on the centre line above the emergency exit.

"ENTER THIS SIDE LOWER SALOON" and "ENTER THIS SIDE UPPER SALOON" was show in black letters in the cream-painted cantrail band on the nearside above the open rear platform, appearing in one line, for example BUT9641Ts, or two lines, for example BUT9611Ts, according to the depth of the band at this point. The application of these boarding instructions ceased around 1958-59.

Adjacent to the rear platform a transferred notice was applied to the waistband ca. 1950 "LOOK RIGHT, THEN LEFT, BEFORE CROSSING THE ROAD" in red lettering on a white background, the first four words being in larger lettering than the last four words.

Plain (4 ins high) gold green edged numerals were mounted on the cream-painted lower deck waistband centrally beneath the driver's cab windscreen and on the near and offside adjacent to the front bulkhead, that is immediately to the rear of the driver's cab; and centrally mounted on the cream-painted cantrail band above the rear platform window.

External paper poster banner advertising, together with a limited number of painted advertisements initially, was carried on the upper deck side panel bays 1-5 (2 axle vehicles) and 1-6 (3 axle vehicles), irregularly on the front panels above the driver's cab windscreen on either side of the indicator box, on the offside rear platform staircase panel (circular "spot") and beneath the rear platform window. As paper poster banner advertisements were only produced in a single length, to suit two axle vehicles, they did not fully utilize the side panels of the BUT9641Ts unlike the sign-written examples.

Detail differences by vehicle type:

455-458 Karrier W4: the cream-painted lower deck waistband beneath the driver's cab windscreen was too narrow to accommodate the front fleet number and this continued to be displayed centrally on the front panel aligned with the top of the headlights using white edged gold numerals.

459-465 Karrier W4, 479-482 Karrier W4: the Karrier maker's symbol mounted at the top of the cream-painted lower deck waistband beneath the driver's cab windscreen left insufficient space for the front fleet number and this continued to be displayed centrally on the front panel aligned with the top of the headlights using white edged gold numerals.

500-601 BUT9641T: initially these vehicles displayed the maximum permitted speed in small green edged block capital gold lettering and numerals at the base of the nearside lower panel immediately in front of the leading rear axle and the unladen weight on the offside lower panel, again immediately in front of the leading rear axle, in small green edged block capital white lettering and numerals.

The only pre-war vehicles to receive this livery style and the title in a single line were:

Karrier E6:	354, 355, 359
Leyland TTB4:	419, 414, 416, 424, 428, 430, 432, 435, 436
AEC 661T:	437, 438, 440,
Daimler CTM4:	441

9) 1962 – 1966

The undertaking's title remained unchanged but was transferred in two lines: NOTTINGHAM being displayed above CITY TRANSPORT with the coat of arms beneath. The General Manager's name and title in gold edged white script lettering was transferred centrally beneath the coat of arms and the head office address on the nearside only following a change of legislation. The offside name and title was painted out.

Plain gold white edged numerals were mounted on the cream-painted lower deck waistband centrally beneath the driver's cab windscreen and on the near and offside adjacent to the front bulkhead, that is immediately to the rear of the driver's cab; and centrally mounted on the cream-painted cantrail band above the rear platform window.

All other livery details were unchanged.

At least the following trolleybuses received the amended layout for the undertaking's title:

504-506, 510, 512, 514, 517-522, 545, 551, 552, 555, 562, 572, 576-578, 595, 599.

The last utility trolleybus to be repainted was 478 following overhaul in December 1961. In 1963 this same vehicle had its lower deck panels and cream bands repainted, becoming the sole example of a utility to receive the fleet name transfer in two-line format. The last two axle trolleybus to be repainted was 493 following overhaul in May 1963 and the final BUT9641T to receive a repaint, again after overhaul, was 576 in January 1964. Until January 1964 it was also a common practice to simply repaint the lower deck panels and cream bands or even just the cream bands to maintain appearances.

Internal Livery, Lettering and Numerals

Throughout the trolleybus era lower and upper saloons, platform and staircase, and the driver's cab were painted in varying applications of green and cream or off-white, accompanied by varnished woodwork. The upper portions of the bulkheads were painted cream or off-white with notices originally transferred in gold with two-tone blue shading and from 1945 in gold with green edging. All seat fittings were painted green. The floors were normally finished in brown linoleum, grey waterproof paint being applied to the open rear platform area. The Second World War "black-out" led to increased use of white paint to aid visibility, for example handrails, the platform and from January 1941 the entire staircase area.

The following exhortations SPITTING STRICTLY PROHIBITED, NO SMOKING ALLOWED, XX STANDING, NO STANDING ALLOWED were transferred in gold letters having cut-off corners and two-tone blue shading. Use of the words "STRICTLY" and "ALLOWED" was discontinued in conjunction with the introduction of the 1939 livery style. From late 1940 the original gold transfers were replaced with greed edged gold letters and numbers.

The fleet number was shown in white on the side of the staircase, on the nearside of the lower saloon front bulkhead and in front of the driver's position above the offside windscreen. The white numbers on the lower saloon front bulkhead and staircase were replaced with black ones when this panel was painted white in conjunction with the introduction of the 1939 livery style. The fleet number was also shown in black on the ceiling of the upper deck front dome above the windows.

From about 1956, the interior transfers such as NO SMOKING, SEATING CAPACITY, etc. were applied in plan green whilst cautionary notices were transferred in white lettering.

There was no internal advertising until 1942 when they were applied to the metal panel on the front bulkhead used for the first aid box then in autumn 1944 advertisements began to be applied to the ceiling cove panels.

Last painting dates for pre-war trolleybuses

337	12/43	361	03/48	380	10/48	399	?	418	02/48
338	04/44	362	?	381	02/49	400	07/42	419	04/47
		363	01/48	382	11/46	401	11/46	420	?
344	12/43	364	01/42	383	07/48	402	?	421	12/46
345	03/48	365	05/44	384	10/48	403	02/49	422	11/48
346	09/43	366	06/46	385	?	404	01/47	423	09/46
347	?	367	06/42	386	09/48	405	10/41	424	05/49
348	09/43	368	06/44	387	08/42	406	06/46	425	?
349	?	369	01/48	388	09/48	407	09/47	426	10/46
351	?	370	09/44	389	?	408	06/47	427	04/46
352	11/48	371	09/46	390	?	409	06/48	428	03/50
353	06/44	372	11/47	391	?	410	05/50	429	?
354	12/49	373	07/47	392	08/48	411	01/49	430	07/49
355	02/50	364	11/46	393	08/45	412	04/47	431	?
356	06/48	375	04/44	394	02/48	413	11/47	432	01/50
357	?	376	?	395	05/47	414	07/50	433	07/48
358	12/48	377	11/46	396	07/43	415	07/47	434	?
359	07/49	378	07/48	397	08/46	416	03/50	435	12/49
360	01/48	379	02/43	398	07/47	417	10/48	436	04/49

BUT 9641T 506, polished for the last day ceremonies, leads a row of trolleybuses over the pits in the final version of the undertakings livery in 1966.
MJ Russell

Appendix D Services and Service Alterations

Service 5

10.04.27 Trolleybus service commenced Queen Street/King Street to Nottingham Road, junction with Vernon Road, Basford via Queen Street, Upper Parliament Street, Milton Street and Mansfield Road, to Gregory Boulevard then via Sherwood Rise and Nottingham Road.
Southbound journeys returned via the reverse route to Upper Parliament Street and then down King Street to the terminus.

05.03.33 Service renumbered 36.

Service H

10.04.27 Trolleybus service commenced Queen Street/King Street to Nottingham Road, junction with Haydn Road via Queen Street, Upper Parliament Street, Milton Street and Mansfield Road to Gregory Boulevard then via Sherwood Rise.
Southbound journeys returned via the reverse route to Upper Parliament Street and then down King Street to the terminus.
Short working of Service 5, peak hours Monday – Saturday only.

06.03.33 Service renumbered 37.

Service 8

29.11.31 Trolleybus service commenced Central Market, Palais de Danse, junction of King Edward Street and Lower Parliament Street to Wollaton Park, Scalford Drive via Upper Parliament Street, Derby Road, Canning Circus, Derby Road and Middleton Boulevard.
Worked as a circular route with Service 9, Central Market to Wollaton Park via Ilkeston Road.

20.03.32 Extended from Central Market to Carlton, Post Office Square via King Edward Street, Bath Street, Handel Street, Carlton Road, Carlton Hill and Main Street.
Westbound journeys deviated from the eastbound route from the junction of Carlton Road with Handel Street and operated via Southwell Road and Lower Parliament Street rejoining the eastbound route at the junction of King Edward Street and Lower Parliament Street at Central Market, Palais de Danse.

05.03.33 Service renumbered 38.

Service 9

29.11.31 Trolleybus service commenced Central Market, Palais de Danse, junction of King Edward Street and Lower Parliament Street, to Wollaton Park, Fairham Drive, via Upper Parliament Street, Derby Road, Canning Circus, Ilkeston Road, Wollaton Road and Middleton Boulevard.
Worked as a circular route with service 8, Central Market to Wollaton Park via Derby Road.

20.03.32 Extended from Central Market to Carlton, Post Office Square via King Edward Street, Bath Street, Handel Street, Carlton Road, Carlton Hill and Main Street.
Westbound journeys deviated from the eastbound route from the junction of Carlton Road with Handel Street and operated via Southwell Road and Lower Parliament Street rejoining the eastbound route at the junction of King Edward Street and Lower Parliament Street at Central Market, Palais de Danse.

05.03.33 Service renumbered 39.

Service 10

23.02.30 Trolleybus service commenced The Wells Road, Kildare Road to Wilford Bridge via The Wells Road, St Ann's Well Road, King Edward Street, Lower Parliament Street, George Street, Carlton Street, Victoria Street, The Poultry, South Parade, Wheeler Gate, Albert Street, Lister Gate, Greyfriar Gate, Wilford Street and Wilford Road.
Northbound journeys deviated from the southbound route from the junction of Wheeler Gate with South Parade and operated via Long Row, Queen Street and Upper Parliament Street to Lower Parliament Street.

05.03.33 Service renumbered 40.

Service 36

05.03.33 Renumbered from trolleybus service 5, operating as before Queen Street/King Street to Nottingham Road, junction with Vernon Road, Basford via Queen Street, Upper Parliament Street, Milton Street and Mansfield Road, to Gregory Boulevard then via Sherwood Rise and Nottingham Road.
Southbound journeys returned via the reverse route to Upper Parliament Street and then down King Street to the terminus.

Early 03.42 City terminus in the apex of the junction between Queen Street and King Street changed to inward alighting point King Street, outward boarding point Queen Street.

16.03.52 Northern terminus curtailed to Nottingham Road, junction with Valley Road.

30.06.06 Last day of operation by trolleybus. Replaced by motorbus service 36.

Service 37

05.03.33 Renumbered from trolleybus service H, operating as before Queen Street/King Street to Nottingham Road, junction with Haydn Road via Queen Street, Upper Parliament Street, Milton Street and Mansfield Road to Gregory Boulevard then via Sherwood Rise.
Southbound journeys returned via the reverse route to Upper Parliament Street and then down King Street to the terminus.
Short working of Service 36, peak hours Monday – Saturday only.

By 02.34 Operations now included Monday – Friday peak hours, including lunchtime, Wednesday afternoon and all day Saturday.

By 05.35 Wednesday afternoon service ceased.

Early 03.42 City terminus in the apex of the junction between Queen Street and King Street changed to: inward alighting point King Street, outward boarding point Queen Street.

By 10.52 Saturday service ceased.

By 08.53 Lunchtime peak hours ceased.

30.06.66 Last day of operation by trolleybus. Replaced by motorbus service 37.

Service 38 (i)

05.03.33 Renumbered from trolleybus service 8, operating as before Carlton, Post Office Square to Wollaton Park, Scalford Drive via Main Street, Carlton Hill, Carlton Road, Southwell Road, Lower Parliament Street, Upper Parliament Street, Derby Road, Canning Circus, Derby Road and Middleton Boulevard.
Westbound journeys deviated from the eastbound route from the junction of Carlton Road with Handel Street and operated via Southwell Road and Lower Parliament Street rejoining the eastbound route at the junction of King Edward Street and Lower Parliament Street at Central Market, Palais de Danse.
Worked as a circular route with Service 39, Carlton, Post Office Square to Wollaton Park via Ilkeston Road.

09.01.37 Service withdrawn. Replaced by trolleybus service 39 (Carlton Post Office Square – City section) and trolleybus service 45 (City – Derby Road – Wollaton Park section).

Service 38 (ii)

06.04.41	Trolleybus service commenced Queen Street/King Street to Carlton, Hooton Road via Queen Street, Upper Parliament Street, King Edward Street, Bath Street, Handel Street, Carlton Road and Carlton Hill. Westbound journeys deviated from the eastbound route from the junction of Carlton Road with Handel Street and operated via Southwell Road and Lower Parliament Street rejoining the eastbound route at the junction of King Edward Street and Lower Parliament Street at Central Market, Palais de Danse. They left Upper Parliament Street at King Street to reach the terminus. Peak hour service Monday – Saturday only.
Early 03.42	City terminus in the apex of the junction between King Street and Queen Street changed to Theatre Square, Elite Cinema (alighting), Upper Parliament Street, Kings Walk (boarding).
06.01.47	City terminus boarding point at Upper Parliament Street, Kings Walk, changed to Lower Parliament Street, Victoria Station Bridge (LNER Bridge).
04.10.47	Saturday service ceased. Operations curtailed to Monday – Friday peak hours only.
By 05.63	Motorbus operation introduced on almost half of all journeys.
11.10.65	All journeys reverted to trolleybus operation.
Late 1965	Motorbus operation reintroduced on many journeys.
Late.01.66	Last day of trolleybus operation. Replaced by motorbus service 38.

Service 39

05.03.33	Renumbered from trolleybus service 9, operating as before Carlton, Post Office Square to Wollaton Park, Fairham Drive to via Main Street, Carlton Hill, Carlton Road, Southwell Road, Lower Parliament Street, Upper Parliament Street, Derby Road, Canning Circus, Ilkeston Road, Wollaton Road and Middleton Boulevard. Eastbound journeys deviated from the westbound route from the junction of King Edward Street and Lower Parliament Street at Central Market, Palais de Danse and operated via King Edward Street, Bath Street and Handel Street rejoining the westbound route at the junction of Handel Street with Carlton Road. Worked as a circular route with service 38, Carlton, Post Office Square to Wollaton Park via Derby Road.
09.01.37	Circular operation with service 38 ceased. Trolleybuses terminate and turn round at Wollaton Park, Fairham Drive operating along Ilkeston Road in both directions.
17.10.43	Inter-working with service 45 commenced. At Wollaton Park alternate vehicles continued via Derby Road and London Road to Trent Bridge, the remainder terminating and turning around at Wollaton Park, Fairham Drive.
22.10.44	Extended from Carlton, Post Office Square to a new terminus at Carlton, Cavendish Road junction with Cemetery Road.
05.11.44	Inter-working with service 45 ceased. All trolleybuses now terminate at Wollaton Park, Fairham Drive operating along Ilkeston Road in both directions.
11.10.59	Curtailed at Wollaton Park from Fairham Drive to Middleton Boulevard, Harrow Road this section of Middleton Boulevard being replaced by an extension of trolleybus service 45.
30.09.65	Last day of trolleybus operation. Replaced by motorbus service 39.

Service 40

05.03.33	Renumbered from trolleybus service 10, operating as before The Wells Road, Kildare Road to Wilford Bridge via The Wells Road, St. Ann's Well Road, King Edward Street, Lower Parliament Street, George Street, Carlton Street, Victoria Street, The Poultry, South Parade, Wheeler Gate, Albert Street, Lister Gate, Greyfriar Gate, Wilford Street and Wilford Road. Northbound journeys deviated from the southbound route from the junction of Wheeler Gate with South Parade and operated via Long Row, Queen Street and Upper Parliament Street to Lower Parliament Street.
19.05.46	Southbound services re-routed from the junction of King Edward Street with Lower Parliament Street to operate via Lower Parliament Street, Upper Parliament Street, King Street and Old Market Square to Wheeler Gate.
10.05.53	Southbound services revert to operate via George Street, Carlton Street, Victoria Street, The Poultry and South Parade to Wheeler Gate.
09.10.65	Last day of trolleybus operation. Replaced by motorbus service 40.

Service 41

5.10.33	Trolleybus service commenced Queen Street/King Street to Cinderhill, Bells Lane via Queen Street, Upper Parliament Street, Milton Street, Mansfield Road to Gregory Boulevard then via Sherwood Rise, Nottingham Road, Valley Road, Church Street, Alpine Street, Percy Street, Stockhill Lane and Nuthall Road. Service timetabled northbound only. Afternoon peak hours Monday – Friday and all day Saturday only augmenting N&D service A1 to Ripley, which opened on the same date, within city boundary.
By 09.34	Separate, timetabled service 41 ceased to operate. It has been suggested that some afternoon peak journeys Monday – Friday may have continued to run, perhaps as extensions of service 37, but the Saturday service ceased completely.
06.04.41	Trolleybus service recommenced Queen Street/King Street to Cinderhill, Bells Lane via Queen Street, Upper Parliament Street, Milton Street, Mansfield Road to Gregory Boulevard then via Sherwood Rise, Nottingham Road, Valley Road, Church Street, Alpine Street, Percy Street, Stockhill Lane and Nuthall Road in both directions. Southbound journeys returned via the reverse route to Upper Parliament Street and then down King Street to the terminus. Peak hours Monday – Friday and all day Saturday.
Early 03.42	City terminus in the apex of the junction between King Street and Queen Street changed to inward alighting point King Street, outward boarding point Queen Street.
26.04.53	Extended from Queen Street/King Street to Trent Bridge, Victoria Embankment, Bunbury Street via Long Row, Old Market Square, Wheeler Gate, Albert Street, Lister Gate, Carrington Street and Arkwright Street. Southbound via King Street, northbound via Queen Street. Becomes an all-day, daily service replacing trolleybus service 48 and N&D trolleybus service A1 within the city boundaries.
30.04.65	Last day of trolleybus operation. Replaced by motorbus service 41.

Service 42

13.05.34	Trolleybus service commenced Bulwell Hall Estate to Trent Bridge, Victoria Embankment via Hucknall Lane, Main Street, Bulwell Market, Highbury Road, Vernon Road, Radford Road, Bentinck Road, Alfreton Road, Canning Circus, Derby Road, Chapel Bar, Angel Row, Old Market Square, Wheeler Gate, Albert Street, Lister Gate, Carrington Street and Arkwright Street.
02.06.35	Inter-working with service 44 commenced. All northbound journeys from Colwick Road Railway Crossing continuing via Colwick Road, Sneinton Hermitage, Manvers Street, Bath Street, King Edward Street, Lower Parliament Street, George Street, Victoria Street, The Poultry, South Parade, Old Market Square to Bulwell Hall Estate displayed service 42.
06.04.41 (assumed date)	Inter-working with service 44 ceased. Trolleybus service 42 curtailed to operate Bulwell Market to Old Market Square, inward alighting point Long Row West, outward boarding point Angel Row, in both directions.
22.08.54	Curtailed to operate Basford, Northern Baths to Old Market Square, inward alighting point Long Row West, outward boarding point Angel Row. Peak hour service Monday – Saturdays only.

10.10.54	Winter Sunday service commenced and extended Basford, Northern Baths to Trent Bridge, Victoria Embankment via Vernon Road, Radford Road, Bentinck Road, Alfreton Road, Canning Circus, Chapel Bar, Angel Row, Old Market Square, Wheeler Gate, Albert Street, Lister Gate, Carrington Street and Arkwright Street.
11.04.59	Saturday peak hour service ceased to operate.
03.04.60	Winter Sunday extension to Trent Bridge ceased to operate.
05.11.63	Motorbus operation introduced on an increasing number of journeys.
	Most journeys reverted to trolleybus operation due to a shortage of motorbuses.
31.05.65	Last day of trolleybus operation. Replaced by motorbus service 42.

Service 43

13.05.34	Trolleybus service commenced Bulwell Market to Trent Bridge, Victoria Embankment via Highbury Road, Vernon Road, Radford Road, Bentinck Road, Alfreton Road, Canning Circus, Derby Road, Chapel Bar, Angel Row, Old Market Square, Wheeler Gate, Albert Street, Lister Gate, Carrington Street and Arkwright Street.
02.06.35	Inter-working with service 44 commenced. All northbound journeys from Colwick Road Railway Crossing continuing via Colwick Road, Sneinton Hermitage, Manvers Street, Bath Street, King Edward Street, Parliament Street, George Street, Victoria Street, The Poultry, South Parade, Old Market Square displayed service 42 if operating to Bulwell Hall Estate or 43 if operating to Bulwell Market.
	Inter-working with service 44 ceased. Trolleybus service 43 operates Bulwell (assumed date) Market to Trent Bridge, Victoria Embankment in both directions.
31.03.65	Last day of trolleybus operation. Replaced by motorbus 43.

Service 44

02.06.35	Trolleybus service commenced Bulwell Hall Estate to Colwick Road Railway Crossing via Hucknall Lane, Main Street, Bulwell Market, Highbury Road, Vernon Road, Radford Road, Bentinck Road, Alfreton Road, Canning Circus, Derby Road, Chapel Bar, Angel Row, Long Row West, Old Market Square, Queen Street, Upper Parliament Street, Lower Parliament Street, King Edward Street, Bath Street, Southwell Road, Manvers Street, Sneinton Hermitage, Hermitage Square and Colwick Road.
	Service operated southbound only. All northbound journeys from Colwick Road Railway Crossing continuing via Colwick Road, Sneinton Hermitage, Manvers Street, Bath Street, King Edward Street, Parliament Street, George Street, Victoria Street, The Poultry, South Parade, Old Market Square displayed service 42 if operating to Bulwell Hall Estate or 43 if operating to Bulwell Market.
12.01.36	Service re-routed between Derby Road and Queen Street to operate along west end of Upper Parliament Street avoiding Old Market Square.
06.04.41	Inter-working with services 42 and 43 ceased. Trolleybus service 44 operates (assumed date) Bulwell Hall Estate to Colwick Road Railway Crossing in both directions.
	Southbound journeys continued to operate along the length of Upper Parliament Street. Northbound journeys deviated from the southbound route from the junction of King Edward Street with Lower Parliament Street and operated via George Street, Carlton Street, Victoria Street, The Poultry, South Parade, Old Market Square, Angel Row and Chapel Bar.
19.05.46	Service re-routed between Upper Parliament Street and Derby Road to operate in both directions along Upper Parliament Street avoiding Old Market Square.
26.07.59	Service re-routed northbound between Upper Parliament Street and Derby Road to operate through the Old Market Square via King Street, Long Row, Angel Row and Chapel Bar. Southbound journeys continued to run along Upper Parliament Street.
31.05.65	Last day of trolleybus operation. Replaced by motorbus service 44.

Service 45

02.06.35	Trolleybus service commenced Trent Bridge, Globe Cinema to Wollaton Park, Scalford Drive via London Road, Pennyfoot Street, Manvers Street, Southwell Road, Bath Street, King Edward Street, Lower Parliament Street, Upper Parliament Street, Derby Road, Canning Circus, Derby Road and Middleton Boulevard. Outward alighting point Turney's Factory at the southern end of London Road, inward boarding point at the Globe Cinema, in the apex of the junction between Arkwright Street and London Road.
18.08.35	Curtailed to operate Trent Bridge, Globe Cinema, to Queen Street/King Street.
	Northbound journeys terminated at King Street. Southbound journeys returned up Queen Street to Upper Parliament Street and then via the reverse route to Trent Bridge.
10.01.37	Re-extended to Wollaton Park, Scalford Drive via Derby Road replacing service 38(i).
17.10.43	Inter-working with service 39 commenced. At Wollaton Park all vehicles continuing via Ilkeston Road, Upper Parliament Street and Bath Street to Carlton, Post Office Square.
05.11.44	Inter-working with service 39 ceased. All trolleybuses terminate and turn around at Wollaton Park, Scalford Drive operating along Derby Road in both directions.
22.02.53	Re-routed to become Trent Bridge, Globe Cinema to Wollaton Park, Scalford Drive via London Road, Lower Parliament Street, Upper Parliament Street, Derby Road, Canning Circus, Derby Road and Middleton Boulevard. (In both directions).
15.03.53	Trent Bridge terminus at the Globe Cinema (boarding point) moved to London Road, Burton's Almshouses.
By 10.54	Trent Bridge terminus at London Road, Burton's Almshouses (boarding point) reverted to the Globe Cinema.
11.10.59	Extended at Wollaton Park from Scalford Drive to Middleton Boulevard, Harrow Road replacing the curtailed service 39. Trent Bridge terminus at the Globe Cinema (boarding point) was moved to Ryehill Street.
15.11.59	Extended at Trent Bridge to Victoria Embankment, east end turning circle (alighting and boarding points).
03.11.62	Last day of trolleybus operation. Replaced by motorbus service 45.

Service 46 (i)

02.06.35	Trolleybus service commenced Old Market Square, Processional Way to Trent Bridge, Victoria Embankment via Wheeler Gate, Lister Gate, Albert Street, Carrington Street and Arkwright Street.
05.09.36	Service withdrawn. Replaced by daily motorbus services 20 and 35.

Service 46 (ii)

23.09.39	Trolleybus service re-commenced Old Market Square, Processional Way to Trent Bridge, Victoria Embankment via Wheeler Gate, Lister Gate, Albert Street, Carrington Street and Arkwright Street.
By 10.50	Service reduced to all day Sunday, and infrequent late evening journeys Monday – Saturday only.
22.08.54	Service further reduced to Summer Sundays only, with occasional peak hour and infrequent late evening journeys Monday – Saturday throughout the year.
31.03.65	Last day of trolleybus operation. Replaced by motorbus service 46.

Service 47

15.06.42	Trolleybus service commenced The Wells Road, Ransom Road to Wilford Bridge via The Wells Road, St Ann's Well Road, King Edward Street, Lower Parliament Street, George Street, Carlton Street, Victoria Street, The Poultry, South Parade, Wheeler Gate, Albert Street, Lister Gate, Greyfriar Gate, Wilford Street and Wilford Road. Northbound journeys deviated from the southbound route from the junction of Wheeler Gate with South Parade and operated via Long Row, Queen Street and Upper Parliament Street to Lower Parliament Street.
19.05.46	Southbound services re-routed from the junction of King Edward Street with Lower Parliament Street to operate via Lower Parliament Street, Upper Parliament Street, King Street, Long Row and Old Market Square to Wheeler Gate.
10.05.53	Southbound services revert to operate via George Street, Carlton Street, Victoria Street, The Poultry and South Parade to Wheeler Gate.
09.10.65	Last day of trolleybus operation. Replaced by motorbus service 47.

Service 48

14 10.45	Trolleybus service commenced Trent Bridge, Victoria Embankment to Nottingham Road, junction with Vernon Road via Arkwright Street, Carrington Street, Lister Gate, Albert Street, Wheeler Gate, Old Market Square, Long Row, Upper Parliament Street, Milton Street, Mansfield Road to Gregory Boulevard then via Sherwood Rise and Nottingham Road. Southbound via King Street, northbound via Queen Street.
16.03.52	Northern terminus curtailed to Nottingham Road, junction with Valley Road.
25.04.53	Last day of trolleybus operation. Replaced by an extension of trolleybus service 41 and an augmented timetable on trolleybus service 36.

Supplementary information

Certain early Sunday morning workings differed from the equivalent Monday to Saturday operations. One service 40 journey operated from Carlton, Post Office Square to Wilford Road for Royal Ordnance Factory (the "gun factory") workers. Some southbound service 40 journeys from Wells Road, Kildare Road and certain journeys entering service from Lower Parliament Street Depot did not work through to Wilford Road, but turned in the city centre by using George Street, Victoria Street, South Parade and then Beastmarket Hill to Long Row East where they would await departure time (often with trolley poles stowed to allow vehicles on other services to overtake). This routing was also followed on Monday – Friday peak hour workings from Wells Road where the final alighting point was South Parade from whence the trolleybus would work back to Lower Parliament Street Depot.

A Sunday morning 44 ran from Bulwell Hall Estate to Lower Parliament Street for postal workers at the nearby sorting office in Huntingdon Street, trolleybuses following a circular route along Lower Parliament Street, Southwell Road, Bath Street and King Edward Street before returning to Bulwell.

Early morning journeys on service 44 originated at Bulwell Market whilst others were advertised as starting from Basford, Northern Baths although they were undoubtedly running out of Bulwell Depot. Equally certain 44 journeys to Colwick Road originated and terminated at Victoria Station Bridge, Lower Parliament Street. Some early Sunday morning journeys on service 44 from Bulwell Hall Estate also only worked as far as the city centre, terminating at Long Row West. Again they would frequently stow their trolley poles to allow overtaking whilst waiting for departure time. They would then use the overhead wiring on the south side of the roundabout at the foot of Market Street erected for service 42 to regain their usual northbound stop at Angel Row.

By the late 1950s some of the peak hour only service 38 trolleybuses to Carlton, Hooton Road, had journeys originating at Wollaton Park working back (showing 38 on the destination blind) via Ilkeston Road, Canning Circus, Derby Road and Upper Parliament Street to join their usual routing at Theatre Square. These "extra" journeys were not shown in the public timetables (which already provided a 3 minute headway between Wollaton Park and Carlton, Post Office Square, with no short workings to Hooton Road) and were presumably intended to serve workers from the Raleigh factory. Other "Raleigh extra" journeys started at Gregory Street as did some 47s for Ransom Road.

The final journey on service 45 on Saturday nights only, operated from Wollaton Park via Derby Road to the City but then worked from the bottom of Derby Road via Chapel Bar, Old Market Square and Arkwright Street to Trent Bridge as service 43 before running in to Trent Bridge Depot.

Appendix E

Destination Displays

As only latter-day destination blinds have survived it has proved impossible to provide a complete review of all displays and the sequence of their appearance on the blinds prior to 1949.

Pre-1931 deliveries

CARTER GATE
KING ST
KING STREET
LONDON RD
HAYDN RD
HAYDN ROAD
WELLS RD
WELLS ROAD
WILFORD BRIDGE
PARLIAMENT ST DEPOT
NOTTINGHAM RD

CARLTON
BULWELL

Note: the additional displays listed below are also known:

CITY
CITY VIA DERBY RD.
WOLLATON PARK/DERBY RD.
SPECIAL

Service numbers were displayed on a separate blind.

1931 – 1935 deliveries

The original indicator blinds on the 1931 deliveries included the outdated destination of Carter Gate Depot, a number of points on the tramway system which were never reached by trolleybuses and Kimberley, some 2 miles beyond the city boundary on the N&D system.

POSTAL
CARLTON POST OFFICE SQUARE
CARLTON WOOTON ROAD
WOLLATON PARK VIA ILKESTON RD
WOLLATON PARK VIA DERBY RD
BULLWELL HALL ESTATE
BULLWELL MARKET
BASFORD ELAND STREET
COLWICK ROAD
CITY
CINDERHILL
NOTTINGHAM ROAD
HAYDN ROAD
WELLS ROAD RANSOM ROAD
WELLS ROAD KILDARE ROAD
WILFORD ROAD

TRENT BRIDGE VIA LONDON RD
TRENT BRIDGE VIA ARKWRIGHT ST
CITY
SPECIAL
TRENT BRIDGE DEPOT
BULWELL DEPOT
PARLIAMENT ST DEPOT
CITY
FOOTBALL GROUND
TRENT BRIDGE VIA NOTTINGHAM RD
NOTTINGHAM RD VIA MANSFIELD RD
TRENT BRIDGE VIA MANSFIELD RD
PRIVATE
CITY
TRENT BRIDGE VIA WOLLATON PARK
CARLTON VIA WOLLATON PARK

Until the ex-Southend vehicles arrived, all trolleybuses, excluding the Leyland TTB3s, could display indicator blinds featuring two rows of lettering, the lower row of letters getting progressively smaller to the right and the upper getting progressively larger to the right, in the narrow indicator box.

The lettered area on the indicator blinds was 27 ins X 5½ ins.

The following latter-day example was removed from 338 prior to withdrawal in 1950:

49 CARLTON MANOR ROAD
39 CARLTON POST OFFICE SQ
39 WOLLATON PARK VIA ILKESTON RD
38 CARLTON HOOTON ROAD
CITY
PARLIAMENT ST DEPOT
44 BULWELL HALL ESTATE
44 COLWICK RD
BASFORD NORTHERN BATHS
BASFORD ELAND STREET
42 BULWELL MARKET
BULWELL DEPOT
43 BULWELL MARKET
43 TRENT BRIDGE VIA ARKWRIGHT ST
46 TRENT BRIDGE VIA ARKWRIGHT ST
CITY
37 HAYDN RD
36 NOTTINGHAM RD VIA MANSFIELD RD

Service numbers were displayed on a separate blind. In the tramcar era, passengers had developed the habit of looking at the upper deck end vestibules for the service number equating to their destination. The unusual position of the service number indicator between the front upper deck windows on the motorbus and trolleybus deliveries of this period was selected as the nearest equivalent location.

Leyland TTB3s

These vehicles introduced a new style of informative blinds to the trolleybus fleet. A complete list of the displays and their sequence on the blinds has not been discovered.

BULWELL MARKET
VIA
OLD MARKET SQUARE
HYSON GREEN
BASFORD

BULWELL MARKET
VIA
BATH ST
OLD MARKET SQUARE
HYSON GREEN

BULWELL HALL ESTATE
VIA
OLD MARKET SQUARE
HYSON GREEN
BULWELL MARKET

BULWELL HALL ESTATE
VIA
BATH ST
OLD MARKET SQUARE
HYSON GREEN

COLWICK RD
VIA
HYSON GREEN
OLD MARKET SQUARE
BATH ST

TRENT BRIDGE
VIA
HYSON GREEN
OLD MARKET SQUARE
ARKWRIGHT ST

TRENT BRIDGE
VIA
HYSON GREEN
CITY
ARKWRIGHT ST

TRENT BRIDGE
VIA
HYSON GREEN
OLD MARKET SQUARE
ARKWRIGHT ST

WOLLATON PARK
VIA
BATH ST
PARLIAMENT ST
DERBY RD

DEPOT
CITY
CITY POSTAL
SPECIAL

Service numbers were displayed on a separate blind.

Wartime deliveries

The second hand purchases from Cleethorpes, Hastings and Southend on Sea were equipped on an ad hoc basis with standard single line blinds as fitted to the 1931-1935 deliveries. Service numbers were displayed on a separate blind.

Daimler CTM 4 441 and the Sunbeam MF2s 447-451 were equipped with large rectangular indicator boxes 36 ins x 24 ins and 36½ ins x 20 ins respectively in size and carried appropriately large blinds displaying a service number to the left of up to 4 lines of information (2 in large lettering, 2 in smaller lettering). Photographic evidence exists of the following examples although their positioning on the blinds is not known:

36 NOTTINGHAM ROAD VIA MANSFIELD RD

39 WOLLATON PARK VIA ILKESTON RD

39 CARLTON POST OFFICE SQUARE

40 WELLS ROAD VIA CITY

43 TRENT BRIDGE VIA ARKWRIGHT ST

C I T Y
S P E C I A L

The utility bodied Karrier Ws were all equipped with blinds displaying a service number to the left of up to 2 lines of written information, the service number was approximately the depth of the 2 lines of information, in a similar style to that adopted as standard post-war.

Post war

A standard blind displaying a service number to the left of up to 2 lines of written information was adopted. The service number was approximately the depth of the 2 lines of information. The content, layout and sequence of individual destination varied a little during the vehicles' lifetime to reflect service revisions. The lettered area on the indicator blinds was 32½ins X 7ins whilst the aperture size was 36ins X 10ins.

When delivered the BUT9641Ts 500-601 carried destination blinds which appeared as follows:

48 NOTTINGHAM RD VIA MANSFIELD RD
48 TRENT BRIDGE VIA MANSFIELD RD
41 CINDERHILL
47 WELLS RD RANSOM RD
40 WELLS RD KILDARE RD

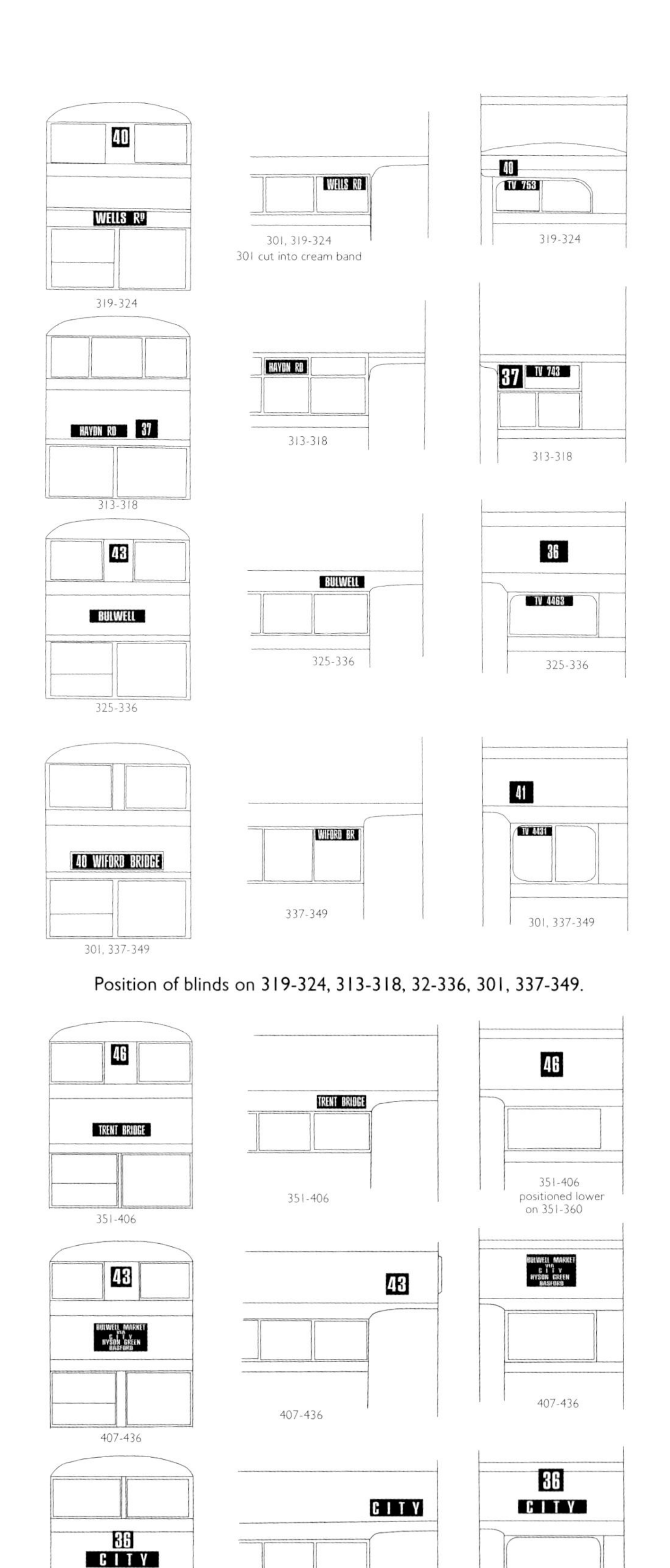

Position of blinds on 319-324, 313-318, 32-336, 301, 337-349.

Position of blinds on 351-406, 407-436, 437-440, 441.

Notes:

1. The "49 CARLTON/MANOR ROAD" display was removed at a later date.
2. Earlier blinds contained a "36 NOTTINGHAM ROAD/VERNON ROAD" display. This was replaced by "36 NOTTINGHAM ROAD/VIA MANSFIELD ROAD".
3. Following the withdrawal of service 48 and its replacement by service 41, the displays "48 NOTTINGHAM RD. VIA MANSFIELD RD." and "48 TRENT BRIDGE/VIA MANSFIELD RD." were removed. The displays "41 TRENT BRIDGE" and "CITY" were inserted between "41 CINDERHILL" and "47 WELLS RD./VIA RANSOM RD.".
4. Following the curtailment of service 42 from Bulwell to Basford, Northern Baths, this latter display received a service number prefix, viz "42 BASFORD / NORTHERN BATHS" and the displays "42 BULWELL MARKET" and "BULWELL DEPOT" immediately thereafter were removed.
5. The display "POSTAL" was in red lettering on the customary black background. It was removed at a later date.

n.b. "/" indicates top line/bottom line.

At each end of the blind there was a black blank, slightly larger than the size of the aperture, followed by a white blank, approximately twice the depth of the aperture, however they were rarely used. Trolleybuses returning to their depot displayed the name of the respective depot whilst those on driver training duties or running to/from Trent Bridge Works would display "NOT ON SERVICE".

Contemporary motor buses with similar style destination boxes did not carry specific trolleybus indicator displays, the sole exception being "43 BULWELL" although "TRENT BRIDGE" was also included but without a service number.

Solely the 1946 Karrier Ws 469-478 of the post-war deliveries were equipped with separate service number blinds, the indicator being on the nearside immediately above the rear open platform. The sequence of numbers on the blind was: 48, then 36-50. Service number 48 appears twice, firstly at the top of the blind together with other Nottingham Road services and then in numerical order. The inclusion of numbers 49 and 50 is interesting as, although there were plans for a service 49 (Carlton, Manor Road) nothing is known of proposals for a service 50.

Position of blinds on 479-495, 500-601, 302-303, 304-309.

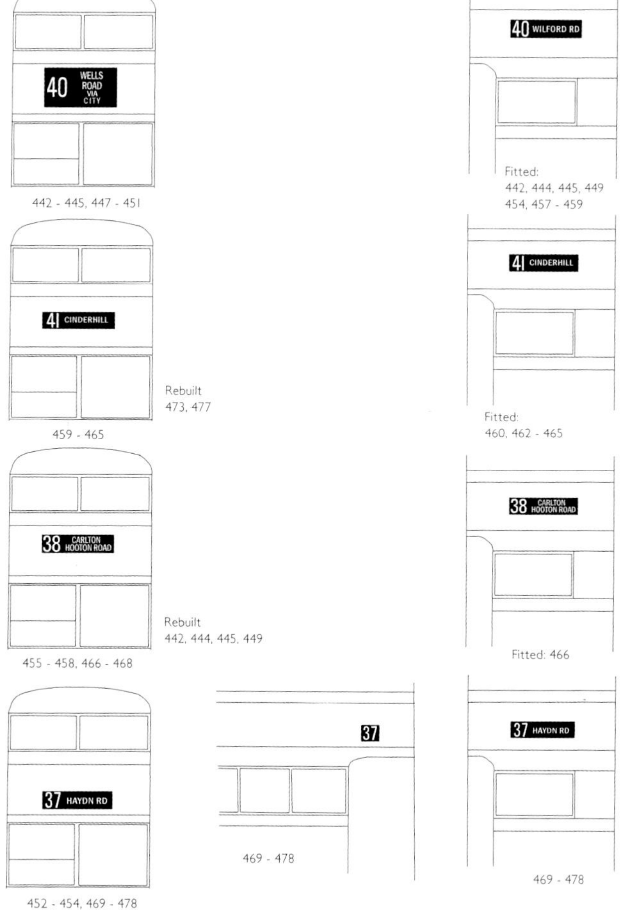

Position of blinds on 442-445, 447-451, 459-465, 455-458, 466-468, 452-454, 469-478.

Appendix F Depots

Trent Bridge Depot packed with BUT9641Ts. *NCT*

Nottingham's trolleybuses operated from 3 different depots, all of which had been built during the tramway era and designed to suit rail-bound vehicles. Bulwell and Trent Bridge Depots were opened in the earliest stages of the construction of the city's first generation electric tramway system at the beginning of the 20th century. Once these depots had been reconstructed for trolleybus operation they tended to suffer from a restricted building maintenance budget.

Individual trolleybuses were allocated to a specific depot, although no indication of such was shown on the vehicles, and it was rare for a trolleybus to move from its "home" base. Each depot was responsible for running a group of services, certain individual services being operated jointly with another depot, leading to vehicles usually spending their entire working lives on the same routes. Exceptions were usually caused by a breakdown, resulting in a substitute vehicle being loaned by another depot but in such cases the "stranger" would be returned as soon as possible to its home base once the first vehicle had been repaired. Only when the size of the fleet began to fall with the abandonment programme did formal vehicle re-allocations commence.

At least in the post-war era there appears to have been a policy of keeping trolleybuses with the same electrical equipment at the same depot(s). The Metropolitan-Vickers equipped BUT 9641Ts were allocated to Bulwell whereas their English Electric equipped counterparts were based at Lower Parliament Street Depot. As each depot carried out running repairs to its allocation, the quantity of spares held in stock could be minimised by grouping the vehicles in this manner. The situation was somewhat different at Trent Bridge Depot as the adjacent Works, which handled all major repairs, held stocks of all types of spares.

A compulsory "leakage" test was carried out daily when each trolleybus returned to its depot by an employee with a large meter hanging from a strap around his neck, an iron bar to earth the system to the tram rails still in situ and a large metal contact, often a headlamp surround, to press against the bodywork.

The pneumatic tyres used during the trolleybus era were not as reliable or sophisticated as today's examples, whilst the rear tyres of 3-axle vehicles suffered additional wear from rear bogie scrub. The result was frequent punctures. Depots handled this by sending out a motorbus with a spare wheel on the rear platform, looked after by a second man, as it was easier to roll the spare on and off a single step platform than to use a breakdown vehicle.

Bulwell Depot

An example of the classical style of tramcar running shed built with brick exterior walls having tall arched windows on the southeast side, facing Piccadilly, raised ground on the northwest side and a light fenestrated girder roof. As constructed, the building was 284ft long and 77ft wide, having a slight bend or curve at the north-east end, with 6-lyes of tram track all equipped with pits and a central row of girder stanchions to support the double-hipped roof. There was accommodation for 45 tramcars. A single track along Piccadilly to/from Highbury Road provided access with a track fan inside the southwest end of the shed.

In early 1934, in preparation for the conversion of the trunk Bulwell – Trent Bridge tram route, work started on an extension to that part of the building beyond the curve and the construction of a new entrance at the northeast end. Trolleybuses used the shed in one direction only, entering at the northeast end and exiting, through the original sole doorway, at the southwest end. The new extension accommodated a single frog, the two pairs of wires therefrom each opening up into 3 lyes within the two bays of the running shed. Office accommodation was limited to a cash office at the southwest end of the running shed whilst there was an oil store at the opposite end of the building in the 1934 extension.

It is believed that Bulwell Depot's initial trolleybus allocation included Karrier E6 51-70. All 30 Leyland TTB3 trolleybuses were allocated to Bulwell upon delivery in mid-1935, possibly representing the depot's entire allocation, and the vehicles displaced were transferred to Trent Bridge. In 1937 Bulwell, until then limited to electric traction, began to operate motorbuses too. After the Second World War some utility and post-war 2-axle trolleybuses were allocated to Bulwell Deport pending the delivery of the BUT9641Ts.

A small canteen was opened in late 1948 adjacent to the exit and towards the end of 1953 a "Februat" brush washing machine, subsequently replaced by a "home made" equivalent, was installed at the running shed exit. Latterly Bulwell vehicles were washed at Lower Parliament Street Depot, reportedly by taking them off service 44 for one journey and returning them afterwards. This no doubt contributed to Bulwell's allocation gaining a reputation for their dirty and unkempt appearance. Management considered the employees there as rather militant.

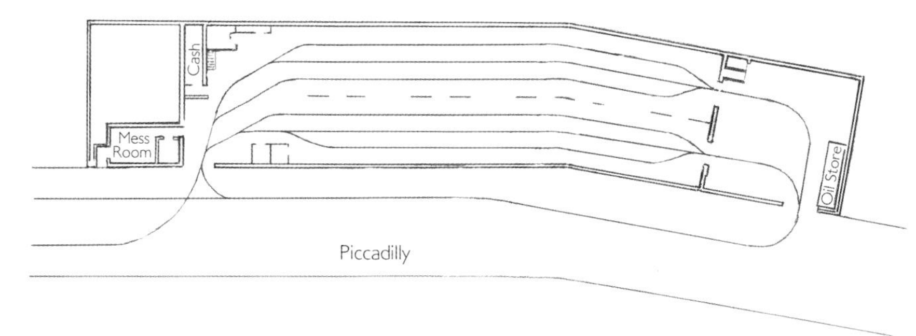

Bulwell Depot plan.

In 1960 Bulwell had the following trolleybus (37 vehicles unchanged from March 1956, when there were also 24 motorbuses) and service allocation:

Trolleybuses:	535-564	BUT9641T (Metropolitan-Vickers equipment, 7ft 6ins wide)
	587-593	BUT9641T (Metropolitan-Vickers equipment, 7ft 6ins wide)
Services:	42	
	43	(jointly operated with Trent Bridge Depot)
	44	
	46	(occasional extra duties)

From November 1963 until 31 March 1965 most journeys on service 42 were operated by Bulwell-based motorbuses, thereafter, until 31 May 1965 when services 42 and 44 were permanently converted to motorbuses, trolleybuses from the remaining Bulwell allocation operated the service. When trolleybus service 43 was withdrawn on 31 March 1965 some of Bulwell's allocation was taken out of service for disposal and others transferred to Lower Parliament Street Depot. This also happened on 31 May 1965 when Bulwell Depot closed to electric traction.

The last trolleybus from the erstwhile Bulwell Depot allocation to remain in service was 535, which was withdrawn on 9 October 1965 following peak hour duties on services 40 and 47 on the final day of these routes.

Although Bulwell was referred to as "life expired" and ripe for closure as early as 1962, the depot continued to operate an increased allocation of motorbuses until March 2001 when the site was put up for sale. Demolition was completed in December 2004 although the retaining wall at the rear of the building, strengthened with buttresses, to support the back gardens of the properties on Ingram Road has survived.

Lower Parliament Street Depot

The availability of a suitable location to the east of the city centre was closely linked with the slum clearances championed in the early years of the 20th century by Dr. P. Boobbyer, Nottingham's Medical Officer of Health. Densely built housing and some 37 streets or yards, had sprung up over an irregular triangle of more than seven acres in the period 1745-1845, during which Nottingham's population increased six-fold without any corresponding increase in area, and by 1912 provided insanitary homes to almost 2,000 people.

Although many properties ceased to be used during the First World War, redevelopment only started in the early 1920s with every old building being demolished. By late 1921 the first new building, premises for the Carter Gate Motor Co., appeared on the corner of Carter Gate and what would be known as Stanhope Street, named after the politician Charles Stanhope, 3rd Earl Stanhope (1753-1816). In March 1926 Trent opened a motorbus garage at the corner of Manvers Street and Stanhope Street, backing on to the Carter Gate Motors premises.

In 1925 it was decided that Nottingham Corporation Tramways should acquire the Southwell Road end of the site as the location for a central base, to be known as Carter Gate Depot, for the growing fleet and a new head office. Construction began in April 1926 and proceeded slowly not least due to the General Strike and its aftermath. Motorbuses and trolley vehicles were housed there from April 1928, together with those trams previously allocated to the original Trent Bridge Depot building which was now converted into an enlarged central works, whilst on 14 June 1928 head office staff were transferred to their new home. The whole building, capable of accommodating 80 trams, just over 45 trolley vehicles and about 70 motorbuses was declared open on 30 April 1929. From the outset, the premises were officially referred to as Lower Parliament Street or colloquially simply as Parliament Street but its earlier title remained in common use, and the 1931 trolleybus deliveries carried "CARTER GATE DEPOT" on their destination blinds.

The architecture is a product of the period of civic pride that gave Nottingham its Council House and was designed by T. Wallis Gordon, City Engineer and Surveyor. The office building consists of a long façade

Inside Bulwell Depot and new BUT9641Ts as far as the eye can see. *NCT*

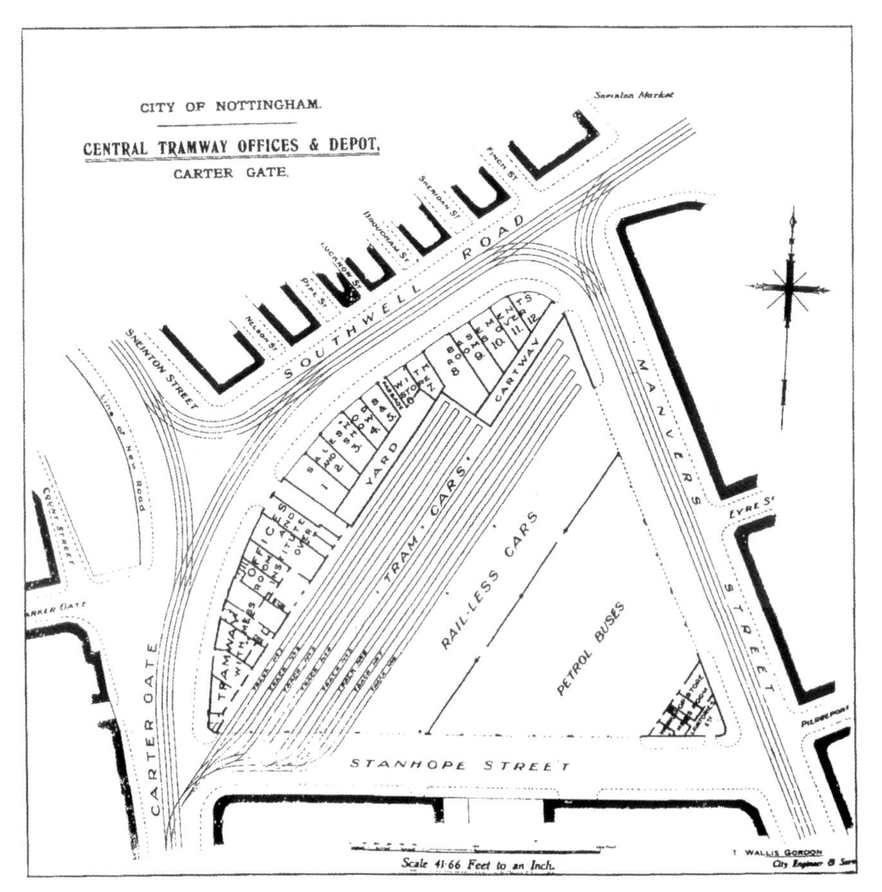

An undated plan of Lower Parliament Street Tram Depot with space for 'Rail-less cars'. *NCT*

following the curve of Lower Parliament Street into Southwell Road, between Stanhope Street and Manvers Street, with the running shed behind.

The main structure of the office building is constructed in brick, enlivened and emphasised by stone-built bays, featuring decorated carved panel and rusticated quoins and sections. Carved into the stonework on the corner of Lower Parliament Street with Stanhope Street can be seen the words 'Nottingham Corporation Tramways 1926' in sans serif capital letters whilst above the leaded fanlight of the main entrance "NCT" appears. Continuing around the façade shops or offices are incorporated into the ground floor, fitted with Georgian-style windows and linked in an elaborate vertical stone composition. During the trolleybus era many businesses so typical of the period, such as the City Clothiers, Meadow Dairy and the Home & Colonial Stores had branches here. On the corner of Manvers Street there is another bay built in stone with an iron gate, which was once the entrance to the depot cartway. One floor above is a round window, possibly intended to accommodate a clock, with the interlaced figures "1927" carved in its surround.

Immediately behind the office accommodation i.e. to the southeast thereof, there were 8 tram tracks. The first 4 lyes (bay 1) abutted shops on Southwell Road and the cartway whilst the other 4 (bays 2, 3) were up to 23ft longer and continued as far as the wall bounding on Manvers Street. There was no exit from any of the tram tracks into Manvers Street, all tramcar movements in or out of the running shed being by way of Stanhope Street and Lower Parliament Street (Carter Gate). Moving further southeast came 4 lyes (bays 4, 5) for railless trolley vehicles. The tram and railless accommodation, comprising bays 1-5, were together known as "No. 3 Depot". Bay 5 was bordered by a longitudinal wall before a number of parking lanes for motor buses, this accommodation being known as "No 1 Depot". Both the trolley vehicle and motorbus lanes were unidirectional, with entry from Stanhope Street and exit by Manvers Street. The triangular nature of the site meant that the lyes and lanes were progressively shorter to the southeast. Finally there were stores and rest rooms in the southeast corner of the complex.

Each of the 4 railless lyes was equipped with inspection pits and a pair of trolley wires in wooden troughs suspended from the roof girders but only within the running shed itself. Access and egress was entirely by use of the offside (positive) trolley pole and a trailing skate, there still being evidence of some sort of light section rail leading into bays 4 and 5 from Stanhope Street for skate use. Once Carter Gate Depot was able to accommodate railless vehicles i.e. April 1928, these ceased to make the long journey to/from Trent Bridge Depot when running into or out of service.

At a tight fit this provided just sufficient accommodation for the entire trolley vehicle fleet, which reached a total of 50 with the 1931-32 Carlton and Wollaton Park extensions. In June 1931, in anticipation of an enlarged trolleybus fleet, pit alterations, demolition of the end wall to bays 2 and 3 used by trams facing Manvers Street and the installation of electric roller shutter doors were approved. It is assumed that this work was carried out in summer 1931 but it is not known when these bays (lyes 5-8) were actually equipped for and regularly used by trolley vehicles. As there was no need for additional depot accommodation until 1934, it is believed that overhead wiring equipment was installed as a part of the preparations for the Bulwell – Trent Bridge conversion. The Passenger Transport Committee Minutes of 27 November 1933 record that "it was necessary to convert a further 4 roads in Carter Gate Depot (sic) for trolley vehicles", the use of the word "further" suggesting that 4 roads had already been converted. Nonetheless it is believed that this referred to tram lyes 5–8 rather than 1-4. It is assumed that, by the time of the conversion of the Carlton tram route to trolleybus operation in March 1932, overhead wiring had been erected from the running shed into Manvers Street and thus Southwell Road.

Some 56 trolleybuses were delivered in 1934 but as 37 of these were housed at Bulwell and Trent Bridge Depots, once their reconstruction was completed, there remained ample depot space at Lower Parliament Street. At the same time the tram fleet was reduced to 83 cars, some of which were based at Sherwood Depot. The resultant considerable reduction in tramcar movements in Stanhope Street, made it practical in 1934-35 to extend the single pair of trolleybus wires in Lower Parliament Street around the corner into Stanhope Street and construct an entry fan to provide access to the overhead wiring already in place inside the depot building.

The 4 remaining tramcar lyes immediately behind the office accommodation survived until the end of tram operations in September 1936 there being no immediate need for additional trolleybus space following the 1935 conversions of Colwick Road and London Road as these routes were operated by Bulwell and Trent Bridge Depots respectively. When trolleybus overhead wiring was erected in bay 1, the layout was complicated by the absence of an exit at the northeast end. A single pair of entry wires led from the Stanhope Street entrance into the building where they divided into two: about 2/3 of the way along the bay these merged together with two terminal stubs and then joined the north westernmost through pair of wires leading into Manvers Street. In addition there were four isolated sidings with inspection pits at the northeast end of bay 1.

The earlier conversions and the original railless lyes involved 4 entries and exits, all of which opened up into two pairs of wires inside the depot building. There were thus a total of 12 trolleybus lyes made up of the former 8 tram lyes and the 4 original lyes foreseen for railless trolley vehicles when the building was originally constructed. In 1954 a Dawson "drive-through" bus washing plant was installed at the northernmost exit into Manvers Street leading to changes in the exit wiring arrangements in bay 2, necessitating the removal of some pits and the installation of concrete flooring in the immediate vicinity. The trolleybuses drove through normally taking power from the overhead wiring.

Once the undertaking had established itself at Lower Parliament Street, it sought to increase the garage accommodation by acquiring surrounding properties although this led to no growth in the space available to trolleybuses after the final tram lyes had been converted for railless traction. In 1933, a little further south along Lower Parliament Street, Trent opened a larger garage for 145 motorbuses and vacated their 1926 premises, which were then acquired by NCT and known as "No 2 Depot" to garage some 40 motorbuses stabled temporarily until then in the former Cammell Laird factory in King's Meadow Road. In the mid-1940s land between "No 2 Depot" and Trent's Manvers Street Garage was levelled to provide open-air parking for motorbuses, known as "MX". In 1961-62 the Manvers Street end of Stanhope Street was roofed to provide further motorbus accommodation.

Between 1938 and 1942 office accommodation was increased by the addition of a second storey on the Stanhope Street end of the office building. Until the arrival of Ben England in 1939 much of the main building was rented out as shop and office space to third parties, the northernmost space used by the Department as a billiard room. Thereafter the offices in Nos. 2, 2a, 4 and 6 Southwell Road were reacquired.

Until Ben England's arrival, all engineering staff were based at Trent Bridge Works but he set about progressively moving all senior staff to Lower Parliament Street as each lease came to an end and additional accommodation became available. The Traffic Department was moved into office space beyond the billiard room that had previously been rented out and the vacated space was re-designated as the Deputy

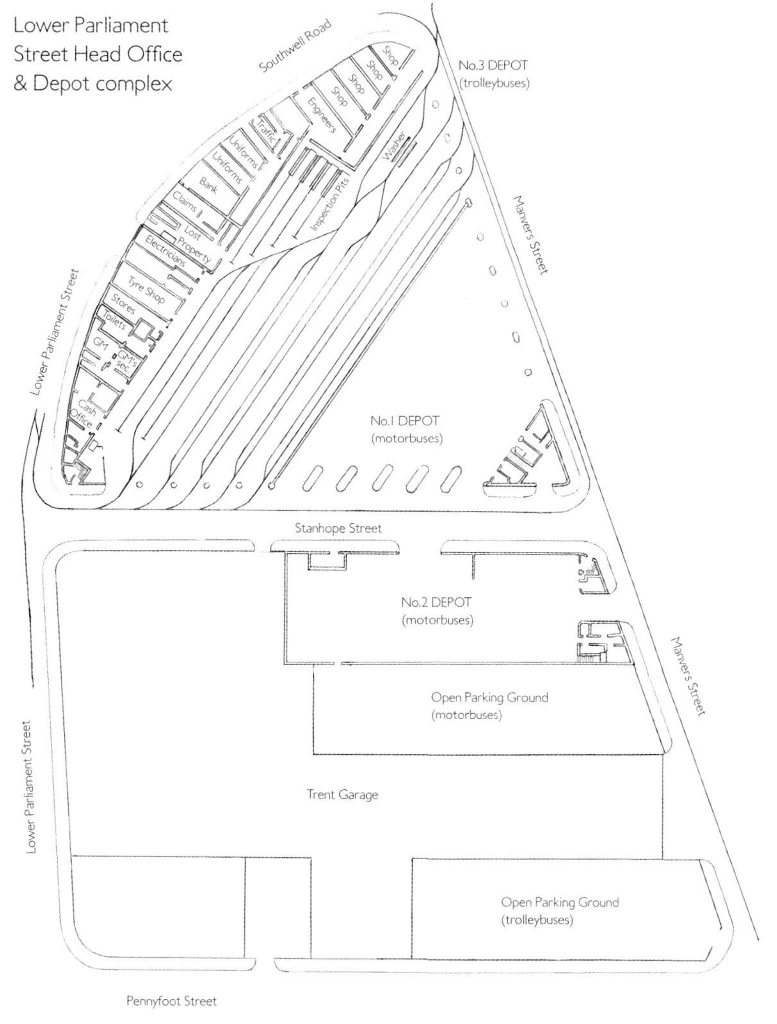

Lower Parliament Street Depot plan.

General Manager's Office. Thereafter the Engineering Department also moved to Head Office.

The mixed trolleybus allocation reflected the complexity of the services run by Lower Parliament Street Depot compounded by the earlier restrictions imposed on the use of 8ft wide vehicles (the entire series of 8ft wide BUT9641Ts being allocated).

The withdrawal of service 45 on 3 November 1962, led to changes in its vehicle allocation although Lower Parliament Street Depot had run no duties on this route.

NCT's "Allocation of Vehicles to Depots" circular of 8 March 1956 details Lower Parliament Street Depots' trolleybus allocation as follows:

Trolleybuses:	442-445	Karrier W (BTH equipment)
	447-451	Sunbeam MF2 (BTH equipment, nominally 8ft wide)
	452-458	Karrier W (English Electric equipment)
	459-468	Karrier W (BTH equipment)
	469-478	Karrier W (BTH equipment)
	479-482	Karrier W (BTH equipment)
	483-495	BUT9611T (English Electric equipment)
	500-524	BUT9641T (English Electric equipment, 8ft wide)
	578-586	BUT9641T (English Electric equipment, 7ft 6ins wide)

By this date 443, 450, 452, 453, 455, 456, 467, 468 were out of use and 460, 461, 475, 476, 468 were in store, giving an operational allocation of 74 vehicles against a total of 87.

In 1960 Lower Parliament Street had the following trolleybus and service allocation:

Trolleybuses:	444	Karrier W (BTH equipment)
	454, 457	Karrier W (English Electric equipment)
	461-466	Karrier W (BTH equipment)
	469-471, 473	Karrier W (BTH equipment)
	475-478	Karrier W (BTH equipment)
	479-482	Karrier W (BTH equipment)
	483-495	BUT9611T (English Electric equipment)
	500-524	BUT9641T (English Electric equipment, 8ft wide)
	576-586	BUT9641T (English Electric equipment, 7ft 6ins wide)
Services:	36, 37 & 41	Mansfield Road, Nottingham Road
	38 & 39	Carlton Road
	40 & 47	St. Anne's Well Road
	46	(occasional extra duties)

By the end of 1962 Karrier W4s 444, 454, 457, 462, 463, 465, 466, 473, 475, 476, 477 had been withdrawn, this being compensated by the transfer of 459-460 and 594-601 from Trent Bridge. The vehicle allocation fell somewhat by 1965 but with the withdrawal of trolleybuses from service 43 (upon which the depot had also run no duties) it was decided to standardise on three axle vehicles and all two axle trolleybuses were withdrawn from passenger service on 31 March 1965. Although some of Lower Parliament Street's three axle vehicles were withdrawn at the same time, replacements were transferred from Bulwell and Trent Bridge depots to compensate.

As further service reductions took place the allocation continued to change with withdrawals and transfers until the closure of services 40 and 47 on 9 October 1965 whereupon it was decided to standardise on 8ft wide BUT9641Ts to see out the system.

The various changes impacted on groups of services as follows:

Service 36 was generally worked with two axle trolleybuses (numbered in the 400 series) during the week with an occasional BUT 9641T of either width. On Saturdays three axle types would predominate with Sunday services being exclusively worked by three axle vehicles. From 3 November 1962 BUT 9641Ts started to take over most weekday duties on service 36.

Service 37 was operated almost exclusively by two axle trolleybuses until their withdrawal on 31 March 1965 with an increasing number of duties run by three axle 7ft 6ins wide vehicles from 3 November 1962 when service 45 was converted to motorbus operation. Use of 8ft wide BUT 9641Ts increased after 31 March 1965.

Service 38 was generally operated by two axle trolleybuses until November 1962 when three axle stock of both widths were introduced. During 1964 many duties were taken over by motorbuses. Following the withdrawal of electric traction from service 39 on 30 September 1965, trolleybuses were reinstated but by now only three axle vehicles remained in the fleet.

Service 39 was operated entirely by three axle trolleybuses of both widths.

Services 40 and 47 were operated exclusively for many years by two axle vehicles and it was not until November 1963 that 7ft 6ins wide BUT 9641Ts began to appear, taking over the entire Sunday service during 1964. During the short period 30 September 1965 (when trolleybus service 39 was withdrawn) until 9 October 1965 (when motorbuses replaced trolleybuses on services 40 and 47) 8ft wide BUT 9641Ts were used for the first time.

Service 41 was operated by three axle trolleybuses of both widths with two axle vehicles being used for peak hour extras. This practice virtually ceased from November 1962.

Service 46 used any type of trolleybus when Lower Parliament Street provided occasional extra vehicles for Saturday afternoon football match traffic.

Trolleybuses terminating at Carlton, Post Office Square or Hooton Road running in to the depot did so via Carlton Road and Southwell Road. However if a driver failed to turn up to relieve one heading for Carlton at "Bath Clock" (Bath Street/Handel Street) the conductor would transfer passengers to the following trolleybus and if no relief driver could be found amongst the "Spotters" (Standbys) or covered with overtime it was necessary for someone, possibly a depot man, to drive the trolleybus to the junction at the east end of Handel Street. A second man (a conductor) would pull the frog to allow the vehicle to use Carlton Road and Southwell Road to the depot.

In 2005 the Lower Parliament Street office building and the depot behind continue to provide the undertaking with its headquarters.

Trent Bridge Depot and Works

The original building, completed in May 1902, bounded by Pyatt Street to the southeast and Turney Street to the north west, comprised an 11-road tramcar running shed, accessed over two 5-track fans from Bunbury Street, and three maintenance workshops to the rear comprising 6-roads and reached by a traverser. Apart from stone corner pillars and facings, the building was constructed in brick with tall arched windows along the side of the running shed. At the front square windows to the mess room and office matched the metal girder stanchions between each entrance track with a plinth above. The running shed was 266ft long and 126ft wide offering accommodation for up to 90 tramcars on "pitted" tracks i.e. the depot floor was 4ft 8ins below rail level. The light fenestrated steel girder roof was built in three spans, the centre one being 54ft 8½ins and the two side spans 36ft 0¾ins; The height from rail level to springing of roof being 21ft 6ins. There were nine entrance openings, the two outermost roads being accessed over points inside the building, equipped with B & S Folding Gate Co. shutter doors.

Beyond the running shed was a repair shop for traction motors 120ft long and 63ft wide, roofed over in two bays, each 31ft 6ins span, the height from rail level to the springing of roof was 24ft 6ins and 19ft from rail level of the shop to the rail level of the travelling cranes. Two tracks were "pitted" to provide access beneath the tramcars. The repair shop was equipped with two 5-ton travelling cranes, vertical and radial drills, lathes, wheel grinding machine, shaping machine, wheel borer and wheel press. There was a gas oven for drying the armatures of electric motors. Behind the repair shop were two store rooms each 31ft 6ins by 30ft with a single store above.

The carpenter's shop was 66ft long by 32ft wide; it contained two tracks and was equipped with suitable equipment for the repairs and maintenance but not construction, of tramcar bodies. The paint shop was also 66ft long but 27 ft 9½ins wide and had two tracks. It was adjoined by a blacksmith's shop having two forges and the building's heating boiler with a sand drying furnace close by. At the rear of the premises there were various stores and sheds, a carriage house, cart shed, stable for three horses and a house for the resident depot foreman. Above the ground floor stores there was an employees' recreation room whilst above the carriage house and cart shed there was a billiard room.

In 1920-21 an additional, smaller running shed depot was built to the north west of Turney Street running shed. This was of utilitarian construction comprising of 3 brick walls and a light girder roof with a brick gable end and entrance facing Bunbury Street. There were 4 storage lyes. As built, the south end had only a small door in the brick wall giving access to a yard behind.

To enter Turney Street drivers had to position their trolleybuses as demonstrated by 568 and then transfer the trolley booms from the through wiring to the tied-off wires. The driver is extracting the bamboo trolley retrieval pole from beneath the vehicle: not a pleasant task in heavy traffic! *Martin Jenkins*

When Lower Parliament Street (Carter Gate) Depot, opened on 30 April 1929, the original Trent Bridge building ceased to be used as a running shed and its allocation of tramcars were transferred to the new depot and headquarters. It was converted into a maintenance and repair workshop with three times its previous capacity by adding 31,500 square feet to the existing 17,000 square feet of workshop space. The smaller newer building remained in use as a running shed for both trams and later trolleybuses, the last trams operating from here on 12 May 1934 concurrent with the withdrawal of tram services from Arkwright Street.

The railless vehicles used on Nottingham's first trolleybus route were accommodated at Trent Bridge (although it is not known which of the two depot buildings available at that time was used), necessitating a long journey to and from the city centre using a trailing skate, from 1927 until April 1928. Thereafter the fleet was based at Lower Parliament Street Depot.

The running shed was converted to house trolleybuses in conjunction with the 13 May 1934 conversion of the trunk Bulwell – Trent Bridge tram route to trolleybus operation however photographs taken shortly after this date show no evidence of overhead wiring leading to/from the building. The 44 tramcars made surplus to requirements, together with 9 earlier withdrawals, were stored in the running shed prior to disposal or dismantleming and it is assumed that the erection of overhead wiring to/from the building was only completed later in the year. It is a matter of conjecture where the 56 new trolleybuses were housed at this time. Photographic evidence of two-way trolleybus overhead wiring at the junction of Bunbury Street with Victoria Embankment and solely one-way (southbound) wiring in Bunbury Street opposite Trent Bridge Works suggests that the pair of wires above Pyatt Street, Fraser Road and Turney Street were initially used in an anti-clockwise direction. It is not known what overhead wiring arrangements existed at this time above the junction of Arkwright Street with Fraser Road.

In the same manner as Bulwell, the Trent Bridge Depot building was reconstructed for unidirectional use by demolishing the rear wall and some of the properties to the rear of the premises. A planked gable, with gaps at the base for the trolleybus overhead wiring, was constructed above the new rear entrance and some years later wooden Esavian folding pairs of sliding doors with windows at the top were added at front and rear (8 pairs). Once the access wiring layout had been erected, trolleybuses returning to the depot proceeded southwest along Turney Street, parallel to the running

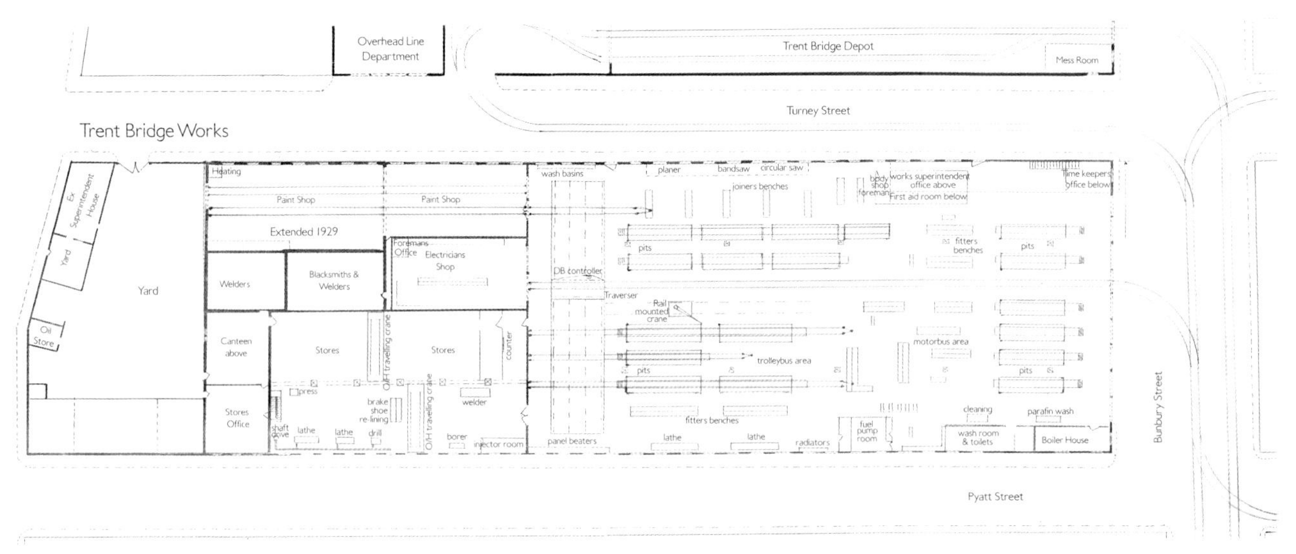

Trent Bridge Works plan.

Trent Bridge Depot & Works

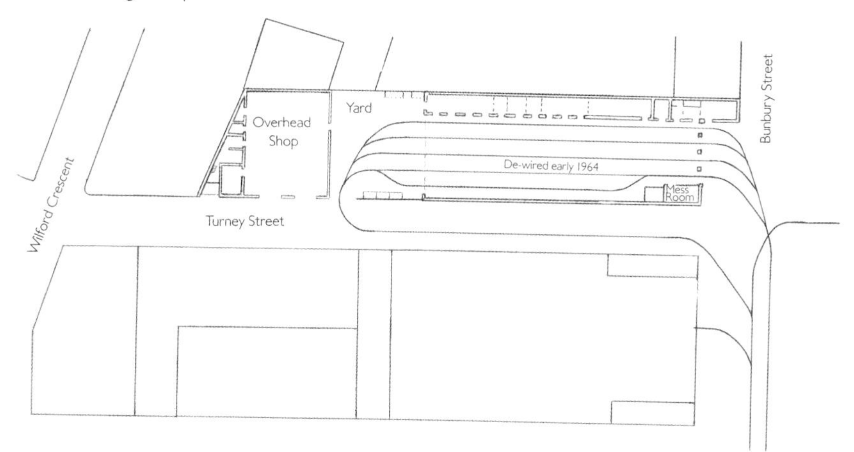

shed, until they reached the rear of the building and then turned right into the yard, which provided an entrance, initially through a completely open end, into the rear of the running shed. Trolleybuses left Trent Bridge Depot at its northeast end and turned right into Bunbury Street. There were 5 lines of overhead wiring above 5 trolleybus lyes that on the south side of shed being shorter than the others due to the presence of a mess room at the Bunbury Street end. It was frogged back into the 4th lye inside the running shed building whereas the main entrance and exit fans were in the rear yard or in Bunbury Street respectively. The doors at front and rear were removed at sometime in the mid-late 1950s but are known to have still been intact in 1954.

There was an auxiliary internal lighting circuit at Trent Bridge Depot and Works supplied from the DC traction supply which proved useful during the post-war power cuts, the lights brightening or dimming in relation to the number of passing trolleybuses!

Although there is no record of the full pre-war trolleybus allocation, it is known that the 1934 Karrier E6 trolleybuses with MCCW metal-framed bodies 51-60 were based at Trent Bridge. After the Second World War some utility and post-war 2-axle trolleybuses were allocated to Trent Bridge Deport pending the delivery of the BUT9641Ts.

Karrier W4 utility trolleybuses 459 and 460 were used on weekday peak hour extra duties on service 43 and occasionally the 45, and sporadically for Saturday afternoon football match traffic on service 46. Apart from these two vehicles it was rare by 1960 for two axle or 8ft wide trolleybuses to appear on services 43 or 45.

Trolleybus operation of service 45 ceased on 3 November 1962, Karrier Ws 459 and 460 and BUT 9641Ts 594-601 being transferred to Lower Parliament Street Depot for further use. As a result of the reduced vehicle allocation, the two southern lyes of Trent Bridge Depot were dewired in early 1964 whilst the overhead wiring along Turney Street, Pyatt Street and Fraser Street had gone by the end of April 1964.Trent Bridge Depot ceased to be used operationally for trolleybuses on 31 March 1965 when service 43 was withdrawn. Again, some of the allocated vehicles were withdrawn and others transferred to Lower Parliament Street Depot for further use.

The last trolleybus that had once been based at Trent Bridge Depot to operate in Nottingham was BUT9641T 572, which suffered a puncture in Mansfield Road on service 36 on 9 October 1965, whilst accident victim 582 was the last trolleybus to be stored there.

There was a single trolleybus overhead line entering Trent Bridge Works and this continued over the traverser as far as the transverse wall at the rear of the building. To the south of this access line, starting about halfway down the length of the building (the front portion was taken up with work benches), were two disconnected lines, with space for two trolleybuses beneath, which also continued as far as the traverser. To the north of the access line, at the rear of the building, were two further lines which enabled trolleybuses to be moved from the traverser into the paint shop. The BUT9641Ts, the only 30ft long vehicles on the system, would only just fit on to the works traverser; a lack of care would result in a smell of burned rubber.

Inside the main entrance was an open-plan overhaul shop covering the width of the building. At the Bunbury Street end motorbuses were overhauled. Moving towards the rear of the building, the trolleybus overhaul shop was situated on the southeast (Pyatt Street) side with the body overhaul shop next to it on the southwest side, immediately before the traverser. There were no physical boundaries between the three overhaul shops. Beyond the traverser were the blacksmiths', electricians', fitting, paint and welding shops, together with the stores. To the rear of the works building was an open yard with various outbuildings used as iron, paint, timber and scrap stores. The former Work's Superintendent's house was also used as a store whilst above the paint and timber stores there was an employees' recreation room, complete with billiard tables and better known as the "Institute". There was a canteen in the main works building above the stores.

In road 3 i.e. behind the second entrance door, a pit commenced some distance down the works building and continued as far as the traverser, being sufficiently long to offer inspection facilities underneath the vehicles for just over two 30ft trolleybus lengths. A pair of overhead wires above enabled trolleybuses to manoeuvre along the full length of the pits and terminated with attachments to the transverse wall immediately southwest of the traverser. Road 4 was equipped with a pit approximately the length of one trolleybus with a commensurately shorter length of overhead wiring above. Road 5 had a similar pit and overhead layout as road 3. The central, sixth road was used until 1956 by a

BUT9641T/Brush 532 turns into the rear of Trent Bridge Depot. The Depot Inspector clearly indicating which road the trolleybus should take. Immediately behind the trolleybus is the Overhead Shop, often known as the "tower wagon garage" whilst behind the tank the roofline of the Works on the other side of Turney Street can be seen. ***Jack Morris***

NCT's "Allocation of Vehicles to Depots" circular of 8 March 1956 shows that 31 trolleybuses were allocated to Trent Bridge Depot:

Trolleybuses:	525-534	BUT9641T (Crompton Parkinson equipment, 7ft 6ins wide)
	565-571	BUT9641T (Allen West equipment, 7ft 6ins wide)
	572-577	BUT9641T (English Electric equipment, 7ft 6ins wide)
	594-601	BUT9641T (Metropolitan-Vickers equipment, 7ft 6ins wide)

In 1960 Trent Bridge had the following trolleybus and service allocation:

Trolleybuses:	459-460	Karrier W (BTH equipment)
	525-534	BUT9641T (Crompton Parkinson equipment, 7ft 6ins wide)
	565-571	BUT9641T (Allen West equipment, 7ft 6ins wide)
	572-575	BUT9641T (English Electric equipment, 7ft 6ins wide)
	594-601	BUT9641T (Metropolitan-Vickers equipment, 7ft 6ins wide)
Services:	43	(jointly operated with Bulwell Depot)
	45	
	46	(with occasional extra duties being run by Bulwell and Lower Parliament Street depots)

Inside Trent Bridge Works with BUT9641T and 9611T types undergoing body repairs beyond the traverser. *NCT*

The DC-powered Trent Bridge Works traverser, now in use at the National Tramway Museum, Crich, Derbyshire. *Neil Lewin*

Trent Bridge Depot rear entrance on 3 January 1965 with 529, 575, 573 and motorbus 316 evident following the removal of the two southern lyes or roads of overhead wiring in early 1964. *Peter Badgery*

rail-mounted crane, running on the tram tracks. This was used to unload heavy spares and lift traction motors, which had been lowered out of trolleybuses, out of the pit.

Only a single pair of trolleybus wires entered the Works from Bunbury Street; these entered through door 6 and continued the length of road 7 as far as the transverse wall on the other side of the traverser. Trolleybuses requiring body repairs could be shunted on to the southwest end of road 8 using the overhead wiring above road 7, in fact there was no overhead wiring at all in the body shop i.e. the southwest ends of roads 8-11, for safety reasons. Inside the paint shop there were two pairs of overhead wires; those above road 10 started on the northeast side of the traverser, continued above the traverser and into the paint shop, whilst those above road 11 were confined to the interior of the paint shop itself. There was no other overhead wiring in the Works.

From an engineer's perspective, trolleybus maintenance was considerably less demanding and thus cheaper than that for motorbuses. The absence of vibration and wearing parts permitted extended periods between vehicle "docking" whilst the paucity of legislation concerning trolleybus mechanical standards and annual checks increased their popularity.

Departmental Vehicles

The following additional vehicles were used in connection with, but not restricted to, the trolleybuses:

Fleet No		Reg	Type	Into Dept	Withdrawn	Note
Original	Last	No		service		
509	809	TV4949	AEC Regent 661 petrol	09/1942	10/1968	1
510	810	TV4955	AEC Regent 661 petrol	by 10/1941	09/1964	2
513	813	431AU	AEC Matador	12/1946	by 12/1970	3

Note:

1 Breakdown lorry. Converted by NCT from 1931 AEC Regent 661 (chassis no. 6611707) double deck motorbus 116 and fitted with an 8-ton Harvey Frost crane. Renumbered 809 in 11/1949. Sold in 08/1969 to Fairley, Newark (dealer) and extant at Boughton, Nottinghamshire. Nicknamed "Mathilda".

2 Open tipper lorry. Converted by NCT from 1931 AEC Regent 661 (chassis no. 6611701) double deck motorbus 122 in 1941. Rebuilt with full width cab and two-part open body only the rear half of which tipped. Renumbered 810 in 11/1949. The preferred vehicle for towing new trolleybuses from the bodybuilders. Sold in 01/1965 to Johnson (dealer), Worksop.

3 Open lorry. Ex-RAF (RAF no. 182414), new in 1945. Used primarily for salting in winter. Renumbered 813 in 11/1949. Sold in 12/1970 to Auto Spares, Bingley, Yorkshire.

AEC Regent 802 tower wagon pulled up at Long Row on Old Market Square, seemingly crewless, on 28th March 1964. *Geoff Lumb*

Appendix G Power Supply & Generation

One of the claimed economies of converting life-expired electric tramways to trolleybus operation was the continued use of the existing traction power supply system with limited additional investment and Nottingham Corporation's trolleybus network was no exception, the current supply arrangements being closely based on that built up in the first decade of the twentieth century for the electric tramways. The trolleybuses like the trams before them received direct current (DC) electric power through overhead wires suspended above the route and supplied by underground cables from the power station and through local substations. A trolleybus system required two overhead wires, one of positive potential carrying current to the vehicle, and the other of negative potential returning the current and completing the connection. The trolley wire closest to the centre of the road was the positive wire. A tramway uses the running rails for its return connection.

Legislation required that the positive wire was interrupted every half mile, the sections each side of the insulating break being entirely separate from each other but connectable through switchgear placed in a cast-iron roadside section pillar often referred to simply as a "box". Identical feeder pillars housed the cables from which the mains power supply was connected to the overhead wiring. Equipment in either pillar could be used to cut off power entirely in an emergency. The negative trolley wire was continuous but at points where negative feeder cables were connected the positive and negative feeds came either from the same pillar or there was a separate negative feeder pillar, which to the onlooker, was identical to a positive feeder pillar.

Nottingham's tramways were noteworthy for their lack of suburban electricity substations, with resultant reduction in voltage towards the extremities of the routes, and long feeder cables, and their successors suffered from the same handicap. In 1908 it was recorded that there were no substations on the tramways but that there was an accumulator station in Isandula Road, Basford about 2½ miles from the St. Ann's power station, "used for steadying the load and keeping up the voltage on the feeders on the longest route to Bulwell". In reducing the available voltage, the distance from a power source also reduced the speed e.g. a current of 125 amps flowing to and from a trolleybus two miles from the supply point fell in "pressure" by 95 volts. The greater rolling resistance of a rubber-tyred trolleybus, particularly over the street surfaces of the period, compared to that of the rail-bound tramcar, enhanced acceleration rates, more powerful traction motors and route extensions together placed greater demands on the power supply and unfortunately this was never sufficiently upgraded to cope. Furthermore the electrical resistance of a negative trolley wire is around fifteen times that of a pair of steel tram rails.

A typical trolleybus drawing away from rest will draw about 200 amps of current, which at a line voltage of 550 volts DC equates to 110 kW, but this drops off rapidly as the vehicle overcomes the initial rolling resistance and gains speed. In comparison a typical domestic electric heater element will use 1 kW or a 60-100 watt lamp bulb 0.06-0.1 kW, wattage being the amount of energy used, calculated by multiplying the voltage by the current flowing (in amperes). This is of course variable dependent on the rate of acceleration, any gradient and the passenger load. The average consumption of electricity per trolleybus was thus reckoned as 3 kWh per mile as opposed to less than 2 kWh for a tram. Nottingham's trolleybuses were noted for their speed but equally there was at least one section, Carlton Road eastbound, where a lack of power hampered their performance.

Traction power needs increased tremendously in the late 1940s as the fleet was modernised with the arrival of the 102 BUT 9641Ts having 120 hp motors and weighing in at almost 10 tons (compared to the Leyland TTB3s of the mid 1930s with 80 hp motors and an unladen weight of 8 tons 17 cwts) whilst passenger loadings soared. Peak traction power requirements often occurred on a Saturday, then still a working or half working day in many businesses, when around lunchtime there would be a rush home, to the shops or to a major sporting event.

Power Stations

The first electric power generating station in Nottingham was built towards the east end of Talbot Street, which runs from west to east two blocks north of Derby Road between Canning Circus and Goldsmith Street. The plot was bordered by Talbot Street, Hanley Street and Wollaton Street. The station was commissioned in September 1894. It became evident during the planning stage of the electric tramways that Talbot Street would have insufficient capacity to generate traction current as well and a suitable location for a new power station was sought.

A slum clearance site of 7,520 sq yds with a frontage to the city end of St. Ann's Well Road at its junction with Huntingdon Street was chosen, the power station being planned to occupy about half the plot. Construction commenced in November 1900 and was practically completed by October 1901 with the chimney being finished in January 1902. In the meantime the generating capacity at Talbot Street was increased to 8,925 hp supplied by 23 steam dynamos of which three 700 hp dynamos were dedicated to the traction load.

Nottingham Corporation had 4 trading departments: gas, electricity, tramways and water. All power supply and transmission issues for the tramways and later the trolleybuses were handled by Nottingham Corporation Electricity Department, the transport undertaking never having its own Mains Department. Until the beginning of August 1902 the tramways' entire power requirement was supplied from Talbot Street, the traction load being completely transferred to St. Ann's on 11 December 1902. By now the tramways had become the Electricity Committee's largest customer requiring 50,000 units per week at a charge of 1¼d per unit. Generating capacity rose from 2,800 hp, when the tramways traction load was transferred from Talbot Street, to 4,200 hp in March 1903. St. Ann's and Talbot Street stations were interconnected by a trunk main. For the year ending 31 March 1904 the Electricity Committee recorded that it had generated 3,768,601 units for traction purposes (about 46.5% of total load). Capacity increased progressively to 9,500 hp in 1913. During the high traffic demands of 1918, the tramways power consumption rose to 6,812,253 units, St. Ann's power station burning 8,157 tons 18cwts of large coal and 20,647 tons of "peas".

After the First World War the government made a review of the nation's electric power industry consisting of over 600 separate undertakings, most of which were too small to operate economically. This led to the Electricity (Supply) Act 1919 which created Electricity Commissioners who could set up voluntary Joint Electricity Authorities for areas with the agreement of the undertakings concerned. It was foreseen that the Authorities would be able to produce electricity more economically by building new larger power stations and that, by linking the various stations, power could be transmitted around their area as supply and demand varied. Few Joint Authorities were created however and as a natural corollary, in 1926 the Central Electricity Board was created to establish an interconnecting network of main transmission lines (the "Grid"), linking the largest generating stations throughout Britain and supplying power to the existing undertakings. The first portion of this network opened in 1935.

Under a government scheme to establish a network of large generating plants, in June 1920 an 80-acre site, adjoining Clifton Colliery on the west bank of the River Trent, almost opposite Wilford Church, was identified as a suitable site for what was to become North Wilford Power Station. At the time Queen's Drive ended at Wilford Toll Bridge and the approach to Clifton Colliery (named after its original owner, Robert Clifton, rather than its geographic location) and North Wilford Power Station was named Colliery Road. Queen's Drive was not extended past Clifton Colliery and the Power Station until 1957-58 in conjunction with the construction of Clifton Bridge. The foundation stone was laid on 14 June 1923 and in preparation, high-tension trunk cables were laid by unemployed labour between North Wilford and Talbot Street in autumn 1923. The first phase with a capacity of 30,000 kW came into service in 1926 and power generation at both Talbot Street and St. Ann's Well Road ceased although the sites continued to be used as substations and switching stations. Generating capacity was progressively increased by 27,500 kW in 1928 and by a further 30,000 kW at the end of 1935 whilst in October 1936 another extension opened. Nottingham Corporation Electricity Department took only a small percentage of North Wilford's total output

On 1 April 1948 the electricity supply industry was nationalised, the British Electricity Authority taking over responsibility for the operation of the nation's power stations and the "Grid", and the supply of electrical energy to the Area Boards. The Nottingham Corporation Electricity Department became one of the 9 sub-areas making up the East Midlands Electricity Board. Under the Electricity Act, 1957 the Central Electricity Generating Board took over the British Electricity Authority's responsibilities.

As a DC substation, St. Ann's remained pivotal in the traction supply until the end of trolleybus operation in Nottingham, indeed parts of the original generating station building albeit with the window's bricked-up remained intact in 2005. The rotary machines at Talbot Street generating station, whose chimneys had been knocked down in the late 1920s, were taken out of service in 1965/66 and the entire complex was demolished in the early 1970s to make way for a car park.

Feeder Cables

A clear division of responsibilities was in place from the construction of the electric tramways: the Nottingham Corporation Electricity Department handled power generation and distribution whereas the Tramways Department dealt with everything from the street feeder pillars onwards. This policy continued until the abandonment of trolleybuses in Nottingham although the Electricity Department's responsibilities passed to their successors, the East Midlands Electricity Board, upon nationalisation.

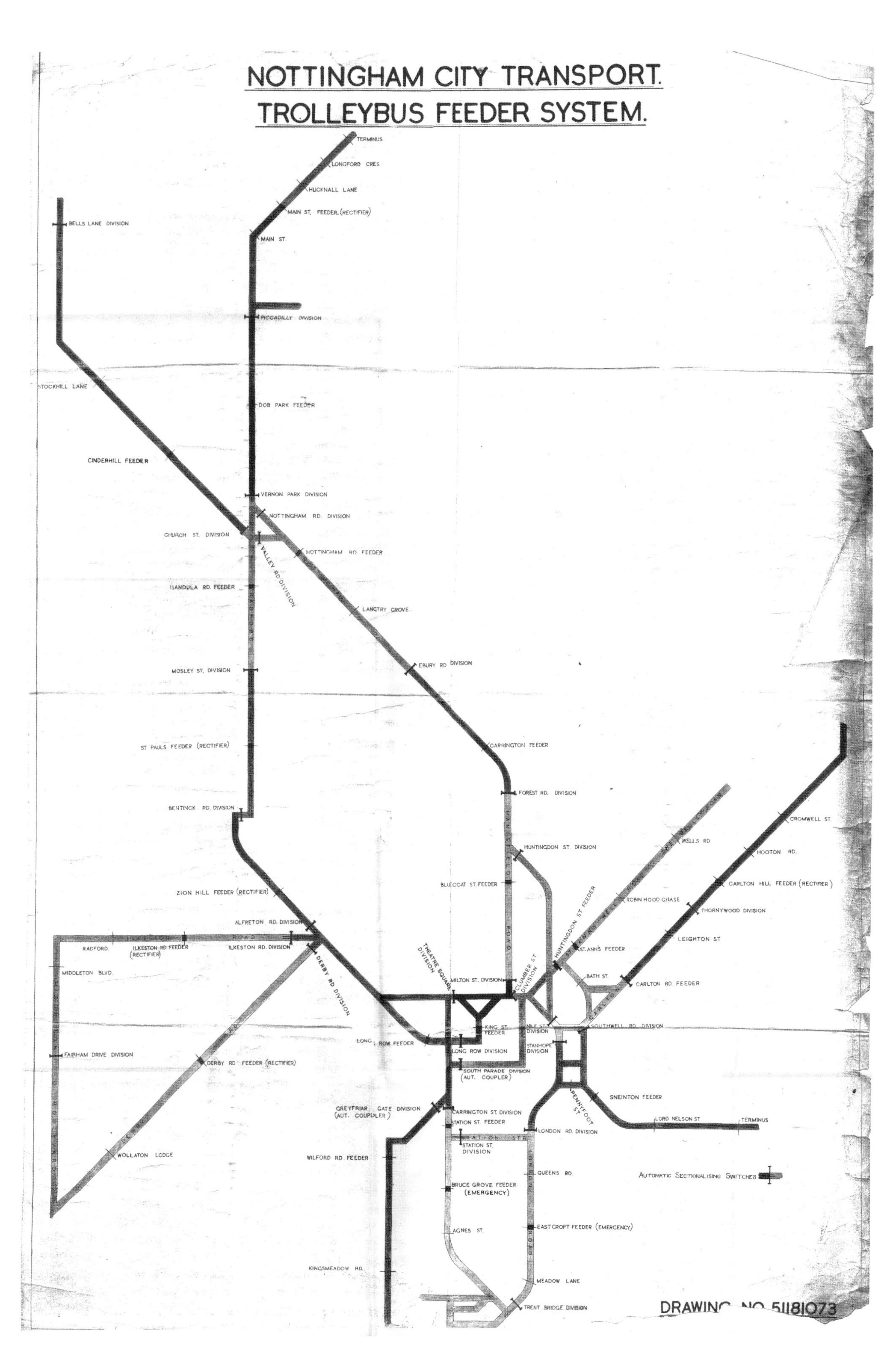
NOTTINGHAM CITY TRANSPORT.
TROLLEYBUS FEEDER SYSTEM.
TERMINUS
LONGFORD CRES
HUCKNALL LANE
MAIN ST. FEEDER, (RECTIFIER)
MAIN ST.
BELLS LANE DIVISION
PICCADILLY DIVISION
STOCKHILL LANE
DOB PARK FEEDER
CINDERHILL FEEDER
VERNON PARK DIVISION
NOTTINGHAM RD. DIVISION
CHURCH ST. DIVISION
NOTTINGHAM RD FEEDER
VALLEY RD DIVISION
ISANDULA RD. FEEDER
LANGTRY GROVE
EBURY RD DIVISION
MOSLEY ST. DIVISION
ST. PAULS FEEDER (RECTIFIER)
CARRINGTON FEEDER
FOREST RD. DIVISION
BENTINCK RD. DIVISION
HUNTINGDON ST. DIVISION
CROMWELL ST.
WELLS RD
HOOTON RD.
BLUECOAT ST. FEEDER
CARLTON HILL FEEDER (RECTIFIER)
ROBIN HOOD CHASE
ZION HILL FEEDER (RECTIFIER)
HUNTINGDON ST FEEDER
THORNYWOOD DIVISION
ALFRETON RD. DIVISION
LEIGHTON ST
RADFORD
ILKESTON RD FEEDER (RECTIFIER)
ILKESTON RD. DIVISION
ST. ANNS FEEDER
THEATRE SQUARE DIVISION
DERBY RD DIVISION
MIDDLETON BLVD.
MILTON ST. DIVISION
CLUMBER ST DIVISION
BATH ST.
CARLTON RD. FEEDER
KING ST. FEEDER
NILE ST. DIVISION
SOUTHWELL RD. DIVISION
LONG ROW FEEDER
STANHOPE DIVISION
LONG ROW DIVISION
FAIRHAM DRIVE DIVISION
DERBY RD. FEEDER (RECTIFIER)
SOUTH PARADE DIVISION (AUT. COUPLER)
SNEINTON FEEDER
PENNYFOOT ST
GREYFRIAR GATE DIVISION (AUT. COUPLER)
CARRINGTON ST. DIVISION
STATION ST. FEEDER
LORD NELSON ST
TERMINUS
LONDON RD. DIVISION
STATION ST. DIVISION
WOLLATON LODGE
WILFORD RD. FEEDER
QUEENS RD.
AUTOMATIC SECTIONALISING SWITCHES
BRUCE GROVE FEEDER (EMERGENCY)
AGNES ST.
EASTCROFT FEEDER (EMERGENCY)
KINGSMEADOW RD.
MEADOW LANE
TRENT BRIDGE DIVISION
DRAWING NO 51181073

Power was supplied to the trams and later the trolleybuses at 550 volts DC through a network of underground feeder cables, insulated with vulcanised bitumen and laid in conduits of vitrified Albion Clay stoneware. Callender's Cable & Construction Co. originally laid 17 feeder cables from the power station of between 0.25 and 0.6 sq ins section and varying in length from 50 to 4,280 yards, the longest being that to Isandula Road accumulator station. Each feeder, which had a corresponding negative return feeder of equal area, ran direct from the generating station to the feeding point. Three of the feeders were connected to both Talbot Street and St. Ann's power stations.

During the trolleybus era there was an 11kW supply cable from Colwick to Chesterfield Road substation. There were also two emergency feeders:

Arkwright Street at its junction with Kirkewhite Street, fed from a substation at Bruce Grove in the Meadows between Arkwright Street and Queens Drive.

London Road (Eastcroft) at its junction with Cattle Market Road and Kirkewhite Street, and also believed to have been fed from Bruce Grove substation.

It should be noted here that Kirkewhite Street was one of two more important thoroughfares running east to west (the other being Waterway Street) that linked London Road with Wilford Road and which were swept away in the 1970s redevelopment of the Meadows. Kirkewhite Street made a junction with London Road immediately opposite Cattle Market Road where the turning circle was situated.

Substations

Around the end of the 19th century DC was preferred for electric traction purposes because the speed of direct current motors and thus that of the vehicle could be simply controlled by varying the voltage applied to them. Alternating current (AC) however was preferable to DC for power distribution and generation because power loss in transmission lines decreases significantly with higher voltages and during the tram and trolleybus era only AC could efficiently be transformed between voltages. Nonetheless electric power for Nottingham's first generation electric tramways was generated and distributed as DC by feeder cables to strategic locations along the routes throughout the city.

Once AC distribution was introduced it was necessary to find a means of converting this energy for use by DC traction motors. Initially a rotary converter, a large, rotating electromechanical device and basically a hybrid of a single winding AC motor and a DC generator (dynamo), was used to convert AC to DC (or vice versa depending on the requirement). These were housed in substations, buildings that varied between exquisite examples of municipal architecture and windowless brick-built cubes, but with no signs of human habitation. Thereafter DC traction current would be transmitted in ducted underground cables to the trolleybus route where it would come up into a cast iron feeder pillar.

The complexity and size of rotary converters required regular attention and maintenance by skilled staff, and any loss of the incoming supply would cause protective switchgear to "drop out" requiring a manual restart. Thus from the late 1920s, coincidental with the growth of Nottingham's railless trolley vehicle system, the needs for additional or replacement equipment was met by the new technology of the mercury arc rectifier. Additionally throughout the 1930s the Electricity Department was in the process of changing their transmission network, not only that for traction power, from DC to AC. In a rectifier substation, the incoming high voltage AC supply was first reduced by transforming to the correct input voltage of approximately 400 volts AC, and thence converted to a nominal 550 volts DC for the overhead line, whereas a rotary converter was an AC motor driving a DC generator that produced a DC current. A mercury arc rectifier had an efficiency of about 93-95%, dependent on load, compared to a rotary converter's efficiency of just over 90%.

The operation of mercury arc rectifiers (also known as Cooper-Hewitt or Hewittic rectifiers after their inventor, the American Peter Cooper Hewitt) was based on the discovery that an electric spark (arc) vaporises mercury contained in a steel tank into a vapour that can only conduct electric current in a single direction between the pool of mercury and a metal anode. AC was fed to the anodes of the octopus-like glass bulbs and an arc was set up between the anodes and a pool of mercury in the bottom of the bulb. Incoming current, alternating at a frequency of 50 cycles a second (the standard frequency of the National Grid supply) flashed 50 times per second between the anodes and the mercury-covered cathodes forming a virtually continuous arc. Multiple anodes were used, fed from a multiple-phase transformer, the arc jumping from the cathode pool to each anode in sequence. The arc glow changed in intensity as the number of trolleybuses moving increased or reduced, or even changed speed. There were three, six or even twelve transformer phases, each feeding one anode. Six and twelve-phase systems used star-connected three-phase transformers with inter-phase transformers between the star common connections. In a six-phase rectifier there were 6 arms on each bulb each connected to a phase of the supply and thus the output was close to being a continuous current but with a slight ripple, that is, the actual voltage waxed and waned by about 20% of the nominal 550 volts DC at a frequency of 300 cycles per second. The windowless substation was filled with a ghostly greenish light, wavering slightly, the mercury bubbling constantly in the bulbs.

Construction was either a glass bulb cooled by an external fan or a steel tank of water for very large units with capacities above about 500 amps. To initiate the arc, an igniting electrode was dipped into the pool of mercury using an external electromagnet thereby drawing a small spark to ionise the mercury vapour, initiating the main arc. These substations had virtually no moving parts and made it practicable to open small substations along the route wherever power was needed. Control circuits within the mercury arc rectifier ensured that if no current at all was being taken from the overhead, the arc within the rectifier did not die out. Mercury arc rectifiers were used until the end of UK trolleybus operation.

The traction current was taken from the rectifiers to the switchboard busbars (bars of solid copper running the length of the rear of the board, their heavy rectangular section offering virtually no resistance to the current and enabling connections to the various switches to be solidly bolted to them). From the busbars, feeder cables went out to various parts of the system, each being connected to the busbars through a heavy-duty circuit breaker and isolating switch.

If the current exceeded a set value, its magnetic effect opened the automatic circuit breaker preventing excessive current from entering a cable and damaging it. A broken positive trolley wire would cut off current if the live ends made a good contact with earth; a dewired trolley head might create a short circuit across the insulators of a frog or crossover, etc. The circuit breakers were equipped with time relays that automatically restored current after a pre-set period. If the fault was still present they reopened. If this cycle of events occurred 3 times, on the fourth occasion the circuit breakers stayed open and an alarm sounded. It was then necessary to locate the fault and isolate the feeder concerned until it was safe to restore current.

In preparation for the trolleybuses two mercury arc rectifiers, 500 kW for Broadholme Street substation and 250 kW for Carlton Hill, were ordered in May 1931 from Hewettic Electric Co. at £2,050 and £1,555 respectively. By 1932 additional rectifier bulbs at Carlton Hill substation had to be installed due to the demands of the augmented trolleybus service whilst after a single winter's experience of trolleybus operation on the Bulwell routes, the Electricity Department suggested an 11,000 volt feeder from Talbot Street to Isandula Street substation via Abbey Bridge distribution centre and new switchgear. In addition they recommended that, in reserve, two 33,000 volt cables be laid at the same time to avoid unnecessary reopening the ground at a later date. These proposals were accepted and the thick feeder cables, enclosed in oil, were laid in new cable ducts.

In June 1944 the City Electrical Engineer reported that a substation would be needed at Trent Bridge Depot and Works to strengthen the existing AC distribution and meet post-war developments which would include changing the Transport Department's DC load to AC. Although the acquisition of a suitable building was agreed, its conversion for use as a substation was placed in abeyance. As far as is known DC power for both machinery and lighting purposes continued to be supplied to Trent Bridge Depot and Works until at least the end of trolleybus operations, indeed the works traverser still used DC power for its conventional tramcar motor and controller when it was removed for further use at the National Tramway Museum, Crich, in 1976.

The following 6 substations were in service during the trolleybus era:

Broadholme Street

Adjacent to Abbey Bridge; AC power was received by aerial power cables direct from North Wilford Power Station to a distribution centre against Abbey Bridge. Broadholme Street rectifier substation was built in connection with the introduction of trolleybuses along both Derby Road and Ilkeston Road to Wollaton Park,

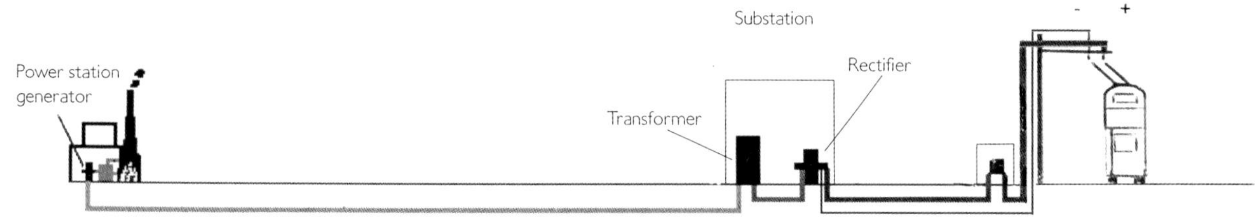

Power supply diagram.

and served the following feeders:

- Derby Road, Lenton Boulevard
- Ilkeston Road, Radford Boulevard

An underground supply line (132kV by the late 1950s) connected the Abbey Bridge distribution centre with Isandula Road substation by way of Lenton, Radford and Gregory Boulevards and Radford Road. On one celebrated occasion this supply line was damaged in the construction of a subway beneath Radford Road linking two portions of Shipstone's Brewery premises.

Bruce Grove

A domestic and industrial supply substation which could also in times of excessive demand e.g. football matches, or when there was a breakdown elsewhere, provide a traction power supply, possibly through rotary converters, to emergency feeders on:

- Arkwright Street, Kirkewhite Street
- London Road, junction with Cattle Market Road and Kirkewhite Street (Eastcroft)

It is known that Eastcroft feeder was switched in whenever Station Street was in use.

Chesterfield Street, Carlton

At the bottom of Carlton Hill (eastern end), this substation received its supply from a distribution centre at Colwick and provided traction power to the eastern end of the Carlton route. The feeder is marked as "independent" on NCT drawing 284 of 20 February 1959, presumably meaning that it was not part of the normal power supply arrangements, and appears to have also supplied the feeder at:

- Carlton Hill, Dale View Road

Isandula Road, New Basford

Housed in a substantial building (still intact in 2005) on the north side of Isandula Road, off Radford Road, next to a police house. The substation premises included the former tramways battery station and were opposite the erstwhile horse tram depot on the south side of the road. This substation is believed to have served the following feeders:

- Bar Lane, Alpine Street (Cinderhill) supplying service 41 and N&D
- Dob Park, Vernon Road (Northern Baths) supplying the Bulwell services
- Isandula Road, Radford Road supplying the Bulwell services
- Main Street, Bulwell
- Nottingham Road (Nottingham Road) supplying services 36, 41 and N&D.

St. Ann's, St. Ann's Well Road

Located in the former power station at the junction of St. Ann's Well Road with Huntingdon Street. St. Ann's was linked by a trunk cable to Talbot Street; the two substations could thus both supply, independently or jointly, the feeders listed under the Talbot Street substation heading.

Talbot Street

The original tramway power station. Talbot Street was linked by a trunk cable to St. Ann's; they could thus both supply, independently or jointly, the following feeders:

- Bluecoat Street
- Carlton Road,
- Carrington
- Huntingdon Street
- King Street
- Long Row
- St. Ann's
- St. Paul's, Radford Road
- Station Street
- Sneinton
- Wilford Road
- Zion Hill, Alfreton Road

The Sunbeam MF2 trolleybuses had regenerative braking, which fed current back into the overhead wires and subsequently to the substations. A rotary converter could absorb regenerated energy but a mercury arc rectifier presented, in effect, an open circuit. This resulted in an over voltage in the traction current supply which could damage other equipment connected to the supply (such as burning-out the high tension bulbs on adjacent trolleybuses) and much reduced braking on the trolleybus concerned if no other vehicles were drawing current in the section at the time. As Nottingham's substations were not equipped with ballast resistances (simulating the presence of another trolleybus) and relays to absorb any over-voltage, a breakdown in the Wollaton Park area occurred in 1942. This led to the introduction of automatic sectionalising switches at Division Points whilst the regenerative braking equipment on the Sunbeam MF2s was disconnected.

Electrical Feeders, Rectifiers, Auxiliary Feeders and Auto Couplers

21 Feeders (7 equipped with rectifiers)

Bluecoat Street	at the junction of Mansfield Road with Bluecoat Street
Carlton Road	on Carlton Road just east of the junction with Handel Street
Carlton Hill, Dale View Road (rectifier)	at the junction of Carlton Hill with Dale View Road
Carrington	on Sherwood Rise near to Clumber Avenue
Chesterfield Street, Carlton (rectifier)	at the junction of Carlton Hill with Chesterfield Street
Cinderhill	at the junction of Alpine Street and Bar Lane
Derby Road, Lenton (rectifier)	at the junction of Derby Road with Lenton Boulevard
Dob Park	on Vernon Road adjacent to Northern Baths
Huntingdon Street	on King Edward Street adjacent to the Salvation Army William Booth Memorial Hall
Ilkeston Road (rectifier)	at the junction of Ilkeston Road with Radford Boulevard
Isandula Road	at the junction of Radford Road with Isandula Road
King Street	on King Street south of the junction with Queen Street
Long Row	on Long Row West
Main Street, Bulwell (rectifier)	on Main Street Bulwell just beyond Bulwell Market
Nottingham Road	at the junction of Nottingham Road with Isandula Road
St. Ann's	on St. Ann's Well Road just past the junction with Bath Street and adjacent to St. Ann's Power Station
St. Paul's (rectifier)	on Radford Road against St. Paul's Church, St. Paul's Avenue
Station Street	on Carrington Street just before the Station Street junction
Sneinton	at the junction of Manvers Street with Newark Street (just past Pennyfoot Street)
Wilford Road	on Wilford Road just south of the LMS railway bridge)
Zion Hill (rectifier)	on Alfreton Road, believed to be near to Newdigate Street

2 Auxiliary or Emergency Feeders

Bruce Grove	at the junction of Arkwright Street with Kirkewhite Street
Eastcroft	at the junction of London Road with Cattle Market Road (operational whenever Station Street was used)

Division Points

A division point, more commonly known as a section insulator, was an electrical break in the trolley wire that electrically isolated one section and its feeder from an adjoining section and its feeder. The resultant length of wire could be isolated by a section switch (contained in a feeder pillar, section pillar or section box). From 1942 onwards some division points were equipped with automatic sectionalising switches following problems with sharp increases in the line voltage within rectifier-fed sections caused by the regenerative braking of the Sunbeam MF2s.

The use of automatic sectionalising switches linking rectifier-fed sections with rotary converter-fed sections prevented overloads. Section ends could be identified by a cast-iron pillar on the pavement nearby. The purpose of the isolation equipment inside, indistinguishable to the passer-by, was always intended to allow the overhead wires on either side of the section insulator to be isolated or fed from either end of the feeder cable.

On a wet autumn day BUT9641T/Brush 534 pulls away from Deby Road, Lenton Boulevard stop en route for Wollaton Park, Harrow Road. Note the pillar and cabling of the Lenton rectifier feeder.
Rod Bramley

Division points were situated at the following locations:
Alfreton Road auto-coupler, automatic sectionalising switch
Bath Street
Bentinck Road positive and negative
Carrington Street
Church Street
Clumber Street
Derby Road auto-coupler, automatic sectionalising switch
Ebury Road positive and negative
Fairham Drive
Forest Road
Greyfriar Gate auto-coupler
Hooton Road
Huntingdon Street
Ilkeston Road auto-coupler, automatic sectionalising switch
King Edward Street
London Road
Long Row (near King Street) auto-coupler
Milton Street
Mosley Street
Nile Street
Piccadilly auto-coupler, automatic sectionalising switch
South Parade auto-coupler
Southwell Road
Stanhope Street
Station Street
Theatre Square
Thorneywood (Swain's Avenue)
Valley Road
Vernon Park

An auto-coupler linked two separate feeds, normally from two separate sources rather than two cables from the same supply. Its purpose was to allow two power sources to back up each other when one was overloaded and the other had energy available. It was an automatic link across the section insulator in the trolley wire, housed in a section pillar adjacent to the supporting traction pole or in a box mounted on the traction pole at the height of the trolley wires. When the trolley wires on both sides of a division point were live i.e. both power sources were supplying power, current could flow through the switch in whichever direction necessary to back-up the overloaded supply. The coupler would open automatically in the event of a failure of one of the power sources or a short circuit on one side, thereby protecting the sound supply. The switch would close again automatically upon restoration of both supplies. It was usual to protect the two feeders, which each terminated at the previous section insulators about a half-mile distant, by replacing the feeder switch with a fuse. A short-circuit on one feeder or overhead line section would induce a heavy current from the sound supply, through the auto-coupler, which would blow that fuse.

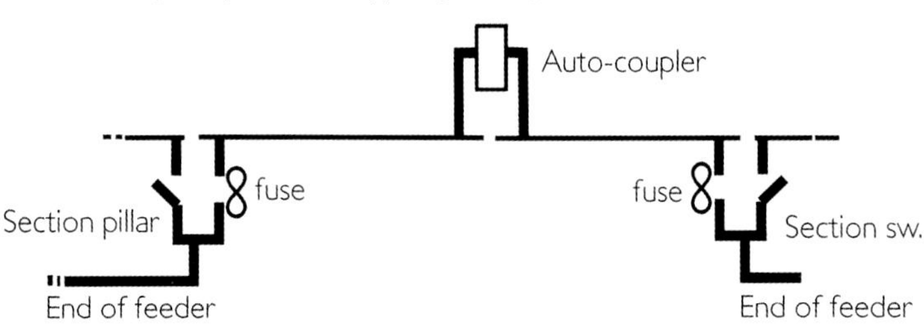

Autocoupler feeder diagram.

Section Breakers

In addition to division points there were also section breakers. Legislation required that the electrical continuity of the positive wire be broken every half-mile. At these points a short length of the positive running wire was replaced by a non-conductive material and the electrical current carried over this break by a "bridge" that was linked by cables to a pole-mounted switch box. The opening of this switch isolated a section electrically. Section breakers were located at the following places:
Arkwright Street, Agnes Street
Bulwell Hall Estate terminus, Hucknall Lane
Carlton Road, Leighton Street
Colwick Road, Lord Nelson Street
Colwick Road terminus
Derby Road, Wollaton Lodge
Hucknall Lane, railway viaduct
Hucknall Lane, Longford Crescent
London Road, Meadow Lane
London Road, Queen's Road
Main Street, Bulwell
Middleton Boulevard, Harrow Road
Nottingham Road, Langtry Grove
Pennyfoot Street
St. Ann's Well Road, Ransom Road
St. Ann's Well Road, Robin Hood Chase
Stockhill Lane
Wilford Road, King's Meadow Road
Wollaton Road, Kennington Road

No limit was laid down on the number of trolleybuses which could operate on a given section at any one time but if several vehicles were all starting away at the same time, the line voltage fell and drivers learned to use their common sense. The vehicles' controls were designed to function at half the normal line voltage but problems developed if this fell below 400 volts, a common occurrence at peak hours. At times when few trolleybuses were operating, line voltage was accordingly high and high speeds could be obtained.

Former trolleybus driver Bernard Jefford recalled that travelling east out of the city along Carlton Road there was a Division Point at Thorneywood, Swain's Avenue separating the section supplied by the Carlton Hill, Dale View Road feeder from that supplied by Carlton Road feeder (situated just east of Handel Street). During busy periods an Inspector was stationed immediately opposite the Manvers School inbound stop to ensure that there were not too many trolleybuses in the section prior to the Division Point as if several vehicles were drawing power at the same time it would be impossible for loaded vehicles to pick up sufficient speed on the rising gradient to coast beneath the breaker without drawing power. The Inspector would despatch vehicles up the hill once he saw the preceding vehicles' flashing indicator lights as it moved away from the Porchester Road stop and passed beneath the breaker. Playful drivers waiting opposite Manvers School would simply apply the first notches of their (electric) footbrake thereby drawing power to create a problem for an unpopular colleague further up the hill until he had passed under the Swain's Avenue Division Point.

This apparent shortage of power on the inner portion of the Carlton route was vehemently denied by the Overhead Department although well known to the Traffic Department and seems to have been a unique feature, there being no similar difficulties on the gradients up Derby Road and Ilkeston Road to Canning Circus. Nonetheless any loaded trolleybuses endeavouring to climb in convoy up Carlton Road could attain little more than a 5 mph crawl whilst the lights would dim and on occasion one vehicle would wait near the garage at Olga Road until the electrical load had been reduced.

The overhead did not remain live 24 hours a day, timer switches cutting off power to each section successively after midnight and reconnecting them again at 5 am.

Appendix H Overhead Wiring

Amongst the memorable features of the Nottingham system were the intense frequencies along most routes and the high service speeds. These could only be achieved by excellent overhead wiring techniques and maintenance provided by the skill of the overhead line crews. The undoubted success and popularity of the trolleybus service in the city remains a tribute to these "Linesmen". There is also no doubt that the speed around curves and under frogs or crossings considered normal in Nottingham were seldom matched by other British trolleybus operators and far exceeded manufacturers' guidelines and recommendations! Sadly, as trolleybus driving standards deteriorated in the 1960s, this practice, on occasions, led to some damaging dewirements.

General

The trolleybuses were indeed the direct successors of their rail-bound predecessors in that they continued to use many items of tramway overhead equipment; in fact this was one of the economic arguments in favour of replacing the trams with railless electric traction.

The initial electric tramway overhead work in Nottingham employed OOO gauge hard drawn copper trolley wire whilst the span wires were of 7/12 and the guard wires 7/14 gauge galvanised steel. By 1908, grooved section trolley wire suitable for use with mechanical supporting ears was being used for replacements and extensions, and by the time railless electric traction commenced it is assumed that British Standard (BS) 4/0 SG cadmium copper wire section of 0.426 ins diameter was employed. The cast metal ears consisted of two side plates which, by tightening clamping screws, gripped the lobe on top of the grooved trolley wire and thus supported the overhead line. On straight portions of trolleybus overhead the mechanical ears were 12ins long but for special work 6ins ears and for curved sections ears up to 24ins long, which tended to conform to the curvature under line tension thus avoiding acute changes in direction, were available. After the Second World War, the MPTA's new standard grooved section trolley wire having a smaller lobe offering a closer fit with the mechanical ears was used for replacements, often necessitating a change in section at a special mid-span splice or splicing ear.

A supporting boss located midway along the length of the ear retained a screw-in moulded compound insulator, widely known as an "insulated bolt", which was itself retained in the hanger or an end fitting. Until the mid-1930s all trolleybus overhead work employed a separate tramway-style hanger to support each trolley wire (a single line hanger) with a strain insulator inserted into the span wire between the positive and negative trolley wires. Thereafter single units supporting both trolley wires (a twin line hanger) were used, an insulated wooden spacer keeping the two wires the designated 24ins apart ensuring triple insulation between the wires. Strain insulators were placed in span wires and catenaries to ensure triple insulation between positive and earth, and double insulation between negative and earth.

The route of the trolley wires was kept as straight as possible, minor deviations and irregularities of the kerb line being ignored to obtain a smooth run. It was assumed that the trolleybus would normally be running more or less beneath the route of the trolley wires and to avoid running with the trolley booms continually at a sideways angle the negative trolley wire was normally not strung more than 7ft from the kerb on roads up to 26ft wide, rising to 11ft for roads between 39 and 45ft in width. A figure of 13ft was never exceeded. Curves were aligned so that the radius of the trolley wire was less than the route of the vehicle beneath wherever possible.

The trolleybus equipment installed in early 1927 for the Nottingham Road conversion was erected by the undertaking's own overhead line department, the trolley wires being new and entirely independent of that used by the trams. Separate wiring was hung between the kerb and the tram overhead enabling trolley vehicles to "overtake" the trams. This was in any case a necessity in Mansfield Road, a wide thoroughfare along which trams continued to operate until September 1936 but at no stage in the tram to trolleybus conversion programme did trams and trolley vehicles regularly share the same positive running wire, as in some cities. There were however short periods prior to a conversion when trams used the positive trolley wire already in place for the trolleybuses e.g. in Carlton Road and Vernon Road.

Conventional tramway-type single line hangers were inserted into the span wire to support the trolley wires with a 30 ins (2ft 6ins) separation and an insulator between negative and positive wires. Subsequent conversions and new routes were initially equipped with trolley wires 18 ins (1ft 6ins) apart. The railless trolley vehicles were equipped with under-running swivel head wheel collectors. Full details of which sections were constructed by contractors and which by the undertaking are not known. Although the overhead line department appears to have erected the equipment for the St. Ann's Well Road – Wilford Road conversion, contemporary newspaper reports tell of delays caused by a sub-contractor. In 1931-32 Estler Bros, of Victoria Docks, London E16, specialist overhead line contractors, installed the trolleybus equipment along the two Wollaton Park routes (Derby Road, Ilkeston Road, Middleton Boulevard) and thereafter from King Edward Street along Bath Street and Handel Street to Carlton Road and Carlton itself.

Pre-war the overhead wiring layout, including crossings and junctions, was constructed on an individual basis from single line hangers and tramway style components e.g. a left hand 25° facing junction would be made up of two single 25° left hand frogs and a 25° left hand insulated crossing. There appears to have been no preferred supplier of overhead equipment, Ohio Brass fittings are known to have been used for example in Bath Street in 1938 whilst the Whitecross Co. Ltd. of Warrington was also a regular, but much smaller, supplier of trolley wire, etc. British Insulated Cables Ltd. (BIC), whose equipment was manufactured at Prescot, Lancashire, had a local office at High Pavement, Nottingham, until at least 1940. In the mid-1930s BIC began to introduce a range of pre-assembled overhead fittings in which rigid spacer bars linked the various parts and from 1941 they became the favoured supplier. In May 1945 BIC amalgamated with Callender's Cable & Construction Co. Ltd. of Belvedere, Erith, Kent, to become British Insulated Callender's Cables Ltd. (BICC).

The undertaking pioneered a catenary suspension system, which reputedly allowed for less rigidity in the overhead than conventional single span wires permitting higher speeds with a reduced risk of dewirements. Each pair of running wires was strung lower on the traction pole nearest to the supported direction of wiring and higher on the traction pole opposite reducing span wire sag. Wiring on the other side was strung similarly and the spans were connected in the centre i.e. above the middle of the road, by a bullring. The "Nottingham Catenary Suspension System" was used for the Wollaton Park, Carlton, Valley Road to Cinderhill and Bulwell conversions in the early 1930's, becoming a common feature of the system.

It was also used on other systems where Nottingham had "influence". In Huddersfield (where the General Manager, Harry Godsmark had been at Nottingham until 1933) this method of suspension was utilised on parts of the Almondbury and Waterloo to Outlane/Lindley routes. However Huddersfield found that when several trolleybuses were running close together the combined upward pressure from the trolley poles could push the trolley wires upwards to the extent that they touched the span wires above and caused a short circuit. A similar outcome was experienced in Kingston upon Hull in 1937 where services 61 and 62 utilised this type of wiring. In an effort to solve this problem, some systems replaced the central bullring with two, one about 18ins above the other and connected by a length of

On a 37 working to Haydn Road Karrier E6/Brush 66 reaches the brow of the hill at the crossroads of Mansfield Road with Forest Road East and Mapperley Road. The open skyline clearly shows the wide 30ins separation between the trolley wires employed for the early conversions, the Nottingham catenary suspension system and the second span wire with street lighting unit. *Roy Marshall*

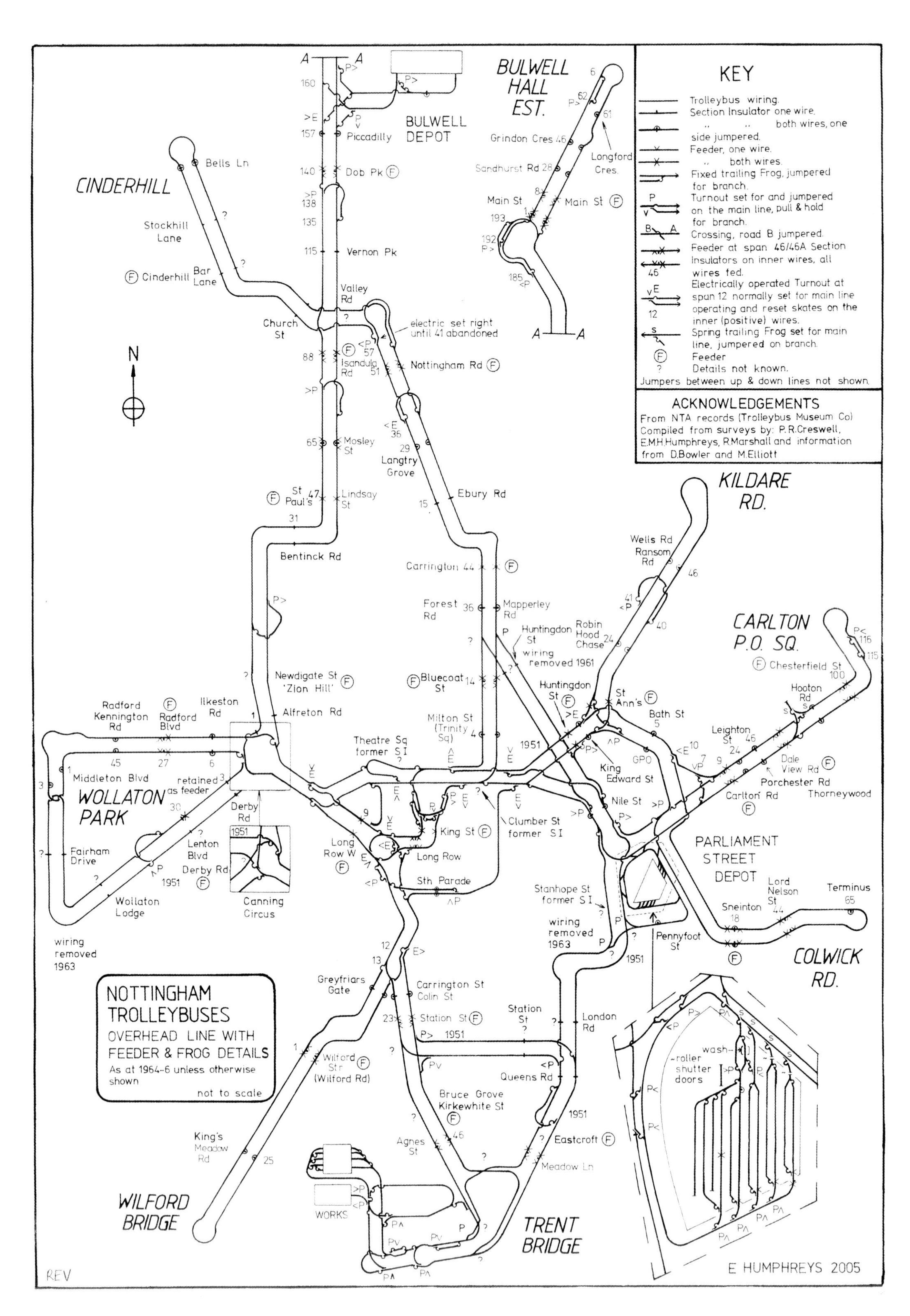
NOTTINGHAM
TROLLEYBUSES
OVERHEAD LINE WITH
FEEDER & FROG DETAILS
As at 1964-6 unless otherwise shown
not to scale
KEY
Trolleybus wiring.
Section Insulator one wire.
both wires, one side jumpered.
Feeder, one wire.
both wires.
Fixed trailing Frog, jumpered for branch.
Turnout set for and jumpered on the main line, pull & hold for branch.
Crossing, road B jumpered.
Feeder at span 46/46A Section Insulators on inner wires, all wires fed.
Electrically operated Turnout at span 12 normally set for main line operating and reset skates on the inner (positive) wires.
Spring trailing Frog set for main line, jumpered on branch.
Feeder
Details not known.
Jumpers between up & down lines not shown.
ACKNOWLEDGEMENTS
From NTA records (Trolleybus Museum Co)
Compiled from surveys by: P.R.Creswell, E.M.H.Humphreys, R.Marshall and information from D.Bowler and M.Elliott
BULWELL HALL EST.
BULWELL DEPOT
Piccadilly
Dob Pk
Vernon Pk
Grindon Cres
Sandhurst Rd
Longford Cres.
Main St
CINDERHILL
Bells Ln
Stockhill Lane
Cinderhill
Bar Lane
Valley Rd
Church St
electric set right until 41 abandoned
Isandula Rd
Nottingham Rd
Mosley St
Langtry Grove
St Paul's
Lindsay St
Ebury Rd
Bentinck Rd
KILDARE RD.
Wells Rd
Ransom Rd
Carrington
Forest Rd
Mapperley Rd
Huntingdon St
wiring removed 1961
Robin Hood Chase
CARLTON P.O. SQ.
Chesterfield St
Hooton Rd
Newdigate St 'Zion Hill'
Bluecoat St
Huntingdon St
St Ann's
Bath St
Leighton St
Radford Kennington Rd
Radford Blvd
Ilkeston Rd
Alfreton Rd
Milton St (Trinity Sq)
Theatre Sq former S I
GPO
King Edward St
Dale View Rd
Porchester Rd
Thorneywood
Carlton Rd
Middleton Blvd
retained as feeder
WOLLATON PARK
Derby Rd
Nile St
Clumber St former S I
King St
Long Row W
Long Row
PARLIAMENT STREET DEPOT
Lenton Blvd
Fairham Drive
Derby Rd
Sth Parade
Lord Nelson St
Terminus
Sneinton
Wollaton Lodge
Canning Circus
Stanhope St former S I
wiring removed 1963
Pennyfoot St
COLWICK RD.
wiring removed 1963
Greyfriars Gate
Carrington St Colin St
Station St
Station St
London Rd
roller shutter doors
wash
Wilford Str (Wilford Rd)
Queens Rd
Bruce Grove Kirkewhite St
King's Meadow Rd
Agnes St
Eastcroft
Meadow Ln
WORKS
WILFORD BRIDGE
TRENT BRIDGE
REV
E HUMPHREYS 2005

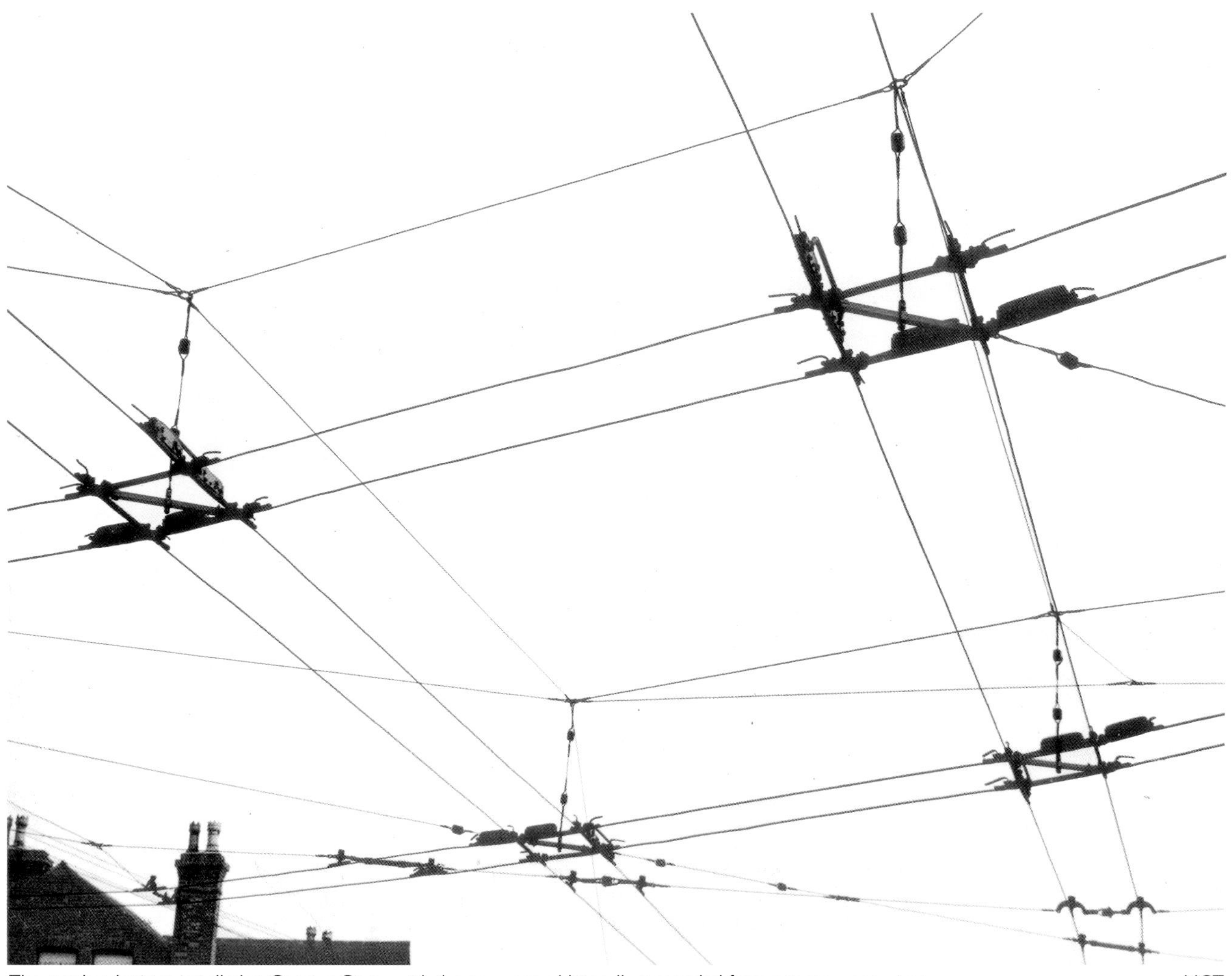

The overhead wiring installed at Canning Circus with 4 crossovers additionally suspended from catenary span wires. *NCT*

galvanised steel span wire. It is not known if Nottingham had similar problems or if they adopted this modification but whilst this system was eventually replaced entirely, sections of the "Nottingham Catenary Suspension System" remained in use until well into the 1950's.

In 1935 an experimental section of "flexible" overhead wiring from a German manufacturer supplied by the Equipment & Engineering Co. was installed at the southern end of London Road, near Meadow Lane, this being the sole UK application. Known as pendulum suspension, the span wires were attached higher up the traction pole than usual and about 9ins above the trolley wires, which were supported by flexible insulated drop hangers. This section was replaced by standard equipment during the Second World War possibly due to difficulties experienced when the replacement of trolley wheels with carbon insert slider heads commenced in January 1940. A modified version has since become normal practice on modern systems throughout the world.

During Chaceley Humpidge's short stay with the undertaking (1939-42), he introduced a policy of repositioning the running wires closer to the centre of the road, in order that trolleybuses could more easily negotiate obstacles, and of re-gauging those sections with an 18ins or 30ins separation between the positive and negative wires to the British standard separation of 24 ins using BICC twin line hangers in place of the less rigid single line hangers. In October 1954 the Trolleybus Society recorded that with the exception of the Basford (Vernon Road – Church Street) to Cinderhill section all service routes had been equipped with BICC twin hangers employing single span wires.

An example of the narrower 18ins separation between the trolley wires, employing single line hangers with an insulator between, together with catenary suspension system outside the Library in Old Bulwell. Beneath Karrier E6 85 and Ransomes D6 95 pass in Highbury Road. *Roy Marshall*

In the case of span wire overhead construction, the galvanised steel supporting wire ran between traction poles planted, normally at the kerb, on each side of the road, and attached to the upper section of the pole by a galvanised mild steel pole strap. MoT regulations required that the height of the trolley wire should not be less than 20ft above the surface of the road except under named low bridges e.g. Arkwright Street. Double insulation between the positive and negative trolley wires was provided by the hangers supporting the trolley wire and between the trolley wire and earth by the hanger and an insulator either in the span wire or between the span wire and the retaining bracket. Wall-mounted rosettes, anchored in roadside buildings, could replace one or both traction poles. Span wire construction provided a flexible support to the trolley wire.

Where side bracket traction poles were employed the insulators supporting the trolley wire were carried by short lengths of span wire thus providing the required double insulation between the positive trolley wire and earth, and also providing a degree of elasticity to the trolley wire support thereby increasing trolley wire life (rigid suspension inevitably caused wire fractures). Further insulation was provided by a section of rubber sheet between the traction pole mounted clamp and the steel tube of the side bracket arm. Part of the weight of the arm, which would normally not exceed a recommended maximum of 16ft in length, although exceptionally 22ft long arms were stipulated on the poling plan for the junction of Middleton Boulevard with Wollaton Hall Drive, was taken by a tie-rod whilst scrollwork could add to the strengthening effect.

Nottingham adopted BIC non-adjustable twin line hangers as the standard method of suspending its trolley wires during the Second World War, the first recorded use, albeit of the adjustable variety (later replaced), being at the junction of London Road with Lower Parliament Street where they replaced equipment damaged in the air raid of 8 – 9 May 1941. Thereafter BICC fittings were used throughout the system replacing the catenary system and the vast majority of tramway type single line hangers. Some of the latter were incorporated into "special" work e.g. the frogs in Southwell Road from the Lower Parliament Street Depot wiring to join service 39 inbound, whilst some remained in the wiring at the rear of Trent Bridge Depot.

The simple span wire suspension inevitably sagged towards the centre of the road and thus the negative trolley wire hung at a slightly higher level than the positive one although this did not create an evident problem for the later slider heads (also known as slipper heads). Latterly, a range of L-shaped twin-line hanger end fittings was introduced whereby the two trolley wires could be brought into vertical alignment. The only portion of overhead wiring designed with vertical "play" to enable the span to be lifted for high loads was in the region of the ring road at the Church Street, Radford Road and Valley Road junction, Basford.

It was normal practice along the main roads in Nottingham where trolleybuses operated to erect a second span wire above that supporting the trolley wires and to attach a street lighting unit. Additionally, until the late 1930s, when telephone lines began to be placed underground in urban areas, thin guard wires were hung between these higher-level spans, above and parallel to the trolley wires, where telephone wires crossed the road to prevent a broken or sagging telephone wire coming into contact with the trolley wires. The guard wires were earthed through a connection to the negative trolley wire at least every five spans and at each end span. Examples of these guard wires could be found in Mansfield Road and in Upper Parliament Street. Protective netting hanging vertically between the traction poles some 15-20 feet above the ground and parallel to the trolley wires immediately above the

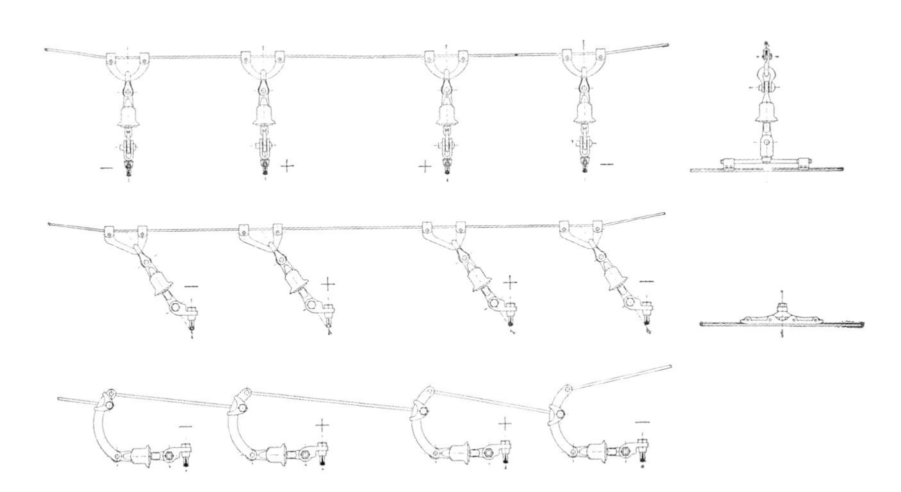

Drawings of flexible overhead fittings by the Rhineland-Westphalia Electrical Company. Published in The Electric Railway, Bus and Tram Journal, August 11th 1933 and thought to have been as used in London Road. The upper fittings were for straights, those in the centre were for large radius curves and those shown at the bottom were for small radius curves. *Rhineland-Westphalia*

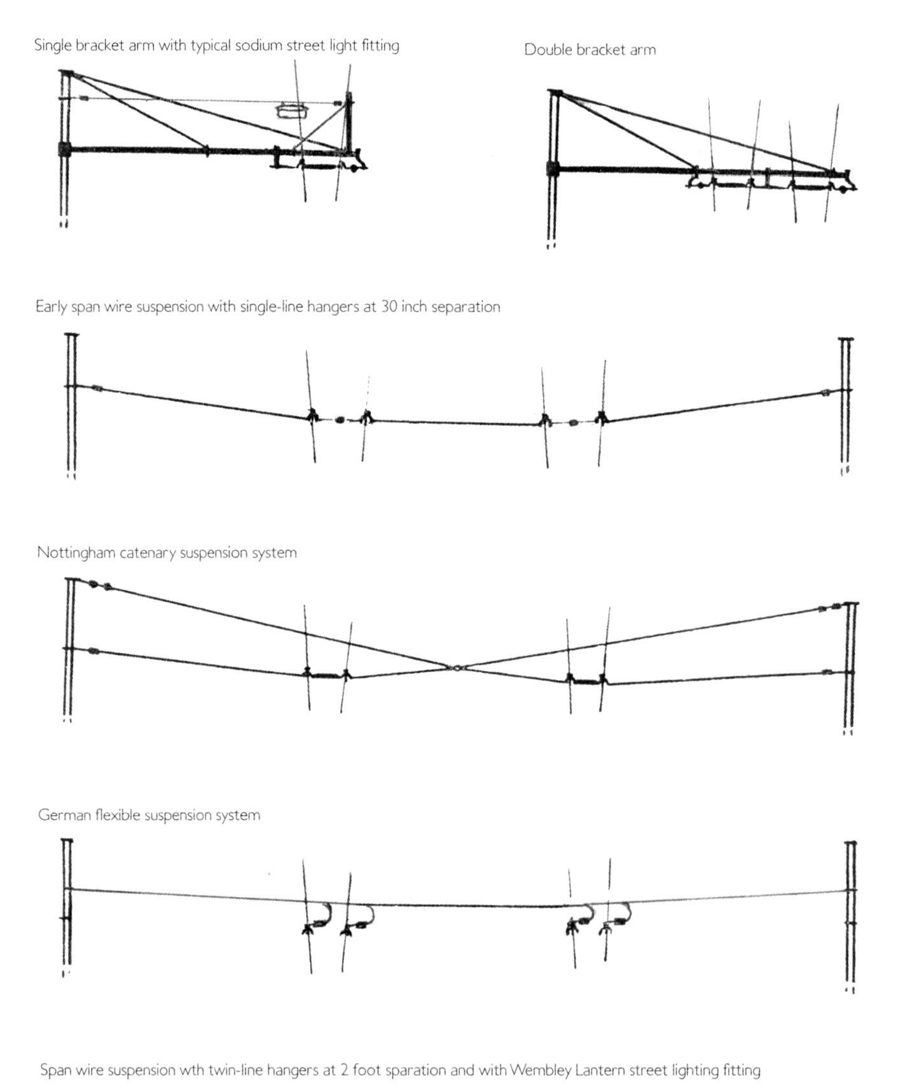

Overhead suspension configurations.

3 crossovers seen at Canning Circus. 4 splices have been inserted either side of the nearest one. *NCT*

A rooftop view of BUT9641T 520 standing at the boarding point of the Nottingham Road services. Note the trailing frog and "overtaking" wiring for services 40, 41 and 47. *MJ Russell*

pavement was installed at points where dewirements were more frequent and where a swinging trolley pole could damage nearby buildings or windows. Installations could be found until the end of trolleybus operation on Carlton Road, on the east side of Carrington Street at the junction with Greyfriar Gate, at Central Market, and in front of the Prudential Building in the apex of King Street and Queen Street adjacent to the crossing where the turning loop access wiring crossed the southbound King Street wires.

The initial cost of overhead equipment excluding special work such as junctions varied considerably according to the geography of the route; a heavily curved or graded section requiring proportionately more traction poles and bridle or pull-off span wires.

Unlike other trolleybus systems Nottingham did not employ any kind of markings or signs, whether at the side of the road, on the road surface or hanging from a span wire, to denote a frog, section breaker or other special work. There was however a signal light at the bottom of Carlton Hill controlling access through a narrow portion of street to the original Post Office Square turning circle and this remained in use until the road was widened in conjunction with the opening of Cavendish Road. Neither were strings of strategically placed "fairy lights" hung from the span wires to provide guidance for drivers at junctions or wide bends in fog. Exceptionally at Colwick Road terminus an arc of square bright metal studs (as then used at pedestrian crossings) were set into the road surface to provide trolleybus drivers with the most suitable turning angle into the turning circle. At this point the road was quite narrow and poorly lit whilst the entry to the turning circle was hidden from other traffic approaching from the east; a potentially dangerous situation if a trolleybus driver misjudged the tight circle and had reversed into the path of this incoming traffic.

There were overtaking or passing loops at several points on the system, specifically Beastmarket Hill westbound, Bulwell Market, Bulwell Hall Estate, Carlton Cavendish Road, Colwick terminus, Lower Parliament Street (LNER bridge), Trent Bridge Victoria Embankment and in the apex of the junction between Queen Street and King Street. In Nottingham these were known as "slip" wires. The loops at Colwick and in Lower Parliament Street were installed for sports specials and were removed by the late 1950s by which time such operations had been taken over by motorbuses.

Similarly, at intermediate turning points sections of parallel wiring were installed to enable waiting vehicles to be overtaken by other trolleybuses proceeding towards the City e.g. at Nottingham Road, Valley Road, where trolleybuses waiting at the 36 terminus could be overtaken by inbound 41s, or towards a more distant terminus e.g. Nottingham Road, Haydn Road, where 37 trolleybuses waiting to use the turning circle could be overtaken by 36s or 41s. Other examples could be found at Basford, Eland Street; Basford, Northern Baths; St. Ann's Well Road, Ransom Road; and of course the elongated "slip" wire at London Road (Cattle Market).

Traction Poles

The tramway overhead wiring equipment was considerably lighter than that necessary for the trolleybuses, not least due to there being just one rather than two trolley wires. Initially traction poles, supplied by John Spencer, Wednesbury, and made from three-section solid-drawn mild steel tube, the sections being welded together under pressure, were erected at the side of the road on single track with passing loop tram routes and, wherever possible, in the middle of the road, on double track routes. The centre pole location however soon proved a hazard to other traffic and many were replaced by side poles on both sides of the road connected by span wires, these poles and those used on route extensions coming from the Mannesmann Tube Co. The traction poles were ornamented with cast iron bases bearing the Corporation coat of arms, cast iron or open spike finials, wrought iron Maltese Cross span wire bracket scrolls and side bracket arm scroll work. The majority of these poles remained in use until the end of the trolleybus era albeit usually bereft of the scroll work which proved difficult to maintain in the rust-provoking pollution laden atmosphere of an industrial community and dated in appearance whilst the cast iron bases were susceptible to minor traffic accidents and heavy blows. In many cases they had been reinforced internally with steel rods and concrete. Nonetheless the bracket arms in King Street retained their ornamental scrollwork until the system's final abandonment whilst one traction pole still with an ornamental base remained in situ at the north end of Nottingham Road in late 2004. Unusually the new bracket arms on the 1931 route along Middleton Boulevard were installed with ornamental scrollwork and bases.

The standard traction pole used on the Nottingham trolleybus system was a 31 foot heavy steel pole, 9½ins in diameter at the base, tapering initially to 8½ins and then again to 7½ins at the top but those manufactured after the early 1940s had fractionally larger dimensions of 9⅝, 8⅝ins and 7⅝ins respectively. They were manufactured by a variety of steel tube manufacturers and were not a specialist item. A variety of pole diameters and lengths e.g. 33 foot or 35 foot, were available to provide greater strength at locations such as curves, junctions or other special work, where the increased weight of the overhead wiring placed additional strains on its supports. The lower 6ft of the traction pole was sunk into the ground, with a backwards rake to compensate for the weight of the overhead equipment, and embedded in concrete. Once the pole was supporting the overhead wiring it was pulled into the vertical. The remains of caves and, in the city centre, cellars extending out from buildings, occasionally led to pole planting difficulties, John Lowrie recalling how in 1960 the base of a traction pole in front of Boots' Wheeler Gate shop had to be extended into their cellar.

On straight sections of road there was a traction pole at least every 35 yards but above curved sections of road where the trolley wire had to be pulled into a series of straights approximating to the desired curves these were more frequent. In such cases of stepped curvature the angle did not exceed 10° to reduce the risk of dewirements. There was a considerable weight of equipment aloft: as an example the two pairs of trolley wires on a straight section between two traction poles, together with the supporting hangers and span wires, weighed about 235 lbs whilst a post-war BICC electrically-operated turnout frog weighed in excess of 80 lbs.

Statutory regulations stipulated a maximum longitudinal span of 120ft with a minimum conductor height of 20ft except under bridges and this separation was retained where existing tramway traction poles were reused. Along routes not previously traversed by trams shorter spans of 105 feet became general to compensate for the increased weight aloft.

Poles and bracket arms were painted at infrequent intervals with green paint which weathered down to a paler, almost olive green, shade over the years. In 1940 or thereabouts traction poles in Wilford Road were experimentally painted aluminium instead of green whilst the impressive double bracket arm pole at the junction of Queen Street and King Street appeared in silver but this was not generally adopted. Each traction pole was numbered in small white figures so that a location could be pinpointed in case of a breakdown or emergency. Although there was no system-wide coding system, each route was numbered from a specific junction or the city centre working outwards to the terminus. On all span wire routes the poles were numbered in pairs, poles on the offside of the road (working outwards) having the same number as that opposite on the nearside but with an "A" suffix e.g. 23 and 23A, or 46 and 46A. At junctions, or on corners and turning circles, where poles had to be placed closer on one side of the road, the suffix lettering could increase e.g. 23B, 23C, 23D.

Examples:

Wells Road (Kildare Road) terminus – final traction poles supporting the circle numbered 67& 68.

Bulwell Hall Estate terminus – final traction pole supporting the circle numbered 66.

Bulwell Market – traction poles numbered from Canning Circus – highest numbered pole in the Market Place (corner of Main Street) 197.

Colwick Road terminus – traction poles numbered from King Edward Street – final pole supporting the circle numbered 67.

Wilford Road terminus – traction poles 36 – 40 were around the east side of the circle, and 40C, 40B, 41 and 36A around the west side, with 40A and 36B in the middle.

On the Carlton route the pole numbers ran from 1 at Sneinton Market to 56 at the city boundary at Lancaster Road, but beyond here the poles, possibly owned by Carlton UDC, displayed no code.

Many traction poles along erstwhile tram routes from the pre-1914 period were replaced in 1956-58, replacements in some cases coming from the erstwhile N&D network in Ilkeston, the Bulwell area being partially re-poled in September 1956.

There were no European-standard road signs in the trolleybus era; those traction poles supporting signs and traffic lights received yellow or black and white bands up to a height of ca. 10 feet.

Single bracket arms could be found at many places on the Nottingham system where the streets were deemed impractically wide for span wires e.g. Derby Road near the Savoy Cinema, along roads having one-way wiring only e.g. Handel Street, or along dual carriageways e.g. Middleton Boulevard. Subject to the width of the road, side bracket arms could support more than one pair of wires e.g. along Sherwood Rise both outbound and inbound wires were supported by poles planted on the west side of the road. They were also used to provide additional support for frogs at some points e.g. the junction of Carrington Street with Station Street. Uniquely, on many side bracket arm equipped traction poles Nottingham suspended a street light from

In the period 1963-65 roadworks necessitated one-way working along Vernon Road for some considerable time. It will be noticed that the overhead crew has temporarily slewed the northbound pair of trolley wires towards the centre of the road thereby easing the reach of the trolley booms and thus reducing the risk of a dewirement. The temporary alignment has been made with "Wiseman adjustable hangers" fitted to the span wires. Upon completion of the road works the trolley wires will be reattached to the original hangers, visible alongside the adjustable version. *Neil Lewin*

In the latter days of the system BUT9641T/Brush 548 climbs past the Royal Oak public house on Nottingham Road citywards from Haydn Road. *MJ Russell*

a short length of span wire strung between the top of the pole and an upright metal tube fixed at right angles at the outer end of the bracket arm. Many examples survived after the trolleybus overhead wiring had been removed!

Single bracket arms were used on:
Bath Street (an isolated example, erected after the route had been closed)
Bunbury Street
Church Street, Basford
Derby Road, from near Elm Avenue to the Boulevards
George Street
Handel Street
King Street
London Road, on the LMS railway bridge south of Station Street
Main Street, Bulwell
Market Street
Middleton Boulevard
Nottingham Road, from the northern end of Sherwood Rise to the junction with Haydn Road
Pennyfoot Street parking area
Poultry
Queen Street
Sherwood Rise, from its junction with Gregory Boulevard to the southern end of Nottingham Road.
Turney Street
Wilford Road, from pole 11 to 35 (just before the terminus).
Wilford Street

Double bracket arms i.e. with a bracket on each side of the traction pole, were uncommon on trolleybus systems but Nottingham had a celebrated example, a survivor from tramway days, in the apex of the junction between King Street and Queen Street in front of the Prudential building. It survived the trolleybus abandonment and was still in situ in May 1968, being removed later for restoration and subsequent display at the National Tramway Museum at Crich, Derbyshire.

Ironically, the final bracket arm to be erected was probably after the last trolleybus had operated on the section of route concerned, namely in March 1966 to support the eastbound pair of wires in Bath Street close to the junction with King Edward Street and St Ann's Well Road. Service trolleybuses last used this section of wiring in December 1965 or January 1966. In order to improve the vehicular access to a business on the south side of the road linesmen cut down a length of the westbound wiring in order that traction pole supporting a span wire, which partially blocked the intended entrance/exit, could be removed and attached a single bracket arm to the traction pole on the opposite side of the road to support the eastbound wiring.

Routes equipped with span wires inevitably had a second span wire hung about 2ft above that supporting the overhead equipment carrying a suspended street light(s). Many traction poles were retained for street lighting purposes after trolleybus operation along the street concerned had ended, some staying in place for 20 or more years, repainted black. This second span wire continued to support a light fitting whilst on bracket arm sections the arm itself, with the short length of span wire above, was retained although all trolleybus-related fittings were removed.

Frogs

Although hand-operated frogs (points or switches in the overhead wiring) were installed throughout as the tramway conversion programme got under way, increasing trolleybus and other traffic, together with consideration of the conductor's workload, encouraged the undertaking to look for alternatives. Until then the conductor had to leap from the rear platform and pull the handle, connected by a sprung steel cable pull and attached at a convenient height to a nearby traction pole to activate the frog mechanism when the trolleybus needed to follow a "branch" line. This system was retained at little-used junctions throughout the life of the system e.g. on Victoria Embankment to provide access to Bunbury Street turning circle and Trent Bridge Depots and Works. Nottingham used solely the conventional hand-operated turnout frog with a pull handle on a nearby traction pole, which had to be pulled and held for the branch or secondary route, and there is no evidence that semi-automatic reset frogs were ever installed. There was an isolated example of a sprung trail or shunt frog at the Hooton Road reversing triangle, enabled a reversing vehicle to open the "tongue" which then sprung back to its normal position permitting egress back onto the main road.

A little too late for Nottingham's tram to trolleybus conversion programme, in the mid-1930s a range of pre-assembled overhead fittings, in which the various parts were already linked by rigid spacer bars, came onto the market. Prior to this, short lengths of span wire, equipped with an insulator, were inserted between the positive and negative trolley wires when the linesmen assembled the equipment. Initially the insulated runners consisted of wooden beams greater in thickness than the trolley wire, and the trolley wheel had to run through the gap in the crossings and frogs on its flanges, both resulting in vertical movement which restricted speed and broke the carbon inserts when slider heads were adopted. Post-war however less obtrusive "wire section" fittings were employed having insulated running strips matching the cross-section of the trolley wire, and moving tongues in both frogs and crossings so that there were no gaps. Combined with the use of slider heads these permitted higher speeds with little risk of dewirement, 30 mph being achieved in tests when following the "main line" beneath frogs (compared to ca. 50 mph beneath the "high speed" frogs with interlaced approaches used on today's modern systems abroad).

The first "auto frogs" probably came into use in 1931, it being noted that 8 hand-operated frogs had been converted to electric operation in the financial year ending 31 March 1935. It was decided to standardize on the automatic frog setter devised by the Forest City Electric Co., Illinois, USA and manufactured in the UK at that company's Stretford, Manchester works. This required a break in the positive trolley wire and the installation of a transfer contact skate ahead of the frog with a direct action restoring contact skate hung about half an inch above the positive wire just beyond the frog to return it to the normal route.

Nottingham's "auto frog" installation policy was "power for the branch" and "coast for straight on", replicating the principle of "power for the curve" used by the tramways and reinforced by a sign inside Lower Parliament Street Depot "THE DRIVER OF THE RAILLESS TAKING THE CURVE MUST TAKE POWER". In principle the services along the busiest route were not required to operate the auto frog thus at Canning Circus outbound, although Derby Road was arguably "straight on", the frequency of services along Alfreton Road and Ilkeston Road took precedence. As the trolleybus approached the setting skate or transfer contact, a driver wishing to take the "branch" line would keep his foot on the power pedal, simultaneously controlling the vehicle's speed with the hand brake thereby drawing current from the positive wire and returning it to the negative wire through the motor. The transfer contact skate thrust the trolley wheel or slider head downwards clear of the trolley wire. The sides of the collector remained in contact with the metal skate, which was live through the operating coil thus completing the circuit. Passing under the transfer contact in the negative wire, current would return through the operating relay installed in a traction pole mounted box about 8ft above the ground which then sent current to the operating solenoid further up the pole. The Forest City setter exerted a pull of ca. 80 lbs and worked a normal hand operated frog, which could be operated or reset manually in case of failure, and lit a confirming signal lamp.

The setting skate was installed 10-15 yards before the frog itself in order that there was sufficient distance to stop the trolleybus if a driver had failed to operate the frog or, indeed, accidentally set it in error. The conductor would then alight to set or re-set the frog manually for the appropriate direction. It should be noted that the trolleybuses were equipped with trolley booms 19ft long and that the driver was some 30ft in front of the trolley heads.

If the driver wished to remain on the "main" line, he would coast under the transfer contact with his foot off the power pedal ensuring that no current was sent into the setter. Drivers were required to learn which auto frogs needed operating for each route as a part of their training. As road traffic continued to increase and turning lanes started to be painted on the road surface, where appropriate and practicable the Overhead Department introduced a policy of installing the transfer contact and frog set back prior to a road junction where the trolleybus' reduced speed passing beneath a frog might prove a disruption to other vehicles e.g. opposite the Albert Hall, Derby Road heading east towards the junction with Upper Parliament Street, and in Upper Parliament Street itself opposite the Elite Cinema heading west towards the junction with Milton Street. The location was usually carefully coordinated with a point where the vehicle was travelling slowly just before or immediately after a trolleybus stop. This resulted in two parallel pairs of wires up to the turn itself thus allowing trolleybuses possibility of selecting the correct traffic lane to the junction. It also allowed other trolleybuses to overtake in another traffic lane. This layout also gave the driver a last chance to avoid dewirement should he or she have incorrectly gained the wrong wiring after the frog by manually transferring the trolley poles using the bamboo retrieval pole carried by every trolleybus, from one pair of trolley wires to the next.

The Forest City auto frog operating relay was contained in an oblong metal box mounted on the traction pole adjacent to the overhead frog with a gently curved top, to provide some protection against the elements, and two separate lenses and indicator lamps although in many cases the second lens was blanked off. When the frog was set for the "main" line there was no indication, the other lamp, normally equipped with an orange lens, gave the "branch" line indication. No lights were illuminated when a trolleybus coasted beneath the setting skate thereby confirming that the frog had not been inadvertently set. All electric frog mechanisms were equipped with a grab handle for manual operation.

In addition both hand-operated and auto frogs were connected to a "repeater" indicator light, normally attached to the nearside traction pole immediately after the frog itself or on an alternative traction pole that was clearly visible to the trolleybus driver. A single white light confirmed that the frog switch tongues had moved to the required position both before and after the trolley heads had passed beneath the frog. If the light went out before they had cleared the frog or if the light did not go out after the trolley heads had cleared the frog, the driver would stop and send his conductor back to pull the frog manually or pull the reset cord if the frog had not restored. All frog repeater indicators were equipped with a pull cord to cancel an illuminated lamp when the frog itself was manually corrected after an erroneous setting by the driver. If a frog setter was missed whether an exchange of trolley booms was required or simply a manual operation of the frog, operating orders instructed the driver to pull on the hand brake tightly, knock out the circuit breakers and place a chock in front of the offside front wheel or behind it as appropriate to the gradient.

Frogs would normally not freeze due to the heating effect of current flowing in the wires however, despite liberal applications of an anti-freeze and glycerine mixture, early morning journeys could suffer as the traction power was cut off at night and auto frogs might require manual operation.

The skate used as a restoring contact for the Forest City machine had a contact strip held down by light springs. As the trolley head passed beneath, the strip was lifted closing the sprung contact thus sending a current at line voltage back to the frog setter relay and restoring the frog to normal. The same skates were used for signalling purposes i.e. at the bottom of Carlton Hill.

During the Second World War white circles were painted on the road surface beneath feeders, frogs, junctions and section breakers to indicate to trolleybus drivers where they should coast to avoid sparks which might give away their location to enemy aircraft. These were "coasting indicators" rather than aids to frog setting. Additionally an asbestos shield was hung above the special work to further reduce the risk. There is no evidence that any kind of road surface indications of special overhead work were provided before the war or, in the increasingly busy traffic conditions, thereafter.

Auto-frog locations and operating direction

Carrington Street/Greyfriar Gate junction (Lister Gate)
 Operate for Greyfriar Gate (service 40)

Old Market Square – Beastmarket Hill/Long Row (James Street)
 Operate for Long Row (services 40/47, 41, 46)

Old Market Square –Long Row West/Processional Walk (Market Street)
 Operate for Processional Walk (services 42, 43, 46)

Old Market Square – service 42 turn round
 Operate for loop (service 42)

Old Market Square – Long Row/Beastmarket Hill (opposite "Griffin & Spaldings")
 Operate for Processional Walk (service 41)

Chapel Bar/Upper Parliament Street (Derby Road outside the Albert Hotel)
 Operate eastbound for Upper Parliament Street (services 39, 44)

Canning Circus operating westbound from Chapel Bar and Upper Parliament Street
 1st setter controlled the frog leading into the continuation of Derby Road
 Operate for Derby Road (service 45)

Canning Circus operating westbound from Chapel Bar and Upper Parliament Street
 2nd setter controlled the frog leading into Ilkeston Road
 Operate for Ilkeston Road (service 39)

Canning Circus operating westbound from Chapel Bar and Upper Parliament Street
 3rd setter controlled the frog leading into Alfreton Road
 Operate for Alfreton Road (services 42, 43, 44)

Theatre Square (turn round)
 Operate for turn around (service 38)

Upper Parliament Street/Milton Street (opposite the Elite Cinema)
 Operate for Milton Street (services 36, 37, 41)

Upper Parliament Street/King Street ("Journal" Building)
 Operate for King Street (services 36, 37, 41, 44)

Lower Parliament Street/King Edward Street (Gas Showrooms)
 Operate for Lower Parliament Street (service 45 & workings to Parliament Street Depot)

Parliament Street/George Street
 Operate for George Street (service 40)

St. Ann's Well Road/Bath Street
 Operate for Bath Street (services 38, 39, 44)

Bath Street/Handel Street
 Operate for Handel Street (services 38, 39)

Nottingham Road/Valley Road ("Futurist" Cinema roundabout)
 Operate for Valley Road (service 41)

Nottingham Road/Haydn Road (turn round)
 Operate for turn round (service 37)

Queen Street (service 41 loop)
 Operate for inside wire (service 41)

Highbury Road/Piccadilly junction (northbound from City providing access to Bulwell Depot)
 Operate for Piccadilly (Depot workings only)

Former trolleybus driver Bernard Jefford recalls that the automatic frog in the eastbound (inwards) wiring on Derby Road for the Chapel Bar/Upper Parliament Street junction, just prior to the Albert Hotel, was a particular challenge. The descending gradient combined with the weight of the passenger load could make frog operation difficult as the driver was required to apply power for the turn out curve into Upper Parliament Street but keep the speed low by use of the handbrake.

In 1953 when the roundabout at the bottom of Market Street in the Old Market Square was installed, the fuse was removed from the auto-frog giving access to the service 46 parking loop leaving the frog to be operated by hand. Unintentional operation had caused numerous dewirements and the entire mechanism was removed in May 1957.

Halfway up the traction pole in the distance (to the nearside of BUT9611T/Roe 487) can be seen the illuminated auto-frog "repeater" indicator light for the Nottingham Road, Valley Road roundabout. The indicator box itself is on the edge of the photograph. It would appear that the frog is erroneously set for the left turn into Valley Road. ***Bernard Jefford***

There remained locations where the installation of auto-frogs would have been an asset; here conductors had to alight in all weathers to pull the "trigger" at an adjacent traction pole to set a frog manually e.g. King Street allowing services 36 and 37 to turn into Queen Street, Trent Bridge terminus of service 43.

Traffic islands or roundabouts were installed at the following locations after the construction of trolleybus equipment at the junctions concerned:

Arkwright Street, at the junction with London Road, Trent Bridge — August 1939
 – Reconstructed as part of a gyratory scheme — November 1959

Bath Street, at the junction with St. Ann's Well Road — 1947

Canning Circus — 1937-38
 – Reconstructed as part of a gyratory scheme — December 1959

Carrington Street, at the junction with Greyfriar Gate and Lister Gate — 1947

Derby Road, at Middleton Boulevard — mid 1938

Derby Road, at the junction with Chapel Bar and Upper Parliament Street — by 1961

Gregory Boulevard, at Mansfield Road — February 1952

Gregory Boulevard, at Sherwood Rise — February 1952

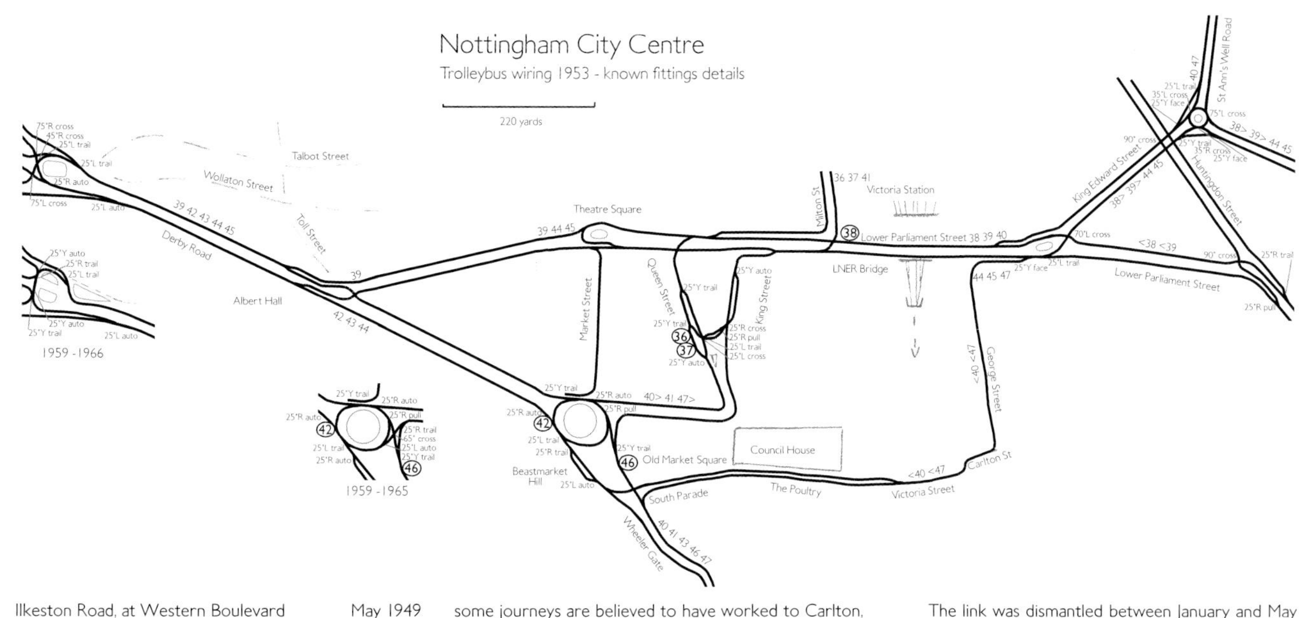

Ilkeston Road, at Western Boulevard May 1949
Ilkeston Road, at Middleton Boulevard May 1949
London Road, at the junction with Canal Street and Lower Parliament Street 1949
– Reconstructed 1955
Lower Parliament Street, at the junction with Huntingdon Street ca 1944
Lower Parliament Street, at the junction with King Edward Street ca 1944
Lower Parliament Street, at the junction with Southwell Road early 1940s
Nottingham Road, at Valley Road a 1933-34
Old Market Square, at the junction with Market Street February 1953
Radford Road, at the junction with Church Street, Valley Road and Western Boulevard by 1938
Theatre Square, Upper Parliament Street by 1941

Little used or unusual sections of overhead wiring and turning circles

Regular trolleybus services did not operate along the following stretches of overhead wiring:

Eland Street, Basford

A turning circle intended for use by peak hour extras and during the Goose Fair, by then held on The Forest, was installed in early 1935 on the east side of Radford Road at the junction with Eland Street just north of the busy Hyson Green area in New Basford. The MoT Inspecting Officer visited the circle on 30 April 1935, official approval for use being received on 22 May 1935.

Although post war trolleybus deliveries included BASFORD (top line) ELAND STREET (2nd line) on their destination blinds no service number was ever allocated and no regular service was scheduled to turn there however there was frequent use by extras starting and/or terminating there. The turning circle remained available for use until 31 May 1965 but it is understood that it was last used by 480 on an enthusiast's tour on 7 March 1965.

Gregory Street

A short-working turning circle for works extras to/from the Raleigh Cycles factory was erected at the southern end of Radmarsh Road, opposite the northern end of Gregory Street, at its junction with Derby Road, Lenton, in 1938. The Derby Road tram service had terminated at this point prior to 16 April 1927 when services were extended to Wollaton Park Gates and a tramway crossover was retained there until June 1930 when trams were cut back to Johnson Road, Lenton, ¼ mile east of Gregory Street.

With the exception of at least one 47 to Wells Road, Ransom Road, the destinations and origins of services to/from Gregory Street are not known although some journeys are believed to have worked to Carlton, Hooton Road as 38s. The journeys were not shown in the public timetable neither was Gregory Street included on the destination blinds. Latterly, the turning circle was rarely used except when an outbound trolleybus, running behind schedule, was required to turn "short" to make up time. The circle was last used, by an enthusiast's tour in 464, on 4 November 1962 and was cut down during 1963.

Huntingdon Street

This ¾ mile section of double wiring, together with new terminal arrangements for Nottingham Road trolleybuses at the junction with Vernon Road, was inspected on 1 October 1935, official approval for use being received on 9 January 1936. Huntingdon Street had been intended by Mr Marks as part of an "inner circle" trolleybus route planned to operate around Canal Street, Castle Boulevard, Lenton Boulevard, Radford Boulevard, Gregory Boulevard, Mansfield Road, Huntingdon Street and Lower Parliament Street back to Canal Street. Changed policies after his departure meant that the link lost its main purpose. The revised layout could have enabled trolleybuses from Bulwell and Cinderhill to join Nottingham Road at Valley Road then follow Mansfield Road, Huntingdon Street and London Road, thereby avoiding city centre congestion, to serve both football grounds and the cricket ground but it was never used as such.

The reluctance of the post-war management to use trolleybuses on special services, combined with the 1952 cut back of the Nottingham Road wiring from Vernon Road to the junction with Valley Road, thereby severing the Bulwell link, removed any traffic potential from Huntingdon Street. In early 1949 there was a proposal to cut back the N&D trolleybus service from Queen Street to a new terminus in Union Street just to the north of Victoria Station which would have necessitated use of the northern end of Huntingdon Street but this came to nothing.

The sole occasion that regular services used this wiring was on Tuesday 28 June 1949 when Princess Elizabeth visited Nottingham as a part of the City's Quincentenary Celebrations, commemorating 500 years since King Henry VI had granted Nottingham its Great Charter, and service 48 ran along Huntingdon Street and London Road and on Wednesday 6 July 1955 when the 41 was diverted to/from Trent Bridge on the occasion of the Queen's visit to the Royal Show in Wollaton Park. Thereafter the route was retained for occasional depot workings to and from Lower Parliament Street Depot for the Nottingham Road services although all journeys were scheduled to start at Queen Street or terminate at King Street.

The link was dismantled between January and May 1961 although the southbound pair of wires between King Edward Street and Lower Parliament Street was retained to permit depot workings from Wells Road to Lower Parliament Street Depot. Even after January 1961 it is known that the occasional late evening trolleybus, returning to the City and then Lower Parliament Street Depot devoid of passengers, in-officially made its way from Mansfield Road down the Huntingdon Street gradient by a combination of gravity and battery power.

London Road, Cattle Market

As part of the London Road tram to trolleybus conversion, which opened on 2 June 1935, a turning circle and long siding was installed on London Road to serve the Notts County Football Ground at Meadow Lane. Pre-war extra journeys to sporting events at Meadow Lane or Trent Bridge (Nottingham Forest Football Ground and Nottinghamshire County Cricket Club, both on the West Bridgford side of the River Trent) ran from Beastmarket Hill via Arkwright Street and Station Street. In post war years, these extras operated from the siding or "slip" line in the eastbound wiring on Victoria Station Railway Bridge on Upper Parliament Street. Trent Bridge was however also served by frequent scheduled trolleybus services 41 or 48 dependent on the period, 43 and 46 along Arkwright Street and service 45 along London Road. In the mid 1950's trolleybuses ceased to be used on "special" services and by the 1960's football services were advertised as being operated by "a special service of motorbuses".

Severe flooding on Wilford Road on 20 March 1947 led to service 40 being diverted south of Greyfriar Gate roundabout along Carrington Street, Station Street and London Road to the Cattle Market loop. This was the sole occasion that a regular service used this turning facility.

The last recorded use of the turning circle was on 4 November 1962 by 464 on an enthusiasts' farewell tour of service 45 and associated wiring. The wiring was cut down by 24 November 1962.

Market Street

A single pair of wires was installed in Market Street in the northbound direction i.e. up the hill from Long Row to Upper Parliament Street at Theatre Square, in connection with the conversion of the Bulwell routes in May 1934, to provide a turn back to the west from the city centre. There was a junction frog in the eastbound wiring along Long Row West outside the Talbot Inn and at Theatre Square a trailing frog enabled trolleybuses to turn west towards Derby Road. Market Street was used for a time by short workings on the 45 from Wollaton Park at Monday to Friday lunchtimes.

On 29 October 1961 BUT9641T/Brush 585 pauses just past the ex-Great Central railway bridge (which crossed both the road and the Midland Station) in Market Street on an enthusiasts' tour. *Rod Bramley*

In March 1941 a turning circle was added on the east side of the traffic island at the south end of Market Street between the north and southbound wiring offering an alternative terminus for vehicles from the west but with the advantage that outbound journeys could then reload at the customary boarding point for Radford Road departures on the north side of the Queen Victoria Statue traffic island. Thereafter the frog providing access from Long Row West into Market Street was removed. Although the rest of the wiring remained in situ it was rarely used, access being achieved by manually transferring the trolley booms. The last known trolleybus to operate up Market Street was 578 on an enthusiasts' tour on 10 October 1965.

Northern Baths, Basford

The City Engineer's Department prepared drawings for a short-working turning circle in the apex of the junction between Bulwell Lane and Vernon Road, immediately to the south of the LNER overbridge at Basford & Bulwell Station, in 1933, in conjunction with the conversion of the Bulwell tram route to trolleybus operation. This was the "off-peak" terminus, then known simply as "Basford", of tram service 4, and it can be assumed that the turning circle was erected as a part of the 1934 conversion scheme.

No services turned here regularly until 22 August 1954 when the northern terminus of service 42 was cut back to Basford, Northern Baths. At that time the circle was accessed by a manual facing frog with the circle crossing over the southbound running wires to provide a section of parallel wiring allowed trolleybuses waiting at the terminus to be overtaken by city-bound 43s and 44s. An NCT clock in a box was attached to the wall of a nearby building. Services ceases on 31 May 1965, the final duty being operated by 537.

Pennyfoot Street

The short section between Lower Parliament Street and Manvers Street was also wired for trolleybus operation at the same time as the London Road to Trent Bridge conversion work, opening for service on 2 June 1935. Service 45 Trent Bridge – Wollaton Park negotiated Pennyfoot Street in both directions.

In summer 1946, additional frogs were erected to allow trolleybuses to turn east out of Pennyfoot Street into Colwick Road to permit the operation of "specials" to the White City (Nottingham's Dog Racing Track). No equivalent facility was provided for vehicles bound for the city centre. However on 22 February 1953 service 45 was re-routed to operate directly between London Road and Upper Parliament Street along Lower Parliament Street, leaving Pennyfoot Street without a regular trolleybus service whilst the number of "Special" services by trolleybus also declined in the 1950's. By the mid-1950s sports specials were operated by motorbuses and there was no longer an operational necessity to retain these frogs, and they were removed, in conjunction with a reconstruction of the road junction, in the late 1950s.

Thereafter Pennyfoot Street saw only occasional use by trolleybuses on test after attention in Parliament Street Depot but following the closure of the London Road trolleybus route on 3 November 1962 the westbound wiring (Manvers Street to Lower Parliament Street), which had also provided power to London Road from the Sneinton feeder, was removed. The eastbound wires were retained until final closure of the system to provide access to the yard at the corner of Pennyfoot Street and Manvers Street used for storing disused trolleybuses after withdrawal. The yard itself had been equipped with overhead wiring in 1946 but this had been removed by 1957 at the latest, although the redundant traction poles were still in place in late 2004. Thereafter withdrawn vehicles reversed into the yard from Manvers Street on battery power. The last trolleybus to use Pennyfoot Street was 518 on an enthusiast's tour on 26 June 1966.

Peveril Street

In early 1941 a turning circle was erected in the apex of the junction between the south end of Peveril Street with Alfreton Road enabling extra trolleybuses operating inwards from Bulwell to turn back to the north. It is believed to have come into regular use from 6 March 1941.The prime source of traffic was the Player's cigarette factory a little to the north on Alfreton Road, it being calculated that northbound trolleybuses running from the City were often full when they reached this point of their journey.

The destinations and origins of services to/from Peveril Street, although limited to points north thereof on the Bulwell route, are not known neither did the turning point appear on destination blinds. The journeys were not shown in the public timetable. Post war the turning circle fell into virtual disuse although it remained available for use until the closure of services 42 and 44 on 31 May 1965. Last recorded use was by an enthusiast's tour using 480 on 7 March 1965

Southwell Road (eastbound)

When the Carlton tram route was converted to trolleybus operation in 1932 only the westbound carriageway of Southwell Road east of Manvers Street was wired. All services from Carlton travelling westbound towards the city followed Carlton Road and Southwell Road to reach Lower Parliament Street however eastbound services followed Bath Street and one-way wiring along Handel Street to reach Carlton Road. The eastbound carriageway of Southwell Road between Lower Parliament Street and Manvers Street was only wired in 1941-42 but no regular trolleybus services ever used it.

Westbound services from Colwick Road turned right out of Manvers Street to follow the eastbound Southwell Road wiring for a few yards before a manually operated frog, set for the turn, allowed them to turn left into Bath Street. Trolleybuses taking up service on the Carlton route from Parliament Street depot pulled out into Manvers Street and turned right into Southwell Road. The conductor would pull the frog-operating trigger to enable the trolleybus to continue straight ahead into Carlton Road, joining the normal route at the junction with Handel Street.

The section of eastbound overhead wiring in Southwell Road between Lower Parliament Street (Price & Beal's corner) and the junction with Manvers Street saw little use but for some early morning journeys on Sundays returning to the city after dropping postal workers at the Huntingdon Street sorting office and for driver training purposes. The right turn out of Handel Street into the westbound carriageway of Southwell Road was also rarely used as most trolleybuses running-in to Parliament Street Depot returned along Lower Parliament Street.

It is believed that trolleybuses last operated beneath the eastbound Southwell Road wiring on 10 October 1965 when an enthusiasts' tour in 578 negotiated this section however the proximity of Parliament Street Depot ensured that the wiring remained aloft until the end of the system.

Station Street

The 500 yard section between Arkwright Street and London Road was wired for trolleybus operation at the same time as the London Road conversion work, being inspected for use on 30 April 1935, with official approval following on 20 May 1935. At this time it was anticipated that the Midland Station to Colwick Road tram service would be converted to trolleybus operation however, the then new General Manager, Mr Gunn, recommended that this service together with those to Lenton and Radford be converted to motorbuses. This took place on 13 May 1934 whilst the Colwick Road trolleybus service was linked with that to and from Bulwell on 2 June 1935, leaving Station Street, newly equipped for trolleybuses, devoid of any trolleybus service.

No scheduled trolleybus service regularly traversed Station Street throughout the life of the system although the wiring was used pre-war for sports specials and during the flooding of early 1947 when service 40 was diverted from Wilford Road to London Road, Cattle Market.

Although surviving feeder diagrams provide no evidence as to how this might have been achieved, it is understood that in latter years the Station Street overhead wiring was not normally energized. Scaffolding was set up above and around the LNER/GCR railway bridge over Station Street in late 1960/early 1961 for BR to carry out repair work safety considerations probably requiring that the trolleybus power be turned off and it is possible that appropriate insulators and switching were installed then. Driver training trolleybuses were seen in Station Street ca. 1960 whilst on 29 October 1961 an enthusiasts' tour in 585 also traversed the wiring. By this date there were section insulators at the London Road end of Station Street that clearly cut off power along the length of the street and linesmen energized the section by inserting a "jumper" cable across the insulators. At the Carrington Street end, all frogs and the crossover had the current breakers towards Station Street and there was no break in power when heading along Carrington Street.

The section was energized a final time, again using temporary "jumper" cables, on 24 June 1962 to enable another tour vehicle 478, to run along Station Street in both directions however a repetition on 4 November 1962, for 464 on the farewell tour of service 45 and associated wiring, was refused apparently due to BR concerns related to the overbridge. 464 managed to run a few yards into Station Street from London Road as far as the section breaker and thus the limit of live wiring, and then reversed to London Road. The last portion of the Station Street wiring was removed during the night of 5-6 May 1963.

Trent Bridge Works and Depot area

In principle there were 3 different turning points for normal services at Trent Bridge. Service 45 trolleybuses turned around the traffic island in the apex of the junction between Arkwright Street and London Road, in front of the Globe Cinema, until the introduction of a one-way system in November 1959 made this impractical. All other journeys, including latterly service 45, turned in a widened portion of Victoria Embankment, immediately prior to a pair of wrought iron gates. Thereafter Victoria Embankment became a private road, the gates being closed once annually for legal purposes on Christmas Day, subject to a 20 mph speed limit. The gates were still in place in spring 2005. In 1946 a second turning circle was installed further west along Victoria Embankment at the junction with Bunbury Street; it was used solely by sports specials until 26 April 1953 when service 41 was extended to Trent Bridge.

In the late 1930s an extension over Trent Bridge and along Radcliffe Road terminating adjacent to Nottingham Forest football ground in connection with plans for a traffic island at the west end of Trent Bridge was considered.

Trolleybuses took over the operation of the Bulwell – Trent Bridge trunk route on 13 May 1934 but photographs taken shortly after this date show no evidence of trolleybus overhead wiring leading to/from Trent Bridge Depot building. However they do show two-way trolleybus overhead at the junction of Bunbury Street with Victoria Embankment and solely one-way (heading southeast) wiring in Bunbury Street opposite Trent Bridge Works suggesting that the pair of wires above Pyatt Street, Fraser Road and Turney Street were initially used in an anti-clockwise direction. It is not known what overhead wiring arrangements existed at this time above the junction of Arkwright Street with Fraser Road.

Once access to/from the Pyatt Street, Fraser Road and Turney Street loop had been modified for clockwise use, the normal trolleybus access to and from Trent Bridge Depot and Works was along the bi-directional wiring following Victoria Embankment and Bunbury Street however, vehicles could also reach Bunbury Street from Arkwright Street by traversing Fraser Road and Pyatt Street in a southwesterly direction. Latterly there was no frog from Arkwright Street into Fraser Road and on the odd occasion access was required in this direction, crews either transferred the booms at the short portion of parallel wiring or proceeded from Victoria Embankment around the corner on battery power re-poling in Fraser Road. One-way, northeast bound wiring was also strung in Turney Street (which its is assumed provided access to Arkwright Street at one time) providing a circuit Turney Street, Fraser Street, Pyatt Street, Bunbury Street for vehicle testing purposes in the immediate vicinity of the works.

The last trolleybus to use the complete circuit was 480 during an enthusiast's tour on 7 March 1965 whilst the last recorded use of any section of this wiring was on 27 March 1965 when 525 returned to the depot by way of Frazer Street and Pyatt Street.

Termini

All trolleybus termini were conventional turning circles into lay-bys at the side of the road, around traffic islands or at wide road junctions; or followed a circular routing around a number of streets, with the following exceptions:

Carlton (Hooton Road)

The sole reversing triangle on the Nottingham trolleybus system came into operation on 6 April 1941 for peak hour short workings on the Carlton route.

Wollaton Park (Harrow Road)

Trolleybuses serving Wollaton Park operated along Middleton Boulevard, a dual carriageway portion of the western ring road. Initially all vehicles followed a circular routing outbound along Derby Road with their return towards the City along Ilkeston Road or vice versa but in 1937 all journeys were amended to terminate at turning circles along Middleton Boulevard. Until 1958, whichever turning circle was in use, trolleybuses turned by leaving

An imaculate one year old Karrier E6 58 with MCCW & F all metal body parked in Bunbury Street outside Trent Bridge Works in March 1935. It will be noted that at this time there was solely one-way (southbound) wiring in this portion of Bunbury Street suggesting that the pair of wires above Pyatt Street, Fraser Road and Turney Street were initially used in an anti-clockwise direction. *GHFA & JMB*

the slow lane on one side of the dual carriageway, through breaks in the central reservation into lay-bys in the opposite carriageway, facing in the direction from whence they had arrived. Separate turning circles for each service were used with a connection for through running being maintained.

The termini of services 39 and 45 were moved to Harrow Road in October 1959 and by May 1960 the through overhead wiring running north/south along Middleton Boulevard at this point was removed and all trolleybuses whether travelling to/from the City along Derby Road or Ilkeston Road terminated there. Two separate but overlapping turning circles were erected through the central reservation with crossovers at each end of the oval shape created in the middle of the wiring. This enabled turning trolleybuses to keep to the correct side of a pair of "keep left" bollards and a traction pole which was also sited within the "oval".

Unfulfilled proposals

A number of drawings still survive showing traction pole location and overhead wiring layout proposals for routes or terminal arrangements that never materialised. These include:

Alfreton Road/Bentinck Road junction, reconstruction for the Bobbers Mill Bridge route

Colwick Road terminus, extension of the overtaking or passing loop to Trent Lane

Colwick Road/Trent Road reverser, 1947 proposals for a terminus dedicated to sports specials

Gregory and Radford Boulevards (circular route), traction poles

Gregory Boulevard/Radford Road junction, for the wartime Gregory Boulevard proposals

Gregory Boulevard/Sherwood Rise junction, for the wartime Gregory Boulevard proposals

Manor Road, Carlton, traction poles

Nuthall Road/Stockhill Lane junction, reconstruction for the Bobbers Mill Bridge route

Standhill Road reverser, vetoed in 1934 by Carlton UDC

Overbridges

A number of low railway overbridges led to the overhead wiring being positioned to the side of the road (usually over the pavement) to maximise the available height required by the trolley poles.

Heights recorded for the lower bridges were:

Arkwright Street	16ft 1in (inwards)
	16ft 3ins (outwards)
Station Street	16ft 2ins
London Road	16ft 3ins
Colwick Road	16ft 7ins and 18ft. 5ins.

Beneath these bridges the trolley wire was attached to a T-iron suspended by porcelain insulators from wooden troughs (intended to catch the trolley in event of a dewirement as contact with the girder work would have been likely to damage and/or rip off a moving trolley head), attached to the underside of the bridge. Similar troughing was attached to the roof girders inside the depots.

The Overhead Department

The Overhead Line Department was based in the former motorbus garage in Turney Street, at the rear of the Trent Bridge running shed, built in 1920 for the resumption of petrol bus services. The building was generally known as the "tower wagon garage" and, following use as the Works' glass fibre shop in the post-trolleybus era, was demolished about 1999.

It took a special breed of men to be out in all weathers, making hasty emergency repairs above a peak hour traffic jam or replacing a complex overhead wiring junction through a Saturday/Sunday night. It was heavy and potentially dangerous work, exposed to the elements some 20 feet above an unforgiving road surface and frequently carried out with the current on. There was always the risk of severe injury from wires, under a ton or more of tension, breaking or being unwisely released

The overlapping turning circles at Middleton Boulevard, Harrow Road installed in October 1959 were unique. In this post-May 1960 view BUT9641T 521 turns back on to the northbound carriageway of Middleton Boulevard before another 39 working to Carlton. *BTS*

AEC Regent tower wagon 803 waits in Lower Parliament Street at Victoria Station Bridge during the 1930s. *BTS*

Dennis tower wagon 801 awaits the next emergency call in Turney Street on 29 July 1953. The rear entrance to Trent Bridge Depot and the roof of a utility bodied Karrier W are visible over the brick wall. *Peter Badgery*

During the trolleybus era, the Overhead Department operated the following vehicles:

Fleet No		Reg	Type	Into Overhead	Withdrawn	Note
Original	Last	No		Dept. service		
1 (?)	1 (?)	AU186	Dennis petrol	02/1921	ca. 12/1934	1
2	801	TO4007	Dennis petrol 40/50 hp	09/1932	ca. 12/1955	2
3	802	TO6094	Dennis petrol 40/50 hp	1931	ca. 12/1952	3
4	803	TV6749	AEC Regent 661 petrol	10/1933	1966-67	4
504	804	Trailer	Chassis only	ca. 1934	1966	5
802	802	FTO614	AEC Regent O661 diesel	01/1953	1970	6

Note:

1 Tower wagon. Dennis 4-ton chassis new in 02/1921.

2 Tower wagon. Converted from 1926 Dennis (chassis no. 40413) double deck motorbus 47 (original number 37) in 1932. Renumbered 501 ca. 1939 and again in 11/1949 to 801. Sold in 07/1956 to R. Hill, Melton Mowbray, Leicestershire.

3 Tower wagon. Converted from 1927 Dennis (chassis no. 45513) single deck motorbus 47 (withdrawn in 1930) in 1931. Renumbered 502 ca. 1939 and again in 11/1949 as 802. Sold in 07/1956 to R. Hill, Melton Mowbray, Leicestershire.

4 Tower wagon. Converted to normal control from 1932 AEC Regent 661 (chassis no. 1857) double deck motorbus 48 in 10/1933 and bus body transferred to TV9435 (as 48). Renumbered 503 ca. 1939 and again in 11/1949 as 803. Sold in 06/1967 to A. Belton and extant at the East Anglia Transport Museum, Carlton Colville, Suffolk.

5 Reel trailer. Converted from 1928 Maudslay ML4 (chassis no. 4224) single deck motorbus 54 in ca 1934. Renumbered 804 in 11/1949. Engine removed.

6 Tower wagon. Converted from 1939 AEC Regent O661 (chassis no. 6460) double deck motorbus 31 in 1952 following an accident in 04/1950. Sold 11/1970 and extant at the Sandtoft Transport Centre near Doncaster, Yorkshire.

Linesmen on AEC Regent tower wagon 802 at work at the junction of Station Street with London Road (looking east) on 29 October 1961. *Rod Bramley*

from their anchorage, high voltage electric shock or a lack of care and attention from other road users. Expediency meant that much of the work was carried out with the "juice" on, yet despite insulation on the tower wagon and rubber gloves, an occasional "belting" was almost inevitable. Reportedly, after such an experience the linesman could only taste copper for several days!

Apart from the continual rolling programme of scheduled inspection, repairs and replacements linesmen had to be available to attend a breakdown or emergency at any time during the normal operating day, in principle from just after 5 am until around midnight. A full 24-hour coverage provided by four crews made up of three men, specifically a Driver, Linesman and Assistant Linesman. In 1954 the Department's establishment was made up of 18 staff as follows:

1 Chargehand (paid as craft grade plus supplement)
7 Linesmen (paid as craft grade)
5 Assistant Linesmen (paid as semi-skilled grade)
5 Drivers (paid as bus drivers)

The crews worked rotating shifts every day of the year except Christmas Day as follows:

6 am – 2 pm
2 pm – 10 pm
10 pm – 6 am
8 am – 4 pm

It will be noted that during much of the day this shift pattern ensured that there were always two crews on duty, one handling routine maintenance and the other on standby to handle any emergency which might materialize. This second crew would wait at the Trent Bridge base cleaning pot insulators and filling oil lamps to bide their time but if called out they would race off like the fire brigade to ensure that any delay to the trolleybus service was kept to a minimum. Major tasks such as the realignment or replacement of a junction would be carried out at night with the power cut off and required the presence of two overhead crews. In such cases it was normal practice for a linesman to personally check at the substation that current had been switched off and the record card signed.

The regular maintenance programme had to consider that normal wear and tear made the trolley wire thin where it led in and out of any rigid fitting. In order to remove and replace a worn or broken length of trolley wire, "come-along" clamps would be attached to the trolley wire, one each side of the section needing repair or replacement, and an unscrewed turnbuckle i.e. an expanding screw with hooks at each end, would be hooked onto the rings attached to each clamp. The turnbuckle was progressively tightened thereby increasing the tension in the trolley wire on the "outer" side of the "come-along" clamps but creating looseness or sag between them. The section to be removed could then be cut out and a new length, with a joining or splicing ear at each end, inserted to a fixing clamp fastened to the trolley wire ends protruding from the "inner" side of the "come-along" clamps. Once the clamping screws within each splicing ear had been securely tightened to ensure mechanical and electrical connection and any kinks removed by the use of special straightening rollers, the tension in the wires would be adjusted to the appropriate figure for that location with a dynamometer or heavy duty spring balance. The turnbuckle would then be gradually opened, allowing the overhead wiring layout to return to its normal position, and the "come-along" clamps removed.

A similar procedure was followed to handle or remove longer distances of trolley wire or frogs. Dependent on the weight, the turnbuckle(s) would be tied off and secured to a traction pole(s) thereby retaining the length under tension. When the overhead wiring network was being dismantled, trolley wire could be dropped in 40-yard lengths and the span wires would either be taken down at the same time or left in situ and removed at a later date.

Some worn parts of equipment such as crossings, frogs and trolleyheads, were reconditioned by the Department by building up using sifbronze welding. Span wires suffered no mechanical wear and tear, and were normally only replaced in conjunction with changes to the road layout or when they were life-expired, the biggest enemy being corrosion.

There was something of a tradition of longevity in the Overhead Department. Jack Morris, who provided personal reminiscences in this section, spent three years with the Transport Department as an Apprentice Electrician before joining the Royal Navy, returning in 1955 when, after a short period as a Fitter's Mate, he joined the overhead line crews. He remained there until final closure and dismantlement of the trolleybus system. Jack's father had joined the tramway overhead maintenance team at the end of World War One but was sadly killed in October 1942 when the raised inspection platform of the tower wagon upon which he was working collided with a span wire as it followed the Highbury Road, Bulwell wiring. Eddie Harper, the Overhead Line Chargehand (Foreman), who lived in Bathley Street, just two blocks away from the Overhead Department's base behind Trent Bridge Depot, was known as a most conscientious gentleman. He made a

The manner in which brackets or extensions were bolted to the upper-deck body pillars to support the girders of the trolley gantry is clearly evident. Traction power cables make their way forward along the roof of BUT9641T 506 from the trolleybases before descending down the inside of the first offside pillar to the control equipment in the driver's cab. Parliament Street Depot on 4 August 1953. *Peter Badgery*

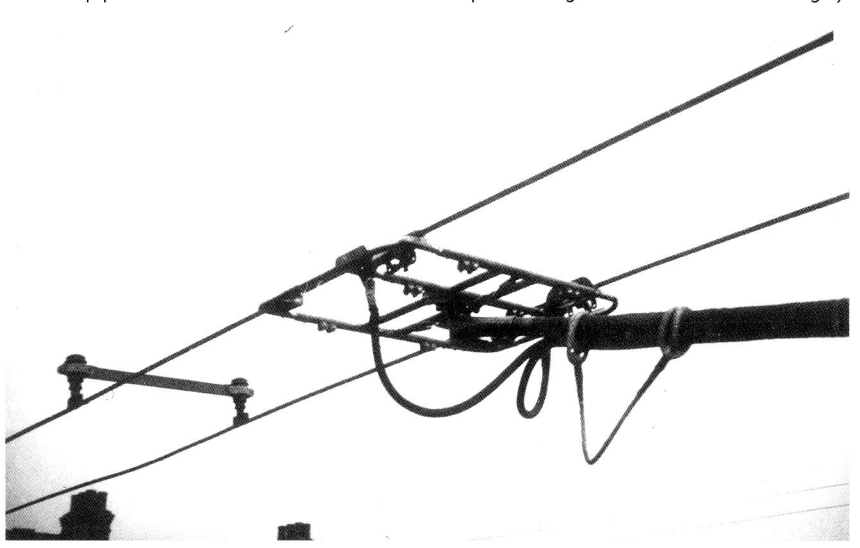

In the late 1930's Karrier E6 50 was experimentally fitted with a single trolley pole having two trolley heads 12ins apart on a metal frame, possibly constructed from a Fischer tramcar bow collector. The separation between the positive and negative trolley wires for some 337 yards around the circuit provided by Pyatt Street, Fraser Street and Turney Street, near Trent Bridge Depot and Works, was narrowed to 12 ins centres but the idea was not pursued. *Roy Marshall*

point of visiting the facilities each evening before retiring to ensure that there was enough work to do! Harry Kirkby, known to everybody as George, Assistant Linesman, worked later in the stores.

In addition to the tower wagons, a trailer, complete with attendant's seat and brakes, for transporting reels of cable or wire and built from a former Maudslay ML4 motor bus chassis, was also based at Trent Bridge. Tower wagon 802 had a bell push on the inspection platform whereby the examining linesman could indicate to the driver where to slow or stop, 803 did not have this luxury and a bang with a hammer had to suffice.

Jack recalls being called out in a blizzard as the auto frog at Canning Circus providing access to Derby Road had ceased to function only to find that the door to the frog indicator box containing the indicator lamps and operating relay was open, and the box packed full of snow. Another recollection is of a spectacular dewirement, caused by excessive speed, on Carlton Hill at Cardale Road, when at least 6ft of a trolley boom broke off and was found hanging on the negative wire!

Vehicle Equipment

The current collectors on the roof of each trolleybus consisted of three main parts, the trolley base carrying the trolley boom and allowing it to swing in a horizontal plane and to rise under spring tension, the boom itself and, at the extreme end of the boom, the trolley head which made contact with the under surface of the power conducting trolley wire. All three parts were insulated from each other, and from at least the 1934 Karrier E6 deliveries the base was also insulated from the trolley gantry by bonded-rubber mountings provided to minimize the transmission of noise to the roof.

The current was carried from the trolley head by a flexible cable running through the hollow trolley boom which narrowed to 1 ins diameter at the trolley head end. The boom, a tapering steel tube was wrapped in black bitumen impregnated insulating tape to minimize the chance of it shorting the trolley wires in the event of a dewirement. The 1927 and 1928 vehicles had trolley masts, similar to those used on open-top tramcars, at the front of the upper saloon, whilst all subsequent deliveries up to fleet number 50 were equipped with the Brecknell Willis "low type" bases with the springs parallel to the vehicles' roof. Thereafter all Nottingham trolleybuses were equipped with the Brecknell Willis "patent lightweight" bases with the springs lying along the trolley boom. The vertical upward pressure of the trolley heads on the wire could be measured by hanging a scale from each boom and adjusted at the springs on the trolley base. Post-war the overall length of the trolley boom from the base swivel to the head swivel was 19ft on both 2-axle and 3-axle vehicles.

From the early days of electric tramway operation, the undertaking renewed, rather than replaced, the trolley wheels which ran along the under surface of the trolley wire. The new wheel, manufactured by the Railway & General Engineering Co. to the design of John Aldworth and his Works Superintendent, was made up of three parts, rather than the customary one, comprising two side flanges and a central grooved collar. When the grooved centre was worn out, the wheel was taken apart, the three portions being simply held together by two small bolts. A fresh centre was put in and the whole bolted together again. The average life of the centre part was 5,500 miles, while the sides were subjected to very little wear.

At the beginning of the Second World War the wheel collector swivel trolley heads were replaced throughout the fleet with slider heads, the entire unit comprising a steel "harp" (which fitted on to the end of the boom and was retained by two bolts) into which sat a swivelling gunmetal globe. On top of the globe there was a phosphor bronze (BICC) or steel (AA) slipper into which fitted a preformed carbon insert skid. The self-lubricating carbon inserts dramatically reduced trolley wire wear, in some cases almost doubling the "wire life", virtually removed the necessity to apply a conductive grease to the trolley wires, reduced the risk of dewirements, permitted higher operating speeds and eliminated the noise (particularly when wet) from the trolley wheels rotating at high speed. Equally importantly in the nation's crisis they much reduced arcing and sparking which would be visible for miles in the "black-out". As the overhead fittings were progressively adapted for the slider heads reduced wear and a further reduction in sparking resulted.

The carbon inserts were inspected for damage and wear daily, an average life being around 800 miles but considerably less in wet or frosty weather conditions. Hoar frost on the trolley wires caused intense arcing which quickly damaged and wore the carbon insert. On frosty mornings the first trolleybus on each route was fitted with a cast-iron insert to remove the ice, these being replaced with a normal carbon insert immediately thereafter as prolonged use of a cast-iron insert would not only remove the frost but would also "shave" the trolley wire.

Appendix J Fares, Fare Tables and Tickets

At the beginning of the electric tramway era the routes were divided into penny (1d) stages with overlapping stages throughout, the average length being 1.68 miles. There were no halfpenny adult fares. The longest through route was from Bulwell Market to Trent Bridge, a distance of 5½ miles, for which the fare in 1908 was 4d. The trolleybuses adopted a similar staged fares list, in principle 1d per stage of equal distance but with a ½d fare for a half stage, fares being charged for a stage or portion of a stage. In principle the trolleybus fares were the same as those prevailing on the tram services they replaced or paralleled between any two points however motorbus fares were more expensive. Only with the appearance of the February 1934 timetable were the first proper fare tables issued. Thereafter detailed fare tables were included in each issue of the combined fare and timetable, separate sheets and notices on the vehicles being used for intermediate amendments.

Reduced workmen's fares were available to all passengers (there being no discrimination between, for example, workmen wearing overalls and others) on journeys commencing before 8 am Monday – Saturday. Pre-war the last morning journey upon which workmen's fares were granted, varying between 7.58 am and 8.15 am, was stipulated in the relevant timetable. Workmen's return fares were double the appropriate workmen's single fares. The return portion of these tickets was available for return on any tramcar and subsequently the trolleybuses up to 9 pm (3 pm on Saturdays). There were no normal return fares.

To combat falling revenue, workmen's return fares, by now referred to as early morning return fares, were abolished on 24 May 1954 and replaced with early morning single fares. A normal single fare had to be purchased for the homeward journey but the fare structure was so designed as to limit the increase for each complete return journey to a maximum of 2d.

Transfer fares had been widely available on the tramway system and this facility was expanded during the 1930s. Lists of Ordinary Single Transfer Stages and Workmen's Return Transfer Stages, showing the boarding and alighting fare stages, permitted transfer point, mode of onward transport e.g. to an "omnibus" (sic), and its service number, accompanied the normal fare tables for each service or group of services shown in the timetable booklet. During the period that the tramway network was being converted to trolleybus operation it was necessary to temporarily split some cross-city services into two, operated by different modes of transport e.g. in connection with the Arkwright Street conversion tram service K (Trent Bridge – Arnold) was cut back to the Old Market Square. Until further progress with the conversion programme made it possible to reintroduce through services, additional transfer fares were introduced.

No transfer fares were available between trolleybuses and motorbuses on the NCT/WBUDC joint services to and from West Bridgford, indeed a surcharge, as for all other instances where motorbuses paralleled a trolleybus route (at one time ½d), applied to local passengers on the joint services between the Old Market Square and Trent Bridge.

The number of transfer fares published reduced considerably in the late 1940s and last appeared in the 1948 timetable booklets.

Bell Punch

Initially trolleybus tickets were of the same Bell Punch geographical fare stage colour-coded type, with

TROLLEYBUS SERVICES 36, 37 and 41
Combined Service
Cinderhill (Bells Lane), Valley Road Junction, Queen Street and Trent Bridge
FARE TABLE

ORDINARY SINGLE

Stage										
(22)	Trent Bridge									
(21)	2	Midland Station								
(20)	2½	2	Queen Street							
(19)	3	2½	2	Woodborough Road						
(18)	4	3	2½	2	Gregory Boulevard					
(17)	4	4	3	2½	2	Falcon Street				
(16)	5	4	4	3	2½	2	Zulu Road			
(15)	5	5	4	4	3	2½	2	Bar Lane		
(14)	6	5	5	4	4	3	2½	2	Stockhill Lane/Nuthall Road	
(13)	6	6	5	5	4	4	3	2½	2	Bells Lane

TROLLEYBUS SERVICES 38 and 39

Service 39—Carlton Post Office, City and Wollaton Park (Harrow Road).
Service 38—Elite and Hooton Road.

FARE TABLE

ORDINARY SINGLE

Stage											
(26)	Carlton Post Office										
(25)	2	Forester Grove									
(24)	2½	2	Standhill Road								
(23)	3	2½	2	Porchester Road							
(22)	4	3	2½	2	St. Matthias' Road						
(21)	4	4	3	2½	2	Central Market					
(20)	5	4	4	3	2½	2	Turkish Baths				
(19)	5	5	4	4	3	2½	2	Canning Circus			
(18)	6	5	5	4	4	3	2½	2	Radford Boulevard		
(17)	6	6	5	5	4	4	3	2½	2	Triumph Road	
(15)	6	6	6	5	5	4	4	3	2½	2	Harrow Road

TROLLEYBUS SERVICES 40 & 47
Combined Service
Kildare Road, Old Market Square and Wilford Bridge
FARE TABLE

ORDINARY SINGLE

Stage							
(24)	Kildare Road						
(23)	2	Ransom Road					
(22)	2½	2	Corporation Road				
(21)	3	2½	2	Central Market			
(20)	4	3	2½	2	Old Market Square		
(19)	4	4	3	2½	2	Waterway Street	
(18)	5	4	4	3	2½	2	Wilford Bridge

TROLLEYBUS SERVICES 42, 43 and 46
Combined Service
Bulwell Market, Old Market Square and Trent Bridge
FARE TABLE

ORDINARY SINGLE

Stage											
(12)	Bulwell Market										
(13)	2	Piccadilly									
(14)	2½	2	Northern Baths								
(15)	3	2½	2	Vernon Avenue							
(16)	4	3	2½	2	Eland Street						
(17)	4	4	3	2½	2	Bobbersmill Road					
(18)	5	4	4	3	2½	2	Bentinck Road Schools				
(19)	5	5	4	4	3	2½	2	Canning Circus			
(20)	6	5	5	4	4	3	2½	2	Old Market Square		
(21)	6	6	5	5	4	4	3	2½	2	Midland Station	
(22)	6	6	6	5	5	4	4	3	2½	2	Trent Bridge

TROLLEYBUS SERVICE 44
Bulwell Hall Estate, Bulwell Market, City and Colwick Road
FARE TABLE

ORDINARY SINGLE

Stage															
(10)	City Boundary														
(11)	2	E. R. Railway Bridge													
(12)	2½	2	Bulwell Market												
(13)	3	2½	2	Piccadilly											
(14)	4	3	2½	2	Northern Baths										
(15)	4	4	3	2½	2	Vernon Avenue									
(16)	5	4	4	3	2½	2	Eland Street								
(17)	5	5	4	4	3	2½	2	Bobbersmill Road							
(18)	6	5	5	4	4	3	2½	2	Bentinck Road Schools						
(19)	6	6	5	5	4	4	3	2½	2	Canning Circus					
(20)	6	6	6	5	5	4	4	3	2½	2	Turkish Baths or Old Market Square				
(21)	6	6	6	6	5	5	4	4	3	2½	2	Central Market			
(22)	6	6	6	6	6	5	5	4	4	3	2½	2	Pennyfoot Street		
(23)	6	6	6	6	6	6	5	5	4	4	3	2½	2	Meadow Lane	
(24)	6	6	6	6	6	6	6	5	5	4	4	3	2½	2	Colwick Road

TROLLEYBUS SERVICE 45
Trent Bridge, City and Wollaton Park (Harrow Road)
FARE TABLE

ORDINARY SINGLE

Stage									
(23)	Trent Bridge								
(22)	2	Station Street							
(21)	2½	2	Central Market						
(20)	3	2½	2	Turkish Baths					
(19)	4	3	2½	2	Canning Circus				
(18)	4	4	3	2½	2	Lenton Boulevard			
(17)	5	4	4	3	2½	2	Hillside		
(16)	5	5	4	4	3	2½	2	Scalford Drive	
(15)	6	5	4	4	3	3	2½	2	Harrow Road

separate sets for each group of services, as used on the trams. The conductor was equipped with a wooden rack holding pre-printed paper tickets, divided by value, under a spring and cancelling punch. The stages were printed along the edges of the ticket with the undertaking's title or abbreviated title, both of which varied considerably during the 20 years the Bell Punch system was used on the trolleybuses, and other information in a central column. Older ticket stock displayed the title "Nottingham Corporation Trys.". The conductor used a cancelling punch to make a small round hole against the fare stage, indicated by geographical name or number, where the passenger had started the journey whilst the fare paid indicated how far the passenger could travel. The cancelling punch recorded the number of holes punched on a secure register inside the machine whilst the small coloured circle of paper punched out of the ticket was retained in the machine (for accounting purposes if required). It also made an audible ring thus ensuring that a fraudulent conductor was not selling a used ticket. At the outer terminus and at the city centre the conductor would record the serial number of the first ticket of each denomination on the rack and enter this on the waybill. This would be checked by inspectors, who would board vehicles at random, to ensure that the conductor was issuing tickets correctly and that passengers had paid the appropriate fare.

By 1932 the original ticket punches were life expired and 550 new replacements were hired from Bell Punch.

Workmen's fare tickets were clearly overprinted in a contrasting colour. During the trolleybus era, the return journey at workmen's return fares was handled by issuing an exchange ticket of the same value as the original one and cancelling it to show the stage boarded. The conductor retained the lower part of the original ticket, both parts showing the fare paid.

Although efficient and successful, the ticketing system was "administration-heavy", slow, required considerable manual dexterity and labour intensive. Nonetheless NCT continued to employ the Bell Punch, despite the use of TIM machines on most trolleybus and erstwhile tram services, until the Ultimate system was adopted as the undertaking's standard in 1947.

The undertaking appears to have purchased tickets for its Bell Punch machines from, in chronological order, Punch & Ticket Co., London, and then the local supplier of Hunt, Hucknall Road, Nottingham (who merged later to become Hunt & Colleys). Hunt did not always show the printer's name on their tickets.

TIM

The faster service speeds of the trolleybuses in comparison to the trams left conductors with less time to collect fares and issue traditional Bell Punch tickets from a ticket rack particularly for short stage journeys within the city centre. Revenue was being lost whilst administrative costs were rising and, following unconvincing experiments with "Verometer" mechanical ticket machines in autumn 1933, trials were carried out with Ticket Issuing Machines Ltd. (TIM), equipment.

The TIM had a dial that allowed the conductor to quickly choose the appropriate fare from 10 different values, the direction of travel and the fare stage boarded. The ticket was printed on a plain roll of paper which also indicated the date of issue. The machine also recorded the number of fares issued for each value for administrative and control purposes.

The trials were deemed successful and 50 TIM machines were put to use from 22 January 1934 on the 38, 39 and 40 trolleybus services and a number of motor bus services. The TIM machines were provided to the undertaking free of charge subject to a commitment to purchase the appropriate blank paper rolls upon which the tickets were printed, sufficient for 250,000 tickets, at a price of 7½d per thousand, per machine per annum for

Ticket colours and styles

Title, variously during the trolleybus era, "NOTTM. CORPN. PASS. TRANSPT. DEPT", "NOTTM. CORPN. PASSENGER TRANSPT. DEPT", "NOTTM. CORPN. PASSENGER TRANSPORT DEPT.", "NOTTM. CORPN. PASS. TRANS. DEPT.", "NOTTINGHAM CITY TRANS" or "NOTTINGHAM CITY TRANSPORT". Geographical or numerical fare stages. All printing in black.

Single tickets were 1¼in X 2½in, in size and had the following colours:

Colour	Denomination	Period	Comment
White	½d	1930s	Child, red overprint. NCPTD era.
Dark blue	½d	pre-1942	) not a deliberate
Medium blue	½d	1942 -	) change
White	1d	early 1930s	
Pink	1d	early 1930s	Child, red overprint
Dark blue	1d	early 1930s	Child, red overprint
Light blue	1d	early 1930s	Child, red overprint
Sage green	1d	1930s -	
Buff	1d	1930s	Workmen's single & return, red overprint
White	1½d	1930s -	Red overprint. Including NCPTD era.
Pink	2d	1930s	Including NCPTD era.
Salmon	2d	1930s -	
White	2d	early 1930s -	Workmen's single & return, red overprint
Lilac	2½d	1930s -	Including NCPTD era.
Cerise pink	3d	1930s -	
White	3d	1930s	Workmen's return, red overprint
Yellow	3½d	1930s -	Including NCPTD era.
Orange	3½d		
Grey	3½d	later	
Bright green	4d	1930s -	
Buff	5d		
Grey	6d		
Pale lilac	6d		

Workmen's return tickets were 1¼in X 2½in, in size and had the following colours. All were overprinted "WORKMEN" in red during the NCPTD era.

Colour	Denomination	Period	Comment
Buff	2d	1930s -	
Medium blue	3d	1930s -	
Vivid yellow	4d	1930s -	
Chocolate brown	5d	1930s -	
Bright green	6d	1930s -	Officially "special" green
Salmon	7d	1930s -	
Orange	8d	1930s -	

The last half-inch was torn off on the return journey and an exchange ticket issued. The exchange tickets were pale mauve (lilac) or pink.

During the period that transfer fares were available the following colours were in use:

Colour	Denomination	Period	Comment
Blue	1½d		Various named transfers
Red	2d		Services 36, 37, 40, 41
Red	2d		Services 39, 45
Red	2d	1938-43	Services 42, 43, 44
Pale blue	2½d		
Green	3d		
Grey	3d	1938-43	Workmen's return, services 39 & 45
Chocolate	3½d		Various named transfers
Yellow	4d	1938-43	Workmen's return, services 39 & 45

Bell Punch transfer tickets were also issued by TIM ticket machine equipped conductors.

(1st line)
4d workmans, transfer on 36, 37, 40, 41; 2d transfer; travel permit;
(2nd line)
1½d white; ½d child; ½d pupil; 1d workman; 3d single;

a period of three years. Thereafter the machines belonged to NCT and the price fell, typically to 3d per thousand tickets. A further 50 TIMs were acquired in March 1934 in time for the conversion of the Trent Bridge – Bulwell trunk services to trolleybus operation. Further machines were acquired as follows: 68 in August 1934, 84 in June 1936 and 80 in June 1937.

In principle the TIMs were used on all trolleybus routes and all former tram services converted to motorbus operation, the sole exception being the Nottingham Road group of trolleybus services (36, 37, 41) which operated in conjunction with the N&D A1 service and which continued to use Bell Punch tickets until the end.

Replacement machines were bought to replace worn-out originals in 1942-43 (24) and in 1945 (30).

The TIM system could not cope easily with fare increases which, once all values were in use or were no longer used, required each machine to be equipped with new printing plates.

Ticket colours and styles

Titles varied according to the date of manufacture of the machine and its printing plates, "NOTTINGHAM CORP. P.T.D.", "NOTTM. CITY TRANS.", "N.C.P.T.D." and "N.C.T." being used indiscriminately. Tickets were 3⅛in X 1½in in size.

Until the end of 1941 workmen's return tickets were printed with pink ink on green paper whilst all other tickets were on white paper. Thereafter workmen's return tickets were printed on white paper with two parallel pink lines inked down the edges of the back of the paper. At the end of 1943, the pink print was replaced by blue and towards the end of 1944 pink paper was introduced for workmen's return tickets.

The printing included a number of boxes or squares headed originally headed "STAGE BOARDED" on the left, "FARE PAID" showing the amount and type of fare on the right, and in between at the base "ROUTE" showing the service number upon which the ticket was issued and "DATE". In the upper central area the undertaking's abbreviated title, machine number and other data was printed. The whole was contained in a rectangular frame with the customary legal disclaimer appearing outside the frame on the left.

During the early part of 1942 "jumping conductors" were introduced and to identify the tickets that they issued from those of the service conductor, the printing ink was transposed i.e. pink ink was used where blue ink was normal and vice versa. Two machines were dedicated to stationary conductors collecting fares from queues at Old Market Square and Trent Bridge, the location being printed in the "ROUTE" box whilst "TIME ISSUED" replaced "STAGE BOARDED". The practice of giving a punch-type ticket as an exchange for TIM workman's returns ceased in September 1943 thereafter a TIM "exchange" was given, the ticket being cancelled on a distinct section denoting the value of the return surrendered. Serrated edge cutters, replacing a straight-edged guillotine, were fitted to these machines, commencing late in 1943, whilst blue ink replaced red in the summer in order to make the tickets more legible in the "black-out".

A collection of Bell Punch, TIM and Ultimate tickets issued by Nottingham City Transport during the lifetime of the trolleybus system.

Ultimate

An experiment with Bell Punch "Ultimate" ticket machines, which basically offered an automated version of the manufacture's traditional pre-printed ticket system, started in March 1946, crews and management being impressed by their fast operation and the colour coding of tickets according to the value issued. It was decided to standardise on the Ultimate machine, replacing both the TIM and Bell Punch systems, once the manufacturing industry was back to normal.

In July 1947 the hire contract for those Bell Punch ticket punches still in use on the services not equipped with TIM ticket machines was replaced by one for 700 Bell Punch "Ultimate" ticket machines. They were progressively introduced on trolleybus services run from Bulwell and Trent Bridge Depots, each conductor or conductress being issued with a personal machine, referred to as the "Ultimate Punch". The changeover was completed by January 1949 and the TIM ticket machines were gradually withdrawn during 1949.

The Ultimate machines used in Nottingham accommodated five compartments each containing a separate fare denomination, pre-printed on to colour coded rolls of 1,000 numbered paper tickets 1¼ ins

A Mycalex and Tim ticket machine from the 1950's.

An Ultimate ticket machine of the type introduced in 1947.

Ticket colours and styles, continued

Title "NOTTINGHAM CITY TRANS."

Tickets were 1¼ins X 1¼ins, in size.

The following Ultimate ticket colours and denominations, limited to a maximum of 5 at any one time, were used on Nottingham's trolleybuses:

Colour	Denomination	Period	Comment
Yellow	½d		Original issues and late 1940s
Light Buff	1d		
Yellow	1d	1949 -	
White	1½d		Original issues and late 1940s
Green	2d		Original issues and late 1940s
Orange	2½d		Original issues and late 1940s
Purple	2½d		Mid to late 1950s
Pale blue	2½d		
Purple	3d		Original issues, late 1940s, early 1950s
Brick red	3d		Early 1950s
Lilac	3d	1957 -	
Blue	3½d	1952 – 10.01.53	
Brown	4d	29.10.52 -	
Lilac	4½d	11.01.53 -	
Blue	5d	19.10.52 -	
Green	6d		
Buff	7d	1964 -	
Yellow	9d	1964 -	

In order to make up additional fare values, double issues of the selected denomination were made in a defined combination. The combinations varied over the years due to fare increases and the number of compartments available on the Ultimate machine:

½d	single ½d ticket
1d	single 1d ticket
1½d	single 1½d ticket
2d	single 2d ticket (later two 1d tickets)
2½d	single 2½d ticket
3d	single 3d ticket
4d	single 4d ticket (later two 2d tickets)
5d	single 5d ticket (later two 2½d tickets)
6d	two 3d tickets
7d	single 7d ticket
8d	two 4d tickets
9d	two 4½d tickets
10d	two 5d tickets

The reason for a defined combination was purely statistical. A counter, known as a "numerator" and recording only the number of double length issues made, was fitted beneath each ticket compartments. As a double 4d ticket was only issued when an 8d fare was taken, the number of double 4d tickets issued represented the number of passengers travelling at that fare. The number of tickets shown on the "numerator" was also recorded on the conductor's waybill at the journey's outer terminus and at the city centre. In 1963 for example the "numerators" for the 2d and 3d ticket compartments recorded double issue 2d (fare value 4d) and double issue 3d (fare value 6d) tickets. The "numerator" beneath the right hand end ticket compartment, as worn by the conductor (in 1963, that beneath the 5d ticket compartment), recorded the total number of tickets sold (the "total numerator") and double issue tickets could not be issued from this compartment. This effectively meant that Nottingham's Ultimate machines could issue tickets to cover a maximum of nine different fares during any one period of time.

As a short term measure to use up obsolete ticket stocks following a fare revision and before new denominations were available, two tickets of different denominations e.g. a 4d and a 5d ticket to cover a 9d fare, were occasionally issued to cover one fare value. More than once NCT ordered ticket stocks for higher valued denominations in anticipation of an application for increased fares being granted in full only to find a partial revision approved.

The undertaking used around 160 million Ultimate tickets annually supplied at different periods by Bell Punch, London; Hunt, Nottingham; Hunt & Colleys Ltd., Nottingham, and Oller Ltd., London, who had submitted a lower tender.

square. The blank tickets were printed in black with three "fare type" boxes or squares originally headed "SINGLE" on the left, blank in the centre, and "RETURN" on the right at the base, sometimes with a herringbone background grid effect, and titled "NOTTINGHAM CITY TRANS.". Different printers omitted a heading above the central "fare type" box or replaced it with a series of dashes. Each new ticket roll had a piece of gummed tape to join it to the end of the old one thus avoiding the conductor having to change rolls mid-journey.

The number of the fare stage at which a passenger had boarded the vehicle was set by turning a knurled wheel on the right hand side of the Ultimate machine. Each ticket compartment had its own operating lever which, when depressed, printed the fare stage boarded number from 00 to 99 in one of three possible "fare type" squares, in purple ink across the base of the ticket. When the lever was released, the ticket was ejected, torn off against a serrated cutter by the conductor and given to the passenger as a receipt for the fare paid. The number of tickets of each value issued was recorded from the printed serial numbers on the ticket roll and visible through a transparent "window" on the top of the machine. When a black button below the operating lever was depressed in the same issuing operation a double length ticket of the required denomination was ejected, in which case the fare stage number was printed in the appropriate square of the first ticket only whilst a cancellation was made across the serial number of the second ticket. As before, the conductor continued to record the number of tickets of each denomination that had been issued and enter this on the waybill at the journey's outer terminus and at the city centre.

Notts & Derby

Trolleybuses of the Nottinghamshire and Derbyshire Traction Co. (N&D) on their Ripley service were permitted to pick up and set down passengers within the city boundaries, local passengers being carried within the city boundaries at applicable Corporation fares. These passengers were issued with NCT Bell Punch tickets, all revenues passing to the Corporation less 10½d per mile working expenses. Passengers travelling across or totally outside the city boundary were issued N&D tickets, all revenues being retained by the company. No other N&D services were permitted to carry local passengers within the boundaries of the city.

Appendix K Timetables and Public Information

Fare and Timetables

It appears that the undertaking did not publish its own timetables during the first thirty years of its existence and that only details of the first and last cars, together with service intervals, were shown in local directories e.g. Allans ABC. Throughout the trolleybus era public fare and timetables, in the form of small "pocket sized" (3½ x 4¾ins) booklets, were issued, except during the Second World War when none appeared and information about service changes was limited to announcements in the local newspapers and the issue of leaflets. A larger format (4½ x 5½ins) was introduced after the war (first issue July 1947). The early post-war booklets did not include fares and a separate faretable booklet was issued in 1949. Until 1954 the booklets were published quarterly and thereafter biannually. Prior to any timetable change detailed information was published in the local newspapers a few days beforehand and traffic notices, printed on brown paper about 4 ins deep and 3ft long, appeared on vehicles in the nearside lower deck window nearest to the platform.

Although NCT prepared the fare and schedule data contained in the booklets, they preferred to invite tenders from specialist publishers or advertising agents for their printing and production. The arrangements varied somewhat over the years but it was assumed that the publishers would produce the timetable booklet free of charge and that their costs would be recovered from the charges for advertisements also included in the booklet. The entire print run passed to the Department for sale to the travelling public and, post-war, for issuance to traffic staff.

These arrangements proved difficult to reintroduce after the War, the publishers arguing increasingly that it was unremunerative for them to produce the timetable and fares booklet free of charge, and receive no portion of the sales revenue. In 1951 it was necessary for the Department to make a contribution towards the printing costs although the publisher continued to benefit from the advertising revenues. From 1953 even this solution proved impossible and the Department took over the publication arrangements themselves (including advertisements which continued to appear throughout the trolleybus era). Thereafter the information within the booklets became noticeably more accurate, however as an economy the number of issues were reduced to twice annually, corresponding to the summer and winter timetables, from April 1954 and October 1954 respectively.

Until about 1938 the undertaking's timetables split cross-town services to appear as two separate services i.e. outer terminus to city, and city to the other outer terminus, although there was through running as evidenced by the fare tables.

The extract (below) from the April 1937 timetable shows how services 38 and 39 were advertised as "dividing" at the Elite Cinema on Upper Parliament Street whereas there were both short-workings to/from this nominal terminus or timing point, and through journeys. Note the references to "Last Workmen's" timings denoting the last journeys upon which reduced Workmen's Fares were available.

As in tramway days selected evening in-bound journeys on some routes were especially annotated in the timetables as "Postal Car" e.g. the 9.45 pm departure from Carlton to the City, 9.32 pm from Bulwell Market, 9.39 pm from Trent Bridge, 9.53 pm departure from Colwick Road, 9.49 pm departure from Vernon Road (April 1937 timetable); and enabled persons along the line of route to post small items to connect with the last mail to London. The special service operated only on Monday-Friday evenings and appears to have covered more routes as the 1930s progressed e.g. the 9.52 pm departure on service 39 from Fairham Drive. The destination display showed "POSTAL" in red lettering on the customary black blind and a red posting box was carried on the rear platform bulkhead adjacent to the used ticket box and collected by a postal worker at the stop closest to the GPO in Queen Street. There was no premium to pay for this service. The service came to an end with the outbreak of the Second World War and was never resumed.

The extract from the April 1937 timetable shows how services 42, 43 and 44 inter-worked 1935-1941 but also how they were advertised as "dividing" at Old Market Square and the Elite Cinema. Note the references to the "Postal Car" timings from Bulwell Market, Colwick Road and Trent Bridge, Monday to Friday.

Individual services were often grouped together within a single timetable e.g. the Arkwright Street group, the Nottingham Road group; which did little to aid clarity when travellers unfamiliar with the city were seeking the service number of a trolleybus to their chosen destination. Post-war this situation was corrected by showing the name of every street traversed by the service or group of services in each timetable, the introduction of an alphabetical list of places served

SERVICES
38 & 39

CARLTON and WOLLATON PARK.

Depart from CARLTON for ELITE.

Monday to Friday.
5.15 a.m. every 15 m. to 6.30 a.m.
6.30 a.m. ,, 5 ,, 7. 0 a.m.
7. 0 a.m. ,, 3 ,, 8.36 a.m.
8.36 a.m. ,, 4 ,, 9. 0 a.m.
9. 0 a.m. ,, 5 ,, 12.20 p.m.
12.20 p.m. ,, 4 ,, 2.20 p.m.
2.20 p.m. ,, 5 ,, 4.15 p.m.
4.15 p.m. ,, 3 ,, 7.42 p.m.
7.45 p.m. ,, 5 ,, 11.5 p.m.
and 11.15 p.m.
Last Workmen's Car 8.0 a.m.
Postal Car 9.45 p.m.

Saturday.
5.15 a.m. every 15 m. to 6.30 a.m.
6.30 a.m. ,, 5 ,, 7. 0 a.m.
7. 0 a.m. ,, 3 ,, 11. 9 p.m.
and 11.15 p.m.
Last Workmen's Car 8.0 a.m.

Sunday.
9. 0 a.m. every 6 m. to 2. 0 p.m.
2. 5 p.m. ,, 4 ,, 10.49 p.m.
and 11.1, 11.17 p.m.

Depart from CARLTON for WOLLATON PARK

Monday to Friday.
6.30 a.m. every 10 m. to 6.50 a.m.
6.55,
7. 0 a.m. every 3 m. to 8.36 a.m.
8.36 a.m. every 4 m. to 9. 0 a.m.
9. 5 a.m. every 5 m. to 12.20 p.m.
12.24 p.m. every 4 m. to 2.20 p.m.
2.25 p.m. every 5 m. to 4.15 p.m.
4.18 p.m. every 3 m. to 7. 0 p.m.
7. 5 p.m. every 5 m. to 11. 0 p.m.
and 11.15 p.m.
Last Workmen's 8.0 a.m.

Saturday.
6.30 a.m. every 10 m. to 6.50 a.m.
6.55,
7. 0 a.m. every 3 m. to 10.54 p.m.
and 11. 0 p.m. and 11.15 p.m.
Last Workmen's 8.0 a.m.

Sunday
9. 0 a.m. every 6 m. to 2. 0 p.m.
2. 4 p.m. every 4 m. to 10.52 p.m.
and 11.0 p.m., 11.16 p.m.

Depart from ELITE for WOLLATON PARK

Monday to Friday.
6.15 a.m. every 10 m. to 6.45 a.m.
6.50, 6.55, 7.5, 7.10 a.m.
7.15 a.m. every 3 m. to 8.51 a.m.
8.55 a.m. every 4 m. to 9.15 a.m.
9.20 a.m. every 5 m. to 12.35 p.m.
12.39 p.m. every 4 m. to 2.35 p.m.
2.40 p.m. every 5 m. to 4.30 p.m.
4.33 p.m. every 3 m. to 7.15 p.m.
7.20 p.m. every 5 m. to 11.15 p.m.
and 11.30 p.m.
Last Workmen's 8.15 a.m.

Saturday.
6.25 a.m. every 10 m. to 7. 5 a.m.
7.10 a.m.
7.15 a.m. every 3 m. to 11.9 p.m.
and 11.15 p.m., 11.30 p.m.
Last Workmen's 8.15 a.m.

Sunday
8.33 a.m., 8.46, 8.52, 8.58, 9.4,
9. 9 a.m.
9.15 a.m. every 6 m. to 2.15 p.m.
2.19 p.m. every 4 m. to 11.7 p.m.
and 11.15 p.m. 11.31 p.m.

67

SERVICES
38& 39

CARLTON and WOLLATON PARK.

Depart from WOLLATON PARK for CARLTON

Monday to Friday.
6.31 a.m. every 10 m. to 7.21 a.m.
7.26, 7.31 a.m.
7.34 a.m. every 3 m. to 9. 7 a.m.
(8.22, 8.25, 8.34, 8.40, 8.49, 8.55,
9.4, 9.14 a.m., to Depot only)
9. 7 a.m. every 4 m. to 9.27 a.m.
9.27 a.m. every 5 m. to 12.57 p.m.
1. 0 p.m. every 4 m. to 2.52 p.m.
(2.0, 2.16, 2.36 p.m. to Depot only).
2.57 p.m. every 5 m. to 4.47 p.m.
4.50 p.m. every 3 m. to 7.32 p.m.
(7.17 7.29 p.m. to Depot only)
7.37 p.m. every 5 m. to 10.52 p.m.
11.2 p.m. and 11.17 p.m.
(10.57, 11.7, 11.12, 11.22, 11.27,
11.32, 11.47 p.m. to Depot only)
Last Workmen's 8.1 a.m.

Saturday.
6.42 a.m., 6.52, 7.1, 7.11, 7.21
7.26 a.m.
7.31 a.m. every 3 m. to 10.53 p.m.
11. 2 p.m., 11.14 p.m., 11.17 p.m.
(10.56, 10.59, 11. 5, 11.8, 11.11,
11.20, 11.23, 11.26, 11.32, 11.47
p.m. to Depot only)
Last Workmen's 8.1 a.m.

Sunday
8.50 a.m., 9.3, 9.9, 9.15, 9.21
a.m.
9.26 a.m. every 6 m. to 2.32 p.m.
2.36 p.m. every 4 m. to 10.52 p.m.
11.0, 11.4, 11.16 and 11.20 p.m.
(10.56, 11.8, 11.12, 11.24, 11.32
11.48 p.m. to Depot only).

Depart from ELITE to CARLTON.

Monday to Friday.
4.55 a.m. every 15 m. to 6.10 a.m.
6.10 a.m. ,, 5 ,, 6.40 a.m.
6.44 a.m. ,, 3 ,, 8.17 a.m.
8.17 a.m. ,, 4 ,, 8.40 a.m.
8.40 a.m. ,, 5 ,, 12 noon
12. 0 noon,, 4 ,, 2. 0 p.m.
2. 0 p.m. ,, 5 ,, 3.55 p.m.
3.59 p.m. ,, 3 ,, 7.23 p.m.
7.25 p.m. ,, 5 ,, 11. 5 p.m.
and 11.15, 11.30 p.m.
Last Workmen's Car 8.15 a.m.

Saturday.
4.55 a.m. every 15 m to 6.10 a.m.
6.10 a.m. ,, 5 ,, 6.44 a.m.
6 44 a.m. ,, 3 ,, 11. 0 p.m.
and 11.15, 11.30 p.m.
Last Workmen's Car 8.15 a.m.

Sunday.
8.40 a.m. every 6 m. to 1.40 p.m.
1.45 p.m. ,, 4 ,, 11. 0 p.m.
and 11.15, 11.30 p.m.

68

Trolleybus route Nos. 38 and 39 timetable (APRIL 1937).

SERVICES
42, 43, 44 Bulwell Hall Estate, Bulwell Market, Trent Bridge and Colwick.

STAGES.	Mon.to Fri. 1st Car	Mon.to Fri. Last Car	Saturday. 1st Car	Saturday. Last Car	Sunday. 1st Car	Sunday. Last Car
	am	pm	am	pm	am	pm
Bulwell Hall Estate to Old Market Sq.	6 9	10 54	6 9	11 16	9 6	11 24
Bulwell Market to Old Market Square	5 0	11 28	5 0	11 38	9 0	11 33
Old Market Square to Trent Bridge	5 20	11 50	5 20	12 1	9 23	11 40
Trent Bridge to Old Market Square	5 30	11 23	5 30	11 23	8 30	11 20
Old Market Square to Bulwell Market	4 45	11 32	4 45	11 32	9 23	11 38
Old Market Sq. to Bulwell Hall Estate	5 25	11 8	5 25	11 8	9 23	11 17

Depart from BULWELL HALL ESTATE to OLD MARKET SQ.

Monday to Friday.
4.54, 5.54, 6.9 a.m., 6.24, 6.39,
6.54 a.m. every 8 m. to 8.54 a.m.
8.54 a.m. „ 12 „ 12.54 p.m.
12.54 p.m. „ 9 „ 2. 6 p.m.
2. 6 p.m. „ 12 „ 4. 6 p.m.
4. 6 p.m. „ 8 „ 6.54 p.m.
6.54 p.m. „ 12 „ 10.54 p.m.
Last Workmen's Car 7.58 a.m.

Saturday.
4.54, 5.54, 6.9, 6.39 a.m.,
6.54 a.m. every 8 m. to 8.54 a.m.
8.54 a.m. „ 9 „ 10.42 a.m.
10.52 a.m. „ 8 „ 11.16 p.m.
Last Workmen's Car 7.58 a.m.

Sunday.
9. 6 a.m. every 12 m. to 2.06 p.m. 2.15 p.m. every 9 m. to 10.57 p.m. 11.15, 11.24 p.m.

Depart from BULWELL MARKET.

Monday to Friday.
5. 0 a.m. every 15 m. to 6.15 a.m.
6.15 a.m. „ 5 „ 7. 0 a.m.
7. 0 a.m. „ 2 „ 8.56 a.m.
8.56 a.m. „ 4 „ 11.36 a.m.
1.36 a.m. „ 3 „ 3.36 p.m.
3.36 p.m. „ 2 „ 6.56 p.m.
6.56 p.m. „ 4 „ 11. 0 p.m.
and 11.8, 11.28 p.m.
Last Workmen's Car 8.2 a.m.
Postal Car 9.32 p.m.

Saturday.
5. 0 a.m. every 15 m. to 6.15 a.m.
6.15 a.m. „ 5 „ 7. 0 a.m.
7. 0 a.m. „ 2 „ 9. 0 a.m.
9. 0 a.m. „ 3 „ 10.54 a.m.
10.54 a.m. „ 2 „ 10.56 p.m.
11.4, 11.6, 11.10, 11.12, 11.14,
and 11.38 p.m.
Last Workmen's Car 8.2 a.m.

Sunday.
9. 0 a.m. every 4 m. to 2. 0 p.m. then every 3 m. to 11.9, 11.21, 11.30, 11.33

73

SERVICES
42 & 43 OLD MARKET SQUARE and TRENT BRIDGE.

Depart from OLD MARKET SQ. for TRENT BRIDGE.

Monday to Friday.
5.19, 5.22 a.m.
5.37 a.m. every 15 m. to 6.07 a.m.
6.24, 6.30, 6.42 6.52, 6.59 a.m.
7.07 7.12 a.m.
7.19 a.m. every 2 and 4 m to 9.10 a.m.
9.18 a.m. „ 8 „ 11.58 a.m.
12.04 p.m. „ 6 „ 3.58 p.m.
4.02 p.m. „ 2 4 „ 7.14 p.m.
7.19, 7.26 „ 8 „ 11.26 p.m.
11.37, 11.40, 11.46, 11.58 and 12.00

Saturday.
5.20 a.m.
5.23 a.m. every 15 m. to 6.44 a.m.
6.47 a.m. „ 10 „ 7.27 a.m.
7.27 a.m. „ 2 4 „ 9.23 a.m.
9.23 a.m. „ 6 „ 11.17 a.m.
11.17 a.m. „ 2 4 „ 11.23 p.m.
11.28, 11.31, 11.33, 11.36, 12.00 mdt.

Sunday.
8.40, 9.0, 9.22 a.m. and every 8 m. to 2.18 p.m.
2.25 „ 6 „ 11.25 p.m.
11.40, 11.43, 11.48, 11.50, 11.52 and 12 midn't

Depart from TRENT BRIDGE for OLD MARKET SQUARE.

Monday to Friday.
5.30, 5.35 a.m.
5.50 a.m. every 5 and 10 m. to 7.0 a.m.
7.06 7.08,
7.11 a.m. „ 6 „ 7.29 a.m.
7.33 a.m. „ 2 4 „ 8.59 a.m.
9.03
9.09 a.m. „ 8 „ 12.11 p.m.
12.18 p.m. „ 6 „ 3.48 p.m.
3.53
3.58 p.m. „ 2 4 „ 7.18 p.m.
7.23 p.m. „ 8 „ 11.23 p.m.
Postal Bus 9.39 p.m.

Saturday.
5.30 5.35 a.m.,
5.50 a.m. every 10 m. to 7. 5 a.m.
7.33 a.m. „ 2 4 „ 9.29 a.m.
9.29 a.m. „ 6 „ 11.17 a.m.
11.17a.m. „ 2 4 „ 11.23 a.m.

Sunday.
8.30, 8.50, 9. 0 a.m. every 8 m to 2.18 p.m.
2.25 p.m „ 6 „ 11.25

74

Trolleybus route Nos. 42, 43 and 44 timetable (APRIL 1937).

SERVICES
42 & 43 BULWELL HALL ESTATE, BULWELL MARKET and TRENT BRIDGE.

Depart from OLD MARKET SQUARE for BULWELL MARKET.

Monday to Friday.
4.45, 5.25, 5.37, 5.44 a.m.
5.59 a.m. every 5 m. to 7.14 a.m.
7.14 a.m. „ 3 „ 7.33 a.m.
7.33 a.m. „ 2 „ 9. 5 a.m.
9. 5 a.m. „ 4 „ 12.11 p.m.
12.11 p.m. „ 3 „ 4.14 p.m
4.14 p.m „ 2 „ 7.36 p.m.
7.36 p.m. „ 4 „ 11.32 p.m.

Saturday.
4.45 5.25, 5.37, 5.44 a.m.
5.59 a.m. every 5. m. to 7.14 a.m.
7.14 a.m. „ 3 „ 7.42 a.m.
7.42 a.m. „ 2 „ 9.42 a.m.
9.42 a.m. „ 3 „ 11.38 a.m.
11.38 a.m. „ 2 „ 11.32 p.m.

Sunday.
9.23 a.m. every 4 m. to 2.35 p.m. then every 3 m. to 11.38 p.m.

Depart from OLD MARKET SQUARE for BULWELL HALL ESTATE.

Monday to Friday.
5.25, 6.4, 6.19, 6.29, 6.44, 6.54, 7.9,
7.17, 7.23, 7.33 7.42 and 7.48 a.m.
7.48 a.m. every 8 m. to 8.20 a.m.
8.20 a.m. „ 12 „ 12.20 p.m.
12.20 p.m. „ 9 „ 1.32 p.m.
1.32 p.m „ 12 „ 3 32 p.m.
3.41 p.m. „ 8 „ 6.20 p.m.
6.32 p.m. „ 12 „ 11.8 p.m.

Saturday.
5.25, 6.4, 6.19, 6.29, 6.44, 6.54 and
7.9 a.m., 7.17, 7.23, 7.33, 7.42, 7.48
7.48 a.m. every 8 m. to 9.28 a.m.
9.28 a.m. „ 9 „ 11.14 a.m.
11.14 a.m. „ 8 „ 11. 8 p.m.

Sunday.
9.23 a.m. every 12 m. to 2.19 p.m. 2.27 p.m. every 9 m. to 11.17 p.m.

75

SERVICES
44,43,42 Old Market Square and Colwick Road Colwick Road and Bulwell Hall Estate. Colwick Road and Bulwell Market.

Depart from ELITE for COLWICK ROAD.

Monday to Friday.
5.45 a.m., 5.57, 6.22, 6.37 a.m.
6.52 a.m. every 6 m. to 8.58 a.m.
9. 6 a.m. „ 8 „ 11.54 a.m.
12. 1 p.m. „ 6 „ 7.22 p.m.
7.30 p.m. „ 8 „ 11. 6 p.m.
and 11.15, 11.30 p.m.

Saturday.
5 45 a.m., 5.57, 6.22, 6.37 a.m.
6.52 a.m. every 6 m. to 11.30 p.m.

Sunday.
8.54, 9.10 a.m. every 8 m. to 2.22 p.m. then every 6 m. to 11.16, 11.30 p.m.

Depart from COLWICK ROAD for OLD MARKET SQUARE.

Monday to Friday.
6.0 a.m., 6.11,
6.30 a.m. every 10 m. to 7. 0 a.m.
7. 7 a.m. „ 6 „ 9. 7 a.m.
9.14 a.m. „ 8 „ 12.10 p.m.
12.16 p.m. „ 6 „ 7.22 p.m.
7.30 p.m. „ 8 „ 11.13 p.m.
and 11.21, 11.30, 11.42 p.m.
Postal Bus 9.53 pm

Saturday
6.0 a.m., 6.11,
6.31 a.m. every 10 m. to 7. 1 a.m.
7. 7 a.m. „ 6 „ 8.55 p.m.
9. 3 a.m. „ 6 „ 11.15 p.m.
11.18, 11.30, 11.45 p.m.

Sunday.
9.11 a.m. every 8 m. to 2.46 p.m. 2.52 p.m. every 6 m. to 11.22 p.m. 11.34, 11.44 p.m.

76

Trolleybus route Nos. 42, 43 and 44 timetable (part2) (APRIL 1937).

accompanied by the relevant service numbers and by the inclusion of a diagrammatic map of the network. Additionally, the heading of each post-war fare and timetable clearly indicated whether it was a motorbus or trolleybus service.

The next extract, taken from the October 1950 issue, shows an example of how services following more or less the same route were grouped together into a single timetable. Service 41, then operating Queen Street/King Street – Cinderhill, Bells Lane and following the route of the services advertised was however shown separately in the timetable booklet.

Supplementary timetable leaflets were issued for every Bank Holiday and special events detailing the amended traffic arrangements on each day within the

TROLLEYBUS ROUTE Nos. 36, 37 and 48

Combined Service

(These services operate in conjunction with the Notts. & Derbys. Traction Co., A1 Service between King Street and the junction of Valley Road and Nottingham Road).

TROLLEYBUS ROUTE No. 36

King Street and Vernon Road Junction

TROLLEYBUS ROUTE No. 37

King Street and Haydn Road

TROLLEYBUS ROUTE No. 48

Trent Bridge, King Street and Vernon Road Junction

Via Arkwright Street, Carrington Street, Lister Gate, Albert Street, Wheeler Gate, Long Row, Queen Street, Parliament Street, Milton Street, Mansfield Road to Gregory Boulevard, then via Sherwood Rise, Nottingham Road to Vernon Road Junction. Returning via same route except King Street instead of Queen Street.

SUNDAY

	a.m.	a.m.	a.m.	a.m.	a.m.	a.m.	a.m.	a.m.		p.m.	p.m.	p.m.	p.m.	p.m.
Trent Bridge ...	—	—	—	—	9.12	9.27	—	9.42	every 15 mins. to	12.27	—	—	12.42	—
King Street ...	7.00	7.40	8.30	9.17	9.27	9.37	9.45	9.52	,, 7½ ,, ,,	12.37	12.45	12.50	12.55	1.00
Haydn Road ...	7.10	7.50	8.40	9.27	9.37	9.47	9.55	10.02	,, 7½ ,, ,,	12.47	12.55	1.00	1.05	1.10
Valley Road ...	7.12	7.52	8.42	9.29	9.39	9.49	9.57	10.04	,, 7½ ,, ,,	12.49	12.57	1.02	1.07	1.12
Vernon Road ...	7.13	7.53	8.43	9.30	9.40	9.50	9.58	10.05	,, 15/7½ ,, ,,	12.50	12.58	1.03	1.08	—

	p.m.		p.m.		p.m.	p.m.	p.m.
Trent Bridge ...	12.55	every 15 mins. to	8.55	every 15 mins. to	10.40	—	—
King Street ...	1.05	,, 5 ,, ,,	9.05	,, 7½ ,, ,,	10.50	10.57	11.05
Haydn Road ...	1.15	,, 5 ,, ,,	9.15	,, 7½ ,, ,,	11.00	11.07	11.15
Valley Road ...	1.17	,, 5 ,, ,,	9.17	,, 7½ ,, ,,	11.02	11.09	11.17
Vernon Road ...	1.18	,, 5/10 ,, ,,	9.18	,, 7½ ,, ,,	11.03	11.10	11.18

	a.m.	a.m.	a.m.	a.m.		p.m.	p.m.	p.m.		p.m.
Vernon Road ...	7.24	8.01	8.50	9.36	every 15/7½ mins. to	12.36	—	12.49	every 5/10 mins. to	8.49
Valley Road ...	7.25	8.02	8.51	9.37	,, 7½ ,, ,,	12.37	12.45	12.50	,, 5 ,, ,,	8.50
Haydn Road ...	7.27	8.04	8.53	9.39	,, 7½ ,, ,,	12.39	12.47	12.52	,, 5 ,, ,,	8.52
King Street ...	7.37	8.14	9.03	9.49	,, 7½ ,, ,,	12.49	12.57	1.02	,, 5 ,, ,,	9.02
Processional Walk	—	—	—	9.50	,, 15 ,, ,,	12.50	—	1.03	,, 15 ,, ,,	9.03
Trent Bridge ...	—	—	—	10.00	,, 15 ,, ,,	1.00	—	1.13	,, 15 ,, ,,	9.13

		p.m.		p.m.
Vernon Road ...	every 7½ mins. to	10.34	every 7½ mins. to	11.26
Valley Road ...	,, 7½ ,, ,,	10.35	,, 7½ ,, ,,	11.27
Haydn Road ...	,, 7½ ,, ,,	10.37	,, 7½ ,, ,,	11.29
King Street ...	,, 7½ ,, ,,	10.47	,, 7½ ,, ,,	11.39
Processional Walk	,, 15 ,, ,,	10.48	—	—
Trent Bridge ...	,, 15 ,, ,,	10.58	—	—

TROLLEYBUS ROUTE Nos. 36, 37 & 48 (Continued)

MONDAY TO FRIDAY

	a.m.	a.m.		a.m.	a.m.	a.m.		a.m.	a.m.	a.m.	a.m.	a.m.
Trent Bridge ...	—	—	—	—	—	7.07	every 10 mins. to	8.37	—	—	—	8.55
King Street ...	5.50	6.00	every 5 mins. to	7.10	7.12	7.17	,, 2½ ,, ,,	8.47	8.50	8.55	9.00	9.05
Haydn Road ...	6.00	6.10	,, 5 ,, ,,	7.20	7.22	7.27	,, 2½ ,, ,,	8 57	9.00	9.05	9.10	9.15
Valley Road ...	6.02	6.12	,, 5 ,, ,,	7.22	7.24	7.29	,, 5 ,, ,,	8.59	9.02	9.07	9.12	9.17
Vernon Road ...	—	6.13	,, 10/5 ,, ,,	7.23	7.25	7.30	,, 5 ,, ,,	9.00	—	9.08	—	9.18

		noon	p.m.	p.m.	p.m.		p.m.	p.m.	p.m.	p.m.
Trent Bridge ...	every 15 mins. to	11.55	—	—	12.07	every 10 mins. to	1.57	—	—	2.09
King Street ...	,, 5 ,, ,,	12.05	12.10	12.15	12.17	,, 2½ ,, ,,	2.07	2.11	2.15	2.19
Haydn Road ...	,, 5 ,, ,,	12.15	12.20	12.25	12.27	,, 2½ ,, ,,	2.17	2.21	2.25	2.29
Valley Road ...	,, 5 ,, ,,	12.17	12.22	12.27	12.29	,, 5 ,, ,,	2.19	2.23	2.27	2.31
Vernon Road ...	,, 5/10 ,, ,,	12.18	12.23	—	12.30	,, 5 ,, ,,	2.20	2.24	—	2.32

		p.m.	p.m.	p.m.	p.m.	p.m.	p.m.	p.m.	p.m.	p.m.	p.m.	p.m.	p.m.	p.m.	p.m.	p.m.
Trent Bridge ...	every 15 mins. to	3.23	—	—	—	—	3.38	—	—	3.48	—	—	3.58	—	—	4.07
King Street ...	,, 3¾ ,, ,,	3.33	3.36	3.39	3.42	3.45	3.48	3.52	3.55	3.58	4.02	4.05	4.08	4.12	4.15	4.17
Haydn Road ...	,, 3¾ ,, ,,	3.43	3.46	3.49	3.52	3.55	3.58	4.02	4.05	4.08	4.12	4.15	4.18	4.22	4.25	4.27
Valley Road ...	,, 7½ ,, ,,	3.45	3.48	3.51	3.54	3.57	4.00	4.04	4.07	4.09	4.14	4.17	4.20	4.24	4.27	4.29
Vernon Road ...	,, 7½ ,, ,,	3.46	3.49	3.52	3.55	—	4.01	4.05	—	4.11	4.15	—	4.21	4.25	—	4.30

		p.m.	p.m.	p.m.	p.m.	p.m.		p.m.		p.m.	p.m.
Trent Bridge ...	every 10 mins. to	6.27	—	—	—	6.40	every 15 mins. to	9.55	every 15 mins. to	10.40	—
King Street ...	,, 2½ ,, ,,	6.37	6.40	6.42	6.45	6.50	,, 5 ,, ,,	10.05	,, 5/10 ,, ,,	10.50	11.00
Haydn Road ...	,, 2½ ,, ,,	6.47	6.50	6.52	6.55	7.00	,, 5 ,, ,,	10.15	,, 5/10 ,, ,,	11.00	11.10
Valley Road ...	,, 5 ,, ,,	6.49	6.51	6.54	6.57	7.02	,, 5 ,, ,,	10.17	,, 5/10 ,, ,,	11.02	11.12
Vernon Road ...	,, 5 ,, ,,	6.50	6.52	6.55	—	7.03	,, 5/10 ,, ,,	10.18	,, 5/10 ,, ,,	11.03	11.13

	a.m.	a.m.	a.m.	a.m.	a.m.		a.m.	a.m.	a.m.	a.m.	a.m.	a.m.	a.m.
Vernon Road ...	—	—	—	—	6.29	every 10/5 mins. to	6.59	—	7.08	7.11	—	7.18	7.21
Valley Road ...	5.35	5.50	6.05	6.20	6.30	,, 5 ,, ,,	7.00	7.05	7.09	7.12	7.15	7.19	7.22
Haydn Road ...	5.37	5.52	6.07	6.22	6.32	,, 5 ,, ,,	7.02	7.07	7.11	7.14	7.17	7.21	7.24
King Street ...	5.47	6.02	6.17	6.32	6.42	,, 5 ,, ,,	7.12	7.17	7.21	7.24	7.27	7.31	7.34
Processional Walk	—	—	—	—	—	—	—	—	—	7.25	—	—	7.35
Trent Bridge ...	—	—	—	—	—	—	—	—	—	7.35	—	—	7.45

		a.m.	a.m.	a.m.	a.m.	a.m.	a.m.	a.m.	a.m.		p.m.	p.m.
Vernon Road ...	every 5 mins. to	8.51	8.56	—	9.01	9.06	9.11	—	9.19	every 5/10 mins. to	12.19	12.24
Valley Road ...	,, 3/2/5 ,, ,,	8.52	8.57	9.00	9.02	9.07	9.12	9.15	9.20	,, 5 ,, ,,	12.20	12.25
Haydn Road ...	,, 2½ ,, ,,	8.54	8.59	9.02	9.04	9.09	9.14	9.17	9.22	,, 5 ,, ,,	12.22	12.27
King Street ...	,, 2½ ,, ,,	9.04	9.09	9.12	9.14	9.19	9.24	9.27	9.32	,, 5 ,, ,,	12.32	12.37
Processional Walk	,, 10 ,, ,,	9.05	—	—	—	9.20	—	—	9.33	,, 15 ,, ,,	12.33	—
Trent Bridge ...	,, 10 ,, ,,	9.15	—	—	—	9.30	—	—	9.43	,, 15 ,, ,,	12.43	—

TROLLEYBUS ROUTE Nos. 36, 37 & 48 (Continued)

MONDAY TO FRIDAY (Continued)

	p.m.	p.m.		p.m.	p.m.	p.m.	p.m.	p.m.	p.m.	p.m.	p.m.	
Vernon Road ...	—	12.31	every 5 mins. to	2.11	—	2.16	—	2.22	2.26	—	2.33	every 7½ mins. to
Valley Road ...	12.30	12.32	,, 3/2/5 ,, ,,	2.12	2.15	2.17	—	2.23	2.27	2.30	2.34	,, 7½ ,, ,,
Haydn Road ...	12.32	12.34	,, 2½ ,, ,,	2.14	2.17	2.19	2.22	2.25	2.29	2.32	2.36	,, 3¾ ,, ,,
King Street ...	12.42	12.44	,, 2½ ,, ,,	2.24	2.27	2.29	2.32	2.35	2.39	2.42	2.46	,, 3¾ ,, ,,
Processional Walk	—	12.45	,, 10 ,, ,,	2.25	—	—	—	2.36	—	—	2.47	,, 15 ,, ,,
Trent Bridge ...	—	12.55	,, 10 ,, ,,	2.35	—	—	—	2.46	—	—	2.57	,, 15 ,, ,,

	p.m.	p.m.	p.m.	p.m.		p.m.	p.m.	p.m.	p.m.	p.m.	p.m.	p.m.	p.m.
Vernon Road ...	3.32	—	—	3.42	every 4/6 mins. to	4.12	4.16	—	4.21	4.24	4.26	—	4.31
Valley Road ...	3.33	—	3.40	3.43	,, 4/3/3 ,, ,,	4.13	4.17	4.20	4.22	4.25	4.27	4.30	4.32
Haydn Road ...	3.35	3.39	3.42	3.45	,, 4 /3/3 ,, ,,	4.15	4.19	4.22	4.24	4.27	4.29	4.32	4.34
King Street ...	3.45	3.49	3.52	3.55	,, 4/3/3 ,, ,,	4.25	4.29	4.32	4.34	4.37	4.39	4.42	4.44
Processional Walk	3.46	—	—	3.56	,, 10 ,, ,,	4.26	—	—	4.35	—	—	—	4.45
Trent Bridge ...	3.56	—	—	4.06	,, 10 ,, ,,	4.36	—	—	4.45	—	—	—	4.55

		p.m.	p.m.	p.m.	p.m.	p.m.	p.m.	p.m.	p.m.	p.m.	p.m.	p.m.	p.m.	p.m.
Vernon Road ...	every 5 mins. to	6.31	—	6.37	6.41	—	6.46	6.49	6.52	6.56	—	7.02	7.06	7.09
Valley Road ...	,, 5/3/2 ,, ,,	6.32	—	6.38	6.42	6.45	6.47	6.50	6.53	6.57	7.00	7.03	7.07	7.10
Haydn Road ...	,, 2½ ,, ,,	6.34	6.37	6.40	6.44	6.47	6.49	6.52	6.55	6.59	7.02	7.05	7.09	7.12
King Street ...	,, 2½ ,, ,,	6.44	6.47	6.50	6.54	6.57	6.59	7.02	7.05	7.09	7.12	7.15	7.19	7.22
Processional Walk	,, 10 ,, ,,	6.45	—	—	6.55	—	—	—	7.06	—	—	—	7.20	—
Trent Bridge ...	,, 10 ,, ,,	6.55	—	—	7.05	—	—	—	7.16	—	—	—	7.30	—

	p.m.	p.m.		p.m.		p.m.		p.m.
Vernon Road ...	—	7.19	every 5/10 mins. to	9.49	every 5/10 mins. to	10.34	every 5/10 mins. to	11.19
Valley Road ...	7.15	7.20	,, 5 ,, ,,	9.50	,, 5/10 ,, ,,	10.35	,, 5/10 ,, ,,	11.20
Haydn Road ...	7.17	7.22	,, 5 ,, ,,	9.52	,, 5/10 ,, ,,	10.37	,, 5/10 ,, ,,	11.22
King Street ...	7.27	7.32	,, 5 ,, ,,	10.02	,, 5/10 ,, ,,	10.47	,, 5/10 ,, ,,	11.32
Processional Walk	—	7.33	,, 15 ,, ,,	10.03	,, 15 ,, ,,	10.48	—	—
Trent Bridge ...	—	7.43	,, 15 ,, ,,	10.13	,, 15 ,, ,,	10.58	—	—

SATURDAY

	a.m.	a.m.		a.m.	a.m.	a.m.		a.m.	a.m.	a.m.	a.m.	a.m.
Trent Bridge ...	—	—		—	—	7.07	every 10 mins. to	8.47	—	—	—	—
King Street ...	5.50	6.00	every 5 mins. to	7.10	7.12	7.17	,, 2½ ,, ,,	8.57	9.00	9.04	9.08	9.10
Haydn Road ...	6.00	6.10	,, 5 ,, ,,	7.20	7.22	7.27	,, 2½ ,, ,,	9.07	9.10	9.14	9.18	9.20
Valley Road ...	6.02	6.12	,, 5 ,, ,,	7.22	7.24	7.29	,, 5 ,, ,,	9.09	9.12	9.16	—	—
Vernon Road ...	—	6.13	,, 10/5 ,, ,,	7.23	7.25	7.30	,, 5 ,, ,,	9.10	—	9.17	—	—

	a.m.		p.m.		p.m.		p.m.	p.m.
Trent Bridge ...	9.02	every 15 mins. to	12.17	every 10 mins. to	9.57	every 10 mins. to	10.47	—
King Street ...	9.12	,, 3¾ ,, ,,	12.27	,, 2½ ,, ,,	10.07	,, 3/2/5 ,, ,,	10.57	11.00
Haydn Road ...	9.22	,, 3¾ ,, ,,	12.37	,, 2½ ,, ,,	10.17	,, 3/2/5 ,, ,,	11.07	11.10
Valley Road ...	9.24	,, 7½/4 ,, ,,	12.39	,, 5 ,, ,,	10.19	,, 5 ,, ,,	11.09	11.12
Vernon Road ...	9.25	,, 7½ ,, ,,	12.40	,, 5 ,, ,,	10.20	,, 5 ,, ,,	11.10	11.13

TROLLEYBUS ROUTE Nos. 36, 37 & 48 (Continued)

SATURDAY (Continued)

	a.m.	a.m.	a.m.	a.m.	a.m.		a.m.	a.m.	a.m.	a.m.	a.m.	a.m.	a.m.
Vernon Road ...	—	—	—	—	6.29	every 10/5 mins. to	6.59	—	7.08	7.11	—	7.18	7.21
Valley Road ...	5.35	5.50	6.05	6.20	6.30	,, 5 ,, ,,	7.00	7.05	7.09	7.12	7.15	7.19	7.22
Haydn Road ...	5.37	5.52	6.07	6.22	6.32	,, 5 ,, ,,	7.02	7.07	7.11	7.14	7.17	7.21	7.24
King Street ...	5.47	6.02	6.17	6.32	6.42	,, 5 ,, ,,	7.12	7.17	7.21	7.24	7.27	7.31	7.34
Processional Walk	—	—	—	—	—	—	—	—	—	7.25	—	—	7.35
Trent Bridge ...	—	—	—	—	—	—	—	—	—	7.35	—	—	7.45

		a.m.	a.m.	a.m.	a.m.	a.m	a.m.		a.m.	a.m.	noon	noon
Vernon Road ...	every 5 mins. to	8.41	—	8.46	—	8.51	8.56	every 7½ mins. to	11.41	—	11.46	—
Valley Road ...	,, 3/2/5 ,, ,,	8.42	8.45	8.47	—	8.52	8.57	,, 7½/4 ,, ,,	11.42	—	11.47	11.50
Haydn Road ...	,, 2½ ,, ,,	8.44	8.47	8.49	8.52	8.54	8.59	,, 3¾ ,, ,,	11.44	11.47	11.49	11.52
King Street ...	,, 2½ ,, ,,	8.54	8.57	8.59	9.02	9.04	9.09	,, 3¾ ,, ,,	11.54	11.57	11.59	12.02
Processional Walk	,, 10 ,, ,,	8.55	—	—	—	—	9.10	,, 15 ,, ,,	11.55	—	—	—
Trent Bridge ...	,, 10 ,, ,,	9.05	—	—	—	—	9.20	,, 15 ,, ,,	12.05	—	—	—

	noon	noon	noon	p.m.		p.m.		p.m.		p.m.	p.m.
Vernon Road ...	11.53	—	—	12.01	every 5 mins. to	9.51	every 5 mins. to	10.41	every 5 mins. to	11.16	11.19
Valley Road ...	11.54	—	12.00	12.02	,, 5/3/2,, ,,	9.52	,, 5 ,, ,,	10.42	,, 5 ,, ,,	11.17	11.20
Haydn Road ...	11.56	11.59	12.02	12.04	,, 2½ ,, ,,	9.54	,,3/2/5 ,, ,,	10.44	,,3/2/5 ,, ,,	11.19	11.22
King Street ...	12.06	12.09	12.12	12.14	,, 2½ ,, ,,	10.04	,,3/2/5 ,,	10.54	,,3/2/5 ,, ,,	11.29	11.32
Processional Walk	12.07	—	—	12.15	,, 10 ,, ,,	10.05	,, 10 ,, ,,	10.55	—	—	—
Trent Bridge ...	12.17	—	—	12.25	,, 10 ,, ,,	10.15	,, 10 ,, ,,	11.05	—	—	—

LAST WORKMEN'S TROLLEYBUSES—MONDAY TO FRIDAY. SATURDAY.

	Monday to Friday		Saturday
King Street to Vernon Road ...	8.47 a.m.	...	8.47 a.m.
Vernon Road to King Street ...	8.46 a.m.	...	8.46 a.m.
Vernon Road to Trent Bridge ...	8.31 a.m.	...	8.31 a.m.
Trent Bridge to Vernon Road ...	8.37 a.m.	...	8.37 a.m.
Trent Bridge to Old Market Square ...	8.37 a.m.	...	8.47 a.m.

HELP THE CONDUCTOR PLEASE TENDER EXACT FARE

period of application. These supplementary timetables also specifically identified arrangements for trolleybus services.

During the 1950s and 1960s the Department also produced an illustrated "handy guide for visitors" entitled "By Bus in Nottingham" including an alphabetical index of places of interest, public buildings, suburbs, etc., details of how to reach them, a complete list of all services and a route map.

It is noteworthy that many of the peak hour frequencies were retained throughout the life of the system. In April 1941 for instance service 39 benefited from a Monday to Friday peak frequency of every three minutes; in April 1962 there was still a three-minute service upon which the 38's peak hour frequency of every six minutes was superimposed. Also in April 1962 there was a two/three minute peak frequency from Wells Road, Ransom Road on the combined 40/47 service, which was even better than the three-minute frequency of December 1944. In August 1954 service 43's two-minute peak headway between Trent Bridge and Bulwell Market was reduced to an alternate two/three minute headway which remained in place until after the abandonment of trolleybus operation however the addition of curtailed service 42 still ensured a combined two minute frequency between the Old Market Square and Basford, Northern Baths. The 44 also followed the same route between the city centre and Bulwell Market with a five-minute service in April 1962 compared to every six minutes in January 1945.

Amongst the "losers" was service 45, which saw its six-minute peak headway of 1945 reduced to every seven and a half minutes by April 1962 whilst the Nottingham Road services, which had offered a combined headway of ever two and a half minutes south of Haydn Road in October 1945, had this cut to an every three/three/four minute headway in August 1953 and again to a three/four/three minute frequency in April 1962.

An analysis of running times taken from the single journey times shown in the public timetables (not working timetables) shows a general trend to cut running times post-war with only minimal allowance made for peak time congestion. Generally speaking the single journey time applied throughout the day, Sunday to Saturday although some early morning journeys had less time and some had more (for whatever reason).

36

Date	Timing Points	Time allowed
1945	Nottingham Road, Vernon Road to King Street	16 minutes
1948	Nottingham Road, Vernon Road to King Street	13 minutes
1953	Nottingham Road, Valley Road to Queen Street	11 minutes
1962	Nottingham Road, Valley Road to Queen Street	11 minutes

37

Date	Timing Points	Time allowed
1945	Nottingham Road, Haydn Road to King Street	13 minutes
1948	Nottingham Road, Haydn Road to King Street	10 minutes
1953	Nottingham Road, Haydn Road to Queen Street	10 minutes
1962	Nottingham Road, Haydn Road to Queen Street	10 minutes

41

Date	Timing Points	Time allowed
1946	Cinderhill, Bells Lane to King Street	22 minutes
1953	Cinderhill, Bells Lane to Trent Bridge	27* minutes
1962	Cinderhill, Bells Lane to Trent Bridge	27* minutes

Note: * an additional one minute was allowed at peak periods.

38

Date	Timing Points	Time allowed
1941	Carlton, Hooton Road to Theatre Square, Elite Cinema	12 minutes
1945	Carlton, Hooton Road to Theatre Square, Elite Cinema	16 minutes
1947	Carlton, Hooton Road to Theatre Square, Elite Cinema	12 minutes
1948	Carlton, Hooton Road to Theatre Square, Elite Cinema	12 minutes
1962	Carlton, Hooton Road to Theatre Square, Elite Cinema	12 minutes

39

Date	Timing Points	Time allowed
1941	Carlton, Post Office Square to Wollaton Park, Fairham Drive	27 minutes
1945	Carlton, Post Office Square to Wollaton Park, Fairham Drive	27 minutes
1947	Carlton, Post Office Square to Wollaton Park, Fairham Drive	27 minutes
1948	Carlton, Post Office Square to Wollaton Park, Fairham Drive	27 minutes
1959	Carlton, Post Office Square to Wollaton Park, Harrow Road	26 minutes
1962	Carlton, Post Office Square to Wollaton Park, Harrow Road	26 minutes

40

Date	Timing Points	Time allowed
1944	Wells Road, Kildare Road to Wilford Bridge	20 minutes
1946	Wells Road, Kildare Road to Wilford Bridge	20 minutes
1958	Wells Road, Kildare Road to Wilford Bridge	19 minutes
1962	Wells Road, Kildare Road to Wilford Bridge	19 minutes

Note: service 47 was granted 2 minutes less for the journey from Wells Road, Ransom Road

42/43/46

Date	Timing Points	Time allowed
1945	Bulwell Market to Trent Bridge	32 minutes
1954	Bulwell Market to Trent Bridge	30 minutes
1954	Trent Bridge to Bulwell Market	29 minutes
1962	Bulwell Market to Trent Bridge	29 minutes
1962	Trent Bridge to Bulwell Market	31 minutes
1954	Basford, Northern Baths to City	18 minutes
1962	Basford, Northern Baths to City	17 minutes
1945	City to Trent Bridge	10 minutes
1946	City to Trent Bridge	10 minutes
1954	City to Trent Bridge	8 minutes
1954	Trent Bridge to City	9 minutes
1962	City to Trent Bridge	8 minutes
1962	Trent Bridge to City	11 minutes

44

Date	Timing Points	Time allowed
1945	Bulwell Hall Estate to Colwick Road Railway Crossing	43 minutes
1945	Colwick Road Railway Crossing to Bulwell Hall Estate	44 minutes
1954	Bulwell Hall Estate to Colwick Road Railway Crossing	37 minutes
1954	Colwick Road Railway Crossing to Bulwell Hall Estate	39 minutes
1962	Bulwell Hall Estate to Colwick Road Railway Crossing	37 minutes
1962	Colwick Road Railway Crossing to Bulwell Hall Estate	39 minutes

45

Date	Timing Points	Time allowed
1945	Trent Bridge, Globe Cinema to Wollaton Park, Scalford Drive	25 minutes
1953	Trent Bridge, Burton's Alms. to Wollaton Park, Scalford Drive	21 minutes
1959	Trent Bridge, Ryehill Street to Wollaton Park, Harrow Road	23 minutes
1962	Trent Bridge, Victoria Embank. to Wollaton Park, Harrow Road	22 minutes

The Peak Vehicle Requirement as at 31 December 1956 was 125 during the morning and 132 during the evening however by August 1959 the overall requirement had fallen to 127 reflecting the trolleybus extras that had either been cancelled entirely or replaced by motorbuses in the interim. In 1962, primarily due to the conversion of service 45 to motorbus operation, some 11 trolleybuses were withdrawn, whilst a further 12 were withdrawn in 1963. Whether this was reflected in a lower Peak Vehicle Requirement or by motorbus operation of trolleybus schedules must be a matter of conjecture. Indeed perhaps the use of motorbuses on services 38 and 42 from 1963 was due to the withdrawal of trolleybuses with accident damage or defects rather than just a shortage of trolleybus drivers. At the start of 1965 there were 111 trolleybuses available for service. Allowing for engineering spares of around 10% this suggests a Peak Vehicle Requirement of around 100 trolleybuses.

Trolleybus Peak Vehicle Requirement (PVR) August 1959

Bulwell		Parliament St.		Trent Bridge	
Service	PVR	Service	PVR	Service	PVR
42	4	36/41	13	43	18
43	12	37	3	45	8
44	18	38	5		
		39	21		
		40/47	18		
Extras	1	Extras	4	Extras	2
Total	35	Total	64	Total	28

Trolleybus Journeys and Extras cancelled or replaced by motorbuses (25 August 1956 - 1 December 1959)

Date	Extra Number	Journey details	Cancelled or Converted
28.08.56	Trolleybus 4 (Parliament St.) Saturday		Cancelled (without replacement)
26.08.57	Four pm Trolleybus extras		Converted to motorbus operation
15.09.58	Trolleybus 1	On services 40/47	Cancelled (without replacement)
20/09/58	Trolleybus 8 (Saturday)	On service 39	Cancelled (without replacement)
01.11.58	Trolleybus 2 (Saturday)	On service 44 – Eland Street to Colwick Road	Cancelled (without replacement)
22.11.58	Trolleybus 9 (Saturday)	On services 40 and 37	Cancelled (without replacement)
14.02.59	Trolleybus extra 2 (Saturday)	On service 38	Cancelled (without replacement)
14.09.59	Four service 42 journeys		Cancelled (without replacement)
02.11.59	Trolleybus 25	Colwick Road to Eland Street	Converted to motorbus operation
02.11.59	Trolleybus 19	Gregory Street to Ransom Rd. & Queen St. to Bell's Lane	Converted to motorbus operation
30.11.59	Trolleybus 23	Wilford Road to City & Queen St. to Cinderhill, Bells Lane	Converted to motorbus operation
01.12.59	Trolleybus 1	Eland Street to City	Cancelled (without replacement)

Running Cards

The running card or running number was a means of identifying workings within the working timetable e.g. the first vehicle on service 43 or tenth vehicle on service 39, usually written as 1(43) and 10(39). Additional workings, which would usually be included in the working timetable, but which were not part of the main public timetabled service e.g. the 47 journey running from Derby Road, Gregory Street, would be covered by extras, with an extra number to identify it, shown in abbreviated form, for example, as 1x; 23x. Designations such as "Trolleybus Extra 1" or "Trolleybus Extra 23" referred to the running card but did not relate to the total of extra journeys operated on any one day.

Matters would be complicated however by the use of extras to cover some working timetable journeys that were part of the public timetabled service and this may have been the case of the early Sunday morning journeys on service 44 from and to Colwick Road, which could have been operated by Parliament Street Depot on extra cards. Unfortunately no Working Timetables are known to survive.

Running cards were not visibly displayed on Nottingham trolleybuses. The running card stayed with the vehicle and there was a holder in the cab for this purpose but it was not uncommon for the conductor to keep the running card in his or her cash bag to facilitate making up the waybill with departure and intermediate times. This would then be passed on to the relieving conductor at crew changeover. Motorbus running cards were a little larger than those used for trolleybuses.

Recorder Clocks

The conductor carried a recorder card, which was inserted into the clock and stamped at the correct departure time (according to the running card) to provide a permanent record of a timely departure or a delay incurred en route. By the early 1960s, recorder clocks used by trolleybus services were situated at:

Bath Street Junction, actually located on St. Ann's Well Road adjacent to St. Catherine's Church: used by services 40, 47 travelling inwards towards the City.

Bath Street Clock, on Bath Street just before Handel Street opposite Victoria Swimming Baths: used by service 38, 39 travelling outwards towards Carlton. It is possible that this clock did not survive in use beyond the 1950s.

Vernon Road, on Vernon Road just before the junction with Western Boulevard/Valley Road: used by services 42, 43, 44 travelling inwards towards the City.

Alma Road, on Carlton Road opposite Alma Road and adjacent to Manvers School: used by services 38, 39 travelling inwards towards the City.

Old Market Square, Processional Way: used by services 41, 43, 46 travelling outwards towards Trent Bridge.

Old Market Square, Beastmarket Hill/Angel Row: used by services 42, 43, 44 travelling outwards towards Bulwell. It is possible that this clock did not survive in use beyond the 1950s.

Derby Road, Hillside, adjacent to Wollaton Hall Lodge situated at the junction of derby Road and Wollaton Hall Drive: used by service 45 trolleybuses (and motorbuses coming from Beeston) travelling inwards towards the City.

Despite the fact that all other services, including part day services such as 38, 42, 46, had at least one "clocking-in" point, it is noticeable that there were no such facilities for services 36 and 37.

Duty sheets

Duty sheets showed the content of each duty and specified whether a trolleybus was to be taken from the depot or relieved "on the road" and on which service, etc. Trolleybus drivers were required to "sign on" for work ten minutes before the allocated duty was scheduled to leave the depot in order that they had sufficient time to check the vehicle for any defects. At the start of duty conductors also had to "sign on" ten minutes before they were due to leave the depot to collect their ticket punch or machine and ticket box. When a conductor started or finished duty "on the road" e.g. Bath Street Junction or Bath Street Clock, rather than at a depot, there was an allowance of time paid to permit them to collect their equipment from the depot and walk to the relieving point or return to the depot and cash up their takings. Drivers starting or finishing "on the road" were paid from the time they were scheduled to take the vehicle over or until their scheduled relief time. When running into the depot drivers had a five-minute allowance to park their trolleybus and conductors a ten-minute allowance to cash up their takings.

Crew changeover points

Bath Street Clock – services 38, 39 eastbound (to Carlton)
Bath Street Junction – services 40, 47
Bulwell, Highbury Road/Piccadilly (Bulwell crews) – services 43, 44
Queen Street/King Street – services 36, 37, 41
Southwell Road (Lower Parliament Street Depot) – services 38, 39 westbound (to City)
Trent Bridge, Victoria Embankment (Trent Bridge crews) – services 43, 45

When no replacement crew was available at a changeover point to take a trolleybus over, the passengers were transferred to the next journey on that service whilst the trolleypoles on the first vehicle were stowed and it was left parked for the Depot Chargeman to come and drive it in to the depot. When this was necessary at Victoria Embankment it was common practice for the Chargeman to leave the trolleypoles stowed and to use battery power to move the trolleybus into Fraser Road before replacing the trolleypoles on the overhead wiring. Trolleybuses parked out of service due to crew shortages could often be seen at Bath Street Clock and Bath Street Junction.

Stop signs

At the time trolley vehicles were introduced to Nottingham's streets, the Department had standardised on conventional metal stop flags, known internally as stop plates, finished in white with a coloured flash or bar and wording to indicate the mode of transport: green for "Railless" and red for motorbuses. Tram flags were finished in yellow with a black flash. It will be noted that the Department advertised their vehicles as "Railless", rather than as Trolley Vehicles (the term "trolleybus" came into common use in the early 1930s), although the public tended to refer to them as "Trackless" i.e. they required no tram tracks. There is however photographic evidence that at least some flags were designated as "TROLLEY VEHICLE" stops. Additional wording beneath the coloured flash indicated whether the flag referred to a compulsory stop ("STOP HERE") or a request stop. The stop signs were usually attached to the nearest

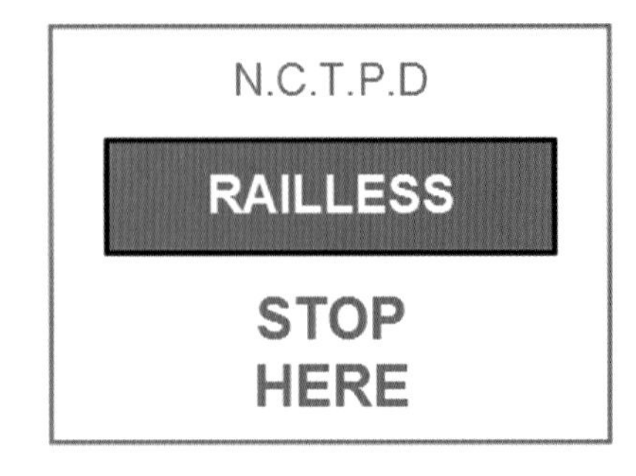

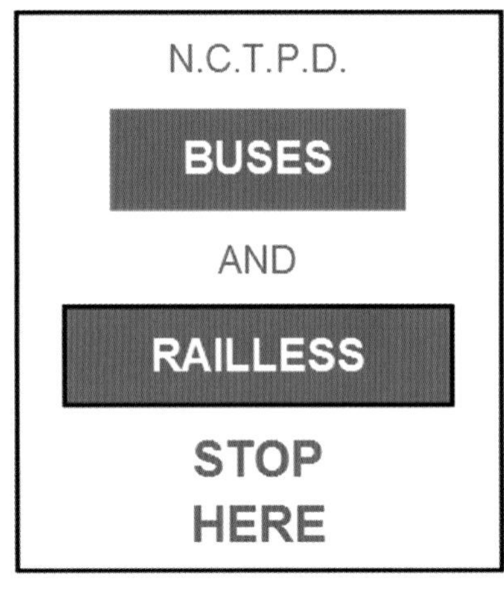

convenient traction pole or exceptionally a separate post.

1. Stop flag used from 1927 until replacement commenced in 1940
2. Stop flag used from 1927 until replacement commenced in 1940
3. Sole example with the additional wording "PLEASE KEEP CLEAR", installed at Old Market Square (removed in 1945)

During the tramway era a limited number of passenger waiting shelters were built at the main junctions or termini, and from the late 1930s these were supplemented by a programme of erecting utilitarian open-sided shelters at important stops throughout the system.

Prior to the Second World War all main city stops had large glass signs featuring silver lettering on a black background fitted to the traction pole rather than metal flags. Commencing in 1941 stops serving more than one service were divided. Again glass signs, approximately 3ft square, were erected with black lettering on a milk white background and a varnished wood frame. As more stops and queue barriers came into used, towards the end of 1942 new glass signs of various sizes with white lettering on a medium green background were used.

Commencing in 1940 a new style of metal bus stop flag featuring plain white lettering on a green background for trolleybus services and on a red background for motorbuses, began to replace the earlier white flags. The programme could not be completed until after war due to a shortage of materials. This style and colour differentiation between trolleybus and motorbus stops was retained until the end of trolleybus operation.

1. Metal stop flag introduced ca. 1940
2. Metal stop flag introduced ca. 1940 (more typically separate green and red flags were used.
3. Glass sign introduced ca. 1942, example at Central Market

The stop flags or plates were 15¾ins wide by 15ins deep. The corners had a 15° radius. The larger lettering e.g. "TROLLEYBUS REQUEST STOP", was 2ins tall and the smaller lettering e.g. "N.C.T." 1⅒ins tall.

The background colour was Light Brunswick Green number 225 from British Standard Colours 381c of 1948. Lettering was White with fare stage lettering being in Golden Yellow number 356 of British Standard Colours 381c of 1948.

Compulsory stops were indicated by flags or plates lettered "TROLLEYBUS STOP", these being used at terminal points or at stops where a recorder clock was situated, or, where this coincided with a fare stage, "TROLLEYBUS FARE STAGE". Only one compulsory stop for safety purposes is known of, located on the sharp descent on Alpine Street inbound just before rounding the bend onto Church Street (by the "White Swan" public house) in Old Basford (service 41), and this was lettered as "TROLLEYBUS STOP".

On the outbreak of war the bottom 3 ft of all bus stop posts, including traction poles used for this purpose, were painted white. A white line was painted on the road surface at each stopping place from September 1939 until 1943 when this practice was discontinued.

White painted queue barriers constructed from small gauge piping were built at a large number of busy stopping places but where these were not available from early 1943 white lines were painted on the pavement, lettered "Q" HERE. Increasingly instruction signs or plates indicating "FORM QUEUE THIS SIDE" or "FORM QUEUE OTHER SIDE" were added to the flags at many stops. These were 15¾ins wide by 6⁷⁄₁₀ins deep with a 15° radius to the bottom corners, all lettering was in upper case.

By late 1944 all the pre-war black background signs and many of the white background signs had been replaced by the green variety although a darker green was used.

In 1954 separate temporary yellow notices with black lettering were attached to the bottom right hand corner of the stop flags to indicate fare stages but these were replaced later with new flags having a green background and orange lettering. At the same time compulsory stop flags were given an orange border but this practice does not appear to have continued long.

Post-war, would-be passengers increasingly had to board both motorbuses and trolleybuses stopped in the main stream of traffic as vehicles parked at or close to the stop itself prevented them from pulling into the kerb. The words "BUS STOP" were painted on the road surface at an increasing number of stops throughout the system during the 1950s and 1960s in an unsuccessful attempt to discourage parking there. In the city centre this was complemented by the introduction of no waiting restrictions, again to little avail.

N.C.T.
TROLLEYBUS
REQUEST
STOP

N.C.T.
MOTORBUS
AND
TROLLEYBUS
REQUEST
STOP

TROLLEYBUSES
FOR
CARLTON 38
HOOTON ROAD
CARLTON 39
POST OFFICE
SQUARE

A standard post war NCT trolleybus stop flag. *A Braddock*

Appendix L Mr Gunn's 1938 Report

GENERAL MANAGER'S REPORT:
– ABANDONMENT OF TROLLEYBUSES

NOTTINGHAM CITY TRANSPORT
Lower Parliament Street,
Nottingham

17 June 1938

To the Chairman and Members of
the Passenger Transport Committee.

Sir and Gentlemen,
At a meeting of the Passenger Transport Committee held on 4th March, 1938, the following Notice of Motion was given:- "Alderman Sir Albert Atkey JP, stated that he would like the Committee to consider at its next meting as to whether the time was now opportune to abolish all trolley vehicle routes and substitute buses thereon and asked for an item to be placed on the Agenda for the next meeting in relation thereto.

RESOLVED that an item be placed on the Agenda for consideration at the next meeting of the Committee and that in the meantime the General Manager be asked to consider the proposals and to submit his report thereon".
I think that it might be advisable to deal with my report in the following order.

(1) The capital expenditure of the Undertaking, the debt outstanding at the end of the past financial year 1937-38 and the redemption of loan debt on the trolleybus system.
(2) (a) The cost of the renewal of trolleybuses when their normal life has expired.
(b) The cost of the substitution of trolleybuses by motorbuses when their normal life has expired.
(3 The actual cost of the operation of oil engine buses as a substitute for trolleybuses.
(4) General observations.

PART 1. FINANCIAL POSITION OF THE UNDERTAKING

The Capital Expenditure and Debt outstanding at 31st March 1938 is as follows:

	Expenditure	Outstanding
Head Office, Parliament St., Trent Bridge, Sherwood and Bulwell Depots	£280,482	£43,076
Trolleybuses (125 vehicles)	£230,732	£95,505
Overhead Equipment (25.55 route miles)	£63,561	£35,112
Motor buses (211 vehicles)	£344,515	£100,138
Plant, Machinery & Other Rolling Stock	£10,505	£1,002
Obsolete Works, Tram track removal, etc.	£69,219	£61,252
	£999,014	£336,085

The Reserve Fund Surplus is small (£45,608) so that any extensive alteration to existing form of transport will have to be met by borrowing.
Included in the above tabulation under "Obsolete Works" is the Loan Debt on the obsolete tramway undertaking £19,333, which will be wholly provided for during the current year.
In Schedule "A" I produce a statement giving the existing fleet of 125 trolleybuses, showing the cost of these vehicles, the loan debt outstanding, how provision for the redemption of the loan debt will be made and when the vehicles fall due for renewal. It will be seen that provision will have been made for the redemption of the debt on the existing fleet by 31st March 1943.
In Schedule "B" I give a statement of the trolleybus overhead installation showing capital cost (excluding feeder cables, sub-stations, etc. provided by the Electricity Department) amounting to £63,561, which sum includes £14,417, for poles transferred from the obsolete tramways undertaking. It will be observed from the Loan Debt on the overhead equipment at the 31st March 1938 amounted to £35,112 and that the poles originally transferred from the Tramways Undertaking and reinforced for the purpose of the trolleybus undertaking are entirely free of debt. The outstanding debt on the existing overhead equipment will be repaid by 31st March 1954.
In connection with the change over from tramways to trolleybuses, you will appreciate the fact that it was necessary to alter the tramway depots in order to accommodate the trolleybuses. The cost of these alterations is given in Schedule "C".
A summary of the aforementioned is given in Schedule "D" viz. Trolleybuses, Overhead Equipment and Trolleybus Depot Alterations, which involved a total cost of £300,241 with a net Loan Debt of £135,428. This tabulation further shows that the loan debt outstanding on existing trolleybuses will not expire until year ended 31st March 1943, while overhead equipment will not be paid off until 1954 and depot alterations until 1955.
All calculations in the attached schedules assume that no further capital expenditure in respect of the Trolleybus system will be incurred and deal only with the redemption of debt on the existing fleet and equipment.

SCHEDULE "A"

TROLLEYBUSES – Existing fleet of 125 vehicles

(1) Total cost of 125 trolleybuses		£230,732
(2) Loan Debt outstanding re the above at	31st March 1938	£95,505
	1939	£69,867
	1940	£43,818
	1941	£22,956
	1942	£2,093
	1943	Nil

(3) Provisions will have been made for redemption as follows:

Vehicle Nos.	Quantity	Loan Debt o/s 31st March 1938	Redeemed
13-18	6	£225	31st March 1939
19-24	6	£571	do.
25-36	12	£5,715	31st March 1940
37-49	13	£6,500	do.
1 & 50	2	£1,154	do.
51-60	10	£8,725	31st March 1941
61-85	25	£20,354	31st March 1942
86-106	21	£17,354	do.
107-136	30	£34,907	31st March 1943
	125	£95,505	

SCHEDULE "B"

TROLLEYBUSES – OVERHEAD EQUIPMENT

(1) Total cost of Overhead Equipment (excluding Feeder Cables, Sub-Stations, etc., provided by Electricity Dept.) — £63,561 (includes £14,417 for poles transferred from Tramways)

(2) Loan Debt outstanding re the above at 31st March 1938 — £35,112 (Poles transferred from Tramways are free of debt)

(3) Provision will have been made for redemption as follows:-

	Loan Debt 31st March 1938	Redeemed
Nottingham Corp. Act 1925 re King St. to Vernon Rd., King St. & South Parade, Parliament St. toKildare Rd., South Parade to Wilford Rd. Terminus.	£5,180	31st March 1949
Nottingham Corp. Act 1929 re South Parade toGeorge St., Valley Road to Nuthall Road.	£3,173	31st March 1951
Nottingham Corp. Act 1930 re Remainder of Existing Trolleybus routes.	£26,759	31st March 1954
	£35,112	

N.B.The Capital Cost and Loan Debt outstanding in respect of Cables, Sub-Stations, etc., provided by the Electricity Department is not included in the above.

SCHEDULE "C"

TROLLEYBUS DEPOT ALTERATIONS

(1) Total cost of Depot alterations for Trolleybuses –	Bulwell	£3,415
	Carter Gate	£1,427
	Trent Bridge	£1,106
		£5,948
(2) Loan Debt outstanding re the above at 31st March 1938		£4,811

(3) Provision will have been made for complete redemption by 31st March 1955.

SCHEDULE "D"

SUMMARY OF TROLLEYBUS LOAN DEBT

The following is a summary of Schedules A, B and C. (i.e. Trolleybuses, Overhead Equipment and Trolleybus Depot alterations) – Total Cost £300,241.

Year Ended	Loan Debt Outstanding	
31st March 1938	£135,428	
1939	£106,117	
1940	£78,381	
1941	£54,820	
1942	£31,246	
1943	£26,426	(Trolleybuses repaid)
1944	£23,686	
1945	£20,931	
1946	£18,162	
1947	£15,376	
1948	£12,575	
1949	£9,968	
1950	£7,623	
1951	£5,262	
1952	£3,126	
1953	£1,002	
1954	£52	(Overhead Equipment repaid)
1955	£Nil	(Depot Alterations repaid)

PART II – RENEWAL OF TROLLEYBUSES OR REPLACEMENT BY MOTORBUSES

(a) If trolleybuses are renewed at such time as the expectant life of the vehicles is reached i.e. 9 years the following table shews (1) when such purchase may be made (2) number of trolleybuses required at an estimated cost of £2,400 each and (3) the capital cost involved.

Financial Year	Trolleybuses to be replaced		Capital cost of renewing Trolleybuses
1939-40	12	(Nos. 13-24)	£ 28,800
1940-41	25	(Nos. 25-49)	£ 60,000
1941-42	2	(Nos. 1 & 50)	£ 4,800
1942-43	46	(Nos. 61-106)	£110,400
1943-44	10	(Nos. 51-60)	£ 24,000
1944-45	30	(Nos. 107-136)	£ 72,000
	125		£300,000

Annual charge for Sinking Fund and Interest (Expectancy of life 9 years) £40,323

(b) If trolleybuses are replaced by motorbuses at such times as the expectant life of the vehicles is reached, the replacement will necessitate additional vehicles to maintain the seating capacity of the replaced vehicles and the following table shews (1) when such purchase may be made (2) number of motorbuses required to replace the existing trolleybus seating capacity at an estimated cost of £1,965 each and (3) the capital cost involved.

Financial Year	Motor Buses required to replace Trolleybus seating		Capital cost
1939-40	13	Motor Buses at £1,965 each	£ 25,545
1940-41	27	Motor Buses at £1,965 each	£ 53,055
1941-42	2	Motor Buses at £1,965 each	£ 3,930
1942-43	53	Motor Buses at £1,965 each	£104,145
1943-44	11	ditto	£ 21,615
1944-45	34	ditto	£ 66,810
	140		£275,100

Annual charge for Sinking Fund and Interest (Expectancy of life 7 years) £45,850

From a comparison of these two tables it is seen that the Capital Cost of Trolleybuses is estimated at £24,900 more than Motor Buses, while the annual provision for redemption is £5,327 less than Motor Buses.

PART III – COST OF OPERATION

Before proceeding to give a general report on the advantages and disadvantages of one form of transport against another, I have made a tabulation of the operating costs (1936-37) of Undertakings operating both trolleybuses and motor buses as under:-

Undertaking	Trolleybus Operating costs per mile	Motor Bus operating costs per mile
	d.	d.
Ashton-under-Lyne	12.985	9.898
Birmingham	12.248	10.967
Bournemouth	10.780	11.290
Chesterfield	8.850	9.010
Derby	12.144	12.826
Doncaster	10.100	7.451
Grimsby	10.219	9.174
Huddersfield	10.209	8.252
Maidstone	11.972	10.437
Newcastle	10.930	9.761
NOTTINGHAM	12.984	10.516
Pontypridd	9.67	9.40
Portsmouth	12.045	11.761
Reading	13.348	12.389
Rotherham	7.520	7.750
St. Helens	9.721	8.287
Southend	12.251	10.333
South Shields	8.275	6.983
Walsall	11.529	10.120
West Hartlepool	9.790	8.200
Wolverhampton	10.354	10.194
AVERAGE	10.854d	9.762d.

The operating costs for Nottingham during the last financial year 1937-38 were-

Trolleybuses	Motor Buses
12.814d.	11.014d.

The Petrol Bus costs were 12.117d. and the Oil Bus costs 10.452d., but it is necessary to point out that the petrol buses are running a low mileage.

For the purpose of comparison between the two systems of transport I have prepared estimated cost on the following lines –

(a) Taking into consideration ascertained increased costs for the current year.

(b) Calculating Motor Bus costs on the assumption that Motor Buses operate on the existing Trolleybus services providing the same seating capacity and operating at a speed ¾ mph higher than trolleybuses.

(c) Calculating Loan Charges on the same basis as stated in Part 2 of this report plus Loan Charges on Overhead Equipment in the case of trolleybuses (Loan Charges on capital expenditure common to both are disregarded e.g. buildings, roads re-instatement, etc.).

The existing Motor Bus services have an average service speed of 1.040 mph greater than that of the Trolleybus services, but I am not assuming that Motor Buses could operate at the same speed on the existing Trolleybus routes which run through densely populated areas. I am, however, of the opinion that some increase of service speed would be obtainable and have assumed an additional ¾ mph.

The operative costs are:-

	Trolleybuses		Motor Buses	
	£.	d.	£	.d.
Operating Expenses	208,437	13.277	201,761	11.482
Capital Charges	43,935	2.799	45,850	2.609
	252,372	16.076d.	247,611	14.091d

showing a balance of £4,761 in favour of Motor Buses made up as follows:-

Motor Buses compared with Trolleybuses

Driving and Conducting	+ £ 2,270
Oiling Vehicles	+ £ 1,930
Licences	+ £ 775
Maintenance	+ £ 5,200
Power or Fuel	- £ 3,450
Rates	- £13,401
Capital Charges	+ £ 1,915
	- £ 4,761

PART IV – GENERAL OBSERVATIONS

It is obvious to me that this report will be considered in the light of the advantages and disadvantages to the ratepayer and in order to be perfectly fair, I have taken an opportunity of discussing this matter with the City Treasurer and find from his estimate that the Local rates will suffer a loss as follows:-

	Assessment		
Nottingham	£16,560	at 15s 8d	= £ 12,972
Carlton	£ 695	at 12s 8d less 2½%	= £ 429
	£17,255		£ 13,401

equivalent to a 1½d. rate in the City.

Trolleybuses pay local rates similarly to a tramways undertaking – the whole undertaking being assessed on a profits basis, whereas in the case of motor buses only the buildings are assessable.

A further point is the loss of income to the Electricity Department and the capital that they have sunk into sub-stations, cables, etc., for traction use only. In the past years the Electricity Department have received a very good return from traction power for any expenditure they have incurred on our behalf and the loss of traction income will have small effect upon their sales as traction is only 4½% of the sales. The price of current is extremely high at the present cost of 0.76d. per unit as the cost to them from the Central Electricity Board is less than ½d. per unit – a ½d. per unit excludes distribution charges to our poles but it must be appreciated that ½d. per unit is an average cost for all purposes and that traction remains a fairly constant source of supply throughout the day.

In the current year, the cost of current will amount to over £34,000 while at 0.65d. per unit the annual cost would amount to £29,000, a saving of £5,000 which would convert the balance in favour of motor buses to a balance in favour of trolleybuses.

The differences between the direct taxation in one form or another for trolleybuses and motor buses area s follows:

	Trolleybuses	Motor Buses
Vehicle Licences	Based upon seating capacity same as trolleybuses. 48-56 seats £86 8s pa 56-64 seats £96 0s pa	
Duty on Fuel	None.	9d. per gallon.
Local Rates	On the whole undertaking, the assessment being arrived at on the profits basis.	On buildings only.
Lubricating Oils	1d. per gallon.	Same as trolleybuses but greater quantity used.
Road Traffic Act & Hackney Carriage, etc., Licences	Hackney Carriage Vehicle Licences 2s pa per bus.	Public Service Vehicle £3 pa per bus. Certificate of
	None.	Fitness £3 per bus for period up to 5 years.
	None.	Road Service Licence £1 pa per service.

The above taxes, divided between National and Local taxation for the existing trolleybus services would amount to:

	Trolleybuses	Motor Buses
National taxation	£12,110	£32,230
Local taxation (Rates only)	£16,850	£ 3,445
	£28,960	£35,67

There is however, a large amount of the national taxation distributed locally.

The following are further material points which the Committee may desire to take into consideration when dealing with this question.

(1) Variation in fuel prices(2)

The effect of War on the question of supplies of fuel (in this connection one must keep in mind that the Naval fleet is operated to a large percentage on fuel oil) and the confiscation of buses by the Government.

(3) The overhead equipment and poles are in good condition. It is anticipated that the poles would remain for centre lighting purposes but the cost of removal of the overhead equipment would probably be met by the value of the scrap.

(4) In the event of a decision being reached to abandon trolleybuses in the city, the question of through running with the Notts and Derby Traction Co. will have to be taken into consideration.

(5) The rate of fares to be charged – at present 1d. per mile Motor Buses and ¾d. per mile trolleybuses.

(6) Other points – employees suitable for trolleybuses only, depreciation of trolleybus stores, tower wagons, etc.

One of the main advantages of Motor Bus operation is the ability of a motor bus to remove localized causes of traffic congestion. Trolleybuses cannot overtake, can only be parked at specially provided points and are slow over crossings where congestion usually arises. Motor Buses can be parked, can turn and operate practically anywhere, totally unlike a trolleybus. For special traffic purposes, extensions of route and new services the flexibility of the Motor Bus is infinitely greater and cheaper.

Another advantage is unification of transport – one type of vehicle can produce economies especially where service alterations and re-arrangements are necessary without duplication, which exists where two types of vehicles are running alongside. The results of unification can only be seen after it has been put into operation for a number of years and it is impossible to estimate the cash value of such a step. However, its importance from a transport viewpoint cannot be over-estimated.

Yours faithfully,
General Manager

Appendix M Legislation

Legislation relating to trolleybuses in Nottingham

This Appendix contains selected extracts from the following items:

1) Bills and Acts of Parliament
2) City of Nottingham Byelaws
3) Transport Department Internal Instructions

Note: These extracts use the same grammar, spelling and style as the original documents. In view of the complex and dated terminology used in the original text, some explanatory additions have been made by the Author. *These are shown in italics.* All paragraphs selected are quoted in their entirety.

1) Bills and Acts of Parliament

Nottingham Corporation Bill, 1913

A Bill to authorise the Mayor Aldermen and Citizens of the city of Nottingham and county of the same city to construct tramways to provide and work a trolley vehicle system to provide and work motor omnibuses and for other purposes.

The Bill was presented and read for the first time on 12 March 1913 but following objections from Nottinghamshire County Council and West Bridgford UDC all references to West Bridgford were struck out.

PART III.- TROLLEY VEHICLES AND MOTOR OMNIBUSES

10. (1) The Corporation may provide maintain and equip but shall not manufacture mechanically propelled vehicles adapted for use upon roads and moved by electrical power transmitted thereto from some external source (in this Act called "trolley vehicles") and may use the same upon the routes hereinafter mentioned and may place erect and maintain in under and along the streets and roads forming such routes cables wires posts poles and any other necessary or convenient apparatus and equipment for the purpose of working trolley vehicles and may supply electrical energy by means of such apparatus and equipment outside the city for that purpose.

(2) The routes hereinbefore referred to are as follows:-

(a) From a point in the Market Place on Beastmarket Hill 130 feet or thereabouts north-west of the north-west side of Friar Lane along Beastmarket Hill the Market Place Wheeler Gate St. Peter's Square Albert Street Lister Gate Carrington Street Arkwright Street and London Road over Trent Bridge to the city boundary at the junction of London Road with Loughborough Road;

(b) From a point in the Radcliffe Road West Bridgford 90 feet or thereabouts east of the front of the County Police Station along Radcliffe Road Holme Road and Trent Boulevard to its junction with Adbolton Grove;

(c) From the city boundary at the junction of London Road with Loughborough Road along Bridgford Road Musters Road and Chaworth Road to its junction with Loughborough Road;

(d) From the city boundary at the junction of London Road with Loughborough Road along Loughborough Road to a point in that road 1,450 feet or thereabouts west of the west side of Old Road.

18. (1) The Corporation may provide (but shall not manufacture) and may run motor omnibuses within the city and outside the city along the following routes:-

(a) Along the routes specified in the section of this Act the marginal note whereof is "Power to provide and work vehicles moved by electricity" and along any other route or routes in the parish and urban district of West Bridgford that may be agreed on between the Corporation and the West Bridgford Urban District Council;

(b) From the city boundary in Carlton Road along Carlton Road Carlton Hill and Main Street East to its junction with Newgate Street;

(c) From the city boundary in Mansfield Road along that road to Daybrook and thence along Nottingham Road (Arnold) and Front Street to its junction with Spout Lane;

(d) From the city boundary in Mapperley Plains Road along that Road to its junction with Spout Lane; and may demand and take such reasonable fares and charges for the conveyance of passengers therein as may be approved by the Board of Trade and may provide such plant appliances and conveniences as may be requisite or expedient for the establishment running and equipment of such motor omnibuses;

(2) The Corporation may make bye-laws for regulating the travelling and for the prevention of nuisance in or upon their motor omnibuses provided that any such bye-law shall be made subject and according to the provisions of the Tramways Act 1870 with respect to the making of bye-laws:

(3) Every motor omnibus moved by electrical power i.e. trolley vehicle, shall be so equipped and worked as to prevent any interference with telegraphic communication by means of any telegraphs of the Postmaster-General;

(4) All provisions of the Conveyance of Mails Act 1893 relating to the conveyance of mails on tramways shall apply and have effect in relation to the motor omnibuses provided under this section as if such omnibuses were carriages on the tramways authorized after the first day of January eighteen hundred and ninety-three:

(5) In this section the expression "motor omnibus" means any carriage moved by mechanical power including in that expression steam electrical and every other motive power not being animal power;

(6) The undertaking authorized by this section shall be deemed to form part of the tramways undertaking of the Corporation Provided that in the accounts of the Corporation relative to their motor omnibus undertaking the receipts and expenditure upon and in connection with the motor omnibuses shall (as far as may be reasonably practicable) be distinguished from the receipts and expenditure in connection with the remainder of such undertaking.

---

3 & 44 Geo.5. [c.cxiv.]

Nottingham Corporation Act, 1913

PART III.- TROLLEY VEHICLES AND MOTOR OMNIBUSES

10. (1) The Corporation may provide (but shall not manufacture) and may run motor omnibuses within the city and may demand and take such reasonable fares and charges for the conveyance of passengers therein as may be approved by the Board of Trade and may provide such plant appliances and conveniences as may be requisite or expedient for the establishment running and equipment of such motor omnibuses:

(2) The Corporation may make bye-laws for regulating the travelling and for the prevention of nuisance in or upon their motor omnibuses Provided that any such bye-law shall be made subject and according to the provisions of the Tramways Act 1870 with respect to the making of bye-laws:

(3) Every motor omnibus moved by electrical power i.e. trolley vehicle, shall be so equipped and worked as to prevent any interference with telegraphic communication by means of any telegraphs of the Postmaster-General:

(4) The Corporation shall perform in respect of the motor omnibuses provided under this section all the services in regard to the conveyance of mails which are prescribed by the Conveyance of Mails Act 1893 in the case of a tramway as defined by that Act and authorized as in that Act stated:

(5) In this section the expression "motor omnibus" means any carriage moved by mechanical power including in that expression steam electrical and every other motive power not being animal power:

(6) The undertaking authorized by this section shall be deemed to form part of the tramway undertaking of the Corporation Provided that in the accounts of the Corporation relative to their tramway undertaking the receipts and expenditure upon and in connection with the motor omnibuses shall (as far as may be reasonably practicable) be distinguished from the receipts and expenditure in connection with the remainder of such undertaking.

11. The Corporation may provide maintain and equip but shall not manufacture mechanically propelled vehicles adapted for use upon roads and moved by electrical power transmitted thereto from some external source (in this Act called "trolley vehicles") and may use the same upon the route hereinafter mentioned and may place erect and maintain in under and along the streets and roads forming such route cables wires posts poles and any other necessary or convenient apparatus and equipment for the purpose of working trolley vehicles and may supply electrical energy by means of such apparatus and equipment for that purpose.

The route hereinbefore referred to is as follows:-

From a point in the Market Place on Beastmarket Hill one hundred and thirty feet or thereabouts north-west of the north-west side of Friar Lane along Beastmarket Hill the Market Place Wheeler Gate St. Peter's Square Albert Street Lister Gate Carrington Street and Arkwright Street to its junction with London Road.

12. Trolley vehicles shall not be deemed to be light locomotives within the meaning of the Locomotives on Highways Act 1896 or of the bye-laws and regulations made thereunder nor shall they be deemed to be motor cars within the meaning of any provisions of the Motor Car Act 1903 (except sub-section (1) of section 1 of that Act and the provisions necessary for enforcing that sub-section) and subject to that exception neither that Act nor the regulations made under that Act nor the enactments mentioned in the schedule to the Locomotives on the Highway Act 1896 nor the Locomotives Act 1898 shall apply to trolley vehicles.

13. Trolley vehicles and the electrical equipment thereof shall be of such form construction and dimensions as the Board of Trade may approve and no trolley vehicle shall be used by the Corporation which does not comply with the requirements of the Board of Trade and no such vehicle (including the weight of its load) shall exceed a weight of five tons.

15. (1) If at any time hereafter the Corporation desire to provide maintain equip and use within the city trolley vehicles upon any road as defined by the Tramways Act 1870 they may make application to the Board of Trade and the Board of Trade shall be and they are hereby empowered to make a Provisional Order authorizing the use of trolley vehicles upon any road or roads to which such application relates and also empowering the Corporation to place erect maintain in under and along such road cables wires posts poles and any other necessary or convenient apparatus or equipment for the purpose of working the trolley vehicles and to supply electrical energy by means of such apparatus for that purpose: And any such Provisional Order may vary modify or render inapplicable provisions of the Locomotives on Highways Act 1896 the Locomotives Act 1898 and the Motor Car Act 1903 or any enactments incorporated therein or bye-laws or regulations made thereunder respectively:

(2) No such application shall be entertained by the Board of Trade unless the Corporation shall-

(a) Have published once in each of two successive weeks in the months of October or November in some newspaper or newspapers circulating in the city notice of their intention to make such application and have published once in one or other of the same months the like notice in the London Gazette;

(b) Have posted for fourteen consecutive days in the months of October or November in conspicuous positions in each of the several streets or roads to which such application relates a notice of their intention to make such application;

and each such notice shall state the time and method for bringing before the Board of Trade any objections to the grant of such application:

(3) The Board of Trade may and they are hereby empowered to prescribe the procedure with respect to any application for a provisional order under this section:

(4) The Board of Trade shall consider any such application and may if they think fit direct an inquiry to be held in the city in relation thereto or may otherwise enquire as to the propriety of proceeding upon such application and they shall consider any objection to such application that may be lodged with them in accordance with the prescribed procedure and shall determine whether or not it is expedient and proper that the application be granted either with or without addition or modification or subject or not to any restriction or condition:

(5) In any case where it shall appear to the Board of Trade expedient and proper that the application be granted they may settle and make a provisional order authorizing the same and shall as soon as conveniently may be thereafter procure a bill to be introduced into either House of Parliament for an Act to confirm the provisional order which shall be set out at length in the schedule to the bill and until confirmation with or without amendment by such Act of Parliament a provisional order under this part of this Act shall not have any operation:

(6) If while any such bill is pending in either House of Parliament a petition is presented against any provisional order comprised therein the bill so far as it relates to the order petitioned against may be referred to a select committee and the petitioner shall be allowed to appear and oppose as in the case of a bill for a special Act:

The Act of Parliament confirming a provisional order under this Act shall be deemed as a public general Act:

(7) The making of a provisional order under this section shall be prima facie evidence that all the requirements of this section in respect of proceedings required to be taken previously to the making of such provisional order have been complied with:

(8) Any expenses incurred by the Board of Trade in connection with the preparation and making of any such provisional order and any expenses incurred by the Board of Trade in connection with any inquiry under this section shall be paid by the Corporation:

PART IV: FINANCIAL AND MISCELLANEOUS

24. (1) The Corporation may from time to time independently of any other borrowing power borrow at interest for the purposes mentioned in the first column of the following table the respective sums mentioned in the second column thereof and they shall pay off all money so borrowed within the respective periods (each of which shall be "the prescribed period" for the purpose of the enactments incorporated herewith) mentioned in the third column of the said table (namely):-

Purpose	Amount	Period of repayment
(a) For and in connection with the construction of the tramways authorized by this Act	£ 19,250	Thirty years from the dates of borrowing.
(b) For the provision of rolling stock for such tramways and for the existing tramways of the Corporation	£ 14,600	Fifteen years from the dates of borrowing.
(c) For the provision of motor omnibuses and trolley vehicles authorized by this Act	£ 17,500	Five years from the dates of borrowing.
(d) For electrical equipment and the construction of other works necessary for the existing tramways of the Corporation and the tramways and trolley vehicles authorized by this Act	£ 10,000	Twenty years from the dates of borrowing.
(e) For the purchase of lands for the purposes of the motor omnibuses and trolley vehicles	£ 900	Sixty years from the dates of borrowing.authorized by this Act
(f) For the construction of buildings for the purposes of the motor omnibuses and trolley vehicles authorized by this Act	£ 3,000	Thirty years from the dates of borrowing.
(g) For paying the costs charges and expenses of this Act as hereinafter provided	The requisite sum	Five years from the passing of this Act

15 & 16 Geo.5. [Ch.cix.]

Nottingham Corporation Act, 1925

27. (1) The Corporation may provide maintain and equip (but shall not manufacture) trolley vehicles and may work the same along the following routes:-

Route A Commencing in Vernon Road at the intersection of the centre lines of Nottingham Road and Vernon Road thence proceeding along Nottingham Road Sherwood Rise Gregory Boulevard Mansfield Road Milton Street Upper Parliament Street King Street and Queen Street and terminating at the junction of King Street with Long Row:

Route B Commencing at the junction of King Street with Long Row thence proceeding along Long Row the Market Place South Parade and Exchange and terminating at the junction of King Street with Long Row:

Route C Commencing in Upper Parliament Street at a point eighty feet or thereabouts measured in a westerly direction from the intersection of the centre lines of Upper Parliament Street and Milton Street thence proceeding along Upper Parliament Street Lower Parliament Street King Edward Street St. Ann's Well Road and The Wells Road and terminating at the junction of The Wells Road with Kildare Road:

Route D Commencing in the Market Place at a point fifty feet or thereabouts measured in a north-westerly direction from the intersection of the centre lines of Friar Lane and Wheeler Gate thence proceeding along the Market Place Wheeler Gate Albert Street Lister Gate Greyfriar Gate Canal Street Wilford Street and Wilford Road and terminating at the junction of Wilford Road with Colliery Road.

Provided that before equipping any trolley vehicle route to include a turning point or before arranging for a new turning point on any route the Corporation shall submit plans of the turning point to the Minister of Transport for approval.

There then followed a paragraph for the protection of the London Midland and Scottish Railway Company in respect of use of bridges, stray currents, etc.

31. (1) The trolley vehicles of the Corporation shall not be deemed to be light locomotives within the meaning of the Locomotives on Highways Act 1896 or of the byelaws and regulations made thereunder nor shall they be deemed to be motor cars within the meaning of any provisions of the Motor Car Act 1903 (except subsection (1) of section 1 and the provisions necessary for enforcing that subsection section 6 and the provisions as amended by the Roads Act 1920 relating to the licensing and licences of drivers) and subject to that exception neither that Act nor the regulations made under that Act nor the enactments mentioned in the schedule to the Locomotives on Highways Act 1896 nor the Locomotives Act 1898 shall apply to the said trolley vehicles.

(2) Section 12 (vehicles not to be deemed light locomotives or motor cars) of the Act of 1913 is hereby repealed.

(3) The trolley vehicles of the Corporation shall not be deemed to be omnibuses within the meaning of the Town Police Clauses Act 1889.

(Section 31 was repealed with the 1947 Act, paragraph 33 (2)).

32. (1) No trolley vehicle (including the weight of its load) used by the Corporation under the authority of this or any other Act shall exceed a weight of ten tons and the said trolley vehicles and the electrical equipment thereof shall be of such form and construction as the Minister of Transport may approve and no trolley vehicle shall be used by the Corporation which does not comply with the requirements of the Minister of Transport.

(The weight limit referred to above was repealed with the 1935 Act, paragraph 15 (3)).

(2) Section 13 (Approval of vehicles by Board of Trade) of the Act of 1913 is hereby repealed.

33. Notwithstanding anything contained in the Act of 1913 the Corporation may carry on their trolley vehicles (1) passengers' luggage and parcels not exceeding fifty-six pounds in weight and may demand and take such rates and charges for the carriage thereof as may from time to time be approved by the Minister of Transport and (2) dogs in the care of passengers the charge for any such dog to be a sum not exceeding the fare payable by the passenger.

---

19 & 20 Geo.5. [Ch.lxi.]

Nottingham Corporation Act, 1929

PART IV.- TROLLEY VEHICLES

39. (1) The Corporation may provide maintain and equip trolley vehicles and may work the same along the following routes in the city:-

Route A Commencing in South Parade by a junction with the authorised trolley vehicle route of the Corporation in that street at a point 350 feet or thereabouts measured in an easterly direction from the intersection of the centre lines of Wheeler Gate and South Parade thence proceeding along South Parade Poultry Victoria Street Carlton Street and George Street to and terminating at the junction of George Street with Lower Parliament Street by a junction with the authorised trolley vehicle route of the Corporation in the last-named street;

Route B Commencing in Nottingham Road at the intersection of the centre lines of Valley Road and Nottingham Road by a junction with the existing trolley vehicle route of the Corporation in the last-named road thence proceeding along Valley Road Church Street High Street Alpine Street Percy Street Thurlow Street Stockhill Lane and Nuthall Road and terminating in Nuthall Road at the city boundary by a junction with the authorised trolley vehicle route of the Nottinghamshire and Derbyshire Traction Company in that road; or convenient to use for the purpose

and with the consent of the Minister of Transport along any other street or road in the city which the Corporation think it necessary or convenient to use for the purpose of providing a turning point of or connecting trolley vehicle routes or of obtaining access thereto from any depôt garage building or work of the Corporation.

(2) Before equipping any trolley vehicle route to include a turning point or before arranging for a new turning point on any route the Corporation shall submit plans of the turning point to the Minister of Transport for approval.

43. The Corporation on the one hand and the Nottinghamshire and Derbyshire Traction Company on the other hand may enter into and carry into effect agreements with respect to the formation of junctions between the trolley vehicle systems of the Corporation and the said company and the Corporation are hereby empowered to carry out all necessary work in connection with the formation of such junctions under any agreement which may be entered into between the said parties.

---

20 & 21 Geo.5. [c.cxiv.]

Nottingham Corporation Act, 1930

An Act to authorise the lord mayor aldermen and citizens of the city of Nottingham and county of the same city to run trolley vehicles on existing and authorised tramway routes and on further routes within the city and to abandon and discontinue tramways and for other purposes, [10th July 1930].

Whereas the city of Nottingham and county of the same city (in this Act called "the city") is under the municipal and local government of the lord mayor aldermen and citizens of the city (in this Act called "the Corporation"):

And whereas the Corporation are the owners of and are working within the city and in the neighbourhood thereof an extensive system of tramways and trolley vehicles (being mechanically propelled vehicles adapted for use upon roads without rails and moved by electrical power transmitted thereto from some external source) and it is expedient to empower the Corporation to work trolley vehicles on the existing and authorised tramway routes of the Corporation and along other routes within the city and to abandon and discontinue their existing tramways within and without the city and to abandon the power to construct such of their tramways within the city as are authorised but not constructed:

And whereas it is expedient that the other provisions contained in this Act be enacted:

And whereas the purposes of this Act cannot be effected without the authority of parliament:

And whereas estimates have been prepared for the purposes hereinafter mentioned and such estimates are as follows:-

For and in connection with the provision of trolley vehicles	£490,000
For and in connection with the provision and adaption of electrical equipment and the construction of other works necessary for working trolley vehicles	£140,000
For buildings for trolley vehicles	£90,000
For reinstatement of roads	£61,000

And whereas the several works included in such estimates are permanent works and it is expedient that the cost thereof should be spread over a term of years:

And whereas in relation to the promotion of the Bill for this Act the requirements of the Borough Funds Acts 1872 and 1903 have been observed:

May it therefore please Your Majesty that it may be enacted and be it enacted by the King's most Excellent Majesty by and with the advice and consent of the Lords Spiritual and temporal and Commons in this present Parliament assembled and by the authority of the same as follows (that is to say):-

1. This Act may be cited as the Nottingham Corporation Act 1930.

2. (1) In this Act the several words and expressions to which meanings are assigned by the Acts wholly or partially incorporated herewith or by the Public Health Act 1875 to 1925 shall have the same respective meanings unless there shall be something in the subject or context repugnant to such construction.

(2) In this Act unless the subject or the context otherwise requires-

"The city" means the city of Nottingham and the county of the same city;

"The Corporation" means the lord mayor aldermen and citizens of the city;

"The general rate fund" and "the general rate" mean respectively the general rate fund and the general rate of the city;

"The county" means the administrative county of Nottingham;

"The road authority" means with reference to any road or part of a road over which any proposed trolley vehicle service will pass the authority in whom such road or part of a road is vested;

"The Act of 1897" "the Act of 1905" "the Act of 1910" "the Act of 1913" "the Act of 1923" "the Act of 1925" and "the Act of 1929" mean respectively the Nottingham Improvement Act 1897 the Nottingham Corporation Act 1905 the Nottingham Corporation Act 1910 the Nottingham Corporation Act 1913 the Nottingham Corporation Act 1923 the Nottingham Corporation Act 1925 and the Nottingham Corporation Act 1929;

"Trolley vehicle" means a mechanically propelled vehicle adapted for use upon roads without rails and moved by electrical power transmitted thereto from some external source;

"Revenues of the Corporation" includes the revenues of the Corporation from time to time arising from any land undertakings or other property for the time being of the Corporation and the rates and contributions leviable by or on the order or precept of the Corporation.

3. (1) The Corporation may work trolley vehicles along the following routes and where necessary may adapt existing tramway poles and apparatus for the purpose of working trolley vehicles:-

(a) Along any tramway route of the Corporation whether within or without the city;

(b) Along the following routes in the city along which Tramways Nos. 1 2A 3 and 4 authorised by the Act of 1923 and the unconstructed portion of Tramway No. 2 authorised by the Act of 1925 were authorised to be constructed-

(i) commencing in Lower Parliament Street 94 feet or thereabouts east of its junction with George Street proceeding along Lower Parliament Street to and along the new street (Street Work No. 3) authorised in the Act of 1923 Sneinton Street Carter Gate the new street (street Work No. 6) authorised by the Act of 1923 to and terminating in London Road 75 feet or thereabouts south of the junction of that road with Leenside;

(ii) commencing in Sneinton Street 95 feet or thereabouts north-west of its junction with Southwell Road thence proceeding in a south-easterly and north-easterly direction to an terminating in Southwell Road 95 feet or thereabouts north-east of the junction of Sneinton Street with Southwell Road;

(iii) commencing in Fisher Gate 60 feet or thereabouts east of its junction with Carter Gate then proceeding in a southerly direction to and terminating in the new street (Street Work No. 6) authorised by the Act of 1923 50 feet or thereabouts south of such junction;

(iv) along Derby Road from its junction with Hillside to a point 200 feet or thereabouts south-west of the junction of Derby Road with Beeston Lane;

(c) Along the following street and roads in the city:-

(v) Sneinton Road from Carlton Road to Dale Street Dale Street Sneinton Dale Cardale Road Thorneywood Lane and Porchester Road from Thorneywood Lane to Woodborough Road;

(vi) Mansfield Street from Huntingdon Street to Windsor Street Windsor Street St. Michael's Street Millstone Lane and Cross Street;

(vii) Leenside and Canal Street;

(viii) Abbey Bridge Abbey Street and Beeston Road from Abbey Street to Greenfield Street;

(ix) Derby Road from a point 200 feet or thereabouts south-west of its junction with Beeston Lane to the city boundary,

(x) Ilkeston Road from its junction with Derby Road to Wollaton Road Wollaton Road and Middleton Boulevard from Wollaton Road to Derby Road;

(xi) Gregory Boulevard from Mansfield Road to Radford Boulevard and Radford Boulevard from Gregory Boulevard to Hartley Road;

(xii) Main Street Bulwell from Bulwell Market Place to Hucknall Lane and Hucknall lane from Main Street to Grindon Crescent;

(xiii) Woodside Road from its junction with Derby Road to the boundary between the city and the urban district of Beeston.

And with the consent of the Ministry of Transport along any other street in the city which the Corporation think it necessary or convenient to use for the purpose of obtaining access to trolley vehicle routes from any depot garage building or work of the Corporation or of connecting trolley vehicle routes and in any street in the city and in the urban district of Arnold the urban district of Carlton and the rural district of Basford for the purpose of providing turning points.

(2 Before equipping any trolley vehicle route to include a turning point or before arranging for a new turning point on any route the Corporation shall submit plans of the turning point to the Ministry of Transport for approval and in the case of turning points in the county shall submit a copy of such plans to the road authority and before approving any such plans the Minister of Transport shall give to the road authority an opportunity of making representations with reference thereto and shall consider any such representations as may be made to him.

5. Notwithstanding anything contained in section 32 (Weight of vehicles and approval of construction by Minister of Transport) of the Act of 1925 a six-wheeled rigid framed trolley vehicle used by the Corporation may be of but shall not exceed such weight as is prescribed by the Heavy Motor Car (Amendment) Order 1927.

(Section 5 was repealed with the 1935 Act, paragraph 15 (3)).

6. The Corporation shall not (unless the Minister of Transport otherwise approves) use on any trolley vehicle run by them any tyres other than pneumatic tyres.

7. (1) The existing tramways of the Corporation within the city on any of the trolley vehicle routes authorised by this Act may be abandoned or discontinued if the Corporation think fit either temporarily or permanently. Provided that no such tramway and portion thereof shall be so abandoned or discontinued by the Corporation until they shall have decided by resolution to use trolley vehicles on the route of such tramway or on the portion thereof so proposed to be abandoned or discontinued.

(2) Nothing in this section shall relieve the Corporation of any liability imposed upon them by section 41 (Tramways to be removed in certain cases) of the Tramways Act 1870 in relation to any tramway or portion thereof in the event of the Corporation discontinuing the working of such tramway or portion thereof otherwise than in accordance with the provisions of this Act.

(3) As from the date upon which a service of trolley vehicles is provided by the Corporation in lieu of a tramway service the revenue of the tramway undertaking of the Corporation shall (to such extent as the Corporation may from time to time by resolution determine) cease to be charged under any statutory enactment relating to that undertaking with expenses incurred by the Corporation upon or in connection with the maintenance and repair of the streets in which such service was run but nothing in this section shall relieve the Corporation from any liability attaching to them in respect of such maintenance and repair.

There then followed paragraphs for the protection of Nottinghamshire County Council and the Urban District Councils of Arnold and Carlton in respect of abandonment of the tramways, reinstatement of the road surface and the equipment of routes outside the city boundary for trolleybus operation.

11. The Corporation may if they think fit abandon the power to construct Tramways Nos. 1 2A 3 and 4 authorised by the Act of 1923 and the unconstructed portion of Tramway No. 2 authorised by the Act of 1925.

(These were:

Tramway 1 (1923) was a 4 furlong 6.85 chains link between the existing tramways in Lower Parliament Street along the new road, later to be known as the Lower Parliament Street extension, to its junction with London Road.

Tramway 2A (1923) was a 2.8 chains link between Tramway 1 and Southwell Road (the Carter Gate –Southwell Road line authorised by the same Act).

Tramway 3 (1923) was a 1.42 chains link between Fisher Gate and Lower Parliament Street extension.

Tramway 4 (1923) was a 3 furlong 1.10 chain from Tramway 1 authorised by the 1920 Act along a new street from Gregory Street to Castle Boulevard as far as the junction with Castle Boulevard

Tramway 2 (1925) was a 1 mile 1 furlong 9.65 chains extension in Derby Road from the junction with Beeston Lane to the junction with Gregory Street and the existing tramways).

12. Notwithstanding anything contained in this Act the Corporation shall not except with the consent of the Nottinghamshire and Derbyshire Traction Company (in this section called "the company") under their common seal at any time prior to the expiry of the period limited by section 14 (Period for completion of trolley vehicle equipment) of the Nottinghamshire and Derbyshire Traction Act 1928 or any extension not exceeding three years of that period which may be authorised by Parliament abandon or discontinue any part of the existing tramways of the Corporation leased to or worked or run over by the company under the agreement dated the twenty-second day of May one thousand nine hundred and eight between the company and the Corporation set out in the First Schedule to and confirmed by the Nottinghamshire and Derbyshire Tramways Act 1908 unless and until the company shall have equipped for the working of trolley vehicles the route of so much of the tramways of the company as is situate between the boundary of the city in Nuthall Road and the village of Kimberley and the Corporation shall have erected the necessary apparatus for the use of trolley vehicle from the said boundary to the junction of Fairfax Street and Nottingham Road on the streets and roads in the city mentioned in subsection (2) of section 10 (As to tramways of Nottingham Corporation leased to company) of the Nottinghamshire and Derbyshire Traction Act 1928 and being Route B authorised by section 39 (Trolley vehicles) of the Act of 1929.

13. (1) If and so long as a service of tramcars or trolley vehicles or a service of tramcars or trolley vehicles is provided by the Corporation or is provided under a working agreement to which the Corporation are parties along any protected route in the city and such service adequately meets the requirements of such protected route it shall not be lawful except as in this section provided or except under a working agreement with the Corporation for any company (except a railway company in pursuance of their statutory powers) or for any other local authority body or person to run omnibuses in competition with the service so provided.

(2) The licensing authority for the city may and shall in order to give effect to the foregoing provisions of this section when licensing an omnibus to ply for hire grant such licence subject to conditions as to the routes upon which such omnibus may or shall not ply for hire. Provided that if any question arises between the Corporation and any company authority body or person as to whether any route in respect of which a licence may be applied for by or may be granted to any such company authority body or person is competitive such question shall on the application of either parties be determined as hereinafter in this section provided. Provided further that the right of the applicant for the licence of appeal to the Minister of Transport from the decision of the licensing authority under section 14 (3) of the Roads Act shall not be affected but the said Minister in making any order under that section shall have regard to the provisions of this section provided also that omnibuses belonging to the same proprietor may be transferred by him from one route to another route along which he is for the time being licensed to run omnibuses so long as he does not at one and the same time allow a greater number of omnibuses to ply for hire on any protected route or any route in competition therewith than the number of licences which he holds for such route.

(3) Any question at any time arising as to whether or not the Corporation are providing an adequate service along any protected route or whether there is or would be any such competition shall be determined by the Minister of Transport on the application of any interested party and the said Minister shall have power to make such order thereon as he thinks fit. Any order made by the said Minister under this section shall be final and binding on the parties affected thereby and shall not be subject to appeal to any court and shall on the application of the said Minister or the Corporation or the applicant for a licence be enforceable by writ of mandamus.

(4) Nothing in this section shall be deemed-

(a) to restrict the running of any omnibus by any such company authority body or person along any protected route or a particular part of any protected route or any other route in competition therewith if no passenger conveyed by such omnibus is both taken up and set down on any one journey on any protected route or any route in competition therewith; or

(b) to prevent the renewal by a licensing authority of any licence to ply for hire with an omnibus along a protected route or route in competition with a protected route if the licence was in force on the twentieth day of November nineteen hundred and twenty-nine and was applicable to any service of omnibuses which was on that date being operated and has since that date been regularly in operation on such protected route or part of a route or route in competition therewith or to prevent the grant of a licence to ply for hire with an omnibus substituted by the licensee for any such first-mentioned omnibus or to restrict the running of any such first-mentioned omnibus or substituted omnibus along any such route or part of a route as aforesaid; or

(c) to prevent the grant or renewal by a licensing authority of any licence to ply for hire with an omnibus on the condition that no passenger conveyed by the omnibus to which the licence relates shall be both taken up and set down on any one journey on any protected route or any route in competition therewith; or

(d) to prevent the grant by a licensing authority of any licence to ply for hire with an omnibus of the Trent Motor Traction Company Limited along a protected route or a particular part of a protected route or a route in competition with a protected route or to restrict the running of any such omnibus along any such route or part of a route. Provided that any omnibus licensed or run as aforesaid shall be run in accordance with the provisions of an agreement dated the eighth day of October nineteen hundred and twenty-eight made between the Corporation of the one part and the Trent Motor Traction Company Limited of the other part which agreement notwithstanding anything therein contained shall not be terminated except by agreement between the parties thereto.

(5) Any company authority body or person who shall run any omnibus along any route in contravention of the provisions of this section shall be liable to a penalty not exceeding five pounds for every day upon which he runs any such omnibus.

(6) In this section the expression "protected route" means any existing tramway or trolley vehicle route of the Corporation in the city or any part of any such existing tramway or trolley vehicle route and any of the trolley vehicle routes in the city authorised by the Act or any part of such a route.

14. (1) The Corporation may from time to time independently of any other borrowing power borrow at interest for and in connection with the purposes mentioned in the first column of the following table the respective sums mentioned in the second column thereof and in order to secure the repayment of the said sums and the payment of interest thereon the Corporation may mortgage or charge the revenues of the Corporation any they shall pay off all moneys so borrowed within the respective periods (which for the purpose of this Act any enactment incorporated therewith or applied thereto shall respectively be "the prescribed period") mentioned in the third column of the said table (namely):-

Purpose.	Amount.	Period for repayment
(a) For and in connection with the provision of trolley vehicles.	£490,000	Ten years from the date or dates of borrowing.
(b) For and in connection with the provision and adaption of electrical equipment and the construction of other works necessary for working trolley vehicles.	£140,000	Twenty years from the date or dates of borrowing.
(c) For buildings for of trolley vehicles.	£90,000	Forty years from the date or dates of borrowing.
(d) For reinstatement of roads.	£61,000	Twenty years from the date or dates of borrowing.
(e) For the payment of the costs charges and expenses of this Act.	The sum requisite.	Five years from the passing of this Act.

(2) (a) The Corporation may also borrow with the consent of the Minister of Transport such further moneys as may be necessary for any of the purposes of this Act.

(b) Any moneys borrowed under this subsection shall be repaid within such period as may be prescribed by the Minister with whose consent the moneys are borrowed and that period shall be the prescribed period for the purposes of this Act and the enactments incorporated therewith or applied thereby.

(c) In order to secure the repayment of any moneys borrowed under this subsection and the payment of interest thereon the Corporation may mortgage or charge the revenues of the Corporation.

24 & 25 Geo.5. [Ch.li.]

Nottingham Corporation (Trolley Vehicles) Order Confirmation Act, 1934

3. (1) The Corporation may use trolley vehicles upon the following routes in the city:-

Route No 1. (1 mile 6 furlongs and 7.42 chains or thereabouts in length) commencing in Alfreton Road at its junction with Bentinck Road thence proceeding along Alfreton Road to and across Bobber's Mill Bridge thence along Nuthall Road to and terminating in that road at its junction with Stockhill Lane.

(2) Before equipping the said route to include a turning point or before arranging for a new turning point thereon the Corporation shall submit plans of the turning point to the Minister of Transport for approval.

(3) If the Corporation shall not have commenced to use trolley vehicles along the said route within five years from the passing of this Act confirming this Order or such extended time as the Minister of Transport may upon the application of the Corporation allow the powers conferred by this Order shall cease to be exercisable.

6. (1) The Corporation shall have power in addition and without prejudice to their powers of borrowing under the Local Government Act 1933 from time to time borrow without the consent of any sanctioning authority for an in connection with the purposes mentioned in the first column of the following table the respective sums mentioned in the second column of the said table and they shall pay off all moneys so borrowed within such periods as the Corporation may determine not exceeding those respectively mentioned in the third column of the said table (namely):-

Purpose.	Amount.	Period for repayment
(a) The provision of trolley vehicles.	£10,000	Ten years from the date or dates of borrowing.
(b) For provision of trolley vehicle equipment and the construction of other works necessary for working trolley vehicles on the trolley vehicle route authorised by this Order.	£10,766	Twenty years from the date or dates of borrowing.
(c) For the payment of the costs charges and expenses of this Order.	The sum requisite.	Five years from the passing of this Order.

(2) The provisions of Part IX of the Local Government Act 1933 so far as they are not inconsistent with this Order shall extend and apply to money borrowed under this section as if it were borrowed under Part IX of that Act and the period fixed for the repayment of any money borrowed under this section shall as respects that money be the fixed period for the purpose of the said Part IX.

(3) In the application of the provisions of the Local Government Act 1933 to the borrowing of any further money for the purposes of this Order the Minister of Transport shall be the sanctioning authority.

25 & 26 Geo.5. [c.cxix.]

Nottingham Corporation Act, 1935

PART III - TRANSPORT

15. (1) All trolley vehicles and the electrical equipment thereof used by the Corporation under the authority of any Act of Order relating to them shall be of such form construction weight and dimensions as the Minister of Transport (in this section referred to as "the Minister") may approve and no trolley vehicle shall be used by the Corporation which does not comply with the requirements of the Minister.

(2) Before applying to the Minister for his approval of the weight of any trolley vehicle to be used upon any road which crosses a bridge belonging to and repairable by a railway company the Corporation shall give to the railway company notice of the weight of the trolley vehicles proposed to be used by them upon such roads and the Minister shall consider and determine after such inquiry as he may think fit any objections which may be submitted by the railway company to him on the ground that the strength of the bridge is insufficient to carry trolley vehicles of such weight. Provided that a copy of the objections shall be sent by the railway company to the Corporation at the same time as they are sent to the Minister.

(3) Section 32 (Weight of vehicles and approval of construction by Minister of Transport) of the Act of 1925 and section 5 (Weight of trolley vehicles) of the Act of 1930 are hereby repealed and notwithstanding any provision to the contrary those sections shall cease to apply to trolley vehicles provided and worked by the Corporation under the Act of 1929 or the Nottingham Corporation (Trolley Vehicles) Order 1934.

16. Notwithstanding the provisions of any Act or Order relating to the procedure for the making of byelaws by the Corporation the provisions of section 250 of the Act of 1933 shall apply to all byelaws to be made by the Corporation in respect of their tramways undertaking and in the application of such last-mentioned provisions the Minister of Transport shall be the confirming authority.

10 & 11 Geo.6. [c.xxxvi.]

Nottingham Corporation Act, 1947

PART IV - TROLLEY VEHICLES

27. The Corporation may subject to the provisions of this Act run trolley vehicles upon the following route in addition to any routes upon which they are already authorised to use trolley vehicles:-

A route in the urban district of Carlton in the county commencing in Main Street East at Post Office Square by a junction with the existing trolley vehicle route thence proceeding along Main Street East to its junction with Manor Road and thence along Manor Road to its junction with Station Road and thence along Station Road to and terminating at the point of commencement in Main Street East. Provided that the Corporation shall run trolley vehicles upon the said route as one-way traffic in a clockwise direction.

28. If the Corporation shall not have commenced to run trolley vehicles along the route authorised by this Act within five years from the passing of this Act or such extended time as the Minister of Transport may upon the application of the Corporation allow the powers conferred by this Act with reference to the running of trolley vehicles along the said route shall cease to be exercisable.

29. The restrictions contained in the enactments relating to the payment of fares in respect of the carriage of passengers upon the tramways of the Corporation applied to the carriage of passengers upon the trolley vehicles of the Corporation shall not extend to any special trolley vehicles or to any special service of trolley vehicles run by the Corporation on extraordinary occasions and in respect of such special trolley vehicles and services the Corporation may demand and take such fares as they shall think fit:

Provided that the running of such special trolley vehicles or special services of trolley vehicles shall in no way curtail the ordinary service of trolley vehicles.

31. The trolley vehicle route and the powers relating thereto authorised by this Part of the Act shall be deemed to form part of the transport undertaking of the Corporation.

32. The trolley vehicles of the Corporation shall not be deemed to be stage carriages for the purposes of sections 13 to 15 of the Railway Passenger Duty Act 1842 but for the purpose of calculating the number of passengers in excess of the seating capacity that may be carried thereon shall be deemed to be public service vehicles.

33. (1) The trolley vehicles of the Corporation shall not be deemed to be omnibuses within the meaning of the Town Police Clause Act 1889.

(2) Section 31 (Vehicles not to be deemed light locomotives) of the Act of 1925 is hereby repealed.

36. The following provisions for the protection of the county council and the urban district council of Carlton (each of whom is in this section referred to as "the road authority") shall notwithstanding anything in this Act contained and unless otherwise agreed in writing apply and have effect (that is to say):-

(1) (a) All posts and apparatus erected or placed by the Corporation in connection with the trolley vehicle route authorised by this Act in over or under any street or road shall be placed in such a position as the road authority may approve;

(b) All posts shall be set back into recesses to be constructed at the expense of the Corporation at the back of the footpaths where so required by the surveyor of the road authority:

(2) The Corporation shall not attach any brackets wires or apparatus to any buildings of which the road authorities are the owners without the consent in writing of the road authority:

(3) All posts and apparatus erected or placed by the Corporation in connection with the trolley vehicle route authorised by this Act in over or under any street or road may be used without any payment being required by the Corporation by the road authority for the fixing thereto or the suspension therefrom of apparatus for lighting the street or road Provided that any apparatus and the method of fixing or suspension thereof shall be previously approved by the Corporation and the work of fixing or suspension shall be carried out to the satisfaction of the Corporation.

15 & 16 Geo.6 & 1 Eliz. 2 [c.xxxiii]

Nottingham Corporation Act, 1952

PART IV - TRANSPORT UNDERTAKING

34. (1) Section 22 (Power to appoint stages) of the Act of 1923 shall have effect as if in subsection (1) the words "two pence" were substituted for the words "one penny" and "three halfpence".

(2) Section 13 (Cheap fares for labouring classes) of the Nottingham Corporation Act 1902 shall have effect as if in subsection (1) the words "three halfpence" were substituted for the words "one halfpenny" and as if the words "two pence" were substituted for the words "one penny".

(3) The provisions of the said section 22 of the Act of 1923 as amended by this Act shall extend and apply to the provision maintenance and running of trolley vehicles under the powers of the Act of 1913.

(4 Section 14 (Fares rates and charges) of the Act of 1913 shall have effect as if subsection (2) were omitted therefrom.

35. (1) (a) If at any time hereafter the Corporation desire to provide equip maintain and use trolley vehicles upon any road dedicated to the public use whether within or outside the city not forming part of any trolley vehicle route for the time being authorised they may make application to the Minister of Transport (in this section referred to as "the Minister") and the Minister is hereby empowered to make an order authorising the use by the Corporation of trolley vehicles subject to such conditions and restrictions (if any) as he may think fit upon any road or roads to which such application relates and containing such incidental provisions as the Minister may deem expedient and subject to the terms of the order the provisions of the Nottingham Corporation Act 1947 shall apply as if the use of trolley vehicles upon such road were authorised by that Act.

(b) The Minister shall not make an order under this section relating to any road outside the city except with the consent of the local authority and of the road authority and subject to such conditions and restrictions as the local authority and the road authority may agree.

(c) Any trolley vehicle route and the powers relating thereto authorised by the Minister under this section shall be deemed to form part of the transport undertaking of the Corporation.

(2) An order made under this section shall be subject to special parliamentary procedure and the First Schedule to the Statutory Orders (Special Procedure) Act 1945 (which sets out the notices to be given and other requirements to be complied with before an order is made) shall in its application to any such order have effect as if paragraph 1 of the said schedule included a provision requiring the Corporation to comply with any direction which may be given by the Minister as to posting and maintaining notices giving the purport of the application in relation to any road or roads to which it relates in that road or in those roads.

(3) The expression "Act of Parliament" in section 7 of the Telegraph Act 1878 (which makes provision as to work done in pursuance of Acts of Parliament involving any telegraphic lines) shall be construed as including any order made under this section authorising the execution of works.

36. The Corporation may make byelaws as to the conduct of persons using public service vehicle and trolley vehicle stations shelters conveniences and other premises forming part of the transport undertaking of the Corporation to which the public have access:

Provided that no such byelaws shall apply to any property or vehicles of the West Bridgford Urban District Council.

2) City of Nottingham Byelaws

CITY OF NOTTINGHAM

BYELAWS AND REGULATIONS
WITH RESPECT TO
THE TRAMWAYS, TRAMCARS AND
TROLLEY VEHICLES OF THE CORPORATION

1934
(REPRINTED 1945)

City of Nottingham At a MEETING of the COUNCIL
And County of the same City of the CITY OF NOTTINGHAM
To Wit: and County of the same City

held at the COUNCIL HOUSE in the City of Nottingham aforesaid on Monday, the 30th day of July, 1934, the following Byelaws and Regulations were made by the said Council in pursuance of the powers conferred on them by the Tramways Act, 1870, the Nottingham Improvement Act, 1897, the Nottingham Corporation Acts, 1905, 1910, 1913, 1920, 1923, 1925, 1929 and 1930, and of every other power enabling them in that behalf, that is to say:-

BYELAWS AND REGULATIONS

Made by the Lord Mayor Aldermen and Citizens of the City of Nottingham and County of the same City acting by the Council (hereinafter referred to as "the Corporation") with respect to the tramways tramcars and trolley vehicles of the Corporation.

1. The Byelaws and Regulations hereinafter set forth shall extend and apply to all carriages of the Corporation and to all places with respect to which the Corporation have power to make Byelaws and Regulations.
2. Throughout these Byelaws and Regulations:
   (1) The expression "conductor" shall include any officer or servant in the employment of the Corporation and having charge of a carriage;
   (2) The expression "carriage" shall include tramcars and trolley vehicles;
   (3) The expression "interior of a carriage" shall not include the upper deck of a covered carriage.
3. Every passenger shall enter or depart from a carriage by the platform or other place of entrance or exit provided for the purpose and not otherwise.
   When a carriage stops, no person shall board the carriage until all passengers desiring to alight therefrom shall have done so.
4. No person shall enter, mount or leave, or attempt to enter, mount or leave any carriage in motion.
5. No passenger shall smoke or carry a lighted pipe, cigar or cigarette in or on any part of the carriage in or on which a notice is exhibited that smoking is prohibited, and no person shall spit in, on, from or against any carriage.
6. No passenger or other person shall, while travelling in or upon any carriage, play or perform upon any musical instrument, or distribute advertisements, pamphlets, notices, handbills or tracts of any kind, or beg or collect money, alms or subscriptions, or sell any article, or play any game, or gamble, or paste notices or handbills or deposit remnants of food or fruit in or upon any carriage.
7. A person in a state of intoxication shall not enter or mount upon any carriage, and if found in or upon any carriage shall leave the carriage immediately on being requested to do so by the conductor, and in the event of refusal to leave it shall be lawful for the conductor or any officer or servant of the Corporation to remove such person from the carriage.

8. No person shall swear or use obscene or offensive language whilst in or upon any carriage, or wilfully interfere with the comfort of any passenger.
9. No person shall commit any nuisance in, on or against any carriage or any premises or property used in connection with the Corporation's tramway or trolley vehicle undertakings.
10. No person shall wilfully cut, tear, soil, or damage the cushions, linings or any part of any carriage, or remove or deface any number plate, printed or other notice in or on the carriage, or break or scratch any window of or otherwise wilfully damage any carriage. Any person acting in contravention of this Byelaw and Regulation shall be liable to the penalty prescribed by these Byelaws and Regulations in addition to the liability to pay the amount of any damage done.
11. A person whose dress or clothing might, in the opinion of the conductor, soil or injure the linings or cushions of the carriage or the dress or clothing of other passengers, or who, in the opinion of the conductor, might for any other reason be offensive to passengers, shall not mount, enter or remain on or in any carriage, and may be prevented from so doing, and, if found on or in any carriage, shall, on request of the conductor, leave the same upon his fare, if previously paid, being returned: Provided that on carriages specially run for artisans, mechanics and daily labourers no person shall be prevented from entering or remaining in or on a carriage under the provisions of this Byelaw and Regulation, on the ground of the condition of his dress or clothing, if such condition is due solely due to the nature of his employment.
12. Each passenger shall, upon demand, pay to the conductor or other duly authorised officer of the Corporation the fare legally demandable for the journey: Provided that no child under the age of three years who is not occupying a seat shall be liable pay a fare.
13. Each passenger shall show his ticket (if any), when required to do so, to the conductor or any duly authorised servant of the Corporation, and shall also, when required so to do, either deliver up his ticket or pay the fare legally demandable for the distance travelled over by such passenger.
14. No person travelling or having travelled in any carriage shall avoid or attempt to avoid payment of the fare. Any passenger paying for a stage less than the whole journey run by the carriage shall be deemed to have completed his journey at the end of the stage paid for; if the passenger remains on the carriage he shall pay the fare legally payable for the remainder of his journey as a new passenger.
14. No artisan, mechanic, daily labourer or other person issued with an artisan's, mechanic's or daily labourer's ticket shall use or attempt to use such ticket except during such hours and at such times as the Corporation may from time to time prescribe.
15. Personal or other luggage carried by passengers (including the tools of artisans, mechanics and daily labourers) shall be placed in such part of the carriage as the conductor may direct. No luggage which from its size or otherwise is in the opinion of the conductor unsuitable for conveyance in or upon a carriage shall be taken in or upon such carriage.
16. No passenger or other person not being a servant of the Corporation shall travel on the steps or platforms of any carriage, or stand on the upper deck, or sit on the railing, guards or buffers of any carriage, and any person so travelling, standing or sitting shall cease to do so immediately on request by the conductor.
17. No person, except a passenger or intending passenger, shall enter or mount any carriage.
18. No person shall hold or hang on by or to any part of any carriage, or travel therein or thereon otherwise than on a seat provided for passengers, except in the interior of the carriage with the consent of the conductor.
19. When any carriage contains the full number of passengers which it is licensed to contain, no additional person shall enter, mount or remain in or on any such carriage when warned by the conductor not to do so.
20. No dog or other animal shall be allowed in or on any carriage except by permission if the conductor, nor in any case in which the conveyance of such dog or other animal might be offensive or an annoyance to passengers. No person shall take a dog or other animal into or on any carriage after having been requested not to do so by the conductor or place any dog elsewhere in or on the carriage than as directed by the conductor. Any dog or other animal taken into or on any carriage in breach of this Byelaw and Regulation shall be removed by the person in charge of such dog or other animal from the carriage immediately upon request by the conductor, and, in default of compliance with such request, may be removed by or under the direction of the conductor.
22. No person shall travel in or on any carriage with loaded firearms, or with dangerous or offensive articles, tools or implements.
23. No passenger shall wilfully obstruct or impede any officer or servant of the Corporation in the execution of his duty upon or in connection with any carriage or tramway of the Corporation, and no person other than the conductor or driver shall change or remove the route indicators or destination boards or interfere with the controllers, brakes, lights, ventilators, trolley cods or any other part of a carriage or its equipment or do or cause to be done anything in such manner as to obstruct any carriage or endanger the lives of persons therein.
24. If at any time a carriage becomes disabled, or in any way damaged, or from any cause unable to proceed, the passengers shall, upon request of the conductor, leave the same, and if such passengers have paid their fares, they shall not be entitled to demand back the amount of their fares so paid, but on production of their tickets shall be allowed to travel by the next available carriage the remainder of the distance in respect of which they have paid their fares. No person shall, except with the consent of the conductor, enter a disabled or damaged carriage.
25. Any person who shall commit, whilst in or on any carriage, any breach of these Byelaws and Regulations, shall if the offence is continued, be liable, in addition to incurring the penalty hereinafter provided, to be immediately removed from the carriage by or under the direction of the conductor, and if such person shall have paid his fare, he shall not be entitled to claim its return.
26. The conductor shall enforce these Byelaws and Regulations and prevent the breach thereof to the best of his ability.
27. Any person offending against or committing a breach of any of these Byelaws shall be liable to a penalty not exceeding forty shillings.
28. There shall be placed and kept in a conspicuous position inside of each carriage in use and in or about any premises or property used in connection with the Corporation's tramway or trolley vehicle undertakings a printed copy of these Byelaws and Regulations.
29. These Byelaws and Regulations shall come into force on the 1st day of December 1934.
30. From and after the date of coming into force of these Byelaws and Regulations the Byelaws Rules and Regulations referred to in the Schedule hereto shall be repealed but without prejudice to any proceedings in respect of any contravention thereof.

THE SCHEDULE above referred to.

Description of Byelaws Rules and Regulations	By whom made	Date of making
Byelaws and Regulations as to the tramways of the Nottingham and District Tramways Company Limited.	The Corporation	6th October 1879
Rules and Regulations as to the tramways of the Nottingham and District Tramways Company Limited.		9th February 1880
The Further Rules and Regulations as to the tramways of the Nottingham and District CorporationTramways Company Limited.		13th August 1883
Byelaws and Regulations with respect to the tramways and tramcars of the Corporation.		6th March 1899

SEALED with the Common Seal of the Lord Mayor Aldermen and Citizens of the City of Nottingham and County of the same City this thirtieth of July, 1934, in the presence of:-

Signed J. FARR
LORD MAYOR

Signed J.E. RICHARDS
DEPUTY TOWN CLERK

I hereby certify that a true copy of the foregoing Byelaws and Regulations has, in accordance with the provisions of section 46 of the Tramways Act, 1870, been laid before the Minister of Transport not less than two calendar months before such Byelaws and Regulations come into operation, and that such Byelaws and Regulations have not been disallowed by the Minister of Transport within the said two calendar months.

Signed E.W. ROWNTREE

ASSISTANT SECRETARY.
MINISTRY OF TRANSPORT

20th November, 1934.

3) Transport Department Internal Instructions

3.1) Instructions to Trolley Vehicle Drivers

Extracts from Nottingham Corporation Passenger Transport Department Rule Book 1934

99. Drivers must report themselves for duty at their respective depots ten minutes before their vehicle is due to leave.

100. (a) Examine coachwork and any fresh damage found must be reported to the Foreman in Charge.
(b) Ascertain that all tyres are fully inflated, that the air brake switch is in the "on" position and pressure registers at gauge.
(c Check air brake compressor motor for "butting in" by making several applications of the brake pedal.
(e) Check positions of main lighting switch.
Important: On the Ransomes twin motor type this switch cuts out the arc brake switch and should always be in the "on" position when the vehicle is on service.

101. Drivers are responsible for keeping themselves fully conversant with details, i.e. switches, fuses, etc. on the different types of vehicle operated by the Department.

102. In the event of breakdown from "no power", the drivers must make the following tests:-
(a) Ascertain that the circuit breakers are in the "on" position;
(b) Check power supply by switching on section of lights;
(c) Examine fuses;
(d) Ascertain that trolley and skate change over switch is making good contact.
(f) Cut out motor (twin motor vehicles only).

103. When changing over from trolley to skate or in the event of a trolley leaving the wires, the main lighting switch must be used in all cases, as this switch cuts out all lighting circuits.

104. When inspecting fuses circuit bases must be in the "off" position.

105. All trolley dewirements must be reported on the report form provided and forwarded to the Traffic Superintendent to reach him not later than 9.00 a.m. on the following morning. If dewirements become frequent, drivers must notify the Motor Inspector to examine trolley heads.

106. Any defect noticed or caused by drivers in the overhead equipment and all damage to same, street lighting, lamp standards and property, must be submitted in a full report, giving the nearest number of standard.

107. Emergency oil lamps must be carried on all trolley vehicles and must be placed in position immediately the ordinary lighting fails or in case of mechanical breakdown during darkness.

108. The speed allowed by the Ministry of Transport are:-

Four miles an hour.

When passing through all trolley wire junctions and crossings and when passing round all turning circles.
Round the curves between:
Parliament Street and King Street;
King Street and Queen Street;
Parliament Street and Milton Street;
Mansfield Road and Gregory Boulevard;
Gregory Boulevard and Sherwood Rise.
When entering and leaving George Street.
At the junction of South Parade and Wheeler Gate.
At the junction of Long Row and Market Street.

Five miles an hour.

When traversing Canning Circus.
In any part of Bulwell Market.
Under the LNER Bridge over Highbury Road.
When crossing Parliament Street to Chapel Bar.
In Council House Square, including Beastmarket Hill.
At Trent Bridge.

Eight miles an hour.

In King Street, Parliament Street and Queen Street.

Ten miles an hour.

Round the curves between:
Middleton Boulevard and Wollaton Road;
Middleton Boulevard and Derby Road.
At the junction of Derby Road and Upper Parliament Street at Park Row.
In Southwell Road.
In Main Street, Carlton.
Round Stockhill Lane Corner.
From Whitemoor Road to the entrance of Basford LMS Goods Yard.
Round the curves at the junction of Alfreton Road with Southey Street and Bentinck Road.

Fifteen miles an hour.

Up Market Street.

Sixteen miles an hour.

In St. Ann's Well Road, King Edward Street and Lower Parliament Street.
In George Street.
In Wilford Road between Kirkewhite Street and the turning circle at Wilford Bridge.
In Nottingham Road and Sherwood Rise.
In Mansfield Road and Milton Street.

Twenty miles an hour.

Between Elliott Street and Canning Circus in Derby Road.
Between Canning Circus and the junction with Upper Parliament Street at Park Row.
In Upper Parliament Street between its junction with Derby Road at Park Row and its junction with Queen Street.
In Ilkeston Road between Ronald Street and Canning Circus.
In Handel Street.
In Carlton Road between Cardiff Street and the Crown Inn.
In Wells Road between Coppice Road and the turning circle at Kildare Road.
Along Percy Street.

Over the bridge from Church Street to Nottingham Road.
Along Main Street, Bulwell, from Ravensworth Road to the Public Library, with the exception of when traversing Bulwell Market.
Along Radford Road from the junction of Beaconsfield Street to the junction of Beaconsfield Street to the junction of Bentinck Road.
Down Chapel Bar.
Along Arkwright Street to Trent Bridge.

Twenty five miles an hour.
In Ilkeston Road, Radford Road and Wollaton Road between Ronald Street and Middleton Boulevard, except when crossing Lenton Boulevard where the speed shall not exceed the rate of ten miles per hour.
In Bath Street.
In Carlton Road, between Handel Street and Cardiff Street, and between the Crown Inn and Carlton Hill.
In Carlton Hill.
In Parliament Street between Southwell Road and King Edward Street.
From the terminus at Longford Crescent, along Hucknall Lane, to Ravensworth Road.
In Highbury Road, from the Public Library to the LNER Bridge.
In Vernon Road.
Along Alfreton Road to Canning Circus.
From Broadmarsh to the Midland Station.

Thirty miles an hour.
In Middleton Boulevard.
In Derby Road, between Elliott Street and Middleton Boulevard, except when crossing Lenton Boulevard, where the speed shall not exceed the rate of ten miles per hour.
From Cinderhill, along Nuthall Road.
Along Stockhill Lane to Percy Street.

Trolley Vehicles shall be brought to a standstill on all occasions before reaching the following points:-
In Wells Road at Coppice Road.
At Commercial Square.
In King Edward Street at Bath Street.
In Victoria Street at Bridlesmith Gate.
In Derby Road, at Middleton Boulevard on the outward journey.

3.2) Speed Limits

From Traffic Circular No. 17, November 1957

8. Trolleybus Speed restrictions

Services 36, 37 and 41
20 mph - In Church Street between its junction with Valley Road and the entrance to the British Railways Basford Goods Station.
20 mph - In Alpine Street, between its junction with Percy Street and Whitemoor Road, until the road is re-surfaced.
15 mph - When rounding the curves of the Gregory Boulevard/Mansfield Road roundabouts.
15 mph - When rounding the curves between Nuthal Road and Stockhill Lane.
10 mph - In Alpine Street, Basford Road and Church Street between the junction with Whitemoor Road and the entrance to the British Railways Goods Station.
10 mph - When passing under the railway bridge in Arkwright Street.
Compulsory Stop
In Alpine Street at its junction with Basford Road (descending vehicles only).

Services 38 and 39
20 mph - In Carlton Hill between its junction with Foxhill Road East and Cavendish Road.
20 mph - In Carlton Hill when rounding the curve at its junction with Dale View Road.
20 mph - In Handel Street, until the road is re-surfaced.
15 mph - When rounding the curves at the junction of Western Boulevard with Wollaton Road.
15 mph - When rounding the curves in Lower Parliament Street at its junction with Barker Gate (inwards only).
15 mph - When rounding the curves between Middleton Boulevard and Wollaton Road.
15 mph - When rounding the Lower Parliament Street/Southwell Road roundabout.

Services 40 and 47
20 mph - In St. Ann's Well Road, between its junction with Ransom Road and Alfred Street Central.
20 mph - In Wilford Road between its junctions with Waterway Street West and King's Meadow Road.

Services 42, 43, 44 and 46
25 mph - In Highbury Road between its junctions with Bulwell Market and Latimer Street.
20 mph - In Main Street, Bulwell between its junctions with Ravensworth Road and Bulwell Market.
20 mph - In Radford Road between its junctions with Eland Street and Gregory Boulevard until the road is re-surfaced.
15 mph - When rounding the curves at the junction of Moor Bridge with Hucknall Lane (inwards only).
15 mph - When passing under railway bridge near Basford and Bulwell Station.
15 mph - When rounding the curves between Radford Road and Bentinck Road.
15 mph - When rounding the curves between Bentinck Road and Alfreton Road.
10 mph - When passing under railway bridge in Colwick Road, near Sneinton Hermitage.
10 mph - When passing under railway bridge in Arkwright Street.

Service 45
20 mph - In Lower Parliament Street when rounding the curves between its junctions with Pennyfoot Street and London Road (outwards only).
15 mph - When rounding the curves in Lower Parliament Street, between its junctions with Pennyfoot Street and London Road (inwards only).
15 mph - When rounding the curves in Lower Parliament Street at its junction with Barker Gate (inwards only).
15 mph - When rounding the curves between Middleton Boulevard and Derby Road.
10 mph - When passing under the railway bridge in London Road.

Other Services
10 mph - When passing under the railway bridge in Station Street.
15 mph - When rounding the Lower Parliament Street/Southwell Road roundabout, after leaving Parliament Street Depot.
8 mph - When passing through all junctions and crossings in the overhead equipment.
8 mph - When rounding all turning circles and right-angled street corners, except where otherwise specified.

3.3) Various operating procedures

Extracts from Traffic Circular No. 17, November 1957

6. Destination Blinds

Drivers and conductors are reminded that destination blinds should not be altered for the next journey until the vehicle leaves the last stopping place prior to the terminus. This also applies to journeys where vehicles are running into the depot from a terminus, and every care must be taken to avoid the display of misleading destinations which often cause great inconvenience to the public.

7. Method of stopping and starting trolleybuses

Every trolleybus driver is aware of the correct procedure to be followed in the use of the handbrake when stopping and starting. The handbrake should be applied as the air brake is released and the vehicle is coming to rest, and it should be released as the drive is taken up after the first notch of the controller has been applied when starting away. It has been observed that some drivers jerk the vehicle badly when stopping and starting, due in most cases to the fact that they are not using the handbrake at all. This practice causes discomfort and possible danger to passengers and conductors, and is also bad for the vehicle: it can and must be avoided.

12. Dewirement Reports

Trolleybus Drivers are not always reporting dewirements as instructed, and this has led to further dewirements and damage to the overhead line and equipment. In every case, drivers must report a dewirement to an inspector at the first opportunity to enable the tower wagon crew to inspect the line as soon as possible, and then follow this up by submitting a dewirement report (Form No. 28) giving full details.

Most dewirements occur at overhead junctions, and I would remind drivers that the speed permitted by the regulations through these points is 8 mph, and must not be exceeded.

13. Reporting vehicle defects for attention

Conductors are particularly asked to inform the driver of any defects noted inside the vehicles, i.e. damage to seats and cushions, loose or broken floor laths, loose handrails, etc., so that these can be noted on the daily running card for attention.

BUT9641T/Brush 507 in the northbound carriageway of Middleton Boulevard, Wollaton Park prior to departure on an eastbound service 39. *EE/Beilby*

Appendix N Enthusiasts' Tours

Date	Vehicle	Hirer	Comments
23 April 1950	493	SCTS	
15 March 1953	N&D 343 N&D 346	OS & SCTS	Covered the N&D system together with the routes followed by N&D trolleybuses and trams within the city boundary. Outbound on carbon insert trolley head equipped 343 via Derby Road, Alfreton Road, Radford Road, Basford, Cinderhill. Inbound on 346 via Nottingham Road to King Street.
15 April 1956	444, 451, 493, 508, 587	Trolleybus Society & DLROS	Tour using a selection of trolleybuses from Lower Parliament Street and one from Bulwell Depots. Included a journey along Huntingdon Street northbound (the sole tour known to have followed this route) and along Station Street.
16 June 1957	587	OS	Included a visit to Lower Parliament Street Depot, Trent Bridge Works and an exhibition of overhead equipment.
19 July 1959	487	SCTS	
14 May 1961	489 (?)	Not known	
29 October 1961	585	NTG	Included the disused Station Street wiring (which had been energised for the occasion) westbound from London Road to Carrington Street.
24 June 1962	478	NTG	Included the disused Station Street wiring (which had been energised for the occasion) in both directions. 478 was the last trolleybus to use this section of overhead wiring.
4 November 1962	464	NTG	Farewell tour of the route of service 45. 464 was the last trolleybus to Wollaton Park via Derby Road, and to Trent Bridge via London Road.
26 May 1963	493	NTG	

The erstwhile Trolleybus Society and DLROS hired five different vehicles for their tour of the system on 15 April 1956. BUT 9611T/Roe 493 is seen heading east along Station Street with the Midland Station on the left and Boots factory on the right. *Peter Badgery*

On 26 May 1963 BUT9611T/Roe 493, chosen due to its celebrity status as an exhibit at the 1948 Commercial Motor Show, stands beneath the Trent Bridge Depot and Works access wiring in Fraser Road on an enthusiasts' tour. In the background can be seen the Globe Cinema standing in the apex of the junction between Arkwright Street and London Road. *Rod Bramley*

On 26 May 1963 BUT9611T/Roe 493 approaches the junction of Pyatt Street with Bunbury Street on an enthusiasts' tour. In the foreground the through wiring in Bunbury Street can be seen. *Rod Bramley*

Date	Vehicle	Hirer	Comments
20 October 1963	514	NTA	Included Eland Street, Peveril Street and Northern Baths turning circles, Market Street and Pyatt Street.
24 May 1964	460 & 562	NTA	
12 July 1964	478	RTS	
7 March 1965	480	NTA	480 was the last trolleybus to use Basford, Eland Street and Peveril Street turning circles.
2 May 1965	500	NTG	Farewell tour of the route of service 41 (closed 30 April 1965). Last trolleybus on the Nottingham Road – Cinderhill section.
10 October 1965	578	NTG	Farewell tour of the routes of services 39 (closed 30 September 1965), 40 and 47 (closed 9 October 1965). Last trolleybus to the Wells Road, Wilford Road and Wollaton Park termini, and on the Hooton Road – Carlton P.O. Square section. The tour was permitted to include the disused Arkwright Street – Trent Bridge section as far as the Works, 578 thus being the last trolleybus to pass through the Old Market Square. This was the last occasion that a 7ft 6ins wide trolleybus operated.
December 1965 or January 1966	515	NUTS	
16 January 1966	522	MTPS	Assumed to have been the last passenger carrying trolleybus at Carlton, Hooton Road.
26 June 1966	518	NTA	Last trolleybus to operate along Pennyfoot Street.
30 June 1966	510	NTG	Farewell tour following a few minutes behind the final Nottingham service trolleybus.

DLROS	Doncaster Light Railway and Omnibus Society
NUTS	Nottingham University Transport Society
MTPS	Manchester Trolleybus Preservation Society
NTA	National Trolleybus Association
NTG	Nottingham Trolleybus Group
OS	Omnibus Society
RTS	Reading Transport Society
SCTS	Southern Counties Touring Society

On the 24 May 1964 NTA enthusiast's tour Karrier W/Roe 460 uses Bulwell Hall Estate terminus looking north up Hucknall Lane, as BUT9641T 588 waits for a Morris Oxford to pass before turning. Another BUT on service 44 is drawn up behind the Regent petrol pumps. *MJ Russell*

Appendix O

Statistics

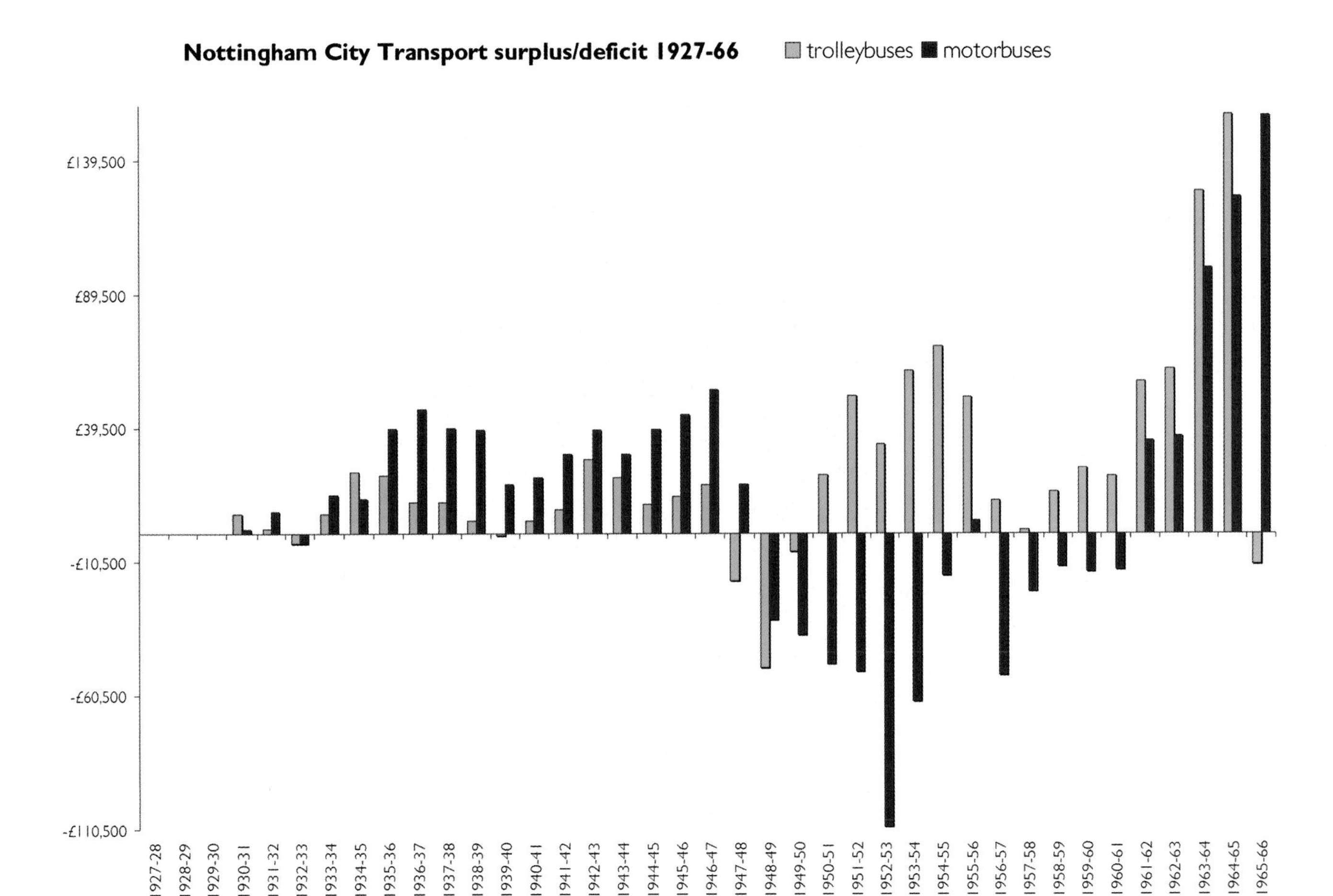

	1927-28				1928-29				1929-30			
	TROLLEYBUSES		MOTORBUSES		TROLLEYBUSES		MOTORBUSES		TROLLEYBUSES		MOTORBUSES	
	Amount	Per Mile	Amount	Per Mile	Amount	Per Mile	Amount	Per Mile	Amount	Per Mile	Amount	Per Mile
Maintenance & Repairs	1,868	1.168	14,133	2.421	3,305	2.014	15,013	1.572	3,902	2.017	27,038	2.205
Traffic Expenses	10,905	6.819	34,577	5.923	11,279	6.875	53,670	5.621	12,850	6.643	61,308	4.999
Power	4,170	2.607	8,685	1.488	3,896	2.375	18,296	1.916	4,211	2.177	29,930	2.44
Rates	1,094	0.684	1,094	0.187	1,103	0.672	1,103	0.116	880	0.455	1,797	0.146
General Expenses	612	0.383	1,748	0.299	601	0.366	2,846	0.298	1,215	0.628	4,840	0.395
(Sub total)	18,649	11.661	60,237	10.318	20,184	12.302	90,928	9.523	23,058	11.92	124,913	10.185
Loan & Bank Interest												
Loan Redemption	(Only incomplete details are available)				(Only incomplete details are available)				(Only incomplete details are available)			
(Sub total)	3,466	2.167	11,218	1.922								
Total Revenue Expenses	22,115	13.828	71,455	12.24								
Total Income	28,284	17.686	62,482	10.703	29,356	17.892	102,136	10.697	34,519	17.844	136,828	11.157
NET SURPLUS(+) or DEFICIT(-)	6,169	3.858	-8,973	-1.537	0	0	0	0	0	0	0	0

	1930-31				1931-32				1932-33			
	TROLLEYBUSES		MOTORBUSES		TROLLEYBUSES		MOTORBUSES		TROLLEYBUSES		MOTORBUSES	
	Amount	Per Mile	Amount	Per Mile	Amount	Per Mile	Amount	Per Mile	Amount	Per Mile	Amount	Per Mile
Maintenance & Repairs	8,467	2.29	33,453	2.253	10,042	2.23	44,435	2.48	11,736	1.556	29,853	1.596
Traffic Expenses	24,588	6.647	77,349	5.209	29,379	6.52	92,875	5.17	47,878	6.348	102,352	5.471
Power	7,815	2.11	30,417	2.048	10,537	2.33	35,526	1.98	18,686	2.478	47,225	2.524
Rates	1,287	0.348	2,032	0.137	1,279	0.28	2,119	0.12	9,298	1.233	1,099	0.059
General Expenses	2,512	0.679	9,054	0.61	3,593	0.8	10,482	0.584	4,210	0.558	10,971	0.586
(Sub total)	44,669	12.075	152,306	10.257	54,830	12.16	185,437	10.336	91,808	12.173	191,500	10.236
Loan & Bank Interest	2,766	0.748	4,196	0.282	3,325	0.737	5,485	0.306	5,602	0.742	23,013	1.23
Loan Redemption	5,363	1.45	21,174	1.426	9,950	2.207	19,439	1.084	15,098	2.002	20,645	1.103
Income Tax	1,911	0.517	4,034	0.272	1,400	0.311	3,994	0.223				
(Sub total)	10,040	2.715	29,404	1.98	14,675	3.255	28,918	1.613	20,700	2.744	43,658	2.333
Total Revenue Expenses	54,709	14.79	181,710	12.237	69,505	15.415	214,355	11.949	112,508	14.917	235,158	12.569
Total Income	62,290	16.839	183,446	12.354	71,433	15.845	222,674	12.413	119,454	15.838	231,529	12.375
NET SURPLUS(+) or DEFICIT(-)	7,581	2.049	1,736	0.117	1,928	0.43	8,319	0.464	6,946	0.921	-3,629	-0.194

	1933-34				1934-35				1935-36			
	TROLLEYBUSES		MOTORBUSES		TROLLEYBUSES		MOTORBUSES		TROLLEYBUSES		MOTORBUSES	
	Amount	Per Mile	Amount	Per Mile	Amount	Per Mile	Amount	Per Mile	Amount	Per Mile	Amount	Per Mile
Maintenance & Repairs	15,460	2.075	35,178	1.877	25,050	1.981	35,821	1.817	29,198	1.898	36,380	1.731
Traffic Expenses	47,361	6.357	98,955	5.281	86,558	6.844	110,839	5.621	104,457	6.79	122,308	5.82
Power	13,569	1.822	45,525	2.429	23,573	1.864	40,082	2.033	29,281	1.904	40,847	1.944
Rates	9,199	1.235	1,403	0.075	14,312	1.132	1,371	0.07	16,416	1.067	1,355	0.064
General Expenses	5,961	0.8	11,710	0.625	10,702	0.847	13,604	0.689	13,574	0.882	15,334	0.73
(Sub total)	91,550	12.289	192,771	10.287	160,195	12.668	201,717	10.23	192,926	12.541	216,224	10.289
Loan & Bank Interest	6,111	0.82	4,406	0.236	8,521	0.67	3,105	0.152	8,715	0.566	2,433	0.116
Loan Redemption	17,685	2.374	27,704	1.468	29,112	2.302	28,224	1.42	34,412	2.237	19,318	0.919
(Sub total)	23,796	3.194	32,110	1.704	37,633	2.972	31,329	1.572	43,127	2.803	21,751	1.035
Total Revenue Expenses	115,346	15.483	224,881	11.991	197,828	15.64	233,046	11.802	236,053	15.345	237,975	11.325
Total Income	122,910	16.498	239,543	12.773	220,814	17.461	246,228	13.176	257,873	16.763	277,350	13.198
NET SURPLUS(+) or DEFICIT(-)	7,564	1.015	14,662	0.782	22,986	1.821	13,182	1.374	21,820	1.418	39,375	1.873

	1936-37				1937-38				1938-39			
	TROLLEYBUSES		MOTORBUSES		TROLLEYBUSES		MOTORBUSES		TROLLEYBUSES		MOTORBUSES	
	Amount	Per Mile	Amount	Per Mile	Amount	Per Mile	Amount	Per Mile	Amount	Per Mile	Amount	Per Mile
Maintenance & Repairs	28,505	1.862	39,424	1.562	28,674	1.826	47,767	1.718	29,424	1.865	47,663	1.636
Traffic Expenses	108,569	7.091	156,872	6.213	111,777	7.12	179,111	6.444	114,902	7.283	190,775	6.549
Power	28,676	1.873	47,357	1.876	31,217	1.989	53,136	1.912	33,016	2.093	51,077	1.754
Rates	19,101	1.248	1,906	0.076	13,979	0.89	2,025	0.073	16,846	1.068	3,075	0.106
General Expenses	13,927	0.91	19,934	0.789	15,511	0.989	24,097	0.867	18,715	1.186	30,069	1.032
(Sub total)	198,778	12.984	265,493	10.516	201,158	12.814	306,136	11.014	212,903	13.495	322,659	11.077
Loan & Bank Interest	7,793	0.509	2,613	0.104	6,926	0.441	4,131	0.149	5,384	0.37	4,705	0.161
Loan Redemption	33,398	2.181	24,062	0.953	33,462	2.131	33,448	1.203	30,937	1.961	36,846	1.265
(Sub total)	41,191	2.69	26,675	1.057	40,388	2.572	37,579	1.352	36,771	2.331	41,551	1.426
Total Revenue Expenses	239,969	15.674	292,168	11.573	241,546	15.386	343,715	12.366	249,674	15.826	364,210	12.503
Total Income	251,652	16.437	338,832	13.421	253,378	16.14	383,285	13.79	254,510	16.132	403,053	13.836
NET SURPLUS(+) or DEFICIT(-)	11,683	0.763	46,664	1.848	11,832	0.754	39,570	1.424	4,836	0.306	38,843	1.333

	1939-40				1940-41				1941-42			
	TROLLEYBUSES		MOTORBUSES		TROLLEYBUSES		MOTORBUSES		TROLLEYBUSES		MOTORBUSES	
	Amount	Per Mile	Amount	Per Mile	Amount	Per Mile	Amount	Per Mile	Amount	Per Mile	Amount	Per Mile
Maintenance & Repairs	30,540	2.006	40,843	1.654	39,731	2.573	43,372	2.055	55,025	3.301	56,274	2.437
Traffic Expenses	118,436	7.781	182,049	7.37	133,715	8.66	183,411	8.891	144,563	8.674	207,763	8.996
Power	30,519	2.005	41,986	1.7	35,340	2.288	44,289	2.099	38,279	2.298	54,147	2.345
Rates	16,015	1.052	3,939	0.159	15,756	1.02	4,011	0.19	15,594	0.936	3,967	0.172
General Expenses	23,564	1.548	37,954	1.537	28,658	1.856	43,315	2.053	32,786	1.967	50,461	2.185
(Sub total)	219,074	14.392	306,771	12.42	253,199	16.397	318,398	15.088	286,247	17.176	372,612	16.135
Loan & Bank Interest	5,504	0.362	5,428	0.22	4,937	0.319	4,789	0.227	4,129	0.248	3,747	0.162
Loan Redemption	29,460	1.935	44,412	1.798	25,318	1.639	43,840	2.077	25,309	1.518	29,213	1.265
Income Tax	157	0.01	253	0.01	464	0.03	692	0.033	15,236	0.914	26,764	1.159
War Damage Contrib									70	0.004	7,384	0.32
(Sub total)	35,121	2.307	50,093	2.028	30,720	1.998	49,547	2.337	44,744	2.684	67,108	2.906
Total Revenue Expenses	254,195	16.699	356,864	14.448	283,919	18.395	367,945	17.425	330,991	19.86	439,720	19.041
Total Income	253,623	16.662	375,396	15.198	288,678	18.695	389,031	18.434	340,003	20.401	469,456	20.328
NET SURPLUS(+) or DEFICIT(-)	-572	-0.037	18,532	0.75	4,759	0.3	21,086	1.009	9,012	0.541	29,736	1.287

	1942-43				1943-44				1944-45			
	TROLLEYBUSES		MOTORBUSES		TROLLEYBUSES		MOTORBUSES		TROLLEYBUSES		MOTORBUSES	
	Amount	Per Mile	Amount	Per Mile	Amount	Per Mile	Amount	Per Mile	Amount	Per Mile	Amount	Per Mile
Maintenance & Repairs	60,601	3.51	69,348	3.003	62,094	3.739	81,150	3.496	63,910	3.774	92,766	3.775
Traffic Expenses	160,648	9.306	228,985	9.914	171,180	10.308	243,746	10.503	197,806	11.678	269,708	10.973
Power	38,428	2.226	56,083	2.428	37,982	2.287	56,862	2.45	42,064	2.484	60,061	2.443
Rates	15,246	0.883	3,880	0.168	14,600	0.879	3,729	0.161	14,625	0.863	3,780	0.154
General Expenses	34,691	2.009	50,816	2.2	36,511	2.199	56,647	2.268	42,031	2.481	59,743	2.432
(Sub total)	309,614	17.934	409,112	17.713	322,367	19.412	438,134	18.878	360,436	21.28	486,058	19.777
Loan & Bank Interest	3,720	0.216	3,057	0.132	2,659	0.16	2,338	0.101	2,898	0.171	1,971	0.08
Loan Redemption	6,859	0.397	15,880	0.688	4,747	0.286	10,594	0.456	4,749	0.28	2,612	0.106
Income Tax	21,290	1.233	33,310	1.442	9,925	0.598	19,757	0.851	390	0.023	12,910	0.525
War Damage Contrib.	92	0.005	2,580	0.112	83	0.005	1,788	0.077	114	0.007	976	0.04
(Sub total)	31,961	1.851	54,827	2.374	17,414	1.049	34,477	1.485	7,371	0.435	18,469	0.751
Total Revenue Expenses	341,575	19.785	463,939	20.087	339,781	20.461	472,611	20.363	367,807	21.715	504,527	20.527
Total Income	369,492	21.402	502,795	21.769	360,979	21.737	502,355	21.645	378,820	22.365	543,667	22.119
NET SURPLUS(+) or DEFICIT(-)	27,917	1.617	38,856	1.682	21,198	1.276	29,744	1.282	11,013	0.65	39,140	1.592

	1945-46				1946-47				1947-48			
	TROLLEYBUSES		MOTORBUSES		TROLLEYBUSES		MOTORBUSES		TROLLEYBUSES		MOTORBUSES	
	Amount	Per Mile	Amount	Per Mile	Amount	Per Mile	Amount	Per Mile	Amount	Per Mile	Amount	Per Mile
Maintenance & Repairs	72,636	3.982	102,999	3.99	76,049	3.942	125,720	4.354	88,217	4.519	133,727	4.275
Traffic Expenses	213,361	11.696	293,281	11.361	233,213	12.089	326,606	11.311	262,611	13.455	381,617	12.2
Power	48,100	2.637	59,033	2.287	50,919	2.64	59,037	2.044	52,167	2.673	66,566	2.128
Rates	17,361	0.952	4,483	0.174	17,394	0.902	4,527	0.157	17,242	0.884	4,727	0.151
General Expenses	39,453	2.162	55,371	2.144	38,120	1.976	53,495	1.853	42,407	2.172	61,385	1.962
(Sub total)	390,911	21.429	515,167	19.956	415,695	21.549	569,385	19.719	462,644	23.703	648,022	20.716
Loan & Bank Interest	2,643	0.145	2,084	0.081	2,714	0.141	2,287	0.079	2,472	0.127	2,020	0.065
Loan Redemption	4,795	0.263	2,566	0.099	4,900	0.254	2,527	0.088	5,000	0.256	2,449	0.078
Income Tax	3,588	0.197	10,115	0.392								
War Damage Contrib.	90	0.005	135	0.005								
(Sub total)	3,940	0.216	14,900	0.577	7,614	0.395	4,814	0.167	7,472	0.383	4,469	0.143
Total Revenue Expenses	394,851	21.645	530,067	20.533	423,309	21.944	574,199	19.886	470,116	24.086	652,491	20.859
Total Income	408,881	22.413	574,596	22.258	441,574	22.891	628,226	21.757	452,538	23.185	671,160	21.456
NET SURPLUS(+) or DEFICIT(-)	14,030	0.768	44,529	1.725	18,265	0.947	54,027	1.871	-17,578	-0.901	18,669	0.597

	1948-49				1949-50				1950-51			
	TROLLEYBUSES		MOTORBUSES		TROLLEYBUSES		MOTORBUSES		TROLLEYBUSES		MOTORBUSES	
	Amount	Per Mile	Amount	Per Mile	Amount	Per Mile	Amount	Per Mile	Amount	Per Mile	Amount	Per Mile
Traffic Operation	)	)	)	)	233,912	11.776	355,239	10.321	230,208	11.483	356,082	10.302
Servicing vehicles & routes	286,872	14.609	426,766	12.889	33,296	1.676	53,244	1.547	31,868	1.59	52,855	1.529
Power	53,121	2.705	76,969	2.325	54,177	2.728	79,016	2.296	57,761	2.881	120,800	3.495
Repairs & maintenance	94,484	4.862	164,725	4.975	88,116	4.436	139,214	4.044	74,992	3.741	133,741	3.87
Licences					13,852	0.697	24,503	0.712	14,626	0.729	23,764	0.688
Rates	17,145	0.873	4,831	0.16	18,228	0.918	5,148	0.15	18,160	0.906	5,298	0.153
General	)	)	)	)	21,985	1.107	38,516	1.119	23,597	1.177	35,681	1.033
Welfare & pensions	46,241	2.355	67,367	2.034	37,347	1.88	52,385	1.522	34,629	1.727	53,101	1.536
Hires							133	0.004			172	0.005
(Sub total)	498,863	25.044	740,658	22.369	500,913	25.218	747,398	21.715	485,841	24.234	781,494	22.611
Loan Interest	8,676	0.442	6,174	0.186	14,930	0.752	42,771	1.243	40,908	2.04	63,882	1.847
Total Revenue Expenses	507,539	25.846	746,832	22.555	516,197	25.988	790,789	22.976	526,749	26.274	845,316	24.458
Total Income	457,385	23.292	714,684	21.585	509,495	25.651	752,981	21.877	548,761	27.372	796,520	23.046
NET SURPLUS(+) or DEFICIT(-)	-50,154	-2.554	-32,148	-0.97	-6,702	-0.337	-37,808	-1.099	22,012	1.098	-48,796	-1.412

	1951-52				1952-53				1953-54			
	TROLLEYBUSES		MOTORBUSES		TROLLEYBUSES		MOTORBUSES		TROLLEYBUSES		MOTORBUSES	
	Amount	Per Mile	Amount	Per Mile	Amount	Per Mile	Amount	Per Mile	Amount	Per Mile	Amount	Per Mile
Traffic Operation	254,363	12.717	398,112	11.477	265,802	13.482	414,963	12.212	273,282	13.928	438,016	12.841
Servicing vehicles & routes	32,909	1.645	54,535	1.572	32,679	1.658	56,128	1.652	26,827	1.372	49,145	1.441
Power	64,795	3.24	153,471	4.424	67,773	3.438	189,904	5.588	68,322	3.495	185,788	5.447
Repairs & maintenance	78,352	3.917	148,378	4.278	80,002	4.058	162,723	4.789	76,316	3.904	157,054	4.604
Licences	14,666	0.733	23,891	0.689	14,771	0.749	23,911	0.704	14,679	0.751	25,247	0.74
Rates	4,977	0.249	5,746	0.166	12,041	0.611	6,085	0.179	14,089	0.721	8,766	0.257
General	23,312	1.165	37,367	1.077	19,256	0.976	36,269	1.067	18,862	0.964	35,426	1.038
Welfare & pensions	36,975	1.849	59,036	1.702	37,792	1.917	58,651	1.726	37,452	1.916	60,236	1.766
(Sub total)	510,349	25.515	880,546	25.385	530,116	26.889	948,634	27.917	528,829	27.051	959,678	28.134
Loan Interest	58,688	2.934	66,746	1.924	71,276	3.616	71,826	2.114	85,337	4.365	83,873	2.459
Total Revenue Expenses	569,037	28.449	947,292	27.309	601,392	30.505	1,020,460	30.031	614,166	31.416	1,043,551	30.593
Total Income	620,401	31.017	895,655	25.821	634,891	32.204	910,902	26.806	675,337	34.545	980,867	28.755
NET SURPLUS(+) or DEFICIT(-)	51,364	2.568	-51,637	-1.488	33,499	1.699	-109,558	-3.225	61,171	3.129	-62,684	-1.838

	1954-55				1955-56				1956-57			
	TROLLEYBUSES		MOTORBUSES		TROLLEYBUSES		MOTORBUSES		TROLLEYBUSES		MOTORBUSES	
	Amount	Per Mile	Amount	Per Mile	Amount	Per Mile	Amount	Per Mile	Amount	Per Mile	Amount	Per Mile
Traffic Operation	278,143	14.809	472,225	13.498	302,074	16.385	521,148	14.707	321,296	17.369	553,551	15.405
Servicing vehicles & routes	22,468	1.196	44,147	1.257	22,680	1.23	44,969	1.269	23,107	1.249	47,359	1.318
Power	68,061	3.624	179,551	5.11	69,718	3.782	181,676	5.127	74,125	4.007	204,184	5.683
Repairs & maintenance	80,076	4.264	146,721	4.176	92,616	5.024	138,288	3.902	101,602	5.492	152,225	4.236
Licences	14,187	0.755	25,247	0.719	14,022	0.76	24,972	0.705	13,934	0.753	25,330	0.705
Rates	14,387	0.766	8,987	0.256	14,192	0.77	9,192	0.259	23,952	1.295	13,933	0.388
General	18,740	0.998	35,853	1.02	20,360	1.104	38,151	1.077	18,407	0.995	34,699	0.966
Welfare & pensions	38,878	2.07	65,610	1.867	40,178	2.179	66,803	1.885	39,463	2.133	68,639	1.91
(Sub total)	534,942	28.482	980,340	27.903	575,840	31.234	1,025,199	28.931	615,887	33.293	1,099,920	30.611
Loan Interest	84,117	4.478	106,721	3.038	81,870	4.441	119,091	3.36	81,629	4.413	134,306	3.738
Total Revenue Expenses	619,119	32.96	1,087,061	30.941	657,710	35.675	1,144,290	32.291	697,516	37.706	1,234,226	34.349
Total Income	689,263	36.243	1,071,397	30.495	708,713	38.442	1,149,568	32.44	710,124	38.387	1,181,470	32.88
NET SURPLUS(+) or DEFICIT(-)	70,144	3.283	-15,664	-0.446	51,003	2.767	5,278	0.149	12,608	0.681	-52,756	-1.469

	1957-58				1958-59				1959-60			
	TROLLEYBUSES		MOTORBUSES		TROLLEYBUSES		MOTORBUSES		TROLLEYBUSES		MOTORBUSES	
	Amount	Per Mile	Amount	Per Mile	Amount	Per Mile	Amount	Per Mile	Amount	Per Mile	Amount	Per Mile
Traffic Operation	342,355	18.744	593,512	16.507	353,487	19.287	612,702	17.032	346,391	20.511	634,143	17.624
Servicing vehicles & routes	24,174	1.323	49,867	1.387	25,823	1.409	50,712	1.41	26,701	1.581	51,975	1.444
Power	73,595	4.029	193,101	5.371	73,413	4.006	178,095	4.951	69,104	4.092	182,073	5.06
Repairs & maintenance	109,972	6.021	155,164	4.315	108,458	5.918	167,506	4.656	100,452	5.948	166,297	4.622
Licences	13,783	0.755	26,103	0.726	13,812	0.754	26,923	0.748	4,859	0.288	11,076	0.308
Rates	7,180	0.393	14,909	0.415	17,346	0.946	16,037	0.446	18,252	1.081	13,399	0.372
General	25,966	1.422	37,484	1.042	22,765	1.242	43,518	1.21	23,332	1.381	43,281	1.203
Welfare & pensions	46,184	2.529	77,924	2.167	47,097	2.57	81,004	2.252	48,411	2.867	88,961	2.473
(Sub total)	643,209	35.418	1,148,064	31.93	662,202	36.132	1,176,498	32.705	637,502	37.749	1,191,205	33.106
Loan Interest	82,191	4.526	117,332	3.263	81,736	4.46	122,730	3.412	76,182	4.511	123,020	3.419
Total Revenue Expenses	725,400	39.944	1,265,396	35.193	743,938	40.592	1,299,228	36.117	713,684	42.26	1,314,225	36.525
Total Income	726,879	40.025	1,243,797	34.592	759,813	41.458	1,287,075	35.779	738,262	43.715	1,300,126	36.133
NET SURPLUS(+) or DEFICIT(-)	1,479	0.081	-21,599	-0.601	15,875	0.866	-12,153	-0.338	24,578	1.455	-14,099	-0.392

	1960-61				1961-62				1962-63			
	TROLLEYBUSES		MOTORBUSES		TROLLEYBUSES		MOTORBUSES		TROLLEYBUSES		MOTORBUSES	
	Amount	Per Mile	Amount	Per Mile	Amount	Per Mile	Amount	Per Mile	Amount	Per Mile	Amount	Per Mile
Traffic Operation	375,766	23.048	702,407	19.647	391,050	24.312	736,468	20.505	392,156	25.371	761,487	20.821
Servicing vehicles & routes	26,902	1.65	52,525	1.47	27,963	1.738	55,553	1.547	28,670	1.855	59,556	1.628
Power	68,933	4.228	182,045	5.092	79,517	4.944	185,880	5.175	76,308	4.937	192,283	5.258
Repairs & maintenance	107,071	6.567	159,864	4.472	103,238	6.418	179,671	5.002	101,579	6.572	186,535	5.1
Licences	4,665	0.286	10,663	0.297	4,701	0.292	10,631	0.296	4,587	0.297	11,652	0.319
Rates	20,252	1.241	17,645	0.494	20,287	1.261	17,905	0.499	20,287	1.313	18,626	0.509
General	24,848	1.525	53,032	1.483	23,788	1.479	53,398	1.486	27,532	1.781	59,333	1.623
Welfare & pensions	50,165	3.077	92,778	2.595	53,143	3.304	98,307	2.737	56,466	3.653	111,181	3.04
(Sub total)	678,602	41.622	1,270,959	35.55	703,687	43.748	1,337,813	37.247	707,585	45.779	1,400,653	38.298
Loan Interest	46,672	2.862	121,172	3.389	26,636	1.656	119,452	3.326	8,362	0.541	116,791	3.193
Total Revenue Expenses	725,274	44.484	1,392,131	38.939	730,323	45.404	1,457,265	40.573	715,947	46.32	1,517,444	41.491
Total Income	746,923	45.812	1,378,783	38.565	787,332	48.948	1,492,274	41.547	777,840	50.324	1,554,041	42.491
NET SURPLUS(+) or DEFICIT(-)	21,649	1.328	-13,348	-0.374	57,009	3.544	35,009	0.974	61,893	4.004	36,597	1

	1963-64				1964-65				1965-66			
	TROLLEYBUSES		MOTORBUSES		TROLLEYBUSES		MOTORBUSES		TROLLEYBUSES		MOTORBUSES	
	Amount	Per Mile	Amount	Per Mile	Amount	Per Mile	Amount	Per Mile	Amount	Per Mile	Amount	Per Mile
Traffic Operation	419,228	28.656	888,534	24.006	433,148	30.337	925,965	25.339	152,209	36.78	1,339,660	29.209
Servicing vehicles & routes	28,624	1.957	67,806	1.832	26,482	1.855	73,013	1.998	6,360	1.537	103,072	2.247
Power	73,458	5.021	192,587	5.203	74,216	5.198	190,217	5.205	23,912	5.778	241,466	5.265
Repairs & maintenance	95,094	6.5	220,930	5.969	83,498	5.848	237,646	6.503	37,811	9.137	282,995	6.17
Licences	4,235	0.29	12,201	0.33	4,029	0.282	12,741	0.349	1,455	0.352	16,034	0.35
Rent & Rates	11,531	0.788	17,242	0.466	12,063	0.845	18,033	0.493	6,928	1.674	27,526	0.6
General	23,228	1.588	56,703	1.532	26,120	1.829	62,332	1.706	9,891	2.39	93,687	2.043
Welfare & medical	2,528	0.173	6,540	0.177	2,006	0.141	5,695	0.156	444	0.107	7,508	0.164
(Sub total)	657,926	44.973	1,462,543	39.515	661,562	46.335	1,525,642	41.749	239,010	57.755	2,111,948	46.048
Loan Interest	2,763	0.189	104,019	2.81	1,536	0.108	80,733	2.209	-	-	101,892	2.222
Total Revenue Expenses	660,689	45.162	1,566,562	42.325	663,098	46.443	1,606,375	43.958	239,010	57.755	2,213,840	48.27
Total Income	788,837	53.921	1,665,932	45.01	819,950	57.429	1,732,417	47.407	227,632	55.006	2,370,285	51.681
NET SURPLUS(+) or DEFICIT(-)	128,148	8.759	99,370	2.685	156,852	10.986	126,042	3.449	-11,378	-2.749	156,445	3.411

Trolleybus total, all years	892,439
Motorbus total, all years	470,559

Nottingham City Transport trolleybus electricity consumption 1927-66

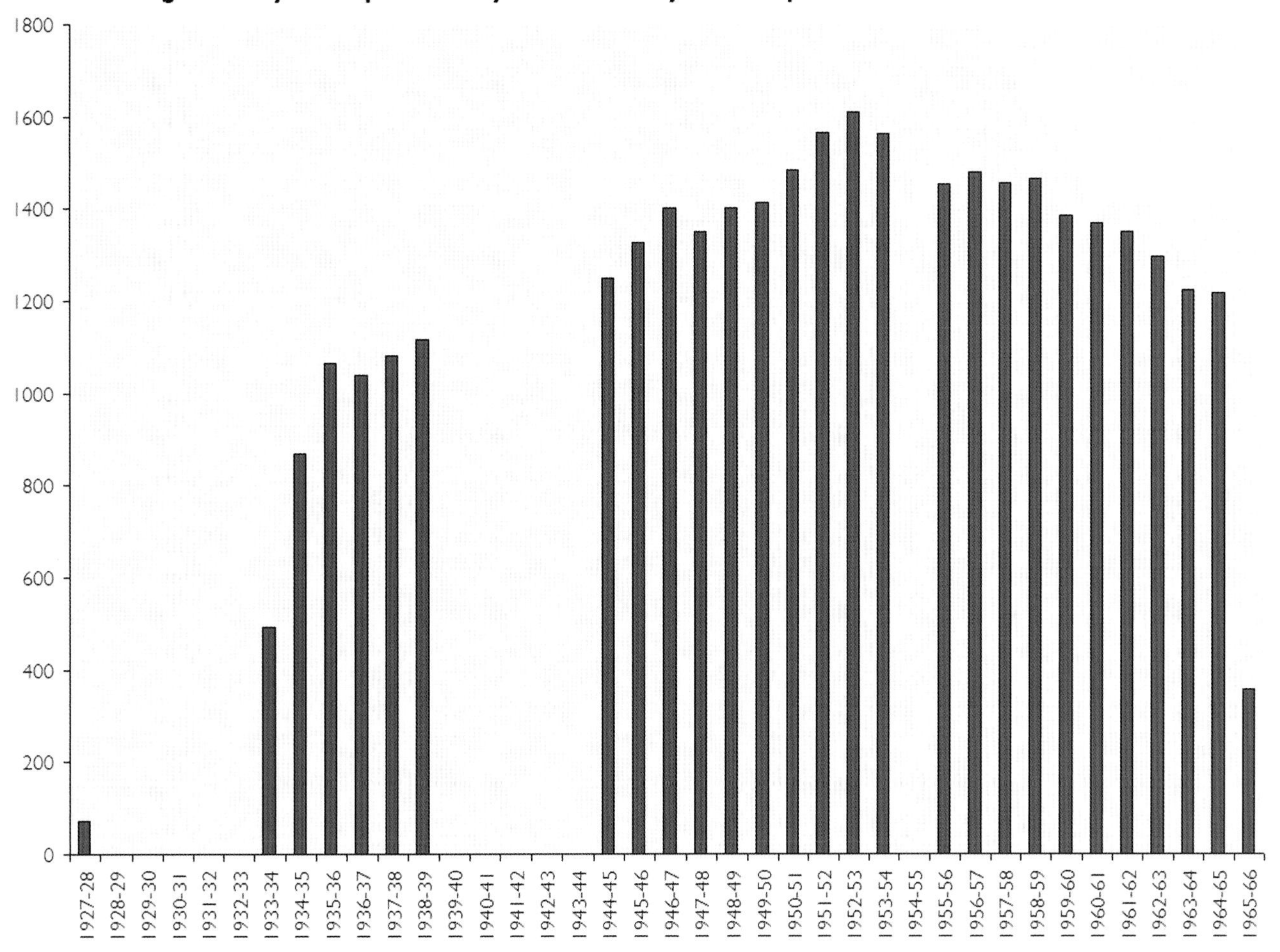

	1927-28	1928-29	1929-30	1930-31	1931-32	1932-33	1933-34	1934-35	1935-36	1936-37
Units used	730,000						4,936,187	8,673,628	10,634,772	10,378,218
Cost per unit (d)	1.37	1.25	1.12	1	1		0.7	0.7	0.7	0.7
Units per mile	1.902						2.761	2.85	2.88	2.824
	1937-38	1938-39	1939-40	1940-41	1941-42	1942-43	1943-44	1944-45	1945-46	1946-47
Units used	10,817,995	11,160,365						12,500,000	13,250,000	14,000,000
Cost per unit (d)	0.73	0.747	0.71	0.8	0.8	0.875	0.794	0.84	0.903	0.914
Units per mile	2.871	2.947						3.075	3.026	3.024
	1947-48	1948-49	1949-50	1950-51	1951-52	1952-53	1953-54	1954-55	1955-56	1956-57
Units used	13,500,000	14,000,000	14,135,000	14,824,000	15,646,000	16,095,000	15,616,000		14,525,000	14,788,000
Cost per unit (d)	0.964	0.957	0.965	0.972	1.03	1.046	1.053		1.152	1.203
Units per mile	2.882	2.988	2.965	3.081	3.259	3.401	3.328		3.283	3.331
	1957-58	1958-59	1959-60	1960-61	1961-62	1962-63	1963-64	1964-65	1965-66	
Units used	14,549,000	14,646,000	13,843,769	13,672,550	13,488,547	12,966,560	12,237,031	12,159,660	3,580,938	
Cost per unit (d)	1.214	1.203	1.198	1.21	1.415	1.412	1.441	1.466	1.598	
Units per mile	3.319	3.33	3.416	3.494	3.494	3.495	3.485	3.522	3.601	

Note: units used includes the power consumption of N&D trolleybuses operating within the NCT area

	1927-28	1928-29	1929-30	1930-31	1931-32	1932-33	1933-34	1934-35	1935-36	1936-37
Miles run	383,801	393,768	464,265	887,776	1,082,004	1,810,111	1,787,940	3,035,132	3,691,982	3,674,399
Passengers carried	5,265,175	5,391,337	6,458,507	12,410,548	14,144,595	22,969,868	23,148,275	40,594,783	47,563,303	46,865,994
Passengers per mile	13.719	13.692	13.911	13.979	13.073	12.69	12.947	13.375	12.833	12.755
	1937-38	1938-39	1939-40	1940-41	1941-42	1942-43	1943-44	1944-45	1945-46	1946-47
Miles run	3,767,695	3,786,398	3,653,219	3,705,839	3,999,829	4,143,300	3,985,546	4,065,097	4,378,150	4,629,781
Passengers carried	47,490,622	47,779,928	47,364,143	51,374,168	60,842,019	66,394,139	65,480,152	68,716,661	73,723,179	78,446,642
Passengers per mile	12.605	12.619	12.965	13.863	15.211	16.024	16.429	16.904	16.839	16.944
	1947-48	1948-49	1949-50	1950-51	1951-52	1952-53	1953-54	1954-55	1955-56	1956-57
Miles run	4,684,366	4,712,738	4,767,050	4,811,562	4,800,497	4,731,554	4,691,891	4,507,637	4,424,661	4,439,701
Passengers carried	79,832,925	80,533,824	77,107,581	72,296,075	72,812,646	73,522,298	73,684,910	69,628,360	68,242,061	67,657,664
Passengers per mile	17.042	17.089	16.175	15.025	15.168	15.539	15.705	15.447	15.423	15.239
	1957-58	1958-59	1959-60	1960-61	1961-62	1962-63	1963-64	1964-65	1965-66	
Miles run	4,358,511	4,398,560	4,053,109	3,912,985	3,860,409	3,709,604	3,511,078	3,426,648	993,195	
Passengers carried	64,197,704	61,211,102	59,241,219	56,166,248	53,217,397	49,878,097	46,161,783	43,382,977	11,864,184	
Passengers per mile	14.729	13.916	14.616	14.354	13.785	13.446	13.147	12.66	11.945	

Analysis of stopping places

Service	Outwards		Inwards		Total		
No.	Stops	Miles	Stops	Miles	Stops	Miles	Yards
36	16	2.232	15	2.191	31	4.423	251
37	13	1.887	12	1.819	25	3.706	261
38	16	2.115	15	2.279	31	4.394	249
39	34	4.911	33	4.889	67	9.8	257
40	20	2.827	19	2.909	39	5.736	257
47	18	2.367	17	2.404	35	4.771	240
41	34	5.179	34	5.297	68	10.476	272
42	18	3.139	21	3.098	39	6.237	281
43	33	5.305	36	5.362	69	10.667	272
44	46	7.308	49	7.18	95	14.488	269
45	30	4.223	27	4.196	57	8.419	260
46	7	1.234	8	1.232	15	2.466	289
Totals	285	42.727	286	42.856	571	85.583	265

Nottingham City Transport trolleybus passengers carried 1927-66

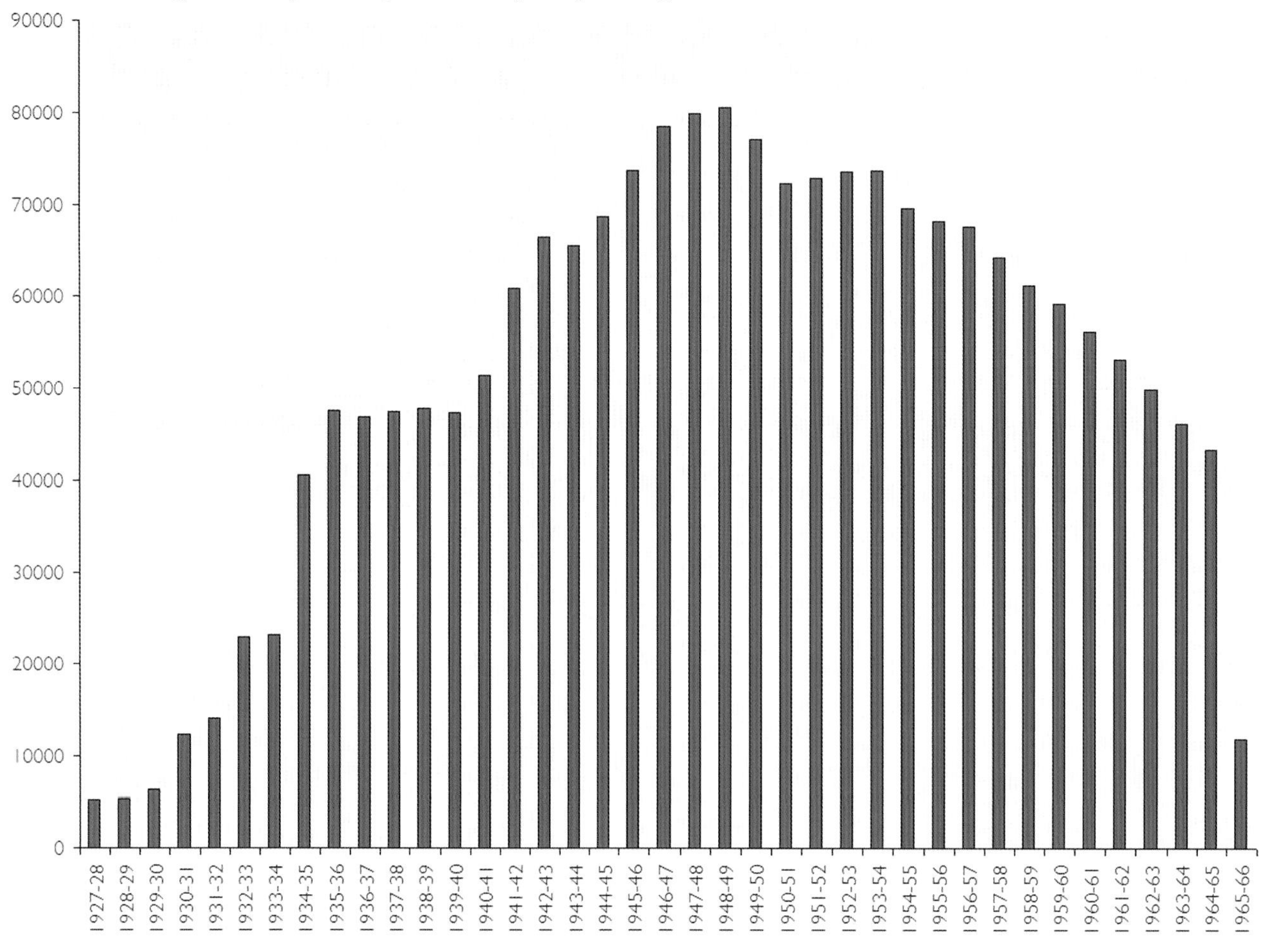

J. Aldworth

Although it is known that John Aldworth was born at Wantage, Berkshire in 1855, it has proved impossible to establish his professional training and early career history. As the worldís first electric tram only ran in 1881 it is possible that he was an electrical engineer by profession and that his first employment was in the power supply and electric lighting industry. Whatever it may have been, John Aldworth had secured a sufficiently high reputation to be appointed Manager of the prestigious pioneer electric tramway undertakings operating along the east coast of the Isle of Man.

The first section of the electric railway between Douglas and Groundle opened on 7 September 1893, with extensions northwards to Laxey on 28 July 1894 and to Ramsey (Ballure) on 2 August 1898.Together with the horse tramway around the bay at Douglas, the Upper Douglas cable tramway (opened 15 August 1896), the Snaefell Mountain Railway (opened 21 August 1895) and the power and lighting utilities on the island, these were all owned by the Isle Of Man Tramways & Electric Power Co. Ltd., which was founded on 30 April 1894. Mr Aldworth was Manager of the combined undertaking from its inception until January 1899. The undertaking was closely linked with Dumbell's Bank, which collapsed under dubious circumstances in February 1900 leading to the disintegration of the Isle of Man Tramways & Electric Power Co. empire. In early 1899 a number of the Companyís officer's, aware of the financial position, resigned and it is assumed that John Aldworth was one of them.

In late 1898 the London County Council, on the verge of becoming a tramways operator in the metropolis, had advertised for a Chief Officer of Tramways. It is understood that Mr Aldworth applied but that the post was offered to John Young of Glasgow Corporation Tramways who refused the position due to the lack of an assistant to help him with the huge task of electrification. The offer then went to Alfred C. Baker, Manager of Nottingham Corporation Tramways and previously the Nottingham and District Tramways Co. Ltd., who accepted the position from 1 February 1899. John Aldworth, who was one of the few professional managers at that time with a thorough working knowledge of electric tramway operation, succeeded him at Nottingham. He was President of the Municipal Tramways Association 1907-1908

John Aldworth managed the tramway undertaking through to his retirement on 31 December 1928 at the age of 74, overseeing the first electric tram, railless trolley vehicle and petrol motor bus. He was noted as being quietly conscientious, genial and a thorough gentleman. He died on 1 December 1936.

A.R. Atkey

Albert Reuben Atkey was brought up in the back streets of St. Annís, Nottingham in 1860. He broke off his training as a water engineer when he discovered an interest in cycling which provided him with an entrÈe into the infant world of motoring. He set up a cycle repair business, and then began selling motorcar and cycle accessories. One of the first motorists on Nottinghamís streets it was a natural step to establish Atkeyís Motor Engineers in 1897. A year later he travelled to South Africa to market his cycle accessories but his stay was prolonged by the Boer War, leading to Albert Atkey setting up the first motorcar agency in Johannesburg and, in 1903, accompanied by Frank Connock, making the first recorded car trip in one day from Johannesburg to Mafeking.

Returning to Nottingham his motor business boomed and there were soon branches throughout the East Midlands. In 1908 he became a city councillor, going on to become a long-term member of the Transport Committee, the Sheriff and the second Lord Mayor of the City of Nottingham (1928-29), as well as an MP (1918-22). His motorcar sales business, Messrs Atkeyís of Nottingham Ltd., in Lower Parliament Street, was a main Austin distributor, which advertised regularly in the NCT fare and timetable booklets. His affection for motoring, combined with his related business endeavours, explain the fervour with which he attacked the trolleybuses through many years of Transport Committee Meetings.

Alderman Sir Albert Atkey died in November 1947 at the age of 80 after a period of ill health.

B. England

Benjamin England was born in Bolton, Lancashire in 1897. He was educated at St. Cuthbert's College, Worksop and in 1913 was apprenticed to railway engine manufacturers Carels Fréres, Gent, Belgium. At the outbreak of World War One he enlisted in the Coldstream Guards, passed the entrance examination for officer training in 1914 and entered the Royal Military College, Sandhurst in 1915. He received a commission in September 1915 in the King's Own Yorkshire Light Infantry but was immediately seconded to the Machine Gun Corps. In 1917 he lost a leg in action at Messines and was invalided out of the forces with the rank of Captain. Early in 1918 he became connected with the Yorkshire (West Riding) Electric Tramways Co. where his father, Harry England, was General Manager and, from 1922, Managing Director. Ben England was engaged variously as the Local Manager of the Castleford area, Assistant Secretary and Traffic Manager. His brother Robert was the Company Secretary.

In 1929 he was appointed General Manager of St. Helens Corporation Transport which soon adopted a policy of converting each tram route to trolleybus operation as the tracks became due for replacement. Here he gained experience of joint trolleybus operations (with South Lancashire Transport), introduced posting boxes on evening services and tried to extend all journeys on the Prescot tram service through to Liverpool. In March 1933 he was appointed General Manager of Southend Corporation Light Railways and Transport. During his short tenure he introduced operating economies to combat falling receipts caused by the depression and also purchased second-hand bogie tramcars and acquired trolleybus operating powers for most of the tram routes. In 1936 he moved to Leicester, as General Manager and Engineer, where the Transport Committee had decided, much to the chagrin of the Electricity Department, that when tramway replacement became necessary, motorbuses rather than trolleybuses would be used. In an effort to match the capacity of a trolleybus, Mr England introduced the 3-axle AEC Renown motorbus into provincial service, however he did not neglect the tramways. They remained in good working order whilst a new livery and side destination boards were introduced; indeed by the time he left Leicester for Nottingham he had overseen the closure of just two short tram routes. The rest of the system survived the Second World War intact.

On 12 June 1939 Ben England, FRGS; MIAE; AMI Mech E.; M.Inst T., was appointed General Manager of Nottingham City Transport at a starting salary of £1,350 pa and 3 months notice on either side. He later committed not to apply for any other position for 3 years.

He is credited with having improved the undertaking's administration. It has been suggested that he was not an enthusiast of trolleybuses but he tolerated their co-existence with motorbuses, realising the importance of this mode of transport in the immediate post-war period when motorbuses were difficult to acquire. Noticeably there were no developments of the system during his period of tenure however it will have been noted that there were many enemies of the trolleybus in the Transport Committee.

Ben England retired in 1962 to live in Cornwall.

H.C. Godsmark

Harry Citford Godsmark was born in 1896 and brought up in Loughborough. He trained as an apprentice at Brush Electrical Engineering and during World War I served with the Railway Operating Engineers in Salonika. Thereafter he joined Cammell-Laird at Nottingham.

Harry Godsmark commenced his transport career as a Technical Assistant with the LCC Tramways, securing promotion to Chief Technical Assistant of the Rolling Stock Department of Manchester Corporation Tramways before coming to Nottingham in 1929 as Assistant Rolling Stock Engineer. He reorganised the repair and stores departments. A staunch enthusiast of the trolleybus, on 1 June 1930 he was promoted to Deputy General Manager however he moved on in spring 1933 to become General Manager of Huddersfield Corporation Transport where the Nottingham influence in trolleybus overhead and vehicle design became most evident. Here he oversaw the experimental introduction of trolleybuses on one tram route before a wholesale conversion of the entire system took place. In spring 1941, by which time the Huddersfield system had grown to almost 47 route miles with 140 trolleybuses in stock, Mr Godsmark left to take charge of the larger Newcastle upon Tyne undertaking where the tram to trolleybus conversion programme had been interrupted by the war. He died in this post on 24 December 1946, following a 6-month illness.

J.L. Gunn

Born in Edinburgh and educated at Leith Academy, James Lowe Gunn joined Leith Corporation Tramways in 1911 and, apart from an interruption of wartime army service, served with them until 1920 when the Leith undertaking was amalgamated with that of Edinburgh when the city extended its boundaries. During World War I he served as an officer in the Royal Garrison Artillery, suffering gas attacks and head wounds. In the enlarged Edinburgh undertaking Mr Gunn rose to the position of Assistant Traffic Superintendent and was heavily engaged with the conversion of the tramways from cable to overhead electric trolley operation.

In 1926 he moved to the Greenock and Port Glasgow Tramways Co. as Manager, reporting to the General Manager. The Company was suffering significant losses due to the high levels of local unemployment and motorbus competition, and Mr Gunn was soon in the midst of tramway abandonment negotiations with the local authorities. Interestingly Greenock Corporation then turned to R. Stuart Pilcher, Mr Gunn's superior and General Manager at Edinburgh, for professional advice. Mr Gunn was then responsible for promoting an Act which created a parliamentary precedent, and conferred on the Company statutory quasi monopoly powers for motor bus operation with certain obligations in Greenock, Gourock and Port Glasgow and within a five mile radius.

In July 1929 he was appointed General Manager of Aberdeen Corporation Tramways and during his 3 years period of tenure it is notable that the Granite City's motorbus services developed rapidly, albeit to compete with aggressive competition from private operators, whereas the modernisation of the tramcar fleet came to a halt and a number of routes were closed. Pilcher had previously been at Aberdeen (1907-1918) and it seems possible that he was Gunn's mentor.

Taking over the management of Nottingham's larger fleet in February 1934 Mr Gunn's enthusiasm for the motorbus undoubtedly influenced the Transport Committee to abandon its tram to trolleybus conversion policy and the further projects of Walter Marks.

Reportedly Mr Gunn suffered from alcoholism, which possibly contributed towards his fall into an inspection pit at Lower Parliament Street Depot on the occasion of the last tram, and from which he never fully recovered. He died in post on 10 April 1939 at the early age of 42.

W.G. Marks

Walter Gray Marks was born in Greenwich in 1883 but grew up in Huddersfield. Apprenticed to a firm of chemists, a family bereavement forced him to earn a wage and he started his transport career in 1900 at the bottom as a conductor with the Imperial Tramway Company at Middlesbrough. He moved to Rotherham in 1903 where the Corporation had just opened electric tramways, rising rapidly to Inspector, Chief Inspector and in 1917 Traffic Superintendent and chief assistant to the General Manager. Rotherham was a pioneer trolleybus operator.

In April 1925 Marks moved to Chesterfield as General Manager. Here he replaced trams on the Brampton – Whittington Moor route with trolley buses (known in Chesterfield as railless electric vehicles or REVs) on 27 September 1927, introduced a new green and white colour scheme, built new workshops, garages and offices, and completely reorganised the undertaking. The REVs were deemed most successful and the route extended beyond the tram terminus to New Whittington.

On 21 November 1928 he tended his resignation and moved to Nottingham effective 1 January 1929. Marks was a heavily built man, well known for his small moustache; 6ft tall, and with a forceful character well able to mould local politicians into his line of thinking. Reportedly he was not happy with the personnel files, detailing each disciplinary matter and misdemeanour, and a new system of records was started which, in principle, gave each employee a clean sheet.

In autumn 1933 he was one of 120 applicants for the post of General Manager of Liverpool Corporation Tramways following the death of P. Priestly and after a long selection process was engaged at £2,200 pa. When he moved to Liverpool in February 1934, that city had a system three times the size of Nottingham and was the fourth largest provincial municipal operator. It was anticipated that he might replace the weary tramway system there with trolleybuses but he promoted a much acclaimed tramway modernisation and retention policy. At its peak the 197 mile network included almost 28 miles of reserved track, whilst Marks superintended the construction of a fleet of 314 new trams.

W.G. Marks was an active member of the Municipal Passenger Transport Association and was its President in 1947-48. He retired as General Manager of Liverpool Corporation Passenger Transport in July 1948 and resided in Southport until his death in 1968.

J.C. Wake

John Cecil Wake was born in Middlesbrough in 1909. On leaving school he joined the Anglo-American Oil Co.,ís transport section before moving into passenger transport some 7 years later with an appointment at Middlesbrough Corporation Transport. He became principal assistant to the General Manager after 18 months service and later, in 1945, was appointed Deputy General Manager and Engineer.

He was then successively General Manager at Burton-on-Trent (1950-52), St. Helens (1952-61), Bradford (3 July 1961 – 30 November 1962) and Nottingham. He first encountered trolleybuses in St. Helens and was instrumental in that system's abandonment on 30 June 1958. The Council had decided in 1951, just prior to Mr Wake's arrival, to gradually replace the trolleybuses over a ten year period as the infrastructure was nearing the end of its useful life. Nonetheless he was considered anti-trolleybus.

Upon his appointment to Bradford City Transport he stopped the redevelopment of the overhead line equipment in the station area for which his predecessor, Chaceley Humpidge, had already purchased the necessary equipment. Having considered 27 applications with a short list of 6, J.C. Wake ACIS, M.Inst.T., MIRTE was appointed at a salary of £3,695 pa rising by annual increments of £125 to £4,070 pa.

It is understood that his ultimate personal aim was to secure the position of General Manager at Manchester but although short listed for the position upon the retirement of Albert Neal in 1965, he was told that he was by then too old. Mr Wake was renowned for his financial prowess as evidenced by the continual improvement in Nottingham City Transport's trading results in the 1960s.

Appendix R Bibliography

Title	Author	Publisher	Date	ISBN number
Books, Brochures and Pamphlets				
Barton (3 volumes)	Alan F. Oxley	Transport Publishing Company	1983	903839 64 4
		Robin Hood Publishing	1986	0 948854 022
		Robin Hood Publishing	1994	0 948854 08 1
British Trolleybuses 1911-1972	Geoff Lumb	Ian Allan Publishing	1995	07110 2347 6
City of Nottingham Transport & West Bridgford UDC Transport (Fleet History PE7)	-	PSV Circle	1982	
Great British Tramway Networks	W.H. Bett & J.C. Gillham	Light Railway Transport League	1962	
History of the British Trolleybus	Nicholas Owen	David & Charles	1974	0 7153 6370 0
History of Nottingham City Transport	Roy Marshall	Nottingham City Transport	1960	
History of the Undertaking	-	Nottingham City Transport	1949	
Llanelly Trolleybuses	Geoff L. Griffiths	Trolleybooks	1992	0 904235 15 7
Midland General (with Notts. & Derby)	Alan F. Oxley	Robin Hood Publishing	1999	0 948854 12 X
Nottingham 1 & 2 (Prestige Series)	G.H.F. Atkins & J. Banks	Venture Publications	2002	
Nottingham City Transport	Philip Groves	Transport Publishing Company	1978	0 903839 25 3
Nottingham's Trams & Trolleybuses	David J. Ottewell	Nottinghamshire County Council	2000	0 902751 33 6
Nottingham's Tramways	Philip Groves	Tramway Museum Society	1978	0 9501045 8 2
Nottingham's Trolleybus System	C.F. Riley	Omnibus Society	1966	
The Electric Trolleybus	R.A. Bishop	Sir Isaac Pitman	1931	
Tramways of the North Midlands	W.H. Bett & J.C. Gillham	Light Railway Transport League	1974	900433 50 7
Trolleybuses of Grimsby & Cleethorpes	Andrew Fieldsend	Andrew Fieldsend	1987	
Trolleybuses of Huddersfield	Roy Brooks	Advertiser Press	1976	
Trolleybus Trails	J. Joyce	Ian Allan Ltd	1963	
Under Two Liveries	I I. Brearley & D.T. Beach	West Riding Transport Society	1970	
50 years of Cleethorpes Trolleybuses	Andrew Fieldsend	Andrew Fieldsend	1987	
Newspapers				
Guardian Journal	Copies held at the Nottingham Local Studies Library			
Nottingham Daily Express	Copies held at the Nottingham Local Studies Library			
Nottingham Evening News	Copies held at the Nottingham Local Studies Library			
Nottingham Evening Post	Copies held at the Nottingham Local Studies Library			
Nottingham Daily Guardian	Copies held at the Nottingham Local Studies Library			
Nottingham Journal	Copies held at the Nottingham Local Studies Library			
Professional Periodicals				
Bus & Coach				
Commercial Motor	In particular February 1927, May 1929 editions.			
Electric Railway, Bus and Tram Journal	In particular March 1931, April 1931, April 1934 editions.			
Light Railway and Tramway Journal	In particular February 1912 and 1930-1934 editions.			
Modern Transport				
Tramway and Railway World	In particular July 1924, February 1927, April 1931, April 1933 editions.			
Transport World	In particular May 1930, December 1936 editions.			
Enthusiasts' Magazines and Periodicals				
Buses Illustrated		Ian Allan Ltd	1949-67	
National Trolleybus Association Newsletter		National Trolleybus Association	1963-67	
Reading Transport Society Newsletter		Reading Transport Society	1961-71	
Trams	Issues No. 2, 24, 29	Tramway Museum Society	1961-68	
Tramway Review	Issue No. 2	Light Railway Transport League	1950	
Trolleybus		British Trolleybus Society	1971-date	
Trolleybus Society Newsletter		Trolleybus Society	1954-55	
Trolleybus Magazine		National Trolleybus Association	1963-date	
Others				
Acts of Parliament				
Commercial Year Book of the Nottingham Chamber of Commerce	(in particular the 1914 issue)			
Municipal Life in Nottingham	(particularly the 1937 issue)			
Minutes of the Electricity Committee	Copies held at the Nottinghamshire Archives			
Minutes of the Tramways Committee	Copies held at the Nottinghamshire Archives			
Minutes of the Passenger Transport Committee	Copies held at the Nottinghamshire Archives			
Minutes of the Transport Committee	Copies held at the Nottinghamshire Archives			
Nottingham City Council Minutes	Copies held at the Nottinghamshire Archives			
West Bridgford Urban District Council Minutes	Copies held at the Nottinghamshire Archives